THE LORD'S SUPPER

OTHER BOOKS IN THIS SERIES:

Vol. 1 James M. Hamilton Jr., *God's Indwelling Presence: The Holy Spirit in the Old and New Testaments*

Vol. 2 Thomas R. Schreiner and Shawn D. Wright, eds., *Believer's Baptism: Sign of the New Covenant in Christ*

Vol. 3 Barry E. Horner, *Future Israel: Why Christian Anti-Judaism Must Be Challenged*

Vol. 4 Timothy M. Pierce, *Enthroned on Our Praise: An Old Testament Theology of Worship*

Vol. 5 Christopher D. Bass, *That You May Know: Assurance of Salvation in 1 John*

Vol. 6 Jason C. Meyer, *The End of the Law: Mosaic Covenant in Pauline Theology*

Vol. 7 Mark F. Rooker, *The Ten Commandments: Ethics for the Twenty-first Century*

Vol. 8 David L. Allen, *Lukan Authorship of Hebrews*

Vol. 9 Michael Rydelnik, *The Messianic Hope: Is the Hebrew Bible Really Messianic?*

NAC STUDIES IN BIBLE & THEOLOGY

THE LORD'S SUPPER

REMEMBERING AND PROCLAIMING CHRIST UNTIL HE COMES

THOMAS R. SCHREINER
& MATTHEW R. CRAWFORD

SERIES EDITOR: E. RAY CLENDENEN

NASHVILLE, TENNESSEE

The Lord's Supper:
Remembering and Proclaiming Christ until He Comes

ISBN: 978-0-8054-4757-6

Published by B&H Publishing Group
Nashville, Tennessee

Dewey Decimal Classification: 264.36
Subject Heading: DOCTRINAL THEOLOGY\LORD'S SUPPER\SACRAMENTS

Printed in the United States of America

2 3 4 5 6 7 8 9 10 11 12 • 17 16 15 14 13 12 11

To

Diane and Brandy

Thank you for your patience

and support.

TABLE OF CONTENTS

LIST OF ABBREVIATIONS

AB	Anchor Bible
ACCS	Ancient Christian Commentary on Scripture, ed. T. C. Oden. OT series (ACCS:OT) or NT series (ACCS:NT).
ANF	*Ante-Nicene Fathers*, ed. A. Roberts, J. Donaldson, P. Schaff, and H. Wace. 10 vols. Eerdmans, 1985.
Ant.	Josephus, *Jewish Antiquities*
AYB	Anchor Yale Bible
b.	*Babylonian Talmud*
BAGD	W. Bauer, W. F. Arndt, F. W. Gingrich, and F. Danker, *Greek-English Lexicon of the New Testament and Other Early Christian Literature*. 2nd ed. University of Chicago Press, 1979.
bar.	*baraita*
BAR	*Biblical Archaeology Review*
BBR	*Bulletin for Biblical Research*
BDAG	W. Bauer, F. W. Danker, W. F. Arndt, and F. W. Gingrich, *Greek-English Lexicon of the New Testament and Other Early Christian Literature*. 3rd ed. University of Chicago Press, 2000.
BDF	F. Blass, A. Debrunner, and R. W. Funk, *A Greek Grammar of the New Testament and Other Early Christian Literature*. University of Chicago, 1961.
BECNT	Baker Exegetical Commentary on the New Testament
BNTC	Black's New Testament Commentary
BTNT	The Biblical Theology of the New Testament
CCCM	*Corpus Christianorum Continuatio Mediaevalis*
CNTC	Calvin's New Testament Commentaries, trans. T. H. L. Parker, ed. D. W. Torrance and T. F. Torrance. Eerdmans, 1988.
CNTOT	*Commentary on the New Testament Use of the Old Testament*, ed. G. K. Beale and D. A. Carson. Baker, 2007.
Congr.	Philo, *De congressu eruditionis gratia*
Contempl.	Philo, *De vita contemplativa*
CTJ	*Calvin Theological Journal*
CTR	*Criswell Theological Review*
Did.	*Didache*

DJG	*Dictionary of Jesus and the Gospels*, ed. J. B. Green, S. McKnight, and I. H. Marshall. Downers Grove: InterVarsity, 1992.
DLNTD	*Dictionary of the Later New Testament and Its Developments*, ed. R. P. Martin and P. H. Davids. InterVarsity, 1997.
DPL	*Dictionary of Paul and His Letters*, ed. G. F. Hawthorne, R. P. Martin, and D. G. Reid. InterVarsity, 1993.
DTIB	*Dictionary for Theological Interpretation of the Bible*, ed. K. Vanhoozer et al. Baker, 2005.
EBC	*Expositor's Bible Commentary*, ed. Frank Gaebelein. Zondervan, 1992.
EBS	Encountering Biblical Studies
esp.	especially
ESV	English Standard Version
ExpTim	*Expository Times*
FC	Fathers of the Church. Catholic University of America Press, 1947–.
GGBB	D. B. Wallace, *Greek Grammar beyond the Basics: An Exegetical Syntax of the New Testament*. Zondervan, 1996.
GGNT	A. T. Robertson, *Greek Grammar of the New Testament*. 4th ed. Broadman, 1934.
GNT	Greek New Testament
HCSB	Holman Christian Standard Bible
Her	Hermeneia
Holmes	*The Apostolic Fathers: Greek Texts and English Translations*, ed. and trans. M. W. Holmes. 3rd ed. Baker, 2007.
HTR	*Harvard Theological Review*
IBC	Interpretation: A Bible Commentary for Teaching and Preaching
ICC	International Critical Commentary
Ign. *Eph.*	Ignatius, *To the Ephesians*
Institutes	John Calvin, *Institutes of the Christian Religion*, ed. J. T. McNeill, trans. F. L. Battles, LCC vols. 21–22. Westminster, 1960.
Int	*Interpretation*
ITQ	*Irish Theological Quarterly*
JBL	*Journal of Biblical Literature*

JBMW	*Journal of Biblical Manhood and Womanhood*
JECS	*Journal of Early Christian Studies*
JEH	*Journal of Ecclesiastical History*
JETS	*Journal of the Evangelical Theological Society*
JRH	*Journal of Religious History*
JSNT	*Journal for the Study of the New Testament*
JSNTSup	Journal for the Study of the New Testament: Supplement Series
JTS	*Journal of Theological Studies*
Jub.	*Jubilees*
J.W.	Josephus, *Jewish War*
KNT	Kommentar zum Neuen Testament
L&N	J. P. Louw and E. A. Nida, eds. *Greek-English Lexicon of the New Testament Based on Semantic Domains*, 2 vols. 2nd ed. UBS, 1989.
LCC	Library of Christian Classics
LCL	Loeb Classical Library
LQ	*The Lutheran Quarterly*
LSJ	H. G. Liddell, R. Scott, H. S. Jones, *A Greek-English Lexicon*. 9th ed. Oxford, 1940.
LW	*Luther's Works*, 55 vols. (American edition)
LXX	Septuagint
m. Pesaḥ.	*Mishnah Pesaḥim*
m. Šabb.	*Mishnah Šabbat*
m. Zebaḥ.	*Mishnah Zebaḥim*
Mansi	J. D. Mansi, ed., *Sacrorum Conciliorum nova et amplissima collectio*. Rev. ed., 31 vols. Petit and Martin, 1899–1927.
Mart. Pol.	*Martyrdom of Polycarp*
Mek.	*Mekilta*
Midr.	*Midrash*
MM	J. H. Moulton and G. Milligan, *The Vocabulary of the Greek Testament*. Eerdmans, 1930.
MT	Masoretic Text
NA^{27}	*Novum Testamentum Graece*, ed. E. and E. Nestle, B. and K. Aland et al. 27th ed.
NAC	New American Commentary
NACSBT	New American Commentary Studies in Bible and Theology

NAS	New American Standard Bible
NICNT	New International Commentary on the New Testament
NIDNTT	*New International Dictionary of New Testament Theology*, ed. Colin Brown. Zondervan, 1975–78.
NIGTC	New International Greek Testament Commentary
NIV	New International Version
NIVAC	NIV Application Commentary
NJB	New Jerusalem Bible
NovT	*Novum Testamentum*
NovTSup	Novum Testamentum Supplement Series
NPNF	*Nicene and Post-Nicene Fathers*, ed. A. Roberts et al. Series one (*NPNF*^{1}) or two (*NPNF*^{2})
NSBT	New Studies in Biblical Theology
NT	New Testament
NTS	*New Testament Studies*
OT	Old Testament
PG	Patrologia graeca [=Patrologiae cursus completus: series Graeca], ed. J.-P. Migne, 162 vols. Paris, 1857–1912.
PGL	*A Patristic Greek lexicon*, ed. G. W. H. Lampe. Oxford, 1961.
PL	Patrologia latina [=Patrologiae cursus completus: Series latina], ed. J.-P. Migne. 217 vols. Paris, 1844–64.
PNTC	Pillar New Testament Commentaries
QE	Philo, *Questions and Answers on Exodus*
Rab.	*Rabbah*
RefR	*Reformed Review*
RevExp	*Review and Expositor*
RSV	Revised Standard Version
Samar.	The Samaritan Version
SBHLA	Southern Baptist Historical Library and Archives
SBJT	*The Southern Baptist Journal of Theology*
SBLDS	Society of Biblical Literature Dissertation Series
SBLMS	Society of Biblical Literature Monograph Series
SBT	Studies in Biblical Theology
SBTS	Southern Baptist Theological Seminary
Schaff	P. Schaff, *Creeds of Christendom, with a History and Critical Notes*. 3 vols.

SE	*Studia evangelica*
SJT	*Scottish Journal of Theology*
SNTSMS	Society for New Testament Studies Monograph Series
Spec.	Philo, *De specialibus legibus*
StPatr	*Studia patristica*
Str-B	H. L. Strack and P. Billerbeck, *Kommentar zum Neuen Testament aus Talmud und Midrasch*, 6 vols. München, 1956.
SwJT	*Southwestern Journal of Theology*
SWBTS	Southwestern Baptist Theological Seminary
t. Ber.	*Tosephta Berakot*
t. Beṣah	*Tosephta Beṣah*
TDNT	*Theological Dictionary of the New Testament*, ed. G. Kittel and G. Friedrich, trans. G. W. Bromiley. 10 vols. Eerdmans, 1964–74.
Tg. Onq.	*Targum Onqelos*
Tg. Qoh.	*Targum Qohelet*
Tg. Yer. I	*Targum Yerušalmi I*
Them	*Themelios*
TNIV	Today's NIV
TNTC	Tyndale New Testament Commentaries
TRE	*Theologische Realenzyklopädie*, ed. G. Krause and G. Müller. De Gruyter, 1977–.
TynBul	*Tyndale Bulletin*
VC	*Vigiliae Christianae*
VE	*Vox Evangelica*
WBC	Word Biblical Commentary
WCF	Westminster Confession of Faith
WTJ	*Westminster Theological Journal*
WUNT	Wissenschaftliche Untersuchungen zum Neuen Testament
y.	*Jerusalem Talmud*
ZNW	*Zeitschrift für die neutestamentliche Wissenschaft und die Kunde der älteren Kirche*

SERIES PREFACE

We live in an exciting era of evangelical scholarship. Many fine educational institutions committed to the inerrancy of Scripture are training men and women to serve Christ in the church and to advance the gospel in the world. Many church leaders and professors are skillfully and fearlessly applying God's Word to critical issues, asking new questions, and developing new tools to answer those questions from Scripture. They are producing valuable new resources to thoroughly equip current and future generations of Christ's servants.

The Bible is an amazing source of truth and an amazing tool when wielded by God's Spirit for God's glory and our good. It is a bottomless well of living water, a treasure-house of endless proportions. Like an ancient tell, exciting discoveries can be made on the surface, but even more exciting are those to be found by digging. The books in this series, NAC Studies in Bible and Theology, often take a biblical difficulty as their point of entry, remembering B. F. Westcott's point that "unless all past experience is worthless, the difficulties of the Bible are the most fruitful guides to its divine depths."

This new series is to be a medium through which the work of evangelical scholars can effectively reach the church. It will include detailed exegetical-theological studies of key pericopes such as the Sermon on the Mount and also fresh examinations of topics in biblical theology and systematic theology. It is intended to supplement the New American Commentary, whose exegetical and theological discussions so many have found helpful. These resources are aimed primarily at church leaders and those who are preparing for such leadership. We trust that individual Christians will find them to be an encouragement to greater progress and joy in the faith. More important, our prayer is that they will help the church proclaim Christ more accurately and effectively and that they will bring praise and glory to our great God.

It is a tremendous privilege to be partners in God's grace with the fine scholars writing for this new series as well as with those who will be helped by it. When Christ returns, may He find us "standing firm in one spirit, with one mind, working side by side for the faith of the gospel" (Phil 1:27).

E. Ray Clendenen
B&H Publishing Group

FOREWORD

David S. Dockery*

It has been aptly observed that the history of Christian theology consists of the flight from one error into the arms of another. One of the greatest challenges we have is to avoid such reaction, for in fleeing the extremes of another, we all too easily cultivate extremes of our own. Throughout the history of the church, different views of the Lord's Supper have influenced both theology and pastoral practice. In this book, Tom Schreiner and Matt Crawford have assembled a stellar line-up of contributors to address the importance of worship and the central place of the Lord's Supper in that worship for our Baptist churches and our Baptist theology.

The contributors join me in their belief that worship is central in and for the life of the church. The ultimate purpose of the church is the worship of God the Father through Jesus Christ as enabled by the Holy Spirit. The functions or purposes of the church are many, but worship seems to be paramount in reference to the others, although it is often neglected as such in practice. A worthy purpose to which we could devote these remarks would be a study of worship in general, including exhortations to restore worship to its proper place in the contemporary church. Worship has not traditionally been one of the strengths of Baptist local church practice. Yet it would seem that the Lord's Supper provides an unusually good opportunity for growth in the practice of worship. The chapters in this volume by Andreas Köstenberger, Jonathan Pennington, and Jim Hamilton help us better understand the biblical teaching in this regard on this important subject.

The highest form of corporate Christian worship is the Lord's Supper. The celebration of the Supper directs our attention backward to the work of Christ on the cross and also encourages a forward look to the second coming of Christ. In addition, it provides a time for believers to examine their own personal relationship with God as well as their relationship with other believers while experiencing communion with the exalted Christ. The observance is one that is so simple

* David S. Dockery received his Ph.D. at the University of Texas at Arlington and is the author or editor of over 30 books. He is president and professor of Christian Thought and Tradition at Union University in Jackson, Tennessee.

a child can partake with a sense of understanding, yet it contains so many theological ramifications that even the most mature believer will not fully comprehend its meaning. While these statements about the Supper are true, the complexity regarding the understanding of the Supper is amplified in the chapters by Michael Haykin, David Hogg, Gregg Allison, Matt Crawford, Shawn Wright, Bruce Ware, Greg Wills, and Brian Vickers. Readers will profit much from a reflective reading of the work of these contributors.

The emphasis in most Baptist church meetings is on the proclamation of the Word of God, as well it should be. Yet at times some pastors are uncomfortable with the ordinance of the Lord's Supper. Many people wonder why we should continue to celebrate this seemingly outdated act, especially if it is only a "symbolic act of obedience." This act of obedience seems often to be the only reason for observing the Supper. The command, however, is not "read about," "preach about," or "meditate upon," but "do this." When and how is this to be done? Some might ask, "How will observing the Lord's Supper help us reach the world for Christ?" Some insightful answers to these challenging questions can be found in the outstanding chapters written by Greg Thornbury and Ray Van Neste.

One aspect of the Lord's commission included "teaching them to observe everything I commanded you" as Christ's followers disciple the nations (Matt 28:19–20). Certainly teaching them to observe "everything I commanded you" would include the practice of the Lord's Supper. Obedience to our Lord's Word in this regard is important, even imperative, but we need to understand these words within a larger context. We need to realize that God is seeking worshippers who will worship him in spirit and in truth (see John 4:23–24).

If one of the central acts of worship in the NT is corporate celebration of the Lord's Supper, should we not give it greater attention? If indeed the regular observance will enhance our love for our Lord, is it not possible that this is how we would answer the earlier question? Would not greater love for the Lord form the foundation for reaching the world for him? Should our practice of the Supper not be more than a mere appendage to the preaching service? Should our practice be done more faithfully and regularly?

Baptists must learn to elevate the place of worship in the believing community. We need to establish a special time for the observance so it is no longer an infrequent practice or hurried appendage to a lengthy sermon. In doing so we must not give up our evangelistic zeal or our growing sense of the importance of edification through expository preaching. We must seek balance and discover the missing jewel of worship. In doing so we must place the Lord's Supper in the center of our understanding of worship, for nothing is able to help us celebrate the work of Christ on our behalf or enable us to experience His presence among us through His Spirit as does the regular observance of the Supper. It also enables the Word to become visible for the community of faith. We might also consider the important potential for pastoral care that can be expanded through self-examination that takes place at the Supper. Certainly celebration of the Supper can help us emphasize unity in our church and in our denomination when we recognize that the apostle's words in 1 Cor 10:17 call us to unity around the ordinance. With these reflections, then, it would seem wise for Baptists in the twenty-first century to renew in a creative way our commitment to the worship of the Lord Jesus Christ by faithfully and regularly participating in His Supper. I am happy to commend this volume as a faithful guide to help us move in that direction.

Many are ready to admit that a regular observance of the Lord's Supper was the practice of the early church and even the patristic period for many generations. The usual objection is that when the Supper is observed so frequently, its meaning is lost. That is a legitimate concern. But the objection could also be raised concerning singing, preaching, praying, and other actions of our worship experience. If meaning is lost, the problem may well be with our hearts rather than with the ordinance itself. The testimony of one of the great Baptist preachers in history maintains that contrary to the previous objection, the opposite can be true and beneficial. Charles H. Spurgeon concluded,

> My witness is, and I speak the mind of many of God's people now present, that coming as some of us do, weekly to the Lord's table, we do not find the breaking of bread to have lost its significance—it is always fresh to us. I've often remarked on the Lord's Day evening whatever the subject may have been, whether Sinai has thundered over our heads or the plaintive notes of Calvary have pierced our hearts, it always seems equally appropriate to come to the breaking of bread. Shame on the church that she would put off to once a month and mar the first day of the week by depriving it of its glory in the meeting together for fellowship and breaking of bread, and showing forth the

> death of Christ till He comes. Those who know the sweetness of each Lord's Day celebrating His Supper will not be content, I am sure, to put it off to less frequent seasons.

In this volume it will be seen that the Lord's Supper is referred to by many names in Scripture. Regardless of the name we prefer for this ordinance, we can all recognize that in the observance past, present, and future are thus gathered in one sacred and joyful celebration following apostolic teaching and practice. Indeed, in this ordinance, the whole of what Christianity means is expressed: one Lord Jesus Christ, incarnate, atoning, and triumphant as the sum and substance of the observance.

Without doubt, the Lord's Supper was observed with considerable frequency in the early church in order that believers might partake and be nourished and strengthened in the life of God. The essence of the experience is the worship of one Lord and fellowship with Him and His people, eating and sharing together, while at the same time conjoining a dynamic remembrance and expectancy of the Lord Jesus Christ. Here we see a dramatic interrelationship between human relationships and relationship with God. Reflecting on Church history in general, and particularly the work of the sixteenth-century Reformers, the seventeenth-century Baptists, and the teaching of the NT, we can gain a new and renewed appreciation for this important practice. A renewal of the apostolic practice and teaching is mandatory for the church of this generation to return to the dynamic worship and ministry of the early church. It is my prayer that this timely volume will serve to strengthen our understanding of the Lord's Supper and enhance our worship of the one true God who has made Himself known to us in our Lord Jesus Christ.

INTRODUCTION

Thomas R. Schreiner and Matthew R. Crawford

One of the most important events that takes place in the weekly gatherings of the church is the celebration of the Lord's Supper. If what takes place during Communion matches the NT, then those gathered are reminded vividly of the gospel. The breaking of the bread symbolizes the breaking of Jesus' body for His disciples (Matt 26:26), and the wine symbolizes Jesus' blood that has been shed for the forgiveness of sins (Matt 26:28). Indeed, in Jesus' death the new covenant is inaugurated (Luke 22:20; 1 Cor 11:25). The significance of what Jesus accomplished is conveyed not only through words but also tangibly and physically. Jesus' death for sinners is so important and fundamental for Christians that our Lord commanded us to continue to observe this meal in His remembrance (Luke 22:19; 1 Cor 11:25). When Christians are gathered together, they must continue to proclaim the Lord's death (1 Cor 11:26), pictured through the eating of the bread and the drinking of the vine, until the Lord returns. As Christians we are sometimes very dim-witted, but even we can see that Jesus Christ wanted us to regularly observe the Eucharist.

We should linger a bit longer to consider the importance of this reality. Proclaiming the significance of what Jesus accomplished in His ministry, death, and resurrection is vital for the health of the church. The church is only the church if it declares the gospel to its members and to the world. But we are not only to say the gospel. We are also summoned to see the gospel. Our new life depends on Jesus' life being torn away from Him. We must remind ourselves that His body was scourged, that He was impaled on a cross with nails, and that He poured out His blood—His very life—that we should live. There must be a horror, a massive evil that resides in us, if such a death is required for our life. The observance of the Supper provokes us to consider why such a sacrifice was necessary, and we begin to realize that there is something terribly wrong with human beings—that there is something terribly wrong with us. We are self-absorbed, proud, self-worshipping creatures. If we knew ourselves, we would know that, given the right circumstances, we would engage in the worst atrocities committed in human history. The stories of evil in history and in the newspaper are part of our story. We need someone to save us from ourselves and to rescue us from the selfishness that distorts and destroys us. We are as sons and daughters of Adam born into the world as those who hate God, so that we refuse to thank and praise Him as we should (Rom 1:21; 5:10).

Our life depends on the torn flesh and bloody sacrifice of the Lord Jesus Christ. We always eat and drink the life of what dies, and so as we eat and drink we are reminded that we derive our very life from the death of our Lord Jesus Christ. Furthermore, the celebration of the Lord's Supper has an eschatological dimension. Jesus promised His disciples that He would drink the fruit of the vine again with them when the kingdom dawns (Mark 14:25). We proclaim through the Supper the Lord's death "until He comes" (1 Cor 11:26). Hence, the Lord's Supper points to "the marriage supper of the Lamb" (Rev 19:9). We do not only look back to what Christ has done for us, but we also look forward to our destiny in the new heavens and the new earth as we eat and drink together in remembrance of Christ.

The Lord's Supper, then, pictures the gospel. If we grasp it truly, we are filled with trembling and joy. We tremble to think of the One who gave His life for us as we reflect on the cost necessary for our life. And we are grateful that He has saved us from ourselves and from the sin that blights our lives. Oh how precious it is to live! Especially when that life is eternal. How joyful we are as we feast on Jesus as the crucified and risen Lord who died so that we might live. How easily we stray from the truth of the gospel, which is that our life was given to us and that we always stand as debtors to His grace. It is not fundamentally what we do for God that is significant, but what He has done for us. The Lord's Supper reminds us concretely of the grace of God, and the life that has been breathed into us via the gospel.

In addition, the Lord's Supper testifies to our unity as Christians. We all partake of one loaf ("one bread," 1 Cor 10:17), and hence we are one body. All of us as Christians feed off Jesus for our life, and hence we are united at the cross. We are the community of the redeemed since we are the community of the needy. Hence, there is no basis for pride or self-exaltation in our fellowship. We are not better than anyone in the world. We are beggars who have eaten of the bread of life, and our life together stands as a testimony to His gracious work. As we commune together we commune in joy, knowing that we belong together by virtue of the love of God in Christ Jesus our Lord. A right interpretation of the Eucharist is important, and yet we want to follow in the footsteps of Radbertus, who as we see in David Hogg's chapter, accepted into the fellowship of the Supper those who were true believers in Jesus Christ but differed from him in their interpretation of its significance.

Since the Lord's Supper is of such vital importance, it warrants careful study. What do the Scriptures teach about what we call the Lord's Supper (1 Cor 11:20), Communion (1 Cor 10:16 KJV; *koinōnia*), or the Eucharist (1 Cor 11:24; *eucharistia,* "thanksgiving")? Do our churches practice it in a way that accords with the Scriptures? Have we reflected as Christians and in our churches on how the Lord's Supper should be practiced and how often we observe it? We are keenly aware that different views of the meal have been propounded throughout Christian history. We would do well, then, to consider not only the biblical texts regarding Communion. We must also be informed by the history of the church and by the thoughtful interaction of Christians who have preceded us. It would be arrogant and foolish to reflect on the Eucharist without learning from and evaluating those who have gone before us. Naturally we are scarcely claiming to present "the final word" about the Eucharist, but our prayer is that our practice of the Supper will honor Christ as we consider the significance of Communion both exegetically and theologically.

The goal of this book, then, is to study the Lord's Supper biblically, historically, theologically, and practically. It is our hope, as we gather together as Christians to observe the Supper, that our practice is rooted in Scripture, with our scriptural exegesis being informed by those who have read the Bible before us.

Naturally we begin with biblical exegesis. Andreas Köstenberger considers whether the Lord's Supper was a Passover meal, and he convincingly demonstrates that it was. Jonathan Pennington and Jim Hamilton examine the biblical texts in the Gospels and Epistles respectively. What do the biblical texts actually teach about the Supper? The Scriptures, after all, are our final authority and the only rule for faith and practice. And yet we do not do biblical exegesis in a vacuum. We are living 2,000 years after the great events of our salvation. Like it or not we are all shaped by those who preceded us. Hence, it is vital to consider the exegesis of Christians who preceded us. Michael Haykin surveys the teaching of the church in the first 500 years, and David Hogg interacts particularly with two scholars who wrote about the Supper during the Carolingian era (ca. AD 800–1000). We also recognize that certain views of the Supper have played a significant role in history. Hence, Gregg Allison considers the Roman Catholic view, Matthew Crawford the contribution of Martin Luther, Bruce Ware the work of Ulrich Zwingli, and Shawn Wright the perspective of John Calvin. The historical chapters are not only descriptive, for we have also asked each of the contributors to evaluate what was being taught about the Supper.

All the contributors to this volume are Baptists, and we have asked Greg Wills to give us soundings of Baptist views. Even though we are Baptists, we freely acknowledge that we must learn from and may even need to be corrected by those who have reflected on the Lord's Supper from other traditions. The theological portion of the book is rounded out with an important essay by Brian Vickers, which represents a theological appraisal of the Lord's Supper for today's church. Finally, what should we do in our churches today? We do not want to make rules where none are needed, but what should the Lord's Supper look like in our churches? How do we reverently and joyfully practice the Supper today? Greg Thornbury considers the implications of the Supper for our life together as Christians. And Ray Van Neste tackles a number of practical questions regarding the Supper.

It should be noted that our contributors do not necessarily agree with one another on everything presented here. For instance, we have different opinions on how often Communion should be celebrated. The sharpest difference in the book centers on open Communion. Ray Van Neste argues for open Communion, but Greg Wills maintains that open Communion became more common among Southern Baptists as liberal theology began to infiltrate the Southern Baptist Convention in the late nineteenth and twentieth century. Wills also observes that not all Baptists defended open Communion for liberalizing reasons. For instance, Charles Spurgeon advocated open Communion. Indeed, open Communion has an ancient heritage among Baptists. The First London Baptist Confession of Faith (1644) allowed open Communion, but this was later revised by William Kiffin (1616–1701) and his friends. Nevertheless, the Second London Baptist Confession of Faith did not draw the line at close Communion in 1677/1689, and famous

Baptists like John Ryland Sr. (1723–92), John Ryland Jr. (1753–1825), Robert Hall Jr. (1764–1831), and Wriothesley Noel (1798–1873) along with others supported open Communion. Wills argues historically that many Southern Baptists in the United States accepted open Communion for liberal reasons, but history also shows (as Wills affirms) that other Baptists promoted open Communion who were biblically and theologically conservative. Hence, acceptance of open Communion does not necessarily point to liberal influence. Both historically and theologically, Baptist scholars who prize the authority and inerrancy of Scripture, may come to different positions on open Communion.

We want to thank our contributors for taking time out of their busy schedules to write on this topic. We think it is a great advantage to have a team of experts instead of relying on one person to do the whole. None of us can master the exegesis, history, and theology necessary to understand the Eucharist adequately. We all benefit greatly, therefore, from scholars who have devoted their expertise to exegesis, history, and theology in studying a topic like the Lord's Supper. We are also grateful to Ray Clendenen at B&H Publishing Group for enthusiastically supporting this work and for helping bring the work to completion with his outstanding editorial skills. Our prayer is that this book will remind us afresh of the gospel, so that our churches will truly remember and proclaim the Lord Jesus as they partake of His body and blood.

WAS THE LAST SUPPER A PASSOVER MEAL?

Andreas J. Köstenberger*

Introduction

For close to 2,000 years, Christians have celebrated the Lord's Supper, an ordinance instituted by Jesus in the Upper Room the night before His crucifixion. That Jesus ate this meal with His disciples is widely acknowledged. What is not as commonly agreed upon, however, is the nature of the meal. Was Jesus' Last Supper the annual Passover meal observed by the Jews, or was it some other kind of meal that sustained no direct demonstrable connection with Israel's Passover? On the surface, this question may seem inconsequential. At a closer look, however, numerous historical, biblical, and theological factors emerge that significantly affect our understanding of the Lord's Supper. This essay examines the biblical data in order to determine what kind of meal Jesus ate with His disciples the night before He died. Was it, or was it not, a Passover meal?

In an effort to address this matter, the following topics will need to be explored. First, in order to gauge the significance of the question, we will investigate the issues at stake in identifying the type of meal Jesus ate with His disciples. Second, we will take a look at the OT background of the Passover in order to acquire the proper historical lens for assessing the NT data. Third, we will address specific arguments by those who suggest that Jesus' Last Supper was not a Passover meal and provide responses that argue for its paschal nature. Finally, we will consider Gospel evidence that favors a paschal interpretation of the Last Supper. The overall picture that will emerge from this investigation will suggest that Jesus did indeed eat a Passover meal with His disciples.

The Issues at Stake

Jesus' Last Supper with His disciples is recorded in all three of the Synoptic Gospels (Matt 26:17–30; Mark 14:12–26; Luke 22:7–38),

* Andreas J. Köstenberger received his Ph.D. from Trinity Evangelical Divinity School. He is founder and president of BIBLICAL FOUNDATIONS®, editor of *JETS*, and professor of NT and Biblical Theology and director of Ph.D. studies at Southeastern Baptist Theological Seminary in Wake Forest, North Carolina.

where it is clearly portrayed as a Passover meal (Mark 14:12: "On the first day of Unleavened Bread, when they sacrifice the Passover lamb, His disciples asked Him, 'Where do You want us to go and prepare the Passover so You may eat it?'"; Luke 22:7–8: "Then the Day of Unleavened Bread came when the Passover lamb had to be sacrificed. Jesus sent Peter and John, saying, 'Go and prepare the Passover meal for us, so we can eat it'"; cf. Josephus, *Ant.* 16.6.2 §§163–64),[1] a meal that took place on the Thursday night before Jesus was crucified the next day (Friday). When one turns the page from Luke's to John's Gospel, however, some contend that the picture appears to change.

According to John's timeline (13:1), Jesus and His disciples celebrated the Last Supper the day before Jesus stood trial before Pilate (18:28–19:16). For John, this trial seems to have taken place prior to the Jewish Passover meal: "It was early morning. They did not enter the headquarters themselves; otherwise they would be defiled and unable to eat the Passover" (18:28b). If the Jews had not yet eaten the Passover when they tried Jesus, it is argued, Jesus could not have eaten the Passover with His disciples the night before. In apparent further confirmation of this, John states that Jesus' Last Supper took place "before the Passover Festival" (13:1) and that Jesus' crucifixion took place on "the preparation day for the Passover" (19:14), that is, on the day before Passover (i.e., Thursday). Thus, for John, it is argued, Jesus ate His Last Supper with His disciples on the Wednesday night of Passion Week (Nisan 14), twenty-four hours before the official celebration of the Passover meal, and Jesus was crucified on Thursday (Nisan 15).

The primary point of tension between the Synoptics and John, then, is readily apparent. The Synoptic writers seem to say that Jesus' Last Supper constituted a Passover meal, which would have fallen on Thursday night of Passion Week, with the crucifixion having occurred the next day (Friday). John, however, appears to suggest that Jesus ate His Last Supper the day before the Passover meal, which would have fallen on Wednesday night of Passion Week, with the crucifixion having occurred on the next day (Thursday). For those who adhere to a high view of Scripture, these apparent contradictions are certainly significant and raise important questions that need to be addressed: Do the accounts of Jesus' Last Supper in the Synoptics

[1] Unless otherwise indicated, Scripture quotations are from the HCSB.

and John contradict one another? If so, did John alter the Synoptic tradition for theological reasons? Or was Jesus' Last Supper with His disciples but a normal meal which the Synoptics and/or John invested with Passover symbolism in order to validate their particular theology of the cross?

The issues at stake, then, are weighty indeed. First, discerning the type of meal Jesus ate with the disciples the night before His crucifixion has a bearing on the issue of biblical inerrancy. If John and the Synoptics are found to contradict one another with regard to the dating of the Last Supper and the type of meal Jesus observed with His disciples, it would follow that John, the Synoptics, or both are in error. Second, there is the related question concerning the historical reliability of the Gospel traditions. If John, the Synoptics, or both are in error, then one or both are historically unreliable, that is, their record of events does not correspond to what actually happened. Third, if the Last Supper was not a Passover meal, it would be necessary to reassess the theological significance of the Passover for the celebration of the Lord's Supper as it has been conceived throughout church history.[2] The first step, then, in addressing this issue involves an investigation of the OT origin of the Passover.

The Old Testament Origins of the Passover

The Passover was a seminal and constitutive event in the formation of Israel's identity as a nation (Exodus 12, esp. vv. 1–13; cf. Deut 16:1–8).[3] While Moses and the Israelites were chafing under Egyptian bondage, God inflicted a series of plagues on the Egyptians in order to compel Pharaoh to release the Israelites. The tenth and final plague brought a death angel over Egypt to kill every firstborn male, except in houses whose doorframes were smeared with lamb's blood. When the angel saw the blood, he "passed over" that particular dwelling, leaving the firstborn male unharmed.[4]

[2] For a recent survey of the Lord's Supper in the various Christian traditions, see G. T. Smith, ed., *The Lord's Supper: Five Views* (Downers Grove: InterVarsity, 2008).

[3] For a helpful discussion of the origins of the Passover as narrated in Exodus 12, see B. Witherington III, *Making a Meal of It: Rethinking the Theology of the Lord's Supper* (Waco, TX: Baylor University Press, 2007), 2–10.

[4] The English word "Passover," recalling the Hebrew *pesach*, may have been coined by William Tyndale (see Witherington, *Making a Meal of It*, 3).

This plague marked a turning point in Jewish history, not only as a historical event that triggered Israel's exodus from Egypt, but also in the tradition that it began. This tradition became known as "Passover" and has been celebrated yearly by Jews on the fourteenth day of the lunar month Nisan, which marked the beginning of the festal calendar and specifically the onset of the Festival of Unleavened Bread. It was no different in Jesus' day. Passover represented an annual celebration in Jerusalem that all men were expected to attend (cf. Deut 16:5–6). As a result, "Large numbers of worshippers from the outlying provinces of Palestine (Luke 2:41–42) and the Diaspora (Acts 2:5) filled the capital city" (cf. Josephus, *J.W.* 2.1.3 §10).[5] This week of festivities, then, provided the setting for Jesus' Last Supper. The question at hand, therefore, is on what particular day of these festivities Jesus ate the Last Supper.

Arguments that the Last Supper Was Not a Passover Meal

In light of the issues at stake and against the above-sketched OT background, we now turn our attention to common arguments that Jesus' Last Supper was not a Passover meal. These arguments are presented in canonical order as they relate to the Synoptics, John, Acts, and Paul. Subsequent to the presentation of a given argument, a response is provided that typically underscores the likelihood that Jesus' Last Supper was in fact a Passover meal.[6]

The Synoptics

Although, as mentioned, the Synoptics clearly call the Last Supper a Passover meal (Matt 26:17–30; Mark 14:12–26; Luke 22:7–38), some scholars still contend that it was not.[7] This argument is based on the premise that Matthew, Mark, and Luke label the Supper a Passover meal, although the actual historical meal did not occur on the night of Passover. The evangelists, some maintain, portrayed the Supper as a Passover because they were either mistaken or took theological

[5] A. J. Köstenberger, *John*, BECNT (Grand Rapids: Baker, 2004), 104.

[6] The following discussion is significantly indebted to J. Jeremias, *The Eucharistic Words of Jesus*, trans. N. Perrin (London: SCM, 1966), 15–88.

[7] For example, see S. McKnight, *Jesus and His Death: Historiography, the Historical Jesus, and Atonement Theory* (Waco: Baylor University Press, 2005), 259–73. For a brief survey of the Gospel references to Jesus' Last Supper, see Witherington, *Making a Meal of It*, 20–28.

liberties when writing their respective Gospels.[8] The following is a list of arguments with accompanying responses.

Argument No. 1: When recounting the story of Jesus blessing the bread (*artos*), the Synoptics do not feature the technical term "unleavened bread" (*azuma*) that was used for a Passover meal (Matt 26:26; Mark 14:22; Luke 22:19).[9] Jesus' serving of leavened instead of unleavened bread, the argument goes, suggests that His last meal was at best a festal meal but certainly not a Passover meal.

Response: Throughout their lexicographical history, *artos* and *azuma* were used interchangeably for both leavened (*artos*) and unleavened bread (*azuma*; Exod 29:2 [cf. MT and LXX]; LXX: Lev 2:4; 8:26; Num 6:15,19; Judg 6:20; Philo, *Spec.* 2.158). Moreover, the showbread (i.e., the "bread of the Presence" kept on the table in the Holy Place; Exod 25:30; Lev 24:5–9; Num 4:7; 2 Chr 2:3), although unleavened (Philo, *Spec.* 2.161; *Congr.* 168; *Contempl.* 81; Josephus, *Ant.* 3.6.6 §142; 3.10.7 §255), is always simply called "bread" (*artos*) in the OT, Mishnah, Targums, and the LXX. Thus the Synoptics' use of *artos* rather than *azuma* proves nothing except that they were most likely aware of the synonymous uses of these terms.

Argument No. 2: Certain elements of the meal were an integral part of every Jewish Passover. Two especially important ingredients were the paschal lamb (Exod 12:3) and bitter herbs (Exod 12:8). Scot McKnight, for example, suggests that had a lamb been consumed in the Upper Room, it would have made more theological sense for Jesus to say something like "this lamb is my body" rather than "this bread is my body." For this reason, McKnight contends that it is "incomprehensible" that Jesus, as well as the Synoptic writers, would have failed to mention the lamb if it had been present.[10] Since the Synoptic accounts mention neither the paschal lamb nor the bitter herbs, the argument goes, the Last Supper could not have been a Passover meal.

[8] McKnight argues that Mark should be given historical precedence over Matthew and Luke since it is "the most primitive account" (McKnight, *Jesus and His Death*, 262–64). This, however, unnecessarily assumes that closer historical proximity *mandates* better accuracy. It also further presupposes that all three Synoptics cannot be simultaneously correct. Especially, in light of Richard Bauckham's recent argument that the NT Gospel writings represent eyewitness accounts (see his *Jesus and the Eyewitnesses: The Gospels as Eyewitness Testimony* [Grand Rapids: Eerdmans, 2006]), the relative close historical proximity of these writings to one another suggests that McKnight's arguments are overstated.

[9] J. Wellhausen, "Ἄρτον ἔκλασεν, Mc 14, 22," *ZNW* 7 (1907): 182.

[10] McKnight, *Jesus and His Death*, 270.

Response: This is an argument from silence. Simply because the Synoptics do not explicitly mention these elements does not mean that they were absent from the meal. Perhaps the evangelists left out these details for personal and/or narrative reasons. Most likely, Mark, for example, did not intend to present a complete description of the Last Supper but rather chose to focus on those "moments which were constitutive for the celebration of the primitive Church."[11] In fact, these elements were so common at Passover meals that to mention them was tantamount to stating the obvious. This was apparently the case in *m. Pesaḥ.* 10:3, where the author refers to the eating of the paschal lamb only in passing.[12] Another possible reason for the lack of explicit reference to these elements is that the primary focus of the Synoptic accounts of the Last Supper is on Jesus and not on the recounting of the details of the Passover meal. In addition, it is possible that Luke mentions the paschal lamb indirectly (22:15)[13] and that Matthew's and Mark's references to "dip[ping] . . . in the bowl" may subtly allude to the eating of bitter herbs (Matt 26:23; Mark 14:20). McKnight's speculation about Jesus' theological motives for focusing on the bread is mere conjecture. It should be noted that Jesus' focus in the present context is on His broken body in light of His imminent crucifixion. Bread—which could easily be broken—lent itself as an eminently suitable metaphor for the message Jesus sought to convey. There is no compelling reason why He must choose to focus on the lamb. In the end, as mentioned, this argument is one from silence, as McKnight himself rightly concedes, and utterly fails to convince in light of more plausible explanations.[14]

Argument No. 3: There are three elements in the Synoptics' description of the Last Supper that are inconsistent with the Passover ritual: (1) Mark portrays Jesus as saying the blessing before breaking the bread, while at the Passover this is reversed; (2) the Synoptics portray Jesus and His disciples as using a single cup, while the use of individual cups was the norm during Passover meals; and (3) at a Passover meal, each person was to have his or her own dish, but at the

[11] Jeremias, *Words*, 67.

[12] Jeremias concludes from *m. Pesaḥ.* 10:3 that we have here "precisely *the same combination of historical report and cultic ritual* as [found] in the texts describing the Last Supper, and in both cases we can observe the same thing happening: [The] cultic ritual overshadows the historical facts and concentrates attention upon the continuing rites" (*Words*, 67; emphasis original).

[13] C. K. Barrett, "Luke XXII.15: To Eat the Passover," *JTS* 9 (1958): 305–7.

[14] McKnight, *Jesus and His Death*, 270.

Last Supper Jesus and His disciples apparently ate from one common dish (Matt 26:23; Mark 14:20).[15]

Response: First, as Jeremias points out, the opposite scenario is actually true for the Jewish Passover: The bread was broken first, followed by a blessing, which is how the events are described in the Synoptics.[16] Marshall further observes that those who suggest otherwise erroneously base their arguments on late Jewish sources.[17] Second, given the lack of first-century data on the order of the Passover service, Marshall rightly suggests that "it seems impossible to conclude with any certainty what the practice in the first century was."[18] That said, Jeremias detects one clue that may shed light on this issue: later protests against the drinking from multiple cups (*t. Ber.* 5.9; 12:9) suggest that the practice of drinking from a single cup had occurred earlier on.[19] Third, this argument may hold true for Passover observance subsequent to AD 70 when the city of Jerusalem was not as crowded during the celebration. Prior to the year 70, however, having one's own table was unlikely in light of the overcrowding of the city. In such cramped conditions, it is unlikely that everyone had his or her own table and individual dishes.[20]

Argument No. 4: The religious leaders in Mark 14:2 do not want to arrest Jesus "during the festival" (*en tē heortē*) because they fear a riot will ensue among the people. Thus the portrait painted by Mark ("not during the festival") seems to put Jesus' arrest in apparent conflict with Matthew and Luke, who place Jesus' arrest on the night of the first day of the festival.[21]

Response: Two considerations cast doubt on the above understanding of Mark 14:2. First, as Jeremias notes, it is unclear whether or not the religious leaders' desire was fulfilled. It is entirely possible

[15] Jeremias, *Words*, 67–71. For a chronological description of the events at a Jewish Passover meal, see W. Barclay, *The Lord's Supper* (Philadelphia: Westminster, 1967), 22–25.

[16] Jeremias, *Words*, 68–69.

[17] I. H. Marshall, *Last Supper and Lord's Supper* (Grand Rapids: Eerdmans, 1980), 62.

[18] Ibid., 63. If Jesus did indeed break the normal custom, Marshall contends, it "is possible that Jesus deliberately adopted a special way of distributing the wine in order to draw an unusual lesson from it" (ibid.).

[19] Jeremias, *Words*, 69. Heinz Schürmann argues that Jesus and His disciples indeed shared a common cup and adopted a new way to distribute the elements in order to deliberately break the normal custom (*Der Paschamahlbericht* [Münster: Aschendorffsche Verlagsbuchhandlung, 1953], 60–61).

[20] Jeremias, *Words*, 70–71.

[21] Ibid., 71–73.

that though the religious leaders did not want to arrest Jesus during the feast, they later decided to do so anyway.[22] Mark may note the intention of the leaders and then recount the opposite taking place to emphasize that prophecy was fulfilled, against the expectations and plans of the religious leaders. One possible scenario is that when Judas came to the authorities and told them where Jesus was, they viewed the opportunity as so ripe that they decided to act, even though initially they had other plans. And hence prophecy was fulfilled. Alternatively, *en tē heortē* may be used locally/spatially ("in the presence of") rather than temporally ("during").[23] If so, the thrust of Mark's statement would be that the religious leaders wanted to arrest Jesus "by stealth" (14:1), that is, remove Him from the public eye quietly rather than "in the presence of the festal crowd" in order to avoid public attention.[24] This would correlate well with the statement in Luke 22:6: "when the crowd was not present."[25]

Argument No. 5: In light of *m. Pesaḥ.* 8:6 ("They may slaughter [the Passover lamb] . . . for one whom they [the authorities] have promised to release from prison"), prisoners who were freed during the festival (Matt 27:15; Mark 15:6; John 18:39) must have been released in time to partake of the Passover meal.[26] Thus, if the prisoner in the Matthean and Markan accounts would have been tried and released on Friday rather than Thursday, he would not have had a chance to eat the Passover meal. According to some, this fits well within the Johannine chronology where Jesus' trial takes place on Thursday before the Passover meal that evening, thus giving the released criminal a chance to partake, but it contradicts the Synoptic chronology where the trial takes place on Friday after the meal.

Response: The weakness of this argument consists in the fact that there can be no certainty that *m. Pesaḥ.* 8:6 refers to a Roman Passover amnesty. In other words, there is no indication that this was a widely imposed Roman policy. Furthermore, as J. Merkel has noted, there is a fundamental difference between *m. Pesaḥ.* 8:6 and the amnesty

[22] Ibid., 71.

[23] Ibid., 71–73. As evidence that τῇ ἑορτῇ can entail a reference to "festal crowds," Jeremias (ibid., 72) cites Ps 73:4 LXX; 117:27 LXX; John 2:23; 7:11; and Plotinus, *Enneades* 6.6.12.

[24] See, e.g., Marshall, who contends that this understanding is "undoubtedly correct" (*Last Supper*, 166, n. 18); see also C. Burchard, "Fussnoten zum neutestamentlichen Griechisch," *ZNW* 61 (1970): 157.

[25] Marshall, *Last Supper*, 64; Jeremias, *Words*, 73.

[26] Jeremias, *Words*, 73.

referred to by the Gospel writers, namely *m. Pesaḥ.* 8:6 promises release while in the Gospels the release actually occurs.[27]

Argument No. 6: Mark 14:17–15:47 records at least ten events that could not have taken place on Nisan 15 (Friday), the first day of the festival of Unleavened Bread, because they contradicted Jewish festal regulations:[28] (1) Jesus visited Gethsemane the night of the Passover (14:32). This is problematic because a Passover adherent was not to leave Jerusalem during the night of Passover; what is more, the meal had to be eaten within the walls of Jerusalem. (2) The temple guards and the disciples carried and wielded weapons at Jesus' arrest (14:43; cf. Matt 26:47, John 18:3), which was not allowed on feast days. (3) In response to Jesus' perceived blasphemy, the high priest tore his clothes (14:63), an action forbidden during the Passover. (4) Removal of Jesus' body from the cross and the rolling of the stone to enclose the tomb (15:46) broke Jewish regulations. (5) Mary and Mary Magdalene prepared spices for Jesus' body (16:1), another act forbidden during feast days. (6) The Jews participated in the Roman trial during the feast (15:1–15). Such participation was forbidden. (7) Jesus was executed on the first day of the feast (15:21–32). (8) Simon from Cyrene, who was forced to carry Jesus' cross, was "coming in from the country" (15:21), which indicates, first, that he apparently traveled a great distance, which was forbidden on Sabbaths and feast days; and second, since he was coming in from the countryside, he was apparently working, which was forbidden as well. (9) Joseph purchased a linen shroud in which to bury Jesus (15:46). (10) The Sanhedrin met and condemned Jesus during the night of the Passover feast (14:53), which broke the Mishnaic code: "None may sit in judgment . . . on a feast day" (*m. Beṣah* 5:2; *t. Beṣah* 4.4).

Response: The first five arguments, Jeremias maintains, "rest upon sheer ignorance of the halakah . . . and should never be mentioned again."[29] (1) Although a Passover adherent could not leave Jerusalem during the night of Passover and the Passover had to be eaten within the walls of Jerusalem, he or she could spend the night in the greater Jerusalem district. Gethsemane was well within this district.[30] (2) It is uncertain whether Nisan 14/15 was subjected to the regulations of

[27] J. Merkel, "Die Begnadigung am Passahfeste," *ZNW* 6 (1905): 306–16.
[28] Jeremias, *Words*, 74–79.
[29] Ibid., 75.
[30] See ibid., 43, n. 2.

feast days. Moreover, according to early halakah, the bearing of arms was permitted on the Sabbath (*m. Šabb.* 6:4).[31] (3) Tearing a robe did not constitute the breaking of a regulation (*m. Šabb.* 13:3). (4) Deuteronomy 21:23 was equally applicable to a feast day: "You are not to leave his corpse on the tree overnight but are to bury him that day, for anyone hung on a tree is under God's curse." (5) Preparations for the dead, even on feast days, were acceptable (*m. Šabb.* 23:5).

The next two arguments, (6) and (7), pertain to the Roman governor and not the Jewish authorities. Execution during a holy time is not completely unprecedented during this era. For example, Polycarp was executed by the Romans in c. AD 155 on the "high Sabbath" (*Mart. Pol.* 21; cf. 8.1). In this account, note that the Jews carried wood to the pile (*Mart. Pol.* 13.1). Luke and John offer two further examples: the residents of Nazareth attempted to execute Jesus on a Sabbath (Luke 4:29), and the Jews planned to stone Jesus during the Festival of Dedication (John 10:22–39). Shedding more light on this issue is Carson, who notes that the Mishnah "insists that the execution of a rebellious teacher should take place on one of the three principle feasts [Unleavened Bread/Passover, Pentecost, and Tabernacles]" in order to deter particular kinds of conduct.[32] Apart from these considerations, those who participated in the trial were apparently not concerned about the other legal aspects of the proceedings. For example, the verdict was predetermined from the outset (Mark 14:1; John 11:50); false testimony was sought and encouraged (Matt 26:59); and the high priest put Jesus under oath, but the Sanhedrin condemned Jesus on the basis of His testimony (Matt 26:63–66). That aspects of the law were broken during the course of Jesus' trial, therefore, does not present a problem with regard to Jesus' final meal with His disciples being a Passover.

(8) The argument about Simon of Cyrene traveling in "from the country," Jeremias rightly avers, rests on arbitrary assumptions.[33] First, Simon probably did not come from working in the fields since it was still early in the morning (Mark 15:25). Second, the field could have been within the distances permitted for travel on a Sabbath. Third,

[31] See Barclay, *Lord's Supper*, 29; C. L. Blomberg, *The Historical Reliability of the Gospels*, 2nd ed. (Downers Grove: InterVarsity, 2007), 225–26; and F. F. Bruce, "The Trial of Jesus in the Fourth Gospel," in *Gospel Perspectives*, ed. R. T. France and D. Wenham (Sheffield: JSOT, 1980), 7–20.

[32] D. A. Carson, "Matthew," in *EBC* 8:532.

[33] Jeremias, *Words*, 76–77.

it is not altogether clear that Simon came in from the fields since *ap' agrou* ("from the country") can possibly connote "from the village" or "from outside the city."[34] If these connotations are plausible, Simon could have resided just outside of Jerusalem and have been on his way to morning prayer (cf. Acts 3:1). Finally, we cannot be certain that Simon was a Jew. For a Gentile, walking long distances on a feast day was an insignificant matter.

The final two arguments, according to Jeremias, are the only ones that should be taken seriously.[35] (9) On the day of Jesus' crucifixion, Joseph "bought some fine linen" (Mark 15:46) in which to bury Jesus. The purchasing of this cloth is problematic if, as Mark states, it occurred on "preparation day" (15:42), since buying and selling was forbidden on such days. By way of response, Jeremias marshals ample evidence to demonstrate that the regulations against buying and selling on rest days were relaxed due to the necessities of everyday life.[36] For example, *m. Šabb.* 23:4 explicitly approves of the buying and selling of food, a coffin, and a shroud on a feast day. Another example from *t. Šabb.* 17.13 confirms this:

> And he said [on the Sabbath] to him: if you cannot get it at the designated place, fetch it from such and such a place; and if you cannot get it for one mina (100 denarii) then get it for 200 (denarii). R. Jose b. Judah [c. AD 180] said: "Only he must not mention the exact price" (cf. *b. Šabb.* 151a).

A particular case specifically related to Passover is recounted in *m. Šabb.* 23:1:

> So, too, in Jerusalem on the eve of Passover when it falls on a Sabbath, a man may leave his cloak [as surety with the seller] and eat his Passover lamb and make his reckoning with the seller after the feast day.

In light of these pieces of evidence, it is certainly reasonable that Joseph purchased a burial cloth without significant practical or religious infractions.

Finally, (10) the Sanhedrin and Jesus' condemnation to execution would not have occurred on the night of the Passover (Mark 14:53–65).[37] This argument is based on a law valid at the time of the Mishnah that forbade such an act: "None may sit in judgment . . . on

[34] Ibid., 77.
[35] Ibid., 77–79.
[36] See ibid., 77–78.
[37] This argument applies equally to the Johannine account (18:12–13,19–24).

a feast day" (*m. Beṣah* 5:2; cf. *t. Beṣah* 4.4 [207.15]; Philo, On the Migration of Abraham 91). By way of response, first, the degree to which given stipulations included in the Mishnah were applicable at the time of Jesus is uncertain.[38] Apart from this issue, Jeremias offers a convincing interpretation of the Deuteronomic mandates concerning legal gatherings on feast days.[39] In essence, he argues that a close reading of Deut 17:8–13 requires that one sentenced to die during the feast be executed on the day of the feast.[40] What is more, it should come as no surprise that since the trial as a whole contained numerous irregularities, its timing was in violation of commonly accepted practice as well.[41]

John

As mentioned above, there are some indications that in John the Last Supper took place one day earlier than in the Synoptics (on Wednesday rather than Thursday night of Passion Week). This apparent contradiction is the most problematic biblical feature for determining the nature of Jesus' last meal with His disciples. Marshall notes that there are three basic solutions to this problem: (1) John's dating is historically accurate and the Synoptics are inaccurate; (2) the Synoptics are historically reliable and John is inaccurate; or (3) both are correct.[42] Those who defend the first solution usually do so because they find the evidence in the Synoptics self-contradictory while John's Gospel is internally consistent.[43] John's account, therefore, is chosen by default.[44] Those who defend the second solution believe

[38] J. Blinzler, *The Trial of Jesus* (Westminster: Newman, 1959), 149–57.

[39] See Jeremias, *Words*, 78–79.

[40] See ibid. for the complete argument.

[41] Marshall, *Last Supper*, 65.

[42] Ibid., 67. Of course, a fourth possibility is that both the Synoptics and John are historically inaccurate. For the relevant bibliography, see the sources mentioned in McKnight, *Jesus and His Death*, 265, nn. 20–22.

[43] Recall arguments from the previous section.

[44] D. A. Carson, *The Gospel according to John*, PNTC 4 (Grand Rapids: Eerdmans, 1991), 455–56. See R. T. France, "Chronological Aspects of 'Gospel Harmony,'" *VE* 16 (1986): 50–54, for a variation of this approach. France concludes that John's chronology is accurate (i.e., Jesus ate the Last Supper on Wednesday evening), and the Synoptics concur. For a summary of France's argument, see Carson, *Gospel according to John*, 456. More recently, McKnight takes this position (*Jesus and His Death*, 271–72).

that John introduces "an historical anomaly in order to gain a theological point."[45] This argument goes as follows:

> Jesus is not only the true temple [in John], the true light, the true vine, but the true paschal lamb: John places Jesus' death at the time of the slaughtering of the paschal lambs [on Thursday instead of Friday] in order to establish this next step in his replacement motif.[46]

Carson is correct to point out, however, that this theory is "theologically flimsy" because John's focus during Jesus' Last Supper was neither on the slaughter of the lambs nor on Jesus as the true Lamb of God. Moreover, as Carson rightly notes, this solution does not address John's alleged historical contradiction with the Synoptics.[47]

The third solution, namely that both John and the Synoptics are correct, best squares with the available data.[48] One popular resolution in this regard is put forth by Annie Jaubert. She argues, based on different calendars used in the first century, that John and the Synoptics are consistent in their portrayal of the Last Supper. While Jesus and His disciples followed the solar calendar of the Qumran community, the Pharisees and Sadducees followed a lunar calendar. These two calendars differed from each other sufficiently to allow for the Synoptics to record accurately the occurrence of the Passover meal on Thursday evening and for John to record it accurately on Wednesday evening.[49] The major weakness of this view is that there is no NT (or other) evidence to suggest that Jesus ever adhered to a Qumran calendar.[50]

[45] Carson, *Gospel according to John*, 456.

[46] Ibid.

[47] Ibid.

[48] Against C. K. Barrett, *The Gospel according to St. John*, 2nd ed. (Philadelphia: Westminster, 1978), 50–51; R. E. Brown, *The Gospel according to John XIII–XXI*, AB 29B (Garden City: Doubleday, 1970), 556; and R. Schnackenburg, *The Gospel according to St. John*, trans. C. Hastings et al. (New York: Crossroad, 1990), 3.36.

[49] A. Jaubert, *The Date of the Last Supper* (New York: Alba House, 1965). Cf. Carson, *Gospel according to John*, 457. Agreeing with Jaubert is E. Ruckstuhl, *Chronology of the Last Days of Jesus*, trans. V. J. Drapela (New York: Desclee, 1965). More recently, I. H. Marshall, in an update of his 1980 *Lord's Supper* volume, suggests that calendrical differences, although only hypothetical, "make[s] the best sense of the evidence" ("Chapter 11 – The Last Supper," in *Key Events in the Life of the Historical Jesus*, ed. D. L. Bock and R. L. Webb, WUNT 247 [Tübingen: Mohr Siebeck, 2009], 559).

[50] For a full critique of Jaubert, see J. Blinzler, "Qumran-Kalendar und Passionchronologie," *ZNW* 49 (1958): 238–51. See also N. Geldenhuys, *Commentary on the Gospel of Luke*, NICNT (Grand Rapids: Eerdmans, 1954), 649–70. For briefer critiques, see Carson, "Matthew," 530–32; L. A. Foster, "The Chronology of the New Testament," in *EBC* 1:599.

Carson rightly concludes that such "calendrical theories all involve delicate historical judgments or a paucity of hard evidence."[51]

Other, less widely held views that seek to harmonize John and the Synoptics include the following:[52] (1) Jesus, knowing that He would be killed at the Passover, celebrated a private Passover with His disciples one day early.[53] (2) Jews in Jesus' day celebrated the Passover on two consecutive days.[54] (3) The vast number of lambs needing to be sacrificed at the Passover caused the Galileans to slaughter their lambs on Nisan 13.[55]

Ben Witherington, finally, boldly proposes that in John, "we have a portrayal of a Greco-Roman banquet complete with closing symposion and the religious rites associated with such a meal. Jesus acts here as the sage, philosopher, and rhetor and offers his after-dinner teaching."[56] This representation, however, unduly neglects the clear Passover setting and symbolism pervading John's Gospel.[57] The harmonization of the Synoptic and Johannine accounts, for its part, depends on an accurate exegetical understanding of the three most problematic passages related to John's rendition of the Last Supper (13:1; 18:28; and 19:14), to which we now turn.[58]

[51] Carson, *Gospel according to John*, 457. Cf. Köstenberger, *John*, 400, n. 1.

[52] See also Marshall, *Lord's Supper*, 71–75; H. Hoehner, *Chronological Aspects of the Life of Christ* (Grand Rapids: Zondervan, 1976), 81–90; and Blomberg, *Historical Reliability*, 222–23.

[53] R. H. Fuller, *The Mission and Achievement of Jesus*, SBT 12 (London: SCM, 1954), 70–71; V. Taylor, *The Gospel according to St. Mark*, 2nd ed. (London: Macmillan, 1966), 664–67. The major problem with this view is that Mark 14:12 places Jesus' Last Supper on the day on which the lambs were slaughtered (but see R. T. France, "Chronological Aspects of Gospel Harmony," *VE* 16 [1986]: 50–54).

[54] D. Chwolson, *Das letzte Passamahl Christi und der Tag seines Todes*, 2nd ed. (Leipzig: H. Haessel, 1908), 20–44. Cf. J. Klausner, *Jesus of Nazareth: His Life, Times, and Teachings*, trans. H. Danby (New York: Allen & Unwin, 1947), 326–28; and M.-J. Lagrange, *The Gospel of Jesus Christ*, trans. Members of the English Dominican Province (London: Burns, Oates & Washbourne, 1947), 193–96. For a modification of Chwolson's theory, see Str-B 3.812–53.

[55] J. Pickl, *The Messias*, trans. A. Green (St. Louis: Herder, 1946), 120–22.

[56] Witherington, *Making a Meal of It*, 65; Witherington contends that the meals narrated in the Synoptics and John "are two different meals" (p. 80; see his treatment of John 13–17 in chap. 4). Witherington's entire discussion is highly idiosyncratic, including his identification of the "disciple Jesus loved" as Lazarus (pp. 68–79). For an adjudication of the historical setting of John's Gospel, see A. J. Köstenberger, *The Theology of John's Gospel and Letters*, BTNT (Grand Rapids: Zondervan, 2009), 51–86.

[57] See the discussion below.

[58] Cf. Köstenberger, *John*, 400–402, 524, 537–38; id., *Encountering John*, EBS (Grand Rapids: Baker, 1999), 146; Blomberg, *Historical Reliability*, 223–24; Carson, *Gospel according to John*, 460–61, 589–90, 603–4.

John 13:1

Argument: John says that the night before Jesus was crucified (and when the Last Supper was eaten) was "before the Passover Festival" (*pro de tēs heortēs tou pascha*; 13:1). Since the meal was eaten before the Passover, it cannot be a Passover meal.

Response: Most likely, the phrase refers to the footwashing only, which took place just before Jesus ate the Passover, not to the meal itself.[59] As Carson notes, "Theologically, the clause alerts the readers to the Passover theme developed throughout the book (2:13,23; 6:4; 11:55; 12:1; cf. 18:28,39; 19:14), inviting them to see in the footwashing an anticipation of Jesus' own climactic Passover act as the Lamb of God who takes away the sin of the world (1:29)."[60] Alternatively, the reference in 13:1 may be to Jesus already knowing prior to the Passover that His hour had come to depart from this world.[61]

John 18:28

Argument: On the morning after Jesus' last meal with His disciples, He was led from Caiaphas to Pilate for an impromptu trial. At this trial, the Jews sought to avoid ceremonial uncleanness by refusing to enter Pilate's Gentile palace so that they would be able to "eat the Passover" (*phagōsin to pascha*; 18:28). Since the Passover meal occurred after the events described in 18:28 (i.e., Jesus' trial), Jesus did not eat a Passover meal the night before with His disciples (13:1).

Response: This argument assumes that the phrase "eat the Passover" (*phagōsin to pascha*) refers only to the Passover meal proper (i.e., the Thursday evening meal). It is more likely, however, that this phrase refers

> not merely to Passover itself but to the Feast of Unleavened Bread, which lasted seven days (note Luke 22:1: "the Feast of Unleavened Bread, called the Passover"), and in particular to the feast-offering (*hagigah*), which was brought on the morning of the first day of the festival (cf. Num 28:18–19).

[59] Carson, *Gospel according to John*, 460.

[60] Ibid., 460–61.

[61] So Geldenhuys, *Luke*, 657; cf. L. Morris, *The Gospel according to John*, rev. ed., NICNT (Grand Rapids: Eerdmans, 1995), 545, who notes that the expression "is perhaps not as precise as most such notes." See also K. A. Mathison, *Given for You: Reclaiming Calvin's Doctrine of the Lord's Supper* (Phillipsburg: P&R, 2002), 206–7; and Jeremias, *Words*, 80, with reference with Zahn, Bauer, and Bultmann.

> "Eat the Passover" probably simply means "celebrate the feast" (cf. 2 Chron 30:21).[62]

In other words, John's use of *phagōsin to pascha* was tantamount to referring to "the many meals and celebrations that week in the Passover season."[63] The Jews in 18:28, then, were not referring to the Thursday night Passover meal. When interpreted in this way, John's chronological account of the trial does not conflict with the Synoptics.

John 19:14 (cf. 19:31,42)

Argument: John says that Jesus' crucifixion took place on "preparation day" (*paraskeuē*; 19:14), which was the day before Passover, that is, the day set aside by the Jews to prepare for the Passover meal. During Jesus' Passion Week, the day of preparation fell on Thursday. Thus, John places the crucifixion on Thursday, which means that Jesus ate His last supper with His disciples the night before on Wednesday (against the Synoptics).

Response: As I have written elsewhere,

> Matthew, Mark, Luke, and Josephus all use παρασκευή to refer to the day preceding the Sabbath.[64] The term therefore should be taken to refer to the day of preparation for the Sabbath (i.e. Friday).[65] If this is accurate, then τοῦ πάσχα (*tou pascha*) means not "of the Passover," but "of Passover week."[66] Indeed, 'Passover' may refer to the (day of) the actual Passover meal or, as in

[62] Köstenberger, *John*, 524. Cf. Geldenhuys, *Luke*, 649–70, see esp. 661–63; Carson, "Matthew," 531; and W. L. Lane, *The Gospel according to Mark*, NICNT (Grand Rapids: Eerdmans, 1974), 498.

[63] G. M. Burge, *The Gospel of John*, NIVAC (Grand Rapids: Zondervan, 2000), 499. Cf. Carson, *Gospel according to John*, 590; C. C. Torrey, "The Date of the Crucifixion according to the Fourth Gospel," *JBL* 50 (1931): 239–40; and T. Zahn, *Introduction to the New Testament*, trans. J. M. Trout et al. (Minneapolis: Klock & Klock, 1977), 3:282–83. L. Morris, *The Gospel according to John*, NICNT (Grand Rapids: Eerdmans, 1971), 778–79, disagrees, suggesting that πάσχα cannot refer to the Feast of Unleavened Bread apart from the Feast of Passover. Carson rightly retorts, however, that John's use of πάσχα does not exclude the Passover meal but refers to the entire Passover festival (*Gospel according to John*, 589–90).

[64] Matt 27:62; Mark 15:42; Luke 23:54; Josephus, *Ant.* 16.6.2 §§163–64.

[65] Cf. *Did.* 8:1; *Mart. Pol.* 7.1. See Torrey, "Date of the Crucifixion" (including his critique of Str-B 2.834–85 on pp. 235–36); A. J. B. Higgins, "Origins of the Eucharist," *NTS* 1 (1954–55): 206–9; C. I. K. Story, "The Bearing of Old Testament Terminology on the Johannine Chronology of the Final Passover of Jesus," *NovT* 31 (1989): 318; Blomberg, *Historical Reliability*, 223–24; Morris, *John*, 708; and H. N. Ridderbos, *The Gospel according to John*, trans. J. Vriend (Grand Rapids: Eerdmans, 1997), 606.

[66] So correctly the NIV (although TNIV has "Passover"). See also Carson, *Gospel according to John*, 604; against Barrett, *John*, 545; Brown, *John*, 882–83, 895. Also against those who, like Morris (*John*, 684–95, esp. 604–95), contend that Jesus and the temple authorities followed different calendars, with the Synoptics using Jesus' calendar (according to which the meal was

> the present case, the entire Passover week, including Passover day as well as the associated Feast of Unleavened Bread.[67] "Day of Preparation of Passover week" is therefore best taken to refer to the day of preparation for the Sabbath (i.e. Friday) of Passover week. Thus, all four Gospels concur that Jesus' last supper was a Passover meal eaten on Thursday evening (by Jewish reckoning, the onset of Friday).[68]

Apart from the above-cited evidence in 13:1; 18:28; and 19:14 that, instead of contradicting the Synoptic accounts, John's depiction of Jesus' Last Supper confirms them, there is substantial additional corroborating evidence in John's Gospel that aligns his account with that of the other canonical Gospels.[69]

Additional Corroborating Evidence in John

Further traces of the Synoptic chronology occur in John 13:2–17. That this is the same scene as the Passover meal in the Synoptics is confirmed by the account of Jesus' interchange with Judas the betrayer at the Last Supper (13:18–30) and the narrative of Judas' betrayal of Jesus and of Jesus' arrest in Gethsemane (18:1–11). John makes at least seven remarks that presuppose a Passover meal: (1) the meal occurred in Jerusalem (11:55; 12:12); (2) it took place at a late hour that lasted into the night; (3) it was celebrated with Jesus' closest circle of disciples (instead of with a larger group, as usual); (4) it was a ceremonial meal (recall the reclining at the table); (5) Jesus did not return to Bethany but stayed in the Garden in the Kidron valley; (6) the meal was taken in a state of Levitical purity (13:10); and (7) the disciples assumed that Judas was to purchase necessities for the feast or to distribute alms (13:29).[70]

Beyond these traces of the Synoptic chronology, John presents Passover symbolism in chaps. 13–17 that is unique to his Gospel:

> (1) Jesus' use of "vine" imagery in 15:1–10 may be predicated upon his and the disciples' partaking of wine just prior to his use of this imagery at the Passover meal.[71]

the Passover) and John using that of the temple authorities (according to whom the sacrificial animals were slain the following day; hence, Jesus was sacrificed as our Passover).

[67] Cf. Josephus, *Ant.* 14.2.1 §21; 17.9.3 §213; *J.W.* 2.1.3 §10; Luke 22:1.

[68] Köstenberger, *John*, 537–38, with reference to Carson, *Gospel according to John*, 603–4.

[69] Jeremias, *Words*, 81. Marshall, without exegetically engaging the Johannine data, argues that an "attempt to re-interpret the Johannine material to make it agree with the Synoptic dating involves a somewhat artificial reading of the crucial texts" ("Last Supper," 559).

[70] These seven points come from Jeremias, *Words*, 81–82.

[71] J. K. Howard, "Passover and Eucharist in the Fourth Gospel," *SJT* 20 (1967): 335.

> (2) The "bearing" and "taking away" language in John 15–17 may hark back to similar terminology in the reference to Jesus as the "Lamb of God" in 1:29. (3) "Glory" language binds together a cluster of motifs that center on Jesus' crucifixion as his glorification, a theology that is significantly indebted to Isaiah's depictions of the Suffering Servant, who . . . "was led like a lamb to the slaughter" (53:7).[72]

In light of the assessment of John 13:1; 18:28; and 19:14 above, and in view of the subtle traces of paschal characteristics in 13:1–17 and elsewhere, it seems amply justified to conclude that the Synoptic and the Johannine accounts concur that Jesus ate a Passover meal with His disciples on the Thursday night prior to His crucifixion on Friday.

Acts

Argument: In Acts 2:42, one finds an early reference to the first Christians' celebration of the Last Supper ("the breaking of bread"). This passage indicates that Jesus' Last Supper was not a Passover meal because the early church celebrated this particular supper daily (Acts 2:42), while the Passover meal was celebrated annually. The question arises as to how faithful Jews, who were taught from childhood to observe the Passover annually, could legitimately celebrate it on a daily basis.

Response: The faulty presupposition underlying this argument is that the early Christians in Acts 2:42 were seeking to replicate Jesus' Last Supper; rather, they sought to relive the "daily table fellowship of the disciples with [Jesus]."[73] "Only gradually," Jeremias observes, "was the early Christian celebration of meals linked with, and influenced by, the remembrance of the Last Supper."[74] In other words, nothing in the text indicates that the disciples or Luke, the author of Acts, intended to portray a Passover or eucharistic meal. What is more, Marshall adds, "[What] Jesus told the disciples to repeat was not the Passover meal [per se] but a particular ritual within that meal."[75]

Paul

Argument No. 1: In the context of a practical discussion on how to deal with an immoral church member, Paul states, "For Christ our

[72] Köstenberger, *Theology of John's Gospel*, 418. See the entire discussion on pp. 417–20.
[73] Jeremias, *Words*, 66.
[74] Ibid.
[75] Marshall, *Last Supper*, 63.

Passover has been sacrificed" (1 Cor 5:7). Paul, doubtless a committed Jew who understood the intricacies of the Passover activities, clearly identified Jesus as the Passover Lamb that was sacrificed. The Passover lamb was always sacrificed on Nisan 14 (on Thursday in the case of Passion Week). Paul, therefore, in comparing Jesus to this sacrificed Passover lamb, implicitly placed Jesus' crucifixion on Thursday rather than Friday. Thus Jesus' Last Supper with His disciples occurred the night before the Passover on Wednesday night, which was not the evening of the Jewish Passover.

Response: Jeremias rightly notes that Paul's comparison of Jesus to the Passover lamb more likely is linked to Jesus' broader sayings about Himself during the meal than to the actual time of His crucifixion.[76] Paul's point was not to present a chronological account of Jesus' last earthly meal. Instead, he more likely focused on the deeper theological implications of the event. No astute first-century Jew could miss the correlation between Jesus' identity and the Passover events. To argue that Paul had in mind the chronology of the specific Passover events, as Marshall rightly argues, "is surely to press the allusion too far."[77]

Argument No. 2: In 1 Cor 15:20, Paul calls Jesus the *aparchē tōn kekoimēmenōn* ("firstfruits of those who have fallen asleep"). Jewish firstfruits were offered on Nisan 16, which fell on the Saturday of Jesus' Passion Week. Paul's statements about Jesus as the firstfruits, then, suggest that Jesus rose from the dead on Saturday rather than on Sunday (against the Synoptics). If Jesus rose from the dead on Saturday, His crucifixion must have taken place on Thursday, with the Last Supper having occurred on Wednesday (Nisan 14), the day before Passover.

Response: This interpretation presses Paul's figurative use of *aparchē* too far. More likely, Paul intends a use of *aparchē* that more directly coincides with *prōtos* ("first").[78] As in 1 Cor 5:7, Paul's concern is not primarily that of Passover chronology.[79] It is exegetically naive to import chronological assertions concerning Jesus' resurrection into Paul's statement when the context suggests that Paul's primary concern was theological.

[76] Jeremias, *Words*, 74.
[77] Marshall, *Last Supper*, 64.
[78] Cf. BDAG 98.
[79] Marshall, *Last Supper*, 65.

Subtle Evidence that Favors a Paschal Interpretation

The discussion above focused on specific exegetical details in the relevant NT documents and concluded that Jesus ate a Passover meal with His disciples before dying on the cross. In this section, attention is focused more broadly on subtle pieces of evidence in the Gospels that are more indirect in nature.[80] The fact that these references are largely incidental, Jeremias suggests, "adds very considerably to their value as evidence," since they serve no particular purpose in the respective Gospel accounts.[81] The following twelve subtle pieces of evidence further demonstrate the paschal nature of Jesus' Last Supper.

(1) According to all four Gospel writers, the Last Supper took place in Jerusalem (Matt 26:18; Mark 14:13; Luke 22:10; John 13:1), which, during the Passover festivities, was direly overcrowded.[82] After entering Jerusalem during the last week of His life, Jesus spent His days teaching and ministering in the city but spent His nights in Bethany and the Mount of Olives (Matt 21:17; Mark 11:11,19; 14:3; Luke 22:39). Why would Jesus, who had friends and acquaintances in Jerusalem, not stay there overnight, which would have been more convenient than traveling to nearby towns? One possibility is that the city was too overcrowded to do so. In light of the cramped conditions in Jerusalem, one rightly wonders why Jesus chose to eat His Last Supper there. The answer, according to Jeremias, most likely is that the Passover lamb was expected to be eaten within the city gates.[83]

(2) Matthew (26:20), Mark (14:17), John (13:30), and Paul (1 Cor 11:23) all observe that the Last Supper took place at night. In Jesus' culture, two meals per day were customary, one between around 10 and 11 o'clock in the morning[84] and one in the late afternoon.[85] The afternoon meals lasted into the night only on special occasions.[86] One particular special occasion is most pertinent to Jesus' Last Supper, namely Passover. All the available data indicates that the Passover

[80] This section is adapted from Jeremias, *Words*, 41–62.

[81] Ibid., 41.

[82] For examples of the living conditions and problems that surfaced due to Jerusalem's overcrowding, see Josephus, *J.W.* 2.1.3 §12; *Ant.* 17.9.3 §217.

[83] *Sipre Num.* 69 on 9.10; *Num. Rab.* 7.8 on 5.2. See Jeremias, *Words*, 43, n. 6.

[84] *b. Šabb.* 10a (*bar.*); *b. Pesaḥ.* 107b; *Tg. Qoh.* 10.16–17. Note that in Acts 2:15, at 9 o'clock in the morning, the people had still not eaten breakfast.

[85] *Mek. Exod.* 18.13; *m. Šabb.* 1:2; *b. Pesaḥ.* 107b. Cf. Jeremias, *Words*, 44–45.

[86] *Deut. Rab.* 9.1 on 31.14; *Midr. Qoh.* on 3.2.

meal was to be eaten at night.[87] Since the Last Supper breaks with the common tradition of eating in the late afternoon, it most likely occurred during a special occasion. This special occasion was in all probability the Passover meal, since the Last Supper took place sometime during the Passover festival.

(3) Matt 26:20 and Mark 14:17 tell us that Jesus celebrated the Last Supper with the Twelve (see also Luke 22:14: "and the apostles with Him").[88] Jesus more often ate with larger groups of people (Mark 2:15; 14:3; Luke 7:36; 11:37; 14:1; cf. Matt 11:19). In light of this common practice, Jesus' limiting His table companions at the Last Supper to the Twelve is telling. The Passover meal had to consist of at least ten people,[89] which was also its average number of participants.[90] This was so because a one-year-old lamb would feed about ten people. Jeremias poses the question, "Is it chance that the small group in some ways corresponds to the Passover practice?"[91]

(4) All four Gospel writers record that Jesus and the Twelve ate the Last Supper while reclining at table (*anakeimai*; Matt 26:20; Mark 14:18; Luke 22:14 [*anapiptō*]; John 13:23,25). That Jesus and His followers reclined at table while eating this meal is significant because when the Gospel writers speak of reclining at meals, they refer to special meals in the open, at a party, a feast, a royal banquet, a wedding feast, or at the end-time banquet.[92] From the Gospel accounts, it is clear that Jesus and His disciples would not have reclined at table

[87] Exod 12:8; *Jub.* 49.1, 12; *m. Zebaḥ.* 5:8; *t. Pesaḥ.* 1.34 (cf. 158.4); 10.9 (cf. 172.27); *y. Pesaḥ.* 5.31d.27; *Sipre Deut.* 133 on 16.6; *Mek. Exod.* 12:6; Josephus, *Ant.* 18.2.2 §29. McKnight rightly asserts that the extant evidence is late and sparse concerning festal meals. In light of this, he suggests that it is "overzealous to think that only a *Pasah* meal could be eaten at night" (*Jesus and His Death*, 268). The evidence may be sparse, but it is a stronger foundation upon which to build a historical reconstruction than McKnight's speculations.

[88] As D. L. Bock, *Luke 9:51–24:53,* BECNT (Grand Rapids: Baker, 1996), 1719, n. 6, points out, "Luke likes to use this term [i.e. 'apostles'] for the Twelve" (with reference to 6:13; see id., *Luke 1:1–9:50,* BECNT [Grand Rapids: Baker, 1994], 541–42). See the thorough discussion in Köstenberger, *Theology of John's Gospel*, 77–78.

[89] *t. Pesaḥ.* 4.3; *b. Pesaḥ.* 64b; *Midr. Lam.* on 1.1; Josephus, *J.W.* 6.9.3 §§423, 425.

[90] According to Jeremias, both Josephus and the Talmud witness to this fact. This number, on occasion, could be exceeded (*m. Pesaḥ.* 8:3).

[91] Jeremias, *Words*, 47. Marshall balances this, however, by reminding us that "this particular point cannot be regarded as a compelling one since we have no proof whatever that Jesus usually ate with a larger company of people, and also since it is possible that some of the women associated with the followers of Jesus were present at the last meal" (*Last Supper*, 59). He does not explain why he thinks women could have been present. And it seems unlikely since the text restricts those present to the apostles or the twelve.

[92] For biblical references and further discussion see Jeremias, *Words*, 49.

during ordinary meals. That they did so during the Last Supper, then, indicates that they had a "ritual duty to recline at table as a symbol of freedom."[93] Such a ritual duty coheres well with the Last Supper being a Passover meal.[94]

(5) John seems to indicate that the Last Supper was eaten in a state of Levitical purity (13:10; cf. Num 19:19). Such Levitical purity was not required of ordinary people for the eating of regular meals. But when a person partook of the Passover, this called for ritual purity.[95]

(6) Matthew (26:21–26) and Mark (14:18–22) indicate that Jesus broke the bread during the course of the meal instead of at its outset. This is telling because ordinary meals in Jesus' day customarily began with the breaking of bread.[96] It was only during the Passover meal that a dish was served prior to the breaking of bread.[97] This is most clearly indicated in a record preserved from antiquity of a young child's question to his father about the Passover meal of which they were partaking: "How is it that on every other evening we dip bread into the dish but on this evening we simply dip (without bread) into the dish" (y. *Pesaḥ*. 10.37d, 4–5)?[98]

(7) Jesus served wine at the Last Supper (Matt 26:29 and parallels). This is notable since water was usually the drink of choice in everyday life and at ordinary meals and since wine was reserved for festive occasions.[99] Drinking wine at Passover was not optional but mandatory, even for the poor (*m. Pesaḥ*. 10:1). Most notable concerning the wine at the Last Supper was the fact that it was red, which is indicated by Jesus' comparison of it to His blood. At least three types of wine were available in Talmudic times: red, white, and black. R. Judah (c. D 150), who, according to Jeremias, represents an older tradition, specifically required that Passover participants drink red wine (*t. Pesaḥ*. 10.1

[93] Jeremias, *Words*, 49 (emphasis original). Extrabiblical literature reveals that such reclining at the Passover symbolized freedom from bondage (y. *Pesaḥ*. 10:37b, 53–54). Exodus 12:11, as Jeremias observes, "was regarded as a rule that was valid only for the actual exodus itself" (*Words*, 49).

[94] Marshall cautions, however, that "reclining was a feature of festive meals in general and was not confined to the Passover meal" (*Last Supper*, 59).

[95] Marshall rightly notes, however, that this is a "somewhat precarious deduction from the text, and it should be received with considerable caution" (*Last Supper*, 59).

[96] See Marshall, *Last Supper*, 21–23, for a description of the Jewish Passover meal.

[97] The festival meals of some upper-class citizens notwithstanding. See Jeremias, *Words*, 49.

[98] This assumes Mark's order can be trusted (Marshall, *Last Supper*, 60).

[99] *b. Pesaḥ*. 109a (Bar.). See Jeremias, *Words*, 50, nn. 8–11.

[172.14]; *b. Pesaḥ.* 108b).[100] In addition, according to R. Jeremiah (c. AD 320), the use of red wine at Passover was binding.[101]

(8) On the night of the Last Supper, some of the disciples thought that Jesus told Judas to "buy what we need for the festival" (John 13:29). The idea of making these purchases at night would make no sense if these events occurred on the evening before Nisan 14 (Wednesday), since all the local businesses would have been open the next day (Thursday). If these events, however, occurred on the evening of Nisan 15 (Thursday, the day before Passover), then the disciples' supposition would make perfect sense; they would assume that Judas must make his purchase "quickly" (John 13:27), because businesses would be closed the next day in celebration of Passover.[102]

(9) When Jesus told Judas, "What you're doing, do quickly" (John 13:27), some of the disciples thought Jesus meant for Judas to "give something to the poor" (13:29). Again, this piece of evidence makes most sense on the assumption that the Last Supper was a Passover meal, because it was customary to give alms to the poor on the night of Passover.[103]

(10) At the end of the Last Supper, Jesus and His disciples sang a hymn (Matt 26:30; Mark 14:26). According to Jeremias, this hymn can only be the second half of the Passover hallel, a common recitation after Passover meals. Marshall concurs: "There seems to be no evidence for a similar occurrence at the end of any other kind of Jewish meal."[104]

(11) Instead of returning to Bethany after the Last Supper where He had spent the preceding nights (Matt 21:17; Mark 11:11), Jesus spent the night on the Mount of Olives (Mark 14:26). Based on an exegesis of Deut 16:7, those observing Passover were required to spend the

[100] Jeremias, *Words*, 53.

[101] Marshall notes that a different color of wine could have been used "if the point of comparison was its fluidity rather than its colour" (*Last Supper*, 60). But this seems more implausible than the wine simply being red.

[102] For an explanation of why businesses would allow purchases on the evening before Passover, see Jeremias, *Words*, 53. E. Schweizer dismisses this argument by suggesting that this was a literary device used by John (*The Lord's Supper according to the New Testament,* trans. J. M. Davis (Philadelphia: Fortress, 1967], 31). But Marshall rightly notes that "even a literary device would have to be convincing to the readers" (*Last Supper*, 61).

[103] See Jeremias, *Words*, 54.

[104] Marshall, *Last Supper*, 61. It is unlikely that this description of the Last Supper was based on the early Christian practice (i.e., in Mark's day) of singing a hymn at the conclusion of the church's observance of the Lord's Supper (E. Schweizer, *The Good News according to Mark,* trans. D. H. Madvig (Atlanta: WJK, 1970], 307; see Marshall, *Last Supper*, 61).

night in Jerusalem. Since, as mentioned, the population of Jerusalem increased dramatically during the Passover festival, the city district was enlarged each year to make obedience to this command possible. Although Bethany fell outside of the enlarged district of Jerusalem, the Mount of Olives, including Gethsemane, was well within it. Jesus' breaking His pattern of returning to Bethany in order to remain within the district of Jerusalem may indicate that He was preparing for the Passover by being obedient to this traditional observance.

(12) While partaking of the Last Supper, Jesus spoke words of interpretation over the bread and the wine (Matt 26:26–29 and parallels). According to Jeremias, "Interpretation of the special elements of the [Passover] meal is a fixed part of the Passover ritual."[105] In other words, it was customary that the head of the family explained certain elements of the Passover meal. In doing so, there were often historical (Philo, *Spec.* 2.158; Josephus, *Ant.* 2.15.2 §316; *Sipre Deut.* 130 on 16.3) or allegorical (Philo, *Spec.* 2.158, 159–61; *Congr.* 161–67; QE 1.15; *Sipre Deut.* 130 on 16.3; *b. Pesaḥ.* 36a; 115b) interpretations placed on the elements of the Passover meal.[106] Most important, however, were the eschatological interpretations of the unleavened bread that were often given (*Midr. Song* on 1.8).[107] In the same way, Jesus, clearly in a ritualistic context, offered an eschatological interpretation of the bread and wine during His Last Supper with the disciples (Matt 26:29 and parallels). In light of the established tradition to offer such interpretations, Jesus' Last Supper was most likely a Passover meal. Jeremias avers that this final piece of evidence represents the most compelling argument.[108]

Conclusion

When Jesus sat down to eat His last meal with His disciples, it was in celebration of the Jewish Passover that commenced on the eve of the Israelites' exodus from Egypt. The Synoptics, John, Acts, and Paul concur in their portrayals of this supper. This unified portrayal is confirmed both by a close exegetical examination of all the pertinent passages and by the subtle pieces of evidences these writers left behind. Proposed historical, theological, and canonical inconsistencies related

[105] Jeremias, *Words*, 56.
[106] Cf. ibid., 58.
[107] Cf. ibid., 59.
[108] Ibid., 55. Against Schweizer, *Lord's Supper according to the New Testament*, 31.

to Jesus' Passover meal prove lacking under close scrutiny. Jesus' last meal, indeed, was in celebration of the Jewish Passover. With this fact secured, we are now in the position to explore its many theological implications.[109]

[109] I would like to acknowledge the competent help of my research assistant, Keith Campbell, in preparing this chapter. Keith was an invaluable help as I worked with him closely in reviewing the available literature and in crafting the argument of the present essay.

THE LORD'S LAST SUPPER IN THE FOURFOLD WITNESS OF THE GOSPELS

Jonathan T. Pennington*

Introduction and Method

The Gospels stand at the head of the NT canon as both the fount from which the apostolic witness flows and also the lens through which the Jewish Scriptures are to be read. For the church, the fourfold witness of the Gospels has always been seen as the fulcrum through which the shaped stones of both the old and new covenant writings are lifted and joined together in their proper places.[1] The relevance of this role is seen in heightened intensity when it comes to such a crucial event as Jesus' last meal with His disciples before His betrayal, arrest, crucifixion, and death. The thickness of meaning in the Lord's Last Supper is great, as it brings together key ideas and aspects from Israel's story and transforms them in a Messianic way in the church.[2] Thus, the fourfold witness of the Gospels to this vital event serves a crucial role in understanding how certain elements of the OT find their consummation in Jesus the Christ *and* how we are to understand the ongoing meaning of one of the church's most regular and important practices, the partaking of the Lord's Supper. One essay cannot of course pull together all such threads nor even gauge the depths of the ocean of significance to all of this. We can, however, attempt to sketch the contours of what the Evangelists would have us to know and understand concerning that last of many fellowship meals between Jesus and His disciples.

But before this exploration can commence we must comment on method. What kind of equipment is best to survey such a deeply

* Jonathan T. Pennington received his Ph.D. from the University of St. Andrews, Scotland. He is associate professor of New Testament Interpretation at The Southern Baptist Theological Seminary in Louisville, Kentucky.

[1] I develop more fully this idea of the Gospels as the fulcrum point or "keystone" of the arch of the Bible in my *The Gospels as Holy Scripture: A Guide to Reading the Gospels Wisely* (Grand Rapids: Baker, forthcoming).

[2] I find Tom Wright's comment not overstated that the Last Supper is "the central symbolic action which provides the key to Jesus' implicit story about his own death" (N. T. Wright, *Jesus and the Victory of God* [Minneapolis: Fortress, 1996], 554). We will return to what this means below.

founded incident as the Last Supper? In seeking to discuss any event or pericope that is shared among the Gospel accounts there is a choice of tools regarding one's approach and method. Namely, should we, as I am inclined to believe, focus on letting each Evangelist have his own voice, concentrating on how he tells his story and how his description of the Last Supper fits into his overall narrative? Following this would necessarily be some sort of description of what the Gospel narratives have in common. Alternatively, should we instead approach the fourfold witness of the Gospels querying the historical and theological function of the Last Supper in Jesus' ministry overall, followed secondarily with comments on some distinct emphases and particular theological *Tendenz* that each of the individual Evangelists seems to be making?[3]

The advantage of the former method is that by it we respect the reality that all history retelling is necessarily interpreted and involves interpretive selection, de-selection, crafting, and arrangement. Consequently, we will be wise to observe and respect the well-crafted point *of each Evangelist* rather than squashing them into a lowest common denominator mold that focuses only on the commonalities of the "event." Related, the disadvantage of the latter approach is that we can too easily fall into the problematic stance of focusing on the event of the Last Supper "behind the text"—i.e., the question of "what really happened on that misty night in Jerusalem?"—rather than on the only thing we actually have, the individual theological witnesses of the Gospel accounts.

Nevertheless, despite the potential dangers of an approach that begins with the overall picture constructed from all four Gospel accounts, I have decided that it is the most practical and heuristically effective way to proceed for this essay. This is because there is so much commonality of description, function, and meaning of the Last Supper across the Gospels that concentrating on the distinct elements within

[3] In large part we could classify these two approaches as the difference between a horizontal and a vertical reading of the Gospels. On another plane of discourse these approaches might also, but not necessarily, be construed as an "in the text" versus "behind the text" approach, respectively. There does seem to be a way, however, to read horizontally, i.e., across parallel accounts in the Gospels, without falling into the danger of a "behind the text" reading that supplants the witness of the Gospels themselves with our reconstruction of "what really happened." On "behind" versus "in" the text approaches, see *inter alia* the excellent essays in C. Bartholomew et al., eds., *"Behind" the Text: History and Biblical Interpretation*, Scripture and Hermeneutics Series, vol. 4 (Grand Rapids: Zondervan, 2003).

Matthew, Mark, Luke, and John would unduly sever the thick rope that ties together their understanding of what the Lord's Last Supper means in Jesus' life and ministry. Consequently, we will focus first on the historical considerations of the event and most on its several common nodes of meaning. This will then be followed by some comments concerning what unique contributions each of the Evangelists make.

Common Historical Considerations

I have registered above the potential danger of focusing too much on the "What really happened?" question in such a way that it excludes or overshadows the more significant textual *telos*: the meaning, function, and evocations of the Last Supper. Nevertheless, with an event such as this one that appears in all four of the Gospels but presents some apparently conflicting details, one is free to ask how we can, if at all, square the various elements of the event. This type of question, of course, is not new nor is it merely a result of the acids of Enlightenment historical criticism. A *primary* focus on this type of question, accompanied by a skepticism and an epistemological stance of the superiority and priority of this kind of knowledge *is* a function of the Enlightenment,[4] but not new is the simple question of putting together the details of the various witnesses within an assumption of its basic "historicality." Such questions are as old as the hills, or at least the Augustinian hills, where we find this kind of question regularly asked and answered.[5] After all, Christianity has always been a faith based on certain historical realities, both in the OT and the NT.[6]

There are three historical questions that arise immediately when one compares the four different accounts of Jesus' Last Supper. The largest one concerns how we are to correlate the accounts as found

[4] See especially Alvin Plantinga's astute taxonomy and challenge to the epistemological analysis of the various forms of Enlightenment historical biblical criticism in his essay, "Two (or More) Kinds of Biblical Scholarship," in Bartholomew et al., *"Behind" the Text*, 19–57.

[5] Augustine's extremely influential *Harmony of the Gospels* had as its main purpose to show how the four Gospels together are at one despite the variety of their accounts. Eusebius had done something similar in the first half of the fourth century in his *Gospel Questions and Solutions*. As an aside, it appears that the regular recurrence of addressing these questions in church history was the result of apologetic need. Some opponents of Christianity (e.g., Celsus) raised as an objection to the truthfulness of Christianity the variance in the accounts of the fourfold witness, and to this a response was required.

[6] One can think not only of many emphases on God's work on behalf of Israel, but also of Paul's strong argument in 1 Corinthians 15 regarding the centrality of the historical reality of the resurrection.

in the Synoptics with the various pieces and places in John that correspond to this same event. The second question is more specific: Was the Lord's Last Supper a celebration of the Passover meal or some other normal meal but invested with great significance? In reality the second question is a subset of the first. That is, there are many apparent differences here between John and the Synoptics, one of which is the chronology that potentially implies in John's account that the meal was *not* the Passover as indicated in the Synoptics. The third question concerns other discrepancies in the details between the accounts, including differences within the Synoptic tradition.

On the second question we may be allowed to comment only briefly as another essay in this same volume is addressed specifically to this topic.[7] In short, good arguments can be made that both John and the Synoptic witness understand this Last Supper to be a celebration—albeit with new, vested theological re-interpretation—of the Passover meal. In my opinion, Jesus intentionally celebrated the Passover meal a day earlier than the official Jerusalem one (and therefore necessarily devoid of a lamb[8]) because He knew of His impending death.[9] As R. T. France notes, "To describe this as a Passover meal correctly conveys Jesus' intention and the context within which his disciples would have understood it, even if it was unavoidably a day in advance."[10]

[7] See A. J. Köstenberger's essay in this volume, "Was the Last Supper a Passover Meal?" Even though my final understanding is not identical to Köstenberger's, he does provide a real service in summarizing the myriad views on this complicated issue.

[8] One of the arguments that Scot McKnight makes against viewing the Last Supper as the Passover meal is that it is "nearly incomprehensible" that Jesus would fail to refer to the "lamb" as His body and instead use the bread (*Jesus and His Death: Historiography, the Historical Jesus, and Atonement Theory* [Waco: Baylor University Press, 2005], 270). Not only is this an argument from silence (as McKnight admits), but it also overlooks the facts that the metaphor of "bread" is significantly more universal and transferable than "lamb"; Jesus had already used the image of "bread" to refer to Himself (cf. John 6); and "bread" is also a readily available and poignant OT image. We may also now add to this response the probability that while this was a Passover meal it was necessarily done without the lamb. Godet argues from the Mishnah that it was possible out of necessity to eat a Passover meal without a lamb, though the unleavened bread was still required (F. Godet, *A Commentary on the Gospel of St. Luke* [New York: Funk, 1881], 464).

[9] N.T. Wright helpfully observes how the symbolic action of the Last Supper correlates with the other great symbolic act of the Passion week, Jesus' actions in the Temple. Wright suggests that the significance of this is that Jesus may have been celebrating Passover early and in a lamb-less way thereby anticipating the coming Diaspora, without recourse to the Temple and its system, whose destruction He had predicted by His actions (Wright, *Jesus and the Victory of God*, 557).

[10] R. T. France, *The Gospel of Matthew*, NICNT (Grand Rapids: Eerdmans, 2007), 985.

The Question of John and the Synoptics

To the other two questions we may now turn. First, the largest one: How are we to understand the many differences between the Synoptic accounts and John concerning the timing and events of the Last Supper? The first and obvious item to note is that what manifests itself as a straightforward and simple event in the Synoptics appears with a seemingly different chronology and is drawn out and expanded in John's account. At the end of John 11 we already find reference to "the Passover of the Jews" being at hand (11:55). Then in chap. 12 we learn that Jesus enters the environs of Jerusalem "six days before the Passover" and has a supper with Lazarus, Martha, Mary, His disciples, and possibly others. On the following day Jesus enters Jerusalem with great fanfare. What follows in chap. 12 is a series of interesting pericopae concerning various responses to Jesus and His own reactions. Then in John 13 we read that "before the feast of the Passover" Jesus was at a supper with His disciples once again and, knowing His time was at an end, He rose and washed His disciples' feet. Typical of John's style, this event and dialogue is expanded and extends all the way through chap. 17 (the famous "Upper Room Discourse"), after which He and His disciples leave for the garden and Jesus' betrayal (18:1). Thus, this is clearly the same Passover festival time at the end of Jesus' life as we find in the Synoptics.[11]

We may note that in terms of relative size and length of the Gospel accounts, this event occurs very early in John in comparison to the Synoptics where the (final) entry into Jerusalem occurs only near the end of the accounts.[12] Also noteworthy is the observation that very little of what appears in John 12–18 can be found in the comparable Synoptic accounts. The one area of overlap most noticeable is the identification of Judas as the betrayer, but little else corresponds. If it were not for John's account, for example, we would be bereft of the

[11] Unless otherwise indicated, Scripture quotations are from the ESV.

[12] Of course, all of the Gospel accounts slow down significantly at the end of Jesus' life. The pace of each Gospel from the entry into Jerusalem on is noticeably slackened. Nevertheless, in terms of relative length John stands apart in the degree to which Holy Week is expanded. For Matthew and Luke this is most obvious, with the entry into Jerusalem and subsequent events making up a smaller portion of the total narrative (Matthew, eight chapters of 28; Luke, four and a half chapters of 24). Closer to John is Mark for whom the matter is weighted more toward the last week of Jesus' life (seven chapters of 16 total). But in all three cases, nothing would prepare one for the reading of John where the final events commence in chap. 12 after a relatively few number of stories and little direct teaching from Jesus. As a result, a full nine chapters of 20 (not counting the epilogue in chap. 21) are given to unpacking Jesus' last week.

image of Jesus washing His disciples feet at the Last Supper. Even more striking is what is absent from John relative to the other Evangelists: the very actions and words of institution concerning the bread and the cup. This is what we think of as constituting the Last Supper, and what apparently becomes the Christian tradition in part, as evidenced as early as 1 Cor 11:23–26. Not only is this seemingly crucial narrative missing in John's account of the Lord's Last Supper, but to add to our perplexity, it does find a parallel in the strongly worded discourse on flesh and blood much earlier in John 6:22–59.

Why the actions and words concerning the bread and the cup are absent in John's Upper Room Discourse is difficult to say. Unfounded is the ignoring of John as if he does not provide us a "Last Supper" account at all simply because the bread and cup language is missing.[13] One proposed solution is that John does not understand this meal as the Passover meal at all, and thus we should not be surprised that the bread and the cup, elements of the Passover celebration, are absent.[14] However, in light of the Synoptics' clear connection of the Last Supper with the Passover and the chronology that will be argued below that fits together the Synoptics with John, it is unlikely that John does not view the Last Supper as a Passover meal. Nor is the absence of the words of institution a smoking gun to this effect. John's frequent mention of the Passover from chap. 12 on sets up the reader to think about the Upper Room Discourse and meal as part of the Passover

[13] This seems the assumption behind Robert Stein's otherwise fine essay on the "Last Supper" in *DJG* and is a common approach in modern critical studies of the Gospels (e.g., McKnight, *Jesus and His Death*, 259). Stein does not discuss John 13–18 at all, only mentioning John 6:25–59 in a list of NT allusions to the Last Supper and briefly addresses the chronology discrepancy between John and the Synoptics. Instead, Stein discusses and classifies the "four accounts of the Last Supper" as falling into two groups—Matthew/Mark and Luke/1 Corinthians. John's absence from this schema is an overly narrow defining of the Lord's Last Supper by the language of the bread and cup.

[14] This view, which may be on the rise in scholarship, can be found in a variety of quarters, as can arguments to the contrary. One recent argument against associating the Last Supper with the Passover can be found in McKnight (*Jesus and His Death*, 260–75). A novel (but too narrow) variation on this theme is that of Ben Witherington who argues that John's Farewell Discourse is intentionally presented as a Greco-Roman meal *rather* than a Jewish Passover celebration because John desires to portray Jesus as Wisdom and to highlight "the more universal aspects of his character and teaching (cf. e.g. John 1), which would work well with Hellenized Jewish Christians in the Diaspora. In other words, Jesus is portrayed as offering teaching that anyone in the Greco-Roman world could make sense of and relate to" (B. Witherington III, *Making a Meal of It: Rethinking the Theology of the Lord's Supper* [Waco: Baylor University Press, 2007], 67). While I think there is something to this reconstruction, this is an unhelpful either/or. John does use more universally recognizable symbols, but he also overtly connects these events with the Jewish Passover.

celebration. The flexibility of letting each Evangelist have his own voice and tell his own story is elastic enough to accommodate this difference between the Synoptics and the Fourth Gospel. John has chosen to emphasize other elements, such as the footwashing and the prayer for unity in the community, while not stating explicitly what was obviously a very early Christian practice of the Lord's Supper.

This may be simply another example of the common phenomenon where the most obvious thing about the meal—the bread and cup—was so well known in Christian tradition by John's time that it was not stated explicitly. It is certainly not the case that John's theological understanding is unable to accommodate the same notion of the bread and the cup, as the expanded discussion along these lines in John 6 makes clear. In fact, there are other clues that John 6 is to be read in conjunction with the Synoptic tradition. The only non-Passion story that appears consistently in all four of the Gospels is this miraculous wilderness feeding, along with its accompanying water crossing. These feeding stories in the Synoptic version are clearly and intentionally connected with their own Last Supper depictions and the words of institution explicitly; the Evangelists expect us to see the overlap between the wilderness feedings and the Last Supper.[15] When we take the fourfold witness as a whole, then, it is not difficult to see multiple strands of interconnectivity which are not easily separated or un-twined. The internal cross-referencing between the Synoptics and John goes both ways. We as readers of the canonical Gospels naturally and rightly see the connections between John 6, Jesus' symbolic wilderness feedings, John 13–17, and the words of institution in Matthew, Mark, and Luke. Only one set on not seeing all these events as connected could possibly come to that conclusion.

The lack of the bread and cup in John may simply be yet another example of the way in which John has built upon the foundation of the Synoptics by assuming some knowledge thereof and both (1) expanding upon this framework with additional and supplemental

[15] It has been long recognized that there is an intentional verbal parallel between the wilderness feedings and the Last Supper, seen through the repetition of the same words in the same order. Matthew 14:19 reads λαβὼν τοὺς πέντε ἄρτους . . . εὐλόγησεν καὶ κλάσας ἔδωκεν τοῖς μαθηταῖς τοὺς ἄρτους. Cf. 26:26—λαβὼν ὁ Ἰησοῦς ἄρτον καὶ εὐλογήσας ἔκλασεν καὶ δοὺς τοῖς μαθηταῖς. With minor differences in tense, Mark 6:41 and 14:22 can likewise be compared, as can Luke 9:16 and 22:19. In all three instances, Jesus' taking and blessing and giving of the bread follows a formulaic, repeated pattern.

material,[16] and (2) taking some thread or theme in the Jesus traditions and expanding and explicating it.[17] There is no need to dichotomize John and the Synoptics on this score; they are speaking to the same event and reality, while speaking in their own, inspired voices.[18]

The Question of Discrepancies of Detail within the Synoptic Tradition

We may now address our last historical question: How are we to understand differences within the Synoptic tradition? Regularly and inevitably within the Synoptic accounts there are minor disparities of wording and emphasis. Such differences are to be expected and those of note will be commented on below in the discussion of the unique contributions of each Evangelist. But here under the topic of historical considerations there is one obvious discrepancy that has stirred debate throughout the centuries: Luke's "second cup" and his presentation of the words of institution that seem to indicate an order of "cup-bread-cup." This is an incongruity because not only does it conflict with Matthew and Mark's order of just two elements, bread and cup, it also does not correspond to the earliest Christian traditions of the Lord's Supper, as witnessed in 1 Corinthians 11 and the churches' widespread practice.[19]

[16] For a brilliant exposition of how John's Gospel "dovetails" with Mark's account, see R. J. Bauckham, "John for the Readers of Mark," in *The Gospels for All Christians: Rethinking the Gospel Audiences*, ed. R. J. Bauckham (Grand Rapids: Eerdmans, 1998), 147–72.

[17] Again, one may refer to R. J. Bauckham, "Historiographical Characteristics of the Gospel of John," *NTS* 53 (2007): 17–36 (republished in R. J. Bauckham, *The Testimony of the Beloved Disciple: Narrative, History, and Theology in the Gospel of John* [Grand Rapids: Baker, 2007], 93–112).

[18] Adolf Schlatter suggests that John's omission of the words may be because he was polemically fighting against the way that the church of his day was "transform[ing] the sacrament into a sanctuary for itself," turning it into something we do as a sacrifice rather than God's gift of love to us in the sacrament. John opposes this "by directing attention away from the mere bread and wine, to the flesh and blood of Jesus which he gave for them unto death and thereby made the bread of life" (A. Schlatter, *The History of the Christ: The Foundation of New Testament Theology*, trans. A. Köstenberger [Grand Rapids: Baker, 1997], 359).

[19] It should be noted that the *Didache* does give instructions in the order of the cup then bread. "And concerning the Eucharist, hold Eucharist thus: First concerning the Cup, 'We give thanks to thee, our Father, for the Holy Vine of David thy child, which, thou didst make known to us through Jesus thy child; to thee be glory for ever.' And concerning the broken Bread: 'We give thee thanks, our Father, for the life and knowledge which thou didst make known to us through Jesus thy Child. To thee be glory for ever'" (*Did.* 9:1–3, trans. K. Lake, *Apostolic Fathers*, LCL [New York: G. P. Putnam's Sons, 1912–13]).

One attempt to solve this dilemma occurred very early and at the textual level. A very few texts, most notably Codex D, contain a shorter reading of only Luke 22:17–19a, thus eliminating the problem of two cups by removing vv. 19b–20 (though it should be noted that this still does not change the order of "cup-bread"). However, both on internal and external grounds, the full reading of 22:17–22, as found in the NA[27] is to be preferred.[20] Thus we are left with an apparent difference between Luke and the rest of the traditions.

Not surprisingly, various interpretations have been offered to explain this discrepancy. Augustine, laboring painfully to show how the four Gospels have "an entire freedom from contradictions," argues that Luke has, according to his habit, introduced the event by anticipation, and that what Luke is saying is "exactly what stands expressed by those other evangelists." It is difficult to know precisely what Augustine is saying here, but it seems to be that there is only one cup and that the cup mentioned in v. 17 is an "anticipation" of the cup in v. 20, added by Luke. Augustine does not give much of a reason as to what Luke's motive in doing so would be, except that this is Luke's habit.[21]

Similarly, Calvin inquires if the double cup is a simple repetition, "as the Evangelists are wont frequently to say the same thing twice," or if Christ, after having tasted the cup, repeated the same thing a second time. The former view may be a reference to Augustine's argument (a regular conversation partner for Calvin), but Calvin argues instead for the latter, saying that this was the ancient practice of the solemn rite of first *tasting* the cup as part of the holy feast. Jesus then follows this by instituting the new mystery, "which was a totally different institution from the paschal lamb."[22] Calvin is insistent that the new ceremony instituted by Jesus was not part of the actual Passover celebration, thus mixing "this new and more excellent supper" with the former banquet. Rather, it was a separate rite that He created after the paschal rites were completed. This is what Luke means by saying

[20] This is a change of opinion from Westcott and Hort and even from the first edition of the RSV (1946), and has now come to be the dominant view, as reflected in the critical editions of the GNT. Among others, one may consult the discussion in D. L. Bock, *Luke 9:51–24:53*, BECNT (Grand Rapids: Baker, 1996), 1721–22.

[21] Augustine, *Harmony of the Gospels*, *NPNF[1]* 6.177. Interestingly, in my edition there is an editor's footnote that reads, "Luke's first reference to the cup belongs to the Passover celebration, in distinction from the Lord's Supper" (ibid., n. 5). This seems to be an attempt to clarify, but does not accord with Augustine's own view.

[22] J. Calvin, *Commentary on a Harmony of the Evangelists, Matthew, Mark, and Luke*, trans. W. Pringle (Grand Rapids: Baker, 1993), 3:203.

that "after he had supped" Christ gave the cup.[23] Thus, in effect there was but one cup that Jesus first tasted and then distributed, and all of this took place after the Passover meal was completed. Fast forward 400 years and a mid-twentieth century scholar in the Reformed tradition, Norval Geldenhuys, argues that the details between the accounts matter not as much as the fact that "on the occasion of the Passover the Savior instituted the Holy Communion by giving bread and also by giving wine." The sequence is not stated, and the church under the guidance of the Spirit generally took the bread then wine, but the NT does not expressly state the sequence in which Jesus instituted it.[24]

Most contemporary scholars are not content with such a generalized understanding nor do they argue along the lines of Augustine or Calvin. Instead, most observe that the Passover ritual involved four cups and that this explains why more than one cup appears in the event. At least the first cup would have been one of the ritual cups from the actual Passover rite; the second cup could be as well or a separate cup after the meal. This is the view, for example, of Craig Blomberg who argues that the original event, as part of the four-cup Passover ritual, involved Jesus saying something about the cup, then bread, then cup. He does not see this as an insurmountable historical discrepancy because "Luke has described what actually happened by referring to an earlier cup which Mark and Matthew failed to mention." Thus, Blomberg understands this example under the category of "Excerpting different portions of a longer original."[25] Joel Green says that the first cup may be the first one of the Passover meal, but Jesus' interpretive words in Luke 22:18 are more appropriate to the second cup.[26] Darrell Bock considers the arguments of some that the cup of 22:17 is the third "cup of blessing" from the Passover meal, maybe doubled and repeated by Jesus so that He can bring His own innovations to the significance of that cup. However, Bock finds it more natural to understand the cup in 22:17 as the first cup of the Passover, with Jesus assuming the headship of the meal (like a Jewish father) and making remarks that lead to the meal's latter portion and produce a "fresh rendering of the imagery in terms of what is about

[23] Ibid., 204.

[24] N. Geldenhuys, *The Gospel of Luke*, NICNT (Grand Rapids: Eerdmans, 1951), 554.

[25] C. Blomberg, *The Historical Reliability of the Gospels* (Downers Grove: InterVarsity, 1987), 133–34.

[26] J. Green, *The Gospel of Luke*, NICNT (Grand Rapids: Eerdmans, 1997), 761.

to take place."[27] Other modern commentators would fall into these same categories.

I find Bock's view most persuasive, that the first cup of Luke 22:17 is actually the first cup of the Passover meal. What is most significant is how this serves both at the event and in Luke's presentation as a summarizing, over-viewing statement. That is, Luke 22:15–18 should be understood as a summary statement framing the whole Passover meal that they are celebrating, showing how it is the last one for Jesus (and by implication, the last regular Jewish Passover for the disciples as well) and is being transformed into a forward-looking meal. This is separate from the actual words of institution that we think of for the Lord's Supper and the order for this which is found consistently in Matthew, Mark, Luke (22:19–20), and John 6. Thus, Luke 22:14–18 are words that are appropriate for the Passover celebration, re-interpreting and redefining it, while vv. 19–20 are emphasizing the new covenant perspective.[28] Moreover, this is not a situation where there is a cup-bread-cup order and therefore no need to appeal to 1 Cor 10:16–17, which is especially odd in light of the clearer connection and reproduction of the tradition in 1 Cor 11:23–26, but rather these are initial, opening comments that frame the whole Passover, followed later by the actual institution of what will become the Lord's Supper.[29]

In sum, the apparent historical differences here between Luke and the rest of the tradition are not insurmountable and indeed reveal a skilled interpretive framing on the part of Luke. As Bock observes, summarizing statements on the many differences within the traditions: "What is clear is that the various renderings portray the significance of what took place; these traditions complement each other with emphases that are clearly associated with the portrayed events. The base of the accounts is fundamentally similar, with Jesus' sacrificial role clearly present. The differences reflect alternative ways to summarize and emphasize the event's implications."[30]

[27] Bock, *Luke 9:51–24:53*, 1723.

[28] Whether the familiar and traditional cup-bread portion was performed as part of the Passover meal or upon its completion I do not know.

[29] In some ways this corresponds to the thrust of Calvin's view, namely, that vv. 16–18 (what he understands as the "tasting" of the cup) serve to introduce the re-interpretation of the Passover.

[30] Bock, *Luke 9:51–24:53*, 1717.

Common Themes within the Gospels

Having addressed these historical considerations regarding the Lord's Last Supper we may now turn our attention to the texts themselves and the important matter of how the fourfold Gospel witness interprets the meaning and significance of this event.

In addition to the arguments made above about the essential similitude of the historical representation of the four Gospel accounts—particularly, that they are referring to the same event and that this event was a celebration of a Passover meal one day earlier than the official one—we may also observe some other common elements found in all four accounts.

At the most basic level it is obvious that the events preceding the Last Supper occur during the last week of Jesus' earthly life, and particularly the last night with His disciples before His betrayal, arrest, trial, and crucifixion. We may also observe that these events clearly occurred in and around the environs of Jerusalem. Moving beyond these mere facts, we may note that in all four accounts the events and Jesus' teaching take the form of a "farewell discourse," a climactic gathering and instruction before a great leader's death. In the ancient world such events were commonly remembered as key times in the life of a community and great significance was placed on the last words of the leader.[31] Also, with the exception of Luke, the Evangelists all connect Jesus' anointing with ointment (for His burial) at a meal in Bethany as a story right before the Passover Last Supper. This shows the theme of Jesus' imminent death as an important set up for the Last Supper.[32]

[31] Jewish examples include Genesis 49; Deuteronomy 33; Joshua 23; *1 Macc* 2:49–70; *Tob* 4:3–12; *Testaments of the 12 Patriarchs*; Josephus, *Ant.* 4.8.1–48; *Testament of Abraham*; *Testament of Job*; *Testament of Moses*; and at Qumran, *Testament of Qahat* (4Q542). Some would see 2 Peter in the NT as an example of testamentary literature. In the more modern period one can think of the great importance placed on the final deathbed words of an influential leader like Jonathan Edwards.

[32] It is unclear why Luke lacks this story which is so closely paralleled in both Matthew (26:6–13) and Mark (14:3–9), and even John (12:1–6). Many commentators have given Luke 7:36–50 as a parallel but at least in the Synoptic tradition this story reads quite differently in terms of the setting, characters, and Jesus-stated point. Complicating and confusing this situation even more, however, is that in the John version there seems to be a conflating of these two different traditions in that it is connected with the geography and chronology of the end of Jesus' life at the Passover time in the Jerusalem area, and Jesus' comments connect it to His coming burial and Judas's indignation (all paralleling Matthew and Mark on these points). Yet at the same time John agrees with Luke that this was an anointing of Jesus' *feet* (not head as in Matthew and Mark) and included a wiping of Jesus' feet with the woman's (in John, "Mary's") hair.

Not surprisingly, when we restrict our examination to what elements are common in the Synoptic tradition, allowing John to stand to the side for a moment, we find many consistent features. The most important one is what we may call the "geographical overlay" of the Synoptic tradition. That is, likely following Mark's schema, Matthew and Luke share with Mark a pattern of events that presents Jesus' ministry in three successive phases of (1) in Galilee, (2) the journey from Galilee to Judea, and then (3) in Jerusalem. This structure, according to R. T. France, "represents a conscious structuring of the story within a geographical framework which owes more to Mark's systematization than to the actual movements of Jesus throughout the period after his baptism."[33] The Synoptic tradition gives the impression that Jesus did not visit Jerusalem at all until the final week of His life, but this conflicts with "the far more historically plausible account of John, who has Jesus, like any other religiously observant Galilean, making regular trips between Galilee and Judea, particularly in connection with the major festivals."[34] In the Synoptic pattern Jesus' experiences in Jerusalem are all withheld from the narrative for the climactic rhetorical and theological effect of Jesus' move from successful ministry in Gentile (and second-class Jewish) Galilee to His rejection in Jerusalem. His Last Supper in Jerusalem, along with the other surrounding events, is part of the strong point made by the Evangelists that while the rest of the world embraced and sought Him, the city of the Jewish leaders instead brought His life to an end.[35]

Nodes of Meaning in the Fourfold Witness

Even more significant than the ways in which the Gospels testify together to common elements historically and narratively, we find several key theological themes that the Evangelists communicate through their retelling of the Last Supper stories. It is important to acknowledge that the Gospel writers are already theologically interpreting and applying for us the significance of this event; this is its "meaning." It is unhelpful to think of the Gospels as the "datum"

[33] France, *Matthew*, 3.

[34] Ibid., 3.

[35] This reading is not to suggest that John and the Synoptic tradition are in irreconcilable conflict. Rather, it is to observe that, as often occurs in ancient historiography, variation in chronological sequence for thematic reasons is accepted within the realm of honest historical reporting.

and the Epistles only as the interpretation and application. There is a sense in which the Epistles are a further, more specific application of the Jesus traditions to particular situations. But we are mistaken if this recognition makes one think of the Gospels themselves as being "just the facts, ma'am" from which the rest of the NT draws its inspiration and application. Rather, the Gospels are the first level of theological reflection upon and application of Jesus' life and teaching.

As with any important event or idea, there is not simply one point or thought or "meaning" being communicated; the most important events and ideas spin off in many avenues of meaning/application. When one strikes the hot metal of significant realities, many sparks fly. This is certainly true with such a weighty, heated incident as the Last Supper.

It will be helpful to think of these various flying sparks as different *nodes* of meaning within the thick, broad structure of ideas that the meaning is. Even as the word "node" has a variety of uses, so too we may think of a text-event as having many nodes or points of outstanding thought that also connect with other ideas. In its use in the realm of computer science, a "node" is a placeholder for some information or a "block of memory" that contains both stored data and references to other nodes. A chain of linked nodes, then, creates a large data structure of interwoven ideas. So too, the Last Supper as presented in the Gospels provides many interconnected nodes of meaning. Our metaphor of a node speaks to the fact that these concentrations of communicative meaning overlap much in content and thrust, while they also can be identified as distinct. We can identify five such thematic nodes—The Last Supper as (1) an enacted parable of Jesus' impending sacrificial death, (2) the fulfillment of the Passover and exodus, (3) the inauguration of the new covenant, (4) the formation of Jesus' community and their identity, and (5) an appetizer for the Messianic eschatological banquet.

(1) An Enacted Parable of Jesus' Impending Sacrificial Death

Godet remarks that "every covenant among the ancients was sealed by some symbolic act."[36] This observation speaks to the significance of symbolic acts or enacted parables in communicating the weight of important events, and one does not have to think very hard to recall

[36] Godet, *Luke*, 466.

many such examples throughout the Scriptures. The prophets would not only speak the word of the Lord in parabolic form, but often they acted out memorable images of God's revelation, such as Ezekiel picturing the siege and plight of Jerusalem and her people (Ezek 4:1–5:4; 12:1–20; 24:15–27), Isaiah walking around naked and barefoot for three years as a sign against Egypt and Ethiopia (Isa 20:2–6), and Nehemiah literally shaking out the folds of his garment as a picture of God shaking out everyone who does not fulfill their promise to Him (Neh 5:13).[37] Enacted parables provide powerful mental snapshots that deepen and extend the effectiveness of the words and events, preserving their memory in the mind's eye. It is not difficult to see that Jesus' words and actions at His Last Supper serve to mark His disciples' memories with an unforgettable picture of His life and teaching. This certainly includes Jesus' self-humiliating act of washing His disciples' feet (John 13:1–17), as well as the very tactile and multi-sensory experiences of the snapping break of the unleavened bread and the taste of the warm, blood-red wine. To appreciate fully the significance of the Lord's Last Supper we must consider that the parabolic enacting of the events—both originally and in their two-millennia-old re-enactment—is a significant part of how they communicate. They make the events of the Last Supper something not just to be reflected upon and proclaimed, but also to be experienced with our senses.[38]

While parables of all sorts do provide experience and not merely information, these are not mutually exclusive goals; indeed, parables provide experience in large part *through* cognition of certain realities. So, we may ask, what is this enacted parable about? What is it communicating? The answer to that is found in many ways by looking at the other four themes or nodes I have identified below. The Lord's Last Supper in all its aspects is a symbolic acting out of multiple theological truths. But particularly, we can identify these events as *live-action metaphors for Jesus' self-chosen, impending death as a sacrifice for His disciples*.

As was mentioned above, the Gospel accounts, despite their many differences, are uniform in placing these events on the very threshold

[37] Cf. the helpful discussion of the OT's extensive use of parables in K. Snodgrass, *Stories with Intent: A Comprehensive Guide to the Parables of Jesus* (Grand Rapids: Eerdmans, 2008), 38–42.

[38] I was happy to find David Wenham argue in a very similar way, calling the Last Supper a multimedia verbal drama that we experience in the Lord's Supper through not only words but also touch, sight, and taste as well (D. Wenham, "How Jesus Understood the Last Supper: A Parable in Action," *Them* 20.2 [Jan 1995]: 14–15).

of Jesus' arrest and death. Everything in the narratives has been leading to this point, and these events find much of their *theological* import by their *chronological* placement. Jesus has been regularly anticipating and speaking of their trip to Jerusalem and His impending betrayal and death.[39] This fellowship meal takes on much of its significance precisely because it is their last of many such meals. These observations point us toward understanding Jesus' death as at the heart of the point of the parabolic picture of the Last Supper.

A closer reading of the texts surrounding the Last Supper also reveals many indicators that Jesus' death should be understood as the focal point. For example, the event is framed and interwoven with the sections about Judas's betrayal of Jesus.[40] This sets up the reader to be thinking about Jesus' impending death. Moreover, Matthew, Mark, and John all retell the story of Jesus' anointing by one "Mary"[41] as part of the buildup to the Passover, and Jesus explicitly comments that this was done in preparation for His burial.[42] Additionally, the Passover-week setting of the Supper, with its high point of the atoning, sacrificial lamb, easily pushes our thoughts toward Jesus' own death as we read the Supper account.[43] Finally, it is interesting to observe how even with John's notorious lack of the technical words of institution,[44] his story of Jesus washing the disciples' feet also serves to highlight Jesus' death as the focus of the Last Supper. In this important event Jesus is teaching many things concerning service and humility, but He is also, as Wenham rightly observes, enacting a parable of His death. His actions in the footwashing are types of what He is about to do on the cross, laying aside His garment (literally and metaphorically) and

[39] For example, Matt 16:21–23; 17:22–23; and 20:17–19.

[40] Judas's agreement to betray Jesus is found in Matt 26:14–15, immediately preceding the Passover in vv. 17–30, and the first part of Jesus' discussion at the table also focuses on this betrayal (vv. 21–25). Identical is Mark's rendering in 14:10–21. Luke likewise sets up the Passover celebration with reference to the plot to kill Jesus (22:1–6). His account varies from Matthew and Mark only slightly in putting the discussion of the betrayer *after* the words of institution.

[41] As is common when comparing John with the Synoptics, the fourth Evangelist gives much more specific detail in terms of times, places, and names. So too here, where John identifies this woman as one of the Mary's, while Matthew and Mark have only "a woman," as does Luke 7, if indeed his story is to be understood as a parallel.

[42] Matt 26:12; Mark 14:8; John 12:7.

[43] Yet again John makes the connection even stronger than the Synoptics by stating that Jesus was crucified and died on "the day of Preparation," which readers would understand as the time when the ritual lambs are sacrificed (cf. this explanation in part in Luke 22:7).

[44] Though these words are missing, it is not difficult to see how they could easily fit into John's narrative in chaps. 13 or 17, in a "John for the readers of Mark" kind of way.

undergoing great humiliation. "In washing the disciples' feet Jesus explains that his death is lowly service for others, that his purpose in dying is to wash them . . . and that they must receive his service. . . . The incident is an acted version of Jesus' saying in Mark 10:45."[45]

If this framing of the Last Supper were not enough to incline us to see Jesus' impending death as central, then we can find further confirmation in the actual images that are used and their accompanying explicit commentary: broken bread as His body "given for you" and poured out wine as His blood. "Blood poured out" is an obvious metaphor for violent death (e.g., Gen 9:6; Lev 17:11; Isa 59:87; Ezek 18:10), and, as Green observes, "'Giving one's body' is potent as an image for giving one's life (in battle) for the sake of one's people."[46] As McKnight points out, even though unleavened bread by itself does not necessarily connote sacrificial death, in combination with the image of the cup, we are right to understand Jesus' offering Himself to His followers as "an act of offering them the protection of a sacrificial death or participation in that death."[47]

Thus, at the core of the theological meaning of the Lord's Last Supper is the self-giving, sacrificial death of Jesus. This is a death that the rest of the NT makes abundantly clear is "for the forgiveness of sins," as Matthew makes explicit as well (Matt 26:28). This by no means exhausts its meaning, however, and is not unrelated to other nodes of meaning, especially the inauguration of the new covenant (through His blood) and the way in which this parabolic act is a fulfillment (and recasting) of the exodus and story of Israel. To these related ideas we can now turn.

[45] Wenham, "How Jesus Understood," 15.

[46] Green, *Luke*, 761. While affirming the insight of this comment, I remain baffled as to Green's statement in the same context that the breaking of the bread itself is "devoid of symbolic significance" and bears no metaphorical weight, but is merely preparatory for the distribution of the bread. Not only is bread already a heavily freighted symbol, but the breaking of the bread is easily connected to Jesus' violent death, even as the image of poured out blood is. Also unclear to me is why Green, following M. Barth, argues that Jesus is *not* enacting His death through His actions here but rather "interpreting through his words the significance of this Passover and, thus, of his death" (p. 762). While the latter is certainly true and important, the former is not a necessary corollary of this nor is this a situation where we must make an either/or choice.

[47] McKnight, *Jesus and His Death*, 281. It should be noted, as McKnight makes clear in his subsequent argument, that he distinguishes this language of "sacrificial death" from the idea of "atoning death," instead preferring the idea of Jesus' death as "protective" from the wrath of God's judgment.

(2) The Fulfillment of the Passover and the New Exodus

As we have discussed above, there is renewed debate about whether Jesus was celebrating a/the Passover meal on the night of His betrayal and arrest. I believe He was, albeit, out of necessity, a night earlier than the official Jerusalem Passover. But even for those who are not inclined to this understanding, virtually all would acknowledge that the Lord's Last Supper occurred during the celebratory week of *Pesach*, a week that was alive with meaning, and therefore, no meal or ritual at this time would be free from these powerful associations.[48]

So, on any account the Passover connection is a central one for understanding the Last Supper. We may ask then, "Why the Passover?" That is, there are many other significant holy days that Jesus could have chosen to associate with His death. For example, Yom Kippur, Rosh Hashanah, Purim, or the Sukkot. Each of these would have been appropriate, and Christ-connections can be (and have been) made for each of them—rich and thick figural connections. We must remember that Jesus clearly chose *when* to enter Jerusalem, and once there He egged on and aggressively sparred with His enemies through both His words and deeds,[49] precipitating His own demise. All of this intentionally aligned His last week with the celebration of Passover. Why? Because Jesus and the Evangelists understand the life, death, resurrection, and ascension of the Messiah to be the fulfillment of the Passover and the corresponding inauguration of the new exodus.

In the stories of the OT there is no more central event than the exodus, by which God rescued His people, delivered them from bondage, covenanted with them, and thereby identified them as His own, all the while promising them a final Messiah to come.[50] In the last 600 years before Christ, the vision and hope for the return of God's reign and

[48] McKnight, *Jesus and His Death,* 275. As we have seen, McKnight argues against the Passover meal interpretation (though with some hesitation and several qualifications), but rightly notes that "every meal that week would be swallowed up in *Pesah* celebrations. . . . The week was alive."

[49] The cleansing/cursing of the Temple being the most obvious example, in one (table-clearing) swoop managing to offend *all* the various Jewish sects at once. He also engaged in verbal debates that left Him standing as irrefutable, followed by His own harsh condemnation of His opponents (cf. Matt 21:23–23:36).

[50] Examples of passages throughout the OT and Second Temple literature which speak to the centrality of the exodus are too numerous to demarcate, but on this last point of the expectation of a Messiah, cf. Deut 18:15–22 with its forward-looking promise of a prophet like Moses with the closing words of the Pentateuch which sadly note that "there has not arisen a prophet since in Israel like Moses" (Deut 34:10).

the restoration of His people becomes the great refrain of the prophets. None proves to be more important in this regard than Isaiah, who pictures the return of God as a new creation and a new exodus, intentionally re-appropriating these events to describe the eschaton.[51] The canonical connections do not stop here, however, as Isaiah's prophetic word proves to be foundational to the NT's self-understanding and witness, being re-appropriated yet again into the stories of Jesus and the church. As has been astutely shown by several scholars, the "Isaianic new exodus" undergirds and structures much of the narrative and theology of Gospels and Acts,[52] not to mention the centrality of Isaiah for Paul's theology.[53]

Thus, the interpretive move to present Jesus' work as the Passover fulfillment and new exodus is not isolated in the Gospels to the Last Supper event. This connection is found throughout the Gospels, but especially in the way in which all four Evangelists intentionally and intimately connect the Last Supper with the feeding of Israel in the wilderness at the exodus. In the Synoptics this is done artfully through a two-step process that first identifies Jesus' water crossing and wilderness feeding as a new exodus, and then second by intra-textually connecting this with the Last Supper.[54] In John, what I affectionately call "the Gospel for dummies," the same sequence of feeding and then water crossing occurs (John 6:1–15 and 6:16–21), but lest anyone

[51] The second part of Isaiah, as introduced by 40:1–11, regularly pictures the eschaton in these ways. Cf. especially 65:17–25 and 49:8–12.

[52] See *inter alia* M. Strauss, *The Davidic Messiah in Luke–Acts: The Promise and Its Fulfillment in Lukan Christology*, JSNTSup 110 (Sheffield: Sheffield Academic, 1995), and especially R. E. Watts, *Isaiah's New Exodus and Mark*, WUNT 2.88 (Tübingen: Mohr Siebeck, 1997) and D. W. Pao, *Acts and the Isaianic New Exodus* (Grand Rapids: Baker, 2000). More generally, in his extensive works N. T. Wright has argued for Jesus' self-understanding to be that of fulfilling the story of Israel, the story which clearly has as its beginning (and end), the exodus. See N. T. Wright, *The New Testament and the People of God* (Minneapolis: Fortress, 1992) and *Jesus and the Victory of God*.

[53] See, for example, J. R. Wagner, *Heralds of the Good News: Isaiah and Paul "In Concert" in the Letter to the Romans* (Leiden: Brill, 2002).

[54] The juxtaposition of water crossings and wilderness feedings in the Gospels (e.g., Matt 14:13–21 and 14:22–33; cp. 15:32–39; Mark 6:30–44 and 6:45–52; cp. 8:1–10) has long been recognized as an intentional allusion to the exodus events being redone and recast by Jesus. Luke does not have the comparable water crossing story, but his account of the miraculous feeding (9:10–17) clearly alludes to the exodus, and this connection is strengthened by the soon-following Transfiguration story in which Luke reports that Jesus was speaking with Moses and Elijah (author's translation) "about His exodus which He was about to fulfill in Jerusalem" (ἔλεγον τὴν ἔξοδον αὐτοῦ, ἣν ἤμελλεν πληροῦν ἐν Ἰερουσαλήμ). Also commonly observed is how the Synoptics use the same sequence of words in the miraculous feedings as will later occur in the Last Supper event. See note 15 above.

miss the exodus connection, John also provides the explicit teaching that Jesus is the bread that came down from heaven, comparing Himself (positively) to the bread that the fathers ate in the wilderness (6:26–59). We have already observed how intimately connected John 6 is with the Last Supper; one need not strain to see the link. Thus, all four Evangelists point the reader to hearing evocations of the exodus even before the culminating event of the Last Supper itself. Then, at the apex of *Pesach* week celebrations, Jesus makes the connection clear through His actions and words of institution.

The theological significance of this inter-connectivity is great. Even as the Passover-Exodus was the calling out and forming of the people of God, their liberation from bondage, and the (re-)establishment of their covenant with God, all through the picture of blood sacrifice, so too was Jesus' Last Supper.[55] Each of these realities finds their fulfillment and consummation in the Christ and His work.

We may also note an important way in which this particular node of meaning overlaps with that of the Last Supper as an enacted parable discussed above. Wright has helpfully observed how Jesus regularly retold, re-appropriated, and re-centered the story of Israel around Himself, often using apocalyptic-prophetic parables.[56] We have argued that the Lord's Last Supper is an enacted parable, much like the prophets' actions. In this particularly Jesus is doing nothing new in that the Passover celebration itself is already a symbolic meal, performed each year as part of the foundational Israel-identity story. What *is* new is how Jesus twists and changes it to be centered on Himself. The key to discerning the significance of such a twist is knowing the "straight" from which it came. Anyone can understand an event or story at a surface level with no previous knowledge. But the greatest colors and hues and shades of meaning come from knowing the way in which this story relates to and subverts the previous stories to which it is connected.

This also helps us see both the continuity with the original exodus, as well as the implied discontinuity: Jesus is not merely another prophet or even another Moses who is calling God's people back to

[55] McKnight, *Jesus and His Death*, 275, succinctly observes that Jesus "assigns to the bread and wine an apparent redemptive meaning that expresses exodus theology." Jesus will endure sufferings not unlike the children of Israel which will lead to a redemption not unlike theirs (280).

[56] See part 2 of Wright, *Jesus and the Victory of God*.

Sinai. He is taking up the foundational story and identity of Israel and drawing it (and them) into His person and work as the eschatological fulfillment of all God promised. The bread and wine are not just presented as symbols of the exodus but are said to be *His* body and *His* blood, thereby establishing the new covenant, a covenant that is inescapably centered on Him.

(3) Inauguration of the New Covenant

We noted above under the discussion on an enacted parable Godet's statement that "every covenant among the ancients was sealed by some symbolic act."[57] We may now focus on the former part of this quote, namely, how the symbolic act of the Last Supper pictures the inauguration of the new covenant in Christ. This also overlaps with our preceding discussion of the Passover and exodus significance of the Last Supper. Schlatter astutely observes that Jesus chose to go to His death at the time of Passover "because in his death he would exercise the office of the Christ, combining its gracious effect with the ancient revelation of God. In a word, he instituted the new covenant on the day commemorating the old."[58]

Interpreters have long seen the connection between the Last Supper and the coming of the new covenant, and justifiably so. There are several clear ways in which these two are connected by the Evangelists. The first and most obvious one is the explicit words to this effect repeated by Matthew, Mark, and Luke. The "words of institution" in the Gospels uniformly identify the cup as the symbol of the blood of the covenant (Matt 26:28; Mark 14:24; Luke 22:20). Matthew and Mark's phrasing is a bit awkward: "this is my blood of the covenant, which is poured out . . . " compared to Luke's smoother and more explicit "this cup is the new covenant in my blood which is poured out . . ." (NIV). But even though only Luke has the qualifying adjective "new," the notion is the same and no less is intended in Matthew and Mark.[59] Because of our familiarity with Christian tradition, it is somewhat surprising to learn that the idea of a "new covenant" or

[57] Godet, *Luke*, 466

[58] Schlatter, *History of the Christ*, 353.

[59] The majority of extant manuscripts do include καινὴ ("new"), but not the weightiest, and this is easily discernible as likely assimilation to Luke and Paul. Allison does not hold back from stating that in Matthew's phrase "the main point seems to be that Jesus' sacrifice is the basis of a new covenant" (W. D. Davies and D. C. Allison Jr., *Matthew*, ICC [Edinburgh: T&T Clark, 1997], 3:472).

even "renewed" covenant is not something explicitly spoken of elsewhere in the Gospels. With the exception of Luke 1:72 and its language of God promising to remember "his holy covenant," the only use of the word "covenant" (*diathēkē*) that occurs in any of the Gospels is here in the parallel passages of the Last Supper. Both Paul and especially the author of Hebrews testify, however, that Jesus' words of institution become central in understanding God's new covenantal work in Christ.

The other main way in which the Last Supper pictures the inauguration of the new covenant is through its thick OT intertextuality. That is, the language of Jesus' words here intentionally evokes at least two important OT passages that point toward the new covenant in Christ. The first is Exod 24:6–8, speaking of "the blood of the covenant" being "poured out," words which undoubtedly inform the phrasing in the Gospels. This is a piece of the strong Moses-Jesus typology and comparison that is made throughout the Gospels.[60] As Allison states,

> There is a typological relationship between the act of Moses and the act of Jesus, a relationship consistent with and reinforced by the Moses typology present elsewhere. As the first redeemer made a sacrifice for the people so that they might enter into a new covenant with God, so does the last redeemer inaugurate another covenant by offering his blood, that is, his life, for the forgiveness of sins.[61]

We might add to this insight the also present typological connection of the Passover lamb. Even as the death of those lambs with their visible blood on the Israelites' lintels provided an escape from death, the opening of deliverance and the road to Sinai, so too the Lamb of God will be sacrificed to bring about a new relationship with God.

Also behind Jesus' words is the familiar and foundational prophecy of Jer 31:31–34 where there is the promise of an eschatological "new covenant" grounded in the forgiveness of sins. Again, this is most clearly connected in Luke (and Paul in 1 Cor 11:25), but it also serves as the background for Matthew and Mark; Luke makes explicit what is implied elsewhere. Interwoven with this is the equally familiar vision of Isaiah 53, which likely also informs the language of "poured out for many" and "for the forgiveness of sins," precisely what the

[60] See D. C. Allison, *The New Moses: A Matthean Typology* (Minneapolis: Fortress, 1993).

[61] Davies and Allison, *Matthew*, 3:473. We may also note that Heb 9:15–22 also cites this text in its argument, and it is likely also alluded to in 1 Pet 1:2.

messianic Servant will do for God's people (Isa 53:4–12).[62] All these thick connections with the OT lead R. T. France to regard the language of the words of institution as "the most comprehensive statement in Matthew's gospel of the redemptive purpose and achievement of Jesus' death."[63] Presumably the same could be said for the other Gospels. In an interesting way, then, while it is the *actual* death and resurrection of Jesus that inaugurates the new covenant between God and humanity, it is the reflection upon them in the Lord's Last Supper that explains and exposits the meaning of those yet-to-happen events, events which get rather brief treatment in the narratives.

Thus, in the midst of the multiple and rich meanings that the Lord's Last Supper is communicating, the meal, in the hands of the Evangelists becomes for us "an occasion to recall and reflect on Jesus' death and the inauguration of the new covenant."[64]

(4) Community/Identity Formation

The previous three nodes of meaning are easily recognizable and overlap extensively with each other as the discussion has shown. There is another point of significance in the thick node-map of the Lord's Last Supper that has not been as commonly observed, namely, how the Supper serves to form and re-form the community and identity of Jesus' disciples. And though it is not as frequently discussed, this idea in fact overlaps quite a bit with our preceding analysis. The connection between community formation, Passover, and new covenant inauguration is very close and more intimately connected than we might at first realize. This is because the celebration of the Passover was an important family and national identity event and because to inaugurate a covenant is to form a community. There is no such thing as an "empty covenant," that is, one devoid of participants. Rather, a covenant is the formation or re-formation of the people in their relationship to God, making them into a community and indelibly forming their identity. As France observes, by describing Jesus' death

> in terms of a "covenant," a relationship between God and his people, Jesus has directed attention to the new community which is to result from his

[62] France, *Matthew*, 994. At least in the case of Matthew we may strengthen this reading with reference to Matt 1:21, which sets up Jesus' mission as to "save his people from their sins," as well as with 20:28, which uses Isaiah 53 to describe Jesus' death as a ransom (cf. Mark 10:45).

[63] Ibid.

[64] Bock, *Luke 9:51–24:53*, 1717–18.

> redemptive death. Here then is the essential theological basis for that new community of the restored people of God which this gospel has increasingly set before us as the result of Jesus' ministry. It is as people are associated with him and the benefits of his saving death that they are confirmed as members of the newly reconstituted people of God.[65]

All this takes on an added measure of significance in light of the formation of this people of God at the family-focused time of the Passover celebration. Not entirely unlike today, but with greater import, Snodgrass explains, meals in the ancient world, especially celebratory banquets, "were among the most important contexts for social relations. They were the primary context in which shame and honor were assigned. Meals were and are a means for organizing society."[66] A Jewish meal such as the Passover was one in which people would gather by families, identifying themselves together. It was "the high point of the annual celebration for Jewish families,"[67] and the head of the household would preside over the ritual aspects of the meal, explaining their significance. In this case Jesus has called out His disciples from their own families and life situations and is identifying them as His own, true family, for "whoever does the will of my Father in heaven is my brother and sister and mother" (Matt 12:50).[68] This is a radical redefinition of identity for the disciples.[69]

The significance of this is great. Not only is Jesus making a covenant with them through His death (now being performed symbolically and proleptically), but He is also forming them into a family, re-orienting their identities around Himself. As Joel Green rightly summarizes, "Sharing a meal has more generally a community-building or boundary-making function, and this function is escalated in this scene in two ways. First, it is explicitly designated as a Passover meal—typically shared among a family or a fictive kin group. Second,

[65] France, *Matthew*, 994–95.

[66] Snodgrass, *Stories with Intent*, 307–8. The honor and shame element of meals may also explain why Jesus chose to emphasize His betrayal (by Judas) at this otherwise sweet fellowship time. Credit for this suggestion goes to Matthew Crawford.

[67] France, *Matthew*, 980.

[68] Wright observes that "Passover would normally be celebrated by families; but Josephus can speak of it being celebrated by what he calls 'a little fraternity,' and in any case, as we have seen, Jesus regarded his followers as a fictive kinship group" (*Jesus and the Victory of God*, 555). France calls Jesus' upper room disciples the "close-knit group of traveling companions" who form the family group and who share in the ceremonial Passover meal (*Matthew*, 979).

[69] For a discussion of how Jesus' redefinition of family identity relates to Christian counseling, one may consult my essay, "Christian Psychology and the Gospel of Matthew," *Edification* 3.2 (2009): 39–48.

Jesus interprets the character of this meal as a foundational, covenant-making event."[70] The idea of having a common cup, given by Jesus to His disciples, underscores this idea.[71]

In this regard we can see again how John's depiction of the Last Supper is not in contradiction to the Synoptics but complements and enhances aspects that are more briefly summarized in the first three Gospels. Particularly, the lengthy teaching of Jesus in the Upper Room Discourse focuses on the mutual love and unity and solidarity of the disciples with Jesus and, by extension as His family/body, with each other. Not only in the content of what is said, but especially in the action of the footwashing, Jesus models for them the nature of this communal life together.[72] His new community is illustrated here as it is elsewhere in Jesus' teachings: the kingdom of heaven is marked by the topsy-turvy ethos of Jesus' ways: sacrificial service toward others—the least as the greatest—all modeled ultimately in Jesus.[73] As Witherington notes, the footwashing episode at the meal, coupled with His prayer for unity in John 17, depicted a social rearrangement of perceptions and practices.[74]

Thus, our main point to make here is that there is not only a crucially vertical (God-humanity covenant) and eschatological (new exodus) aspect to the enacted parable of the Last Supper, but there is equally a horizontal, new covenant community aspect. And particularly, taking the fourfold witness of the Gospels together, this community is identified as the followers of Jesus who are known by their love for one another and solidarity. Confirmation of this reading can be found in part by considering the earliest recorded application of

[70] Green, *Luke*, 756. Green understands the Last Supper as a Passover meal constructed along the lines of a Greco-Roman symposium, following M. Barth who says that in the Hellenistic era the Passover evolved into a Greek festival meal or symposium. It should also be noted that here "fictive kin" does not mean "fictional" or "imaginary" as some readers might assume. Rather, this is a term used to refer to people who are not related by birth but who live and function as a family.

[71] "If, as seems probable, Jesus' instructions to his disciples to share a common cup are unconventional, [citing H. Schurmann, *Der Paschamahlbericht* (Münster: Aschendorffsche Verlagsbuchhandlung, 1953), 60–61] this would underscore all the more the solidarity of those gathered, with regard both to the meal and to what it signifies" (Green, *Luke*, 761).

[72] We may also observe how this model of humility finds parallel in Matthew 18 with its corresponding teaching on community identity, there focusing on the related idea of forgiving one another graciously.

[73] Cf. also Green's comments: The Last Supper heightens the relevance of all subsequent Christian meals as "times of celebration and eschatological anticipation, characterized by a reversal of normal status-oriented concerns and conventions" (*Luke*, 761).

[74] Witherington, *Making a Meal of It*, 65.

the Last Supper to the Christian churches. In his first canonical letter to the Corinthians, the Last Supper serves for Paul as illustrative of this same point. In 1 Cor 10:14–22 the unity of the body of Christ in the Lord's Supper is used as part of Paul's argument against partaking in the table of idols. Even more expansively, 1 Cor 11:17–34 with its reiteration of the words of institution, has as its purpose not so much to teach or outline what was widely known and practiced about the Last Supper, but to *apply* it to horizontal unity among believers. The Last or Lord's Supper is used by Paul to exhort believers to unity and mutual forgiveness, thus confirming and applying the pictures of community given to us in the Gospels' Last Supper accounts.

(5) Appetizer of the Eschatological Banquet

We may finally consider one more node of theological meaning inherent in the Lord's Last Supper. And yet again we will see that this idea overlaps significantly with the others. The Last Supper is meant to picture not only the fulfillment of past promises of God and the present impending death of Jesus, but just as much the assured future of an even greater meal in the coming kingdom of God. Each of the four Evangelists makes this point. In Matthew and Mark the words of institution end with this climactic statement that Jesus will not drink of the fruit of the vine again until the coming of God's kingdom (Matt 26:29; Mark 14:25). Luke is even more emphatic, choosing to front this theme in his summary of the event *before* the parallel words of institution and doubling this idea by connecting the kingdom to both the bread and the wine (Luke 22:15–18).[75] And John is not to be left out. In John 6:51–58 Jesus makes the eating of His flesh and drinking of His blood necessary if one is to have "eternal life" and be raised up "on the last day," both phrases that are John's preferred way of talking about the Synoptics' coming "kingdom."[76]

[75] Further evidence that we are reading Luke's emphasis correctly can be found in Paul's use of the Lukan version of the Jesus tradition here, to which Paul amends this concluding commentary: "For as often as you eat this bread and drink the cup, you proclaim the Lord's death *until he comes*" (1 Cor 11:26, my emphasis).

[76] It appears that John, conscious of the Synoptic Jesus traditions, intentionally identifies certain phrases that he prefers with others used by the Synoptics. For example, in Mark 9:42–10:31 there are several texts that use "kingdom of God" and "life" or "eternal life" in parallel and interchangeably. Likewise, in John 3 we find that "kingdom of God" is used in parallel with "eternal life." This is our literary clue that these are to be understood as the same, and by making this connection early on in his Gospel, John is freed up to use "eternal life" the rest of the time,

This future kingdom language in the Last Supper should not be a surprise in light of the dominance and centrality of this theme in Jesus' ministry. Indeed, it would be surprising if an event of such weighty significance as the Last Supper did *not* touch on the theme of the eschatological kingdom. And again, Jesus' choice of timing to bring this theme of the kingdom to a climax at the Passover is no mere coincidence. Jesus is taking up the celebration of the past deliverance of God and translating it into an image of "the eschatological advent of God's dominion."[77] The Last Supper reiterates the hope that Jesus' disciples have for the ultimate eschatological banquet feast.

But it is not only the Last Supper that points in this direction. The importance of the eschatological banquet aspect of the Last Supper is heightened when one considers the broader context for this theological idea. At least as far back as Isaiah, the image of a feast has served as a potent image for God's restoration of His people.[78] The book of Revelation is not writing *de novo* when it speaks of the eschaton as "the marriage supper of the Lamb" (Rev 19:9). In the Gospels this theme proves important. Jesus' wilderness feedings, as we have seen, are intentionally connected with the Last Supper, and in them Jesus is providing a foretaste of God's provision for His people in the last days. Along with His healing ministry, Jesus' provision of food is intended to confirm that in Jesus the kingdom of God has come. In addition to these events, Jesus' teaching also regularly uses the idea of a future kingdom banquet. For example, in Matt 8:11–12; Luke 13:28–30, and 22:28–30, Jesus promises to reward the faithful with a place at His table. In response to someone's proclamation that "Blessed is he who shall eat bread in the kingdom of God!" (Luke 14:15 NKJV) Jesus proceeds to tell a story which serves as a warning about those who will not "taste my banquet" (Luke 14:16–24). One can also think of a parabolic image such as the king who throws a wedding feast for his son, a parable whose end is as clearly eschatological in meaning as it is disturbing (Matt 22:1–14). Thus, when we get to the Last Supper itself the talk of eating this meal again in the coming kingdom makes more and deeper sense.

including in it the notion of the kingdom. Cf. Bauckham, "Historiographical Characteristics of the Gospel of John," 35.

[77] Green, *Luke*, 761.

[78] See Isa 25:6–9; cf. also 55:1–5.

In his profound reflections, Adolf Schlatter observes that the Last Supper was a "farewell and love meal" in which Jesus raised the thoughts of His disciples beyond just the current moment or the past celebration. "The meal he shared with them now was not their last, since he described for them the coming new communion as a table fellowship characterized by the use of the festive cup, which he would drink with them again."[79]

Conclusion

The banquet of the Lord's Last Supper as presented by the Evangelists is as rich and deeply aged as the finest wine that could be imagined. Foundational, varied, and overlapping grand themes are brought together into the polyvalent nodes of meaning that the Last Supper contains. An overall view of the Last Supper as it comes to us in the fourfold witness of the Gospels reveals that it is temporally tri-perspectival: It looks back to the cross as the place of Jesus' broken body and poured out blood; it looks around at the present with its emphasis on Communion with each other and the presence of the risen Lord with His people; and it looks forward to the day when this meal will be seen as a mere tidbit from the banquet buffet of the eschaton.

Distinctive Voices from Each of the Evangelists

As was discussed at the beginning, I have chosen to focus our analysis of the Lord's Last Supper on those aspects and elements that are common to the fourfold witness. This is because in this event and its interpretation the Evangelists sing with much accord. This is not to say, however, that they do not differ at points. At times one will step to the front to sing a particular recitative or will add in a new line of harmony. While we do not want to so focus on these moments that the common melody is overpowered, we will find benefit in listening a bit to the particular voice of each of the Evangelists as they retell and interpret the Last Supper.

Matthew

For Matthew the most important distinction can be found in two little phrases that are unique to his presentation. These two phrases

[79] Schlatter, *History of the Christ*, 357.

are freighted with much Matthean theology and are mutually interpretive. They are "for the forgiveness of sins" in 26:28 and "with you" in v. 29.

I have suggested above that Jesus' (Synoptically consistent) language of "blood poured out" and "(new) covenant" entails the idea of forgiveness of sins as it evokes the images of Exodus 24, Jeremiah 31, and Isaiah 53. Thus, the fact that it is Matthew alone that contains the whole phrase, "this is my blood of the covenant which is poured out for many *for the forgiveness of sins*," does not mean that he alone is intimating this interpretation.[80] Rather, the significance of this fuller and explicit statement is found in how it triggers insight into the frequency of this theological theme in the first Gospel.

Matthew's prologue already contains the programmatic statement that this miraculous child is to be named "Jesus, for he will save his people from their sins." This sets up a frequented theme in Matthew, wherein not only is Jesus shown to be the One who is able to forgive sins (especially, 9:1–8), but Jesus' disciples are constantly exhorted to forgive one another; this is an essential mark of being a Christian.[81] Thus, when we get to 26:28 this theme is already much on the reader's mind. And it works the other way as well. As Ulrich Luz observes, "The passages in Matthew that summon to the forgiveness of sins . . . receive their depth from the Lord's Supper. To forgive others their guilt is to participate in the mission of Jesus and to reflect the gift received from him."[82] Therefore, we may note that Jesus' entire earthly ministry as depicted in Matthew is framed with reference to this theme of forgiveness of sins.[83]

The other related framing reference is the overlapping idea of "God with us." Back in the story of Jesus' naming, we not only find the notion of salvation from sins, but also the dovetailed idea of God's (covenantal) presence. Matthew comments on the naming of Jesus

[80] Schlatter observes that because of the firm link already there in Jeremiah 31 the enacting of the new covenant entails the idea of the forgiveness of sins. "It would be a vapid notion to propose that Jesus had never considered what Jeremiah said about the new covenant, and that Matthew was the first to see this link" (*History of the Christ*, 356, n. 37).

[81] For example, 5:23–24; 6:14–15; 18:15–22 and its supporting parable in 18:23–25. Cf. the request for the forgiveness of our sins in 6:12.

[82] U. Luz, *Matthew 21–28: A Commentary*, trans. J. E. Crouch, Her (Minneapolis: Fortress, 2005), 3:383–84.

[83] Cf. the helpful summary of this in M. Hasitschka, "Matthew and Hebrews," in *Matthew and His Christian Contemporaries*, ed. D. C. Sim and B. Repschinski (London: T&T Clark, 2008), 92–97.

that this "fulfills" the words of Isa 7:14 that the name of the son will be "Immanuel, . . . which is translated, 'God with us'" (Matt 1:23 HCSB). At first glance this may seem a poor connection to make, but further reflection discloses the intimate link between the dual gift of God forgiving sins and giving His own presence. For God to be with His people is to favor and bless them and forgive them. This is nothing less than the communion of God with His people, the great goal of creatures ever since we have been east of Eden.

For Matthew, as with forgiveness of sins, the idea of God's presence becomes a framing and overarching truth. It is not accidental that the programmatic statement from 1:23 finds its corresponding bookend in the climactic promise in the Great Commission: "Behold, I will be with you always, even unto the consummation of the age" (28:20, author's translation). But this idea is not only there, but is also found in other crucial places, most notably in 18:20, which describes the church's functioning, as well as here in the Last Supper (26:29).[84] The communal emphasis on partaking of the same cup together becomes a proleptic promise that will find its fulfillment in the coming of the Father's kingdom.

To sum up, in the Last Supper Matthew chooses to particularly highlight God's gracious forgiving of our sins and its correlative giving of Himself in communal presence. "According to Matthew the reason behind Jesus' entire earthly life and ministry lies in the salvation from a situation of sin as a distorted relationship with God."[85]

Mark

In terms of unique contributions from Mark there is not a great deal to say. This is because Mark and Matthew are nearly identical in their presentations, and when they do rarely differ it is Matthew who has the fuller phraseology. The only exception to this is the phrase in Mark 14:23, "they all drank of it." This emphasizes the disciples' solidarity, maybe a bit stronger than Matthew, though this idea is certainly not absent in Matthew's parallel rendering as a command rather than a statement: "Drink of it, all of you" (Matt 26:27).

[84] One may also rightly note the connection with Jesus' self-revelation to His sea-tossed and scared disciples in 14:27: θαρσεῖτε, ἐγώ εἰμι.

[85] Hasitschka, "Matthew and Hebrews," 97.

There is one way that Mark seems to emphasize a particular theme, and this is discernible by recognition of this motif throughout his Gospel. It is the theme of discipleship failure. This theme is not unique to Mark, but it has been recognized as playing a prominent role there. It appears once again in the Last Supper narrative through his intercalation or sandwiching of certain pericopae around the meal story. Mark's meal scene is surrounded by two pictures of discipleship failure—Judas's betrayal (14:17–21) and the denial of Peter and the flight of the rest (14:26–31).[86] While these stories are not absent in Matthew, their poignancy is heightened by the discipleship failure theme that has been building throughout his narrative. As France observes, "the whole narrative buildup to Jesus' trial and death is thus interspersed with the theme of betrayal and desertion on the part of his followers, predicted and fulfilled."[87]

Luke

We have already had occasion to mention above some of the ways in which Luke stands apart from the rest of the Synoptic tradition. A couple of very obvious examples include the *two* cups of Luke and the explicit identification of the wine-represented covenant as "new."[88] Additionally, we may note the simple fact that the Lucan version is three times as long as its Synoptic counterparts. In these and in other differences Luke can be seen as strikingly more explicit in his theological interpretation of the events.

Beyond these comments, a consideration of Luke overall reveals that his account of the Last Supper has several nuances and depths of meaning that contribute a unique voice. First, as Raymond Brown has observed, Luke's predictions of things to come are more positive, with the result that "the supper dialogue taken as a whole is less foreboding and tilts toward victory."[89] This is seen in Luke's addition of Jesus' promise of the disciples' future reigning with Him (Luke 22:28–30),[90]

[86] D. Senior, *The Passion of Jesus in the Gospel of Mark* (Wilmington: Michael Glazier, 1984), 49; also R. T. France, *The Gospel of Mark: A Commentary on the Greek Text*, NIGTC (Grand Rapids: Eerdmans, 2002), 573.

[87] France, *Mark*, 573.

[88] Cf. also the common observation that it is Luke's version of the account that most closely matches and is likely interacting with the Pauline version in 1 Cor 11:23–26.

[89] R. E. Brown, *The Death of the Messiah: From Gethsemane to the Grave* (New York: Doubleday, 1994), 1:121.

[90] The parallel to this in Matthew (19:28) is set in a very different context, as a promise to the disciples of their reward for leaving everything to follow Him.

a note not found here in Matthew or Mark, as well as the positive expansion of the prediction of Peter's denial to include the word that when he has turned again he will strengthen the brethren (Luke 22:32), again a note missing in the other accounts.

Second, we may observe that in Luke especially the theme of meals is very common and important.[91] This highlights and heightens the meaning of the Last Supper and helps us see its connections throughout Luke's account. When discussing one such meal scene, the parable of the banquet in 14:15–24, Snodgrass notes that "eating and meals are major themes in Luke's Gospel. Virtually every chapter contains something relevant to the subject. Already in 1:53 there are hints of the themes of this parable."[92] As noted above, meals have a very important societal function, providing group identity and organizing society. By the time the reader gets to the Last Supper, Jesus' use of meals in these ways is already well established.

In addition to these pre-passion meals, Luke's Gospel and its companion volume, Acts, provide several examples of post-resurrection meals among Jesus' followers. One can think especially of the story of Cleopas and his fellow disciple encountering the risen Christ on the road to Emmaus and their subsequent recognition of the Lord "in the breaking of the bread" (Luke 24:13–35). "There was something familiar about the pattern of the risen Christ's activity,"[93] and this points the reader back to the Lord's Last Supper. This phrase "the breaking of the bread" (Luke 24:35) is picked up and used several times in Acts to describe other, clearly related fellowship meals (Acts 1:4 [NIV "while he was eating with them"[94]]; 2:42,46; 20:7; 27:35). Even though these are not explicitly called celebrations of the Last Supper, the Last Supper event heightens the relevance of all subsequent Christian meals as "times of celebration and eschatological anticipation."[95]

[91] In his very thorough treatment of how meals in the NT serve as pictures of eschatological utopian abundance, Peter-Ben Smit has a lengthy discussion of the various eschatological meals in Luke. P-B Smit, *Fellowship and Food in the Kingdom: Eschatological Meals and Scenes of Utopian Abundance in the New Testament*, WUNT 2 (Tübingen: Mohr-Siebeck, 2008), 113–200.

[92] Snodgrass, *Stories with Intent*, 306.

[93] G. Cole in *DTIB*, s.v. "Lord's Supper," 464.

[94] Green argues well for a reading of this verse to mean "while eating with them" rather than "while staying with them," based on the likely root of the form συναλιζόμενος (*Luke*, 760, n. 55).

[95] Ibid., 761.

Third, there is in Luke's version a strong emphasis on the "epochal character of the scene."[96] This is accomplished through accenting the kingdom and new exodus themes. Reference to the coming kingdom is doubly emphasized in the meal by Luke's fronting of this idea and its repetition (22:16,18). It appears again later in the conversation as a future promise of eating and drinking "at my table in my kingdom" (22:30). Related to this is the clear statement that this is part of the "new" covenant (22:20), an expression that also evokes the theme of the new exodus. The new exodus theme has already been hinted at in Luke's retelling of the Transfiguration wherein we learn the content of Jesus' discussion with Moses and Elijah: "They were talking about His exodus which He was about to fulfill in Jerusalem" (9:31, author's translation). All this flows together into a particularly strong emphasis in Luke's version of the Last Supper on the new age dawning through Christ's death and resurrection in Jerusalem.

Finally, we may note that Luke adds to his Last Supper retelling an important note of the theme of humility and sacrificial service. He does this most clearly by including here the account of the disciples disputing among themselves about who was the greatest (maybe stimulated by seating arrangements at this last and important meal), followed by Jesus' response that He was the servant of them all (22:24–28). This scene and these words, which are familiar to us as examples of human pride and the radical nature of Jesus' upside-down kingdom, are found elsewhere in Matthew (20:24–28) and Mark (10:41–45). This idea plays an important role in all its appearances in the Gospels, but Luke's choice to connect this teaching with the Last Supper is very significant and reveals something of his interpretive stress. The most interesting thing about this observation is how it reveals the way in which Luke's retelling corresponds more closely to John's than it does to the Synoptics. As we will see below more fully, John's themes focus very much on mutual love and unity between the disciples, modeled most perfectly through Jesus' washing of the disciples' feet. Luke likewise, along with the apostle Paul, weights the meaning of the Last Supper toward the emphasis on humble service at the horizontal level between the disciples.

[96] Ibid., 757.

John

Under the first sections of this essay we discussed a number of differences between John and the Synoptic tradition. The matter at hand here is how John contributes uniquely to a full-orbed understanding of the witness of the Last Supper in the Gospels. The most obvious difference in John is the greater complexity and length of the surrounding story and the extended dialogue of the Upper Room Discourse. I have already argued that the upper room is indeed the Supper room, even though the event and words of institution do not explicitly appear. The question is how John complements the well-known Synoptic presentation.

There are three observations to make about John's voice in the Last Supper. First, we may note again that it is appropriate that we read John 6 in conjunction with his Last Supper narrative. This is because this same connection between the wilderness feedings and the Last Supper has already been made in the Synoptic tradition and because John 6 itself reflects the same thematic teaching as both the Synoptic Last Supper accounts and John's Upper Room Discourse. In John 6 Jesus' sayings about eating His flesh and drinking His blood, enclosed with references to the bread of life, is a call for any to come and draw near to Him without stumbling, to abide with Him (v. 56) and to *believe* (see especially v. 29). Intertwined with this call is the promise of satisfaction (v. 35) and resurrection into eternal life (vv. 33,40,54,57,58), along with the corresponding warning that those who do not believe will be condemned (v. 53). The point here is that many of these same themes and emphases appear in the Upper Room Discourse, enabling the reader to see the intended connection once again. It is unique to John that he has separated these events, but John 6 and John's extended Last Supper account are to be read together.

Second, as we observed regarding Luke, but with a greater emphasis, John's presentation of the Last Supper emphasizes humility and sacrificial service to others. This is seen most evidently through Jesus' act of footwashing, a story unique to John. Markus Barth questions tying John 6 too closely with the institution texts as the history of interpretation has done, especially because, he argues, in John's account of the Last Supper, "the foot washing stands in the center."[97] I believe

[97] M. Barth, *Rediscovering the Lord's Supper: Communion with Israel, with Christ, and Among the Guests* (Atlanta: John Knox, 1988), 19.

Barth is mistaken on his main point here, as I have suggested already that we are meant to read these passages together (as the history of interpretation has done). However, his observation about the centrality of the footwashing in John's Last Supper account is astute. The footwashing incident greatly marks John's whole presentation of the Last Supper. Jesus' subsequent discourse and "high priestly prayer" confirm this reading, with their teaching that focuses on love for one another and unity among the disciples, the great witness to the transforming power of Jesus' Gospel. Yet again we may note that the theological interpretation of the Last Supper finds concord not only in Luke but also in the apostle Paul, who uses the Last or Lord's Supper to exhort believers to unity and mutual love (1 Corinthians 11). Jesus' virtuous model serves for the disciples as "the constitutive law for their relationship with him and with one another."[98]

Finally, John's expansive Last Supper account emphasizes the continual presence and abiding of the risen Christ with His disciples. We have observed above that this is also a theme for Matthew, but once again, John uses an extended discourse to communicate the same idea, tying into John's overall theme of "abiding." Schlatter states that much of Jesus' teaching here shows the ongoing Christian community (which could have trouble believing in a dead person or having an invisible person as one's Lord and leader) "that Jesus' [impending] death did not bring an end to his association with them. It rather provided the basis for it."[99] It is true in all the Gospels that Jesus' death does not abolish His union with the disciples, but John "indicate[s] more strongly than others that Jesus' death completed his communion with the disciples."[100]

From the Last Supper to the Lord's Supper

The greatest witness to the meaning and significance of the Lord's Last Supper is the way in which it becomes so foundational for the Christian community through its transformation into the Lord's Supper. As McKnight notes, "These two elements (bread, wine) *distinguished* the early Christian communities from all other Jewish communities and did so from the very beginning. There is no time period

[98] Schlatter, *History of the Christ*, 354.
[99] Ibid., 359.
[100] Ibid., 361.

of earliest Christianity that does not know of the Lord's Supper, and there is no better explanation for its origins than the one given by the church itself: Jesus' last supper."[101]

It is important to note that the Last Supper and the Lord's Supper are not identical, even though they overlap much in meaning. The Last Supper was a Passover meal, celebrated annually in the month of Nisan, and including unleavened bread, kosher wine, etc. The Lord's Supper becomes something more akin to a love-feast. It is not constrained by the ritualistic foods; and as we see in Acts, it is celebrated regularly as "the breaking of bread." The Lord's Supper is the Christian remembrance and eschatological re-appropriation of the significance and meaning of the Last Supper. It is organically related but not the same thing.[102]

So how does the Last Supper inform the Lord's Supper? First, the Lord's Supper gets from the Last Supper its emphasis on service and love within the community of the saints. Partaking of the Lord's Supper "in remembrance of me" is following Jesus' model to share meals together in a way that "recalled the significance of his own life and death in obedience to God on behalf of others. This recollection should have the effect of drawing forth responses reminiscent of Jesus' own table manners—his openness to outsiders, his comportment as a servant, his indifference toward issues of status, honor, and the like . . . ."[103]

Second, the Lord's Supper also gets from the Last Supper the foundational understanding that our celebration is one of receiving grace, not performing a religious rite through our partaking. Schlatter astutely argues that in the Last Supper it was a *sacrament* not a *sacrifice* which originated. This is because "sacraments are acts by which God's love is manifested to us and his gift is mediated to us. Sacrifices are acts by which we testify our love to God by our gift."[104] The Lord's Supper is a testimony from God of His love for us, not our religious devotion to Him. As Schlatter goes on to say, "It had fundamental

[101] McKnight, *Jesus and His Death*, 276.

[102] One implication of this is that we are not required, as some have suggested, to use unleavened bread any more than we would be to use kosher wine. While it is certainly fine to use cracker-type breads for our Communion rather than leavened bread, to require this fails to understand the eschatological and new covenant difference between the Last Supper and the Lord's Supper.

[103] Green, *Luke*, 762.

[104] Schlatter, *History of the Christ*, 358, n. 38.

significance for the religious history of his disciples that the center of their common cult was not a sacrifice but a sacrament. . . . By not placing the value of the Last Supper in what they did there but in what Christ did, the disciples proved that they celebrated their Last Supper as a sacrament. The meaning of their action was that it granted them the share in what Christ's death provided for them."[105]

Finally, the Lord's Supper is primarily a forward-looking, future-hoping celebration, even as the Last Supper was. And even as there was a Lord's Last Supper, so too there will one day be a last Lord's Supper, when the remembering and the future hoping will have no need, even as Jerusalem will have no need of the sun. Instead, the Last Supper and the Lord's Supper will both be seen as the mere prelude to the great wedding feast of the Lamb and His bride.[106]

[105] Ibid., 358–59.

[106] I would like to thank my research assistant H. Clift Ward for his help in tracking down various sources for this essay.

THE LORD'S SUPPER IN PAUL: AN IDENTITY-FORMING PROCLAMATION OF THE GOSPEL

James M. Hamilton Jr.*

In a strange twist of God's providence, we find ourselves grateful for the ways that the Corinthian church struggled. We are not grateful that they sinned but grateful that their problems provoked Paul to apply the gospel to their lives in ways that continue to instruct. Paul's letters are occasional, and scholars often observe that if the Corinthians had not provoked Paul to address their abuse of the Lord's Table, the Lord's Supper might not have been directly addressed in his letters.[1]

Paul's words in 1 Cor 11:17–34 explain that the Lord's Supper is a proclamation of the gospel made by those who embrace the gospel, those whose identity is shaped by the gospel.[2] In order to establish this thesis we must understand the abuses of the Lord's Supper in the church in Corinth, and these abuses are tangled up with the other problems in the church that Paul addresses. Throughout 1 Corinthians, Paul addresses Corinthian error with Christian gospel. The fact that the Lord's Supper is a proclamation of the gospel made by those who embrace the gospel makes what Paul says about the Lord's Supper in 1 Corinthians 10–11 relevant to the issues Paul addresses in 1 Corinthians 1–9.

* James M. Hamilton Jr. received his Ph.D. from The Southern Baptist Theological Seminary. He is associate professor of Biblical Theology at The Southern Baptist Theological Seminary in Louisville, Kentucky.

[1] Cf. T. R. Schreiner, *Paul, Apostle of God's Glory in Christ: A Pauline Theology* (Downers Grove: InterVarsity, 2001), 39; I. H. Marshall, "Lord's Supper," in *DPL*, 570; I. H. Marshall, *Last Supper and Lord's Supper* (Carlisle: Paternoster, 1997 [1980]), 16. R. B. Hays writes, "Strangely, we are indebted to the Corinthians for messing up their celebration of the Lord's Supper. . . . the Corinthians' trouble serves for our instruction" (*First Corinthians*, IBC [Louisville: John Knox, 1997], 203).

[2] For brief expositions of the Lord's Supper, see T. R. Schreiner, *New Testament Theology: Magnifying God in Christ* (Grand Rapids: Baker, 2008), 730–34; P. J. Gentry, "The Lord's Supper, *BF&M* Article 7b," in *An Exposition from the Faculty of The Southern Baptist Theological Seminary on The Baptist Faith and Message 2000* (Louisville: The Southern Baptist Theological Seminary, 2001), 25–28, available online: http://www.sbts.edu/pdf/bfmexposition.pdf, and J. M. Hamilton Jr., "The Meaning and Significance of the Lord's Supper," *Gospel Witness* (August 2008): 6–7.

The first section of this essay, then, will survey the problems in the Corinthian church and the way that Paul addresses these with the gospel. The second part focuses in on 1 Corinthians 10–11,[3] where Paul explains the Lord's Supper as an identity-shaping proclamation of the gospel. The essay will then conclude with brief reflections on what Paul's teaching in 1 Corinthians means for contemporary church practice.

Problems in the Corinthian Church

In 1 Corinthians Paul addresses what he has heard from the Corinthians[4] about the difficulties facing the church: schisms, immorality, idolatry, and then the misbehavior when the church gathers for worship. Paul confronts each of these threats to the Corinthian church with the truth of the gospel. Thus, if Romans is the letter where Paul most systematically explains his gospel, 1 Corinthians might be the one that most directly applies the gospel to Christian life in a church.

Paul addresses the divisions in the Corinthian church in 1 Corinthians 1–4, the sexual sin and confusion in the church in chaps. 5–7, the appropriate response to food offered to idols and avoiding idolatry in chaps. 8–10, inappropriate behavior when Christians gather for worship in chaps. 11–14, mistaken thinking on the resurrection in chap. 15, and then in chap. 16 he prepares the church for his next visit.[5] This summary of the nature of the problems Paul addresses in 1 Corinthians 1–10 seeks to highlight the way that Paul confronts each of these issues with the good news of Jesus Christ, crucified and risen.

[3] First Corinthians 10 functions as a transitional section of the letter in which the Lord's Supper is introduced as a decisive consideration in the discussion of idol meat in 1 Corinthians 8–10. At the same time, because the Lord's Supper is an element of Christian worship, introducing the topic paves the way for Paul's discussion of Christian worship in 1 Corinthians 11–14. Cf. E. E. Ellis, "ΣΟΜΑ in First Corinthians," in E. E. Ellis, *Christ and the Future in New Testament History*. NovTSup 97 (Boston: Brill, 2001), 165; repr. from *Int* 44 (April 1990): 32–44.

[4] Cf. what seem to be Paul's references to reports he has received from Corinth in 1 Cor 1:11; 5:1; 11:18; 15:12, and the wording of 7:1,5; 8:1; 12:1; 16:1,12, which seems to indicate Paul is addressing a list of questions posed to him by the Corinthians.

[5] Cf. the summary of "The Structure of 1 Corinthians" in R. E. Ciampa and B. S. Rosner, "I Corinthians," in *CNTOT* 695–96.

1 Corinthians 1–4, The Gospel Against Factionalism

The factionalism seen in the first four chapters seems to have arisen from worldly standards of evaluation that, Paul asserts, would empty the cross of its power (1 Cor 1:17). The members of the Corinthian church were identifying themselves with particular Christian teachers—whether Paul, Apollos, Cephas, or even Christ Himself (1 Cor 1:12). This preference for one teacher over another perhaps had to do with the distinctive strengths and emphases of the particular teachers, and by identifying with such strengths, whether the suffering of Paul, the eloquence of Apollos, the boldness of Cephas, or even the piety and perfection of Jesus Himself, the members of the Corinthian church became "puffed up" (4:6), evidently esteeming themselves superior to others in the congregation who identified with a different set of strengths seen in a different teacher.[6]

Paul dismantles this proud, divisive way of thinking by explaining that by worldly standards—the kind that result in their boasting over one another (1 Cor 4:6–7,10)—the gospel is a stumbling block because it appears to be folly and weakness (1:18,23). If one is drawn to the gospel by the eloquence or wisdom of the one proclaiming the gospel, the cross could be emptied of its power (1:17). How? Because someone drawn to eloquence might confess Christ merely because they felt the appeal of an eloquent, wise orator. Such a person is in danger of trusting human wisdom rather than God's power (2:4). In such a case, the power would be in the speaker's ability rather than in the cross of Christ. Moreover, Paul asserts that people do not come to know God by wisdom but through "the folly of what we preach" (1:21), which means that no one can boast that they were wise enough to find their way to God (1:29).

Paul's saving message is offensive to different kinds of people for different kinds of reasons: the idea of a crucified Messiah seems foolish to Gentiles and scandalous to Jews. For Jews, the concept of a crucified Messiah is a contradiction in terms. It looks like proof that the crucified one was not, in fact, the Messiah (cf. Acts 5:36–37). For Gentiles, the idea that a god might become human would represent a foolish decision to surrender power in exchange for weakness, as can be seen from Origen's account of the objections of Celsus[7] and

[6] In this essay Scripture quotations are the author's translation.

[7] Origen reports that Celsus objected to the incarnation on the grounds that "if he came

Tertullian's reply to Marcion.[8] Thus, from human perspectives, Jesus' mission looks like a failed project. And this is exactly Paul's point, because what looks foolish and weak to the eyes of the world is in fact the wisdom and power of God.

The truth of the gospel is not something discovered by those with secret or elevated insight but given to those who are called (1 Cor 1:24). Those who are called are not the wise, powerful, and noble by worldly standards, but the foolish, shameful, and weak (1:26–28).[9] God did it this way so that no one could boast before Him (1:29). God did it this way so that Christ would be everything to those who embrace the gospel (1:30),[10] with the result that those who embrace the gospel identify themselves with Christ and boast only in Him (1:31; 4:6).

Paul's argument in 1 Corinthians 1–4 is that the gospel is not a message that one receives by virtue of one's individual strengths and distinctive advantages. Rather, the gospel is a message that declares all people bankrupt before God, all people unable to understand the message apart from the revealing power of the Holy Spirit (2:10–14). This means that the distinctive appeal of the personalities who proclaim the gospel is irrelevant (3:5; 4:6). God has set things up so that no one can take credit for their own salvation, but by identifying with particular teachers, the Corinthians are acting as though they have

down among men, he must undergo a change, and a change from good to evil, from virtue to vice, from happiness to misery, and from best to worst. Who, then, would make choice of such a change?" (Origen, *Contra Celsum*, 4.14, cf. also 4.18; 5:2 [*ANF* 4.502, 504, 543]).

[8] Tertullian asks, "Will you find anything to be so 'foolish' as believing in a God that has been born, and that of a virgin, and of a fleshly nature too, who wallowed in all the beforementioned humiliations of nature? . . . according to the world's wisdom, it is more easy to believe that Jupiter became a bull or a swan, if we listen to Marcion, than that Christ really became a man. . . . For which is more unworthy of God, which is more likely to raise a blush of shame, that *God* should be born, or that He should die? . . . . And the Son of God died; it is by all means to be believed, because it is absurd. And He was buried, and rose again; the fact is certain, because it is impossible" (Tertullian, *De carne Christi*, 5.4, 5.1, 4 [*ANF* 3.524–25]). I owe these references to Origen and Tertullian to O. Skarsaune, *In the Shadow of the Temple: Jewish Influences on Early Christianity* (Downers Grove: InterVarsity, 2002), 323–25.

[9] Not for a moment denying that "if Paul says that there were not many in the Corinthian congregation who were wise, powerful, and wellborn, then this much is certain: there were some. As early as Origen this passage was cited as an objection to Celsus's opinion that in Christian gatherings one would find only the lower classes" (G. Thiessen, "Social Stratification in the Corinthian Congregation: A Contribution to the Sociology of Early Hellenistic Christianity," in *The Social Setting of Pauline Christianity: Essays on Corinth*, ed. and trans. J. H. Schütz [Philadelphia: Fortress, 1982], 72, citing Origen, *Contra Celsum* 3.48).

[10] See the lucid discussion of 1 Cor 1:30 in B. Vickers, *Jesus' Blood and Righteousness: Paul's Theology of Imputation* (Wheaton: Crossway, 2006), 200–205.

something other than Christ in which they can boast (1:31; 3:21; 4:6,18–20). Paul presents the gospel to the Corinthians in these chapters as a message that will unite the church because it nullifies all the things that divide worldly minded people from one another. Christians have nothing but what they have received, and thus they cannot boast as though they somehow earned what they have (4:7). Paul seeks to undermine the factionalism in Corinth, then, by demonstrating that the gospel of Jesus Christ is a leveler of persons. Those who embrace the gospel will boast only in Christ, and they will be inclined to celebrate their own folly and weakness that Christ might be seen as strong and wise (3:18; 4:8–13).

1 Corinthians 5–7, The Gospel Against Sexual Immorality

Having addressed the factionalism in Corinth with the humility-producing, leveling influence of the gospel, Paul moves on to address their sexual immorality and confusion. The leaven of sexual immorality has no place in the church because the church is a new, unleavened lump since Christ, the Passover lamb, has been sacrificed (1 Cor 5:1–8). This means that "anyone who bears the name of brother" (5:11), i.e., anyone who identifies him or herself as a believer, yet who refuses to repent of sin, is to be put out of the church (5:9–13). The lawsuits Paul addresses in 1 Cor 6:1–8 may or may not be related to sexual immorality,[11] but the response Paul commends has to do with the gospel. Rather than wronging and defrauding the brothers (6:8), the Corinthians should, like Christ, suffer wrong and be defrauded (6:7). Similarly, the Corinthians should not join themselves to prostitutes because they "were bought with a price" (6:20, cf. 6:12–20). This idea that they "were bought with a price" is also applied to the question of marital and societal status (7:23). The Corinthians are to be identified as those purchased at the price of the death of Jesus, which

[11] For possible connections between 1 Corinthians 5–6, see J. A. Fitzmyer, *First Corinthians*, AYB 32 (New Haven: Yale University Press, 2008), 232. Thiessen ("Social Stratification in the Corinthian Community," 97) suggests, "The object of such suits are βιωτικά, probably affairs of property or income." By contrast, B. W. Winter ("Civil Law and Christian Litigiousness [1 Cor 6:1–8]," in *After Paul Left Corinth: The Influence of Secular Ethics and Social Change* [Grand Rapids: Eerdmans, 2001], 65) connects the lawsuits to the divisiveness in 1 Corinthians 1–4 and writes, "This 'strife and jealousy' arising out of the issue of Christian leadership was also expressed in litigation, with one of the leading Christians taking another leading Christian to court."

means they identify themselves as those to whom the gospel has been applied. That identity is to shape their behavior.

1 Corinthians 8–10, The Gospel Against Idolatry

From factionalism (1 Cor 1–4) and immorality (1 Cor 5–7) Paul turns to idolatry in 1 Corinthians 8–9. Having raised the issue of food offered to idols, in chap. 8 he addresses the "knowledge" of some, which appears to be causing them to disregard the needs of those with weaker consciences (1 Cor 8:1–2,7). Again the gospel informs Paul's reply: by their knowledge, the brother for whom Christ died is destroyed (8:11). There is a clear contrast here between Christ, the strong who surrendered His rights and died for the weak, and the Corinthians, whose "authority" proves to be "a stumbling block to the weak" (8:9). Paul then defends his own freedoms and rights (9:1–12a,13–14) in order to highlight the ways he surrenders his rights and freedoms as he seeks to serve others and thereby win them to faith in Christ (9:12b,15–27). In this Paul is building to his call for the Corinthians to follow him as he follows Christ (11:1). Just as Jesus forsook fleshly standards of privilege and authority, significance and wisdom, so also Paul does "all on account of the gospel" in order that he might "partake of it" (9:23).

As noted above, 1 Corinthians 10 is a transitional chapter in the argument of the letter. On the one hand, Paul concludes his discussion of food offered to idols. On the other hand, the way he concludes this discussion opens the door to the matter of Christian worship in chaps. 11–14. From the argument that Paul makes in 1 Corinthians 10, it seems that the Corinthian Christians had drawn false conclusions from their baptism and participation in the Lord's Supper. Thus, 1 Corinthians 10 sheds light on the problems in the Corinthian church that will be addressed by Paul's exposition of the identity-shaping proclamation of the gospel, the Lord's Supper, in chap. 11 (see the next section of this essay).

From what Paul says in 1 Corinthians 10, it seems that either the Corinthians were assuming they would escape judgment because they had been baptized and were partaking of the Lord's Supper, or perhaps Paul anticipated this assumption and sought to combat it in

1 Cor 10:1–13.[12] In 1 Cor 10:1–5, Paul explains that Israel was typologically baptized and ate the Lord's Supper but did not please God: they "were baptized into Moses" (1 Cor 10:2) and they "ate the same spiritual food" and "drank the same spiritual drink" (10:3–4). Perhaps the identification of the rock from which Israel drank as Christ ("and the rock was Christ," 10:4)[13] is meant to guard against a Corinthian objection that Israel was judged because Israel's "baptism" and "Lord's Supper" were not as effective as what the Corinthians experienced. Paul's proof that Israel's version of baptism and the Lord's Supper did not protect them from judgment is stated in 10:5, "But God was not pleased with most of them, for their bodies were strewn in the wilderness."

Paul states plainly in 1 Cor 10:6 that "these became types of us," then warns the Corinthians not to sin and face judgment as Israel did (10:6–10). Typology consists of historical correspondence and escalation between persons, events, and institutions in the stream of Israel's salvation historical experience.[14] The points of correspondence in view between Israel and the Corinthian church include their experience of baptism, their partaking of the Lord's Supper, and their sin. Paul details the sins of Israel, which resulted in judgment, in 10:6–10. The upshot of the typological comparison is then stated in 10:11, and the note of escalation is sounded as well: "Now these things happened

[12] Cf. G. D. Fee, *The First Epistle to the Corinthians*, NICNT (Grand Rapids: Eerdmans, 1987), 443: "The nature of this argument strongly suggests that those who 'think they stand' (v. 12) do so on the basis of a somewhat magical view of the sacraments." Similarly J. E. Smith, "1 Corinthians," in *The Bible Knowledge Word Study: Acts–Ephesians*, ed. D. L. Bock (Colorado Springs: Cook, 2006), 273; Schreiner, *Paul*, 376–77; J. D. G. Dunn, *The Theology of Paul the Apostle* (Grand Rapids: Eerdmans, 1998), 614.

[13] See G. K. Beale's treatment of this text, in discussion with the views of Peter Enns, in "Did Jesus and the Apostles Preach the Right Doctrine from the Wrong Texts? Revisiting the Debate Seventeen Years Later in the Light of Peter Enns' Book, *Inspiration and Incarnation*," *Them* 32.1 (2006): 32–37.

[14] Arguing for the pre-existence of Christ on the basis of "ΧΡΙΣΤΟΣ in 1 Cor 10:4,9," and citing Goppelt, E. E. Ellis asserts, "The passage explicitly identifies the . . . events . . . as 'types . . . for us, as happening 'typically' . . . and 'written for our admonition' (10:6,11). It uses the terms 'technically [as an] advance presentation' intimating eschatological events" (*Christ and the Future in New Testament History*, 90). For my efforts to flesh out typological interpretation, see "The Virgin Will Conceive: Typological Fulfillment in Matthew 1:18–23," in *Built upon the Rock: Studies in the Gospel of Matthew*, ed. J. Nolland and D. Gurtner (Grand Rapids: Eerdmans, 2008), 228–47, and "Was Joseph a Type of the Messiah? Tracing the Typological Identification between Joseph, David, and Jesus," *SBJT* 12.4 (2008): 52–77. See also my Julius Brown Gay Lecture presented at The Southern Baptist Theological Seminary on March 13, 2008, "The Typology of David's Rise to Power: Messianic Patterns in the Book of Samuel," available online in audio: http://www.sbts.edu/MP3/JBGay/20080313hamilton.mp3 or text format: http://www.sbts.edu/pdf/JBGay/the_typology_of_davids_rise_to_power2008–03–101.pdf.

to them typologically, but they were written for our instruction, on whom the ends of the ages have come" (10:11). The fact that the ends of the ages have come in the dawning of the already-not yet kingdom of Jesus[15] means that the significance of these events is increased in God's economy. Paul argues that just as God judged the Israelites who sinned, even though they were baptized into Moses and partook of the "type" of the Lord's Supper, so also God will judge the Corinthian Christians who sin, even though they have been baptized and partake of the Lord's Supper (10:12–13).[16]

Because God will judge, Paul urges the Corinthians to "flee from idolatry" (10:14), and he presents an argument—"as to sensible people" (10:15)—that they do so. This argument consists of two premises and a conclusion:

> *Premise 1*: Paul explains in 1 Cor 10:16–17 that partaking of the cup and the bread at the Lord's Supper unites Christians in fellowship with Christ by partaking of His body and blood in the bread and cup.
> *Premise 2*: Paul explains in 1 Cor 10:18–20 that the OT teaches that those who eat sacrifices partake in the altar, which means that those who eat food offered to idols fellowship with the demons to whom the idol meat was offered.
> *Conclusion*: in 1 Cor 10:21–22, Paul concludes from these two premises that one cannot partake in the Table and cup with both Jesus and demons, because to do so is to provoke the Lord to jealousy and He cannot be overcome.

Paul then seems to turn from meat that would be eaten in the temple of an idol (1 Cor 10:14–22) to meat sacrificed to an idol, sold in the market, and eaten in homes (10:23–11:1).[17] He may be responding to Corinthian slogans ("all things are lawful for me") in 1 Cor 10:23,[18] but

[15] For the already-not yet in Paul, see Schreiner, *New Testament Theology*, 97–108, 734.

[16] Schreiner (*Paul*, 287) writes, "Thus in 1 Corinthians 10 he reminds the 'knowers'—who feel free to eat even in idols' temples—that even though the Israelites were freed from Egypt, though they experienced a baptism of sorts at the Red Sea, though they experienced an anticipation of the Lord's Supper in eating manna and water from the rock, though they had Christ's presence in their midst, they were still judged by God. . . . Israel's destruction is a type of God's eschatological judgment (1 Cor 10:11) and functions as a warning to the church. . . . One cannot partake of the benefits of Christ's sacrifice by eating at his table and then proceed to eat at the table of idols and share in the 'benefits' of demonic powers. God will not tolerate such idolatry."

[17] Cf. Fee, *First Corinthians*, 441, 475–78; D. E. Garland, *1 Corinthians*, BECNT (Grand Rapids: Baker, 2003), 486–87.

[18] Fee (*First Corinthians*, 479) suggests that "everything is permissible" in 1 Cor 10:23 is a Corinthian slogan. So also Smith, "1 Corinthians," 277; D. Burk, "Discerning Corinthian Slogans through Paul's Use of the Diatribe in 1 Cor 6:12–20," *BBR* 18.1 (2008): 99–121; J. E. Smith, "The Roots of a 'Libertine' Slogan in 1 Cor 6:18," *JTS* 59.1 (2008): 63–95.

in any case his point in 1 Cor 10:23–24 is that the Corinthians should seek what benefits and edifies others. In 10:25–31 Paul instructs the Corinthians that since the earth belongs to the Lord, they are free to eat without bothering about the source of the meat—unless doing so will harm the conscience of another. They are to live for God's glory, whether eating or abstaining (10:31), and they are to follow Paul as he follows Jesus—and that means inconveniencing themselves as they seek the benefit of others that they may be saved (10:31–11:1).

The issues Paul has been dealing with in the first 10 chapters of 1 Corinthians do not vanish once we arrive at chap. 11. The factionalism (1 Cor 1–4) and problems with sexuality (1 Cor 5–7) continue to be addressed with the gospel that overturns such behavior. The immorality confronted in chaps. 5–7 reflects a failure to honor and obey God where issues of sex and gender are concerned, and in 1 Cor 11:2–16 Paul teaches the Corinthians how they are to honor God with respect to gender when the church is gathered for worship.[19] Similarly, the factionalism seen in chaps. 1–4 is to have no place at the Lord's Supper, which Paul addresses in 11:17–34. Paul's instructions on what is proper during the worship of God all through 1 Corinthians 11–14 serve as a kind of antidote to the idolatry challenging the church at Corinth, which Paul dealt with in chaps. 8–10. False worship (1 Cor 8–10) is to be replaced with true worship (1 Cor 11–14). We have seen that Paul has opposed factionalism, immorality, and idolatry with the truth of the gospel in 1 Corinthians 1–10. We are now ready to consider Paul's explanation of the Lord's Supper as an identity-shaping proclamation of the gospel.

[19] See especially T. R. Schreiner, "Head Coverings, Prophecies, and the Trinity: 1 Cor 11:2–16," in *Recovering Biblical Manhood and Womanhood*, ed. J. Piper and W. Grudem (Wheaton: Crossway, 1991), 117–32, available online: http://www.cbmw.org/rbmw/rbmw.pdf, and id., "A Review of 'Praying and Prophesying in the Assemblies: 1 Cor 11:2–16' by G. Fee," *JBMW* 10.1 (2005): 17–21, available online: http://www.cbmw.org/Resources/Book-Reviews/Praying-and-Prophesying-in-the-Assemblies-by-Gordon-D-Fee-from-Discovering-Biblical-Equality. For my attempt to synthesize the gender passages in the NT, see "What Women Can Do in Ministry: Full Participation within Biblical Boundaries," in *Women, Ministry and the Gospel*, ed. M. A. Husbands and T. Larsen (Downers Grove: InterVarsity, 2007), 32–52.

The Lord's Supper: An Identity-Shaping Proclamation of the Gospel

The earliest church seems to have met on a daily basis in the homes of believers to break bread (Acts 2:46). As time passed and the church settled into normal patterns, they moved to a weekly meeting. On the first day of the week, the church would gather to break bread (Acts 20:7).[20] Just as Jesus instituted the Lord's Supper in the context of a meal, so the early Christian celebration of the Lord's Supper seems to have taken place in the context of a meal.[21]

Not only is it important to understand that the early Christians took the Lord's Supper on the Lord's day in the context of a meal, but it is also important to recognize that they did so in homes.[22] Scholars generally follow Jerome Murphy-O'Connor's analysis of what this would entail.[23] In what follows I will summarize some of these conclusions and interpret what Paul says in light of them, but from the outset I must stress that the main lines of the argument here are not dependent upon any particular reconstruction. The argument here is that the Corinthians should identify themselves as those who have been redeemed by the death of Jesus and are united to Him and other

[20] For worship on the first day of the week, see Skarsaune, *In the Shadow of the Temple*, 378–85. I. H. Marshall identifies "the Breaking of Bread" as part of "The New Testament Vocabulary" for the Lord's Supper, citing Acts 2:42,46; 20:7,11; 1 Cor 10:16, and referencing also Ign. *Eph.* 20:2 and *Did* 14:1 (*Last Supper and Lord's Supper* [Carlisle: Paternoster, 1997], 14–15, 158). F. F. Bruce writes on Acts 20:7, "The breaking of the bread was probably a fellowship meal in the course of which the Eucharist was celebrated (cf. 2:42)" (*The Book of Acts*, rev. ed., NICNT [Grand Rapids: Eerdmans, 1988], 384). See also E. J. Schnabel, *Early Christian Mission* (Downers Grove: InterVarsity, 2004), 414; Schreiner, *New Testament Theology*, 699.

[21] B. B. Blue ("Love Feast," in *DPL* 579) writes, "The separation of the meal/*agapē* from the Lord's Supper, or Eucharist, was made in the second century. Justin Martyr (c. 150) indicates that by his time the common meal and Eucharist (as sacrament) were separate observances. . ." Citing Justin Martyr *1 Apol.* 65–66. Cf. Fitzmyer, *First Corinthians*, 428–29. Skarsaune helpfully traces the line of development from the Jewish Passover meal to the early Christian celebration of the Lord's Supper (*In the Shadow of the Temple*, 399–421). E. E. Ellis writes that Paul's comments in 1 Cor 11:17–34 "initiate, quite unintentionally no doubt, a process that in time will eliminate the meal altogether from the observance of the Supper" (*Pauline Theology: Ministry and Society* [Grand Rapids: Eerdmans, 1989], 113). Ellis's point only stands if when Paul recommends eating in one's own home, he separates the meal from the Lord's Supper rather than making a comment about the spiritual state of the Corinthians.

[22] See B. B. Blue, "Architecture, Early Church," in *DLNTD*, 91–95.

[23] J. Murphy O'Connor, *St. Paul's Corinth: Texts and Archeology*, 3rd ed. (Wilmington: Glazier, 2002 [1983]). A. C. Thiselton (*The First Epistle to the Corinthians*, NIGTC [Grand Rapids: Eerdmans, 2000], 860) speaks of O'Connor's work as "a foundation . . . which has transformed exegesis since the early 1980s. . . ." Fitzmyer (*First Corinthians*, 428) calls attention to the fact that some recent scholars have disputed this reconstruction.

Christians by faith. Instead of their actions declaring these realities, their behavior at the Lord's Supper was pointing to status distinctions recognized by Roman culture, and the observance of these status distinctions amounted to a denial of their unity as the body of Christ. Paul confronts this misbehavior with an explanation of the way the Lord's Supper proclaims the death of Jesus, unifying all those who proclaim it as they confess their common need for and equal standing under the mercy of God at the foot of the cross. Moreover, the identity of those redeemed by Jesus is to be shaped by this gospel such that they follow Christ in laying down their lives for others. The Corinthian Christians were not doing this, and Paul therefore rehearses for them what he had taught them earlier: that the Lord's Supper is an identity-shaping proclamation of the gospel.

As we consider the behaviors reflected in what Paul wrote to the Corinthians, we can be helped toward a clearer picture by what has been discerned of the architectural and social realities of Roman Corinth. Then as now, wealthier people could afford private homes as opposed to dwelling in apartments. As Fee points out, this would mean that the host of the Christians gathering for worship would be the patron of the meal.[24] Schnabel writes,

> Jerome Murphy-O'Connor concludes on the basis of the architectural features of the Roman atrium house and the Greek peristyle house . . . , whose largest room could accommodate between thirty and forty people, that the Christian house churches had about that same number of members. In some exceptional cases it was possible that up to one hundred people could gather in private houses with large rooms.[25]

This is relevant to our consideration of the Lord's Supper because, as Fee points out, "The triclinia average about 36 square meters (about 18 x 18 ft.). If they actually reclined (triclinium = a table with three sides on which to recline) at such meals, there would be room for about 9 to 12 guests at table."[26] And as Schnabel observes, "The early Christian house churches existed in the context of the hierarchical social structures of Roman society."[27] Both architectural and social realities are relevant for what Paul says to the church in Corinth in 1 Cor 11:17–34. Richard B. Hays writes,

[24] Fee, *First Corinthians*, 533.
[25] Schnabel, *Early Christian Mission*, 1304.
[26] Fee, *First Corinthians*, 533, n. 11.
[27] Schnabel, *Early Christian Mission*, 1304.

> The host of such a gathering would, of course, be one of the wealthier members of the community. It is reasonable to assume, therefore, that the host's higher-status friends would be invited to dine in the *triclinium*, while lower-status members of the church (such as freedmen and slaves) would be placed in the larger space outside.
>
> Furthermore, under such conditions it was not at all unusual for the higher status guests in the dining room to be served better food and wine than the other guests . . . A number of surviving texts from this period testify to this custom among Romans (and Corinth was, we must recall, a Roman colony).[28]

The situation we find in 1 Cor 11:17–34, then, is another instance of Paul addressing Corinthian sin with Christian gospel. The passage seems to break down into four parts:

A 11:17–22 Corinthian anti-gospel divisions at the Lord's Supper
  B 11:23–26 Proclaiming the Lord's death until He comes
  B´ 11:27–32 Partaking in a worthy manner
A´ 11:33–34 Receiving one another at the Lord's Supper[29]

The remedy for the problematic behavior outlined in 1 Cor 11:17–22 is proposed in 11:33–34, and the worthy manner in which the Corinthians are to proclaim the Lord's death as they partake of the Lord's Supper (11:23–26) is outlined in 11:27–32. We will consider these each in turn.

Anti-gospel Divisions

If the architectural and social picture sketched above does indeed inform what was happening in Corinth,[30] we can immediately

[28] Hays, *First Corinthians*, 196, citing Pliny the Younger, *Letters* 2.6. Fee (*First Corinthians*, 542, n. 55) also cites relevant texts from Juvenal (*Satire* 5) and Martial (*Epigram* 3.60). Similarly Smith, "1 Corinthians," 286. Part 1 of O'Connor, *St. Paul's Corinth* lays out and discusses an array of potentially relevant texts from antiquity (3–147).

[29] Cf. Fee, *First Corinthians*, 532. This structure better captures the thought of the passage than does the tri-partite division (A 11:17–22; B 11:23–26; A´ 11:27–34) put forward by Garland (*1 Corinthians*, 535) because it reflects the two occurrences of Ὥστε, "therefore/so then" (11:27,33) and it captures the way that 11:27–32 matches 11:23–26 in teaching the Corinthians how to partake worthily, while 11:33–34 provides the remedies to the problems outlined in 11:17–22. Cf. Fitzmyer, *First Corinthians*, 426, who divides the text into five parts: 11:17–22,23–25,26–28,29–32, and 33–34.

[30] When bringing background considerations such as these to bear on our interpretations, we should bear in mind that these things *might* inform what was happening in the church in Corinth. What we have in the text of 1 Cor 11:17–34 does not explicitly declare that the church met in the homes of wealthy members, that wealthy members of the church brought their own private meals (see below), and that the host and patron invited his elite friends into the triclinium, leaving those of lower ranks in the atrium or elsewhere. The interpretation proposed

understand what Paul says in 11:17—"not for the better but for the worse you come together."[31] Paul has pointed to the unifying nature of the Lord's Supper in 10:16–17:

> The cup of blessing which we bless, is it not participation in the blood of the Messiah? The bread which we break, is it not participation in the body of the Messiah? Because there is one bread, we the many are one body, for we all partake of the one bread.

As Jay Smith writes, "the Lord's Supper is a *koinōnia*, 'a communal participation, a sharing together' in Christ's redemptive work and identity and all that this solidarity with him means and entails."[32] This term *koinōnia*, which means "fellowship" or "participation," is used elsewhere by Paul to describe his "fellowship" in the sufferings of Christ and conformity to His death (Phil 3:10). Paul also uses the term to describe the way the Macedonians shared in the ministry to the saints by their generous gifts (2 Cor 8:4). Participating in the body and blood of the Messiah, then, would appear to point to union with Christ in His death and resurrection (cf. Gal 2:20; Eph 2:5–6). Those who bless the cup and break the bread are celebrating their participation in Christ's death and the benefits it achieved (1 Cor 10:16). Moreover, since they are united to Christ, they are also united to one another—they are "one body" partaking of "one bread" (10:17). This means that the celebration of the Lord's Supper enacts the solidarity of the members of the church and her Messiah, in whose body and blood, death and resurrection, she participates. This solidarity with Christ entails another: the solidarity of the members of the church with one another in the body of Christ as they partake of the one bread. But

here fits these circumstances, but as noted above, the reading adopted herein is not ultimately dependent upon them and they are not the main point Paul is making. The issue Paul has with the church in Corinth is simply that their conduct at the Lord's Supper is in conflict with what they are ostensibly proclaiming in the Lord's Supper. Participation in the Lord's Supper declares that their identity is determined by the gospel and that the gospel is a message of One who was rich becoming poor so that others could be rich by His poverty (cf. 2 Cor 8:9). The behavior of the Corinthians at the Lord's Supper instead affirms social distinctions between those who have and those who do not have, and this denies the gospel and demonstrates that their identity has not been reshaped by it.

[31] The verb συνέρχομαι, "come together," occurs five times in this passage, the first three instances (11:17,18,20) highlighting the disjunction between the physical "coming together" and the church's failure to realize a corresponding spiritual "coming together," and the last two calling for it (11:33,34). Hays (*First Corinthians*, 194) cites an interesting parallel describing "the many" "coming together" as "one personality" for the "better" in Aristotle, *Politics* 3.6.4.

[32] Smith, "1 Corinthians," 276.

rather than affirming the unity of the body, that is, the church, the actions of the Corinthians are divisive:[33] "For first,[34] indeed, when you come together as a church, I hear that there are divisions among you, and in part I believe it" (1 Cor 11:18). Paul's comments that follow elaborate on the nature of the divisions he addresses. Here we note a verbal link between 11:18 and 1:10, established by the use of the word "divisions" (*schismata*) in both places.[35] Paul's statement that he believes what he has heard "in part" means, as Fee writes, "that he really does believe it but also acknowledges that his informants are scarcely disinterested observers."[36]

Paul then indicates that the hard work of church life—plowing, planting, sowing, watering (cf 1 Cor 3:6–9)—not only means that those who serve will get dirt under their fingernails, it also reveals who is approved: "For it is even necessary for there to be factions among you, in order that the approved might be manifest among you" (11:19). Schreiner correctly concludes that those who are not approved "are not truly believers."[37] The crucible of church life reveals

[33] Fitzmyer, *First Corinthians*, 433.

[34] C. K. Barrett (*The First Epistle to the Corinthians*, BNTC [Peabody: Hendrickson, 1968], 260) observes that no "secondly" follows the "first," but A. T. Robertson (*GGNT* 1152) suggests "the contrast is implied in verses 20 ff." This would seem to indicate that Robertson takes Paul to mean: first, there are divisions among you (11:18), and second, it is not the Lord's Supper that you eat (11:20). Alternatively, Robertson and Plummer write, "Possibly there is no antithesis; but some find it in the section about spiritual gifts (xxii.1 f.)" (A. Robertson and A. Plummer, *A Critical and Exegetical Commentary on the First Epistle of St Paul to the Corinthians*, 2nd ed., ICC [Edinburgh: T&T Clark, 1914], 239).

[35] See Thiselton, *First Corinthians*, 850.

[36] Fee, *First Corinthians*, 537. The position Hays endorses, that this is a rhetorical way for Paul to highlight his incredulity at the Corinthians' outrageous behavior, seems strained in light of the more direct ways Paul expresses his indignation elsewhere in the letter (see below) (Hays, *First Corinthians*, 295; similarly Barrett, *First Corinthians*, 261). Fee's view is superior to others that have been proposed because Paul does argue as though he believes that the abuses that have been reported are indeed occurring. Robertson and Plummer suggest that Paul "will not believe that all he hears to their discredit is true" (*First Corinthians*, 239), a view which does not fit well with Paul's statements about human nature and the behavior of the Corinthians elsewhere—would he have believed the report addressed in 1 Cor 5:1–5 if this view were correct? Thiselton (*First Corinthians*, 858) writes, "Paul avoids unnecessary confrontation and especially rash, overly hasty speech," but this hardly matches Paul's vigorous interaction with ideas he disputes (cf. 1 Cor 4:8–21; 5:3–5; 6:5; 11:22. Cf. 15:35–36, "But someone will ask . . . ? Fool!"). Nor am I convinced by Winter's argument that the phrase should be rendered "I believe a certain report" (*After Paul Left Corinth*, 159–63), since the summaries of the usage of μέρος in LSJ (s.v., 1104–05), MM (s.v., 389–99), L&N (s.v., 2:160), and BDAG (s.v., 633–34) all seem to indicate that the word signifies "part/portion," with meanings such as "matter/business" being derived from "one's portion in the business;" meanwhile, the adverbial accusative reflected in the rendering "in part I believe it" seems very well established.

[37] Schreiner, *New Testament Theology*, 733.

whether the participants have received God's Spirit and been enabled to understand the gospel and its implications for how they should conduct themselves (2:12). The contextual implication of 1 Cor 11:19 is that those who are "approved" will adhere to Paul's teaching on the Lord's Supper.

Paul's words in 1 Cor 11:20 probably would have been shocking to the members of the Corinthian church. Again, if the architectural and social scene that scholars have put together informs this passage, the members of the Corinthian church were conducting themselves according to expected and accepted patterns of behavior in Roman Corinth in their celebration of the Lord's Supper. Paul declares that they are not, in fact, eating the Lord's Supper because they are acting according to what was accepted custom among human beings: "When you come together in the same place, then, it is not to eat the Lord's Supper" (11:20).

Paul begins to underscore the fundamentally counter-cultural nature of the Lord's Supper as a proclamation of the Lord's death in 11:21: "for in the eating each one devours his own supper, and one goes hungry while another gets drunk." In this translation I have rendered the term *prolambanō* "devours." This translation assumes that the prefixed preposition *pro-* is serving to intensify the meaning of the verb (take vigorously = devour) rather than indicating temporal priority (take beforehand).[38] The temporal aspect of the preposition *pro-* is widely recognized,[39] but it does not seem to fit the context, where some six phrases in 11:18–21 point to the church being gathered when this action takes place: (1) "when you come together" (11:18);[40] (2) "as a church" (11:18); (3) "divisions among you" (11:18); (4) "when you

[38] BDAG, s.v., 872, places the use of προλαμβάνω in 1 Cor 11:21 under the first subheading, with text in bold that reads "to do someth. that involves some element of temporal priority." By contrast, BAGD, s.v., 708, places the use of this verb in 1 Cor 11:21 under the second subheading, with the explanatory comment (lacking in BDAG), "in uses where the temporal sense of προ- is felt very little, if at all." I owe this observation to the discussion in Smith, "1 Corinthians," 285–88. For a discussion of linguistic evidence, with the pertinent observation that in Gal 6:1 the verb simply means "taken/caught," see O. Hofius, "The Lord's Supper and the Lord's Supper Tradition: Reflections on 1 Cor 11:23b–25," in *One Loaf, One Cup: Ecumenical Studies of 1 Cor 11 and Other Eucharistic Texts*, ed. B. F. Meyer (Macon, GA: Mercer University Press, 1993), 91. See also Garland, *1 Corinthians*, 540–42; Hays, *First Corinthians*, 197.

[39] See, e.g., BDAG, s.v., 864; A. T. Robertson, *GGNT*, 620–22; BDF § 213.

[40] D. B. Wallace (*GGBB*, 655) states that "about 90% of the time" the genitive absolute participle (here συνερχομένων ὑμῶν, also in 11:20) is temporal. Fitzmyer (*First Corinthians*, 433) sees a concessive nuance in the participle ("Although you hold your meetings in one place") but also acknowledges the temporal nuance.

come together" (11:20); (5) "in the same place" (11:20); (6) "in the eating" (11:21).[41] These phrases indicate that the problem is one that happens once all the members have gathered, rather than one that begins before some members of the church arrive.[42]

The picture of what was happening is given a little more detail in 1 Cor 11:22: "For do you not have houses for eating and drinking? Or do you despise the church of God, and do you shame those who have not? What do I say to you? Shall I praise you? In this I do not praise you." This salvo of questions seems directed at "those who have" rather than at "those who have not."

The question about the homes they have where they can eat and drink is suggestive, and when we combine it with Paul's observation in 11:19 that divisions are necessary and the command to eat at home if one is hungry in 11:34, the question suggests that the Corinthians should evaluate their actions. They are eating their own supper rather than the Lord's Supper (11:20–21), and they should do that in their own homes, not in the church (11:22).

Paul understands the behavior of "those who have" to be such that it both despises the church and shames "those who have not." It seems, then, that cultural norms were controlling what happened when the Corinthian church gathered to partake of the Lord's Supper.

[41] On the phrase ἐν τῷ φαγεῖν, which I have rendered "in the eating," cf. D. Burk, *Articular Infinitives in the Greek of the New Testament: On the Exegetical Benefit of Grammatical Precision*, New Testament Monographs 14 (Sheffield: Sheffield Phoenix, 2006), 95–96: "BDF suggests that ἐν τῷ plus the present infinitive denotes contemporaneous time while ἐν τῷ plus the aorist infinitive denotes antecedent time [§404 and (2)]. . . . Ernest Burton has rightly rejected this view of the aorist tense in ἐν τῷ plus the infinitive [*Syntax of the Moods and Tenses of New Testament Greek*, 50]. . . . Simply put, the infinitive uses tense morphemes not to grammaticalize time, but verbal aspect. . . . The articular infinitive emphasizes the *locative* use of the dative case." This would seem to indicate that the "*temporal* 'location'" (Burk, *Articular Infinitives*, 92) is in view with the whole church gathered to eat at the same time. Similarly Hofius, "The Lord's Supper," 89. See also BAGD, s.v. ἐν, II.3, 260, discussing ἐν τῷ plus the aorist infinitive, "the meaning is likewise *when*. Owing to the fundamental significance of the aor. the action in such a construction is not thought of as durative, but merely as punctiliar." BDAG has changed the last phrase to read, "Owing to the fundamental significance of the aor. the action is the focal point" (BDAG, s.v. ἐν, 10.c, 330).

[42] Hofius makes a similar observation about ἕκαστος "each one" and ὃς μὲν . . . ὃς δὲ "one goes hungry, another gets drunk" ("The Lord's Supper," 89–90, cf. 92). *Pace* Fitzmyer, *First Corinthians*, 434–35, who maintains that temporal nuances are in view in both 11:21 ("goes ahead with his own meal") and 11:33 ("wait for one another"). For discussion of relevant lexical evidence, see B. W. Winter, "'Private' Dinners and Christian Divisiveness (1 Cor 11:17–34)," in *After Paul Left Corinth*, 144–48 (142–58). Fee also claims "there is no clear evidence of the verb *prolambanō*'s being used this way [temporal priority] in the context of eating" (*First Corinthians*, 542).

The "haves" were perhaps eating superior food and greater quantities of it. Evidence for the superior food of the wealthier members of the church might be seen in the statement, "each one devours *his own* supper" (11:21, emphasis added).[43] This understanding sees Paul's reference to drunkenness in 11:21 as a hyperbolic characterization of the way the "haves" disregarded the inferior, insufficient provisions of the "have nots."[44] So if those in the church of higher social standing and greater means were enjoying a sumptuous feast in the triclinium, while those of lower status—a judgment that itself denies the leveling influence of the gospel—were left in an outer room such as the atrium or court to make do with food of lower quality, we can understand why Paul would say such behavior despises the church and shames the "have nots."[45]

To be specific: this behavior shames the church because rather than depicting the need common to all—rich and poor, slave and master, male and female, Jew and Gentile—the need for the gospel that is proclaimed in the Supper, the observance of what seem to amount to class distinctions at the Supper enacts the socio-economic distinctions of the pagan Roman culture.[46] This behavior of the Corinthians shows that their identity has not been reconfigured by the gospel. As Paul has done throughout the letter of 1 Corinthians to this point, so he does here: he confronts Corinthian error with Christian gospel.

Proclaiming the Lord's Death

Paul introduces his description of the Lord's Supper with words that mark what follows as traditional material: "For I received from the Lord what I also delivered to you" (1 Cor 11:23).[47] Paul then

[43] For a concise summary of the evidence, see Smith, "1 Corinthians," 285–86. For further discussion, see Winter, "'Private' Dinners and Christian Divisiveness," 154–58. For a summary of the proposals that favor Winter's view, see Fee, *First Corinthians*, 540–41. If B. B. Blue is correct that a famine struck Corinth soon after Paul left, the situation would have been exacerbated by food shortages ("The House Church at Corinth and the Lord's Supper: Famine, Food Supply, and the *Present Distress*," *CTR* 5.2 (1991): 221–39.

[44] So also Smith, "1 Corinthians," 286; Fee, *First Corinthians*, 542–43.

[45] Similarly V. P. Furnish, *The Theology of the First Letter to the Corinthians*, New Testament Theology (Cambridge: Cambridge University Press, 1999), 79.

[46] So also Furnish, *Theology of First Corinthians*, 83: "Instead of demonstrating the new life that is established in the gift and claim of the cross, its celebrations demonstrate, rather, that considerations of social status continue to prevail even among those who profess to belong to the company of Christ."

[47] Cf. 1 Cor 15:3. Larry Hurtado writes, "Paul's recitation of early tradition in 1 Cor 11:23–26

recounts the words and actions of Jesus at the Last Supper in terms that correspond most closely to Luke's Gospel,[48] and Luke was one of Paul's traveling companions who might have been with Paul in Corinth.[49] The statement, "what I also delivered to you," in 11:23 establishes that Paul had previously taught these traditions to the Corinthians.[50] As Paul retells the story in the context of this letter, the self-giving of Jesus, which Christians are to remember as they partake of the Lord's Supper, exposes and rebukes the selfish behavior of the Corinthians at the Supper.

Jesus and His disciples were apparently celebrating the Passover when Jesus instituted the Lord's Supper.[51] From Paul's account of what Jesus said and did that night, it appears that Jesus interpreted what was about to take place (His death, resurrection, ascension, and the building of the church) through the framework provided by Israel's

indicates that the cultic significance of Jesus in the meal was not a Pauline innovation, but stemmed from earlier Christian circles" (L. W. Hurtado, *Lord Jesus Christ: Devotion to Jesus in Earliest Christianity* [Grand Rapids: Eerdmans, 2003], 146). Paul's is the earliest account of these events that we have (Robertson and Plummer, *First Corinthians*, 244; Fitzmyer, *First Corinthians*, 429). For a wider study of "Traditions in 1 Corinthians," see E. E. Ellis, *The Making of the New Testament Documents* (Boston: Brill, 2002), 69–94.

[48] For easy comparison of the Synoptic accounts of the Last Supper, see K. Aland, ed., *Synopsis Quattuor Evangeliorum*, 4th ed. rev. (Stuttgart: Deutsche Bibelgesellschaft, 1995 [1963]), 436–37 (§311). Elements of the account that are unique to Luke's Gospel among the Synoptics but are also recounted by Paul include the following: "'. . . which is for you; do this for my remembrance.' . . . So also the cup, after supper saying, 'This cup is the new covenant in my blood.'" For the possible OT texts that influenced the accounts in the Gospels and in 1 Corinthians, see C. J. Collins, "The Eucharist as Christian Sacrifice: How Patristic Authors Can Help Us Read the Bible," *WTJ* 66 (2004): 2, 18–19.

[49] The "we" passages begin in Acts 16:10, but the next first person plurals are used in 20:5 and following, so we cannot be sure that Luke was with Paul in Corinth during the visit narrated in Acts 18:1–17.

[50] Osvaldo Padilla writes, "With his usual meticulousness, Martin Hengel . . . argues that in the unusual chronological detail inserted by Paul in 1 Cor 11:23 ('in the night that Jesus was betrayed') it is possible to deduce that Paul related the entire passion narrative to the congregations he founded" (review of Christian Grappe, ed., *Le Repas de Dieu/Das Mahl Gottes: 4. Symposium Strasbourg, Tübingen, Upsala, 11–15 septembre 2002*, WUNT 169 [Tübingen: Mohr Siebeck, 2004], in *BBR* 18.1 [2008]: 178–79) Cf. M. Hengel, "Das Mahl in der Nacht, 'in der Jesus ausgeliefert wurde' (1 Kor 11,23)," in *Le Repas de Dieu/Das Mahl Gottes*, 115–60.

[51] See Thiselton's excursus, "Was the Last Supper a Passover Meal? Significance for Exegesis" (*First Corinthians*, 871–74), where having discussed the relationship between John and the Synoptics, he concludes, "Jesus presided at a Passover meal which proclaimed his own broken body and shed blood as the new Passover for Christian believers." Collins ("The Eucharist as Christian Sacrifice," 3 and n. 6) urges that the Eucharist be interpreted in light of OT peace offerings, and that the early fathers understood this, while later fathers failed to distinguish between various OT sacrifices, resulting in the misconception of the Eucharist as a propitiatory sacrifice (ibid., 8–9). For the Lord's Supper as a Passover meal, see also Köstenberger's essay in this volume.

history. In order to appreciate the interpretive moves Jesus made, and in order to see the way that Paul carried forward the interpretive strategy he learned from Jesus,[52] we must briefly recount salient elements of the exodus from Egypt and the Passover celebration.

As the climactic plague, Yahweh promised to slay every firstborn in Egypt (Exod 11:4–5). The Israelites were to kill a lamb and place its blood on the doorposts and lintel of their homes (12:6–7,21–23). Seeing the blood on the doorpost, Yahweh passed over the homes covered by the blood (12:13,23). The deliverance was to be commemorated yearly by the Festival of Unleavened Bread (12:14,24–27; 13:3–10). For seven days, the Israelites were to remove leaven from their homes, on pain of being cut off from the people (12:15). The people fled in haste, with no time for the leaven to work through the dough (12:34). Yahweh then claimed the firstborn of Israel for Himself, who were to be redeemed by sacrifice (13:1–2,11–16). Yahweh led Israel out by a pillar of cloud and flame (13:21), and He parted the waters of the Red Sea for Israel to pass through on dry land (14:21–22). As the people moved through the wilderness, Yahweh provided bread from heaven (16:4) and water from a rock (17:6) for the journey to the promised land.

Celebrating the Passover feast commemorating these events with His disciples on the night He was betrayed, Jesus took the symbolism of the hasty departure from Egypt—the unleavened bread—and turned it in a new direction.[53] Paul relates "that the Lord Jesus, on the night in which he was delivered up,[54] took bread, and having given

[52] E. E. Ellis does not cite the connections I will draw here between, for instance, Paul's assertion in 1 Cor 5:7–8 and the teaching of Jesus recounted in 11:23–26, but I am following the lines of his argument in "Jesus' Use of the Old Testament and the Genesis of New Testament Theology," in *Christ and the Future*, 20–37. Similarly D. Wenham, *Paul: Follower of Jesus or Founder of Christianity* (Grand Rapids: Eerdmans, 1995), 158–59.

[53] Gentry, "The Lord's Supper," 26. There is no basis in the text for Hans Conzelmann's assertion, "In contrast to the Synoptics, the Supper in the Pauline version is not characterized as a Passover meal" (*A Commentary on the First Epistle to the Corinthians*, trans. J. W. Leitch, Her [Philadelphia: Fortress, 1975], 197).

[54] The same verb is used in the statements "what I also *delivered* to you" (παρέδωκα) and "in the night he was *delivered up*" (παρεδίδετο). Though translations typically render this "in the night he was *betrayed*" (ESV, HCSB, KJV, NAS, NIV, NJB), commentators seem to prefer "delivered up," which preserves the possible allusion to Isa 53:6, where the same verb is used. See J. Ziegler, *Septuaginta: Vetus Testamentum Graecum Auctoritate Societatis Litterarum Gottingensis editum XIV: Isaias* (Göttingen: Vandenhoeck and Ruprecht, 1939, 1983). Hofius writes, "The passive παρεδίδετο describes the act of God and the verb is used in the sense of Rom 4:25; 8:32. Cf. Isa 53:12" ("The Lord's Supper," 76, n. 4). Robertson and Plummer (*First Corinthians*, 243) write, "To translate 'was betrayed' confines the meaning to the action of Judas; whereas

thanks, he broke it[55] and said, 'This is my body, which is for you; this do for my remembrance'" (1 Cor 11:23–24).[56] Whereas the unleavened bread at the Passover reminded Israel of their hurried flight from Egypt, Jesus identifies the bread with His body. This indicates that Paul learned his interpretive method from Jesus Himself: Jesus explained His death and resurrection as typologically fulfilling what was celebrated in the Passover—the exodus from Egypt. Taking his cue from this, Paul interprets the events of Israel's history as types of Jesus and those He redeems (e.g., 1 Cor 10:1–13). That is to say, Jesus presents His body, broken for His people, as the new exodus replacement of the bread eaten in the Passover feast commemorating the exodus from Egypt.[57] Just as Israel was instructed to *remember* what took place at the exodus by celebrating the Passover (Exod 12:14;

the Father's surrender of the Son is included, and perhaps is chiefly meant, and the Son's self-sacrifice may also be included." Hays argues that God is the one handing Jesus over rather than Judas being the one betraying Jesus (*First Corinthians*, 198). Fitzmyer, *First Corinthians*, 436 follows this view, asserting that Paul never refers to Judas or what he did (but, as Prof. Schreiner has pointed out to me, Paul's comments on the Lord's Supper are also rare). Barrett (*First Corinthians*, 266) also prefers this view. Cf. Conzelmann, *1 Corinthians*, 197, n. 44: "It must not be taken too narrowly in the present passage, i.e. merely of Judas' betrayal." On the other hand, arguing that the treachery of Judas is in view, Fee (*First Corinthians*, 549) writes, "Paul is here referring to the 'tradition,' and the Gospel traditions place the announcement of the betrayal at the time of the Supper."

[55] Thiselton (*First Corinthians*, 875) observes that "in the context of the Last Supper and the Lord's Supper all four accounts include the same pair of Greek words ἄρτον . . . ἔκλασεν (Matt 26:26; Mark 14:22; Luke 22:19; 1 Cor 11:23b,24a)."

[56] For a modern Roman Catholic perspective defending the idea of the "Real Presence," see Fitzmyer, *First Corinthians*, 438–39, 444, 446. Contrast Fitzmyer's view with that of Thiselton, *First Corinthians*, 876–77, Hays, *First Corinthians*, 199, and Fee, *First Corinthians*, 550. Gentry ("The Lord's Supper," 27) gives four concise reasons transubstantiation is a misunderstanding: (1) figurative language is used; (2) the Lord's Supper is rooted in the Passover, which used symbols to memorialize what took place at the exodus; (3) festivals in pagan religions were also symbolic, so a literal understanding of "this is my body" would have required further explanation; and (4) Jesus twice said, "Do this in remembrance of me." See also Hofius, "The Lord's Supper," 100: "just as the cup or its content *is not* the new covenant in the sense of substance, neither is the bread in a substantial sense the body of Christ." So also Schreiner, *New Testament Theology*, 734.

[57] I am suggesting that Paul learned his typological interpretation from Jesus. For an early Christian homily that carries forward the typological interpretation of the Passover being fulfilled in the death of Jesus, see Melito of Sardis (d. ca. 180) "On Pascha." The first part (§§ 1–45) is conveniently available in R. A. Whitacre, ed., *A Patristic Greek Reader* (Peabody, MA: Hendrickson, 2007), 79–98 (introduction and Greek text), 220–27 (English translation). For the full (§§ 1–105) critical text, see S. G. Hall, ed. and trans., *Melito of Sardis: On Pascha and Fragments* (Oxford: Clarendon, 1979). Such a view might also be reflected in *Did* 9:4 if the "broken bread" that "was gathered together and became one" is a reference to exiled Israel being regathered in the person of Jesus.

Deut 16:3), so Jesus instructs His disciples to continue to partake of the bread that is His body for His "remembrance."[58]

Paul continues to narrate what Jesus said and did: "Likewise also the cup, after supper,[59] saying, 'This cup is the new covenant in my blood; this do, as often as you drink it, for my remembrance'" (1 Cor 11:25). The Supper that was eaten, again, was a celebration of the Passover meal. Jesus takes the cup that followed the Supper, and as He had done with the unleavened bread, transforms its symbolism. He identifies the cup as the symbol of the new covenant that He is entering into with His people (cf. Jer 31:31–34). The covenant with the nation of Israel was inaugurated with the blood of sacrificial animals (Exod 24:5–8) in the context of a covenantal feast (24:9–11). The new covenant is inaugurated by the blood of Jesus in the context of the Passover, which Jesus transforms into a celebration of the new exodus accomplished by His own death and resurrection (1 Cor 11:23–26). As Ridderbos writes, "Christ's self-surrender is now, as hitherto the exodus of Israel out of Egypt, the new and definitive fact of redemption which in the eating of the bread and in the drinking of the wine the church may accept as such again and again from the hand of God."[60]

Paul's recitation of the institution of the Lord's Supper confronts what was happening in the Corinthian celebration of the Lord's Supper on two levels: first, the Corinthians are confronted at the level of the simple gospel message, which, second, confronts their conception of their identity as reflected in their behavior.

At the first level, the simple gospel message is presented in the retelling of what Jesus did on the night He was betrayed. This reiterates the need every member of the church has for the sacrifice of

[58] Fitzmyer, *First Corinthians*, 441. Against suggested Hellenistic backgrounds for the remembrance in view, H. Ridderbos writes, "There is much more to be said for a link with the element of *anamnesis* in the ritual of the Jewish feast days, especially in the Passover meal. . . . The Lord's Supper is herewith qualified as a redemptive-historical commemorative meal" (*Paul: An Outline of His Theology*, trans. J. R. De Witt [Grand Rapids: Eerdmans, 1975], 421).

[59] For discussion of the cup, with an argument that there are no pointers "to the particularities of a Passover meal," see Hofius, "The Lord's Supper," 80–86. But the combination of Paul's identification of Jesus as the Passover lamb in 1 Cor 5:7 and the clear connections between 1 Cor 11:23–26 and Luke's Gospel, which Hofius acknowledges to be "clearly oriented to the sequence of a Passover meal" (83, n. 45), place the burden of proof on the case against Paul presenting the Lord's Supper as being instituted in the context of the Last Supper, which was a Passover meal.

[60] Ridderbos, *Paul*, 421.

Christ. Before God, every member of the church in Corinth stood condemned. Neither wealth nor social standing placed some nearer to God than others. First Corinthians 11:23–26 clearly states the significance of Jesus' death as the sacrifice that delivers His people: Jesus *broke* the bread He identified as His body, told His disciples that His broken body was *for them*,[61] and then said that the covenant was *in His blood* (1 Cor 11:24–25).[62] Those who embrace this message embrace the idea that they have nothing but Christ that can commend them to God (cf. 1 Cor 1:30). Thus, anything that distinguishes human beings as superior or inferior by worldly standards of measure is rendered *irrelevant* by the truth of the gospel.

At the second level, Richard B. Hays has it right: "Paul's missionary strategy in his confrontation with pagan culture repeatedly draws upon eschatologically interpreted Scripture texts to clarify the identity of the church and to remake the minds of his congregations."[63] As Hays says at another point, Paul "is calling for a conversion of the imagination—an imaginative projection of their lives into the framework of the Pentateuchal narrative."[64] Paul wants the Corinthian Christians "to understand that they live at the turning point of the ages . . . . they are to see in their own experience the typological fulfillment of the biblical narrative."[65] The upshot of this is that "the Corinthians who still prize [the wisdom of the world] are oblivious to God's apocalyptic delegitimation of their symbolic world."[66]

To see how Paul reshapes the symbolic universe in the minds of the Corinthians, we must again remind ourselves that a letter like 1 Corinthians is occasional. Paul is not systematically explaining the way he sees the world. Rather, he is making assertions on the basis of what he previously taught the Corinthians, and these assertions arise from the narrative storyline that Paul wants the Corinthians to embrace as their own. In seeking to show how the statements Paul

[61] Fitzmyer (*First Corinthians*, 440) writes, "The vicarious sense of the prep. *hyper* can be found in 1 Cor 15:3,29; 2 Cor 5:14; Rom 5:6; 8:32. See also Sir 29:15; 2 Macc 7:9; 8:21 . . ." Thiselton adds Rom 5:8 and Gal 3:13 (*First Corinthians*, 878). Fee writes, "The words 'for you' are an adaptation of the language of Isa. 53:12, where the Suffering Servant 'bore the sin for many'" (*First Corinthians*, 551).

[62] See Hofius, "The Lord's Supper," 98–99.

[63] R. B. Hays, *The Conversion of the Imagination: Paul as Interpreter of Israel's Scripture* (Grand Rapids: Eerdmans, 2005), 5.

[64] Ibid., 10.

[65] Ibid., 11.

[66] Ibid., 14.

makes arise from this underlying thought structure, we are pursuing Pauline theology. In this case, Paul's statements reflect an appropriation of the pattern of events typified at the exodus from Egypt. Paul evidently intends the Corinthian Christians to identify themselves as redeemed slaves who follow Paul as he follows Christ in giving Himself for others. In their behavior at the Lord's Supper, the Corinthians are denying this identity and living out another, the one native to Roman Corinth rather than the Jerusalem above.

In fact, this conception of Christ and the church as the typological fulfillment of the storyline of Israel strengthens the idea that the Lord's Supper is in view when Paul mentions not eating with "one who is called a brother" yet continues in unrepentant sin in 1 Cor 5:11.[67] In 5:7 Paul declared to the Corinthians that "Christ, our Passover lamb, has been sacrificed." Such a declaration implies that just as the slain blood of the Passover lamb on the lintel (Exod 12:21–22) shielded those in the house from Yahweh, who passed over that house (12:23), so also the blood of Christ covers His people, removing from them the threat of God's wrath. In 1 Cor 5:7 Paul also urges the Corinthians to "clean out the old leaven." At the exodus the Israelites were instructed to remove leaven from their homes for seven days, and anyone who ate leaven was to be cut off from the people (Exod 12:14–15). The benefits of the Passover were not applied to anyone who disregarded the command and ate leaven (12:15). They were not shielded from God's wrath but cut off from the people. So also, Paul calls the Corinthian church to "celebrate the feast not in the old leaven" (1 Cor 5:8), calling the church to cleanse itself from the one who has indulged in the "leaven" of sexual immorality (5:1–2). In the light of the Passover imagery throughout 1 Cor 5:1–11, it seems that when Paul says "not even to eat with such a one" in 5:11 he is referring to the exclusion of those who have partaken of the "old leaven" from the new Passover—the Lord's Supper.

The typological fulfillment of the exodus from Egypt in the new exodus of the death and resurrection of Jesus probably also informs Paul's comments about the Corinthians being the temple of the Holy

[67] Cf. Fitzmyer, *First Corinthians*, 243–44: "Not only is one not to share the Lord's Supper with such a wrongdoer, but one should not be found in social contact with him, or even dine with him." Similarly Barrett, *First Corinthians*, 132: "This prohibition will evidently include (though it will not be confined to) his exclusion from the church's common meal (cf. Gal. ii.12; and see x. 16–21; xi. 17–34) . . ."

Spirit (1 Cor 3:16; 6:19) and his references to them being "bought with a price" (6:20; 7:23). Paul makes the typology between Israel and the church explicit in 1 Cor 10:1–13 (esp. 10:6,11). Through the events of the Passover, Yahweh redeemed Israel from slavery, brought them through the waters of the Red Sea, entered into a covenant with them at Sinai, took up residence among them in the tabernacle, and accompanied them as they journeyed through the wilderness on their way to the land of promise. It seems that the undercurrent of Paul's statements to the Corinthians—the narrative framework that results in him saying what he says—is that the Corinthians have experienced the new exodus: Christ is the new Passover lamb whose blood covers them and removes God's wrath; the waters of baptism match the waters of the Red Sea; they have entered into a new covenant; God has tabernacled in them by His Spirit, making them His temple;[68] and they journey through the wilderness toward the kingdom of God, partaking of the Lord's Supper as Israel partook of the manna and celebrated the feasts of God's deliverance.

It seems that Paul provides this narrative to the Corinthians as a way for them to understand who they are, what has happened to them, where they are going, and how they must behave. They are typologically reliving the story of God's redemption of His people, and Paul is calling them to identify themselves with those who believed and were delivered, those whose behavior corresponded with what God had done for them. The problem is that in the Corinthian celebration of the new Passover, the Lord's Supper, their behavior indicates that they are identifying themselves as Romans of social standing rather than as slaves rescued from the house of bondage.

The way that Jesus selflessly sacrificed Himself for others directly repudiates the way that fallen human beings seek to exalt themselves over others. But by observing the social distinctions of Roman culture at the Lord's Table the Corinthians were doing precisely that (11:17–22). Earlier in the letter Paul detailed the way that he laid aside his own rights and preferences for the benefit of others (9:1–23), and then he called the Corinthians to follow him as he follows Christ (11:1). The recitation of what Jesus did on the night He was betrayed rehearses the way that Jesus laid aside His rights and privileges and

[68] On this theme, see my study, *God's Indwelling Presence: The Holy Spirit in the Old and New Testaments*, NACSBT (Nashville: B&H, 2006).

gave Himself for others, and this has implications for the way the Corinthian Christians are to conduct themselves at the Supper.

Before taking up those implications, Paul summarizes the significance of what takes place in the Lord's Supper in 1 Cor 11:26, "For as often as you eat this bread and drink the cup, you proclaim the Lord's death until he comes." It is clear from 1 Cor 10:16–17 that eating the bread and drinking the cup is participating in the body and blood of Christ. This means that in eating the bread and drinking the cup the Corinthians were by faith claiming for themselves the benefits of the death of Christ and identifying themselves with the body of Christ—the church. To proclaim the Lord's death is to celebrate His life-giving sacrifice of Himself, looking back to the cross, and at the same time forward to His return—"until he comes" (11:26).[69]

Partaking in a Worthy Manner

Having proclaimed the Lord's death in the retelling of the institution of the Lord's Supper, Paul presents the church in Corinth with two main implications for behavior at the Lord's Table, each marked with the inferential conjunction *hōste*, which several translations render "therefore" in 11:27 and "So then" in 11:33. These two occurrences of *hōste* mark the two main inferences Paul draws from what he has said to this point: first is the broad application that the Corinthians are to partake of the Lord's Table in a worthy manner (11:27–32), and second are instructions that apply specifically to what was happening in Corinth: they are to receive one another (11:33–34).

Whether or not Paul intended a chiastic structure to 1 Cor 11:17–34, the text seems to fall out that way. The first section, 11:17–22, describes the Corinthians' problematic behavior, and the last section, 11:33–34 provides the specific remedy to that abuse. Similarly, the two middle sections correspond to one another, with the recitation of the institution of the Lord's Supper in 11:23–26 matched by general instructions on taking the Supper in 11:27–32.

Paul's first concluding thought is on taking the Supper worthily: "As a result, whoever eats the bread or drinks the cup of the Lord

[69] Hofius ("The Lord's Supper," 107–8) suggests that the proclamation in view should be understood as a reference to "the Eucharistic prayers spoken over bread and cup." Cf. also Furnish, *Theology of First Corinthians*, 84: "Paul's reference to the Lord's coming is one more expression of the eschatological expectation that surfaces repeatedly in this letter, from the opening thanksgiving (1.7–8) to its closing lines (16.22, 'Our Lord, come!')."

unworthily, he will be guilty of the body and blood of the Lord" (1 Cor 11:27). To be "guilty of the body and blood of the Lord" is nothing less than being guilty of having "crucified the Lord of glory" (2:8, cf. Heb 6:6).[70] Thus, Paul declares in 1 Cor 11:27 that those who partake unworthily identify themselves with those who crucified Christ rather than with those for whom He was crucified. Those who partake unworthily are not with the "approved" (11:19). They neither proclaim the gospel nor is their identity shaped by it. They are unbelievers. They reject Jesus and put Him on the cross. They are guilty of His body and blood. This reading is confirmed by the references to drinking judgment to oneself in 11:29, experiencing God's judgment in 11:30, and being condemned with the world in 11:32.

To clarify, I am arguing that those who have already died (11:30) were not Christians. Some hold that they were Christians whom the Lord killed in discipline,[71] perhaps in line with a similar (mis)interpretation of 1 John 5:16–17.[72] Against this, I am suggesting that a better parallel text is Rev 2:21–23. There Jesus threatens to throw unrepentant Jezebel and those who sin with her "onto a sickbed" and "into great tribulation," and their only hope is to "repent of her works" (Rev 2:22, ESV). If they do not repent, they show themselves to be Jezebel's children, and Jesus promises to "strike her children dead" (2:23, ESV). This matches what Paul says in 1 Cor 11:30–32. In 11:30 he says that many are weak and ill and some have died because of the way they have partaken of the Supper. Jesus has thrown some on the sick bed, and some of Jezebel's children have already been killed. In the next verse, 1 Cor 11:31, Paul states that those who judge themselves rightly will not be judged. I would suggest that judging oneself

[70] So also Garland, *1 Corinthians*, 550–51; F. W. Grosheide, *Commentary on the First Epistle to the Corinthians*, NICNT (Grand Rapids: Eerdmans, 1953), 274. *Pace* BDAG, s.v. ἔνοχος, 338–39, where 1 Cor 11:27 is glossed "sin against the body and blood" under 2.b.γ "to denote the pers. (or thing) against whom the sin has been committed." The reading adopted here would place 1 Cor 11:27 under 2.b.β., "to denote the crime," such that "guilty of the body and blood" refers to the crime of rejecting and crucifying Christ. Obviously Paul is not charging the offenders with the literal death of Christ, but this charge is similar to the one in Heb 6:6 where those who reject Christ "crucify *for themselves* the Son of God"—the idea being that by rejecting Him they are casting their lot in with those who crucified Jesus.

[71] Fee (*1 Corinthians*, 565) says the judgment "does not have to do with their eternal salvation." Hays (*First Corinthians*, 201) speaks of "lapsed Christians."

[72] For an argument that the sin unto death in 1 John 5:16–17 "will amount to specific manifestations of unregenerate conduct," see R. Yarbrough, *1–3 John*, BECNT (Grand Rapids: Baker, 2008), 308.

rightly leads one to conclude that repentance is necessary. The disciplinary action to which Paul refers in 1 Cor 11:32, then, appears to be the sickness and weakness designed to provoke repentance. Being condemned along with the world (1 Cor 11:32) appears to be the killing of an unrepentant, unregenerate person, which is only a foretaste of the "second death" that awaits those whose names are not written in the Lamb's book of life (cf. Rev 20:14–15). In my judgment, the various references in this passage to those who are unrepentant confirm this interpretation: they are unapproved (1 Cor 11:19); they despise the church (11:22); they eat in an unworthy manner and profane the Lord's body and blood (11:27); they eat and drink judgment on themselves (11:29); and Paul tells them to stay home (11:34). Of course, Paul knows that only God knows the heart, so in saying these things he hopes to provoke repentance. He hopes to prompt the Corinthians to judge themselves rightly (11:31), to be moved by the Lord's discipline to avoid condemnation (11:32).[73] It seems likely that he even hopes for some of the unrepentant and unregenerate Corinthians to be converted by this direct confrontation with the gospel.

To avoid the guilt of unrepentance which results in death, Paul counsels the Corinthians, "But let a man examine himself and thus let him eat of the bread and drink from the cup" (1 Cor 11:28). In view of the immediate context, in which Paul has recited the proclamation of the Lord's death (1 Cor 11:23–26), it seems that 1 Cor 11:28 is a call to examine one's life in the light of the gospel. Paul here urges the Christians to ask themselves if they are by faith placing themselves under the blood of Christ in the way that the Israelites placed themselves under the blood of the Passover lamb. Are they recognizing their bankruptcy before God, with Christ as the only thing that can commend them to God, or are they relying on their status in the Roman world? Moreover, they are then to take the further step of evaluating their treatment of others, especially others in the church, by the standard of Christ's self-giving of Himself: has their identity been so shaped by the gospel of Jesus Christ that they now treat others the way that Jesus has treated them?

[73] Though they do not discuss this passage, I am applying the perspective articulated by T. R. Schreiner and A. B. Caneday, *The Race Set Before Us: A Biblical Theology of Perseverance and Assurance* (Downers Grove: InterVarsity, 2001), arguing that 1 Cor 11:27–32 functions the way that other warnings do: to preserve the elect. Garland also treats the warning as functioning this way (*1 Corinthians*, 554).

It is not only the immediate context of this passage, however, that cues us to the indicators Paul gives regarding what constitutes partaking unworthily and how he would have the Corinthians examine themselves. We must pursue what Paul intended by the references to eating and drinking unworthily and self-examination from what Paul has said throughout 1 Corinthians to this point.[74]

According to Fee, "Because the paragraph has had a long history of being read at the Lord's Supper independent of its original context, its interpretation has also been independent of that context."[75] In his view, "Paul's concern is related directly to vv. 20–22, where some are abusing others at the Lord's Table by going ahead with their own private meals. Such conduct is unworthy of the Table where Jesus' death is being proclaimed until he comes."[76] Thus, he sees the introspection that has been based on this passage as a "tragedy."[77] In my view, Fee's interpretation—which would apparently do away with the idea that "People are 'unworthy' if they have any sin in their lives, or have committed sins during the past week,"[78]— focuses too narrowly on the immediate context to the exclusion of the broader context.

There are other places in 1 Corinthians where Paul has addressed the Lord's Supper, and it seems unlikely that the deviant behavior addressed there should be left out of consideration when we seek Paul's view on what it means to partake in an unworthy manner. Paul brought the bread and the cup into his argument that the Corinthian Christians should flee idolatry (10:14–22, esp. 10:16–17). Surely Paul would regard unrepentant participation in idolatry as partaking unworthily.

It seems that Paul also has the Lord's Supper in view in 1 Corinthians 5. He refers to Christ, the Passover Lamb being sacrificed in 1 Cor 5:7, followed by the reference to celebrating the feast not with old leaven in 5:8. Since Jesus transformed the Passover into the Lord's

[74] For a rather different interpretation that focuses on "identification with Christ and the cross in the Lord's Supper [as being] at the same time a dialectical passing through judgment as 'guilty' and 'accepted' or 'rightwise,'" see Thiselton, *First Corinthians*, 898.

[75] Fee, *First Corinthians*, 559.

[76] Ibid., 560.

[77] Ibid., 560, n. 10. Cf. 561 on 11:28, "which along with v. 27 has been the cause of untold anxieties within the church. This is not a call for deep personal introspection to determine whether one is worthy of the Table." Against this, see Garland, *1 Corinthians*, 551: "the Supper is to be eaten in an atmosphere of self-examination."

[78] Fee, *First Corinthians*, 560, n. 10.

Supper on the night He was betrayed, the feast in view would seem to be the Lord's Supper. All this is followed by the call in 5:11 not to eat with professing Christians who continue in unrepentant sin. These observations indicate that anyone who refuses to repent of the sins Paul mentions in 1 Corinthians 5 (sexual immorality, greed, swindling others, idolatry, reviling others, and drunkenness [5:1–2,9–11]) partakes unworthily. Indeed, Paul calls the church to "purge the evil person from among you" (5:13, quoting Deut 17:7). This indicates that individual members of the church should not only be concerned to partake in a worthy manner themselves, but the church as a whole should seek to keep unrepentant individuals from partaking in an unworthy manner.[79]

It would seem, then, that at least everything Paul writes to the church in 1 Corinthians is relevant for what he says in 11:28, "But let a man examine himself and in this way let him eat from the bread and drink from the cup." Is it likely that Paul would limit the self-examination he calls for here to the specific actions addressed regarding the way the Corinthian church is abusing the Supper? No doubt those things are included—surely he means for the Corinthian Christians to examine their hearts to make sure they are trusting in the death of Christ as the definitive sacrifice to reconcile them to God. Surely he also means for them to measure themselves by the self-sacrificial behavior of Jesus—are they following Him in laying down their lives for others just as He did? But the burden of proof would seem to be on anyone who would suggest that Paul did not intend the Corinthian believers to examine themselves with reference to what he said about the gospel being wisdom to the mature but foolishness to the world (1:23; 2:6), about wood, hay, and stubble approaches to ministry (3:10–17), about sexual immorality, homosexuality, and prostitution (6:9–10,15), about proper marital relations (7:1–40), about building others up (10:23), and about appropriate behavior during Christian worship (11:3–16).

The gravity of these issues can be seen in 1 Cor 11:29, where Paul writes, "For the one who eats and drinks, eats and drinks judgment to himself, not discerning the body." The risk of eating and drinking judgment to oneself would seem to commend a thoroughgoing self-examination, rather than a less rigorous approach to the Supper. The

[79] Cf. Fitzmyer, *First Corinthians*, 241; Hays, *First Corinthians*, 201–2.

idea of corporate personality, whereby the one stands for the many and the many are represented in the one, informs the reference to "the body" in 11:29. No distinction should be drawn between the body of Jesus and the church.[80] Both are in view. The one who does not examine himself does not recognize the significance of Christ nor of the body of Christ.

In what he says next, Paul seems to apply the interpretive strategy he modeled in 1 Cor 10:1–13 to the situation of the Corinthians in 11:30: "On account of this many among you are weak and sick and a good number sleep." This assertion is reminiscent of the reference to the bodies of the Israelites being "strewn in the wilderness" in 10:5. Like the Israelites, the Corinthians have been baptized—but with a greater baptism into Christ—and they are partaking of superior spiritual food and drink in the Lord's Supper. And like the Israelites, the Corinthians have engaged in idolatry and sexual immorality, and God is not pleased with them. Like the Israelites, unbelieving Corinthians who associated with the church but lacked genuine faith have experienced God's judgment.

Paul's comments in 1 Cor 11:31–32 continue in this vein: "But if we judge ourselves rightly, we would not be judged; but being judged by the Lord, we are disciplined, so that we might not be condemned with the world." When Paul refers to judging oneself rightly in 11:31, it would seem that he has in view a self-examination (11:28) that rightly discerns the body (11:27,29). This would include discerning that all members of the body of Christ, the church, are on equal footing before the cross, which would exclude the kind of favoritism that reflects relative worth or status by the standards of Roman Corinth. So the church in Corinth is no doubt called here to what Paul will make explicit in 11:33–34.

In addition to this, however, it seems that Paul's comments about celebrating the feast not with old leaven in 5:8 are relevant, and there he identifies "old leaven" as particular sins. Perhaps, then, Paul is calling the church in Corinth to judge whether or not they have sufficiently dealt with the leaven of sin in their lives before they partake of the Lord's Supper. If we ask whether this would ever mean

[80] In keeping with his Roman Catholicism, Fitzmyer prefers the view that "acknowledging the body would mean taking stock of oneself in order to eat the bread and drink of the cup worthily as 'the body and blood of the Lord'" (*First Corinthians*, 446).

that a believer should abstain from partaking in the Lord's Supper, we might have a relevant example from an instance in Israel's history. In Numbers 9 there is an account of some who were unclean and could not keep the Passover at the appointed time, and the Lord directed Moses to have them celebrate the Passover one month later, when they were clean (Num 9:6–12). A NT analog to this may be found in Jesus' teaching in the Sermon on the Mount, when He instructed His disciples that if they are offering a gift at the altar and recognize that a brother has something against them, they should go and be reconciled and then come and offer the gift (Matt 5:23–24). Given the way that Paul has described sin in the life of the believer as "leaven" in the context of the celebration of the feast—the feast that celebrates the sacrifice of Christ, our Passover Lamb (1 Cor 5:6–8)—perhaps a believer recognizing that he has the "old leaven" of sin that he must deal with should abstain. We can also say that the cleansing out of the old leaven that Paul describes in 1 Cor 5:7 is probably a call to repent of sin. Perhaps, then, abstention from partaking of the Lord's Supper should be limited either to a recognition that one is unrepentant on some point, or to a situation in which one must be reconciled to a brother—something that cannot be handled before the rest of the body partakes. This interpretation seems to be reflected in the *Didache*:

> On the Lord's own day gather together and break bread and give thanks, having first confessed your sins so that your sacrifice may be pure. But let no one who has a quarrel with a companion join you until they have been reconciled, so that your sacrifice may not be defiled (*Did* 14:1–2).[81]

In the context of the mention of those who have suffered the Lord's judgment in the form of weakness, sickness, and death (1 Cor 11:30), the way to avoid judgment in 1 Cor 11:31 is to judge oneself rightly. This seems to entail recognizing sin and repenting of it, or, if one is either unrepentant or unable to be reconciled with an offended brother,

[81] While this text is not authoritative, it does reflect the practice of at least one group within early Christianity. I am grateful for fruitful discussion of this passage with Prof. Michael Haykin. Cf. also Collins, "The Eucharist as Christian Sacrifice," 6: "The early Christians required that believers be at peace with one another before they partook of the Eucharist." Similarly I. H. Marshall, "The Last Supper," in *Key Events in the Life of the Historical Jesus: A Collaborative Exploration of Contexts & Coherence*, ed. D. L. Bock and R. L. Webb, WUNT (Tübingen: Mohr Siebeck, 2009), 522.

abstaining.[82] Fee writes, "One does not have to 'get rid of the sin in one's life' in order to partake,"[83] but surely the proclamation of the Lord's death in the elements and the call to examine oneself are an occasion to take stock of one's life and repent of all known sin. Judging oneself in this way delivers one from the Lord's judgment. Indeed, this is itself a form of judgment from the Lord, whose kindness leads to conviction and repentance (Rom 2:4), and this kind conviction unto repentance would seem to be what Paul means when he speaks of the Lord's discipline in 1 Cor 11:32. Those who experience this discipline that provokes repentance avoid the condemnation that comes upon the unrepentant world.

Receiving One Another

Having given general instructions on how to partake of the Lord's Supper in a worthy manner in 1 Cor 11:27–32, Paul addresses the specific abuses of the church in Corinth directly in 11:33–34: "As a result, my brothers, when coming together to eat, receive one another. If anyone is hungry, let him eat at home, so that you might not come together for judgment. Now I will arrange the rest when I come." Above I followed those who understand the verb *prolambanō* in 11:21 to mean *devours* rather than seeing a temporal nuance that would communicate *eating beforehand*. So also in 11:33, I follow those who take the verb *ekdechomai* to mean "receive one another" rather than "wait for one another." As noted above, at least six items in 11:18–21 point to the problematic behavior in Corinth taking place with the whole church gathered rather than before some of the members of the church arrive, and "receive/welcome" is an established meaning of this verb (3 *Macc* 5:26; Josephus, *Ant.* 7.351).[84] In giving this instruction, Paul seems to be calling the "haves" to welcome the "have nots" into their company. Rather than perpetuating the socio-economic distinctions of Roman culture, the Corinthian church is to display the radically unified identity of the body of Christ at the Lord's Supper. They are to proclaim in their actions that they are identified with one

[82] Similarly C. Blomberg, *1 Corinthians*, NIVAC (Grand Rapids: Zondervan, 1994), 234–35.

[83] Fee, *First Corinthians*, 566–67.

[84] See Hofius, "The Lord's Supper," 93–94; Winter, "'Private' Dinners and Corinthian Divisiveness," 151–52; Smith, "1 Corinthians," 287–88 (Smith cites several other passages in Josephus: *Ant.* 11.340; 12.138; 13.104; 13.148; *J.W.* 2.297; 3.32); Hays, *First Corinthians*, 202–3; Fee, *First Corinthians*, 567–68, citing also Tebtunis Papyrus I.33 from MM and LSJ.

another by means of their common need for Christ and their union with Him by faith.

The interpretation of v. 34 has gone in at least two directions. Fitzmyer writes, "If hunger really becomes a problem, there is another way of handling it, apart from eating at the common gathering ahead of others. Consumption at home would eliminate solitary or private eating in a common setting."[85] Against this, however, it does not seem likely that Paul would suggest that the Corinthians have to follow Christ and concern themselves with others when they gather with the church, but when they are at home they can indulge their appetites.[86] No, Paul is telling them that if they want to act like unbelievers they should not gather with the believers because to do so is to "come together for judgment" (1 Cor 11:34). If they want to eat their own dinners rather than the Lord's Supper they should do so in their own homes (11:20–22), identifying themselves with pagan Rome rather than Christ and His kingdom. Reading the passage this way sees Paul's words in 11:34 as a refusal to tolerate selfishness and a call to repent of such behavior.[87] Those who do not identify themselves as being in need of Christ's sacrifice, as redeemed slaves mercied by God, should not gather because to do so only places them under judgment.

Implications for the Contemporary Church

In 1 Cor 11:17–34 the selfishness of the members of the Corinthian church at the Lord's Supper is confronted with the gospel of Jesus' giving of Himself on behalf of others. Paul calls the Corinthians to proclaim this gospel and have their identity and behavior shaped by it. They are to know their bankruptcy before God, to feel mercied and redeemed, and they are to follow Christ by giving themselves for others. When they are thus identified and shaped by the gospel, their celebration of the Lord's Supper will be an identity-forming proclamation of the gospel. They will be proclaiming the Lord's death.

From what Paul says in 1 Cor 11:17–34, it seems that the church partook of the Lord's Supper when they "came together," and from

[85] Fitzmyer, *First Corinthians*, 448. So also Fee, *First Corinthians*, 568: "If you want to satisfy your desire for the kinds of meals that the wealthy are accustomed to eat together, do that at home, but not in the context of the gathered assembly, where some 'have nothing' and are thereby humiliated (vv. 21–22)."

[86] Schreiner, *New Testament Theology*, 733.

[87] Garland, *1 Corinthians*, 555.

1 Cor 16:2, it seems that the Corinthian church "came together" on the first day of the week. When combined with a text like Acts 20:7, which indicates that Paul's practice was to celebrate the Lord's Supper with the church when it gathered for worship on the first day of the week, this seems to be the early church's practice. It is not clear to me why churches that seek to model themselves by the pattern of church life and structure seen in the NT would not also partake of the Lord's Supper on the first day of the week. If it is objected that this would diminish its significance, my reply is simply that those who make this argument typically do not claim that weekly observance diminishes the significance of the preaching of the Word, the prayers of God's people, the singing of Psalms, hymns, and spiritual songs, and I doubt they would be disappointed to have weekly baptisms! The same practices and attitudes that keep preaching, praying, singing, and baptizing from having their significance diminished could surely be applied to the weekly celebration of the Lord's Supper.

In the Lord's Supper, we are proclaiming the Lord's death: heralding that Jesus died for our sins. The gospel has more power to humble than any other force in the world. It places all on equal footing before the cross. This humbling power of the gospel then enables us to proclaim the Lord's death as we live out the self-inconveniencing love for others modeled by Jesus, even unto death.

Just as the kind of idolatry that Paul urged the Corinthian Christians to flee was normal behavior in the wider culture of Roman Corinth, so there are idolatrous behaviors in contemporary culture that are considered normal. Just as there was rampant immorality in Roman Corinth, so all manner of sexual deviancy is considered normal in our day. And just as the Corinthians exalted themselves by identifying with those they thought were superior, so there is no lack of hero-worship and super-star Christianity today, to say nothing of rampant materialism and vainglorious displays of economic privilege. There are no favorites at the Lord's Table. The only cure for factionalism, immorality, idolatry, and favoritism, then as now, is the gospel. Christ covers our sins, transforms our identity and self-conception, and leaves us an example that we should follow in His steps (cf. 1 Pet 2:21–25).

As we come to the Table, we must examine ourselves. If the pendulum has swung too far in the direction of introspection in the past, that is not our problem today. In our flippant culture we are not reflective enough. Self-examination, however, is not an end to itself. It should be spurred by our awareness of the behavior of Christ, which in turn should lead to repentance and celebration of the sufficiency of Christ's death. Self-examination should be prompted by our understanding of Christ's love, and it should then be swallowed up in our awareness of God's mercy to those of us who believe—for the things about ourselves of which we become aware in our examination are all nailed to the cross of Christ. Let us proclaim His death until He comes![88]

[88] A previous version of this essay was presented at the national meeting of the Evangelical Theological Society in November 2008. I wish to thank Professor Thomas R. Schreiner for his careful reading and stimulating interaction on this study.

"A GLORIOUS INEBRIATION": EUCHARISTIC THOUGHT AND PIETY IN THE PATRISTIC ERA[1]

Michael A. G. Haykin*

It is commonplace to say that because the nature of the Lord's Supper was never the subject of a formal controversy in the ancient church, the amount of literature pertaining to it is somewhat limited. Although there was indeed no such controversy, there is such a plethora of material related to this subject that it makes it difficult to know what to treat in a survey like this one. The renowned patristic scholar Everett Ferguson, when writing a similar survey, restricted himself to the question of the real presence as found in the Latin-speaking tradition, and even then he only took what he called "soundings at strategic places" in this tradition's history of eucharistic theology.[2] This present essay, although also focused on some key pastor-theologians—five to be precise (Justin Martyr, Irenaeus of Lyons, Cyprian of Carthage, Ambrose of Milan, and Basil of Caesarea)—takes a somewhat different approach. While it includes some discussion of questions that later generations in the ninth and sixteenth centuries, when there was profound controversy over the Lord's Table, found interesting, it also reflects on the experiential piety of these five men so as to better understand what the non-literate Christian of this era might have experienced when he sat down to eat and drink at his Lord's Table in the churches of one of these men.[3] It

* Michael A. G. Haykin received his Th.D. from Wycliffe College and the University of Toronto. He is professor of Church History and Biblical Spirituality and director of The Andrew Fuller Center for Baptist Studies at The Southern Baptist Theological Seminary in Louisville, Kentucky.

[1] The phrase quoted in the title is from Ambrose, *On the Sacraments*, 5.3.17. See below for its context.

[2] "The Lord's Supper in Church History: The Early Church Through the Medieval Period," in *The Lord's Supper: Believers Church Perspectives*, ed. D. R. Stoffer (Scottdale, PA/Waterloo, Ontario: Herald, 1997), 21–45. It should be noted that Ferguson was also dealing with a much larger expanse of time than this essay.

[3] For some helpful synthetic essays of patristic thought and practice, see G. W. H. Lampe, "The Eucharist in the Thought of the Early Church," in *Eucharistic Theology Then and Now*, ed. G. W. H. Lampe et al. (London: SPCK, 1968), 34–58; E. G. Hinson, "The Lord's Supper in Early Church History," *RevExp* 64 (Winter, 1969): 15–24; G. Kretschmar, "Abendmahl. III/1. Alte Kirche," *TRE* 1:59–89; R. J. Halliburton, "The Patristic Theology of the Eucharist," in *The Study of Liturgy*, ed. C. Jones, G. Wainwright, and E. Yarnold (London: SPCK, 1978),

is this essay's partial focus on eucharistic piety, then, that explains the choice of three of the figures examined, namely, Cyprian, Ambrose, and Basil, all of whom explained the Lord's Supper in ways that open up significant vistas on patristic piety. If the questions of later eras had been the main guiding principle for the choice of individuals studied, then it would have been appropriate to include an author such as Augustine of Hippo (354–430), some of whose statements were central to the eucharistic debates at the time of the Reformation.[4] Justin and Irenaeus are included since they offer two very important early witnesses to patristic thought about the Table.

"Fouler than any sacrilege": Roman Accusations about the Christian Eucharist

In what is the earliest pagan Roman description of Christianity, the imperial governor Pliny the Younger (61/62–c. 113) mentions in a letter to the emperor Trajan (reign 98–117) that Christians in Bithynia and Pontus, whom he had placed on trial for their beliefs, were in the habit of meeting on a weekly basis "to partake of food—but common and harmless food [*cibum, promiscuum tamen et innoxium*]."[5] Pliny's evident surprise that the food consumed by these Christians was both "ordinary and harmless" seems to reveal that he expected to find something quite different, namely, "deviate and sinister meals."[6] Such meals as were supposedly consumed by Christians were luridly

201–8; A. I. C. Heron, *Table and Tradition* (Philadelphia: Westminster, 1983), 59–79; D. Sheerin, "Eucharistic Liturgy," in *The Oxford Handbook of Early Christian Studies*, ed. S. A. Harvey and D. G. Hunter (Oxford: Oxford University Press, 2008), 711–43.

[4] For a brief, but very helpful, summary of Augustine's eucharistic thought, see C. Markschies, "Eucharist/Communion. II. Church History. 1. Early Church," in *Religion Past & Present: Encyclopedia of Theology and Religion*, ed. H. D. Betz et al. (Leiden/Boston: Brill, 2008), 4:624.

[5] Pliny, *Letter* 10.96. All translations of Greek and Latin in this chapter are those of the author, unless otherwise indicated. On the date of this letter, see A. N. Sherwin-White, *The Letters of Pliny: A Historical and Social Commentary* (Oxford: Clarendon, 1966), 693. For its interpretation, also see J. C. Salzmann, "Pliny (ep. 10, 96) and Christian Liturgy—A Reconsideration," *StPatr* 20 (1989): 389–95. For an English translation of this letter, see B. Radice, *The Letters of the Younger Pliny* (Harmondsworth, Middlesex: Penguin Books, 1963), 293–95.

[6] J. Engberg, *Impulsore Chresto: Opposition to Christianity in the Roman Empire c.50–250 AD*, trans. G. Carter, Early Christianity in the Context of Antiquity 2 (Frankfurt am Main: Peter Lang, 2007), 188. For a similar opinion, see A. Henrichs, "Pagan Ritual and the Alleged Crimes of the Early Christians: A Reconsideration," in *Kyriakon: Festschrift Johannes Quasten*, ed. P. Granfield and J. A. Jungmann (Münster: Verlag Aschendorff, 1970), 1:19–20. For a different reading of this text, see L. R. Lanzillotta, "The Early Christians and Human Sacrifice," in *The Strange World of Human Sacrifice*, ed. J. N. Bremmer (Leuven: Peeters, 2007), 84–85.

described in a speech from the mid-second century that some scholars attribute to the Roman grammarian and rhetorician Marcus Cornelius Fronto (c. 100–166/176) and that was cited by the Christian apologist Minucius Felix (fl. 200–35) in his rebuttal of attacks on the Christian faith:

> The story of their [i.e. Christian] initiation of novices [is] as horrible as it is well known. A baby covered with pastry, so as to deceive the unwary, is set before the initiate in their rites. The novice is encouraged by the pastry crust to give it seemingly harmless jabs and the baby is killed by the unseen and hidden wounds. Thirstily—O for shame!—they lick up his blood, compete in sharing out his limbs, league themselves together by this victim, pledge themselves to mutual silence by this complicity in crime. These rites are fouler than any sacrilege.[7]

Given the number of Christian apologists in the second century who responded to this charge of cannibalism, there seems little doubt that this accusation about Christians was widespread.[8] It is, of course, a garbled misunderstanding of the dominical command to "eat his body" and "drink his blood" as well as mere slander. But if the early Christians were not engaged in such reprehensible deeds, what was actually happening in their assemblies when they took the Lord's Supper?

"We do not receive . . . ordinary bread or ordinary drink": The View of Justin Martyr

An excellent entry-point into second-century eucharistic praxis and piety is the discussion of the rite by the apologist Justin Martyr (c. 100/110–c. 165) in his *First Apology* (151/155).[9] According to

[7] *Octavius* 9.5, trans. M. Whittaker, *Jews and Christians: Graeco-Roman Views* (Cambridge: Cambridge University Press, 1984), 174. For Minucius's rebuttal of this charge, see *Octavius* 30.1–2. Minucius Felix is notoriously difficult to date. For one argument that places his writing *Octavius* during the Severan dynasty, see G. W. Clarke, "The Historical Setting of the Octavius of Minucius Felix," *JRH* 4 (1966–67): 265–86. P. J. Cousins argues for a date after 260: "Great Lives in Troubled Times: The Date and Setting of the Octavius by Minucius Felix," *VE* 27 (1997): 45–56.

[8] See, for instance, Justin Martyr, *First Apology,* 26; id., *Second Apology,* 12; Athenagoras, *Plea for the Christians,* 3.35; Tertullian, *Apology,* 7.1; Eusebius, *Ecclesiastical History,* 5.1. See the excellent and provocative discussions of this issue in Henrichs, "Pagan Ritual and the Alleged Crimes of the Early Christians," 18–35, and A. McGowan, "Eating People: Accusations of Cannibalism Against Christians in the Second Century," *JECS* 2 (1994): 413–42.

[9] For a recent collection of essays on Justin's life and thought, see S. Parvis and P. Foster, eds., *Justin Martyr and His Worlds* (Minneapolis: Fortress, 2007). See also P. Parvis, "Justin Martyr," *ExpTim* 120 (2008): 53–61.

Justin's *Second Apology*, it was the sight of the martyrs that initially drew him to Christianity in the early 130s.[10] Twenty or so years later, he was ministering as a teacher in Rome and busy drawing up his *First Apology*. Justin's statements about the Lord's Supper are very significant, for he is the earliest witness outside of the NT to the words of the Supper's institution, and, according to Andrew Brian McGowan, his discussion of the Lord's Supper in the *First Apology* is "perhaps the single most important witness to the ritual form of a eucharistic meal for fifty years on either side."[11]

Justin moves into a discussion of the celebration of the Lord's Supper after his treatment of the practice of Christian baptism. He outlines two eucharistic celebrations: the first customarily followed the baptism of believers and the second was the regular weekly Communion.[12] At the former, there was first prayer and then the kiss of peace. Afterward, Justin said, the elements of "bread and a cup of water and wine mixed with water" were brought to the "ruler [*proestōs*] of the brethren" who offers up prayer and thanksgiving (*eucharistian*) to "the Father of the universe through the name of the Son and the Holy Spirit." The deacons distributed the elements and all present who were believers partook of "the eucharistized bread and wine and water [*tou eucharistēthentos artou kai oinou kai hudatos*]."[13] What Justin understands by the term *eucharistēthentos*, he now explains:

> Now, this food is called by us "the eucharist," from which no one is allowed to partake except the one who believes what we teach to be true, and who has been washed with the washing that is for the forgiveness of sins and regeneration, and who lives in exactly the way Christ handed down to us. For we do not receive these things as ordinary bread or ordinary drink [*koinon arton oude koinon poma*]; but, just as Jesus Christ our Savior was made flesh by a word of God and took flesh and blood for our salvation, so also we have been taught that the food for which thanks has been given [*eucharistētheisan trophēn*] by a word of prayer [*di' euchēs logou*] that is from him,[14] from which

[10] *Second Apology,* 12. For the date of Justin's conversion, see L. W. Barnard, "Introduction" to his trans., *St. Justin Martyr: The First and Second Apologies* (New York/Mahwah, NJ: Paulist, 1997), 4–5.

[11] "'Is there a Liturgical Text in this Gospel?': The Institution Narratives and Their Early Interpretive Communities," *JBL* 118 (1999): 80.

[12] *First Apology,* 65 and 67. For the Greek text of Justin, I have used E. J. Goodspeed, ed., *Die ältesten Apologeten* (Göttingen: Vandenhoeck & Ruprecht, 1915).

[13] *First Apology,* 65. For the translation of προεστώς, see T. G. Jalland, "Justin Martyr and the President of the Eucharist," in *Studia Patristica, Texte und Untersuchungen* 80, ed. F. L. Cross (Berlin: Akademie-Verlag, 1962), 5:83–85.

[14] For the translation of this phrase "by a word of prayer that is from him," see G. J. Cuming,

> our flesh and blood are nourished by a transformation [*kata metabolēn*], is the flesh and blood of that Jesus who became incarnate. For the Apostles, in the memoirs produced by them, which are called Gospels, thus handed on what they were commanded: Jesus took bread, gave thanks [*eucharistēsanta*], and said, "Do this in remembrance of me, this is my body"; and likewise he took the cup, and giving thanks, said, "This is my blood."[15] And he shared it with them alone.[16]

Justin begins by stressing that the Eucharist is only for those who have embraced the Christian faith, have been baptized as believers, and who are living in obedience to the teaching of Christ.[17] The bread and the wine consumed in the Lord's Supper, he continues, are not to be regarded simply as bread and wine, but after thanks has been given for them, they are the "flesh and blood" of Christ. Understandably Justin's realistic language here has been interpreted in the light of later eucharistic debates, such as those of the ninth and sixteenth centuries, but what is noteworthy is not only the realism of Justin's eucharistic doctrine but also the restraint with which he writes.

He does not spell out what he means by the phrase *kata metabolēn*, for instance. Is this phrase a description of an ontological change in the bread and the wine? Or is it describing a transformation in the person partaking of the Eucharist?[18] There is also a distinct lack of clarity about the clause *di' euchēs logou*. Does this indicate that the change in the bread and wine comes about through the actual word of institution, which would entail the preposition *dia* governing *logou*?[19] Or is *logou* a subjective genitive, which would imply that the divine Word, invoked in the *epiclesis*, that is, the invocation of the Spirit,

"ΔΙ' ΕΥΧΗΣ ΛΟΓΟΥ (Justin, *Apology*, i.66.2)," *JTS* 31 (1980): 80–82 and A. Gelston, "ΔΙ' ΕΥΧΗΣ ΛΟΓΟΥ (Justin, *Apology*, i.66.2)," *JTS* 33 (1982): 172–75.

[15] This quotation does not reproduce exactly any of the statements by Jesus in the canonical Gospels. Rather it seems a loose rendering of Matt 26:26–8 and 1 Cor 11:23–25.

[16] *First Apology*, 66.

[17] L. W. Barnard, *Justin Martyr: His Life and Thought* (Cambridge: University Press, 1967), 145.

[18] Ferguson, "Lord's Supper in Church History," 23–4; J. Pelikan, *The Emergence of the Catholic Tradition (100–600)* (vol. 1 of *The Christian Tradition;* Chicago/London: University of Chicago Press, 1971), 169; Barnard, *St. Justin Martyr: The First and Second Apologies*, 181, n. 407; C. Buchanan, "Questions Liturgists Would Like to Ask Justin Martyr," in Parvis and Foster, eds., *Justin Martyr and His Worlds*, 152–59. See also P. H. Jones, *Christ's Eucharistic Presence: A History of the Doctrine* (New York: Peter Lang, 1994), 29.

[19] The views of Cuming, "ΔΙ' ΕΥΧΗΣ ΛΟΓΟΥ (Justin, *Apology*, i.66.2)," and Gelston, "ΔΙ' ΕΥΧΗΣ ΛΟΓΟΥ (Justin, *Apology*, i.66.2)."

is the agent of transformation?[20] No clear answer is forthcoming to any of these questions, either in the larger context of this text nor in Justin's other main references to the Eucharist in his *Dialogue with Trypho*, where he sees the Eucharist as a fulfillment of the "pure sacrifice" of Mal 1:11.[21] Justin appears content to generally allude to the spiritual blessings of the Lord's Supper without specifying the exact way in which those blessings come through the bread and the wine. Later attempts to argue from the realism of his language to a specific eucharistic theory are both anachronistic and futile.[22]

"Consisting of two realities": The Eucharistic Thought of Irenaeus of Lyons

Prior to going to Rome, Justin had taught in Ephesus, not far from Smyrna, the native town of Irenaeus of Lyons (c. 130–c. 200), the leading Greek theologian of the last quarter of the second century.[23] It is very likely that Irenaeus studied under Justin either in Ephesus or later at Rome.[24] In Smyrna, Irenaeus was also privileged to sit under the preaching and teaching ministry of Polycarp (c. 69/70–155/156).[25] At some point before the martyrdom of Polycarp, Irenaeus moved to Rome and then later to Lyons as a missionary teacher. It says much for Irenaeus's passion for planting mature, biblical churches that he learned the language of the native people, Gaulish, a Celtic tongue now extinct. According to his own report Irenaeus so concentrated

[20] M. Heintz, "δι' εὐχῆς λόγου τοῦ παρ' αὐτοῦ (Justin, *Apology*, 1.66.2): Cuming and Gelston Revisited," *Studia Liturgica* 33 (2003): 33–36. See also Barnard, *Justin Martyr*, 147.

[21] *Dialogue with Trypho*, 41. For a brief discussion of this text, see Barnard, *Justin Martyr*, 144. On the importance of Mal 1:11 in the development of patristic reflection on the Lord's Supper, see Heron, *Table and Tradition*, 74–5; D. A. Adams, "Augustine's Doctrine of the Eucharist" (Unpublished M.A. thesis, The University of Western Ontario, 1990), chap. 2.

[22] Pelikan, *The Emergence of the Catholic Tradition*, 167; D. Bridge and D. Phypers, *Communion: The Meal That Unites?* (Wheaton: Harold Shaw, 1981), 51; Ferguson, "Lord's Supper in Church History," 24.

[23] On Irenaeus and his thought, see especially D. Minns, *Irenaeus* (London: Geoffrey Chapman, 1994); R. M. Grant, *Irenaeus of Lyons* (London: Routledge, 1997); and E. Osborn, *Irenaeus of Lyons* (Cambridge: Cambridge University Press, 2001). For an excellent brief overview, see D. Minns, "Irenaeus," *ExpTim* 120 (January, 2009): 157–66, and for a significant critique of Grant, *Irenaeus of Lyons*, see J. R. Payton Jr., "Condensing Irenaeus: A Review Article," *CTJ* 33 (1988): 175–85.

[24] See M. Slusser, "How Much Did Irenaeus Learn from Justin?" *StPatr* 40 (2006): 515–20.

[25] *The Martyrdom of Polycarp*, 22.2 and Appendix IV.1–2 (The Moscow Epilogue); Irenaeus, *Letter to Florinus* (cited in Eusebius of Caesarea, *Church History*, 5.20); Irenaeus, *Against Heresies*, 3.3.4.

on mastering this language that he later felt that he had lost much of his facility with his own language.[26] After the death of the bishop of Lyons, Pothinus, in a vicious bout of persecution in 177, Irenaeus was appointed bishop of the church in Lyons.

It was in the final period of his life, during the 180s, that Irenaeus wrote his magnum opus, *The Refutation and Overthrow of the Knowledge Falsely So Called*,[27] though the five-volume work has become more popularly known as simply *Against Heresies*. It was originally written in Greek—hence Irenaeus's concern regarding his facility in his mother tongue—but the Greek version is only partially preserved. The whole text has come down to us solely in Latin.[28] Principally it is a spirited reply to the two major heretical movements of the second century: that of Marcion (fl.120s–150s)[29] and Gnosticism, in particular, the views of Valentinus (fl.130s–60s) and his disciples.[30] Marcion, Valentinus, and most Gnostics were committed to a radical dualism of immateriality and matter. The former was divine and wholly good, while the latter was irredeemably evil. Through a cosmic upheaval, bits of immateriality became trapped in material bodies as human souls. Since this entrapment in the human body was hidden, knowledge of one's true state was needed, which, for most Gnostic systems, involved Jesus as the Revealer, and hence His role as Savior.[31]

Like Justin, Irenaeus found in the "pure sacrifice" (*sacrificium purum/kathara thusia*) of Mal 1:11 a foreshadowing of the church's

[26] *Against Heresies*, 1, Preface 3. There is nothing to justify Robert Grant's remark that Irenaeus's mission among the Celts was a failure and that the "Celtic population remained resolutely non-Christian" (*Irenaeus of Lyons*, 5).

[27] For the date, see R. M. Grant, *Greek Apologists of the Second Century* (Philadelphia: Westminster, 1988), 182–83. The title of the treatise is based on the wording of 1 Tim 6:20.

[28] For the Greek and Latin text of *Against Heresies*, I have used *Irénée de Lyon: Contre les heresies*, 5 vols., ed. A. Rousseau et al., Sources chrétiennes, vols. 100.1–2, 152–3, 210–11, 263–4, 293–4 (Paris: Les Éditions du Cerf, 1965 [vol. 4], 1969 [vol. 5], 1974 [vol. 3], 1979 [vol. 1], 1982 [vol. 2]).

[29] For a recent overview of the life and teaching of Marcion, see P. Foster, "Marcion: His Life, Works, Beliefs, and Impact," *ExpTim* 121 (March 2010): 269–80.

[30] For a sympathetic portrayal of Valentinus and his followers, see I. Dunderberg, *Beyond Gnosticism: Myth, Lifestyle, and Society in the School of Valentinus* (New York: Columbia University Press, 2008). In an interesting venture into virtual history, Dunderberg has also written an article about what "Christianity" would have looked like if Valentinus's heresy had been successful in subverting orthodoxy. As with all virtual history, the further away in time Dunderberg's speculations are from Valentinus's actual lifetime, the more "sci-fi-ish" they get. See his "Valentinus and His School: What Might Have Been," *The Fourth R*, 22, no. 6 (November–December 2009), 3–10.

[31] For this mini-sketch of Gnosticism, I am indebted to R. A. Segal, "Religion: Karen L. King, What Is Gnosticism?" *Times Literary Supplement* (November 21, 2003), 31.

Eucharist.[32] The church's Eucharist is "pure" as long as it is done "with a pure mind, and in faith without hypocrisy, in well-grounded hope, in fervent love."[33] Irenaeus contrasts the church's eucharistic worship with the offerings of the Jews, which are not pure because "they did not accept the Word through whom offering is made to God."[34] Nor are the eucharists of the Gnostics acceptable to God,[35] for they disparage Him when they claim that the very elements used in the Eucharist, the bread and the wine, have been created not by Him but by a lesser being, the *Dēmiourgos*, or are a result of "ignorance and passion"—a reference to two leitmotifs in Gnostic cosmogonies.[36] In other words, how can the Gnostics employ aspects of the created realm in their worship when they believe they are part of a creation that is fundamentally evil?

On the other hand, Irenaeus is confident that there is a solid theological fit between the church's theology of creation and her perspective on the Eucharist:

> Our opinion agrees with the eucharist, and the eucharist, in turn, establishes our opinion, for we offer to him what is his own, proclaiming fittingly the fellowship and union of the flesh and the spirit. For as the bread, which is produced from the earth, after it has received the invocation of God [*tēn epiklēsin tou theou*], is no longer common bread [*koinos artos*], but the eucharist, consisting of two realities [*eucharistia ek duo pragmatōn sunestēkuia*], the earthly and the heavenly, so also our bodies, when they receive the eucharist [*metalambanonta tēs eucharistias*], are no longer corruptible, but have the hope of resurrection.[37]

[32] *Against Heresies,* 4.17.4–4.18.3.

[33] *Against Heresies,* 4.18.4, trans. A. Roberts and J. Donaldson in *The Apostolic Fathers with Justin Martyr and Irenaeus*, rev. and arr. A. C. Coxe, *ANF* 1.485; and *The Eucharist, Message of the Fathers of the Church*, rev. D. J. Sheerin (Wilmington, DE: Michael Glazier, 1986), 7.249. Translations from this work will henceforth be cited with the pagination in vol. 1 of *ANF* and in Sheerin, *Eucharist.*

[34] *Against Heresies,* 4.18.4, trans. *ANF* 485–6; Sheerin, *Eucharist*, 249.

[35] On the Eucharist among the various Gnostic groups, see, e.g., Irenaeus, *Against Heresies,* 1.13.2; *Acts of Thomas,* 26–7, 49–50; *The Gospel of Philip,* 53, 68, 98, 100, 108. Also see E. Segelberg, "The Coptic-Gnostic Gospel according to Philip and Its Sacramental System," *Numen* 7 (1960): 195–7; W. C. van Unnik, "Three Notes on the 'Gospel of Philip'," *NTS* 10 (1963–64): 468–9; A. H. C. van Eijk, "The Gospel of Philip and Clement of Alexandria: Gnostic and Ecclesiastical Theology on the Resurrection and the Eucharist," *VC* 25 (1971): 94–120, passim; A. McGowan, *Ascetic Eucharists: Food and Drink in Early Christian Ritual Meals* (Oxford: Clarendon, 1999), 162–67.

[36] *Against Heresies,* 4.18.4. See P. Frederiksen, "Hysteria and the Gnostic Myths of Creation," *VC* 33 (1979): 287–88.

[37] *Against Heresies,* 4.18.5, trans. *ANF* 486; Sheerin, *Eucharist*, 249, altered. Irenaeus's use of

During the Lord's Supper, bread and wine—from wheat and grapes that are ultimately from the hand of a good Creator—are offered back to the One who made them. But now they are not only bread and wine. They also contain a heavenly reality. Irenaeus makes no attempt to explain how this transpires. Here he simply identifies the *epiklēsis* as the moment when the addition of that which is "heavenly" happens.[38] In a later passage, Irenaeus states that it is through "the word of God" that the wine and the bread "become the eucharist of Christ's body and blood."[39] Moreover, as we saw with Justin, his predecessor, it would be anachronistic to attempt to locate Irenaeus within the various streams of eucharistic thought during and since the Reformation on this issue.[40]

Against Heresies' overall anti-Gnostic thrust also prompts Irenaeus to draw a parallel between what transpires in the Eucharist and what happens to the bodies of believers. Just as ordinary substances, bread and wine, become the vehicles of God's grace, so too our earthly bodies are made capable of resurrection, which is a direct riposte to the general denial of a bodily resurrection by the Gnostics. What is striking, though, is Irenaeus's parenthetical statement about the effect of the Lord's Supper with regard to the bodies of believers. Those partaking[41] of the Eucharist are no longer the bearers of bodies destined for corruption, but have the hope that their bodies will rise again.

A second Irenaean text that associates the Eucharist with the salvation of the body occurs in *Against Heresies* 5. The bishop of Lyons has just stated that those who deny the possibility of the body's resurrection are foolish, for

> if this flesh is not saved, then the Lord has not redeemed us by his blood, and the cup of the eucharist is not a communion in his blood, and the bread which we break is not a sharing in his body.[42] . . . Since, therefore, both the mixed cup and the prepared bread receive the word of God, and become the eucharist of Christ's body and blood, from which the substance of our flesh

the phrase κοινὸς ἄρτος seems to be indebted to Justin Martyr. See Ferguson, "Lord's Supper in Church History," 25.

[38] Ferguson, "Lord's Supper in Church History," 25.

[39] *Against Heresies,* 5.2.3, trans. *ANF* 528; Sheerin, *Eucharist*, 252.

[40] D. van den Eynde, "Eucharistia ex duabus rebus constans: *S. Irénée, Adv. Haereses*, IV, 18, 5," *Antonianum* 15 (1940): 13–28.

[41] Μεταλαμβάνω is frequently used by the Fathers to refer to the reception of the Eucharist. See *PGL*, s.v. B.2. Also see Basil of Caesarea, *The Morals,* 21.1; *Letter,* 93. For a discussion of the latter text, see below.

[42] Cp. 1 Cor 10:16.

> is strengthened and supported [*sunistatai*], how, then, can they say that the flesh, which is nourished by the body and blood of the Lord, and is one of his members, is incapable of receiving the gift of God which is everlasting life?[43]

Doubtless Mary Ann Donovan is right to see "a literal physicality" in this text, for Irenaeus is seeking once again to show the reasonableness of the biblical conviction that the human body can be redeemed.[44] If the human body has no future beyond the grave, then Christ's redemptive work has failed, for Irenaeus cannot conceive of a redemption that fails to encompass the body.[45] For the bishop of Lyons, as for Scripture, the human body is an essential part of what constitutes a person. Moreover, if the body is shut out from participation in eternal life, 1 Cor 10:16 is utterly enigmatic. This Pauline text states that the Lord's Supper involves sharing in the blood and body of Christ, but if the humanity of Jesus has not been raised from the dead, there can be no Communion with His risen humanity and its power. The Eucharist, containing a heavenly reality—as Irenaeus had argued in *Against Heresies*, 4.18.5—is thus spiritual nourishment for believers,[46] and, because of the Eucharist's earthly reality, a pledge that the very body that eats the bread and drinks the wine will be raised into everlasting life.

At an earlier juncture, Irenaeus had asserted that the means of communion between believers and Christ is the Holy Spirit, "the pledge of immortality, the strengthening of our faith, and the ladder of ascent to God," and that it is the presence of the Spirit in the church that provides her with "every kind of grace" (*omnis gratia*), among which would have been the Lord's Supper. The critical factor is the Spirit's life-giving presence, for "those who do not partake of the Spirit are not nourished for life at their mother's breasts, nor do they experience the most brilliant fountain that issues from the body of Christ."[47] Thus, any blessing from the Lord's Supper must ultimately come from

[43] *Against Heresies*, 5.2.2, 3, trans. *ANF* 528; Sheerin, *Eucharist*, 252, altered.

[44] "Irenaeus' Teaching on the Unity of God and His Immediacy to the Material World in Relation to Valentinian Gnosticism" (Unpublished Ph.D. thesis, University of St. Michael's College, 1977), 230.

[45] For a succinct statement of Irenaeus's belief in the salvation of the flesh, see *Against Heresies*, 5.14.1. For a discussion of Irenaeus's soteriology, see Donovan, "Irenaeus' Teaching on the Unity of God," 213–43; Osborn, *Irenaeus of Lyons*, 95–140, passim.

[46] Donovan, "Irenaeus' Teaching on the Unity of God," 229–30; id., *One Right Reading? A Guide to Irenaeus* (Collegeville, MN: Liturgical, 1997), 111.

[47] *Against Heresies*, 3.24.1.

the fact that it is celebrated within the church where the Spirit is regnant with power. Yet the physical experience of eating bread and wine is of great significance for Irenaeus, for it bears witness to two great Christian truths: the reality of the incarnation of the Lord Jesus and the promise of the bodily resurrection.

"Your cup . . . is intoxicating": Cyprian and Eucharistic Experience

The "first authentic eucharistic treatise" in the pre-Constantinian era is the way *Letter* 63 of Cyprian of Carthage (c. 200–258) has been described.[48] Its author had been converted in 246 from an aristocratic background and, partly due to his training as a rhetorician, was appointed a mere two years later as bishop of Carthage, which made him the leading bishop in Latin Africa and an influential voice in the development of North African Christianity.[49] Although initially opposed by more senior elders in Carthage because of his too rapid advance to the episcopate and the fact that he seemed to be still too much the secular Roman patron dispensing favors to his clients, Cyprian proved to be, in the empire-wide persecutions of the late 240s and 250s, a wise and balanced Christian leader. He was martyred during the reign of the emperor Valerian for refusing to perform ritual sacrifice to the Roman gods.[50]

Letter 63 was written to Caecilius, bishop of Biltha,[51] probably in the autumn of 253,[52] to address the error of an aquarian Eucharist, that is, the use of water alone instead of a mixture of wine and water in the Lord's Supper.[53] Cyprian began with the basic principle that

[48] A. Hamman, "Eucharist. I. In the Fathers," in Angelo Di Berardino, ed., *Encyclopedia of the Early Church*, trans. A. Walford (New York: Oxford University Press, 1992), 1:293; Sheerin, *Eucharist*, 256.

[49] J. P. Burns, "Cyprian of Carthage," *ExpTim* 120 (2009): 469. On his life and thought, see especially P. Hinchliff, *Cyprian of Carthage and the Unity of the Christian Church* (London: Geoffrey Chapman, 1974); M. M. Sage, *Cyprian*, Patristic Monograph Series, no. 1 (Philadelphia: Philadelphia Patristic Foundation, Ltd., 1975); J. P. Burns, *Cyprian the Bishop* (London/New York: Routledge, 2002); and id., "Cyprian of Carthage," 469–77.

[50] See *The Acts of St. Cyprian* in *The Acts of the Christian Martyrs*, ed. H. Musurillo (Oxford: Clarendon, 1972), 168–75.

[51] For the few details known about Caecilius, see E. W. Benson, "Caecilius (6) Bishop of Biltha," in W. Smith and H. Wace, eds., *A Dictionary of Christian Biography* (Boston: Little, Brown, and Co., 1877), 1:369, col.2.

[52] For the date of the letter, see Sage, *Cyprian*, 291 and 366; and Sheerin, *Eucharist*, 256.

[53] For this issue, see A. Hovey, "Patristic Testimonies as to Wine, especially as used in the Lord's Supper," *The Baptist Quarterly Review* 10 (1888): 78–93; G. W. Clarke, *The Letters of*

Christians were not at liberty to change "what the Lord Jesus Christ did and taught" unless they wanted to offend their Master.[54] When it came to the eucharistic cup, this specifically meant that "the chalice that is offered in memory of him should be offered mixed with wine. For since Christ pronounces: 'I am the true vine,' the blood of Christ without qualification is not water."[55] Christ's own use of wine at the Last Supper as an illustration of his blood instructs the church that "the chalice should be mixed by commingling water and wine."[56] And this is what was handed down by the apostles. To use water alone is thus to go against dominical, "evangelical and apostolic practice."[57] The Carthaginian bishop finds support for his argument from various OT examples that he regards as types[58] of the passion of Christ and its representation in the bread and the wine: the inebriation of Noah,[59] the offering of bread and wine by Melchizedek, Lady Wisdom in Proverbs 9, the blessing of Judah, and an Isaianic prediction of the Messiah in Isaiah 63.[60] Cyprian then notes that it is the initiatory rite of baptism that is "in water alone."[61] The Eucharist, though, must

St. Cyprian of Carthage, Ancient Christian Writers 46 (New York/Mahwah, NJ: Newman, 1986), 3:288–90; McGowan, *Ascetic Eucharists*, passim and especially 204–11; M. M. Daly-Denton, "Water in the Eucharistic Cup: A Feature of the Eucharist in Johannine Trajectories through Early Christianity," *ITQ* 72 (2007): 356–70.

[54] *Letter,* 63.1, trans. A. Brent, *St Cyprian of Carthage: On the Church: Select Letters* (Crestwood, NY: St Vladimir's Seminary Press, 2006), 173. Henceforth this translation will be cited simply as Brent, *St Cyprian* with the appropriate pagination.

[55] *Letter,* 63.2, trans. Brent, *St Cyprian*, 173, altered. The quote is from John 15:1. See also *Letter* 63.10, 14, 16, 18. In *Letter* 63.18 Cyprian cites Matt 28:18–20 to buttress his appeal to dominical authority and by implication includes the use of water and wine in the Lord's Supper as one of the things that Christ commanded His apostles to teach to disciples.

[56] *Letter,* 63.9, trans. Brent, *St Cyprian*, 179.

[57] *Letter,* 63.11, trans. Brent, *St Cyprian*, 180.

[58] Cyprian uses the term *sacramentum*, that is, "pledge" or "sign," to describe these examples.

[59] This is a most curious type, which led Edward White Benson to speak about the "wildness . . . of the Biblical interpretations and the looseness of the logic" in Cyprian's letter. See his *Cyprian: His Life, His Times, His Work* (London: Macmillan, 1897), 291. And yet the overall thrust of Cyprian's typological exegesis here is common to the Fathers, namely, "to situate Christ himself within the sacred narratives of the past in the sense that he both participates in and fulfills those narratives" (J. J. O'Keefe and R. R. Reno, *Sanctified Vision: An Introduction to Early Christian Interpretation of the Bible* [Baltimore/London: Johns Hopkins University Press, 2005], 73). Like most pre-critical exegetes, Cyprian was eager to discover what any given biblical passage meant for him and the believing community of his day.

[60] *Letter,* 63.3–7. For a discussion of various aspects of Cyprian's typological exegesis, see Clarke, *Letters of St. Cyprian*, 3:292–4. For a listing of other types of the Lord's Supper found by the Fathers in the OT, see Sheerin, "Eucharistic Liturgy," 723.

[61] *Letter,* 63.8, trans. Brent, *St Cyprian*, 177.

employ both water and wine, for its purpose is to recall the shedding of Christ's blood.

Cyprian also buttresses his argument with a phrase from Ps 22:5 (23:5) as it appeared in the Old Latin translation of the Psalms. In the version of this psalm known to Cyprian, there was a statement, "your cup, though the finest, is intoxicating" (*calix tuus inebrians perquam optimus*), that the bishop interprets as a reference to the Lord's Supper.[62] As Cyprian notes, water alone never causes inebriation. For drunkenness to occur, there must be wine. Of course, partaking of the cup in the Eucharist produces an insobriety entirely different from that of this world's wine. Eucharistic insobriety makes men and women "sober, in the sense that it restores hearts back to a spiritual wisdom, in the sense that each person returns to his senses about his understanding of God from tasting the experience of this age."[63] What is fascinating about this interpretation is that it provides us with a vantage-point to reflect upon the richness of Cyprian's experience of the Lord's Table.

For the North African theologian, the Lord's Supper is a place of spiritual wisdom, for it helps to recall men and women from their temptation of being infatuated with the world. As Cyprian goes on to note, "drinking the blood of the Lord and his saving cup" is a means of forgetting this world's pattern of living. And just as "ordinary wine" initially has a relaxing effect and a way of dispelling sadness, so it is that the Lord's Supper, conducted as the Lord directed—which, in this context, means wine mixed with water—relieves the believer of those "choking sins" that had overwhelmed him or her. The Eucharist is thus a place where the believer knows afresh the forgiveness of the Lord and as a result is suffused with joy.[64] In relation to this, elsewhere Cyprian can encourage Christians as "soldiers of Christ" to drink "the cup of the blood of Christ" so that they might be enabled to renounce the world even to the point of shedding their blood for Christ.[65]

[62] *Letter,* 63.11, trans. Brent, *St Cyprian*, 180. For the Latin, see PL 4.382B.

[63] *Letter,* 63.11, trans. Brent, *St Cyprian*, 180. The theme of *sobria ebrietas* was a favorite one with the Fathers. See below for its development by Ambrose.

[64] *Letter,* 63.11, trans. Brent, *St Cyprian*, 181.

[65] *Letter,* 58.1–2. I owe this reference to A. McGowan, "Rethinking Agape and Eucharist in Early North African Christianity," *Studia Liturgica* 34 (2004): 175. On this passage, also see John D. Laurance, *"Priest" as Type of Christ: The Leader of the Eucharist in Salvation History according to Cyprian of Carthage*, American University Studies, Series VII, vol. 5 (New York: Peter Lang, 1984), 185–88.

The Eucharist also speaks of the union of the people with their Lord. Cyprian suggests that the water in the cup represents the people of God, while wine, of course, is indicative of the shed blood of the Savior. When the water is mixed with wine in the cup, then, it depicts the unbreakable union of love that Christians have with one another and with their Lord. Given what the cup therefore represents, it is improper to use either water alone or wine by itself. Similarly, the bread that is broken consists of "wheat gathered and ground down and kneaded together" with water to form one loaf. For Cyprian, the Eucharist is a powerful experiential witness to the "sworn bond" (*sacramentum*) that binds together believers as one body in Christ.[66] This was especially important for Cyprian as he sought to deal with schismatics in the North African churches who refused to offer full restoration to those who had apostasized in the Decian persecution (249–51) and who, afterward, were sincerely repentant.[67] As J. Patout Burns notes, for Cyprian, the "uniting of the community in Christ became the major function of the Eucharist."[68]

This letter is also noteworthy for it contains, in the estimation of the incisive Congregationalist theologian P. T. Forsyth (1848–1921), "an absolutely unscriptural change." After linking the biblical affirmation about the offering of Christ, the high priest of God, "as a sacrifice to the Father" with His command to His disciples to celebrate the Lord's Supper in His remembrance, Cyprian concludes that Jesus is asking His disciples to do exactly as He did. This means that the one presiding at the Eucharist "imitates that which Christ did," when he "offers a true and full sacrifice in the Church to God the Father."[69] In making this exegetical move, Cyprian became, according to Forsyth, "the chief culprit in effecting the change from a *sacrificium laudis* by the Church to a *sacrificium propitiatorium* by the priest."[70] Whether or not Forsyth is right to designate Cyprian as the "chief culprit" in this regard is moot.[71] What Cyprian's words do reveal is that earlier

[66] *Letter,* 63.13, trans. Brent, *St Cyprian*, 181–82.

[67] For a helpful outline of this persecution and its impact on the churches in North Africa and Rome, see Brent, "Introduction" to his trans., *St Cyprian of Carthage: On the Church*, 17–38.

[68] "Cyprian of Carthage," 474. See also A. Kreider, "Worship and Evangelism in Pre-Christendom (The Laing Lecture 1994)," *VE* 24 (1994): 23: "The eucharist was a unitive rite. . . ."

[69] *Letter,* 63.14, trans. Brent, *St Cyprian*, 183–84.

[70] P. T. Forsyth, *The Church and the Sacraments*, 4th ed. (London: Independent Press Ltd., 1953), 272. Also see E. G. Hinson, "The Lord's Supper in Early Church History," *RevExp* 64 (1969): 18–19.

[71] See Heron, *Table and Tradition,* 75–6, for similar statements by Tertullian and Origen.

usage of the term "sacrifice" with regard to the Eucharist—as found, for example, in the exegesis of Mal 1:11 by Justin and Irenaeus, an interpretation with which Cyprian generally agrees[72]—has probably helped prepare the way for the significant change reflected in this letter of Cyprian. Whereas Justin and Irenaeus, however, saw the people of God corporately offering up the sacrifice of the Eucharist in purity of heart, Cyprian identifies the bishop or minister as the one who is uniquely called to do this and who, in this aspect of his ministry, imitates the high priestly sacrifice of Christ Himself.[73] Fundamental to this shift in focus is Cyprian's use of the term "priest" (*sacerdos*) as a description of the one presiding at the Eucharist. Prior to Cyprian, this term is never used to designate Christian ministry per se, but Cyprian, as in the letter under consideration, continually calls the one presiding at the Eucharist, whether bishop or elder, a *sacerdos*.[74] And just as there are types of Christ's passion in the history of God's people preceding the incarnation, as Cyprian outlines in this letter, so in the history of the church since the death and resurrection of Christ there are priests who imitate Christ's priesthood and who are vehicles for His presence in the church's worship.[75]

"A glorious inebriation": Ambrose of Milan as a Eucharistic Pioneer

The public embrace of Christianity by a Roman emperor, namely Flavius Valerius Constantinus, otherwise known as Constantine I (272–337), in the second decade of the fourth century AD, had such far-reaching effects that by the time he died there was scarcely any facet of the public life of the Empire or that of the church which had not been impacted by his policy of official Christianization. Constantine genuinely perceived himself to be a friend and ally of the church, who was used by God to bring an end to the imperial persecution of God's people.[76] Yet, the long-term impact of his reign on Christianity was not always for the best. For instance, not long after Constantine's

[72] *Three Books of Testimonies Against the Jews*, 1.16.

[73] Heron, *Table and Tradition*, 76.

[74] Laurance, *"Priest" as Type of Christ*, 195–200.

[75] Ibid., 223–30.

[76] For a convincing argument in this regard, see T. D. Barnes, *Constantine and Eusebius* (Cambridge, MA/London: Harvard University Press, 1981). See also H. Doerries, *Constantine the Great*, trans. R. H. Bainton (New York: Harper Row Publications, 1972).

death, his son, the Arian emperor Constantius II (317–61), was persecuting supporters of the Nicene Creed, such as Athanasius (c. 299–373), and thus setting a precedent for the later extensive involvement of the state in the life of the church.

Among the key defenders of Nicene orthodoxy in the West against Arian-instigated persecution was Ambrose (c. 339–97), a provincial governor before being appointed bishop of Milan in 374.[77] Used to the exercise of power, Ambrose did not find it easy to adjust to his new role, and his relationships with those like the Arian empress Justina (d. 388) or the decidedly orthodox Theodosius I (347–95), who made Nicene Trinitarianism the official religion of the Roman Empire, illustrate the dangers faced by influential church leaders in a society now committed to the Christian faith.[78] Although Ambrose was not a brilliant theologian, his deep knowledge of Greek gave him access to the riches of the Greek patristic tradition, which he passed on to the West through his various works. Ivor Davidson rightly notes that Ambrose's role in the formation of Latin Christianity was both "remarkable and complex."[79] This is clearly the case with regard to eucharistic thought and piety, where Ambrose was a pioneer of new ways of thinking about the Lord's Supper.[80]

The heart of Ambrose's eucharistic thought and reflection is to be found in his *On the Sacraments* and *On the Mysteries*. Like Cyprian, Ambrose sees prefigurations of the Eucharist in such OT texts as the Genesis account of Melchizedek's offering bread and wine to Abraham.[81] Again, like Cyprian and other earlier authors, Ambrose uses

[77] On the life and thought of Ambrose, see N. B. McLynn, *Ambrose of Milan: Church and Court in a Christian Capital* (Berkeley: University of California Press, 1994) and D. H. Williams, *Ambrose of Milan and the End of the Nicene-Arian Conflicts* (Oxford: Clarendon/New York: Oxford University Press, 1995). For selections of his writings, see B. Ramsey, *Ambrose* (London/New York: Routledge, 1997). The classic study is F. H. Dudden, *The Life and Times of St. Ambrose*, 2 vols. (Oxford: Clarendon, 1935).

[78] As Ramsey notes, "Ambrose was above all a man of the spirit, whose activities in the public forum were guided overwhelmingly by spiritual considerations, however ill conceived they occasionally were. It is impossible . . . not to posit a deep spirituality in a man in whose writings the mystical meaning of the Song of Songs plays so prominent a role, and who was capable of composing such extraordinary hymns" (*Ambrose*, x).

[79] I. Davidson, "Ambrose," in P. F. Esler, ed., *The Early Christian World* (London/New York: Routledge, 2000), 2:1175.

[80] R. Johanny, *L'eucharistie, centre de l'histoire du salut chez saint Ambroise de Milan* (Paris: Beauchesne, 1968); Davidson, "Ambrose," 1197; G. Macy, *The Theologies of the Eucharist in the Early Scholastic Period: A Study of the Salvific Function of the Sacrament according to the Theologians c. 1080–c. 1220* (Oxford: Clarendon, 1984), 19.

[81] *On the Sacraments*, 4.3.10–12; 5.1.1; *On the Mysteries*, 8.45–6.

realistic language about the bread and wine: when consumed in the Lord's Supper they are the body and blood of Christ.[82] He goes beyond earlier authors, however, by identifying Christ's words of institution as the means by which a change is effected in the elements of bread and wine:

> Before [the bread] is consecrated, it is bread; but when Christ's words have been added, it is the body of Christ. Finally, hear him as he says: "Take and eat of this, all of you; for this is my body" [cp. Matt 26:26–7]. And before the words of Christ, the chalice is full of wine and water; when the words of Christ have been added, then blood is effected [*efficitur*], which redeemed the people. So behold in what great respects the expression of Christ is able to change [*convertere*] all things.[83]

Fourth-century theologians were generally more explicit than previous authors in spelling out details of the change that happens to the bread and the wine at the celebration of the Lord's Supper.[84] For a Greek-speaking author like Cyril of Jerusalem (c. 315–87), it is the *epiclesis* that brings about a change in the elements.[85] The West would follow Ambrose in locating the power to effect change in the elements in the words of Christ.[86] To those who found the idea of such a change hard to believe, Ambrose brought forward a whole array of biblical examples, from Moses' rod which was changed into a serpent and back again, to Elijah's iron axe head being made able to float.[87] Ambrose is able to avoid a crass materialistic interpretation of the changes that take place in the elements by emphasizing that

> Christ is in that sacrament, because it is the body of Christ; therefore it is not bodily food, but spiritual. Whence also the Apostle says of the type of it that "our fathers ate spiritual meat, and drank spiritual drink" [1 Cor 10:3–4]. For the body of God is a spiritual body; the body of Christ is the body of a divine Spirit, because Christ is Spirit [cp. 1 Cor 15:45; 2 Cor 3:17].[88]

[82] *On the Sacraments,* 4.4.14, 19–20.

[83] *On the Sacraments,* 4.5.23 (PL 16.444A-B), trans. R. J. Deferrari, *Saint Ambrose: Theological and Dogmatic Works*, FC 44:305. See also Ambrose, *On the Sacraments,* 4.4.14, 19; *On the Mysteries,* 52.

[84] Halliburton, "Patristic Theology of the Eucharist," 207; Ferguson, "Lord's Supper in Church History," 28.

[85] See, e.g., Cyril of Jerusalem, *On the Mysteries,* 5.7. For discussion of this text, see Heron, *Table and Tradition*, 66; Ferguson, "Lord's Supper in Church History," 28–29.

[86] Heron, *Table and Tradition*, 66–67.

[87] *On the Sacraments,* 4.4.11; *On the Mysteries,* 51–52.

[88] *On the Mysteries,* 9.58, Ambrose, *On the Sacraments and On the Mysteries*, ed. J. H. Srawley, trans. T. Thompson (London: SPCK, 1950), 150. See also the comments of C. W. Dugmore,

Nevertheless, he can still say that in the mystery of the Lord's Supper believers adore the flesh of Christ, which might lead to confusion between the bread and the wine and that which they signified.[89]

Ambrose is also a pioneer in one other important area relating to the Eucharist, namely, the use of the Song of Songs to express the believer's experience at the Table.[90] It is Christ, Ambrose remarks, who calls the believer, cleansed of sin, to come to His "marvelous sacraments" (*sacramenta mirabilia*) with the words "Let him kiss me with the kiss of his mouth" (Song 1:2), which Ambrose interprets to mean "Let Christ impress a kiss upon me."[91] The reception of the Lord's Supper is here likened to the joyous experience of being kissed by one's beloved. This loving communion that Christ has with His people through the Eucharist Ambrose further likens to the beloved coming into his garden and drinking his wine with milk (Song 5:1). This is nothing less, Ambrose maintains, than Christ giving His people forgiveness of sins through the Supper and their subsequent rejoicing or inebriation in the Spirit.[92] To be so inebriated with the Spirit, Ambrose continues, is to be "deeply rooted in Christ" (*radicatus in Christo est*) and as such is a state that Ambrose can only describe as "a glorious inebriation" (*praeclara ebrietas*).[93]

Ambrose's emphasis on the transformation of the bread and the wine into the body and blood of Christ would increasingly make the Lord's Supper not so much a community celebration, as it was for earlier Christians, but a place of adoration, reverent awe, and fear lest something be done wrong.[94] His use of the Song of Songs, however, tempered this development, for by it Christians were reminded that the Table was ultimately meant to be a place of exuberant spiritual joy over sins forgiven and union with Christ.

"Sacrament and Sacrifice in the Early Fathers," *JEH* 2 (1951): 35–36; Lampe, "Eucharist in the Thought of the Early Church," 52–53.

89 *On the Holy Spirit*, 3.79 (PL 16.794D–795A).

90 Hamman, "Eucharist. I. In the Fathers," in Berardino, *Encyclopedia of the Early Church*, 1:293. The employment of the Song of Songs as an expression of eucharistic piety would come to full fruition much later in the writings of such medieval authors as Bernard of Clairvaux (1090–1153) and Puritan pastors like Edward Taylor (1642–1729).

91 *On the Sacraments*, 5.2.5–7 (PL 16.447C–D).

92 *On the Sacraments*, 5.3.15–17 (PL 16.449A–C).

93 *On the Sacraments*, 5.3.17 (PL 16.449C–450A).

94 Macy, *Theologies of the Eucharist*, 19–20; Lampe, "Eucharist in the Thought of the Early Church," 52.

"An indelible commemoration": The Eucharist in the Life and Thought of Basil

Among Ambrose's episcopal colleagues in the Eastern Roman Empire was his fellow-bishop Basil of Caesarea (c. 329–79), who had undergone a powerful conversion to Christ and to the monastic life in 356 through the witness of his elder sister Macrina (c. 327–80).[95] Macrina had confronted him with the way that he was wasting his life upon the wisdom of this world, for he had spent many years pursuing a first-class education in rhetoric and had just returned to Cappadocia to teach rhetoric. He came to realize, as he would later say, that "human wisdom is illusory, for it is a meagre and lowly thing and not a great and pre-eminent good."[96] After his baptism in 356 he initially immersed himself in a semi-monastic environment of simplicity, silence, and meditation. In the 360s, though, he was drawn into local church life in Caesarea, and eventually became bishop of Caesarea in 370. During the 370s his defence of the deity of the Holy Spirit proved to be absolutely vital to the triumph of Trinitarian orthodoxy at the Council of Constantinople (381), two years after his death. He was also a reformer of the early monastic movement that was taken up with the admiration of spectacular feats of asceticism and a preoccupation about fighting Satan. Taking Acts 4:32 as his watchword, Basil sought to reform monasticism so that it would be communal in focus with a stress on the development of Christian character, especially with regard to humility and love. To this end Basil drew up a monastic rule, *The Morals*, around 360 to guide those who wanted to follow this path of life, and it was in this context that he made some extensive comments on the Lord's Supper.[97]

In Rule 21 of *The Morals*, for instance, Basil first noted that reception of the body and blood of Christ was "necessary for life

[95] For the life and thought of Basil, see especially P. J. Fedwick, *The Church and the Charisma of Leadership in Basil of Caesarea*, Studies and Texts 45 (Toronto: Pontifical Institute of Mediaeval Studies, 1979) and id., ed., *Basil of Caesarea: Christian, Humanist, Ascetic: A Sixteen-Hundredth Anniversary Symposium*, 2 vols. (Toronto: Pontifical Institute of Mediaeval Studies, 1981). See also the brief summary of his life by S. M. Hildebrand, *The Trinitarian Theology of Basil of Caesarea: A Synthesis of Greek Thought and Biblical Truth* (Washington, D.C.: The Catholic University of America Press, 2007), 18–29. For the life of Macrina, see Gregory of Nyssa, *The Life of Saint Macrina*, trans. K. Corrigan (repr. ed.; Eugene, OR: Wipf & Stock, 2005).

[96] *Homily*, 20.2, trans. M. M. Wagner, *Saint Basil: Ascetical Works*, FC 9:478. Henceforth this translation will be cited as Wagner, *Saint Basil* with the appropriate pagination.

[97] For the date, see J. Ducatillon, "Introduction" to her trans., *Basile de Césarée: Sur le Baptême* (Paris : Les Éditions du Cerf, 1989), 23.

everlasting," and he cited John 6:54–55 to support this assertion.[98] Basil evidently did not conceive of this benefit being *ex opere operato*, for he goes on to lay down the conditions for a worthy reception of the bread and the wine. The only proper way in which someone can partake of the Lord's Supper is with a heart mindful of "the obedience of the Lord even unto death" and a corresponding determination to no longer live for self, but for Christ who died for that individual and rose again. Listening to the words recited at the celebration of the Lord's Table—passages like John 6:52–63, 1 Cor 11:23–29, and Luke 22:19–20—should be a powerful reminder of what Christ has done for the believer.[99]

The same emphasis occurs in the conclusion of this rule, *Morals* 80—a text that Paul J. Fedwick has described as "a magnificent summary and synthesis" of this monastic rule and which he rightly considers to be Basil's spiritual testament.[100] Basil asks, "What is the mark of a Christian?"[101] His answer to this query stresses, among other things, that a Christian is a person who lives a holy life and has been cleansed of sin "by the blood of Christ" and, as such, he can "eat the body of Christ and drink his blood."[102] The Lord's Table is for believers, then, who are walking in communion with their Lord. And their eating and drinking at the Lord's Table should be a perpetual reminder to them of the crucified and risen Christ so that "they live not for themselves but for him who died for them and rose again."[103]

This theme of the Lord's Supper as a key vehicle for the re-affirmation of one's total commitment to Christ is also prominent in Basil's *Concerning Baptism*, written either in the mid-360s or at some point between 372 and 375.[104] Baptism, Basil notes, is a "confession . . . that we are dead to sin and to the world, and alive to righteousness."[105]

[98] *The Morals*, 21, trans. Wagner, *Saint Basil*, 101. Hinson views Basil's statement here as an exaggerated claim about the power of the Eucharist ("Lord's Supper in Early Church History," 24). It might appear so, if viewed in isolation. However, this statement needs to be seen in the larger context of Basil's eucharistic thought.

[99] *Morals*, 21.2, trans. Wagner, *Saint Basil*, 102–3.

[100] *Basil of Caesarea*, 1:18, n. 96.

[101] *Morals*, 80.22.

[102] *Morals*, 80.22. For the Greek, see PG 31.869A.

[103] *Morals*, 80.22 (PG 31.869A), trans. Wagner, *Saint Basil*, 204–5.

[104] For the mid-360s, see Ducatillon, "Introduction" to her trans., *Basile de Césarée: Sur le Baptême*, 21–4. For 372–75, see Fedwick, *Basil of Caesarea*, 1:14–15 and n. 83.

[105] *Concerning Baptism*, 1.3.1. The Greek translated here is from the critical edition of U. Neri, found in Ducatillon, *Basile de Césarée: Sur le Baptême*, 190, henceforth referred to simply as Ducatillon, *Sur le Baptême* with the appropriate pagination.

After such an entry into the Christian life, the believer needs ongoing spiritual nourishment, "the food of eternal life" (*trophēn zōēs aiōniou*), which is found in the Eucharist.[106] Basil goes on to cite John 6:53–56,60–69, along with the institution texts from Matthew 26 and 1 Corinthians 11, and asks, "How then do these words benefit us?" He answers,

> That as we eat and drink we always remember the One who died and was raised for us, and thus learn necessarily how to keep before God and his Christ the doctrine that has been entrusted to us by the Apostle when he said, "For the love of Christ constrains us since we have determined this, that if one has died for all, then all have died; and he died for all in order that those who live might no longer live for themselves, but for the One who died and was raised for them" [2 Cor 5:14–15].[107]

The Lord's Supper for Basil is, therefore, a critical time to recall the nature of what was pledged in baptism: absolute and total dedication to Christ as one's Lord. For Basil this appears to be the central meaning of what he calls the "indelible commemoration [*anexaleipton mnēmēn*] of Jesus Christ our Lord."[108] The Cappadocian bishop thus goes on to emphasize that the person who partakes of the Lord's Supper but fails to be so controlled by love that he is living for Christ eats and drinks "unworthily" (*anaxiōs*),[109] "without any benefit" (*anōphelōs*), and "profoundly grieves the Holy Spirit" (*perissoterōs lupountos to Pneuma to hagion*).[110] To approach the Table one must then be "pure from all defilement of flesh and spirit" and "actively" (*energōs*) devoted to the Lord Jesus.[111]

One other Basilian text on this subject that needs noting is Basil's *Letter* 93, in which Basil discusses practical issues regarding reception of what he calls "the communion" (*to koinōnein*). Daily communion is both "good and helpful" (*epōpheles*), he tells a certain Caesaria.[112]

[106] *Concerning Baptism*, 1.3.1 (Ducatillon, *Sur le Baptême*, 192).

[107] *Concerning Baptism*, 1.3.2 (Ducatillon, *Sur le Baptême*, 194, 196).

[108] *Concerning Baptism*, 1.3.2 (Ducatillon, *Sur le Baptême*, 196).

[109] Basil is alluding to 1 Cor 11:27.

[110] *Concerning Baptism*, 1.3.3 (Ducatillon, *Sur le Baptême*, 198). The final clause is a loose citation of Eph 4:30.

[111] *Concerning Baptism*, 1.3.3 (Ducatillon, *Sur le Baptême*, 198). For the same argument, see also *Concerning Baptism*, 2.3. Sheerin doubts the authenticity of this letter ("Eucharistic Liturgy," 720).

[112] For the Greek text, see Y. Courtonne, ed., *Saint Basile: Lettres* (Paris: Société d'Édition "Les Belles Lettres," 1957), 1:203–4, henceforth cited as Courtonne, ed., *Lettres*, I with the appropriate pagination. There is nothing within the text of this letter that enables a pinpoint dating. Courtonne (*Lettres*, 1:203, notes) suggests the letter was written around 372, but he

Basil notes that he received the Lord's Supper at least four times a week—"on the Lord's day, Wednesday, Friday, and on the Sabbath." Since Christ said that "the one who eats my flesh and drinks my blood has eternal life" (John 6:54), to partake (*metechein*[113]) of the Lord's Supper continually, Basil reasons on the basis of this Johannine text, is to be filled with life in manifold ways.[114] How the Lord's Supper does this Basil does not say.

Now, what is most intriguing about Basil's eucharistic thought is that in his magisterial defense of the Spirit's deity, *On the Holy Spirit* (376), where he had ample opportunity to mention the Spirit's work in the Lord's Supper, he says nothing about this subject. There is a long section on baptism and understandably so because of the baptismal formula in Matthew 28 that includes the Holy Spirit as One who is fully equal to the Father and the Son.[115] There is nary a word about the Lord's Supper, however—how the bread and wine become vehicles of the Spirit's activity, for example, which seems to be presumed in *Letter* 93.[116] Basil's brother Gregory of Nyssa (c. 335–c. 396) developed a whole theory of how the bread and the wine became the body and blood of Christ.[117] And while it is possible that Basil would not have disagreed with his brother, nothing further can be said with any degree of finality beyond noting that what was important for Basil was the impact the Lord's Supper should have on the partaker in terms of living wholeheartedly for Christ.

gives no reasons for this dating. On the other hand, Fedwick (*Basil of Caesarea*, 1:19) does not assign a date to the letter. For Caesaria, see Wolf-Dieter Hauschild, trans., *Bailius von Caesarea: Briefe*, Bibliothek der Griechischen Literatur 32 (Stuttgart: Anton Hiersemann, 1990), 217–18, n. 406.

[113] Basil also uses the verb μεταλαμβάνω in this letter with regard to the reception of the Lord's Supper. See above, n. 41.

[114] Basil also argues that it is not improper to give oneself Communion during a time of persecution (Courtonne, *Lettres*, 1:204).

[115] *On the Holy Spirit*, 10–15.

[116] B. Bobrinskoy, "Liturgie et ecclésiologie trinitaire de saint Basile," *Verbum Caro* 23 (1969): 14. In *On the Holy Spirit*, 27.66 Basil does maintain that historically the church has not allowed the unbaptized to be present at the Lord's Supper, and that there were certain unwritten traditions with regard to the celebration of the Supper.

[117] *Catechetical Oration*, 37. For a helpful summary of Nyssen's view, see Markschies, "Eucharist/Communion. II. Church History. 1. Early Church," 623.

Summing Up

During the course of the patristic era there is little doubt that the Eucharist became a central aspect of the worship of the church.[118] For the earliest authors examined in this chapter—Justin and Irenaeus—it is an act of profound thanksgiving and a source of spiritual blessing. Due to his concern to respond to the Gnostics, Irenaeus also ties the Eucharist to such key Christian truths as the incarnation of Christ and the bodily resurrection. Participation in the Lord's Supper is a confession of the reality of those events. There is thus a stress on the materiality of the bread and the wine. At the same time, Irenaeus is conscious that the consecrated bread and wine serve as vehicles of spiritual nourishment, though he does not attempt to specify how this is so.

Cyprian well represents certain shifts in eucharistic thought and praxis that were taking place during the third century. For him, having to battle schism in the midst of empire-wide persecution, the Eucharist is a pledge of the unity of the body of Christ. He also reaffirms the centrality of the Table for Christian experiential piety by using the image of "sober intoxication" as a summary way of describing the experience of eating the bread and drinking the wine. In a distinct break from earlier perspectives, though, Cyprian employs the term "priest" (*sacerdos*) to describe the one presiding at the Table, which would provide ground for later, strongly sacerdotal interpretations of the Lord's Supper.

Along with the significant changes that came into the life of the church and its worship in the fourth century with the toleration of Christianity, there came a movement toward more exact specification of how the bread and the wine served as the body and blood of Christ. In the East, Cyril of Jerusalem appears to have been the first to specify the details of this conversion,[119] and in the West it is Ambrose who was the main conduit of this line of thinking. Ambrose can thus speak of adoration of the flesh of Christ during the Eucharist, which would lead to the medieval emphasis on the Eucharist as a place of reverence and awe-inspiring rite. At the same time, Ambrose employs the Song of Songs to describe the believer's eucharistic experience as intimate

[118] Srawley, "Eucharist," in Ambrose, *On the Sacraments and on the Mysteries,* 548; Sheerin, "Eucharistic Liturgy," 723.

[119] Srawley, "Eucharist," 550.

communion with Christ. For Ambrose, this experience appears to be open to all who partake of the bread and the wine.

Finally, Basil of Caesarea stressed that the Eucharist is of no value unless it be accompanied by a determination to live wholeheartedly for the One whose death it commemorates. Basil is thus deeply concerned to distinguish the sign of the Eucharist from its meaning and to highlight the importance of what the Eucharist signifies. The future of eucharistic praxis and piety, however, lay not with such an emphasis, but with Ambrose's thought, which would inexorably lead to a confusion of symbol and meaning.[120]

[120] In the East, the thinking of Basil's brother Nyssen about the conversion of the elements played a deeply influential role on later Eastern Orthodox thought.

CAROLINGIAN CONFLICT: TWO MONKS ON THE MASS

David S. Hogg*

In the first few centuries following the apostolic era the church suffered persecution in various ways and to varying degrees. To be sure, persecution and oppression were neither uniform nor constant, but they were ever-present possibilities. During those years it would have been difficult to conceive of a time when the leaders of the church would replace or supplant the very officials who caused such harm. Dare one even dream of a time before the second coming when bishops, who pastored the pastors, would care not only for the flock of God, but oversee the affairs of pagans who fell within the bounds of their authority? Prior to the reign of Constantine in the early fourth century, such a dream would have been just over the horizon of what the church could have either asked or imagined. Constantine did not, of course, make Christianity the state religion (that was the work of Theodosius I), but he did favor leniency toward Christians.[1] While Constantine's desire to establish toleration for Christians was more likely the product of a shrewd political mind than a compassionate regenerate soul, the result was the burgeoning of a new context in which the church could carry out its divinely appointed mandate to labor in the exegesis of and reflection on Scripture that produces theology. In short, the *confessio dei* of the church was moving from defending the faith amidst hostility to declaring the faith amidst curiosity.

One of the church's practices that had been viewed with suspicion by unbelievers and as a cause for punishment was the Lord's Supper. Misunderstanding about what took place during this rite was widespread throughout the early Roman Empire. When the leader of a congregation stated unequivocally that what was about to be ingested and imbibed was the body and blood of Jesus Christ, questions were

* David S. Hogg received his Ph.D. from the University of St. Andrews. He is associate professor of Theology and Medieval Studies at Southeastern Baptist Theological Seminary in Wake Forest, North Carolina.

[1] While numerous sources could be cited here, the recent and very readable volumes by Ivor Davidson are a good place to begin. For information on the credibility of Constantine's faith see Davidson's *The Birth of the Church, from Jesus to Constantine AD 30–312* (Grand Rapids: Baker, 2004), 343–46. For information on Theodosius I's relationship to the church see id., *A Public Faith, from Constantine to the Medieval World AD 312–600* (Grand Rapids: Baker, 2005), 93–95.

raised as to the possibility of cannibalism. Documents from both the churches and the authorities in the Empire evince believers' consistent and continual denial of this misinterpretation. In light of this and with the added knowledge that the fourth century brought significant changes for the church under Constantine, we might be tempted to think that as the Western Roman Empire gave way to the multiplicity of kingdoms and dominions we now more readily associate with the European Middle Ages, the question of the meaning of the Lord's Supper came to an end. Since there were no more persecutors to misinterpret the practice, and since Christianity was spreading quickly throughout every strata of society, surely such a central aspect of Christian worship could be considered settled. As we move through the ancient church toward the Middle Ages we discover that this was not the case, and that two views in particular became even more entrenched. What were these opposing, even contradictory views? One view was that the bread and the wine were symbols of the body and blood of Christ. To be sure, these were powerful symbols of Christ's atoning sacrifice that should not be taken lightly for they signify a present spiritual reality, but what began as bread and wine never became something more than bread and wine. The other view was that the bread and the wine were not merely symbols of the body and blood of Christ, as though abstract mnemonic devices, but were somehow transformed from their mundane substance by a divine miracle. Through the elements, the very body and blood of Christ were made real to the communicant.[2]

At this juncture modern readers must take care not to read more into the second of these two views than is warranted. There is a tendency to move quickly to the assumption that what has been described is transubstantiation. The term "transubstantiation" was not used in debates over the nature of the Lord's Supper until the twelfth century, and it is not until the Fourth Lateran Council of 1215 that the term

[2] For more information see J. N. D. Kelly, *Early Christian Doctrines* (New York: Harper Collins, 1978), 440–55. Some insightful, though brief, comments are included in J. Pelikan, *The Emergence of the Catholic Tradition (100–600)* (vol. 1 of *The Christian Tradition;* Chicago: University of Chicago Press, 1971), 166–71. Pelikan, in summarizing his findings, says, "Yet it does seem 'express and clear' that no orthodox father of the second or third century of whom we have record either declared the presence of the body and blood of Christ in the Eucharist to be no more than symbolic (although Clement and Origen came close to doing so) or specified a process of substantial change by which the presence was effected (although Ignatius and Justin came close to doing so)" (p. 167).

was officially defined. Moreover, it was only later in the thirteenth century that a helpful and more precise definition of what was meant by this term was given. By that time, the finer Aristotelian distinctions that undergirded this term were teased out. What was changing was the substance of the bread and wine, but not the accidents. The substance is, at the risk of oversimplifying, the fundamental nature of a thing, and the accidents are the outward, visible manifestation of the nature of a thing. Consequently, the argument is that through a divine miracle the substance of the bread and wine change into the very nature of the body and blood of Christ; the visible, sensible accidents of the elements are, nevertheless, preserved. In this way, the communicant is genuinely partaking of the body and blood of Christ, but is spared both the gruesome reality and sin of eating flesh and drinking blood.

As already stated, this understanding of the Lord's Supper was a later development in the Middle Ages and should, therefore, not be imported into an earlier time. True, there were Christians in the ancient and early medieval period who believed in the reality of Christ's presence at the Table, but that does not mean they explained or understood this belief in the same way as later believers. It is for this reason that we will describe the two views that began in the ancient period and passed into the Middle Ages as the real presence view and the spiritual presence view. Using this terminology helps us not only to avoid anachronism, but also to conform to the terminology historical theologians employ. In order to be clear, then, the *real presence* view is the view that Christ's body is somehow actually present in the bread and wine of the Lord's Supper. The *spiritual presence* view is the view that while there is great significance in the sacramental bread and wine, that significance is not the corporeal presence of Christ in the elements, but His spiritual presence.

It should be clear even from this brief description that views on the Lord's Supper were not uniform during the Middle Ages. There was a divergence of opinion in addition to differing ways of explaining similar positions. In addressing the topic of the church's belief about the Lord's Supper during this long period, then, we necessarily need to hone our perspective and narrow our field for examination if we are to gain any appreciable level of understanding. It will not do to be superficial, for that more often than not continues to breed misunderstanding rather than clarity. Consequently, our focus in this chapter will be on two monks who were involved in a prominent debate over the interpretation of the Lord's Supper in the tenth-century Carolingian Empire (the Carolingian Empire lasted from, roughly, the eighth to the tenth century).[3] The monks both lived at the monastery in Corbie (modern-day France) and, unfortunately for us, had very similar names. The monk named Radbertus defended the real presence view of the Lord's Supper, while the monk named Ratramnus defended the spiritual presence view. It is to the more senior of the two men that we now turn.

Radbertus and Real Presence

It does not take the reader long to realize that Radbertus's work *The Lord's Body and Blood* is a sustained defense of the belief that the body and blood of Christ are present in the bread and wine of the Lord's Supper. The opening sentence (after the greetings and dedications to the appropriate people) states unequivocally that there is no reason anyone ought to doubt that it is the true body and blood of Christ that is present at Communion.[4] To the skeptic who may wonder at the possibility of the true body and blood of Christ being present in the sacramental elements, Radbertus hastily notes that the presence of which He is speaking is a mystery. Nevertheless, even though the flesh of Christ incarnate is present as a mystery, as something that cannot be discerned by sight or taste, it is no less to be believed for the simple reason that this mystery comes to us by the command of God. After the consecration of the bread and wine, the elements are truly, though mysteriously, transformed.[5] The initial biblical warrant

[3] For some introductory reading on the Carolingian Empire the reader may wish to consult R. McKitterick, ed., *The Frankish Kingdoms Under the Carolingians, 751–987* (London: Longman, 1983); id., *Charlemagne: The Formation of Carolingian Identity* (Cambridge: Cambridge University Press, 2008).

[4] "Christi communionem uerum corpus eius et sanguine esse non dubitandum." Pascasius Radbertus, *De Corpore et Sanguine Domini*, in *Corpus Christianorum Continuatio Mediaevalis* 16, ed. B. Paulus O.S.B. (Turnholt: Brepols, 1969), 13, lines 1–2. All Latin citations are taken from this edition of Radbertus's work and will be abbreviated as *CCCM* 16. For a good, though incomplete, English translation of Radbertus's treatise see G. McCracken and A. Cabaniss, eds. and trans. *Early Medieval Theology*, LCC 9 (London: SCM, 1957), 94–108.

[5] "Et quia uoluit licet figura panis et uini haec sic esse, omnino nihil aliud quam caro Christi et sanguis post consecrationem credenda sunt." "And because he willed he may remain in the figure of bread and wine, but these must be believed to be wholly nothing other than the flesh and blood of Christ after consecration," *CCCM* 16.14–5 lines 47–49.

for making this assertion is John 6:51 where Jesus says, "The bread that I will give for the life of the world is My flesh." The casual reader may wonder if Radbertus means that what is present in the sacramental bread and wine is somehow equivalent to the incarnate body of Jesus. It certainly sounds as though he is asserting and defending this idea, but perhaps he is simply overstating his case in order to press the point of the spiritual significance of the Lord's Supper upon his readers. While it cannot be denied that Radbertus is doing his best both to bolster the faith of those sympathetic to his position and to compel those not so sympathetic to his position, his conviction is that the very flesh and blood of the One who died on the cross is what is present during the sacrament. Anticipating a negative reaction from some, to say the least, Radbertus quickly adds two further supporting arguments. First, he reminds everyone that this is a mystery; second, he contends yet again that this mystery comes to us by no less than the will and power of God. If indeed God has willed the presence of this mystery in the life of the church, then it can be neither impossible nor evil.[6] The Word of God stands as witness along with the Holy Spirit who works through the sacrament of the Eucharist so that the real presence of Christ in the elements is part of the mysterious work of salvation within the church.

At this stage, Radbertus adds further force to his argument in an almost casual or inadvertent manner. He reminds his readers that it was Christ who left this sacrament for His church along with the sacrament of baptism.[7] The point intended by Radbertus is that just as baptism is soteriologically significant, just as it is irrefutably tied to salvation, so too is the celebration of the Lord's Supper. The sacrament

[6] " . . . quia in sapientia sua omnia vult, immo ipsa sapientia eius voluntas est et propterea nihil mali, nihil quod non posit, vult." " . . . because in his wisdom he wills all things, indeed, his very wisdom is his will and therefore he wills nothing evil, nothing which he is not able to do," *CCCM* 16.17 lines 107–9.

[7] It may strike the reader as strange that a medieval theologian would name only two sacraments. A little later in the work Radbertus will again affirm his belief that baptism and the Lord's Supper are the sacraments of the church (*CCCM* 16.24 lines 14–16). This does not necessarily mean that Radbertus denied that there were more than two sacraments, however. The modern reader should be aware that agreement on the number of sacraments was not achieved until the middle of the twelfth century through the work of Peter Lombard (*Sentences*, bk. 4, dist. 1, num. 2). Lombard's conclusion that there are seven sacraments was later affirmed by Thomas Aquinas and then, most importantly, by the Council of Trent (1545–63). Some theologians both prior to the twelfth century and even after the sixteenth century, emphasized baptism and the Eucharist so as to give the impression that these two sacraments carry greater weight in the lives of believers.

of baptism is an outward sign of the inward participation of the believer in Christ. The sacrament of the Lord's Supper is also an outward sign of the inward participation of the believer in Christ. The difference between the two is that baptism happens once to mark the beginning of Christ's work in an individual, whereas the Lord's Supper is celebrated repeatedly as a mark of the continued life of the believer in Christ.[8] In this way, the celebration of and participation in the Lord's Supper are expressions of the faithful to the object of faith, Jesus Christ. This point is no less important for Radbertus because the Lord's Supper is not efficacious for unbelievers. Although he does not delve into the details of how the transformed bread and wine are effective for the one who partakes in faith while simultaneously ineffective for the one who partakes without faith, Radbertus is adamant that the mystery applies only to those who come to the altar on account of their faith. It may be that the transformation of the bread and wine into the body and blood of Christ is a mystery, but even though a mystery cannot be explained, its purpose and effect can still be understood and appropriated by faith. Thus, the communicant does not approach the altar in the hope of receiving faith for the first time, as though someone is made a Christian through the Lord's Supper; rather, communicants come by faith with the expectation that their faith will be strengthened by the ever closer bond that is forged between them and Christ through the ingestion of the very body and blood of their Savior.[9]

In addition to the analogy with baptism, Radbertus draws a second analogy with the tree of life in the garden of Eden. It was from eating

[8] "Nihil enim Christus ecclesiae suae maius aliquid in mysterio reliquit quam hoc baptismique sacramentum, necnon et Scripturas Sanctas in quibus omnibus Spiritus Sanctus qui pignus totius ecclesiae est, interius mystica salutis nostrae ad inmortalitatem operator. . . . in fide et in intellectu divinis redoleant mysteriis et in eisdem aeternitas mortalibus et participation Christi in unitate corporis concedatur." "For Christ left for his church, in a mystery, something greater than the sacrament of baptism and the holy scriptures in all of which the Holy Spirit who is a pledge to the whole church is working the interior mysteries of our salvation to immortality. . . . in faith and understanding that these mysteries may be a pleasing odor and that in them men might be granted eternity and participation in Christ and in the unity of the body," *CCCM* 16.17 lines 114–18; 16.18 lines 122–24.

[9] "Et ideo vera Christi caro et sanguis quam qui manducat digne, habet vitam aeternam in se manentem. Sed visu corporeo et gustu propterea non demutantur, quatenus fides exerceatur ad iustitiam et ob meritum fidei merces iustitiae consequatur." "Therefore, the true flesh and blood of Christ, which anyone eats in a worthy manner, has eternal life remaining in them even though the physical appearance and taste has not changed, as long as faith is exercised for justification and on account of the merit of faith, the reward of justification will follow," *CCCM* 16.18 lines 129–34.

the fruit of this tree that Adam and Eve had the promise of immortality. Here is a fine example of eating something that is unassuming in its outward appearance, yet accomplishes more than one could either hope or imagine. Just as eating the fruit of the tree would have sustained the first couple in immortality had they remained faithful in their obedience, so eating the body of the One who hung on a tree will sustain into eternity those who take it by faith.[10]

In Radbertus's theology, then, the mystery of the eucharistic transformation is assured chiefly by the command of Christ contained in Scripture, but also by analogy with baptism as well as by analogy with the tree of life at the beginning of creation. But an inquisitive reader may ask, what of those who participate in the Lord's Supper without the knowledge or understanding that a mystery is taking place? To put it more poignantly, are believers who either do not know or do not believe that the body and blood of the Lord are truly though mysteriously present in the bread and wine receiving the promised blessing of salvation and growth in faith as claimed by Radbertus? This question was certainly not an academic one considering the fact that Ratramnus, one of his fellow monks at Corbie and a noteworthy theologian in his own right, disagreed with Radbertus. Was Ratramnus outside the fold and wasting away in spiritual turpitude because he upheld a spiritual presence view rather than the real presence view? No. Radbertus contends that as long as the sacrament is approached properly and received prayerfully in faith, there yet remains pardon for anyone who, through laziness or ineptitude, does not realize or understand the mystery of the Eucharist. What is lost is not their salvation, but their knowledge of what the mystery is doing within them.[11] Ignorance deprives the believer of the joyful knowledge of what God is accomplishing in them.

In connection with this concern, Radbertus is careful to draw a distinction between those who receive the sacrament as believers,

[10] "Ita siquidem et in isto communionis sacramento visibili divina virtus ad inmortalitatem sua invisibili potentia, quasi ex fructu ligni paradysi, nos et gustu sapientiae sustentat et virtute, quatinus per hoc inmortales in anima, quamdiu ex hoc digne sumimus, demum in melius transpositi ad inmortalia feramur." "Thus it follows that in that visible sacrament of communion divine power sustains us to immortality by its invisible power as if [we had eaten] from the fruit of the tree of paradise, by the taste of wisdom and virtue, to the extent that we are made immortal in spirit, inasmuch as we accept it worthily, so that eventually we are carried away to immortality," CCCM 16.19 lines 148–53. Radbertus returns to the analogy of the tree of life in Eden in *CCCM* 16.54 lines 65ff.

[11] *CCCM* 16.23 lines 88–90.

however ignorant or unlearned they may be, and those who receive the sacrament as unbelievers either in ignorance or outright defiance of the teaching of the church. To this end, Radbertus relates the story of a Jew who, so the story goes, was incited by an evil spirit to make a mockery of the Eucharist by receiving it with the intention of spitting it out onto a dunghill (*sterquilinium*). The man joined the throng of worshippers and opened his mouth to receive the bread only to discover that the moment it entered his mouth he could neither close his mouth nor move his tongue. He began screaming in pain and trying to speak but to no avail as both his jaw and his tongue were held steadfastly in place. At first, the congregation was shocked by this sight, but then those who were closest to the man saw the figure of Christ's body in his mouth and began praising God for working such a miracle which showed the veracity of the biblical truth that God is not mocked. Eventually, the bishop had the man come forward and he removed the Eucharist from his mouth. The pain stopped. His jaw could move. His tongue was freed that he might speak again. The Jewish man immediately threw himself down before the bishop and professed faith in Christ and expressed his desire to be baptized without delay.[12]

While this story is, sadly, part and parcel of ninth-century attitudes toward Jews, we can still draw something of value from it. First, Radbertus undoubtedly believed that the sacred nature of the Eucharist would be defended by Christ Himself, for who but Christ could know the inner thoughts and intentions of the communicants? Second, we learn that when Radbertus speaks of those who try to participate in the Lord's Supper in an unworthy manner, he has unbelievers in view rather than ignorant or ill-informed believers. This is confirmed somewhat later in the treatise when he addresses the question of the grounds on which a communicant receives either judgment or reward.[13] Those who receive the mystery in faith receive the reward of eternal life; those who receive the mystery apart from faith or unworthily receive judgment.

There are several other issues and questions to which Radbertus directs his attention, such as why bread and wine are used, why water is mixed with the wine in the chalice, why there is no change in

[12] *CCCM* 16.36–7 lines 51–108.

[13] This issue is taken up in *CCCM* 16.40–52.

the color or taste of the sacramental elements after they have been transformed, but the answers to these queries invariably draw on the material introduced in the opening sections of the work. The sum of his theology of the Lord's Supper is that there is a real though mysterious transformation in the bread and wine which, by the working of the Spirit, provides eternal life to the communicant who, by faith, attends to the sacrament in a manner worthy of the miracle performed for their salvation. This is the position Radbertus defended to King Charles the Bald as the one worthy of acceptance and maintained by all those faithful to the truth. It was not the position, however, that was upheld by his colleague Ratramnus.

Ratramnus: Getting Here from There

Although the view expressed above by Radbertus was the view that eventually dominated the next half millennium,[14] Ratramnus's defense of a spiritual and noncorporeal presence in the Eucharist enjoyed popularity and support beyond his own day. Men such as Flodoard of Reims (c. 894–966), Hériger of Lobbes (c. 925–1007), Aelfric of Eynsham (c. 955–1020), Berengar of Tours (1010–88), Sigebert of Gembloux (c. 1035–1112), though little known now, were significant figures in their own time, and all knew and made reference to Ratramnus's work.[15] Granted, the use of *Christ's Body and Blood* ranges from little more than a favorable reference to a clear appropriation of his ideas, but his work was, nonetheless, known, read and appreciated.

[14] The literature on the Eucharist throughout the Middle Ages and especially in the eleventh century and beyond is vast. There are doubtless many reasons for this, among them the growth of accounts of visions related to the eucharistic body of Christ, ecstatic experiences of various kinds reported during the celebration of the Mass, the emergence to greater prominence of mystics such as Julian of Norwich who desired greater intimacy than the church or the sacraments could provide, the development of mystery plays associated with Easter celebrations, not to mention the ever-increasing significance of blood cults. Some significant resources addressing these and related matters include, C. W. Bynum, *Wonderful Blood, Theology and Practice in Late Medieval Northern Germany and Beyond* (Philadelphia: University of Pennsylvania Press, 2007); F. C. Bauerschmidt, *Julian of Norwich and the Mystical Body Politic of Christ* (Notre Dame: University of Notre Dame Press, 1999); E. Duffy, *The Stripping of the Altars, Traditional Religion in England 1400–1580* (New Haven: Yale University Press, 1992); A. J. MacDonald, *Berengar and the Reform of the Sacramental Doctrine* (London: Longmans, Green and Co., 1930); M. Rubin, *Corpus Christi: The Eucharist in Late Medieval Culture* (Cambridge: Cambridge University Press, 1991).

[15] Cf. McCracken, *Early Medieval Theology*, 111–13. Although McCracken wrote his introduction in the mid-twentieth century, what details he does provide remain agreed upon by Carolingian scholars to this day.

What is perhaps more worthy of note is that throughout the next two centuries Ratramnus's view was not deemed heretical. Eventually, however, *Christ's Body and Blood* fell out of favor and even Ratrmanus's name was forgotten while the position represented by Radbertus gained the ascendency. All was not lost, though, as the tectonic plates of intellectual and spiritual change slowly began to produce a readership once again in the fifteenth century. After an initial, though brief, mention in the works of the Benedictine abbot Joannes Trithemius of Spanheim (c. 1462–1516) and later, in a work on the Eucharist by the bishop of Rochester, John Fisher (c. 1459–1535), Ratramnus's treatise was published in 1531.[16] In fact, not only were Ratramnus's views published in Latin for the educated to read, but within a year of its first printing his *De Corpore et Sanguine Domini* was translated into German for a much wider audience.[17] Perhaps the most telling comment on the influence Ratramnus's work could have on sixteenth-century Reformers comes from no less than Bishop Nicholas Ridley during his trial for heresy in 1555. He said of Ratramnus,

> This man was the first that pulled me by the ear, and forced me from the common error of the Roman church to a more diligent search of Scripture and ecclesiastical writers on this matter.[18]

None of this should surprise us, of course, since one of the hotly debated points of religious disagreement and cause of considerable unrest in the sixteenth century was the nature of the Lord's Supper. Was the substance of the incarnate body of Christ present in the elements as the reigning powers of the church in that day argued? Was Christ tied to the elements in some spiritual or mystical way quite apart from a bodily presence? Was the Lord's Supper a simple memorial of His death and resurrection and a reminder of His second coming? The questions and arguments abounded, but what is significant for our purposes here is that those who chose to articulate a position contrary to the real presence view (referred to more commonly as transubstantiation by the sixteenth century), had historical precedent upon which to draw. To be sure, they could draw on the Fathers to help show that they were not creating a new doctrine or deviating

[16] Ibid., 113–14.

[17] Ibid., 114.

[18] Glocester Ridley, *Life of Dr. Nicholas Ridley* (London, 1763), 685, cited in McCracken, *Early Medieval Theology*, 115.

altogether from the faith handed down and once for all entrusted to the saints. What was more helpful was that they could point to, among others, a theologian such as Ratramnus who not only represented a sizable portion of opinion in the church during the ninth century, but whose opinion was not immediately condemned but left open for consideration. In other words, there was a time when discussion on the nature and meaning of the Lord's Supper could be debated without fear of censure or worse. Moreover, there was a line of interpretation that stretched from the Fathers to the sixteenth century that lent credence to the spiritual presence view even if there was not agreement at all points. In light of the attention and excitement that surrounded Ratramnus's theology of this sacrament during the sixteenth century, our interest should be all the more piqued as to the contents of this little treatise.

Ratramnus on Spiritual Presence

Ratramnus opens his work by acknowledging that it is only on account of the request of royalty (Charles the Bald) that he has decided to put pen to paper and express his views on the nature of the Eucharist.[19] Such an opening foray is not the outworking of an arrogant heart, but was imperative for at least three reasons. First, it was important that Ratramnus grip his audience's attention. This treatise is not a work borne out of the meandering mind of a bored monk. Second, given the fact that Ratramnus was setting out to disagree and even publicly disparage the work of his fellow monk and abbot (recall that both men lived at the monastery in Corbie), he needed to set everyone straight on the driving force behind his efforts. Third, an exposition on the nature of something so fundamental to the belief and practice of the church is a delicate matter, and thus one best placed in the context of a direct royal request.

Having set the context, Ratramnus moved immediately to summarize the current state of affairs in ninth-century liturgical practice and belief as it pertains to the daily celebration of the mystery of the body and blood of Christ.[20] He informs us that there are some in the church

[19] "Jussistis, gloriose princeps ut quid de sanguinis et corporis Christi mysterio sentiam . . . " "You command me, glorious prince, that I should make known the mystery of the blood and body of Christ..." Ratramni Corbeiensis Monachi, *De Corpore et Sanguine Domini* in PL 121.125D.

[20] " . . . quod in Ecclesia quotidie celebrator . . . " " . . . which is celebrated in the church today . . . ", PL 121.128A. It is worth noting here that the Lord's Supper was celebrated daily.

who believe that there is no mysterious change in the elements of the sacrament, while there are others who believe there is some change even if we cannot see it. Hiding behind his royal patron's request, Ratramnus somewhat playfully alludes to 1 Cor 1:10 and claims that the whole church should be in agreement and not divided. To this end the truth must be sought out with all diligence so that those who have deviated might be recalled to the truth.[21]

The crux of the matter, as far as Ratramnus is concerned, is whether or not "that very body which was born of Mary, and suffered, died and was buried, which rose again and ascended into heaven to sit at the right hand of the Father" is in the elements of the Lord's Supper.[22] In order to guard against imprecision, Ratramnus contends that, first and foremost, the terminology commonly employed in this debate must be carefully defined. The two terms that demand attention are "figure" (*figura*) and "truth" (*veritas*). What does each mean? A figure is the means by which an intention is made known under a kind of veil, when one thing is spoken, but something else or something more is meant. Thus, when Jesus referred to Himself as the vine and His disciples as the branches, He was speaking of vines and branches, but clearly intending to convey something more than horticultural information. In contrast to this, truth does not use veils, but is a way of speaking plainly. When we read that Jesus was born of a virgin, for example, the text is telling us that He was born of a virgin. This description is not a metaphor or analogy.[23] Quite apart from trying to set out a clear exposition, Ratramnus had to make this clarification because Radbertus had used these terms and asserted that the mysterious change that takes place at the consecration of the elements can be thought of as both figure and truth.

This would have been the practice in monasteries as well as in cathedrals, but as for smaller country churches, the celebration of the sacrament, let alone a peasant's participation, would have been much more uneven. For a gentle introduction to this situation see H. S. Bennett, *Life on the English Manor* (Cambridge: Cambridge University Press, 1989). For some excellent and more critical scholarship see R. McKitterick, *The Frankish Church and the Carolingian Reforms, 789–895* (London: Royal Historical Society, 1977); J. M. Wallace-Hadrill, *The Frankish Church* (Oxford: Clarendon, 1983).

[21] ". . . ut ad eam deviantes revocare posit" ". . . so that it might be possible to recall those who have wandered," PL 121.129A.

[22] ". . . et utrum ipsum corpus quod de Maria natum est, et passum, mortuum et sepultum, quodque resurgens et coelos ascendens, ad dexteram Patris consideat." ". . . and whether it is the very body which was born of Mary, and suffered, and died, and was buried, which rose again and ascended to heaven, and sits at the right hand of the Father," PL 121.130A.

[23] PL 121.130A–C.

In *The Lord's Body and Blood* Radbertus drew heavily from Jesus' words in John 6. In that chapter John reports Jesus' instruction: "Truly, truly, I say to you: unless you eat the flesh of the Son of Man and drink His blood, you will not have eternal life in you."[24] Radbertus infers from this that Jesus must be speaking about His very own incarnate flesh and blood. What Jesus spoke, He spoke in truth. Even so, reasons Radbertus, we know that the elements are administered under a figure since they do not change in any physical way. Herein lies a dilemma for it seems impossible to say that Jesus was speaking simultaneously in figure and in truth. The proposed solution is that the eucharistic elements are a figure in so far as the senses cannot penetrate any further than bread and wine, but those same elements are, in fact, the very incarnate body of Christ—in truth—when considered from the perspective of the believing participant because truth is anything "rightly understood or believed inwardly."[25] In light of this assessment Ratramnus has determined that the appropriate method with which to begin is to define what a figure is, juxtapose it to truth (speaking plainly) and then ascertain whether one or both readings are supported by a careful reading of Scripture.

To the reader who already believes in a version of the spiritual presence view, indeed to many Protestants, the temptation is surely to jump to the conclusion that there is an inherent incompatibility in holding that the bread and wine are simultaneously figuratively and actually the body of Christ. Surely the former is the only tenable position? The bread and wine are symbols. While it is clearly anachronistic to speak of Ratramnus responding to a Protestant interest, he does answer the concern, though from a different perspective. One way to resolve the dilemma of a double intention (interpreting the Eucharist as a figure and as a truth) is to maintain that the elements are, as just noted, solely figures. This appears to be one of the options of which

[24] "Amen, amen dico vobis: nisi manducaveritis carnem filii hominis et biberitis eius sanguine, non habebitis vitam aeternam in vobis." Radbertus's text differs little from the Vulgate currently in use. Perhaps the most significant departure is the use of the future at the end of the verse, "will not have" (*non habebitis*) instead of the present "do not have" (*non habetis*). The astute reader will also notice that the form of the verbs for eat (*manducaveritis*) and drink (*biberitis*) could be either future perfect indicative or perfect active subjunctive. Since the Greek text uses the aorist active subjunctive, it seems more likely that the Vulgate is reflecting the Greek mood.

[25] " . . . veritas vero quicquid de hoc mysterio interius recte intellegitur aut creditor." " . . . truth, as it pertains to this mystery, is anything rightly understood or believed inwardly," Radbertus, *CCCM* 16.29 lines 45–6.

Ratramnus is aware, but one he does not favor. Ratramnus asks what place faith would have in the Lord's Supper if there were no element of mystery at all. Quoting from Heb 11:1, he argues that since faith is the evidence of things not seen, there must be something that is not seen in the Eucharist, otherwise the celebration could not be said to relate to our faith in any meaningful way.[26] Accordingly, there must be something more going on than just a service of remembrance, but we must take care not to claim there has been any change in the elements. Ratramnus grounds his position in the patristic authority by alluding to Ambrose's assertion that the bread and wine do not go through any change at all. They do not become something other than what they are, and they do not become nothing, and they do not become something as though they were nothing! Ratramnus covers every conceivable form of change and states at the conclusion that the bread is still bread and the wine is still wine.[27]

The thrust of this line of thought is to challenge any notion that the elements undergo a change "in truth." By definition, if the elements have undergone a change in truth, that change must be evident to the senses. Since no one who has ever participated in the Lord's Supper has, to Ratramnus's knowledge, ever claimed that the consistency or smell or taste of the bread became that of flesh (or that similar changes occurred in the wine) the claim that the elements turn into the incarnate body and blood of Christ "in truth" is unwarranted and false.[28] The only option remaining given the dichotomy Ratramnus set

[26] "Et cum fides, secundum Apostolum, sit rerum argumentum non apparentium, id est non earum quae videntur, sed quae non videntur substantiarum, nihil hic secundum fidem accipiemus, quoniam quidquid existit, secundum sensus corporis dijudicamus." "And since faith, according to the Apostle, is the evidence of things not appearing, that is, not of substances which are visible, but invisible, we will receive nothing according to faith since we determine what it is according to the bodily senses," PL 121.132A.

[27] PL 132B–C. Ratramnus returns to Ambrose's *De Sacramentis* later to argue compellingly that what the body takes in physically cannot of itself be the true body of Christ since the participant's body is manifestly not made incorruptible and eternal by eating and drinking the bread and wine. "Est ergo in illo panis vita, quae non oculis apparet corporis, sed fidei contuetur aspectu." "There is, therefore life in that very bread, which does not appear to the bodily eyes, but is seen by the vision of faith," PL 121.148B.

[28] " . . . negant quod affirmare creduntur, et quod credunt destruere comprobantur. Corpus etenim sanguinemque Christi fideliter confitentur: et eum hoc faciunt, non hoc iam esse quod prius fuere procul dubio protestantur: et si aliud sint quam fuere, mutationem accepere." " . . . they deny what they believe they affirm, and what they believe they destroy, they prove. For they faithfully confess the body and blood of Christ, and when they do this, they testify that these are not what they were to begin with, and if they are other than what they were, they admit a change," PL 121.134A.

up between figure and truth, is that the eucharistic elements should be understood figuratively. Here modern readers must take care to bear the context in mind. We have already noted that, on the analogy of Heb 11:1, Ratramnus does not agree with the idea that the elements are merely symbols as though given for mnemonic purposes alone. Moreover, Ratramnus's definition of a figure indicates that although a distinction must be maintained between the signifier and the thing signified, nevertheless, the thing signified is real and in this case really present.[29] Consequently, the bread and wine are the physical veils that convey the spiritual body and spiritual blood of Christ. What Radbertus believed is actually or truly present in the elements (though mysteriously), Ratramnus believed is present spiritually. This is why the designations of real presence and spiritual presence are so apt.

How does Ratramnus defend his position? He does so with a litany of examples with which he expects his audience to connect, wherein the signifier (the physical part) undergoes no change at all, but signifies something spiritually real. The first and most obvious example for a ninth-century theologian is baptism. In the waters of baptism the signifier is the water and the thing signified is new life. In Ratramnus's day this was the most effective analogy to his spiritual presence view of the Eucharist because of the almost universal agreement that while the waters of baptism are not themselves changed, what is understood to take place is the very real spiritual work of the Holy Spirit who alone can cleanse humanity of sin and work sanctification in the soul.[30] This position is summed up in a rather clever turn of phrase when Ratramnus writes, "*Non ergo sunt idem quod cernuntur et*

[29] " . . . necesse est iam ut figurate facta esse dicatur; quoniam sub velamento corporei panis corporeique vini spirituate corpus spiritualisque sanguis existit . . . . Secundum namque quod utrumque corporaliter contingitur, species sunt creaturae corporeae; secundum potentiam vero quod spiritaliter factae sunt, mysteria sunt sorporis et sanguinis Christi." " . . . it is necessary that what was said [that the elements turn spiritually into the body and blood of Christ] was done figuratively, since under the cover of physical bread and wine his [Christ's] spiritual body and blood are present. . . . According to the physicality of both they are of things created corporeally; according to power, in so far as they have been spiritually made, they are the mysteries of the body and blood of Christ," PL 121.134B–135A.

[30] "Si requires quod superficietenus lavat, elementum est; si vero perpendas quod interius purgat, virtus vitalis est, virtus sanctificationis, virtus immortalitatis. Igitur in proprietate humor corruptibilis, in mysterio vero virtus sanabilis." "If you ask what washes superficially, it is the element; if you carefully assess what cleanses the inward parts, it is the power of life, the power of sanctification, the power of immortality. Therefore, in its innate property it [water] is corruptible, but in the mystery it has power to cure," PL 121.136A.

quod creduntur" ("What is seen and what is believed are not the same thing").[31]

Ratramnus moves naturally from baptism as it is known and experienced by the church to the baptism of Israel to which Paul referred in 1 Corinthians 10. There Paul speaks of "our fathers" who were baptized in the cloud and in the sea. In addition to this, Paul also refers to the water that flowed from the rock, and the rock was Christ. Without pausing to delve into a full exegesis of Paul's larger purpose, Ratramnus simply notes that this is another example of how physical things (the Red Sea, the cloud that led the people of Israel, the rock from which the people drank in the desert) signify a greater spiritual reality without themselves being changed. Just as the waters of baptism signal the internal spiritual cleansing of the one baptized, so the waters of the Red Sea and the cloud signaled the internal spiritual cleansing of Israel in the desert.[32]

After spending considerable space fleshing out more examples that support his spiritual presence view, Ratramnus follows Radbertus's lead and turns to address the question of why bread and wine, in particular, were chosen as the symbols. The answer he gives is very much in keeping with the thinking of his day, and here we discover more similarity between Ratramnus and his theological opponents than difference. Even so, Ratramnus shows his brilliance by using an accepted explanation to his own advantage. Put simply, the common explanation in the Middle Ages (on this point there is little difference from century to century) as to why bread was chosen is because just as bread is made up of many different grains of flour, so the church, the body of Christ, is made up of many different people. Furthermore, just as the bread is a whole that is broken, so it represents Christ's whole body broken for us. By this symbol not only is the body of Jesus Christ signified, but so too is the church. What Ratramnus pauses to point out is that no one believes that the bodies of the faithful are, in truth, present in the eucharistic bread or wine. It was commonly held that in this regard the bread and wine were but symbols of a greater reality. Seizing on this, Ratramnus argues that just as the bread with

[31] PL 121.136A.

[32] "Igitur et mare et nubes non secundum hoc quod corpus exstiterant, sanctificationis munditiam praebuere, verum secundum quod invisibiliter sancti Spiritus sanctificationem continebant." "Therefore, the sea and the cloud provided the purification of sanctification not according to their physical existence, but as they contained the sanctification of the Holy Spirit which was invisible," PL 121.137A.

its many grains is a symbol of the spiritual reality of the church made up of many people, so the bread is a symbol of the body of Christ ingested spiritually.[33]

The final argument Ratramnus makes in favor of the spiritual presence is eschatological. He begins by citing the liturgy which says in one place, "By taking the pledge of eternal life, we humbly ask that of what we touch in the image of the sacrament we may obtain a clear share."[34] In another place the liturgy says, "O Lord, we ask that your sacraments may perfect in us what they contain, so that what we have in appearance now we may take hold of in truth."[35] In both places Ratramnus explains that the church's confession is that the bread and wine are images or pledges of what believers hope to realize "in truth" in some measure now through an ever-growing likeness to Christ, but completely in the eschaton. For Ratramnus, this final piece is significant because the goal of the gospel is that believers will one day know and see "in truth" what we now only know and see through a figure. The very nature of the figure is that it is fleeting and transient and therefore inferior to what is permanent and eternal. We rejoice in what we have now, yet we long for what we will possess then.[36] To return to one of Ratramnus's opening points, were we to have Christ "in truth" through the Eucharist now, to what would our faith look forward and on what would our hope be set?

A Central Text: John 6

There can be no doubt that Radbertus and Ratramnus had their differences over the interpretation of the Lord's Supper. Despite these differences, however, one striking similarity between them is their use of John 6. The use of this passage is striking because they both appeal to it, but for entirely different reasons. Radbertus appeals to John 6 as

[33] "Qua de re, sicut in mysterio panis ille Christi corpus accipitur, sic etiam in mysterio membra populi credentis in Christum intimantur; et sicut non corporaliter sed spiritualiter panis ille credentium corpus dicitur, sic quoque Christi corpus non corporaliter sed spiritualiter necesse est intelligatur." "Concerning this, just as in the mystery the bread is received as the body of Christ, so also is the mystery of the members of the people who believe in Christ revealed; and just as the bread is called the body of those who believe, though not physically but spiritually, so the body of Christ must be understood as something spiritual and not physical," PL 121.159B.

[34] "Pignus aeternae vitae capientes humiliter imploramus ut quod in imagine contingimus sacramenti, manifesta participation sumamus," PL 121.162D.

[35] "Perficiant in nobis, Domine, quaesumus, tua sacramenta quod continent: ut quae nunc specie gerimus, rerum veritate capiamus," PL 121.164A.

[36] PL 121.169A–B.

proof that his position is correct, while Ratramnus appeals to this passage in favor of his position. It seems prudent, therefore, to examine this passage since it is a portion of Scripture to which not only these theologians referred, but subsequent theologians have continued to refer even to our present day.

While many evangelicals and, more broadly, Protestants may be itching to correct Radbertus's exegesis and to engage him in lively hermeneutical debate, it would behoove such to pause for a moment to consider an oft-neglected positive point that emerges from his writing. We observed earlier that Radbertus addressed the question of whether or not a Christian who did not believe in his theology of the real presence of Christ in the Eucharist could still benefit from, let alone participate in, that Christ-appointed rite of the church. His answer was in the affirmative. How remarkable that a theological position that has divided Christians for centuries should be espoused and rigorously defended during the Middle Ages, but in such a way as to include rather than exclude those who disagree. Granted, there are many issues and concerns that must be addressed when approaching the question of who may be included in the celebration of the Lord's Supper. Nevertheless, surely Radbertus gives the modern church something to ponder. Even when stridently disagreeing with his fellow monk Ratramnus, Radbertus does not deny him fellowship.

Radbertus opens his work with a citation of Jesus' words in John 6:51 to support his real presence view. Jesus says there that His body is given for the life of the world. At first glance, this passage in John is an odd one. Jesus says quite plainly that He is the living bread from heaven, and anyone who eats this living bread, which is His flesh, will live forever. Could the Bible be any clearer? Surely, this is evidence enough to demonstrate that, in some mysterious though immutable way, the very body and blood of the incarnate Christ is ingested by His followers.[37] How that might be expected to occur from the perspective of those listening in John 6 would have proven something of a puzzle, but one to which the answer is given by the end of the Gospel, with the Last Supper. Our desire here, however, is to stay close to the contours of John 6, so let us take stock of the content and context of this

[37] Radbertus, *CCCM* 16.27 lines 3–13.

chapter alone in order to assist our appreciation and assessment of the credibility of Radbertus's interpretation.[38]

John 6 begins with an account of the feeding of the 5,000. The miraculous nature of what took place was not lost on the people, nor were their intentions missed by the Messiah. When the feeding had finished, Jesus withdrew to a mountain so that He might escape the crowd's ambition to forcibly make Him their king. After a brief interlude in which Jesus walked on water to His disciples' boat during the evening, the crowds became aware the next day that Jesus was not returning to the place where they were fed. Upon embarking in boats, they eventually found Him and began to inquire after His itinerary. It is as this point that Jesus turns the tables on the crowd.

Jesus informs the crowd that what matters most to them are their stomachs. Jesus fed them, and they wanted more food. Jesus warns the people not to work for the food that perishes, but to work for the food that endures into everlasting life. It is this food that the Son of Man provides. The obvious question here is what work is required to gain the food of everlasting life, to which Jesus replies that the work of God is to believe in the One God has sent. At this stage in the dialogue, the people clearly recognized that Jesus was speaking about Himself, and so they asked for a sign that He really is sent by God. Now, at first glance, such a request might sound ridiculous since Jesus had just fed them in a miraculous manner. What the people were requesting, however, is a sign that accords with the promise of eternal bread. In other words, they had already seen and accepted the sign that qualified Jesus as a prophet; now they wanted to see the sign that qualified Jesus to fulfill His promise that He was sent from God and had the very seal of the Father on Him. Moses gave our forefathers bread from heaven, what can you do?

Jesus seized on this reference immediately. First, He clarified for the people that it was not Moses who gave the people bread from heaven, but God. More important than that, however, is the point that

[38] For far more enlightening comments and greater detail on this chapter from an evangelical point of view see the commentaries by H. Ridderbos, *The Gospel of John, a Theological Commentary,* trans. J. Vriend (Grand Rapids: Eerdmans, 1997), 208–44; D. A. Carson, *The Gospel According to John* (Grand Rapids: Eerdmans, 1991), 267–99. To get a flavor for the interpretation of this passage in the ancient church see J. C. Elowsky, ed. *John 1–10,* ACCS:NT 4a (Downers Grove: InterVarsity, 2006), 208–43. For comments on the interpretation of Scripture in general, consult the older but indispensable B. Smalley, *The Study of the Bible in the Middle Ages* (Oxford: Blackwell, 1952).

while Moses' bread was given some time ago (note the past tense in v. 32a), the true bread which the people need to eat is currently available (note the present tense in v. 32b). How is it that eternal bread is currently available to the people? It is available because the true bread of God, the true bread given from heaven, is Jesus who says, "I am the bread of life" (John 6:35). Jesus then states clearly in the succeeding verses that anyone who comes to Him and believes in Him will no longer be hungry or thirsty. In line with Ratramnus's interpretation of this passage, what is taught here is that the desire to satisfy hunger is achieved by believing in Him.[39]

Jesus' deft use of the people's reference to food from heaven has resulted in His appropriation of that reference into a metaphor. In spite of this, v. 51 raises a question that, to some, has been lurking in the depths if not simmering under the very surface of the text. With all of the language of eating and drinking the body or flesh of Christ, not to mention the focus on His blood that comes in the ensuing verses, surely Radbertus was right to see a reference here to the Eucharist. Are not the words of our Lord, "This is my body" echoed in Jesus' final statement that "I will give my flesh . . . for the life of the world" (John 6:51)? Certainly, it may be argued that there are echoes here, but it is difficult to sustain the notion that there are more than echoes here. Consider, for example, that in all the accounts of the Lord's Supper in the NT it is, particularly, the Lord's *body* that is mentioned and not His flesh. Had John wanted to make a clear connection between this part of Jesus' teaching and the Lord's Supper, choosing different diction at a crucial juncture is not the way to go about it. But wait, we might hear Radbertus retort, what about the statements regarding the drinking of blood in addition to the eating of flesh in John 6:53–54?

Again, this is not the place to enter into an extended discussion, but several comments will suffice. First, it is worth remembering the context in which John 6 is taking place. There was no way for the original audience to conceive of Jesus' words referring to what the church would later call the Eucharist or Lord's Supper. For them, the only way Jesus' teaching could be understood against the backdrop of OT law forbidding cannibalism would be to understand that Jesus was using a metaphor. Were His disciples and the Jews at large not inclined to interpret Jesus' words in this way, their response would not

[39] Ratramnus, PL 121.139A–B.

simply have been to walk away grumbling that this is difficult teaching. The only appropriate response would have been to usher Jesus into the courts and to try Him for inciting people to break the law. This is a perspective that Radbertus, along with like-minded theologians, appear to forget.

Second, the reader would do well to pay attention to the force of Jesus' statement in v. 54. Jesus says there that whoever eats His flesh and drinks His blood has eternal life and will be raised on the last day. Here is a startling promise that is given without reservation or condition. Can we believe that Jesus would have promised salvation to those who partake in the Lord's Supper, as though it is the eating and drinking that bring salvation? This countermands the very foundation of Jesus' gospel, not to mention the immediate context of these verses. As we have already seen, the idea of believing in the Son of God is paramount in this pericope. The work of God is to believe (v. 29). The desire of the people is to believe in Jesus on the basis of a sign (v. 30). The one who believes in Jesus will never thirst again (v. 35). The one who believes in the Son will have eternal life and be raised up on the last day (v. 40). He who believes has eternal life (v. 47). Most profoundly, at the end of the chapter, Peter tells Jesus that the disciples will not desert Him, for Jesus alone has the words of life and they believe that Jesus is the Holy One of God (v. 69). Everything in this chapter points toward Jesus' words being understood metaphorically, the crowd grasping the great cost of the salvation that comes through the Son of Man, and the disciples becoming all the more aware of the necessity of believing in Jesus. Truly, the Holy One of God descended to take on flesh that He might give Himself, in His flesh, for the life of the world, and having done so to ascend to where He was before as a demonstration of what lies ahead for those who believe.

In sum, then, while John 6:51 may at first appear to lend support to Radbertus's idea that the body, the very flesh of Jesus, is somehow present in the eucharistic elements, a careful consideration of the context of that passage does not lend itself to the same conclusion. This passage denies a real presence view and its later development in transubstantiation.

Implications: From Medieval to Modern

There is much even in this brief exchange between medieval monks that warrants extended reflection. Perhaps the most obvious point that can be made is that these men took the Lord's Supper seriously. Regardless of the nature of the celebration, both men and those they represented recognized that a proper understanding and practice of this part of the liturgy was a weighty matter. The gravity of the moment came not only from the fact that this ecclesial rite was instituted by Christ Himself, but also from the fact that it is a celebration that draws on multiple facets of biblical revelation in order to bring unity to the participants. The Lord's Supper is not segregated from the doctrines of the church or of Christ or of salvation. The activity Christ commanded we carry out is an activity of the church, not an activity for the individual. What we celebrate, we celebrate corporately. What we declare about the person and work of the incarnate Christ we declare most effectively as the body of Christ. What we proclaim about the application of redemption to humanity, we can only proclaim in the context of the presence and power of the gospel of Jesus Christ. When believers fail to remember that what they are doing is more than remembering, they remove themselves not only from the main stream of the church's confession, but also from the depth of the riches of the glorious gospel that draws believers to unity in the faith and so "to the measure of the stature which belongs to the fullness of Christ" (Eph 4:13).

Building on this, we can also learn from our medieval forebears that the Lord's Supper is a vital expression of salvation. Although we did not delve into some of the peripheral discussions that developed as part of this debate, one of those discussions had to do with the relationship between the Lord's Supper and the atonement. The archbishop Hincmar of Reims who believed in the real presence view as Radbertus did, asserted that the redeeming blood of Christ is offered to all through the cup that contains the very blood of the incarnate Christ. Not that the participant is saved by merely receiving the sacrament apart from faith, but that the universal offer of salvation is visibly represented before the people in the fact that the wine has mysteriously turned into the infinitely redeeming blood of Christ. In this sense, salvation full and free is available to all through the sacrament. Against this Ratramnus certainly had no difficulty with the proclamation of the gospel to the ends of the earth, but, along with the monk Gottschalk, contended that the offer of the sacrament only to those who by faith understood and believed in what the elements represented, mirrored the limited nature of the atonement based on the electing purposes of divine predestination.[40] Regardless of the position taken, it is good to be reminded that the content and form of our worship should be carefully thought out in relation to our theology. Is our liturgical practice consistent with our theological profession?

Finally, Radbertus and Ratramnus did not take for granted something that the evangelical church today has, for the most part, lost sight of. They recognized that the Eucharist is a sign of God's grace. While they would doubtless express themselves differently than we might now, their thinking moves along distinctly biblical lines. When we think of God's activity in and for humanity, what do we see? We see God providing an outward, visible sign of the inward grace He is dispensing to His people. When God made His covenant with Abraham, that through His seed blessing would come to all the families of the earth, He gave Abraham the sign of circumcision (Gen 17:11). After God led the people of Israel out of Egypt to Mount Sinai, He made a covenant there with them of which the Sabbath was the sign (Exod 31:16–17). When we come to the new covenant which Jesus ratified through the shedding of His blood, we see that the sign of this new covenant is the Lord's Supper (Luke 22:20; 1 Cor 11:25).

Therefore, when Protestants in general or evangelicals in particular assess what they believe to be the medieval view of the Lord's Supper (by now it should be clear that until the tenth century, at least, the notion of a single medieval view is inaccurate), they ought to take greater care in accounting for why that view is held. Yes, there is disagreement on whether the incarnate body of Christ is somehow present in the Communion elements, but what of the desire to express the reality of the intimate union declared in those elements that led to the sealing of the new covenant? The Lord's Supper is not a time to indulge in introspection as though a thorough cleaning of the heart is up to each individual. To be sure, all must examine themselves, but that self-examination takes place in the context of the Savior, on the one hand, who gave Himself for us and will return again bodily, and,

[40] C. Chazelle, *The Crucified God in the Carolingian Era* (Cambridge: Cambridge University Press, 2001), 224–25.

on the other hand, the body of Christ which is the church. In other words, the self-examination as instructed by Paul must be carried out in relation to the dispensation of grace made available in Christ as well as in relation to the dispensation of grace made known in the church. It is precisely because the Lord's Supper is suffused with grace that it is a proclamation of the Lord's death until He comes (1 Cor 11:26). We are not saved because we partake of the elements, but in partaking of the elements the church gives witness to its foundation, its unity, its hope, and its conviction; all of which is exclusively grounded in the grace of the new covenant inaugurated by Christ on the cross.

THE THEOLOGY OF THE EUCHARIST ACCORDING TO THE CATHOLIC CHURCH

Gregg R. Allison*

Introduction

Setting forth the theology of the Eucharist according to the Catholic Church is no easy task for an evangelical like me. As I will demonstrate in this chapter, Catholic theology is a significantly different framework from a Protestant[1] worldview, which makes it quite difficult to grasp. Moreover, presenting and understanding one aspect of Catholic theology—like its eucharistic theology, the focus of this essay—cannot be severed from a presentation and understanding of Catholic theology in general, as the entire theological system hangs together. Furthermore, many evangelicals, though perhaps mildly familiar with Catholic theology through attendance at a Catholic wedding or going to a Catholic Mass with a friend, are not well acquainted with this area. For these reasons and others, my task is quite formidable.

Though not raised as a Catholic, I have had plenty of experience working within various Catholic contexts. Accordingly, I hope to be a reliable guide for my readers. As a staff member of Campus Crusade for Christ, I worked in campus ministry at the University of Notre Dame, and the majority of students involved in our movement were Catholic. Through this ministry I developed a burden for working in a Catholic context in Europe, and this hope became a reality when my next ministry assignment was Rome, Italy. I was embedded in a nascent Catholic lay evangelization movement, Alfa Omega,[2] in which I served as its initial training center director. This platform provided friendships and working relationships with Catholic laypeople and priests and many opportunities to share the gospel, lead Bible studies, disciple, and teach in a wide variety of Catholic contexts.

* Gregg R. Allison received his Ph.D. from Trinity Evangelical Divinity School. He is professor of Christian Theology at The Southern Baptist Theological Seminary in Louisville, Kentucky.

[1] I will use the terms "evangelical" and "Protestant" interchangeably in this essay, though significant differences exist between them.

[2] Alfa Omega: *perché Cristo sia tutto in tutti* ("that Christ may be all in all").

Furthermore, during my graduate studies at Trinity Evangelical Divinity School, I took a class, "Documents of Vatican II," at St. Mary's of the Lake Catholic Seminary in Mundelein, Illinois. Because of this background, I regularly taught the course on Catholic theology at Western Seminary and continue to teach it at The Southern Baptist Theological Seminary. I trust that this rich experience helps me fairly represent and critique the Catholic theology of the Eucharist.

In this chapter, I will first describe the celebration of the Eucharist as it is carried out in the Catholic Church today. Next, relying upon the presentation in the *Catechism of the Catholic Church*,[3] I will discuss the theology of the Eucharist. I will then outline the historical development of the doctrine of the Eucharist from the early church to the time of the Reformation, ending with the Council of Trent. Next, because Catholic eucharistic theology is part of a broader theological framework, I will discuss several other Catholic doctrines that impinge on the presentation and understanding of its doctrine of the Eucharist. Finally, I will offer an evangelical assessment of this Catholic theology of the Eucharist.

The Celebration of the Eucharist

Following the Liturgy of the Word and the initial stages of the Liturgy of the Eucharist, the Catholic Mass reaches the *anaphora*,[4] "the heart and summit of the celebration."[5] "In the *epiclesis*,[6] the Church asks the Father to send his Holy Spirit" to transform the elements of bread and wine.[7] The priest requests, "Be pleased, O God, we pray, to bless, acknowledge, and approve this offering in every respect; make it spiritual and acceptable, so that it may become for us the Body and Blood of your most beloved Son, our Lord Jesus Christ."[8] He then

[3] *Catechism of the Catholic Church* (New York: Image Book/Doubleday, 1995). Just how different this contemporary *Catechism* is from the *Catechism of the Council of Trent*, both generally speaking and in regard to their theology of the Eucharist, is beyond the scope of this chapter. Given that the contemporary *Catechism* expresses current Catholic theology, it will be the focus of my attention.

[4] Literally, "carrying up"; thus, an offering. Naturally, this chapter only presents a summary of the eucharistic liturgy.

[5] *Catechism*, 1352. As there are numerous editions of the *Catechism* (including online versions), all references to it will indicate the section numbers (which are standard and thus common to all editions) rather than the page numbers (which may vary from version to version).

[6] Literally, "call upon"; thus, an invocation.

[7] *Catechism*, 1353.

[8] *Roman Missal*, Eucharistic Prayer I (Roman Canon) (International Committee on English

recites the institution narrative.[9] As he announces, "On the day before he [Jesus] was to suffer," the priest elevates the bread slightly above the altar, then continues, "he took bread in his holy and venerable hands [the priest raises his eyes] and with eyes raised to heaven to you, O God, his almighty Father, giving you thanks he said the blessing, broke the bread, and gave it to his disciples, saying [the priest bows slightly], 'Take this, all of you, and eat of it, for this is my body, which will be given up for you.'" The priest displays the consecrated host (the wafer) to the congregation, places it on the paten (the tray), and genuflects (bends one knee) in adoration.[10] Continuing, as he announces "In a similar way, when supper was ended," he elevates the chalice (the cup of wine with a bit of water intermixed)[11] slightly above the altar, then continues: "he took this precious chalice in his holy and venerable hands, and once more giving you thanks, he said the blessing and gave the chalice to his disciples, saying [the priest bows slightly], 'Take this, all of you, and drink from it, for this is the chalice of my blood, the blood of the new and eternal covenant, which will be poured out for you and for many for the forgiveness of sins. Do this in memory of me.'" The priest displays the chalice to the congregation, places it on the corporal (the linen cloth covering the altar), and genuflects (bends one knee) in adoration.[12] He then says, "The mystery of faith."[13] "In the institution narrative, the power of the words and the action of Christ, and the power of the Holy Spirit make sacramentally present under the species [elements] of bread and wine

in the Liturgy, 2006, 2008), 88.

[9] The words of Jesus during His Last Supper with the disciples, as found in the (Synoptic) Gospels, by which He instituted the Lord's Supper.

[10] *Roman Missal*, Eucharistic Prayer I, 89.

[11] The Catholic Church adds water to the wine in accordance with ancient tradition. This practice probably extends back to Christ Himself at the Last Supper, as it was the gastronomical custom for the people of His day to drink a mixture of wine and water. In his mid-second century snapshot of the early church's celebration of the Lord's Supper, Justin Martyr acknowledged that the rite involved bread and a cup, which contained "wine mixed with water" (Justin Martyr, *First Apology*, 65, 67 [*ANF* 1.185, 186]). A century later, Cyprian defended the practice as originating with Christ Himself (Cyprian, *Letter* 62.9 [*ANF* 5.360–61]). Thus, as Jesus Himself celebrated the first Communion with bread and a cup containing both wine and water, so the church must "maintain the plan of evangelical truth and of the tradition of the Lord" (Cyprian, *Letter* 62.1 [*ANF* 5.359])

[12] *Roman Missal*, Eucharistic Prayer I, 90.

[13] Ibid., 91.

Christ's body and blood, his sacrifice offered on the cross once for all."[14]

This part of the Mass is followed by the *anamnesis*[15] and offering, in which "the Church calls to mind the Passion, resurrection, and glorious return of Christ Jesus; she presents to the Father the offering of his Son which reconciles us with him."[16] The priest prays, "Therefore, O Lord, as we celebrate the memorial of the blessed Passion, the Resurrection from the dead, and the glorious Ascension into heaven of Christ, your Son, our Lord, we, your servants and your holy people, offer to your glorious majesty from the gifts that you have given us, this pure victim, this holy victim, this spotless victim, the holy Bread of eternal life and the Chalice of everlasting salvation."[17]

As the actual Communion rite begins, the priest leads the congregation in the recitation of the Lord's Prayer, then instructs the faithful to exchange the sign of peace. He then takes the host, breaks it, and places a small amount in the chalice, saying, "May this mingling of the Body and Blood of our Lord Jesus Christ bring eternal life to us who receive it."[18] The congregation prays, "Lamb of God, you take away the sins of the world, have mercy on us. Lamb of God, you take away the sins of the world, have mercy on us. Lamb of God, you take away the sins of the world, grant us peace."[19] Genuflecting, the priest displays the host as he elevates it slightly above the paten (or above the chalice), and announces, "Behold the Lamb of God, behold him who takes away the sins of the world. Blessed are those called to the supper of the Lamb." Together, the priest and the faithful pray, "Lord, I am not worthy that you should enter under my roof, but only say the word and my soul shall be healed."[20] Facing the altar, the priest says, "May the Body of Christ keep me safe for eternal life," then he consumes the Body of Christ. In the same way, taking the chalice, he prays, "May the Blood of Christ keep me safe for eternal life," then he consumes the Blood of Christ.[21] He next offers the host to

[14] *Catechism*, 1353.

[15] Literally, "remembering"; thus, the memory of Jesus' death, resurrection, and ascension.

[16] *Catechism*, 1354.

[17] *Roman Missal*, Eucharistic Prayer I, 92.

[18] Ibid., 129.

[19] Ibid., 130. The reference to Jesus as the Lamb of God is taken from John the Baptist's words (John 1:29; cf. v. 36).

[20] Ibid., 132. The profession of unworthiness reflects the centurion's humility before Jesus (Matt 8:8).

[21] Ibid., 133.

the faithful, saying "the Body of Christ" before he gives it to them. Similarly, the cup is offered to the faithful, preceded by the saying "the Blood of Christ."[22]

At the conclusion of the Liturgy, the priest announces, "Go forth, the mass is ended" (*Ite, missa est*).[23] The second word *missa* is the foundation for referring to the Liturgy as "the Mass," as it implies "mission."[24] Accordingly, having participated in the Mass, and being nourished by the Body and Blood of Christ in the celebration of the Eucharist, the members of the Church embark on their mission.

The Theology of the Eucharist

This celebration of the Eucharist—indeed, every aspect of the Mass—is grounded on (the Catholic interpretation of) Scripture, Church tradition, and Catholic theology. As a guide to the theology of the Eucharist, I will discuss the relevant sections in the *Catechism of the Catholic Church.*[25]

The sacrament of the Eucharist is one of the seven sacraments of the Catholic Church. These seven, divided into three categories, are: the sacraments of initiation (baptism, confirmation, the Eucharist); the sacraments of healing (penance, the anointing of the sick); the sacraments at the service of Communion (holy orders, matrimony).[26] All Catholics who have been baptized and confirmed—in other words, have participated in the first two sacraments of initiation—may participate in this sacrament.[27] But the Eucharist is not just one of the sacraments; rather, "[t]he other sacraments . . . are bound up with the Eucharist and are oriented toward it." Specifically, the Eucharist is considered to be "the source and summit of the Christian life" because

[22] Ibid., 134.

[23] The deacon may make this announcement. Ibid., 144.

[24] As Pope Benedict XVI explained, "These words help us to grasp the relationship between the Mass just celebrated and the mission of Christians in the world. In antiquity, *missa* simply meant 'dismissal.' However in Christian usage it gradually took on a deeper meaning. The word 'dismissal' has come to imply a 'mission.' These few words succinctly express the missionary nature of the Church" (Pope Benedict XVI, *Sacramentum Caritatis* [22 February 2007]: 51).

[25] *Catechism*, "Part Two: The Celebration of the Christian Mystery; Section One: The Sacramental Economy; Chapter One: The Paschal Mystery in the Age of the Church; Article 3: The Sacrament of the Eucharist," 1322–1419.

[26] *Catechism*, 1211.

[27] Ibid., 1322. The Eastern Orthodox Church unites the sacraments of baptism and confirmation, which are followed by the sacrament of the Eucharist. The Catholic Church separates the first two sacraments of initiation, allowing for children to take the sacrament of the Eucharist before they reach "the age of discretion" and receive the sacrament of confirmation.

"in the blessed Eucharist is contained the whole spiritual good of the Church, namely Christ himself, our Pasch."[28] As such, it is necessary for the Church's existence; indeed, by the Eucharist "the Church is kept in being."[29]

This sacrament is known by various names, each of which contributes to our understanding of the rite. It is called the Eucharist,[30] the Lord's Supper,[31] the Breaking of Bread,[32] the Eucharistic Assembly,[33] the Memorial,[34] the Holy Sacrifice,[35] the Holy and Divine Liturgy,[36] Holy Communion,[37] and Holy Mass.[38] These various names for this sacrament are highly significant and enable us to understand important aspects of the theology of the Eucharist.

Although the Church emphasizes the institution of this sacrament at Christ's Last Supper, it also detects numerous OT forerunners—harbingers that made use of bread and/or wine—of the Eucharist.[39] New Testament predecessors include the multiplication of the loaves

[28] *Catechism*, 1324. "Pasch," or "Paschal," is an adjective commonly used to describe the mystery of Christ's work and refers to His passion (or suffering), death, resurrection, and ascension.

[29] Ibid., 1325.

[30] "Eucharist, because it is an action of thanksgiving to God" (ibid., 1328). Specifically, the Greek word εὐχαριστήσας, "giving thanks," is found in the institution narratives (Matt 26:27; Mark 14:23; Luke 22:17,19).

[31] "The Lord's Supper," because it was instituted during Christ's Last Supper with His disciples and "because it anticipates the wedding feast of the Lamb in the heavenly Jerusalem" (ibid., 1329).

[32] "The Breaking of Bread," because of Jesus' action, part of the Passover feast, of breaking the loaf and distributing it to His disciples while investing it with new meaning. This name was also the early church's designation for "their Eucharistic assemblies" (Acts 2:42,46; 20:7,11) (ibid., 1329).

[33] "The Eucharistic assembly (*synaxis*), because the Eucharist is celebrated amid the assembly of the faithful, the visible expression of the Church" (ibid., 1329).

[34] "The memorial," because by it the Church remembers Christ's death and resurrection (ibid., 1330).

[35] "The Holy Sacrifice, because it makes present the one sacrifice of Christ the Savior and includes the Church's offering" (ibid., 1330).

[36] "The Holy and Divine Liturgy," because it is the apex of the entire Mass. Similarly, the celebration is called "the Sacred Mysteries" and "the Most Blessed Sacrament because it is the Sacrament of sacraments" (ibid., 1330).

[37] "Holy Communion," because the members of the Church unite themselves to Christ, through sharing in His Body and Blood, and to one another to form one body (ibid., 1331).

[38] "Holy Mass" (*Missa*) because, as noted above, the Liturgy "concludes with the sending forth (*missio*) of the faithful" (ibid., 1332).

[39] The first was "the gesture of the king-priest Melchizedek, who 'brought out bread and wine" [Gen 14:18], a prefiguring of her [the Church's] own offering." Other precursors include the unleavened bread of the Exodus (Exod 13:3–10), which the Jews celebrate in their annual Passover festivals (Deut 16:1–8); the manna in the wilderness (Exodus 16); and the cup of blessing at the conclusion of the Passover (ibid., 1333–34.

in the feeding of the 5,000 and the 4,000 (Matt 14:13–21; 15:32–39); the miracle of turning the water into wine at the wedding of Cana (John 2:1–11); and Jesus' "first announcement of the Eucharist" (John 6:25–71).[40]

These forerunners anticipated and pointed to Jesus' institution of the Eucharist, as recounted in the Synoptic Gospels and 1 Corinthians. "At the Last Supper, on the night he was betrayed, our Savior instituted the Eucharistic sacrifice of his Body and Blood. This he did in order to perpetuate the sacrifice of the cross throughout the ages until he should come again, and so to entrust to his beloved Spouse, the Church, a memorial of his death and resurrection."[41] Moreover, Jesus "commanded his apostles to celebrate it until he comes; 'thereby he constituted them priests of the New Testament.'"[42] As priests, they are responsible for "the liturgical celebration . . . of the memorial of Christ."[43] Following closely the historical pattern for the Mass developed over many centuries,[44] this celebration "displays two great parts that form a fundamental unity:" (1) the Liturgy of the Word, which commonly features three readings—from the OT, the NT, and one of the Gospels—and a homily, or brief sermon; and (2) the Liturgy of the Eucharist. These two elements "together form 'one single act of worship'; the Eucharistic table set for us is the table both of the Word of God and the Body of the Lord."[45]

[40] Ibid., 1336.

[41] Ibid., 1323.

[42] Ibid., 1337. The citation is from the Council of Trent.

[43] Ibid., 1341.

[44] Indeed, the Church contends that there have been no substantive changes in the eucharistic celebration since its first institution by Jesus. As John Paul II explained: "Beginning with the Upper Room and Holy Thursday, the celebration of the Eucharist has a long history, a history as long as that of the Church. In the course of this history the secondary elements have undergone certain changes, but there has been no change in the essence of the 'Mysterium' instituted by the Redeemer of the world at the Last Supper" (John Paul II, *Dominicae cenae* [24 February 1980]: 8; cited from A. Flannery, gen. ed., *Vatican Council II: Volume II: More Post-Conciliar Documents* [Northport, NY: Costello, 1998], 73).

[45] *Catechism*, 1346. The Church underscores the connection between these two elements: "Pastors should therefore 'carefully teach the faithful to participate in the whole Mass,' showing the close connection between the liturgy of the Word and the celebration of the Lord's Supper, so that they can see clearly how the two constitute a single act of worship. For 'the teaching of the Word is necessary for the very administration of the sacraments, in as much as they are sacraments of faith, which is born of the Word and fed by it'" (*Eucharisticum Mysterium* [25 May 1967]: 10; cited from A. Flannery, gen. ed., *Vatican Council II: Volume 1: The Conciliar and Post-Conciliar Documents* (Northport, NY: Costello, 1998), 109. *Eucharisticum Mysterium* cites the Vatican II document *Constitution on the Sacred Liturgy*, 56).

Though the liturgy is celebrated by the Church, "[a]t its head is Christ himself, the principal agent of the Eucharist. He is high priest of the New Covenant; it is he himself who presides invisibly over every Eucharistic celebration." This mystery is made possible by the priest representing Christ, the celebrant "acting in the person of Christ the head."[46] As He commanded it, the Church celebrates "the memorial of his sacrifice. In so doing, we offer to the Father what he has himself given us: the gifts of his creation, bread and wine which, by the power of the Holy Spirit and the words of Christ, have become the body and blood of Christ. Christ is thus really and mysteriously made present."[47]

Within this trinitarian structure, the Eucharist must be considered as three realities: thanksgiving (to the Father), sacrifice (of the Son), and presence (by the Holy Spirit). As for the first reality, and in keeping with the sense of the Greek word, "[t]he Eucharist is a sacrifice of thanksgiving and praise to the Father, a blessing by which the Church expresses her gratitude to God for all his benefits, for all that he has accomplished through creation, redemption, and sanctification."[48]

In terms of the second reality, "[t]he Eucharist is the memorial of Christ's Passover, the making present and the sacramental offering of his unique sacrifice."[49] Because this aspect is of particular importance as well as difficult for Protestants to grasp, several comments are in order. Catholic theology does not teach that the sacrifice on the cross of Calvary is repeated over and over again, each time the Eucharist is celebrated. This common misconception is unfortunate and refuted by the Catholic Church. Appealing to Israel's understanding of its liberation from Egypt, celebrated in its Passover, the Church affirms that the notion of a memorial in Scripture "is not merely the recollection of past events."[50] Rather, "[w]hen the Church celebrates the Eucharist, she commemorates Christ's Passover, and it is made present: the sacrifice of Christ offered once for all on the cross remains ever present."[51] The reason for this present reality is that the sacrifice on

[46] *Catechism*, 1348. Cf. John Paul II, *Dominicae cenae* (24 February 1980), 8; *Vatican Council II: Volume II*, 73.

[47] *Catechism*, 1357.

[48] Ibid., 1360.

[49] Ibid., 1362.

[50] Ibid., 1363.

[51] Ibid., 1364. Biblical support for this notion is Heb 7:25–27, a passage that emphasizes the once-for-all nature of Christ's work on the cross. Cf. *The Companion to the Catechism of the*

Calvary participates in the divine eternity or atemporality: Just as God is not located in, restricted by, or confined within time, so the work of Christ on the cross is not located in, restricted by, or confined within that moment nearly 2,000 years ago.[52] As a memorial, Christ's death is not just to be remembered; rather, it is re-presented in the eucharistic liturgy.

A crucial implication is drawn from this framework: "Because it is the memorial of Christ's Passover, the Eucharist is also a sacrifice."[53] The institution narrative underscores this sacrificial character: "'This is my body which is given for you' and 'This cup which is poured out for you is the New Covenant in my blood.'"[54] Interpreted literally, these words of Jesus emphasize the sacrificial nature of His actions during His Last Supper. Accordingly, "[I]n the Eucharist Christ gives us the very body which he gave up for us on the cross, the very blood which he 'poured out for many for the forgiveness of sins.'"[55] Specifically, "The Eucharist is thus a sacrifice because it re-presents [makes present] the sacrifice of the cross, because it is a memorial and because it applies its fruits."[56] Thus, the Church does not believe in many, repeated sacrifices. On the contrary, "The sacrifice of Christ and the sacrifice of the Eucharist are one single sacrifice. 'The victim is one and the same: the same now offers through the ministry of priests, who then offered himself on the cross; only the manner of offering is different.' 'In this divine sacrifice which is celebrated in the Mass, the same Christ who offered himself once in a bloody manner on the altar of the cross is contained and is offered in an unbloody manner.'"[57] The atonement of Christ took place as He shed His blood on the cross, once for all, 2,000 years ago, but it is not time-bound to

Catholic Church: A Compendium of Texts Referred to in the Catechism of the Catholic Church (San Francisco: Ignatius, 1994), 491.

[52] "His Paschal mystery is a real event that occurred in our history, but it is unique: all other historical events happen once, and then they pass away, swallowed up in the past. The Paschal mystery of Christ, by contrast, cannot remain only in the past, because by his death he destroyed death, and all that Christ is—all that he did and suffered for all men—participates in the divine eternity, and so transcends all times while being made present in them all. The event of the Cross and Resurrection *abides* and draws everything toward life" (*Catechism*, 1084).

[53] Ibid., 1365.

[54] Ibid., 1365. The citation is from Luke 22:19–20.

[55] Ibid., 1365. The citation is from Matt 26:28.

[56] Ibid., 1366.

[57] Ibid., 1367. The citations are from the Council of Trent.

that moment. Indeed, that sacrifice is made present when the priest celebrates the Liturgy of the Eucharist.

The third eucharistic reality is "the presence of Christ by the power of his word and the Holy Spirit." While acknowledging that Christ "is present in many ways to his Church," the Church emphasizes that "he is present . . . most especially in the Eucharistic species."[58] Specifically, the mode of Christ's presence is unique: "In the most blessed sacrament of the Eucharist 'the body and blood, together with the soul and divinity, of our Lord Jesus Christ and, therefore, the whole Christ is truly, really, and substantially contained.'"[59] These adverbs are significant: "This presence is called 'real' . . . because it is presence in the fullest sense; that is to say, it is a substantial presence by which Christ, God and man, makes himself wholly and entirely present."[60]

This true, real, and substantial presence of Christ in the eucharistic celebrations occurs by means of transubstantiation. From two Latin words—*trans* (change) and *substantia* (substance; that which makes something what is it)—transubstantiation is the change of the substance of the consecrated bread into the body of Christ, and the change of the substance of the consecrated wine into the blood of Christ. "It is by the conversion of the bread and wine into Christ's body and blood that Christ becomes present in this sacrament."[61] The Church contends that both its tradition—e.g., John Chrysostom and Ambrose[62]—and Scripture affirm transubstantiation. The Council of Trent, referring to the biblical basis, "summarizes the Catholic faith by declaring,"

> Because Christ our Redeemer said that it was truly his body that he was offering under the species of bread, it has always been the conviction of the Church of God . . . that by the consecration of the bread and wine there takes place a change of the whole substance of the bread into the substance of the body of Christ our Lord and of the whole substance of the wine into the substance of his blood. This change the holy Catholic Church has fittingly and properly called transubstantiation.[63]

[58] Ibid., 1373. The latter citation is from *Sacrosanctum concilium*, 7.

[59] Ibid., 1374. The citation is from the "Decree Concerning the Most Holy Sacrament of the Eucharist," 1. *The Canons and Decrees of the Council of Trent*, 13th session (11 October, 1551).

[60] *Catechism*, 1374.

[61] Ibid., 1375.

[62] Ibid., 1376.

[63] Ibid., 1376. The citation is from the "Decree Concerning the Most Holy Sacrament of the Eucharist," 4. *The Canons and Decrees of the Council of Trent*, 13th session (11 October, 1551).

As will be explained more fully in the historical section, transubstantiation relies on a philosophical idea that things are composed of both substance and accidents. A thing's substance is its nature, that what makes it what it is.[64] A thing's accidents are its external characteristics, that which can be perceived by the senses.[65] Applying this notion of substance and accidents to the Eucharist, transubstantiation is the change that the substance of the bread and wine undergoes while the accidents of these elements remain the same. What before the consecration was bread becomes the body of Christ, and what before the consecration was wine becomes the blood of Christ. Thus, He is truly, really, and substantially present after the consecration of the host and the chalice.

There are two more important points regarding this transubstantiation: "The Eucharistic presence of Christ begins at the moment of the consecration and endures as long as the Eucharistic species subsist."[66] This change is effected when the priest engages in the *epiclesis* and pronounces the words of institution, and the presence of Christ effected by this change is a continuing rather than a momentary presence.[67] Moreover, "Christ is present whole and entire in each of the species and whole and entire in each of their parts, in such a way that the breaking of bread does not divide Christ."[68] This point depends on the orthodox doctrine of Christ: In the incarnation, the divine Son of God took on human nature, so that the God-man was both fully divine and fully human, two natures united into one person.[69] It is this God-man who is "present whole and entire" in the Eucharist. Christ is not present in His divine nature alone, nor in His human nature alone, but in the totality of both His divine and human natures. Moreover,

[64] For example, a human being has a complex nature consisting of both a material component (the body) and an immaterial component (the soul or spirit).

[65] For example, a human being may have blond hair or brown, blue eyes or hazel, more or less darkly pigmented skin, and the like.

[66] *Catechism*, 1377.

[67] Thus, "in the sacrifice of the Mass our Lord is immolated [sacrificed] when 'he begins to be present sacramentally as the spiritual food of the faithful under the appearance of bread and wine'" (*Eucharisticum Mysterium*, Introduction, 3b; *Vatican Council II: Volume 1*, 102–103; the citation is from Pope Paul VI, *Mysterium fidei* [3 September 1965], 34).

[68] *Catechism*, 1377.

[69] The Catholic Church affirms the Creed of Nicea, the Nicene (or Nicene-Constantinopolitan) Creed, the Apostles' Creed, and the Chalcedonian Creed, the early creeds that articulated orthodox Christology.

in the totality of both His divine and human natures, He is present in the bread and in each of its grains, and in the totality of both His divine and human natures, He is present in the wine and in each of its drops. Accordingly, one does not receive more or less of Christ if the consecrated host is larger or smaller, and one does not receive more or less of Christ if the quantity of the wine consumed is larger or smaller. Furthermore, one who takes Communion in one kind—that is, one takes the wafer only and not the wine—receives all of Christ.[70] Finally, if some consecrated elements remain after the sacrament has been distributed, Christ remains present.

This last point prompts ongoing worship of the Eucharist: "The Catholic Church has always offered and still offers to the sacrament of the Eucharist the cult of adoration, not only during the Mass, but also outside of it, reserving the consecrated hosts with the utmost care, exposing them to the solemn veneration of the faithful, and carrying them in procession."[71] Accordingly, after the distribution of the sacrament during the Mass, if any consecrated elements remain, they are placed in the tabernacle—a container consecrated for holding the eucharistic elements and "located in an especially worthy place in the church"—and reserved for both distribution to the sick (*viaticum*) and silent adoration by the faithful who gather there.[72]

To the "Paschal banquet" of the sacrament of the Eucharist, the Catholic faithful are called to come.[73] Indeed, this invitation comes

[70] The scandal that the Church's practice of administering Communion in one kind evoked at the time of the Reformation will be covered in the historical section. Following Vatican II, up to which Communion in one kind was the normal way of celebrating the sacrament, the Church has moved to preferring the administration of Communion in both kinds. See: *Eucharisticum Mysterium*, 32; *Vatican Council II: Volume 1*, 121.

[71] *Catechism*, 1378. At this point the *Catechism* cites Pope Paul VI, *Mysterium fidei* (3 September 1965), 56.

[72] *Catechism*, 1379. Cf. *Eucharisticum Mysterium*, 49–58; *Vatican Council II: Volume 1*, 129–33. *Viaticum*, literally "passing over," is the name given to the Eucharist that is part of the sacrament of the Anointing of the Sick. As such, "the Eucharist is here the sacrament of passing over from death to life, from this world to the Father" (*Catechism*, 1524; cf. ibid., 1517).

[73] Participation in the sacrament is forbidden to Protestants, for the following reason: "Ecclesial communities derived from the Reformation and separated from the Catholic Church, 'have not preserved the proper reality of the Eucharistic mystery in its fullness, especially because of the absence of the sacrament of Holy Orders.' It is for this reason that Eucharistic intercommunion with these communions is not possible for the Catholic Church" (ibid., 1400). The citation is from the Vatican II document *Decree on Ecumenism*, 22. The Church does allow for one exception to this rule: in the case of "grave necessity"; *Catechism*, 1401. For further discussion, see: *Dans ces derniers temps* (7 January 1970); *Vatican Council II: Volume 1*, 502–7. *Quibus Rerum Circumstantiis* (1 June 1972); *Vatican Council II: Volume 1*, 556–559. *Dopo la publicazione* (17 October 1973); *Vatican Council II: Volume 1*, 560–63.

from Christ Himself: "Truly, I say to you, unless you eat of the flesh of the Son of man and drink his blood, you have no life in you."[74] They must prepare themselves for this sacrament, meaning that "[a]nyone conscious of a grave sin must receive the sacrament of Reconciliation before coming to communion."[75] By means of this sacrament, those who have committed mortal sin, and thus lost divine grace, confess to a priest, who absolves them of sin, enabling them to once again participate in the sacrament of the Eucharist. Such participation is ongoing; indeed, the faithful should "receive communion each time they participate in the Mass."[76] Actually, few Catholics observe their obligation to participate regularly ("on Sundays and feast days, or more often still, even daily"); still, they are obligated "to receive the Eucharist at least once a year, if possible during the Easter season."[77]

Participation in the Eucharist provides many benefits for faithful Catholics. It augments union with Christ; specifically, such union "preserves, increases, and renews the life of grace received at Baptism. This growth in Christian life needs the nourishment of Eucharistic Communion."[78] Moreover, it separates the faithful from sin; specifically, it cleanses from past sins and preserves from future sins.[79] With regard to the first element, "[t]he Eucharist is not ordered to the forgiveness of mortal sins [grievous sins by which grace is forfeited]—that is proper to the sacrament of Reconciliation. The Eucharist is properly the sacrament of those who are in full communion with the Church."[80] As such, "the Eucharist strengthens our charity [love] . . . and this living charity wipes away venial sins" (less grievous sins by which grace is wounded but not forfeited).[81] With regard to the second element, "[b]y the same charity that it enkindles in us, the Eucharist preserves us from future mortal sins."[82] Furthermore, "the Eucharist makes the Church," because by it the faithful are more united to Christ and thus united in one body.[83] Finally, it commits the Church to the poor.[84] The

[74] *Catechism*, 1384, citing John 6:53.
[75] Ibid., 1385.
[76] Ibid., 1388.
[77] Ibid., 1389.
[78] Ibid., 1392.
[79] Ibid., 1393.
[80] Ibid., 1395.
[81] Ibid., 1394.
[82] Ibid., 1395.
[83] Ibid., 1396.
[84] Ibid., 1397.

degree of fruitfulness of these benefits for the individual participants is dependent on the life and attitude of those participating: "Like the passion of Christ itself, this sacrifice, though offered for all, 'has no effect except in those united to the passion of Christ by faith and charity . . . To these things it brings a greater or lesser benefit in proportion to their devotion.'"[85]

Having presented the theology of the Eucharist, I will now outline how this eucharistic theology and the practice of the celebration of the Mass developed from the early church until the time of the Reformation. Because other essays in this volume treat this historical development, I will present only the briefest outline.

The Historical Development of Eucharistic Theology and Practice[86]

The early church understood the Lord's Supper in a variety of ways.[87] The concept of it as a sacrifice is found very early on.[88] While it is clear that sacrificial language was associated with the Lord's Supper, it is not as clear what the early church believed about the nature of the sacrifice. According to Irenaeus, the sacrifices are the bread and the cup of wine, the first fruits of the divine creation.[89] Yet, in arguing against the heresy of Docetism, which denied the reality of the incarnation and the resurrection of the body, Irenaeus also spoke of the Lord's Supper in terms of the actual body of Christ: "The bread, which is produced from the earth, when it receives the invocation from God,

[85] *Eucharisticum Mysterium*, 12; *Vatican Council II: Volume 1*, 111. The citation is from Thomas Aquinas, *Summa Theologica*, part 3, q. 79, art. 7.

[86] The following presentation is adapted from my forthcoming book: G. R. Allison, *Historical Theology: An Introduction to Christian Doctrine* (Grand Rapids: Zondervan, 2011).

[87] For further discussion, see the fine essay in this volume by Michael Haykin, "'A glorious inebriation': Eucharistic Thought and Piety in the Patristic Era."

[88] Some linked the eucharistic sacrifice to the prophecy of Malachi, who rebuked the people of Israel for their worthless offerings and looked forward to a true sacrifice—"incense and pure offerings"—among the Gentiles (Mal 1:10–11). E.g., the *Didache* appealed to this passage to encourage proper participation in the "sacrifice" of the Lord's Supper: "On the Lord's own day gather together and break bread and give thanks, having first confessed your sins so that your sacrifice may be pure. But let no one who has a quarrel with a companion join you until they have been reconciled, so that your sacrifice may not be defiled. For this is the sacrifice concerning which the Lord said, 'In every place and time offer me a pure sacrifice, for I am a great king, says the Lord, and my name is marvelous among the nations'" (*Did.*, 14 [Holmes, 267; cf. *ANF* 7.381]). Cf. Justin Martyr, *Dialogue with Trypho the Jew*, 41 (*ANF* 1.215); Irenaeus, *Against Heresies*, 4.17.5 (*ANF* 1.484).

[89] Irenaeus, *Fragment* 37 (*ANF* 1.574).

is no longer common bread, but the Eucharist, [and] it consists of two realities, earthly and heavenly."[90] This idea rested on a belief in the reality of the presence of Christ in the Eucharist. Addressing the heresy of the Docetists, Ignatius noted a crucial error: "They abstain from the Eucharist and prayer, because they refuse to acknowledge that the Eucharist is the flesh of our Savior Jesus Christ, which suffered for our sins and which the Father by his goodness raised up."[91] Thus, just as these heretics denied the reality of the body of Jesus in His incarnation, so they denied the reality of His body in the Eucharist. Ignatius, however, held to a one-to-one correspondence between the bread and cup and the body and blood: "I want the bread of God, which is the flesh of Christ who is of the seed of David; and for drink I want his blood, which is incorruptible love."[92] Others made this identification as well. Justin Martyr explained the church's teaching on the elements: "We do not receive these as common bread and common drink. But in like manner as Jesus Christ our Savior, having been made flesh by the Word of God, had both flesh and blood for our salvation, so likewise we have been taught that the food which is blessed by the prayer of his word, and from which our blood and flesh by transmutation are nourished, is the flesh and blood of that Jesus who was made flesh."[93]

[90] Irenaeus, *Against Heresies*, 4.18.5 (*ANF* 1.486). Cyprian made a parallel between Christ the High Priest and the church's ministers as priests: As Christ the High Priest offered Himself a sacrifice to the Father, so the priests offer a real sacrifice to God when celebrating the Lord's Supper. As Cyprian reasoned, "If Jesus Christ, our Lord and God, is himself the chief priest of God the Father, and has first offered himself a sacrifice to the Father, and has commanded this to be done in commemoration of himself, certainly that priest truly discharges the office of Christ, who imitates that which Christ did; and he then offers a true and full sacrifice in the church to God the Father, when he proceeds to offer it according to what he sees Christ himself to have offered" (*Letter* 62.14 [*ANF* 5.362]). For Cyprian, this parallel was warranted because "the Lord's passion is the sacrifice which we offer" (*Letter* 62.17 [*ANF* 5.363]).

[91] Ignatius, *Letter to the Smyrneans*, 7.1 (Holmes, 189; cf. *ANF* 1.89).

[92] Ignatius, *Letter to the Romans*, 7.3 (Holmes, 175; cf. *ANF* 1.77).

[93] Justin Martyr, *First Apology*, 66 (*ANF* 1.185). Irenaeus associated this transformation of the bread and the cup with the "consecration from God" during the eucharistic celebration. He further explained that the wine and the bread, "having received the Word of God, become the Eucharist, which is the body and blood of Christ" (*Against Heresies*, 5.2.3 [*ANF* 1.528]). He also associated this change with the Holy Spirit, who was called upon after the church gave thanks for the elements and offered them to God: "we invoke the Holy Spirit, that he may exhibit this sacrifice, both the bread—the body of Christ—and the cup—the blood of Christ—in order that the receivers of these antitypes may obtain remission of sins and life eternal" (Irenaeus, *Fragment* 37 [*ANF* 1.574]). Thus, through the Word and the Spirit of God, the elements became associated with the body and blood of Christ. Additionally, this belief in the reality of Christ's presence was tied to the act of commemoration, a key aspect of the rite. Justin Martyr saw the

The Lord's Supper was also viewed by some in symbolic terms. Tertullian used the eucharistic elements to demonstrate the wrongness of the heretic Marcion's denial of the true body of Jesus Christ:

> Having taken the bread and given it to his disciples, Jesus made it his own body, by saying, "This is my body," that is, the symbol of my body. There could not have been a symbol, however, unless there were first a true body. An empty thing or phantom is incapable of a symbol. He likewise, when mentioning the cup and making the new covenant to be sealed "in his blood," affirms the reality of his body. For no blood can belong to a body that is not a body of flesh.[94]

Still, for Tertullian, the elements were not empty symbols, for he also affirmed that "the flesh—the human body—feeds on the body and blood of Christ."[95]

Augustine's contribution to the theology of the sacraments was determinative for the church for centuries to come. He defined a sacrament generally as an outward and visible sign of an invisible yet genuine grace.[96] Furthermore, the sacraments are effective in communicating this grace *ex opere operato*—literally, by the work performed.[97] Accordingly, God's grace is effectively channeled through those sacraments. For this reason, the sacraments of baptism and the Lord's Supper are necessary for salvation.[98]

eucharistic elements alluded to in Isa 33:13–19: "Now it is evident that in this prophecy [allusion is made] to the bread which our Christ gave us to eat, in remembrance of his being made flesh for the sake of his believers, for whom he also suffered; and to the cup which he gave us to drink, in remembrance of his own blood, with giving of thanks" (*Dialogue with Trypho the Jew*, 70 [*ANF* 1.234]). Thus, Justin emphasized the commemorative aspect of the Eucharist, "the celebration of which our Lord Jesus Christ prescribed, in remembrance of the suffering which he endured on behalf of those who are purified in soul from all iniquity" (*Dialogue with Trypho the Jew*, 41 [*ANF* 1.215]). In the midst of realistic language about the bread and cup, even Cyprian underscored that Christ "has first offered himself a sacrifice to the Father, and he has commanded this to be done in commemoration of himself" (Cyprian, *Letter* 62.14 [*ANF* 5.362]).

[94] Tertullian then gives examples of wine as a symbol for blood (Tertullian, *Against Marcion*, 4.40 [*ANF* 3.418]). I have rendered the text more clear, especially substituting the word "symbol" for "figure."

[95] Tertullian, *On the Resurrection of the Flesh*, 8 (*ANF* 3.551).

[96] Augustine, *On the Catechizing of the Uninstructed*, 26.50 (*NPNF*[1] 3.312).

[97] This perspective stood in stark contrast with heretics like the Donatists, who insisted that sacraments are valid only when administered in a true church by a duly ordained minister. Augustine argued instead that Christ Himself is actually the One who baptizes, serves the Lord's Supper, and administers other grace.

[98] "No one will enter into his kingdom who is not born again of water and the Spirit; nor shall anyone attain salvation and eternal life except in his kingdom—since the man who does not believe in the Son, and does not eat his flesh, shall not have life, but the wrath of God remains upon him" (Augustine, *On the Merits and Forgiveness of Sins, and On the Baptism of Infants*, 1.33 [*NPNF*[1] 3.28]). I have rendered the text more clearly.

Specifically, Augustine offered two perspectives on the Lord's Supper. On the one hand, he maintained that Christ is truly present in the elements: "That bread that you see on the altar, sanctified by the Word of God, is Christ's body. That cup, or rather the contents of that cup, sanctified by the Word of God, is Christ's blood. By these elements the Lord Christ willed to convey his body and his blood, which he shed for us."[99] On the other hand, he held a symbolic position, in accordance with his view of what a sacrament is. Augustine denied that the body and blood of the Lord's Supper are identical with Christ's historical body, as seen in his interpretation of the words Jesus spoke to His disciples at the institution of the Supper: "Understand spiritually what I said; you are not to eat this body which you see, nor to drink that blood which they who will crucify me shall pour forth. . . . Although it is needful that this be visibly celebrated, yet it must be spiritually understood."[100] Indeed, Christ explained "what it is to eat his body and to drink his blood. . . . This it is, therefore, for a man to eat that meat [food] and to drink that drink, to dwell in Christ, and to have Christ dwelling in him."[101]

Augustine's view held sway for several centuries, but in the ninth century a controversy involving two monks, Radbertus and Ratramnus, erupted over the nature of the presence of Christ in the Lord's Supper.[102] Hogg summarizes the two opposing positions:

> One view [that of Ratramnus] was that the bread and the wine were symbols of the body and blood of Christ. To be sure, these were powerful symbols of Christ's atoning sacrifice that should not be taken lightly for they signify a present spiritual reality, but what began as bread and wine never became something more than bread and wine. The other view [that of Radbertus] was that the bread and the wine were not merely symbols of the body and blood of Christ, as though abstract mnemonic devices, but were somehow transformed from their mundane substance by a divine miracle. Through the elements, the very body and blood of Christ were made real to the communicant.[103]

[99] Augustine, *Sermon* 227 (cited in J. N. D. Kelly, *Early Christian Doctrines*, rev. ed. [San Francisco: HarperCollins, 1978], 447).

[100] Augustine, *Exposition of the Psalms*, 99.8 (*NPNF*[1] 8.485–86).

[101] Augustine, *Tractates on the Gospel of John*, 26.18 (*NPNF*[1] 7.173).

[102] For further discussion, see the fine essay in this volume by David Hogg, "Carolingian Conflict: Two Monks on the Mass."

[103] Ibid., 132.

A similar controversy flared up in the eleventh century. Berengar of Tours opposed the identification of the bread and the wine in the Lord's Supper with the historical body and blood of Christ.[104] His denial that "the empirical . . . bread consecrated on the altar is, after the consecration, truly the body of Christ that exists above"[105] sounded like heresy and was quickly opposed by the church.[106] In 1059, he was forced to repudiate his view by signing a statement affirming that "the bread and wine which are placed on the altar are, after consecration, not only a sacrament but the true body and blood of our Lord Jesus Christ, and that these are sensibly handled and broken by the hands of priests and crushed by the teeth of the faithful, not only sacramentally but in reality."[107]

This development resulted in much discussion concerning how the elements become the body and blood of Christ.[108] The word *substance* came to hold special significance in the church's doctrine of the Lord's Supper. In particular, Aristotle's use of the term *substance* to refer to the essence or defining nature of a thing was employed: The change that took place at the words of institution was a change in the substance of the bread and wine. According to Lanfranc, "earthly substances are changed in the essence of the Lord's body," and Baldwin

[104] In support of his view, he appealed to the early church fathers (Berengar of Tours, *Epistle to Adelmannus*; cited from J. Pelikan, *The Growth of Medieval Theology, 600–1300*, vol. 3 of *The Christian Tradition: A History of the Development of Doctrine* [Chicago and London: University of Chicago Press, 1978], 192). E.g., he noted Ambrose's view that Christ, who has been resurrected and ascended into heaven, is in an exalted state and cannot undergo any change. Thus, He cannot once again become a suffering victim in the Eucharist (Berengar of Tours, *Epistle to Adelmannus*, 192).

[105] Berengar of Tours, *On the Holy Supper* 21; Pelikan, *The Growth of Medieval Theology*, 192.

[106] He was "accused of saying that the Eucharist is not the true body of Christ nor his true blood, but some sort of figure and likeness" (Adelmannus of Brescia, *Epistle to Berengar*, in Pelikan, *The Growth of Medieval Theology*, 186]).

[107] Berengar of Tours, *Fragments*, appearing in Lanfranc of Bec, *On the Body and Blood of the Lord*, 2 (Pelikan, *The Growth of Medieval Theology*, 187). Berengar later repudiated this recantation, and was again condemned in 1079.

[108] Berengar articulated a view called *impanation*, that in a hidden manner the body and the blood of Christ are truly contained in the bread and wine, which remain as they are in substance. The church did not accept this theory. Rather, it held that "before the consecration, the bread set forth on the Lord's table is nothing but bread, but in the consecration, by the ineffable power of God, the nature and substance of the bread are converted into the nature and substance of the flesh of Christ" (*Life of Saint Maurilius* 11, in Pelikan, *The Growth of Medieval Theology*, 199). ~his transformation takes place when the words of consecration are pronounced, resulting in ~ bread and wine ceasing to exist as such and the body and blood of Christ being present in ~ sacrament.

of Ford explained "the substance of the bread is changed into the substance of the flesh of Christ."[109]

Aristotle had spoken of both *substance*—the essence or nature of a thing—and *accidents*—the characteristics of a thing that can be perceived by the senses; thus, their appearance, taste, smell, texture, and sound. Guitmond of Aversa parlayed this distinction into the definitive formula for the eucharistic transformation: While the *accidents* of the bread and wine remain the same—the elements still look like, taste like, smell like, and feel like bread and wine—their *substance* is transformed into the body and blood of Jesus Christ. Rolando Bandinelli, later to become Pope Alexander III, coined the term *transubstantiation* in 1140 to refer to this substantial change.[110]

The Fourth Lateran Council in 1215 made the official pronouncement of the church's position regarding the eucharistic presence of Jesus Christ, "whose body and blood are truly contained in the sacrament of the altar under the forms of bread and wine. The bread is transubstantiated into the body and the wine into the blood by the power of God, so we may receive from him what he has received from us."[111] Thus, the doctrine of transubstantiation was officially affirmed in the church. This Council also established the law that people should participate in the sacrament at least once a year after the confession of sins.[112]

Following the official decree of the Fourth Lateran Council, Thomas Aquinas offered the definitive theological and philosophical framework to support transubstantiation. He explained how conversion of one substance into another—something that is naturally impossible—can take place by divine power with the Eucharist. Though

[109] Lanfranc of Bec, *On the Body and Blood of the Lord*, 18 (Pelikan, *The Growth of Medieval Theology*, 203); Baldwin of Ford, *The Sacrament of the Altar*, 2.1.3 (ibid., 203).

[110] Alexander III, *The Sentences of Roland* (ibid., 203). The term also appeared in the writing of Stephen of Autun about the same time (*On the Sacrament of the Altar* [ibid., 203]).

[111] Fourth Lateran Council, canon 1 (cited from R. C. Petry, ed., *The Early and Medieval Church* [vol. 1 of *A History of Christianity: Readings in the History of the Church*; Grand Rapids, MI: Baker, 1990], 322–23).

[112] Fourth Lateran Council, canon 21 (Petry, *The Early and Medieval Church*, 323). Though proclaimed by this Council, the rule stipulating participation in Communion at least once a year was not followed by other councils in the thirteenth century. For example, the Council of Toulouse in 1229 and the Council of Albi in 1254 ruled that the faithful should participate in the Eucharist at least three times a year—Christmas and Pentecost, in addition to Easter (*The Council of Toulouse*, canon 13; Mansi, 23.197. *The Council of Albi*, canon 29; Mansi, 23.840 (G. P. Fisher, *History of Christian Doctrine* [New York: Charles Scribner's Sons, 1896], 101).

the substance changes, the accidents of the bread and wine remain.[113] By joining Aristotelian philosophy with the church's theology of the Lord's Supper, Aquinas set forth the definitive Catholic view of the presence of Christ during the celebration of the Eucharist.

> God is infinite act; thus, his action extends to the whole nature of being. Therefore, he can work not only formal conversion, so that diverse forms succeed each other in the same subject; but also the change of being itself, so that the whole substance of one thing be changed into the whole substance of another. And this is done by divine power in this sacrament. For the whole substance of the bread is changed into the whole substance of Christ's body, and the whole substance of the wine into the whole substance of Christ's blood. Thus, this is not a formal, but a substantial conversion; nor is it a kind of natural movement. Rather, with a name of its own, it can be called *transubstantiation*.[114]

In the thirteenth century, the church began to give the bread but not the cup to the laity. This practice was justified theologically by the doctrine of *concomitance*, which was explained by Bonaventura: "Because the blessed and glorious body of Christ cannot be divided into its parts and cannot be separated from the soul or from the highest divinity, so under each species there is the one, entire, and indivisible Christ—namely, body, soul, and God. Thus, in each is present the one and most simple sacrament containing the entire Christ."[115] Because the entire Christ is present in each of the elements, taking only one of them still provides the faithful with all of Christ. Thus, the laypeople were given only the consecrated bread, and the drinking of the cup of wine was restricted to the priest celebrating the Mass. This practice was called *communion in one kind* (*communion sub una*) because only one element—the bread—was given to the laity.

While the medieval Church settled into its observance of the Eucharist with the understanding of transubstantiation, several voices raised strong opposition to its belief. Chief among these was John Wycliffe, who attacked the church's view with a fury[116] and offered several reasons for his rejection of transubstantiation. First and fore-

[113] Thomas Aquinas, *Summa Theologica*, part 3, q. 75, art. 5.

[114] Ibid., art. 4.

[115] Bonaventura, *Breviloquium*, 6.9 (5). E. E. Nemmers, *Breviloquium of St. Bonaventura* (St. Louis: B. Herder Book Co., 1946), 199–200.

[116] "I maintain that among all the heresies which have ever appeared in the church, there was never one that was more cunningly smuggled in by hypocrites than this [transubstantiation], or which in more ways deceives the people; for it plunders them [the people], leads them astray into idolatry, denies the teaching of Scripture, and by this unbelief provokes the Truth himself

most, he decried the lack of a biblical and rational foundation for the idea.[117] A second reason was the fact that transubstantiation did not enjoy the support of church history.[118] Thirdly, transubstantiation was defeated by the recognition of the senses and human judgment that the bread is bread before being consecrated and remains bread after it is consecrated.[119] Finally, Wycliffe drew attention to the disastrous consequences of belief in transubstantiation. He was particularly critical of the idolatry that resulted from the idea, which he saw in two areas: people's worship of the consecrated bread, and the absolute power claimed by the priests to transform the bread into the body of Christ.[120]

On another front, the Catholic Church's practice of Communion in one kind was attacked by John Hus and his followers. Hus decried the giving of the eucharistic bread to laypeople while withholding the eucharistic cup from them. He urged the Church to rehabilitate the practice of Communion of both species, supporting his idea with the conviction that "not custom, but the example of Christ"[121] must be authoritative.[122] The critiques of Wycliffe and Hus were but precursors to the more virulent attacks against the eucharistic theology of the Church by the Protestant Reformers.

With the publication of *The Babylonian Captivity of the Church* in 1520, Martin Luther[123] attacked the sacramental system and the eucharistic practices of the Catholic Church.[124] In particular, he addressed

oftentimes to anger" (John Wycliffe, *Trialog*, 4.2.248; cited from G. Lechler, *John Wycliffe and His English Precursors* [London: The Religious Tract Society, 1878], 343).

[117] "Neither upon Scripture nor reason nor revelation can the [Catholic] Church base . . . transubstantiation. Therefore, we are not any more obligated to believe this than was the primitive church" (John Wycliffe, *On the Eucharist*, 3.13; in *Advocates of Reform*, ed. M. Spinka, LCC 14 [Philadelphia: Westminster, 1953], 81).

[118] John Wycliffe, *On the Eucharist*, 2.31 (Spinka, *Advocates of Reform*, 73).

[119] John Wycliffe, *Trialog*, 4.4.257 (G. Lechler, *John Wycliffe*, 346).

[120] John Wycliffe, *Trialog*, 4.5.261; 4.6.264; 4.7.279 (G. Lechler, *John Wycliffe*, 347).

[121] John Hus, *Epistle* 141 (cited from J. Pelikan, *Reformation of Church and Dogma, 1300–1700* [vol. 4 of *The Christian Tradition: A History of the Development of Doctrine*; Chicago and London: University of Chicago Press, 1984], 123).

[122] His follower John of Rokycana echoed Hus on this, underscoring that "the communion of the divine Eucharist under both species, namely, bread and wine, is of great value and aid to salvation and is necessary for the entire people of believers, and it was commanded by our Lord and Savior" (John of Rokycana, *The Position that Communion under Both Kinds Is Necessary and Commanded by the Lord Our Savior*, in Pelikan, *Reformation of Church and Dogma*, 123).

[123] For a more detailed discussion of Luther's contribution to the doctrine and practice of the Lord's Supper, see Matt Crawford's fine essay in this volume, "On Faith, Signs, and Fruits: Martin Luther's Theology of the Lord's Supper."

[124] "To begin with, I must deny that there are seven sacraments, and for the present maintain

three "captivities" to which the Church had subjected the Lord's Supper. The first captivity was the Church's withholding of the cup from the laity and the administration of Communion in one kind.[125] The second captivity was the Church's decree that transubstantiation—based on Aquinas' use of Aristotle's philosophy—was the only legitimate view of the presence of Christ in the Eucharist. Like Wycliffe before him, Luther underscored the lack of biblical evidence for this position, concluding, "What is asserted without the Scriptures or proven revelation may be held as an opinion but need not be believed."[126] Moreover Luther, knowing that Aristotle held substance and accidents to be inseparable, criticized Aquinas for misunderstanding and misusing Aristotelian philosophy to explain the "miracle" of transubstantiation.[127] More importantly, at the heart of his rejection of transubstantiation was the essential principle of interpreting the words of Scripture according to "their grammatical and proper sense."[128] Applying this to the discussion of the Lord's Supper, Luther noted, "It is an absurd and unheard-of juggling with words to understand 'bread' to mean 'the form or accidents of bread,' and 'wine' to mean 'the form or accidents of wine. . . .' [It is not] right to enfeeble the words of God in this way, and by depriving them of their meaning to cause so much

that there are but three: baptism, penance, and the bread. All three have been subjected to a miserable captivity by the Roman curia, and the church has been robbed of all her liberty" (Martin Luther, *The Babylonian Captivity of the Church*, *LW* 36.18). When he said "for the present," Luther was nearly exaggerating, because by the end of this writing he had excluded penance from being a sacrament: "Nevertheless, it has seemed right to restrict the name of sacrament to those promises which have signs attached to them. The remainder, not being bound to signs, are bare [mere] promises. Hence there are, strictly speaking, but two sacraments in the church of God—baptism and the bread. For only in these two do we find both the divinely instituted sign and the promise of forgiveness of sins" (ibid., 36.124). Thus, the Protestant position that there are only two sacraments, not seven, was originated.

[125] Luther passionately opposed this practice. He underscored Jesus' insistence that the cup be drunk by "all" of His disciples (his appeal was to Matt 26:27 and Mark 14:23). He also dissented logically, reasoning that if the Lord's Supper is given "to the laity, it inevitably follows that it ought not to be withheld from them in either form." Most importantly, Luther focused on the fact that "the blood is given to all those for whose sins it was poured out. But who will dare to say that it was not poured out for the laity?" (his appeal was to Matt 26:28 with Luke 22:20). Finally, Luther questioned why the Church, if it concedes that the laity receive divine grace (the more important matter) through the sacrament, would not concede the sacrament itself (a lesser matter). He called for a general council of the Church to put a halt to this tyranny (ibid., 36.20–23).

[126] Ibid., 36.29.

[127] Thus, he criticized Aquinas because he built "an unfortunate superstructure [philosophical, rather than biblical, support for transubstantiation] upon an unfortunate foundation [a misunderstanding of Aristotle's philosophy]" (ibid., 36.29).

[128] Ibid., 36.30.

harm."[129] He also appealed to church history: "The church kept the true faith for more than twelve hundred years, during which time the holy fathers never, at any time or place, mentioned this transubstantiation (a monstrous word and a monstrous idea), until the pseudo philosophy of Aristotle began to make its inroads into the church in these last three hundred years."[130] Luther could not subscribe to such a recent doctrine. To conclude the matter, he pointed out that "[t]he laymen have never become familiar with their fine-spun philosophy of substance and accidents, and could not grasp it if it were taught to them."[131] The third captivity was the Church's view of the Lord's Supper as "a good work and a sacrifice."[132] As a result, "this abuse has brought an endless host of other abuses in its train, so that the faith of this sacrament has become utterly extinct and the holy sacrament has been turned into mere merchandise, a market, and a profit-making business."[133]

Like Luther, Huldrych Zwingli dissented from the Catholic idea of transubstantiation, offering several arguments against it.[134] First, relying on Augustine, Zwingli noted that Christ's body, as a truly human body, can be and is located in only one place.[135] In particular, "according to its proper essence, the body of Christ is truly and naturally seated at the right hand of the Father. It cannot therefore be present in this way in the Supper."[136] From this line of reasoning, Zwingli concluded that the eucharistic elements cannot be transubstantiated

[129] Ibid., 36.31.

[130] Ibid.

[131] Ibid.

[132] Ibid., 36.35.

[133] Ibid.

[134] Huldrych Zwingli, *An Exposition of the Faith* (G. W. Bromiley, ed., *Zwingli and Bullinger*, LCC 24 [Philadelphia: Westminster, 1979], 254–55).

[135] "The body of Christ has to be in some particular place in heaven by reason of its character as a true body. And again: Seeing that the body of Christ rose from the dead, it is necessarily in one place. The body of Christ is not in several places at one and the same time any more than our bodies are" (ibid., 255). His appeal to Augustine was from the latter's *Tractate on the Gospel of St. John*, 30.1. Zwingli strengthened this point by focusing on the promise of Christ in John 17:11 and its fulfillment in His ascension: "'Again, I leave the world and go to the Father.' Truth itself compels us to refer this saying primarily and quite literally to Christ's humanity. . . . Which nature is it that leaves the world? Not the divine, for the divine nature is not confined to one place and therefore does not leave it. Consequently, it is the human nature that leaves the world. . . . [A]s regards a natural, essential and localized presence, the humanity is not here, for it has left the world. Hence, the body of Christ is not eaten by us naturally or literally . . . but sacramentally and spiritually" (ibid., 257).

[136] Ibid., 256.

into the body and blood of Christ.[137] For his second point, Zwingli defined a sacrament as "the sign of a holy thing. . . . Now the sign and the thing signified cannot be one and the same. Therefore the sacrament of the body of Christ cannot be the body itself."[138] Thus, there is no one-to-one correspondence between the eucharistic elements and the body and blood of Christ. Thirdly, Zwingli underscored the proper way to interpret the words of institution. They should not be taken literally, but figuratively, as proved by Christ's own words in John 6:63: "The flesh profits nothing."[139] In the Lord's Supper, therefore, "the words of Christ cannot refer to physical flesh and blood."[140] Like his contemporary Luther, Zwingli attacked Catholic eucharistic theology.

John Calvin added his criticism to those of Luther and Zwingli.[141] Expressing contempt for that "fictitious transubstantiation," Calvin referred to it as a great superstition, a perverse error, a deceitful subtlety, a monster, and a trumped-up illusion.[142] Because of this, he denounced the Catholic mass in no uncertain terms: "Inasmuch as the mass of the pope was a reprobate and diabolical ordinance subverting the mystery of the Holy Supper, we declare that it is damnable to us, an idolatry condemned by God; for so much is it itself regarded as a sacrifice for the redemption of souls that the bread is in it taken and adored as God."[143]

[137] For his apparent separation between the human nature and divine nature of Christ, Zwingli was charged by his opponents with the ancient heresy of Nestorianism, or the division of the divine and human natures in Christ (Luther, *Confession Concerning Christ's Supper, LW* 37.212–13).

[138] Huldrych Zwingli, *On the Lord's Supper*; Bromiley, *Zwingli and Bullinger*, 188.

[139] Ibid., 189–90.

[140] Ibid., 191.

[141] "We must not dream of such a presence of Christ in the sacrament as the craftsmen of the Roman court have fashioned—as if the body of Christ, by a local presence, were put there to be touched by the hands, to be chewed by the teeth, and to be swallowed by the mouth. We do not doubt that Christ's body is limited by the general characteristics common to all human bodies, and is contained in heaven (where it was once for all received) until Christ will return in judgment [Acts 3:21]. Thus, we deem it utterly unlawful to draw it back under these corruptible elements of bread and wine or to imagine it to be present everywhere" (*Institutes* 4.17.12).

[142] *Institutes* 4.17.12–15.

[143] John Calvin, *The Genevan Confession*, 16 (in J. K. S. Reid, ed. and trans., *Calvin: Theological Treatises*, LCC 22 [London: SCM Press, 1954], 30). When asked by a recent convert from Catholicism to the Reformed faith if it were possible to participate in the Lord's Supper in a Reformed church, Calvin agreed, "provided that you are asking about Christ's Supper. When you examine the matter, you will find that there is no more agreement between the Lord's Supper and the papist Mass than between light and darkness. Men's wickedness and ignorance certainly cannot weaken anything ordained by the Lord, but I deny that the Mass can be ascribed to

In addition to their denunciation of the Catholic Church's theology and practice of the Eucharist, Luther, Zwingli, and Calvin offered their own doctrines of the Lord's Supper. Their perspectives are recounted elsewhere in this volume.

In reaction to Protestant attacks against its eucharistic theology, and in opposition to the various Protestant views of the Lord's Supper, the Council of Trent reaffirmed the traditional Catholic belief in the real presence of Christ: "In the august [sacred] sacrament of the holy Eucharist, after the consecration of the bread and wine, our Lord Jesus Christ, true God and true man, is truly, really and substantially contained under the appearance of those sensible things."[144] The Council went on to explain the basis for this affirmation—transubstantiation:

> Because Christ, our Redeemer, declared that which he offered under the species of bread to be truly his own body, therefore has it ever been a firm belief in the Church of God . . . that by the consecration of the bread and of the wine, a conversion is made of the whole substance of the bread into the substance of the body of Christ our Lord, and of the whole substance of the wine into the substance of his blood; which conversion is, by the holy Catholic Church, suitably and properly called Transubstantiation.[145]

An important corollary of this transformation was that Christ should be worshipped when the consecrated elements are displayed to the public after the Mass is completed, and the Council underscored the propriety of such adoration.[146] Trent also reaffirmed that the mass is a sacrifice that appeases the wrath of God:

Christ as its originator. On the contrary, I say that it was devised by Satan himself to destroy the Holy Supper. Certainly it is diametrically opposed to the Lord's Supper when, under the name of a sacrificial rite, the power and effectiveness of the Lord's sufferings are turned into a contrived act. Open idolatry is part of the Mass too, not only when the bread is worshipped but when there are prayers for the dead, and when the merits and intercessions of the saints are prayed for, and when many other things of that sort take place, which the Lord expressly condemns. The faithful are not allowed to share in that superstition. . . . It is absolutely inconsistent with the confession of faith that the Lord requires of us" (John Calvin, "So That a Pious Man May Withdraw from the Superstitions of the Papacy," in M. Beaty and B. W. Farley, trans., *Calvin's Ecclesiastical Advice* [Louisville: Westminster/John Knox, 1991], 63).

[144] "Decree Concerning the Most Holy Sacrament of the Eucharist," 1. *The Canons and Decrees of the Council of Trent*, 13th session (11 October 1551) (Schaff, 2.126).

[145] Ibid., 4 (Schaff, 2.130).

[146] "All the faithful of Christ may, according to the custom ever received in the Catholic Church, render in veneration the worship of latria, which is due to the true God, to this most holy sacrament. For not therefore is it the less to be adored on this account, that it was instituted by Christ, the Lord, in order to be received" (ibid., 5; Schaff, 2.131).

> As in this divine sacrifice which is celebrated in the mass, that same Christ is contained and immolated [sacrificed] in an unbloody manner who once offered himself in a bloody manner on the altar of the cross, the Holy Synod teaches that this sacrifice is truly propitiatory. . . . For the victim is one and the same, the same now offering by the ministry of priests, who then offered himself on the cross, the manner alone of offering being different.[147]

Over against Protestant beliefs about the Lord's Supper, the Council pronounced *anathemas*, curses excommunicating and damning to hell all who subscribed to erroneous views. It specifically condemned those who did not hold to transubstantiation[148] and did not believe that the mass is a sacrifice.[149] It also pronounced anathemas against errors in administering the rite, including a condemnation of Communion in two kinds.[150]

The Council of Trent reemphasized and rearticulated the historic position of the Catholic Church with regard to the theology and practice of the Eucharist. Though important developments in this Catholic doctrine took place in the centuries following Trent, they have thus far culminated in the *aggiornamento* ("bringing up to date") proposed by the Second Vatican Council and enacted by the Church since then. As earlier sections of this chapter have treated both the celebration of the Mass and the theology of the Eucharist as set forth in the

[147] "Doctrine of the Sacrifice of the Mass," 2. *The Canons and Decrees of the Council of Trent*, 22nd session (17 September 1562) (Schaff, 2.179). As noted earlier, by no means does this re-presentation of the sacrifice of Christ detract from His once-and-for-all sacrifice on Calvary.

[148] "If anyone says, that in the sacred and holy sacrament of the Eucharist, the substance of the bread and wine remains conjointly [together] with the body and blood of our Lord Jesus Christ, and denies that wonderful and singular conversion of the whole substance of the bread into the body, and of the whole substance of the wine into the blood—the species only of the bread and wine remain—the Catholic Church most aptly calls Transubstantiation: let him be anathema" ("Decree Concerning the Most Holy Sacrament of the Eucharist," canon 2; Schaff, 2.136).

[149] "If anyone says that, in the mass a true and proper sacrifice is not offered to God: . . . let him be anathema. . . . If anyone says, that the sacrifice of the mass is only a sacrifice of praise and thanksgiving; or, that it is a bare commemoration of the sacrifice on the cross, but not a propitiatory sacrifice . . . or that it should not be offered for the living and the dead for sins, pains, satisfactions and other necessities: let him be anathema" ("Doctrine of the Sacrifice of the Mass," canons 1, 3; Schaff, 2.184–85).

[150] "If anyone says, that, by the precept of God, or by the necessity of salvation, all and each of the faithful of Christ should receive both species of the most holy sacrament of the Eucharist, let him be anathema" ("Doctrine Concerning the Communion in Two Kinds, and of Little Children, canon 1; *The Canons and Decrees of the Council of Trent*, 21st session [16 July 1562]; Schaff, 2.174).

Catechism, reflective of these post-Vatican II developments, I end this historical section at the Council of Trent.

Eucharistic Theology and Practice Set within an Overview of Catholic Theology in General

Presenting and understanding Catholic eucharistic theology cannot be severed from a presentation and understanding of Catholic theology in general, as the entire theological system hangs together. In this section I will address several key Catholic doctrines that impinge on its eucharistic doctrine and practice.

Divine Revelation and Its Interpretation (Scripture, Tradition, and the Magisterium)

Catholic theology of the Eucharist is not derived from Scripture alone, but is also based on Church tradition. As Vatican II summarized the doctrine of divine revelation: "Sacred Tradition and sacred Scripture make up a single sacred deposit of the Word of God, which is entrusted to the Church."[151] Sacred Scripture is the written Word of God, or Bible.[152] Church tradition is the teaching of Jesus that He orally communicated to the apostles yet was not written down, and which in turn the apostles orally communicated to their successors, the bishops. This living tradition continues in the Church today and at times has been proclaimed as official Catholic doctrine.[153] The result of this view of divine revelation is "that the Church does not draw her certainty about all revealed truths from the holy Scriptures alone. Hence, both Scripture and Tradition must be accepted and honored

[151] *Dogmatic Constitution on Divine Revelation* (Vatican II, *Dei Verbum*, 18 November 1965), 10. This single yet two-part source of tradition and Scripture is so because "both of them, flowing out from the same divine well-spring, come together in some fashion to form one thing, and move towards the same goal" (ibid., 9). The difference between the two parts is explained: "Sacred Scripture is the speech of God as it is put down in writing under the breath of the Holy Spirit. And Tradition transmits in its entirety the Word of God which has been entrusted to the apostles by Christ the Lord and the Holy Spirit. It transmits it to the successors of the apostles so that, enlightened by the Spirit of truth, they may faithfully preserve, expound and spread it abroad by their preaching" (ibid.).

[152] It should be recalled that the Catholic canon of Scripture is more extensive than that of the Protestant Bible, because it contains additional books not found in the Protestant Bible, and additional sections in books that it shares in common with the Protestant Bible.

[153] Specifically, Pope Pius IX promulgated the dogma of the Immaculate Conception of Mary in his bull *Ineffabilis Deus* (8 December 1854), and Pope Pius XII promulgated the dogma of the Bodily Assumption of Mary in his bull *Munificentissimus Deus* (1 November 1950).

with equal feelings of devotion and reverence."[154] Catholic theology also insists that the *Magisterium*, or teaching office of the Church, has the sole prerogative to determine the proper and authoritative interpretation of this divine revelation.[155]

Combining the last few points of discussion, Vatican II underscored that "in the supremely wise arrangement of God, sacred Tradition, sacred Scripture and the Magisterium of the Church are so connected and associated that one of them cannot stand without the others. Working together, each in its own way under the action of the one Holy Spirit, they all contribute effectively to the salvation of souls."[156] And, together, the three contribute to the Church's theology and practice of the Eucharist.

Doctrine of Salvation (Law, Grace, Justification, Cooperation, Merit, and Sanctification)

Catholic theology of the Eucharist is intimately tied to its doctrine of salvation. Though "God created man a rational being" in the divine image "so that he might of his own accord seek his Creator and freely attain his full and blessed perfection by cleaving to him,"[157] man abused this freedom and "freely sinned."[158] "Called to beatitude but wounded by sin, man stands in need of salvation from God. Divine help comes to him in Christ through the law that guides him and the grace that sustains him."[159] The law, consisting of the natural moral law, the law of Moses, and the law of the gospel,[160] "prescribes for man the ways, the rules of conduct that lead to the promised beatitudes."[161] Keeping this law is an essential aspect of salvation.

[154] *Dogmatic Constitution on Divine Revelation*, 9.

[155] Again, Vatican II summarized the Church's position: "But the task of giving an authentic interpretation of the Word of God, whether in its written form or in the form of Tradition, has been entrusted to the living teaching office of the Church alone" (ibid., 10). This position was first articulated by the Council of Trent in reaction to the growing Protestant threat. See *The Council of Trent*, 4th session, "Decree Concerning the Canonical Scriptures" (8 April 1546).

[156] *Dogmatic Constitution on Divine Revelation*, 10.

[157] *Catechism*, 1730. Elsewhere, the *Catechism* affirms: "The Beatitudes reveal the goal of human existence, the ultimate end of human acts: God calls us to his own beatitude" (ibid., 1719).

[158] Ibid., 1739.

[159] Ibid., 1949.

[160] Ibid., 1954–74. This law of the gospel includes the evangelical councils, the vows of chastity, poverty, and obedience (ibid., 914–16).

[161] Ibid., 1950.

Grace for salvation comes through the Holy Spirit who "has the power to justify us, that is, to cleanse us from our sins and to communicate to us 'the righteousness of God through faith in Jesus Christ' and through Baptism."[162] Specifically, "[t]he first work of the grace of the Holy Spirit is conversion, effecting justification."[163] Of great importance is the Catholic doctrine of the latter: "Justification is not only the remission of sins, but also the sanctification and renewal of the interior man."[164] As a fruit of justification, "faith, hope, and charity are poured into our hearts, and obedience to the divine will is granted us."[165] "Justification is conferred in Baptism, the sacrament of faith. It conforms us to the righteousness of God, who makes us inwardly just by the power of his mercy."[166] Accordingly, baptismal justification (which dovetails with what Protestants call "baptismal regeneration") introduces sinful people into the Church's life of grace.

But there is more: "Justification establishes cooperation between God's grace and man's freedom."[167] Though "no one can merit the initial grace of forgiveness and justification, at the beginning of conversion, [m]oved by the Holy Spirit and by charity, we can then merit for ourselves and for others the graces needed for our sanctification, for the increase of grace and charity, and for the attainment of eternal life."[168] What is expected in regard to human cooperation in salvation is that one *facere quod in se est*—does what is in one to do, which includes participation in the Church and its sacraments. By so doing, one achieves merits before God and attains eternal life.[169] Accordingly,

[162] Ibid., 1987. The reference is to Rom 3:22.

[163] Ibid., 1989.

[164] Ibid. The citation is from the "Decree on Justification," 7 (*The Canons and Decrees of the Council of Trent*, sixth session [13 January 1547]).

[165] *Catechism*, 1991.

[166] Ibid., 1992.

[167] Ibid. Divine grace comes in various kinds, including prevenient grace, justifying grace, sanctifying grace, habitual grace, actual grace, sacramental grace (for which point see the next section on the sacramental economy), and the grace of final perseverance (ibid., 1996–2005, 2016).

[168] Ibid., 2010.

[169] Catholic theology affirms that, "[w]ith respect to God, there is no strict right to any merit on the part of man." Thus, though He did not have to establish a cooperative enterprise with man, God did institute such an arrangement by which He would reward man. Thus, "[t]he merit of man before God in the Christian life arises from the fact that God has freely chosen to associate man with the work of his grace" (ibid., 2007–8). Accordingly, Catholic theology distinguishes between two types of merits: (1) *Condign merits* are real merits, or merits of worthiness, accomplished by a righteous person through divine grace. (2) *Congruous merits*, or merits of fitness, are not strictly merits; rather, they are human works reckoned as merits because in

sharing in the Eucharist is an essential aspect of salvation. Yet even this "sacrament of sacraments" is part of a broader framework called the sacramental economy.

The Sacramental Economy (The Role of the Church as a Means of Grace)

Catholic theology insists that the Church is a means of grace and thus necessary for salvation. At the heart of the Catholic doctrine of the Church is the idea of the *sacramental economy*: Jesus Christ is both redeemer and high priest. As redeemer, He "accomplished [note the past tense] his work principally by the Pascal mystery of his blessed Passion, Resurrection from the dead, and glorious Ascension."[170] This salvific work occurred in history, nearly 2,000 years ago. From this sacrifice on the cross "there came forth 'the wondrous sacrament of the whole Church.' For this reason, the Church celebrates in the liturgy above all the Paschal mystery by which Christ accomplished the work of our salvation."[171]

As redeemer and high priest, Jesus Christ "continues [note the present tense] the work of our redemption in, with, and through the Church."[172] This ongoing effort has particular reference to the apostles and their successors, the bishops, who teach, govern, and sanctify the Church.[173] Specifically, Christ "acts through the sacraments in . . . 'the sacramental economy'; this is the communication

doing them, people do what is in them to do. Considered in and of themselves, good works do not achieve any real merit—condign merit—before God, because those who do good works have received everything—especially grace—from Him in the first place. But as long as people do what is within their ability to accomplish—according to the way God has designed them to use their free will to do good—they are rewarded with congruous merit.

[170] Ibid., 1067.

[171] Ibid.

[172] Ibid., 1069.

[173] "She [the Church] continues to be taught, sanctified, and guided by the apostles until Christ's return, through their successors in pastoral office: the college of bishops, 'assisted by priests, in union with the successor of Peter, the Church's supreme pastor [the Pope]'" (ibid., 857). Elsewhere: "'In order that the mission entrusted to them might be continued after their death, [the apostles] consigned, by will and testament, as it were, to their immediate collaborators the duty of completing and consolidating the work they had begun. . . . They accordingly designated such men and then made the ruling that likewise on their death other proven men should take over their ministry.'. . . . Hence the Church teaches that 'the bishops have by divine institution taken the place of the apostles as pastors of the Church, in such wise that whoever listens to them is listening to Christ and whoever despises them despises Christ and him who sent Christ'" (ibid., 861–62). The two citations are taken from the *Dogmatic Constitution on the Church* (Vatican II, *Lumen Gentium*, 21 November 1964), 20; *Vatican Council II: Volume*

(or 'dispensation') of the fruits of Christ's Paschal mystery in the celebration of the Church's 'sacramental' liturgy."[174] Increase in grace, separation and protection from sin, and unity with Christ and His faithful are dispensed, and personal and corporate sanctification is augmented, as Christ continues His salvific work through the liturgy. "The liturgy then is rightly seen as an exercise of the priestly office of Jesus Christ. It involves the presentation of man's sanctification under the guise of signs perceptible by the senses and its accomplishment in ways appropriate to each of these signs."[175] Specifically, the Church's liturgy celebrates the seven sacraments.[176]

The goal of this ongoing work of the redeemer and high priest Jesus Christ through the sacramental economy of the Church—particularly its celebration of the Eucharist—is the salvation of the entire world.[177] What Jesus Christ, the redeemer and high priest, accomplished—past tense—through His death, resurrection, and ascension, He accomplishes—present tense—in an ongoing manner through His Church.[178] Its eucharistic theology is firmly situated at the center of this sacramental economy.

1, 371–72. As for the three responsibilities of the office of bishop—teaching, sanctifying, and governing—see *Catechism*, 888–96.

[174] Ibid., 1076.

[175] Ibid., 1070.

[176] *Baptism* regenerates a sinful person, who in most cases is an infant, and removes original sin. *Confirmation* confers the empowerment of the Holy Spirit. The *Eucharist* is what we are discussing. *Reconciliation* provides forgiveness for and cleansing from all post-baptismal sins. *Marriage* unites a man and a woman in an enduring and monogamous covenantal relationship. *Holy Orders* consecrates and ordains qualified men to the priesthood. *Anointing of the Sick* readies those who are sick or dying, or who are for other reasons in mortal danger, for their passage from death into eternity. For a full discussion of each of these sacraments, see ibid., 1066–1666.

[177] "As a sacrament, the Church is Christ's instrument. 'She is taken up by him also as the instrument for the salvation of all,' 'the universal sacrament of salvation,' by which Christ is 'at once manifesting and actualizing the mystery of God's love for men.' The Church 'is the visible plan of God's love for humanity,' because God desires 'that the whole human race may become one People of God, form one Body of Christ, and be built up into one temple of the Holy Spirit'" (ibid., 776). The citations are from the *Dogmatic Constitution on the Church* (Vatican II, *Lumen Gentium*, 21 November 1964); the *Pastoral Constitution on the Church in the Modern World* (Vatican II, *Gaudium et Spes*, 7 December 1965), 45; and the *Decree on the Church's Missionary Activity* (Vatican II, *Ad Gentes Divinitus*, 7 December 1965), 7.

[178] To be more precise, the sacramental liturgy is not the only means given to the Church to effect its work for the salvation of the world. Evangelization and preaching of the gospel (*Catechism*, 1070, 1072), works of charity (ibid., 1070), prayer (ibid., 1073), and catechesis (ibid., 1074–75) are other elements of the Church's sacramental economy.

An Evangelical Assessment of the Catholic Theology of the Eucharist

In this final section, I will set forth an assessment of the eucharistic theology of the Catholic Church, organized by general topics. While space limitations permit only a measured assessment, much more could be said about each topic.

The first area concerns the biblical support for the Catholic theology of the Eucharist. Whereas the Catholic interpretation of the words of institution[179] is literal, both Zwingli and Calvin demonstrated that such an interpretation of these passages is not demanded. Indeed, a figurative interpretation is well warranted. Jesus commonly employed figurative language when speaking of His person and work,[180] and the context of the institution narrative weighs heavily in favor of taking His words in a figurative sense. Jesus was pressing on toward His crucifixion, the act by which He would atone for the sins of the world, and He used the occasion of His Last Supper, the final Passover celebrated with His disciples, to foretell once again His upcoming death.[181] Furthermore, the establishment of a new covenant with His people required new signs, both to distinguish this covenant from its predecessor (the Mosaic covenant) and to provide a lasting memorial of His sacrificial death on the cross for His church. Taking the loaf of bread and the cup of wine, elements of the Passover celebration at the heart of the old covenant, Jesus invested them with new meaning: the one would symbolize His broken body, the other, His shed blood. Together, these tokens would constitute a sign of His new covenant.[182] That His disciples could have understood His words literally and grasped them in any way approaching the developed Catholic theology of actual presence, strains these words of institution and their context. A literal interpretation of the institution narratives, which constitutes key biblical support for the Catholic theology of the Eucharist, is not warranted.

[179] Matt 26:26–29; Mark 14:22–25; Luke 22:14–23.

[180] To keep with the theme of bread, an example of Jesus' use of figurative language was His interchange with His disciples concerning the "leaven of the Pharisees and Sadducees" (Matt 16:5–12).

[181] Earlier references to His death in Jerusalem, in the Gospel of Matthew, are 16:21–23; 17:22–23; and 20:17–19.

[182] The other sign, introduced by Jesus after His resurrection, at His giving of the Great Commission, is baptism.

The other key text offered in support of the Church's eucharistic theology is John 6:22–71. Jonathan Pennington adeptly treats this passage elsewhere in this volume.[183] I will treat it briefly.

By appealing to the realistic nature of Jesus' words (He speaks of His flesh as "real food" and His blood as "real drink," 6:55), the benefits promised to the one who "eats My [Jesus'] flesh and drinks My blood" (i.e., "eternal life" and resurrection, 6:54; being united with Christ, 6:56), and the parallelism between this passage ("The bread that I will give for the life of the world is My flesh," 6:51) and the words of institution ("This is my body") in the Synoptic Gospels, the Church understands this passage as eucharistic teaching.[184] However, several points stand against this interpretation. The presence of realistic language does not prove that the words must be taken literally (and hence sacramentally). Elsewhere in John's Gospel (10:1–18), Jesus' vivid portrayal of the plight of sheep at the hands of a marauder is not an indication that His words "I am the door of the sheep" should be interpreted literally. As noted in the historical section, Augustine understood this passage in a symbolic manner; a literal interpretation is not required. Regarding the benefits promised to the one who consumes Christ, elsewhere in this Gospel Jesus promises eternal life (3:15,16,36), resurrection (11:25–26; cf. 5:25), and unity with Him (17:20–21) to those who "believe in" Him.[185] Given that John's volume is "the Gospel of belief" (20:30–31), it appears that Jesus' words in John 6 are intended to be interpreted metaphorically, not literally (and hence sacramentally).[186] As for the parallelism with the institution narratives, one notes that whereas the Synoptic Gospels use the word *sōma*, John's Gospel employs *sarx*, which "suggests (though it does not prove) that John is not making any *direct* reference" to the

[183] See Pennington's chapter, "The Lord's Last Supper in the Fourfold Witness of the Gospels."

[184] These are not the only reasons for interpreting this passage as a reference to the Eucharist, but for sake of space limitations, I will limit my comments to these three points. Scripture here and elsewhere is from the HCSB.

[185] Interestingly, in His conversation with the woman at the well, Jesus spoke of "living water" (4:10) while promising "eternal life" to "whoever drinks of the water that I will give him" (4:14). Though the benefit promised here by Jesus parallels the fruit of the Eucharist, no one suggests that the water to which Jesus referred is the water added to the wine of the sacrament. Jesus' is clearly using metaphorical language. If this is the case in this passage, it may also be the case in John 6.

[186] For further discussion, see D. A. Carson, *The Gospel According to John* (Leicester, UK: InterVarsity, and Grand Rapids, MI: Eerdmans, 1991), 276–82.

Lord's Supper.[187] Furthermore, if one is looking for parallelism, the clearest parallel is (con)textually close at hand:

> "Anyone who eats My flesh and drinks My blood has eternal life, and I will raise him up on the last day" (6:54).
> " . . . everyone who sees the Son and believes in Him may have eternal life, and I will raise him up on the last day" (6:40).

As Carson underscores, "The only substantial difference is that one speaks of eating Jesus' flesh and drinking Jesus' blood, while the other, in precisely the same conceptual location, speaks of looking to the Son and believing in him. The conclusion is obvious: the former is the metaphorical way of referring to the latter."[188] Other reasons may be marshaled against a literal or sacramental interpretation of this passage: the context in which Jesus delivered this teaching was certainly not the occasion of His Last Supper;[189] in John's narrative flow, the miracles that are recounted are Jesus' feeding of the 5,000 (6:5–13) and His walking on the water (6:16–21), not the "miracle" of the Eucharist;[190] and at the conclusion of His discourse, Jesus warned against taking His words literally (6:63).[191]

Other biblical support includes Paul's discussion of the Lord's Supper in 1 Corinthians. The two passages, 10:14–22 and 11:17–34, are

[187] Ibid., 295. Moreover, as Carson rightly notes, "But the alert reader will think of [John] 1:14: the Word became 'flesh' (*sarx*). 'It is as the incarnate logos that Jesus is able to give his "flesh" for the life of the world.'" His citation is from F. J. Moloney, *The Johannine Son of Man*, 2nd ed., Biblioteca di Scienze Religiose 14 (Rome: Libreria Ateneo Salesiano, 1978), 115.

[188] Carson, *The Gospel According to John*, 297.

[189] Following the Synoptic Gospels' ordering of events, the narrative of the Lord's Supper would fit around chap. 13 of John's Gospel. For his purposes, however, John did not write about that event. That this fact results in John's Gospel "lacking" an account of the Lord's Supper does not constitute good evidence for interpreting John 6 as the apostle's rendition of the Eucharist.

[190] Indeed, if the Gospel of John centers around seven miracles—changing the water into wine (2:1–11), healing the official's son (4:46–54), healing the invalid (5:1–15), feeding of the 5,000 (6:5–13), walking on the water (6:16–21), healing the blind man (9:1–7), and raising Lazarus from the dead (11:1–44)—as proof of the identity of Jesus Christ, His discourse in 6:22–71 cannot be taken as the "miracle" of the Eucharist.

[191] As Carson explains, "To take the words of the preceding discourse [6:22–58] literally, without penetrating to their symbolic meaning, is useless. It causes offence; it does not arrive at Jesus' meaning, for *the flesh counts for nothing*. Although this clause does not rule out all allusion in the preceding verses to the Lord's supper, it is impossible not to see in 'flesh' a direct reference to the preceding discussion, and therefore a dismissal of all *primarily* sacramental interpretations" (Carson, *The Gospel According to John*, 301).

thoroughly discussed by Jim Hamilton elsewhere in this volume.[192] I will treat them briefly.

In 1 Cor 10:14–22, Paul issues a warning to flee from idolatry (10:14), a dreadful sin in which the Corinthians engaged through their practice of attending feasts in pagan temples. This ritual involved demons and consequently resulted in spiritual danger (10:20). Paul raises two rhetorical questions for the Corinthians to judge sensibly (10:15): "The cup of blessing that we bless, is it not a participation in the blood of Christ? The bread that we break, is it not a participation in the body of Christ?" (10:16). Of great importance for our purpose is the nature of the church's participation in the body and blood of Christ. Catholic theology maintains that this passage offers support for its doctrine of the real presence of Christ: The Church participates in the body and blood of Christ because He is "truly, really, and substantially contained" in the eucharistic elements.[193] But to make this assertion from this passage proves too much.[194]

In his discussion, Paul parallels three events: what takes place in the celebration of the Lord's Supper by the church, what took place in ancient Israel when members of the community made their peace offerings on the altar in the temple (Leviticus 3; 15), and what takes place when pagans offer food and drink to idols at their banquets:

Lord's Supper	Israelite Altar	Pagan Banquets
cup: participation in the blood of Christ	eat sacrifices: participation in the altar	drink offered to idols/cup of demons: participation with demons
bread: participation in the body of Christ		food offered to idols/table of demons: participation with demons

The operative word linking these activities is *koinōnia*, rendered "participation" (or, derivatively, "participants"). Through eating the sacrifices, the Israelites were "participants in the altar" (10:18). Through eating the food and imbibing the drink sacrificed to idols, pagans are participants with demons, because "what pagans sacrifice they offer

[192] See Hamilton's chapter, "The Lord's Supper in Paul: An Identity-Forming Proclamation of the Gospel."

[193] "Decree Concerning the Most Holy Sacrament of the Eucharist," 1. *The Canons and Decrees of the Council of Trent*, 13th session (11 October 1551) (Schaff, 2.126).

[194] The following is adapted from G. R. Allison, *The Assembly of "The Way": The Doctrine of the Church*, Foundations of Evangelical Theology, J. S. Feinberg, gen. ed. (Wheaton: Crossway, forthcoming).

to demons and not to God" (10:20). Through blessing the cup of blessing and breaking the bread, Christians participate in the blood and the body of Christ (10:15–16). The notion of participation links these activities. If it is true, according to the Catholic theology, that the Church's participation in the body and blood of Christ is due to His being "truly, really, and substantially contained" in the eucharistic elements, then the same explanation would need to avail for the Israelites' participation in its sacrifices on the altar and the pagans' participation in their sacrifices offered to idols/demons.[195] Such is clearly not the case, nor would Catholic theology agree with the idea; indeed, it insists that Christ's presence in the Eucharist is unique. Appeal to the divine eternity or atemporality, in which the sacrifice of Christ on Calvary shares, is made only in regard to the Eucharist. But to claim uniqueness for this event, by which the Church participates in the body and blood of Christ, leaves Paul's parallelism with two other events in shambles. Accordingly, this passage does not constitute biblical support for Catholic theology of the Eucharist.

Paul's discussion of the Lord's Supper in 1 Cor 11:17–34 focuses on the abuse of that celebration by the wealthier members of the Corinthian church. Though the Supper was intended to unite its diverse elements, the church's actual manner of observation served only to heighten the stratification already present among its members. Several important points relevant to our discussion are made in the midst of Paul's rebuke. Following Luke's institution narrative (Luke 22:14–23), the apostle emphasizes the memorial aspect of the Lord's Supper and closely links it to a proclamatory function. That is, Jesus' actions and announcement accompanying the bread conclude with His instruction, "Do this in remembrance of me" (11:24). Similarly, His action and pronouncement concerning the cup conclude with the instruction, "Do this, as often as you drink it, in remembrance of me" (11:25). Paul then explains ("for") how this memorial element is made possible as the church gathers to "eat this bread and drink the cup": By engaging in these designated actions, "you [the church] proclaim the Lord's death until he comes" (11:26). Proclamation (a visible, tangible re-enactment of Christ's institution of the Lord's Supper, involving the breaking of a loaf of bread and the drinking of a cup

[195] Accordingly, the substance of the peace offerings would have changed so as to become the altar (or, the Lord?), and the substance of the drink and food offered to idols would be changed so as to become demons.

of wine) facilitating remembrance (of the Lord's death that establishes a new covenant)—not a re-presentation of Christ's bloody sacrifice in a bloodless manner—is the significance of this celebration, according to Paul.

But what is to be made of the dreadful consequences attached to the Corinthians' abuse of this celebration, divine judgments that included weakness, illness, and even premature death (11:30)? Do these not point to the very presence of Christ the Avenger in/of His holy sacrament? According to this interpretation, then, the divine discipline was meted out on the church of Corinth for its failure to grasp the fullness of Christ's presence in the bread and the cup.[196] But the reason for punishment that is given in the text is not a breakdown in discerning the eucharistic presence of Christ, but participation in the Lord's Supper "in an unworthy manner" (11:27): the wealthier members of the church disregarded its poorer members, rushing ahead of them in the preceding agape feast and so consuming all the food and drinking all the wine to the point of gluttony and drunkenness. Divine judgment was poured out not because the Corinthians failed to discern the presence of Christ in the Lord's Supper, but because they failed to discern the fellowship of Christ's body and act in ways appropriate to that unity as they celebrated together. This passage, then, does not constitute biblical support for the Catholic theology of the Eucharist. Accordingly, the biblical evidence for the Church's theology of the Eucharist is not strong.

The Church also appeals to historical precedent for its theology of the Eucharist. While it is true that the themes of sacrifice and the reality of the presence of Christ in the Eucharist resounded in the early church, a note of symbolism also echoed, even from such an important theologian as Augustine. Moreover, at least some of the early church's insistence on the actual presence of Christ was due to its battle against the heresy of Docetism. An emphasis on the real presence of Christ was a ready ally in this fight: If it was true that the body and blood of Jesus Christ were actually present when the church celebrated the Eucharist, then surely this fact confirmed the true humanity of the Son of God in the incarnation, consequently defeating Docetism. Ignatius, who combated this heresy by insisting on the

[196] This was the contention of the *Catechism of the Council of Trent*. "The Holy Eucharist," *Catechism of the Council of Trent*, trans. J. A. McHugh and C. J. Callan (New York: Joseph F. Wagner, 1934), 229–30.

real presence, also countered factionalism in the churches to which he wrote, and innovations that he introduced to stave off those divisions lacked biblical support and, indeed, contradicted Scripture.[197] Though high regard should be paid to Ignatius for his stellar faith and link with the apostle John, his views are not above critique.[198] This includes his perspective on the Eucharist.[199]

Furthermore, the fact that medieval controversies flared up involving Radbertus, Ratramnus, Berengar of Tours, and others confirms that the early church was not settled on this belief, unlike many other crucial doctrines (e.g., the Trinity; the deity and humanity of Christ). Even a practice of the early church with which I as an evangelical Baptist disagree—infant baptism—developed very quickly, especially in comparison to the church's doctrine of the Last Supper. As Luther underscored, the church existed for well over twelve hundred years without a dogma of transubstantiation, indicating the lateness of its development. Finally, the importance one places on historical precedent as evidence for one's theology must be carefully investigated and weighed. By no means is historical development infallible, and ultimately all of the church's theology and practice must be evaluated against the touchstone of Scripture.

In further support of its theology of the Eucharist, the Catholic Church points to philosophical undergirding, specifically transubstantiation. The important critiques of transubstantiation by Wycliffe, Luther, Zwingli, and Calvin have already been noted: it lacks biblical support; it contradicts Scripture's affirmation that Christ's human nature is located in one space, at the right hand of the Father, and is not ubiquitous; it lacks the support of church history; it is based on a misunderstanding of Aristotelian philosophy by Aquinas; it cannot be a binding belief; it defies reason, is counterintuitive to the senses, and is too complex for laypeople to understand; it leads to disastrous consequences, including the adoration of the consecrated bread in the tabernacle; and as signs of the new covenant, the bread and the cup cannot be the real body and blood of Jesus Christ, because a sign is never the thing signified itself.

[197] See e.g., Ignatius, *Letter to the Smyrneans,* 8 (Holmes, 190–91; cf. *ANF* 1.89–90).

[198] Cf. Carson, *The Gospel According to John*, 277–78.

[199] The same caution holds for all theologians, biblical scholars, and leaders of the early church (and the church in subsequent eras).

To this list of problems articulated by my Protestant forerunners, I add three concerns. First, ongoing debate about transubstantiation has produced a great deal of discussion that is far removed from the biblical presentation of the Lord's Supper. Here are some examples of these issues, put into question format:[200] What becomes of the substance of the bread and the substance of the wine at the moment of consecration—are they annihilated or dissolved into their original matter?[201] Does the atmosphere become the substance of the accidents of the bread and wine after they are consecrated?[202] What happens to the water that has been added to the wine—does it remain unchanged after the consecration, does it change into the water that flowed from Christ's side, or does it change first into wine, which then changes into the blood of Christ?[203] Bizarre issues, like whether a mouse that eats the consecrated host by breaking into the tabernacle is nourished physically—by the mere accidents of the bread—or miraculously, were raised as well.[204] And contemporary matters—how does eucharistic theology and its metaphysical underpinnings of substance and accidents relate to particle physics, quantum mechanics, and other current scientific theories?—also clamor for attention. My point is this: These issues are so far removed from Scripture that they have lost all connection to it. Depending on the topic, these corollaries of transubstantiation are of more or less importance for Catholic theology, but for evangelicals, their distance from Scripture's presentation of the Lord's Supper underscores the wrongness of transubstantiation.

A second concern, echoing that of Luther, regards the intelligibility of the doctrine of transubstantiation. Even within an Aristotelian framework as interpreted by Aquinas, the notion is incoherent, because "transubstantiation demands that we take the distinction between substance and accidents as a *dissection*, and so treat them as so

[200] These examples are developed in P. J. Fitzpatrick, "Present and Past in a Debate on Transubstantiation," in *The Philosophical Assessment of Theology: Essays in Honour of Frederick C. Copleston*, ed. G. J. Hughes (Kent, UK: Search, and Washington, D.C.: Georgetown University Press, 1987), 131–53.

[201] Thomas Aquinas, *Summa Theologica*, part 3, q. 75, art. 3.

[202] Ibid., part 3, q. 77, art. 1.

[203] Ibid., part 3, q. 74, art. 8.

[204] Alan of Lille, *De fide catholica*. In H.-J. Jorissen, *Die Entfaltung der Transsubstantiationslehre bis zum Beginn der Hochscholastik*, Münsterische Beiträge zur Theologie, Heft 28, 1 (Münster, Westfalen: Aschendorffsche Verlagsbuchhandlung, 1965). Referenced in Fitzpatrick, "Present and Past in a Debate on Transubstantiation," 145.

many *things*."[205] While for Aristotle substance and accidents may be distinguished as terms but not separated in reality—and Aquinas notes this inseparability of the two is the case in the natural order[206]—in one instance—the transubstantiation of the bread and wine into the body and blood of Christ—this inseparability is suspended. Thus, the consecrated bread and wine have no substance, yet they continue to exist. And they continue to exist as things, which contradicts the inseparability of substance and accidents, making the notion unintelligible.

Aquinas's explanation for how the unintelligible can be actual is an appeal to the "Divine power,"[207] and this appeal is my third concern:

> This change is not like natural changes, but is entirely supernatural, and effected by God's power alone. . . . And this is done by Divine power in this sacrament; for the whole substance of the bread is changed into the whole substance of Christ's body, and the whole substance of the wine into the whole substance of Christ's blood. Hence this is not a formal, but a substantial conversion; nor is it a kind of natural movement: but, with a name of its own, it can be called "transubstantiation."[208]

Appeal to the power of God to effect miracles may certainly be warranted: the creation of the universe *ex nihilo*, and the conception of the Son of God in the womb of the Virgin Mary, are clear examples of divine power at work.[209] A significant difference exists, however, between the appeals to divine power to explain creation and the virgin birth, and the appeal to divine power to explain transubstantiation: The first two have clear biblical warrant; the latter does not. This lack of scriptural grounding for the miracle of transubstantiation makes it unacceptable to Protestants.

The final area of assessment focuses on the broader theological framework in which the Church's theology of the Eucharist is rooted and flourishes. The doctrine of divine revelation influences the very foundation from which the Church develops its eucharistic theology: Not from Scripture alone, but also from Church tradition, and as both elements of the one source of divine revelation are interpreted by the

[205] Fitzpatrick, "Present and Past in a Debate on Transubstantiation," 138. This second concern follows Fitzpatrick's presentation.

[206] Aquinas, *Summa Theologica*, part 3, q. 74, art. 4.

[207] Ibid., part 3, q. 77, art. 1.

[208] Ibid., part 3, q. 75, art. 4.

[209] Indeed, Aquinas appeals to these miracles in support of the divine power at work in transubstantiation (Thomas Aquinas, *Summa Theologica*, part 3, q. 75, art. 4 [in which he cites Ambrose, *De Mysterium*, 4] and 8).

Magisterium. By means of this triptych structure, several conclusions are reached. First, the words of institution are interpreted literally. Second, John 6:22–71, along with Paul's discussion in 1 Corinthians 10 and 11, are considered to be support for the real presence of Christ in the Eucharist. Third, the early church's writings that viewed the celebration of the Lord's Supper as a sacrifice involving His actual body and blood are taken as reliable developments of the sacrament. And finally, conciliar decisions are regarded as authoritative pronouncements regarding transubstantiation. A Protestant assessment questions the interpretation of these texts, the consideration of certain passages as unfolding eucharistic teaching, the theological reliability of the early writings, and the authority of conciliar declarations, all the while insisting on its formal principle: *sola Scriptura* (Scripture alone).[210]

The formal principle of Protestantism is Scripture only; its material principle is justification by grace through faith alone.[211] This doctrine also clashes with the Catholic doctrine of salvation and its insistence that the call to God's beatitude is experienced through (1) keeping the law; (2) justification, consisting not only of the reception of forgiveness of sins and the divine righteousness, but including also the renewal of sinful human nature; (3) cooperation with grace so as to love and engage in good deeds, by which sanctification is increased and eternal life is merited; and (4) involvement in the sacramental economy of the Church, especially through participation in the seven sacraments by which grace is communicated. From an evangelical perspective, (1) no one can keep the law and be justified before God (Rom 3:20; Gal 2:16–21); (2) justification is the forensic declaration of God that one is not guilty, but righteous instead, not because of any intrinsic righteousness of one's own or infused righteousness from the sacraments, but because the righteousness of Christ is imputed to one's account (Rom 3:21–4:8); and (3) the synergy at the heart of the Catholic notion of human cooperation with divine grace destroys grace and merits nothing more than condemnation, for salvation leading to eternal life is the gift of God apart from human works (Eph 2:1–10).

As for (4) the sacramental economy of the Catholic Church, this concept is so far removed from Scripture (and even early church

[210] Space limitations preclude me from offering a defense of this principle, but I hope to do so in G. R. Allison, *Intrigue and Critique: An Evangelical Assessment of Roman Catholic Theology and Practice* (Wheaton: Crossway, forthcoming).

[211] Again, defense of this principle awaits the publication of my forthcoming book.

history) that no Protestant denomination or church has an ecclesiology that even remotely resembles it. The explanation for how Christ's sacrifice on the cross nearly 2,000 years ago is re-presented each time the Liturgy of the Eucharist is celebrated—an appeal to the Paschal mystery's participation in the eternality of God—is a theological construct without biblical warrant.[212] Moreover, apostolic succession is one of the most critical differences between the Catholic Church and Protestant churches: The former insists that because Protestantism lacks apostolic succession, none of its ecclesial communities is a church;[213] the latter protests that the alleged biblical basis for apostolic succession—Jesus' words to Peter (Matt 16:13–20 and the disciples (John 20:21–23)—is based on a faulty interpretation of those passages and thus has no scriptural warrant. Furthermore, Protestants have always denounced the notion of seven sacraments, maintaining that only two—baptism and the Lord's Supper—were ordained by Christ (Matt 26:26–29 and parallels; 28:19; 1 Cor 11:17–34) and have accompanying tangible signs (water; bread and wine).

To offer these pointed criticisms is not to overlook or deny the many cardinal doctrines Protestants and Catholics gratefully hold together. But as both sides readily admit, with regard to the presence of Christ in the Eucharist, Protestants reject absolutely the dogma of transubstantiation and Catholics insist absolutely that the Church participates in the body and blood of Christ because He is "truly, really, and substantially contained" in the eucharistic elements through a change in their substance. This essay has presented an evangelical assessment of the Catholic theology of the Eucharist, showing why this difference continues rightly to separate Catholicism and Protestantism.

[212] The appeal to the Israelites' understanding of their liberation from Egypt, by which the Church infers that the idea of a memorial in Scripture "is not merely the recollection of past events" (*Catechism*, 1363), is still not biblical evidence for re-presentation. The Jewish celebration of the Passover was and continues to be a memorial of the exodus events, and this remembrance never approaches a re-presentation of those events.

[213] Pope Benedict XVI, "Responses to Some Questions Regarding Certain Aspects of the Doctrine of the Church" (29 June 2007). The Pope's address reaffirmed traditional Catholic teaching that Christ established only one true Church on earth, and this Church subsists in the Catholic Church. As for Protestant churches, "According to Catholic doctrine, these Communities do not enjoy apostolic succession in the sacrament of Orders, and are, therefore, deprived of a constitutive element of the Church. These ecclesial Communities which, specifically because of the absence of the sacramental priesthood, have not preserved the genuine and integral substance of the Eucharistic Mystery cannot, according to Catholic doctrine, be called 'Churches' in the proper sense."

ON FAITH, SIGNS, AND FRUITS: MARTIN LUTHER'S THEOLOGY OF THE LORD'S SUPPER

Matthew R. Crawford*

Introduction

In 1530, not even two decades into the Reformation, Martin Luther lamented the way that Christians viewed the sacrament of the Lord's Supper, stating that "people now regard the holy sacrament of the body and blood of our Lord so lightly and assume an attitude toward it as if there were nothing on earth which they needed less than just this sacrament."[1] Luther laid the blame for this attitude at the feet of church leaders who failed to execute their divinely given task, namely, the oversight of souls, by allowing their congregants to persist in theological ignorance and wayward conduct. He thus stated his plea that "all pastors and preachers . . . would diligently look after the people whom God has purchased as his possession through the blood of his Son and has called and brought to baptism and into his kingdom."[2] Luther understood that "looking after" the people of God required that the pastor instruct his congregation in the right understanding and use of the Lord's Supper. He did much during his lifetime to recover the right doctrine and practice of the Supper among the churches of the Reformation, and his writings on the Supper can serve pastors today as they attempt to instruct their congregations regarding this sacred observance.

Luther's eucharistic theology is instructive at several points, but his greatest insight about the Lord's Supper was that the Supper must be understood in light of the gospel. Tied to this insight is Luther's Reformation principle *sola Scriptura*. He returned the Word to primary place in corporate Christian worship.[3] In fact, it might be stated that,

* Matthew R. Crawford received an M.Div. from The Southern Baptist Theological Seminary and is pursuing a Ph.D. in patristics from Durham University in Durham, England.

[1] Martin Luther, *Admonition Concerning the Sacrament of the Body and Blood of Our Lord*, *LW* 38.98.

[2] Ibid., 100.

[3] Luther, *Concerning the Order of Public Worship*, *LW* 53.11.

for Luther, the Word was the only means of grace.[4] The Lord's Supper is a sacrament only because it is the Word repackaged in a distinct form.[5] The content of the Word is the gospel, that is, forgiveness of sins. Thus, the content of the sacrament is also the gospel. In his work critiquing Catholicism, *The Babylonian Captivity of the Church*, Luther stated, "Now the mass is part of the gospel; indeed, it is the sum and substance of it. For what is the whole gospel but the good tidings of the forgiveness of sins? Whatever can be said about the forgiveness of sins and the mercy of God in the broadest and richest sense is all briefly comprehended in the word of this testament."[6] The purpose of this chapter is to understand Luther's theology of the Eucharist as he himself did—through the lens of the gospel.

Luther defined the Lord's Supper as consisting of three parts: faith in the promise of God, the presence of the physical sign accompanying the promise, and the fruits resulting from the sacrament.[7] This distinction occurs as early as 1519 in Luther's *The Blessed Sacrament of the Holy and True Body of Christ, and the Brotherhoods*, and again in 1526 in *The Sacrament of the Body and Blood of Christ—Against the Fanatics*.[8] Accordingly, these three parts form the structure of this

[4] H. Bornkamm, *Luther's World of Thought*, trans. M. H. Bertram (St. Louis: Concordia, 1958), 95.

[5] Luther said regarding the Lord's Supper, "Here the sign is added as if it were the Word, concrete and before the eyes, so that the sign might teach the same thing that the Word teaches" (Luther, *Lectures on Isaiah: Chapters 1–39*, *LW* 16.168).

[6] Luther, *The Babylonian Captivity of the Church*, *LW* 36.56. This point is noted by Hermann Sasse in his seminal study of Luther's eucharistic theology. He calls the Supper "the Gospel in action" (*This Is My Body: Luther's Contention for the Real Presence in the Sacrament of the Altar* [Minneapolis: Augsburg, 1959], 108). Sasse's volume is the best full-length monograph on Luther's view of the Lord's Supper that is available in English.

[7] B. Lohse notes that this is "a unique definition of the sacraments that is without precedent in all the tradition" (*Martin Luther's Theology*, trans. and ed. R. A. Harrisville [Minneapolis: Fortress, 1999], 128). Lohse's book is the best one-volume treatment of Luther's theology. Lohse's work is divided into two parts, the first detailing the chronological development of Luther's theology as he engaged in controversies with Rome and his fellow Reformers, and the second giving a systematic exposition Luther's theology in its final form. This approach is how Lohse deals with one of the most difficult questions when studying Luther, namely, whether to present his theology as it developed or in a systematic fashion. In this chapter I attempt to balance the two approaches, since both are necessary to fully understand Luther's theology of the Lord's Supper. Luther's view is here presented in systematic fashion, but historical developments are noted when appropriate.

[8] Luther, *The Blessed Sacrament of the Holy and True Body of Christ, and the Brotherhoods*, *LW* 35.49. Luther was not always consistent in mentioning all three elements. In a later work against Zwingli, he did not mention the fruits of the sacrament, but this is because they were not what was primarily at stake in the debate at the time (id., *The Sacrament of the Body and Blood of Christ—Against the Fanatics*, *LW* 36.335). In a sermon from 1528 he mentioned all three but did

chapter. This structure thus gives primary emphasis to the Reformer's own understanding of his theology. Moreover, it provides a useful framework within which to place Luther's polemical writings. As Luther himself stated, his controversy with the Catholic Church was primarily concerning the meaning of faith and his controversy with the so-called "fanatics" centered on the sign itself.[9] Thus, his polemical writings will be placed within the larger purview of Luther's doctrine. By structuring this study according to Luther's own understanding of the sacrament, and by looking at examples from several genres of Luther's works, the overall cohesiveness of his view will be evident.

"Given for You": Promise and Faith in the Sacrament

Forgiveness of Sins and the Lord's Supper

Martin Luther's sacramental theology flowed out of his own experience of God's grace. The source of Luther's angst while a monk was how he, a convicted sinner before God, could obtain forgiveness. This acute awareness of his sin was not alleviated until around the year 1514 as Luther struggled with the meaning of the "righteousness of God" while lecturing through Romans.[10] Pondering how God could punish men, causing them such great suffering for their transgression of the divine law, Luther was struck by the phrase in Rom 1:17, "The just shall live by faith."[11] It was then that he realized that Paul taught salvation was possible through faith alone, rather than through faith joined with good works, and that God's righteousness was obtained by the work of Christ and was imputed to the unrighteous sinner. For Luther, the question of God's justice was not merely an abstract inquiry, but "an *existential quest* that concerned the *whole* human being, encompassing thought and action, soul and body, love and suffering."[12]

not distinguish between faith and the sign in his exposition (id., *Ten Sermons on the Catechism*, *LW* 51.190).

[9] At the beginning of the controversy with Zwingli in 1526 Luther wrote, "Up to now I have not preached very much about the first part [the sign], but have treated only the second [faith itself]," and that he was now beginning to focus on the first part because it is being attacked by the Zwinglians (Luther, *The Sacrament of the Body and Blood of Christ—Against the Fanatics*, *LW* 36.335).

[10] Lohse, *Martin Luther's Theology*, 92–94.

[11] H. A. Oberman, *Luther: Man between God and the Devil*, trans. E. Walliser-Schwarzbart (New Haven: Yale University Press, 1989), 165.

[12] Ibid., 151. Oberman says that it was the transformation of this abstract question into an

This existential quest for divine forgiveness eventually led Luther to reformulate his eucharistic theology as an existential reminder of the forgiveness he had found.

The experience of being forgiven by God coupled with Luther's close study of the Scriptures was the driving force behind his new formulation of the Lord's Supper.[13] According to Luther the bread and the wine are a sign that God has promised this forgiveness of sins in Christ, and the response of the believer should be faith in the finished work of Christ. Luther's earliest work laying out his eucharistic theology along these lines was *A Treatise on the New Testament, That Is, the Holy Mass*, written in 1520. The phrase "New Testament" in the title is not a reference to the corpus of writings, but to the testament, or promise, made by Christ to His followers. Luther's central idea in the work was that the mass is not simply a reenactment of the new testament, but is the very essence of the new testament, or new covenant. For this reason, Luther's goal was to return as closely as possible to the first mass of Christ.[14] Thus, Luther spilled much ink in his treatise expounding the accounts of the Last Supper recorded in the gospels, stating that "everything depends . . . upon the words of this sacrament."[15] So important was the Word that the loss of the words of the institution meant the loss of the sacrament, and the presence of the Word brought the presence of Christ and blessing to the believer.

In his *Treatise on the New Testament*, Luther closely examined the words of the institution of the Supper, but he also placed the new covenant in its context within redemptive history. Throughout redemptive history, God had taken the initiative to make promises to His people, including the protoevangelium of Gen 3:15, the promises to Abraham, the covenant with Noah, and promises to David.[16] The new

existential quest that gave Luther a wide hearing.

[13] On this point see Lohse, *Martin Luther's Theology*, 313; B. Hall, "*Hoc est Corpus Meum*: The Centrality of the Real Presence for Luther," in *Luther: Theologian for Catholics and Protestants*, ed. G. Yule (Edinburgh: T&T Clark, 1985), 115.

[14] Luther, *A Treatise on the New Testament, That Is, the Holy Mass*, *LW* 35.81. Elsewhere Luther stated, "The Word of God is the chief thing in the sacrament," quoting Augustine's statement that "the Word comes to the element, and it becomes a sacrament" (*Ten Sermons on the Catechism*, *LW* 51.189). Augustine's statement came in his *Tractates on the Gospel of John*, 80.3 (*NPNF*[1] 7.344).

[15] Luther, *A Treatise on the New Testament*, *LW* 35.88.

[16] Luther always placed the primary emphasis on God's actions in salvation rather than on man's. He wrote, "If a man is to deal with God and receive anything from him, it must happen

testament, Luther taught, is a promise greater than any that preceded it because of the surpassing value of that which is promised. In the Supper Christ says to His followers,

> See here, man, in these words I promise and bequeath to you forgiveness of all your sins and the life eternal. In order that you may be certain and know that such a promise remains irrevocably yours, I will die for it, and will give my body and blood for it, and will leave them both to you as a sign and seal, that by them you may remember me.[17]

The new testament is a promise of the forgiveness of sins, and the promise is guaranteed because of the death of Christ.

The proper response of the Christian to the promise of the new testament was faith. Luther defined faith as "a firm trust that Christ, the Son of God, stands in our place and has taken all our sins upon his shoulders and that he is the eternal satisfaction for our sin and reconciles us with God the Father."[18] Luther's conception of faith thus presupposed an awareness of one's sin. Faith was essential in order for the believer to benefit from the sacrament. Therefore, the sacrament does not help those who are not in adversity or sin; rather "this sacrament demands souls that are desirous, needy, and sorrowful."[19] When the Christian approaches the Lord's Supper he is saying, in effect, "Though I am a sinner and have fallen, though this or that misfortune has befallen me, nevertheless I will go to the sacrament to receive a sign from God that I have on my side Christ's righteousness, life, and sufferings, with all holy angels and the blessed in heaven and all pious men on earth."[20] Luther, keenly aware of his own sin before God, undoubtedly experienced a great sense of consolation through observing the Lord's Supper, and expected others to have a similar sense of their own sin if they were to partake of the Supper correctly so as to benefit from it. Therefore, he held that the Supper should not be observed unless there are some present who truly desire the benefit of it.[21]

in this manner, not that man begins and lays the first stone, but that God alone—without any entreaty or desire of man—must first come and give him a promise" (ibid., 82).

[17] Ibid., 85.

[18] Luther, *Eight Sermons at Wittenberg*, *LW* 51.92.

[19] Luther, *Blessed Sacrament of the Body of Christ*, *LW* 35.55–56.

[20] Ibid., 54.

[21] Luther wrote, "For the sacrament should never be celebrated except at the instigation and request of hungry souls, never because of duty, endowment, custom, ordinance, or habit" (*Receiving Both Kinds in the Sacrament*, *LW* 36.256–57). Luther identified this point as one of the steps toward instituting the right observance of the Supper in churches still in the process of being reformed.

Nevertheless, a mere desire for the fruits of the sacrament was insufficient. While faith presupposed an awareness of one's own sin, Luther also demanded that Christians demonstrate some holiness of life in order to partake of the Supper, although this requirement did not stipulate that Christians must do penance in order to partake. In his work, *The Misuse of the Mass*, Luther wrote, "To this mass all those should come who hunger and thirst after this food, that is, all devout, believing Christians, contrite and fearful consciences who desire with all their hearts to become righteous and whole. All who lead a carnal life should be excluded from it."[22] Luther thus expresses well the tension that the Supper is intended for sinners, but only for those who long for righteousness and pursue holiness of life.

In 1520 Luther penned his landmark critique of the Catholic Church, *The Babylonian Captivity of the Church*, in which he again highlighted the primacy of faith in the observance of the sacrament. Luther quoted Augustine's statement, "Believe and you have eaten," implying that faith takes precedence over the partaking of the bread and wine.[23] Or, to use different terminology, spiritual eating is of greater importance than physical eating. The believer, Luther taught, was to rely in faith upon the finished work of Christ, rather than trying to merit God's favor as the Catholic Church taught.[24] In Luther's

[22] Luther, *The Misuse of the Mass*, *LW* 36.198. Luther's typical practice was to make confession several times before observing the sacrament. Once, in a particularly desperate spiritual state, he partook without the typical confessions, and found that "if a person has no longing or reverence for the sacrament and yet earnestly makes the effort to participate in it, then such thoughts and the action itself bring forth sufficient reverence and longing and do a good job of driving away the lazy and morose thoughts which hinder a person and make him unfit" (*Admonition Concerning the Sacrament*, *LW* 38.127). Elsewhere Luther exhorted pastors to examine their church members yearly in order to make sure they understood the sacrament before receiving it. Those who "sin brazenly and without fear while they boast glorious things about the gospel" should be barred from the Table (id., *An Order of Mass and Communion for the Church at Wittenberg*, *LW* 53.33).

[23] Luther, *The Babylonian Captivity*, *LW* 36.44. Luther never denied this emphasis on spiritual eating, although it retreated into the background during the debates over the presence of Christ. In one of his works directed against Zwingli he again quotes this passage from Augustine to highlight the primacy of spiritual eating (id., *That These Words of Christ, "This Is My Body," etc., Still Stand Firm Against the Fanatics*, *LW* 37.124). The original quote can be found in *Homilies on the Gospel of John* 25.12, trans. J. Gibb and J. Innes, *NPNF*[1] 7.164.

[24] In 1519 Luther decided that there were only three true sacraments among the seven proclaimed by the pope—baptism, the Lord's Supper, and penance. That year he preached a sermon on each of the sacraments (*The Sacrament of Penance, The Holy and Blessed Sacrament of Baptism*, and *The Blessed Sacrament of the Holy and True Body of Christ, and the Brotherhoods*; all are found in *LW* 35). That same year Luther wrote to Spalatin stating that he could not recognize the rest of the medieval sacraments as legitimate (Lohse, *Martin Luther's Theology*, 128). A year

eyes, the Catholic view of the sacraments dishonored the uniqueness of the work of Christ and cheapened God's forgiveness by denying the sovereign freedom of God.[25] Following logically from his view of the Supper as "God's gracious condescension," Luther disagreed with Rome over two primary points. The first was the notion of the mass as a sacrifice and the second was the necessity of faith for the proper observance of the sacrament.

The Mass as a Sacrifice

The sacrifice of the body and blood of Christ was an essential element in the Catholic doctrine of the sacrament, and remains so to this day.[26] According to Luther, the Catholic Church taught that the altar of the sacrament was a repetition of what happened on the cross, in other words, that the sacrifice of Christ was offered anew.[27] For example, in the first part of the canon spoken at the mass the priest prayed, "We humbly beseech Thee, most merciful Father, through Jesus Christ, Thy Son, our Lord, that Thou wilt deign to be pleased with and bless these gifts, these presents, these holy and unspotted sacrifices, which we offer Thee especially for Thy holy universal

later in *The Babylonian Captivity*, Luther argued that there are only two sacraments—baptism and the Supper. This reduction in the number of sacraments is due to Luther's contention that the two essential parts of a sacrament are the word of God and an outward sign (A. McGrath, *Reformation Thought: An Introduction* [New York: Basil Blackwell, 1988], 119–20). Penance has no outward sign and is therefore not a sacrament (Luther, *The Babylonian Captivity*, *LW* 36.124; cf. Bornkamm, *Luther's World of Thought*, 101).

[25] T. J. Davis acknowledges that the "faith/testament schema" is the basis upon which "communion under one species, transubstantiation, and the concept of *opus operatum* are all attacked" ("'His Completely Trustworthy Testament': The Development of Luther's Early Eucharistic Teaching, 1517–1521," *Fides et Historia* 25 [1993]: 13; republished in T. J. Davis, *This Is My Body: The Presence of Christ in Reformation Thought* [Grand Rapids: Baker, 2008]). In other words, this new schema was what drove Luther to break from Roman eucharistic theology.

[26] H. Oberman states that the two key questions discussed during the late medieval period regarding the Lord's Supper were the relation between the sacrifice of Christ on the cross and the sacrifice on the Communion Table and the mode of Christ's presence in the sacrament (*Forerunners of the Reformation: The Shape of Late Medieval Thought Illustrated by Key Documents*, trans. P. L. Nyhus [New York: Holt, Rinehart and Winston, 1966], 243–44).

[27] Note, however, that as Gregg Allison perceptively points out elsewhere in this volume, the Catholic Church actually does not teach that the sacrament is a repetition of the sacrifice of Christ, but a participation in the timeless, once-for-all sacrifice of Christ on the cross. He states, "Catholic theology does not teach that the sacrifice on the cross of Calvary is repeated over and over again, each time the Eucharist is celebrated" ("The Theology of the Eucharist according to the Catholic Church," 162). For the purposes of this chapter, I am restricting myself to Luther's own understanding of the Catholic doctrine. Whether or not this accurately reflects the Catholic eucharistic theology of his day or of the Catholic Church today is beyond the scope of this chapter.

Christian Church."[28] The bread and wine offered in the mass appeased the anger of God by serving as a sacrifice for sins. In *The Babylonian Captivity* aimed at the Catholic Church, as well as in his later writings directed against his fellow Reformers, Luther consistently argued that this corruption of the Lord's Supper was the greatest.[29] He realized that the Reformation gospel was incompatible with the notion of the mass as a sacrifice.

In *The Babylonian Captivity*, Luther's method of countering the doctrine of the mass as sacrifice was to focus once again on the words of the institution as recorded in the gospels and Paul, summarizing the several recorded accounts into a single statement. He argued that the very meaning of "testament" apparent in these passages contradicted the Catholic doctrine of the Eucharist, for a testament is a promise, not a good work or a sacrifice. If it is a promise, it is accessed not by works, but by faith alone.[30] Moreover, as J. Pelikan has pointed out, Luther made an important distinction between sacrifices of thanksgiving and sacrifices of atonement. Corruption in the church came about by the confusion of these two.[31] The only true sacrifice of atonement was the work of Christ on the cross. Sacrifices of thanksgiving, such as the Lord's Supper, were made by those who already stood reconciled to God, and were a result, not a cause of that reconciliation. Furthermore, the Lord's Supper was not a sacrifice of atonement because the words of the institution emphasized the grace of God, not

[28] Quoted by Luther in *The Abomination of the Secret Mass*, *LW* 36.314. In contrast to the Catholic canon, Luther taught that "Christ has made us righteous and holy through that sacrifice [of Christ on the cross] and has redeemed us from sin, death, and the devil and has brought us into his heavenly kingdom" (ibid., 313).

[29] Luther, *The Babylonian Captivity*, *LW* 36.35. Luther first lodged his criticism against this Catholic doctrine in *A Treatise on the New Testament* (written in 1520), but only devoted a few pages to it. By the time he wrote *The Babylonian Captivity* later the same year, he elaborated on the significance of this point, devoting the most space in his section on the Supper to argue against the idea that the mass is a sacrifice (*The Babylonian Captivity*, *LW* 36.35–57). See also id., *The Adoration of the Sacrament*, *LW* 36.288; id., *Confession Concerning Christ's Supper*, *LW* 37.371. See also the same view presented in id., *The Smalcald Articles*, in *The Book of Concord: The Confessions of the Evangelical Lutheran Church*, ed. R. Kolb and T. J. Wengert, trans. C. Arand et al. (Minneapolis: Fortress, 2000), 301. Consequently, Luther wrote, "if the Mass falls, the papacy falls" (*The Smalcald Articles*, 303). Furthermore, Luther identified the notion of the mass as a sacrifice with the "abomination of desolation" in Matt 24:15 (id., *Lectures on Genesis: Chapters 38–44*, *LW* 7.297).

[30] Luther, *The Babylonian Captivity*, *LW* 36.39.

[31] J. Pelikan, *Luther the Expositor: Introduction to the Reformer's Exegetical Writings*, *LW*, companion volume (St. Louis: Concordia, 1959), 238. See Luther's discussion of sacrifices in his *Lectures on Genesis: Chapters 1–5*, *LW* 1.247–50.

His anger. In the phrase "which is given for you," there is no hint of an angry God needing to be appeased by sacrifice, but of a gracious God giving a gift.[32]

The Necessity of Faith

The second great change from Rome that Luther made in his understanding of the meaning of the sacrament was his emphasis on faith. According to Luther, the sacrament accomplishes nothing without faith. In holding to this position, Luther rejected the Catholic doctrine of *opus operatum* ("the work performed") in favor of the position *opus operantis* ("the work of the worker").[33] *Opus operatum* refers to a work that is complete and pleasing to God in itself, without regard to the interior disposition of the doer, while *opus operantis* is a work that is considered with reference to the doer.[34] In Luther's theological context, *opus operatum* meant that the sacrament conveys grace to the worshipper unless he "locks the door against it" with a mortal sin.[35] Grace was conferred merely through the performance of the act

[32] Luther, *The Misuse of the Mass*, *LW* 36.177.

[33] Luther, *A Treatise on the New Testament*, *LW* 35.102. Note, however, that Luther's understanding of the role of faith in regard to the sacrament developed over time. In fact, in his writings from the years 1518–19, there seems to be some sense in which Luther's view is a form of *opus operatum*, since he focuses so much on the Eucharist as a finished work, and the role of the communion of saints to mediate that work. In this early period, Luther thought that personal faith was not required to rightly receive the sacrament, since the corporate faith of the church could be enough to help a struggling believer to benefit from the sacrament. As Luther's eucharistic theology shifted to a primary emphasis on testament and promise in 1520, personal faith, not merely corporate faith, became essential to the right observance. See the very helpful discussion of this transition in Davis, "His Completely Trustworthy Testament," 6–11.

[34] Oberman, *Forerunners of the Reformation*, 244. The full Latin phrases are *ex opere operantis* ("by the work of the worker") and *ex opere operato* ("by the work performed"). See also R. A. Muller, *Dictionary of Latin and Greek Theological Terms: Drawn Principally from Protestant Scholastic Theology* (Grand Rapids: Baker, 1985), s.v. "*ex opere operantis*" and "*ex opere operato*." The distinction arose originally in order to emphasize the superiority of the sacraments of the NT over those of the OT, with the former being *opus operatum* and the latter being *opus operantis*. Thirteenth-century theologians who held to *opus operatum* such as Aquinas and Bonaventura still presupposed faith as a necessary condition to receive the sacrament. However, by the fourteenth century in the theology of Duns Scotus and then in the fifteenth-century theology of Gabriel Biel, faith was removed one step further as being expendable to the proper use of the sacrament (Luther, *Blessed Sacrament of the Body of Christ*, *LW* 35.64, n. 39). Another original intent of the doctrine was to insist on the efficacy of the sacrament regardless of the priest's state of grace, an idea that Luther accepted as true throughout his life. He wrote, "Even though a scoundrel receives or administers the sacrament, it is the true sacrament" (id., *The Large Catechism*, in *The Book of Concord*, 468; cf. Lohse, *Martin Luther's Theology*, 132–33).

[35] P. Althaus, *The Theology of Martin Luther*, trans. R. C. Schultz (Philadelphia: Fortress, 1966), 348; cf. Sasse, *This Is My Body*, 83.

regardless of the presence or absence of faith. In contrast, Luther declared that it is not enough for the sacrament to be merely completed, but "it must also be used in faith."[36]

Luther's overriding emphasis on faith also led him to attack the practice of priests muttering the words of the sacrament so quietly that a layman could not hear them. If the Christian cannot hear the words of the institution, how can he possibly be exhorted to believe the promise? In 1525 Luther wrote a treatise on the topic, titled *The Abomination of the Secret Mass*, attacking what he termed the *Stillmesse* ("secret mass"), that is, the canon that the priest read in a whisper due to its holiness.[37] Luther pointed out that the priests not only added their own erroneous words to the words of Scripture, but when they did quote the words of Jesus they said it so softly that no one could understand them, and even left out one of the most crucial phrases, "which is given for you." So that the laity might have access to the words of Christ, and so have faith in this promise, Luther argued early on in his career that the mass should be in German, not Latin.[38] Luther's goal was that the laity have a direct experience with the words of Christ, that their faith in His promise might be strengthened.

Luther the Conservative

Even though Luther's view differed in fundamental ways from the Catholic tradition that he inherited, he was also willing to retain many parts of the Catholic mass.[39] He tended to view some elements as nonessentials, and was therefore willing to leave room in the reformed camp for those who disagreed with him. For example, Luther said that he would not argue about certain details like the vestments and proper chalices. These concerns were mere human accretions to the

[36] Luther, *Blessed Sacrament of the Body of Christ*, *LW* 35.63–64. Luther was willing to use the technical theological terms if necessary, but he also said "in short, such expressions . . . are vain words of men, more of a hindrance than a help" (ibid.). The Council of Trent condemned Luther's definition of the sacrament, pronouncing anathema anyone who "says that faith alone is a sufficient preparation for receiving the sacrament of the most Holy Eucharist" (J. H. Leith, *Creeds of the Churches: A Reader in Christian Doctrine from the Bible to the Present*, 3rd ed. [Louisville, KY: John Knox, 1982], 437).

[37] Luther, *The Abomination of the Secret Mass*, *LW* 36.310, 314.

[38] Luther, *A Treatise on the New Testament*, *LW* 35.90. Luther said that the words of the institution should be sung loudest of all during the mass; cf. id., *Sermon on the Worthy Reception of the Sacrament*, *LW* 42.173; id., *An Order of Mass and Communion*, *LW* 53.21.

[39] Sasse notes that Luther was the most conservative of the Reformers and "preserved the Catholic heritage as far as possible" (*This Is My Body*, 83).

mass as recorded in the NT, and as such could not be either forced upon or denied to Christians. Every Christian is lord over all human teachings and commandments, and was thus free to either accept or reject them. Another practice common at the time was the adoration of the sacrament. Once the priest consecrated the elements, he would lift them up before the congregation and the partakers of the sacrament would kneel or bow before the sacrament, out of reverence for the true body and blood of Christ. On this matter as well, Luther said that each Christian should have the freedom to follow his or her own conscience. He nevertheless stated clearly what true adoration of the sacrament was.[40] "In short, the proper honor for the Word is nothing else than a genuine faith from the bottom of one's heart, a faith that holds the Word to be true, that trusts it and stakes its life upon it for eternity."[41] The thing of primary importance was that the Word be fixed in the heart of the believer in faith.

Luther's boldness in rejecting Catholic theology and practice was tempered with pastoral wisdom as well. While Luther was away at Wartburg Castle, insurrectionists in Wittenberg began insisting that the laity partake of both elements of the Lord's Supper. Although he was sympathetic with the idea that the laity should partake of both kinds, Luther nevertheless did not think it wise to force this practice too quickly upon the church. In his response to the event, he pointed out, "We must let the old misuse of the sacrament go on for a while yet, until the vessels, at least most of them, have become new and the gospel has taken root among the people."[42] Luther then adumbrated ten steps to bring about the needed change among the laity.

[40] Luther, *Receiving Both Kinds in the Sacrament*, *LW* 36.241. Luther did, however, caution that there is danger in adoring the sacrament, because humans by nature so easily begin to trust in their own works rather than the work of God (ibid., 297). Eventually Luther would abolish the elevation of the elements in Wittenberg, leading some to charge him with being a Zwinglian. Luther explained why he earlier allowed the elevation of the elements: "Because our teaching was at that time new and exceedingly offensive to the entire world, I had to proceed with forbearance and accommodate myself a great deal for the sake of the weak, which I afterward no longer did" (id., *Brief Confession Concerning the Holy Sacrament*, *LW* 38.314).

[41] Luther, *The Adoration of the Sacrament*, *LW* 36.278–79. It should be noted that in this context Luther explicitly said that the real presence is one of the articles in which the Christian must have faith, a point that became increasingly important for him as the focus of his polemical works shifts from the papacy to Zwingli.

[42] Luther, *Receiving Both Kinds in the Sacrament*, *LW* 36.252. Sasse remarks that the rule that Luther followed in his entire work as a Reformer was "to take into account the weak brother's conscience" (*This Is My Body*, 96). Cf. Luther, *Eight Sermons at Wittenberg*, *LW* 51.90–91, which were preached when he returned to Wittenberg.

While letting the old practice continue, pastors should emphasize in their sermons the words of the sacrament, avoiding every word in the canon that refers to the mass as a sacrifice.[43] Thus Luther exhibited pastoral wisdom by realizing that all the changes of the Reformation would take time. Far from being a fanatical radical, Luther stood firm for the gospel. He sought reformation, not revolution.

Evaluation

The first thing that must be observed in evaluating Luther's understanding of the meaning of the Lord's Supper is his courage in disagreeing with the Catholic Church at a time when doing so could mean death. His fortitude was rooted in the Reformation principle of *sola Scriptura*. Moreover, his return to the words of the institution was a breath of fresh air amid the staleness of much of the scholastic discussions of the Supper. Luther recovered the biblical teaching that the Lord's Supper is intimately tied to the work of Christ, but it is not a re-sacrifice of the body of Christ. Moreover, Luther correctly realized that the center of the gospel, forgiveness of sins and justification by faith alone, must be the center of the Lord's Supper. However, in his strong emphasis on justification, Luther did not highlight other legitimate theological emphases, for in the Supper Christians also celebrate the Lord's victory over sin, Satan, and death. In addition the Lord's Supper foreshadows the new creation. The forgiveness of sins is the heart of the gospel and of the Lord's Supper, but it does not exhaust the meaning of either.

Following from his emphasis on the gospel, Luther's understanding of how a Christian should partake of the Lord's Supper is particularly instructive. He struck the biblical balance between the truth that the Lord's Supper is a holy event, and the truth that the Supper was intended for those who are sinners. The Christian thus comes to the Supper with the realization that he is a sinner, and, with an awareness of the cost of his salvation, clings to Christ for forgiveness. The worthiness required to partake of the Supper is not found in doing penance, but in an awareness of one's need and a confidence in the

[43] Luther, *Receiving Both Kinds in the Sacrament*, *LW* 36.254. A decade later Luther's position on this issue had further developed: a priest who withholds the cup and drinks it only himself is partaking of mere wine because it is not the proper sacrament (id., *The Private Mass and the Consecration of Priests*, *LW* 38.205).

promise of salvation in Christ.[44] Contemporary evangelicals would do well to regain this particularly *evangelical* understanding of the Lord's Supper, and to follow Luther in meditation upon the words of Christ at the institution of the Supper.

"This Is My Body": The Sign of the Sacrament

The Role of "Signs" in Salvation History

In Luther's theology, signs were an essential component of God's dealings with humans throughout redemptive history. Because humans tend to have weak faith, it is necessary that there be physical signs that remind God's people of His faithfulness to fulfill His promises. In his lectures on Genesis, Luther stated, "God in His divine wisdom arranges to manifest Himself to human beings by some definite and visible form which can be seen with the eyes and touched with the hands, in short, is within the scope of the five senses."[45] In fact, every promise of God given in Scripture was accompanied by a sign.[46] The sacrifices of Cain and Abel in Genesis 4 constituted a sign in salvation history. Similarly, God gave to Noah the sign of the rainbow and to Abraham the sign of circumcision.[47] Luther said that in the new covenant, God has given believers the signs of baptism and the

[44] Oberman, *Luther: Man Between God and the Devil*, 242. As Oberman writes, "The call of the words of the institution liberates the Christian from the clutches of self-analysis" (243). Davis summarizes Luther's thought on the worthy reception of the sacrament in three words: recognition, desire, and faith ("His Completely Trustworthy Testament," 15). That is, the believer must recognize his sin, desire the grace offered in the sacrament, and have faith that Christ is true to His promise (cf. Luther, *The Large Catechism*, 470). Also, for Luther even this preparation is done by God, as God gives the word to burden man with his sin, gives the promise of forgiveness, and engenders faith in the heart of the believer. Nevertheless, Luther counseled pastors to create a hunger and thirst in the Christian for the sacrament by "showing him his frailty and his need so that he will see his wretched condition and feel the desire to be delivered from it," since "the greater and more fervent this desire is in you, the better fit you are to receive the sacrament (id., *Sermon on the Worthy Reception*, *LW* 42.172–73; in this sermon Luther gives 13 points on the worthy reception).

[45] Luther, *Lectures on Genesis: Chapters 15–20*, *LW* 3.109. Luther also described the sacrament as a "token" in *A Treatise on the New Testament*, *LW* 35.100.

[46] Ibid., 35.91.

[47] Luther, *Lectures on Genesis: Chapters 1–5*, *LW* 1.248.

Lord's Supper.[48] These signs serve to remind Christians that God "is with us, takes care of us, and is favorably inclined toward us."[49]

If the outline of Luther's understanding of the Supper was promise and faith, then the signs of the bread and wine, united with the body and blood of Christ, represent the promise and thus strengthen the Christian's faith. The reality of Christ's bodily presence in the bread and the wine meant that the sign of the Eucharist was of unique value, and it made the Lord's Supper especially potent and precious as a reminder of the promise of forgiveness.[50] If the sacrament was a testament, the truth of the real presence meant that the Testator was there to bespeak the testament at each observance.[51] In the Supper Christians thus meet God face-to-face, as the work of God in human history is taken out of the abstract and placed concretely before the assembled congregation.[52] Moreover, the physicality of Christ's presence in the Supper was something that the Devil could not assume, making the Supper a particularly powerful weapon in the battle of faith.[53] Luther could not conceive of the Lord's Supper without assuming the real presence of Christ, because the efficacy of the Lord's Supper rested on the reality of Christ's presence. Together they formed

[48] However, Luther sometimes expanded the list of "signs" for the Christian beyond simply baptism and the Supper. See ibid., 249 ("Word, Baptism, and the Eucharist" are "dependable tokens of the sun of grace"); ibid., 250 ("Baptism, the Eucharist, and absolution" are "visible signs of grace"); id., *Psalm 45*, *LW* 12.262 ("Baptism, the Gospel, and the Eucharist" are "signs and pledges"); ibid., 266 ("Baptism, the Eucharist, the Gospel, Holy Scriptures, pastors, and the gifts of the Holy Spirit" are called "promises"); ibid., 269 ("Word, Baptism, and Eucharist" are "signs"); and id., *Sermons on the Gospel of St. John: Chapters 1–4*, *LW* 22.66 ("the ministry, Baptism, the Lord's Supper, and absolution" are "agents, ordained by God to direct us to the Light").

[49] Luther, *Lectures on Genesis: Chapters 1–5*, *LW* 1.309.

[50] Luther, *A Treatise on the New Testament*, *LW* 35.86.

[51] Davis, "'The Truth of the Divine Words': Luther's Sermons on the Eucharist, 1521–28, and the Structure of Eucharistic Meaning," *The Sixteenth Century Journal* 30 (1999): 331; republished in Davis, *This Is My Body*.

[52] D. Wells, *The Person of Christ: A Biblical and Historical Analysis of the Incarnation* (Westchester, IL: Crossway, 1984), 122. That Christians meet God face-to-face depends upon Luther's doctrine of the *communicatio idiomatum*. More about this point will be discussed below. For Luther, the presence of the Word insured the presence of Christ in the Supper. He wrote, "It is the Word, I say, that makes this a sacrament and distinguishes it from ordinary bread and wine so that it is called and truly is Christ's body and blood" (Luther, *The Large Catechism*, 468). This sentiment is in keeping with the previously noted quotation from Augustine: "When the Word is joined to the external element, it becomes a sacrament (quoted in *The Large Catechism*, 468).

[53] Oberman, *Luther: Man between God and the Devil*, 243. Writing of the eucharistic controversy, Oberman states, "The idea that God is genuinely 'there,' outside the person, and can be found beyond the individual powers of thought and strength of faith is what the controversy of that time bestowed on posterity" (ibid., 245).

a unity in his mind. Tying together the various elements of his view, Luther summarized the necessity of the real presence:

> See, then, what a beautiful, great, marvelous thing this is, how everything meshes together in one sacramental reality. The words are the first thing, for without the words the cup and the bread would be nothing. Further, without bread and cup, the body and blood of Christ would not be there. Without the body and blood of Christ, the new testament would not be there. Without the new testament, forgiveness of sins would not be there. Without forgiveness of sins, life and salvation would not be there. Thus the words first connect the bread and cup to the sacrament; bread and cup embrace the body and blood of Christ; body and blood of Christ embrace the new testament; the new testament embraces the forgiveness of sins; forgiveness of sins embraces eternal life and salvation. See, all this the words of the Supper offer and give us, and we embrace it by faith.[54]

Luther's view of the real presence, like so much of his theology, was developed in the course of his controversy over the topic. This controversy must now be examined in greater detail.

The Rejection of Transubstantiation

As a Catholic theologian, Luther accepted in his early years the Catholic view of transubstantiation.[55] The first evidence that Luther was questioning transubstantiation came in 1517, in his work *Disputation against Scholastic Theology*. There Luther made clear his rejection of Aristotelianism as practiced by the scholastic theologians, stating that "no one can become a theologian unless he becomes one without Aristotle."[56] Since transubstantiation rested on the Aristotelian

[54] Luther, *Confession Concerning Christ's Supper*, *LW* 37.338. Some have argued that during the eucharistic controversies, the presence of Christ replaced the Word of Christ as central to Luther's theology (Sasse, *This Is My Body*, 104). This quotation, coming as it does in the height of the controversy over the presence is evidence that the presence always depended on the Word in Luther's thought. The presence may have been the most distinctive part of Luther's theology during this period, but it was not the most foundational (Davis, "The Truth of the Divine Words," 324).

[55] Transubstantiation is the view that, in the observance of the mass, the substance of the bread and wine are replaced by the substance of the body and blood of Christ, while the accidents of the bread and wine remain. It became official church doctrine in 1215 at the Fourth Lateran Council. See the previous chapter in this volume by Gregg Allison for a fuller exposition of this Catholic doctrine.

[56] Luther, *Disputation Against Scholastic Theology*, *LW* 31.12. McGrath refers to Luther's "total" rejection of Aristotelianism in this disputation (*Reformation Thought*, 120), but one must question how total Luther's rejection was, since he later used scholastic categories in his debate with Zwingli. I assume that the ambiguity on this point lies with Luther, not McGrath. Nuance is required here. It seems that in his *Disputation*, Luther did not reject Aristotelianism wholesale,

categories of substance and accidents, Luther's repudiation of Aristotle and scholastic theology implied a different understanding of the presence of Christ in the Supper. However, Luther's rejection of transubstantiation was not immediate, as it took him four years to work out fully the implications of his rejection of Aristotelianism. Two years after his *Disputation* Luther could still state that "the bread is changed into his true natural body and the wine into his natural true blood,"[57] a statement that seems to assume transubstantiation. In 1520, just one year later, Luther spoke of the real presence, but did not use the language of transformation.[58] Finally, the following year Luther presented his first sustained attack on transubstantiation in *The Babylonian Captivity*.

The Babylonian Captivity is a watershed work for Luther's theology of the Supper, for in his critique of transubstantiation lie several key hermeneutical principles that would come to the fore again in his battles with Ulrich Zwingli and the other Reformers. Luther's rejection of transubstantiation rested on biblical and philosophical grounds. His guiding hermeneutical principle was "what is asserted without the Scriptures or proven revelation may be held as an opinion, but need not be believed."[59] Transubstantiation was not taught by the Scriptures, according to Luther, but was a speculative attempt to explain a question the Scripture did not ask, namely, how the body and blood of Christ could be present in the bread and the wine. Therefore, Christians were free to hold differing answers to this question, so long as they did not press others to accept them as articles of faith.[60] Luther,

but only as it was practiced by the scholastic theologians. Luther rejected any theology that was done outside of the bounds of the Bible.

[57] Luther, *The Blessed Sacrament of the Holy and True Body of Christ*, *LW* 35.59. Later in this work Luther said that Christians should not worry about the "how" and the "where" of the change that takes place in the elements. What is most important is to know that Christ is present (ibid., 62).

[58] Luther, *A Treatise on the New Testament*, *LW* 35.86.

[59] Luther, *The Babylonian Captivity*, *LW* 36.29.

[60] Ibid., 36.35. Lohse points out that Luther's criticism of transubstantiation does not get to the heart of the matter (*Martin Luther's Theology*, 135). In a letter from 1524 Luther revealed some of his personal struggles regarding the presence of Christ in the Supper during the period when he was moving from the position of transubstantiation to the position of the real presence. He wrote, "I confess that if Dr. Karlstadt, or anyone else, could have convinced me five years ago that only bread and wine were in the sacrament he would have done me a great service. At that time I suffered such severe conflicts and inner strife and torment that I would gladly have been delivered from them. I realized that at this point I could best resist the papacy" (Luther, *Letter to the Christians at Strassburg in Opposition to the Fanatic Spirit*, *LW* 40.68; cf. Althaus, *The Theology of Martin Luther*, 377). This quote reveals that Luther was tempted to deny completely

always eager to bring the salve of the gospel to the consciences of men and women, advocated putting aside questions about the mode of Christ's presence and instead clinging in simplicity to the words of Christ at the institution of the Supper.

Although Luther insisted that Christians should simply trust the words of Christ at the Supper, he did offer some explanation for how Christ could be present in the Supper. In *The Babylonian Captivity* Luther illustrated his view by describing a red-hot iron in which both fire and iron are mingled together. Accordingly, in the Supper the substance of the elements and the substance of the body and blood of Christ are present intermingled.[61] Even though he conceded, "It is undeniably true that two diverse substances cannot be one substance," Luther stated that "against all reason and hairsplitting logic I hold that two diverse substances may well be, in reality and in name, one substance."[62] He likened this union of substances to the union in the Trinity and in the incarnation.[63] Accordingly, any objection lodged against his view could equally be brought against the incarnation itself. The phrase Luther used to describe his view was *unio sacramentalis* ("sacramental unity"), a more appropriate term than the more common term "consubstantiation."[64]

the physical presence of Christ in the Supper, in order to make as great a break from Rome as possible. The reason he gives in the letter why he could not go that far was the word of the institution which "is too powerfully present, and will not allow itself to be torn from its meaning by mere verbiage" (68).

[61] Luther, *The Babylonian Captivity*, *LW* 36.32. It is interesting to note that Luther employed the hot-iron illustration elsewhere to describe the union of the two natures in the person of Christ (id., *Sermons on the Gospel of St. John: Chapters 6–8*, *LW* 23.123–24). Luther saw a similarity between the union of the two natures in Jesus Christ, and the union of the elements with the body and blood of Christ in the sacrament. Lohse says that Luther did not clearly argue for the real presence until 1523 in *The Adoration of the Sacrament* (*Martin Luther's Theology*, 170). However, in *The Babylonian Captivity* Luther clearly argued for the real presence, although he did not give the extensive theological foundation for his theory that he articulated later.

[62] Luther, *Confession Concerning Christ's Supper*, *LW* 37.295–96. Lohse says, "In its theological content, Luther's view of the real presence was not so far removed from the doctrine of transubstantiation." Nevertheless, the Council of Trent pronounced anathema all who held that "the substance of the bread and wine remains conjointly with the body and blood of our Lord Jesus Christ, and denies that wonderful and singular change of the whole substance of the bread into the body and the whole substance of the wine into the blood, the appearances only of bread and wine remaining" (Leith, *Creeds of the Churches*, 435).

[63] Luther, *Confession Concerning Christ's Supper*, *LW* 37.297; cf. id., *The Babylonian Captivity*, 32.

[64] Luther, *Confession Concerning Christ's Supper*, *LW* 37.298 (cf. Lohse, *Martin Luther's Theology*, 309). Lohse points out that Luther never used the term consubstantiation, and the Lutheran view was not described as such until the 1550s, in the writings of Reformed theologians (Lohse, *Martin Luther's Theology*, 309). Consubstantiation was one of the scholastic

The Early Controversy over the Real Presence

Not long after Luther rejected transubstantiation, he had to respond to critics arising from his own camp.[65] He was caught between two apparent extremes—the Catholics on the one hand, and those who denied the real presence on the other hand. The battles over the real presence were some of the most heated of Luther's career. The first important event in the controversy was the writing of a letter by Cornelisz Hoen in 1522 that presented the case for a figurative interpretation of the phrase, "This is my body."[66] Hoen's letter was well received by Ulrich Zwingli who quickly adopted its arguments for his own view and published the letter in 1525.[67] Though Luther mentioned the issue in some of his earlier writings, it was certainly not the main focus of his work. It was not until his view came under attack from his fellow Reformers[68] that he devoted his attention to it, first in *The Sacrament of the Body and Blood of Christ—Against the Fanatics*, then further in *That These Words of Christ, "This Is My Body," etc., Still Stand Firm Against the Fanatics*,[69] and finally most thoroughly in his

positions, represented by Peter d'Ailly. Luther referred to d'Ailly in *The Babylonian Captivity* as an example of a Roman Catholic who did not hold to transubstantiation, but the Reformer did not advocate d'Ailly's view (Luther, *The Babylonian Captivity*, *LW* 36.28–29; noted by Sasse, *This Is My Body*, 103–4). Since consubstantiation properly refers to a scholastic position on the Lord's Supper, it is probably not the best term for Luther's eucharistic theology.

[65] Luther consistently held that the denial of the real presence was a more serious error than transubstantiation. In *The Babylonian Captivity* Luther primarily rejected not transubstantiation per se, but elevating it to an article of faith. In *Confession Concerning Christ's Supper* Luther said, "I have often enough asserted that I do not argue whether the wine remains or not. It is enough for me that Christ's blood is present; let it be with the wine as God wills. Sooner than have mere wine with the fanatics, I would agree with the pope that there is only blood" (*LW* 37.317).

[66] The full text of the letter is in Oberman, *Forerunners of the Reformation*, 268–76. Hoen's interpretation was not original. He drew upon the tract *De sacramento Eucharistiae* written by Wessel Gansfort (1489), and the view was widespread in Dutch humanist circles (Lohse, *Martin Luther's Theology*, 170).

[67] A summary of Zwingli's view of the Supper up to 1527 is available in his *On the Lord's Supper*, in *Zwingli and Bullinger*, LCC 24, ed. and trans. G. W. Bromiley (Philadelphia: Westminster, 1953), 176–238. This work, originally written in German, was intended as a popular-level treatise to communicate Zwingli's view to the church at large. See also Bruce Ware's chapter in this volume, "The Meaning of the Lord's Supper in the Theology of Ulrich Zwingli (1484–1531)".

[68] A list of these writings is given in the introduction to Luther, *That These Words of Christ Still Stand Firm*, *LW* 37.8.

[69] Ibid., 16. In this work Luther attributed the growing controversy to Satan. In fact, throughout the 150-page treatise, he consistently addressed his arguments and rebuttals to Satan, rather than to his opponents by name, believing that Satan was at work behind Zwingli and his compatriots. The subtitle to Oberman's biography—*Man between God and the Devil*—points to the prominent role that the Devil played in Luther's thought and experience.

200-page *Confession Concerning Christ's Supper*.[70] The culmination of the controversy with Zwingli came in 1529 at the Marburg Colloquy.

When he was pressed by the so-called fanatics to state his view with greater precision, Luther further developed his theology based upon two foundations. The first was his interpretation of the words of Christ, "This is my body" (*hoc est corpus meum*). Luther insisted on an essentially literal interpretation of these words, arguing that any other interpretation did violence to the text. The second foundation of Luther's view of the presence was his Christology. This point was derivative, arising as a necessary corollary to Luther's view of the presence of Christ.[71] Christ could be present in the Supper because His body was omnipresent.

As in his writings against the Catholics, the words of the institution formed the central motif in Luther's arguments against his opponents Zwingli, Oecolampadius, and Karlstadt. Zwingli, following Hoen's letter, argued in his writings that *est* actually meant *significat*; Oecolampadius said that the word *corpus* was meant metaphorically; and Karlstadt proposed the unlikely solution that when Jesus spoke the words He was pointing to His own body, and that they had no reference to the bread and wine. Luther's hermeneutical principle was, "Every single word should be permitted to stand in its natural meaning; no deviation should be allowed unless faith compels it."[72] Accordingly, he wrote regarding the words of the institution of the Supper,

> Now, here stands the text, stating clearly and lucidly that Christ gives his body to eat when he distributes the bread. On this we take our stand, and we also believe and teach that in the Supper we eat and take to ourselves Christ's body truly and physically. But how this takes place or how he is in the bread, we do not know and are not meant to know. God's Word we should believe

[70] Luther closed the *Confession Concerning Christ's Supper* by stating, "For if in the assault of temptation or the pangs of death I should say something different—which God forbid—let it be disregarded; herewith I declare publicly that it would be incorrect, spoken under the devil's influence. In this may my Lord and Savior Jesus Christ assist me: blessed be he for ever, Amen" (*LW* 37.372). Luther never did say anything different from what he confessed in this work, and the *Confession Concerning Christ's Supper* would later be quoted more than any other treatise in the Formula of Concord.

[71] Luther's eucharistic theology and his Christology mutually informed one another. The Lord's Supper controversy did not lead Luther to an entirely new Christology, but caused him to draw out implications and to accentuate certain aspects of his view of Christ (Althaus, *The Theology of Martin Luther*, 398; cf. Bornkamm, *Luther's World of Thought*, 108–9).

[72] Luther, *The Adoration of the Sacrament*, *LW* 36.281.

> without setting bounds or measure to it. The bread we see with our eyes, but we hear with our ears that Christ's body is present.[73]

Luther's battle over the words of the sacrament was thus a battle over language. The Reformer denied that language ever is used with the figurative sense imposed upon it by Zwingli and the others. In response, Zwingli and Oecolampadius mentioned such texts as John 15:1 (Jesus: "I am the true vine") and 1 Cor 10:4 ("the Rock was Christ"), which they argued presented a figurative use of the copulative verb. Luther responded by shifting the locus of the metaphor. He insisted on an equative function of the verb, but redefined the predicate nominative in both cases as a spiritual reality, a linguistic device known as a trope. Thus, Christ really is the true spiritual vine, and the rock in the wilderness was Christ spiritually.[74] Although Luther conceded that Scripture does employ tropes, he never saw a convincing reason why the words of Christ at the Supper should be interpreted as a trope. The Reformer further pointed out that his opponents did not even understand the terms they were using, since Oecolampadius interpreted the words of Christ as a backward trope. In a true trope the new meaning of the word always surpassed the old meaning. Such was not the case when one interpreted "body" as "sign of the body," since the body of Christ was greater than any sign that pointed to it.[75] Moreover, as Hebrews teaches, "He who has the figure of the new testament cannot yet have the new testament itself."[76] Thus, the development of redemptive history makes signs out of place in the new covenant. To assert that the Lord's Supper is merely a sign of the new testament is to revert back to the old covenant.

The second locus of Luther's debate with Zwingli was Christology. How could the body of Christ be present worldwide, everywhere that the Supper was observed, if His body was circumscribed to a

[73] Luther, *That These Words of Christ Still Stand Firm*, *LW* 37.28–29.

[74] Ibid., 37.36–38. Elsewhere, Luther says that if one were to say "Christ is a flower," the word *is* still means *is*, but the word *flower* has acquired a new meaning. See id., *Confession Concerning Christ's Supper*, *LW* 37.172. In the heat of controversy the number of metaphors in Scripture seemed to dwindle in Luther's view. The result was "to make the recognition of genuinely figurative language in the Scripture extraordinarily difficult, if not impossible" (M. D. Thompson, "*Claritas Scripturae* in the Eucharistic Writings of Martin Luther," *WTJ* 60 [1998], 34).

[75] Luther, *Confession Concerning Christ's Supper*, *LW* 37.254–55. Luther said, "When Scripture makes tropes or new words, it takes an old word, which is the likeness, and gives it a new meaning, which is the true reality" (ibid., 37.254–55).

[76] Ibid., 37.325. Luther learned this point from Aquinas (J. Stephenson, "Martin Luther and the Eucharist," *SJT* 36 [1983]: 452).

single place? Luther's view required that Christ be present physically everywhere, every time that the Lord's Supper was celebrated according to the Scriptures.[77] In other words, he held to the ubiquity of the body of Christ. For Luther this was not a difficulty, since he held to a "Word-flesh" Christology that emphasized the doctrine of *communicatio idiomatum* ("sharing of proper qualities"). Because the union occurred in Christ's person, and not merely in His two natures, what could be predicated of one nature could also properly be predicated of the other nature as well.[78] Since Christ, in His divinity was omnipresent, His humanity also inhabited all space. Zwingli's view failed, in Luther's estimation, because it divided Christ who was everywhere from His body which was not everywhere.

Luther realized that the difference between himself and Zwingli was over Christology. Presenting his own view, he stated, "Since the divinity and humanity are one person in Christ, the Scriptures ascribe to the divinity, because of this personal union, all that happens to humanity, and vice versa."[79] Here it is once again evident that, in Luther's eyes, these debates were over the heart of the gospel itself, for if Christ were not truly divine and truly human, He could not serve as Savior. Luther condemned Zwingli's view because "it will finally construct a kind of Christ after whom I would not want to be a Christian, that is, a Christ who is and does no more in his passion and life than any other ordinary saint. For if I believe only the human nature suffered for me, then Christ would be a poor Savior for me, in fact, he himself would need a Savior."[80] Only the suffering of the complete God-man could suffice for salvation. Thus, one could not speak of the actions or attributes of a single nature of Christ in isolation.

The ubiquity of Christ's body seemed to be at odds with the statement of Scripture that the Christ was at the "right hand of God" (Luke 22:69; Acts 2:33; Col 3:1; Heb 1:31; 1 Pet 3:22), an inconsistency that Zwingli was quick to point out. Luther replied by redefining the phrase. God's right hand is not a specific place, but is "the almighty power of God, which at one and the same time can be nowhere and

[77] Davis convincingly makes the case that "instead of being part and parcel of eucharistic meaning, ubiquity stands as a guaranty and explanation for that meaning" ("The Truth of the Divine Words," 325).

[78] Wells, *The Person of Christ*, 122.

[79] Luther, *Confession Concerning Christ's Supper*, *LW* 37.209.

[80] Ibid. This statement is also quoted in the Formula of Concord. See *The Book of Concord*, 623.

yet must be everywhere. . . . it must be essentially present at all places, even in the tiniest tree leaf."[81] Thus, Luther and Zwingli had differing understandings of the ascension. Zwingli saw it as Christ's removal from human space and time. Luther saw it as merely a change in the mode of Christ's presence, not a complete removal.[82]

In discussing the ubiquity of the body of Christ, Luther fell back on something that he had earlier repudiated—Aristotelian philosophy. Although it is not essential to his argument, Luther nevertheless found it helpful to use the scholastic distinctions in order to explain how Christ's body is present in the Supper. Despite deriding them as sophists, he nevertheless followed the Occamist scholastics who distinguished between three modes of presence. Objects could be present locally, definitively, and repletively.[83] In the first sense, an object is present in a circumscribed manner like a wine in a casket, in the second sense an object is present but could occupy greater or lesser space such as angels and demons, and in the third sense an object is present in all places yet without being measured or circumscribed in any place. This last mode "is altogether incomprehensible, beyond our reason, and can be maintained only with faith, in the Word."[84] The body of Christ is present in the Supper in an uncircumscribed mode, but He can appear circumscribed when He so pleases.

Luther's reliance on scholastic discussions of presence should not be overstated. As Pelikan and others have pointed out, Luther's doctrine of the ubiquity of Christ's body rested primarily on his exegetical method, not on an *a priori* commitment to a theological or philosophical system.[85] As one modern scholar of Luther says, "[Luther] finds what the terms intend are already available in Scripture. . . . For Luther these scholastic explanations are possibilities only, they propose means to an end which can be reached by other means."[86] Although

[81] Luther, *That These Words of Christ Still Stand Firm*, *LW* 37.57.

[82] D. Steinmetz, *Luther in Context* (Grand Rapids: Baker, 1995), 81.

[83] Lohse points out that Luther is following the work of Occam and Biel, but altering it by positing that the "right hand of God" is not a particular place in heaven (*Martin Luther's Theology*, 174).

[84] Luther, *Confession Concerning Christ's Supper*, *LW* 37.215–16. Earlier in this treatise, Luther criticized Zwingli for confusing accidents with substance (196), two categories that he had earlier in his career rejected along with the theory of transubstantiation.

[85] Pelikan, *Luther the Expositor*, 141. Stephenson says that Luther was careful not to base his view of the real presence on a Christological syllogism, and that the theory served for the Reformer as "an apologetic device" ("Martin Luther and the Eucharist," 457).

[86] Hall, "*Hoc est Corpus Meum*," 143, n. 65.

these scholastic explanations are not essential to Luther's position vis-à-vis Zwingli, it is nevertheless significant that he brought them up. Luther was apparently ambivalent about using scholastic philosophy, since he later at the Marburg Colloquy refused to enter into discussions about such "mathematics."[87] The best explanation for Luther's return to Aristotelianism in his debate with Zwingli is that he, like most theologians, fell back on his training when in the thick of controversy.

A final point to note in the Christological debate between Luther and Zwingli is the way each theologian addressed John 6:63—"It is the Spirit who gives life; the flesh is of no avail." Zwingli introduced this text, supposing that it served to invalidate Luther's contention for the real presence.[88] Zwingli assumed that John 6 was a discussion of the Lord's Supper, and inferred from the aforementioned text that eating the flesh of Christ profits nothing. What is important is the spiritual eating, which for Zwingli was remembering the work of Christ on behalf of the believer.[89] Luther also taught a spiritual eating, but explained the adjective "spiritual" not as referring to the object of the eating, but as referring to the manner of eating. Luther intuited that Zwingli's exegesis implied a Gnostic disregard for the body and docetism, and that the biblical concept of "flesh" was a reference to "the old Adam," not to a physical body.[90] Luther understood the biblical terms "soul," "body," "spirit," and "flesh" to refer to the human person as a whole in its various relations, not as composite parts of the person, as did Zwingli. Accordingly, the passage in question "simply means that the self-centered self is unable to reconstitute its broken relationship to God or become the principle of its own spiritual renewal."[91] Finally, instead of disregarding the physical, as

[87] M. E. Lehmann, ed., *The Marburg Colloquy and the Marburg Articles*, *LW* 38.45.

[88] As early as 1520, prior to the debate with Zwingli, Luther argued that this passage does not pertain to the discussion of the Supper (*The Babylonian Captivity*, *LW* 36.19; noted by Lohse, *Martin Luther's Theology*, 172).

[89] Note, however, that some scholars see a shift in the post-Marburg Zwingli to a proto-Calvinist view of the Lord's Supper. See Bruce Ware's chapter in this volume for evidence of this shift.

[90] Luther, *That These Words of Christ Still Stand Firm*, *LW* 37.82–83, 96. Althaus notes that "Zwingli and his followers were teaching the dualism and the spiritualism of late classical antiquity" (*The Theology of Martin Luther*, 395). The degree of anti-physicalism inherent within the Zwinglian camp is evident in Oecolampadius's statement at Marburg that "we ought not to adhere to the humanity of Christ so closely but be lifted up to his divinity" (Lehmann, *The Marburg Colloquy and the Marburg Articles*, *LW* 38.82).

[91] Steinmetz, *Luther in Context*, 76.

did Zwingli, Luther held that the physical was precisely where man and God met. Against Zwingli he wrote, "The Spirit cannot be with us except in material and physical things such as the Word, water, and Christ's body and in his saints on earth."[92] These volleys over the meaning of John 6 and the ubiquity of the body of Christ were mere precursors to the showdown that lay ahead, one that would prove to be among the most significant meetings in the history of the church.

The Marburg Colloquy

The debate between Luther and Zwingli came to a head in 1529 at a colloquy in the German city of Marburg. Philip of Hesse, a politically important German prince who had accepted the Lutheran Reformation, convened the colloquy in order to create a united federation of Reformers to counterbalance Catholic political strength. Zwingli was in favor of such a meeting, believing along with Philip that only a federation of Protestant territories could save the fledgling cause of the Reformation.[93] A first attempt in 1528 to organize a colloquy failed due to Luther's refusal to participate.[94] Luther's refusal stemmed from his belief that further discussion of the issue would do nothing to move matters forward, since he had stated his final position in his *Confession Concerning Christ's Supper*, and the Zwinglians had rejected it. However, once Philip had won over Luther's ruler, the elector John, to the idea, Luther reluctantly agreed to go, warning that the colloquy could even make matters worse.[95] Carrying with him the recently written Schwabach Articles, Luther traveled to Marburg to meet Zwingli and the other leaders of the Reformation.

[92] Luther, *That These Words of Christ Still Stand Firm, LW* 37.95. Althaus says regarding Zwingli's view, "Despising bodiliness shows that one does not take seriously the true historicity of God's revelation" (*The Theology of Martin Luther*, 397).

[93] Sasse, *This Is My Body*, 199–200. Zwingli was both a preacher and a politician, believing that the latter could serve the former. The monument of Zwingli at Zurich shows him with a Bible in one hand and a sword in his other (Sasse, *This Is My Body*, 204).

[94] Sasse, *This Is My Body*, 192. The year 1528 was a tumultuous time for the nascent Reformation movement. Germany appeared to be on the brink of religious war, with Switzerland about to follow suit; the Turks nearly conquered Vienna; and the emperor was expected to return soon to Germany and deal with the Lutheran movement (ibid., 201). It is understandable why Philip wanted to solidify political strength. It is noteworthy that during this period Luther penned his well-known hymn "A Mighty Fortress Is Our God," demonstrating where his confidence for the preservation of the Reformation lay (ibid.; translated as "Our God He Is a Castle Strong," *LW* 53.283–85).

[95] Introduction to Lehmann, *The Marburg Colloquy and the Marburg Articles, LW* 38.8.

At Luther's request and to Zwingli's objection, no official minutes of the colloquy were kept. As a result, seven different accounts are extant, all written and distributed following the event.[96] Zwingli wished for the debate to be open to all who wished to attend, but Philip and Luther disagreed. Furthermore, Zwingli desired that the debate take place in Latin since he had a Swiss German dialect, but it was decided that the colloquy would be conducted in German so that the laymen present could understand the proceedings.[97] The first day, September 30, was devoted to personal meetings between the delegates. The following day preliminary discussions were held between Luther and Oecolampadius, and Zwingli and Melanchthon. Finally, on October 1, 1529, the colloquy proper began in the morning and lasted through the afternoon of the following day.

Luther's prescience that the colloquy would do little to change anyone's views proved true. No new arguments appear in the notes from the meeting, merely a rehashing of the disputed points discussed already in print. Each side began with what they considered to be the most important text for the debate. Oecolampadius and Zwingli started with John 6 and proceeded to argue that the words of the institution should be interpreted figuratively. Luther began with the words of the institution and refused to budge from them. In fact, Luther wrote the words "This is my body" on the table at the beginning of the debate so that "he might not allow himself to be diverted from these words."[98] A discussion of the church fathers also took place. Luther conceded that Augustine and Fulgentius were on the side of Zwingli, but claimed that all the other fathers were on his side.[99] The debate grew heated at points and ended with Zwingli in tears as he exclaimed how greatly he desired Luther's friendship. The Lutherans agreed to call Zwingli and Oecolampadius friends, but said that they could not

[96] The seven accounts are recorded in English in Lehmann, *The Marburg Colloquy*, *LW* 38.3–89. Sasse combines the seven accounts into a single record of the exchange in *This Is My Body*, 223–72. The seven accounts include varying degrees of detail, but all reflect substantially the same events.

[97] Introduction to Lehmann, *The Marburg Colloquy*, *LW* 38.10.

[98] Ibid., 38.52. In one of the more intense moments of the debate, Zwingli declared that John 6 was going to break Luther's neck. Luther retorted "Don't boast too much. You are in Hesse and not in Switzerland. Necks do not break so easily here" (ibid., 38.57).

[99] Ibid., 62. This is an oversimplification to be sure. For an introduction to the Fathers' views on the Lord's Supper, see Michael Haykin's essay in this volume, "'A Glorious Inebriation': Eucharistic Thought and Piety in the Patristic Era."

consider them as brothers and members of the church.[100] Despite the attempts of Philip, an agreement on the presence of Christ in the Supper was not reached at the colloquy.

When it became apparent that no agreement was possible between the Swiss and the Germans, Philip requested that the Lutherans draw up a brief confession of faith. The resulting document was largely based upon the Schwabach Articles, and became known as *The Marburg Articles*. The attendees to the meeting agreed to fourteen of the fifteen articles. The fifteenth article stated

> We believe . . . that the Sacrament of the Altar is a sacrament of the true body and blood of Jesus Christ and that the spiritual partaking of the same body and blood is especially necessary for every Christian. . . . Although at this time, we have not reached an agreement as to whether the true body and blood of Christ are bodily present in the bread and wine, nevertheless, each side should show Christian love to the other side insofar as conscience will permit, and both sides should diligently pray to Almighty God that through his Spirit he might confirm us in the right understanding.[101]

To the surprise of the Lutherans, the Swiss agreed to sign the articles. This agreement was a superficial one, since, as Sasse notes, each side understood the articles in a different way. The Lutherans thought that Zwingli was willing to yield in some of these theological matters, but Zwingli and his friends viewed it as a political success, since the articles could serve as a foundation for common political action and fellowship.[102] Zwingli showed his lack of adherence to the Marburg Articles by later publishing them with appended notes.[103]

Two years after the meeting at Marburg, Zwingli died unexpectedly in a battle at Kappel, followed immediately by the sudden death of Oecolampadius. Luther interpreted the death of Zwingli as the judgment of God for his errant views. Moreover, Luther judged Zwingli's

[100] Ibid., 79.

[101] Ibid., 88–89.

[102] Sasse, *This Is My Body*, 275. Sasse argues that it was not merely the fifteenth article that Luther and Zwingli disagreed upon. The two theologians scarcely understood a single one of the other fourteen in the same way, and the difference between them was a fundamental difference in the understanding of the gospel (Sasse, *This Is My Body*, 278, 281). Lohse takes a more favorable reading of the Marburg Articles and thinks that several genuine agreements were made (*Martin Luther's Theology*, 176).

[103] Hall, "*Hoc est Corpus Meum*," 138. Hall states, "Each side had signed with a different intention; Luther signed what was essentially a statement of faith, Zwingli gave his signature to no more than a demonstration of a common front against Rome in which individual choice of interpretation of the Articles was of no consequence" (138–39).

motives in signing the Marburg Articles to be less than sincere, since in 1531 Zwingli published his *Exposition of the Christian Faith to the Christian King* in which he maintained his former view. Because Zwingli died with this disposition, Luther stated that he harbored serious doubts regarding the salvation of his opponent's soul.[104] Further attempts to unite the Protestant factions were temporarily successful, but in the end the political cost of the eucharistic controversies was the failure to form a lasting alliance of all Protestants.[105]

Evaluation

Regarding Luther's view of the physical sign, there is much to affirm and some points that must be rejected. He rightly realized the crucial role of signs in salvation history, and that the Lord's Supper was not just a sign, but *the* sign of the new covenant in Christ. Moreover, Luther's insistence that the Lord's Supper was intended to appeal to the five senses is accurate. It must be asked why God instituted a Supper at all. Why did Jesus not simply tell Christians to meet together and recite the words of the institution? Surely the reason is that the physicality of the Supper adds potency to the words of the gospel. It does not add to the content of the gospel, but grants greater weight to the gospel truth. Without the Supper, the word of Christ may seem distant and abstract to the worshipper. The physicality of the Supper serves to remind Christians that the truths of the gospel are rooted in historical reality—a dirty manger surrounded by cattle, dusty feet on a road in the Judean desert, and the splintered wood of a cross on Golgotha. Those who wish to hold to a Zwinglian view of the Supper must take care that they are not doing so out of a Gnostic disregard for such physical realities. Too sharply distinguishing between the deity and humanity of Christ jeopardizes the unity of Christ's person as the incarnate Son of God who accomplished salvation for humanity.[106] The Son of God Himself actually experienced the created world through His hypostatic union with the human body and soul.

[104] Luther, *Brief Confession Concerning the Holy Sacrament*, *LW* 38.289, 302. The text of Zwingli's work can be found in *Zwingli and Bullinger*, LCC 24, 239–79.

[105] Oberman, *Luther: Man between God and the Devil*, 240. In 1531 the Schmalkaldic League was formed, uniting the Lutherans and the Zwinglians, but this union would only last for 16 years.

[106] This is the error of Nestorianism.

Nevertheless, Luther's rock solid commitment to the real presence must be rejected on at least two counts. First, his commitment to the literal interpretation of the words of Christ at the institution of the Supper, though demonstrating an admirably high view of the Word of God, is in error. The Lord's Supper, being instituted during the Last Supper, surely is modeled after the Passover feast from Israel's history. The Passover meal was filled with symbolism that served to remind Israel of her exodus from Egypt, and so it would seem plausible that Jesus followed in this pattern by establishing a meal for His followers that was filled with rich symbolism. The burden of proof therefore rests on the one who claims that the language of the Supper should not also be interpreted metaphorically.

Second, the notion of the ubiquity of Christ's body must also be rejected. By asserting that the properties of one nature of Christ can be predicated of the other nature, Luther comes dangerously close to Eutychianism, that is, the mixing of the two natures of Christ such that a third nature is formed that is neither God nor man. In fact, as Karl Barth noted, it seems that the Lutheran view of the ubiquity of the body is actually a theological innovation that departs from the earlier tradition of the church, while the so-called *extra Calvinisticum* which the Reformed theologians asserted in opposition to Lutheran Christology stood in continuity with the greater tradition.[107] Even those early and medieval theologians who held to the real presence of Christ in the Supper did not express such a view in terms of the ubiquity of Christ's body. Moreover, Luther's view of ubiquity threatens to undermine the very value that he rightly places on bodiliness. For, if the resurrected body of Christ is the firstfruits of the general resurrection that all Christians will enjoy, then there is some similarity between the resurrected body of Christ and the resurrected bodies of His followers. If this is the case, then Luther's view seems to imply that all Christians will enjoy ubiquity of body in their glorified state. Such a ubiquitous body is not truly a human body at all, but rather is

[107] *Church Dogmatics*, trans. G. W. Bromiley, G. T. Thomson, and H. Knight (New York: T&T Clark, 2009), I/2, 168–69. Especially helpful is Barth's discussion of the *anhypostasis* and *enhypostasis* on this issue (see I/2, 159–71 for the full discussion). For a statement of the *extra Calvinisticum*, see Calvin, *Institutes* 4.17.30. Though Calvin himself doesn't use the phrase, the *extra Calvinisticum* came to be the standard way of referring to the Reformed notion that the divine Son is not spatially restricted to His human body (which is spatially confined), in opposition to the Lutheran doctrine of the ubiquity of Christ's body. See Barth for several passages from the Fathers that support the *extra Calvinisticum*.

a disembodied state. These concerns are sufficient to give one pause when considering the Christology that undergirded Luther's reflections on the Eucharist.

"Whoever Feeds on This Bread Will Live Forever": The Fruits of the Sacrament

According to Luther the third part of the sacrament of the Supper is the benefit it confers on the communicant, or, as it is also called, the fruits of the sacrament. The Lord's Supper, in his estimation, was a central part of Christian worship, and an indispensable element of the Christian's spiritual life. So important was the Supper in his own spirituality that Luther could say, "If some minister of a church were to deny me absolution and keep me from Holy Communion, even though it were done for some trivial reason, I nevertheless believe that I would run away in despair with Judas and hang myself."[108] What was it about the Lord's Supper that meant so much to Luther? In his writings on the Supper he mentions three benefits of the sacrament—the building of community, assurance of forgiveness, and renewed life in Christ.[109]

Perhaps Luther's most devotional work on the Lord's Supper is his treatise from 1519 titled *The Blessed Sacrament of the Holy and True Body of Christ, and the Brotherhoods.*[110] It is unfortunate that the major

[108] Luther, *Lectures on Genesis: Chapters 21–25, LW* 4.48. See also Luther's personal anecdote in *Admonition Concerning the Sacrament, LW* 38.127. Luther describes a period in which the Devil kept him busy so that he missed observing the sacrament for several weeks. Luther eventually realized the Devil's "cleverness" and quickly went to participate in the observance. That Luther thought Satan was conniving to keep him from the sacrament is evidence that he saw the right reception of the sacrament as essential to a Christian's perseverance in the faith. Too many Christians today would have difficulty imagining why the Devil would try to keep anyone from the sacrament, since in their estimation it has such little significance for the life of faith.

[109] Stephenson lists only two of these three as benefits of the Lord's Supper ("Martin Luther and the Eucharist," 458). He leaves out fellowship, which is inexplicable given the fact that this theme is most prominent in Luther's writings on the subject.

[110] Althaus writes, "These thoughts of 1519 are to be found—as far as I can see—only up to the year 1524. It is significant that they cease at the very point at which the battle about the real presence begins. There can be no question that this development restricted and impoverished the doctrine of the sacrament of the Lord's Supper" (*The Theology of Martin Luther*, 321–22). Althaus's estimation is wrong. Davis examines Luther's sermons from 1521–28 in which he finds the Word of God to be central to Luther's thought as it had been prior to the controversy ("The Truth of the Divine Words," 324–25). Davis also points out that in 1528 Luther preached again his sermon on the Eucharist from 1519 ("The Truth of the Divine Words," 337). Moreover, in 1530, just one year after the meeting at Marburg, Luther wrote the *Admonition Concerning the Sacrament of the Body and Blood of Our Lord*, in which he once again highlighted the themes he

emphases of this work do not surface in his later polemical writings, but they are at least evident in his sermons from the period of controversy. Moreover, in 1530, just one year after the meeting at Marburg, Luther wrote *Admonition Concerning the Sacrament of the Body and Blood of Our Lord*, in which he once again highlighted the themes he first mentioned in 1519. It seems that times of controversy called forth such strong responses from his pen that other legitimate emphases faded into background, although they were never forgotten.

In *The Blessed Sacrament* Luther defined the effect of the sacrament as the fellowship of the saints, focusing on the word *communio* ("fellowship"). The Lord's Supper served to assure the Christian that he is a part of the church, just as a document might verify that a person is a citizen of a city. Central to Luther's concept of fellowship are the themes of sharing and love. When Christians come together at the Table, the "spiritual possessions" of Christ and the church become common property, available to all who receive the sacrament. All sufferings and sins also become common property, and this sharing engenders love that unites the saints.[111] The church was designed by God to assist the Christian to face adversity, such as the flesh, evil spirits, the world, and one's own conscience, and nowhere is this assistance more available than in the sacrament of the altar. Luther writes that if anyone is "in despair, distressed by a sin-stricken conscience or terrified by death or carrying some other burden upon his heart" he should "go joyfully to the sacrament of the altar and lay down his woe in the midst of the community [of saints] and seek help from the entire company of the spiritual body."[112] Furthermore, the *communio* of the Supper is not merely a passive fellowship, but impels the Christian to action. It calls Christians to love one another, to help all those who are suffering unjustly, to feel the misery of Christendom, and to

first mentioned in 1519. Just because Luther did not explicitly mention an aspect of his theology of the Supper in a polemical work does not mean that he had completely forgotten or abandoned that part of his doctrine.

[111] Luther, *The Blessed Sacrament*, *LW* 35.51 (cf. id., *Eight Sermons at Wittenberg*, *LW* 51.95–96 where Luther describes *communio* as love among Christians). The idea of *communio* came from Augustine (Lohse, *Martin Luther's Theology*, 132). Davis observes that in this treatise, there is "nothing here that would set Luther apart from the Church of his day; indeed, . . . Luther articulated in eloquent fashion emphases fully acceptable to the Church" ("His Completely Trustworthy Testament," 10). Davis also points out that, although Luther never abandoned the doctrine of *communio*, it did shift in the hierarchy of meaning in the Supper, as the promise-faith theme became Luther's controlling idea (11).

[112] Luther, *The Blessed Sacrament*, *LW* 35.53.

bear one another's burdens.[113] Luther castigated those who wished to share in the profits of the sacrament but not the costs attendant to loving one another, stating that for such persons the sacrament offers no benefit. Luther illustrated his idea of *communio* with a vivid metaphor. Just as many grains are mixed to make up a single loaf of bread and many drops combine to form a cup of wine, so in the sacrament many Christians come together to make up one fellowship, holding all things in common. "In this way we are changed into one another and are made into a community by love."[114] Christians do not come to the Supper perfectly exemplifying this kind of love, but they are instructed by partaking. "This sacrament is a taskmaster by which we order our lives and learn as long as we live."[115]

Alongside this emphasis on community, Luther also taught that the Lord's Supper provided to the individual believer assurance of the gospel, that is, forgiveness of sins. The word of God came to the believer in a variety of forms, including preaching, baptism, and the Lord's Supper, but the Lord's Supper was unique in that it particularized the word for the individual Christian. In the Lord's Supper the Christian knew, not merely that Christ forgives sins generally, but that Christ forgives his sins. The troubled Christian will find that the

[113] Ibid., 35.54. It is worth noting that Luther thought Christians should partake of the Lord's Supper frequently so that they do not forget this fellowship (ibid., 35.56). Nevertheless, Luther thought that Christian liberty should rule in the question of the frequency of the Supper. He encouraged Christians to abstain if they were not partaking willingly and gladly (id., *Admonition Concerning the Sacrament*, *LW* 38.101), but also warned those who were "so strong" that they had not participated in five years, stating that such people needed it most of all (id., *Ten Sermons on the Catechism*, *LW* 51.191). Luther suggested that once a week or once a month might be an appropriate frequency, so long as there were those present who were spiritually hungry for the sacrament (id., *Receiving Both Kinds in the Sacrament*, *LW* 36.256–57), but he approved of those who might go for six months without it (*Eight Sermons at Wittenberg*, *LW* 51.94). What he primarily opposed was on the one hand the compulsion of Christians to come to the sacrament, as the pope did every Easter (ibid., 51.93), and on the other hand Christians who felt that they had no need of the sacrament (id., *The Large Catechism*, 471). Those Christians who go for a long period of time without it are not to be considered Christians, according to Luther (*The Large Catechism*, 471).

[114] Luther, *The Blessed Sacrament*, *LW* 35.58. See also id., *The Sacrament—Against the Fanatics*, *LW* 36.353, where he uses the same metaphor. Pelikan points out that the metaphor comes from the church fathers (*Luther the Expositor*, 192). It goes back at least to the second century in the *Didache*, although Luther did not know of this work. The author of the *Didache* wrote "Just as this broken bread was scattered upon the mountains and then was gathered together and became one, so may your church be gathered together from the ends of the earth into your kingdom" (9:4; in Holmes, 359). Also see the essay ("Carolingian Conflict: Two Monks on the Mass") by David Hogg in this volume.

[115] Luther, *The Sacrament—Against the Fanatics*, *LW* 36.353.

Lord's Supper is a "precious royal feast" that "benefits, satisfies, and fills a hungry and empty soul."[116] Even though Christ is present everywhere, in the Supper He is particularly present in a saving sense, so that Christians might lay hold of Him.[117] Luther insisted that this benefit of the sacrament was the greatest one. He wrote,

> Therefore, this is the primary benefit and fruit which accrues to you from the use of the sacrament that you are reminded of such favor and grace and that your faith and love are stimulated, renewed, and strengthened so that you might not reach the point of forgetting or despising your dear Savior and his bitter suffering and the great, manifold, eternal need and death out of which he has rescued you. Dear fellow, do not regard such benefit as trifling.[118]

Constant opposition from the flesh, the world, death, and Satan might cause the Christian to doubt God's goodness and care, but the sacrament served as a powerful reminder of God's benevolence.[119] Luther said that, with the Lord's Supper Christians should be content "whether there is good fortune or misfortune. For why do I fear the plague, the Turk, danger, or the death of a child? Why am I so insane when I have a propitious, protecting, favoring, and consoling God?"[120] The forgiveness of sins was a stark reminder of the tender mercy of God, and as the physical symbol of that forgiveness, the Lord's Supper graphically depicted the mercy of God toward His people.

At times, Luther went even further than this and said that not merely assurance but forgiveness itself is available through the Lord's Supper. Indeed, Zwingli pushed Luther on precisely this point, for to him it sounded like the Catholic doctrine that mere physical eating of the Supper brings forgiveness of sins. Luther responded by distinguishing between the merit of Christ and the distribution of merit. Forgiveness of sins was merited by the work of Christ on the cross, and wherever Christ is savingly present, there He distributes this forgiveness. Luther

[116] Luther, *The Misuse of the Mass*, *LW* 36.226.

[117] Luther, *The Sacrament—Against the Fanatics*, *LW* 36.326. Luther said "it is one thing if God is present, and another if he is present for you" (*That These Words Still Stand*, *LW* 37.68). D. Steinmetz says about Luther's view that the Word and the will of God are necessary to distinguish between Christ's presence and His saving presence (*Luther in Context*, 81).

[118] Luther, *Admonition Concerning the Sacrament of the Body and Blood of Our Lord*, *LW* 38.125–26. Cf. id., *Ten Sermons on the Catechism*, *LW* 51.190, where in defining the fruit of the sacrament he said, "Therefore I use the sacrament for the forgiveness of my sins."

[119] Luther, *Admonition Concerning the Sacrament of the Body and Blood of Our Lord*, *LW* 38.131. Luther describes ways for the Christian to remind himself of the opposition from these forces so that he might sense his need for the sacrament.

[120] Luther, *Lectures on Genesis: Chapters 38–44*, *LW* 7.304.

wrote, "We know that Christ has died for us once, and that he distributes this death through preaching, baptizing, the Spirit, reading, believing, eating, and in whatever way he wishes, wherever he is, and whatever he is, and whatever he does."[121] In Luther's understanding, the forgiveness of sins was communicated anew to the communicant each time he partook of the sacrament.[122] Pelikan states that Luther refused to identify forgiveness with the channels of forgiveness, as did Catholicism, but he also refused to separate them, as did Zwingli. As he describes Luther's sacramental theology, "God in His freedom might confer His forgiveness whenever and however He pleased, but men were obliged to cling to the channels which He had selected and designated 'for the forgiveness of sins.'"[123] Pelikan concludes that the best English word to describe this component of Luther's theology is "communicate."[124] The Supper communicates the forgiveness of sins to the believer in Christ.

The church father Ignatius of Antioch is famous for calling the Lord's Supper the "medicine of immortality."[125] This notion, that partaking of the Lord's Supper confers physical benefits on the communicant, was current in Luther's day, and it was one that the Reformer affirmed. Toward the end of the Catholic canon, the priest would pray, calling the mass a "healing potion," one of the few phrases that Luther quoted approvingly in his critique of the canon.[126] Luther described this benefit of the mass using a metaphor. When the Christian partakes

[121] Luther, *Confession Concerning Christ's Supper*, *LW* 37.193 (cf. id., *The Large Catechism*, 469). Compare with this statement of the Council of Trent: "Appeased by this sacrifice [of the mass], the Lord grants the grace and gift of penitence and pardons even the gravest crimes and sins" (22nd session, chap. 2; in Leith, *Creeds of the Churches*, 439). Thus, Catholic doctrine was that pardon of sins is distributed in the sacrament, a position close to what Luther articulates here. However, Luther's statement about merit must be tempered by the following quotation from *The Smalcald Articles*: "Christ's merit is not acquired through our work or pennies, but through faith by grace, without any money and merit—not by the authority of the pope, but rather by preaching a sermon, that is, God's Word" (305). The difference between Rome and Luther was not over the reality of Christ's merit, but how that merit is distributed. Disagreeing with Catholic dogma, Luther thought the merit could not be distributed through good works. The sacrament is not a good work, but a gift given by God.

[122] Stephenson, "Martin Luther and the Eucharist," 458.

[123] Pelikan, *Luther the Expositor*, 161.

[124] Ibid., 173.

[125] The statement comes in Ignatius's letter *To the Ephesians*. The full quote is that the church should obey its bishop and presbyters "breaking one bread, which is the medicine of immortality [φάρμακον ἀθανασίας], the antidote [ἀντίδοτος] we take in order not to die but to live forever in Jesus Christ" (20:2; in Holmes, 199).

[126] Luther, *The Abomination of the Secret Mass*, *LW* 38.325.

of the bread and wine, it is as if a wolf ate a sheep that was so powerful the wolf was turned into a sheep. "So, when we eat Christ's flesh physically and spiritually, the food is so powerful that it transforms us into itself and out of fleshly, sinful, mortal men makes spiritual, holy, living men."[127] Because the bread and the wine are joined with the body and the blood of Christ, this "eternal food" enables those who receive it to "live eternally."[128] The exegetical basis for Luther's understanding of the Lord's Supper as a healing potion was the Gospel of John. When Jesus described Himself as the bread of life, He also said, "If anyone eats of this bread, he will live forever" (John 6:51). Luther understood "life" in John's Gospel as a term meaning life in the fullest sense—biological, mental, spiritual, encompassing the whole man. In salvation the believer in Christ participated in the entire work of redemption, including both the death and resurrection of Christ. Just as the death of Christ was efficacious for the forgiveness of sins, so the resurrection of Christ was efficacious for the resurrection of the Christian.[129]

Evaluation

Luther provided a great service to the church by expounding on the effect of the Lord's Supper on Christians. That he wrote on this topic demonstrates that the great Reformer was concerned with more than merely obtuse theological debates, but sought to bring to every Christian the same help he had received from the Supper. Luther's emphasis on the idea of *communio* is a welcome antidote to the rampant individualism of the modern West. Sometimes the Lord's Supper is approached as if it were simply an act of individual worship, with apparent disregard for the rest of the church. This error is not helped when pastors encourage their congregants to close their eyes and meditate on their own personal relationship with Jesus. Such an attitude tends

[127] Luther, *That These Words Still Stand*, *LW* 37.101; cf. ibid., 115–20. See also *The Large Catechism*, 474: the sacrament is "a soothing medicine that aids you and gives life in both soul and body. For where the soul is healed, the body is helped as well."

[128] Luther, *That These Words Still Stand*, *LW* 37.132. Where Luther disagreed with the Catholics was on his insistence on the necessity of faith. He asserted that the Lord's Supper was not only a healing potion to the Christian, but also a poison to the one who partook of it unworthily, that is, without faith (id., *Confession Concerning Christ's Supper*, *LW* 37.238).

[129] Pelikan writes regarding Luther's view, "Where the death of Christ, conveyed through the means of grace, had granted the forgiveness of sins, there this 'life' came as a result of this death" (Pelikan, *Luther the Expositor*, 183).

to divorce the reality of individual forgiveness of sins from the reality that Christ came to die for His *church*. It is instructive that Luther, the great champion of individual forgiveness of sins, nevertheless also emphasized so strongly the communal aspect of the Supper. Following his theological wisdom, Christians should approach the Lord's Supper always with a view, not simply to themselves, but to the community of saints redeemed by Christ of which they are a part. As Luther wrote, the Lord's Supper should impel Christians to help one another in the battle of faith and to love all those around them. If Christians are partaking of the Lord's Supper while ignoring the various struggles of their fellow believers in Christ, they are failing to partake rightly.

Moreover, in his understanding of how forgiveness relates to the Supper, Luther corrected a Catholic error. As seen in the canon, according to Catholic dogma the distribution of Christ's merit in the Supper was tied to the renewed sacrifice of Christ at each observance.[130] Having rejected the continual sacrifice of Christ at each observance of the mass, Luther grounded the forgiveness offered in the sacrament in Christ's original atoning death, precisely where it should be. Those who come to the sacrament in faith, confessing their sins and trusting in Christ, find renewed forgiveness flowing from the once-for-all work of Christ on the cross.

Finally, Luther's idea about the physical benefit of the Supper is unbiblical. If in the Supper the bread and wine are not joined to the physical body and blood of Christ, as I have argued, the physical benefits of the Supper must also be rejected. The Supper prepares the believer for the resurrection by helping him or her persevere in the faith, but not by somehow renewing the very flesh of the communicant. Life in John's Gospel does mean life in its fullest sense, both spiritual and physical, but the physical life referred to does not become the possession of the Christian until after the resurrection. For the renewal of their physical bodies Christians must await the renewal of all things in Christ in the new heavens and new earth.

[130] At the end of the canon, the priest prayed, "Grant that the sacrifice which I have offered . . . may be pleasing to Thee and through Thy mercy atone for me together with all for whom I have offered it" (Luther, *The Abomination of the Secret Mass*, *LW* 36.327). See also the chap. 2 of the twenty-second session of the Council of Trent which declares that the sacrifice of the mass is "propitiatory" (Leith, *Creeds of the Churches*, 439).

Conclusion

Luther maintained much of the Catholic tradition that he inherited, certainly more than those in the Baptist tradition would be willing to keep. Nevertheless, when it came to the really significant issues, such as his insistence on the gospel of justification by faith alone in Christ alone, he courageously stood for the cause of biblical truth. Where Luther was right, he was *really* right. No matter how much they disagree with Luther on matters of liturgy, the proper use of philosophy, or the details of sacramental theology, Protestants of all types stand indebted to Luther's rediscovery of the gospel of the grace of God. Every time they partake in Christ's Supper as a celebration of the gospel, evangelicals do so because of Luther's theological reflections.

As has been demonstrated in this chapter, one of Luther's greatest insights regarding the sacraments, and specifically the Lord's Supper, was that they must be understood according to the Word of God. If the sacrament is tied to the Word, that means it must also be tied to the gospel, for the message of the Word is the gospel. Accordingly, Luther said if someone were to ask, What is the gospel? "You can give no better answer than these words of the New Testament, namely, that Christ gave his body and poured out his blood for us for the forgiveness of sins."[131] Luther was right. The next time that a child asks his parent why everyone at church observes the Lord's Supper, the best answer is an explanation of the gospel of Christ. Similarly, the next time a visitor to church is wondering what the gospel is, he should hear and see the answer as the Christians around him together observe the Supper in worship and thankfulness to God. If the gospel is central to evangelical identity, then the Supper must also be, for the Supper is nothing more than "the gospel in action."[132]

[131] Luther, *The Misuse of the Mass*, *LW* 36.183.

[132] Sasse, *This Is My Body*, 108.

THE MEANING OF THE LORD'S SUPPER IN THE THEOLOGY OF ULRICH ZWINGLI (1484–1531)

Bruce A. Ware*

Ulrich Zwingli's understanding of the Lord's Supper is often called the "memorial view." While this label for Zwingli's view is not wrong or inaccurate, it is partial and imprecise. Indeed, as we shall see, Zwingli clearly and certainly meant more by the Lord's Supper than that it was a symbolic memorial of the broken body and shed blood of Jesus who died on the cross for sin; but at the same time, he never meant less or other than this. When we see the textured character of Zwingli's view, we must marvel at both its relative richness, when compared to popular reductionist (mis?)understandings of his position, and the striking similarities he shared with John Calvin's view of the Supper when compared to that of Martin Luther or of the Roman Catholic Church.

In what follows, I will develop the key themes that Zwingli appealed to when defending his view of the Lord's Supper. While this begins with the "memorial" theme, the reader will soon see that it broadens to incorporate other complementary themes which give Zwingli's view far greater breadth and depth than is often thought. And as we put together the fullness of what Zwingli stressed on the Lord's Supper, we can see his endeavor to honor the teaching of Scripture as clearly as he can while also providing for the church what is pastorally needed for those who come to the Table wanting to meet afresh with the Christ who died in their place. We see in Zwingli nearly equal parts of biblical theologian and pastor in his insistence to uphold the view he championed with great passion, especially in his heated disagreements with the venerable, and only slightly older, Martin Luther.

* Bruce A. Ware received his Ph.D. from Fuller Theological Seminary. He is professor of Christian Theology at The Southern Baptist Theological Seminary, Louisville, Kentucky.

The Lord's Supper as a Memorial to Christ's Once-for-All Sacrifice

We begin with the theme that runs through all of Zwingli's writings on the Lord's Supper. His earliest discussions of the Eucharist come in some brief descriptions written in 1522–23. In his first disputation in January 1523, he wrote, "That Christ, having sacrificed himself once, is to eternity a certain and valid sacrifice for the sins of all faithful, wherefrom it follows that the mass is not a sacrifice, but is a remembrance of the sacrifice and assurance of salvation which Christ has given us."[1] For Zwingli, the thought of Christ's physical presence in the elements of the mass would be a violation of the once-for-all nature of that sacrifice. Surely, since the mass is not and cannot be a sacrifice, it then must serve the purpose of reminding the faithful of the saving sacrifice Christ has already accomplished for them, bringing His broken body and shed blood to their memory as they partake of the elements in the mass. In arguing this way, Zwingli had in mind first and foremost the Roman Catholic practice of re-presenting the sacrifice of Christ in the mass in an overt and deliberate fashion. But he saw Luther's view as also deeply problematic. If Christ's literal body and blood are present in the elements of the mass, one risks seeing the mass not for what it is fundamentally—calling to mind and trusting in the once-for-all accomplishment of Christ in His historical death on the cross—but rather a "new" presence of Christ's atoning work as His body is once again broken and blood spilt in the masticating of His literal flesh and the pouring out of His literal blood. Zwingli saw, then, the commemorative function of the Lord's Supper both to focus on what is most central to the meaning of that Supper while also avoiding any possible misunderstanding of the Eucharist as a continuation of the sacrifice of Christ's literal body or the pouring out of His literal blood. So, while Zwingli's main concern at this point is the denial of the mass as sacrifice, he also understands his commemorative view, as opposed to any bodily presence view, as necessary to avoid seeing the Eucharist as some form of continued sacrifice of Christ.[2]

A few years later, Zwingli took the encouragement of a friend to write out a summary of many key beliefs of the Christian faith. Thus,

[1] Zwingli, *Selected Works*, 112, quoted in W. P. Stephens, *Zwingli: An Introduction to His Thought* (Oxford: Clarendon, 1992), 95.

[2] W. P. Stephens, *The Theology of Huldrych Zwingli* (Oxford: Clarendon, 1986), 219, 221.

his *Commentary on True and False Religion* contains some of his most developed discussions on the Lord's Supper. Commenting on Paul's instructions in 1 Cor 11:25–26, he writes,

> Does not the saying, "Do this in remembrance of me," plainly indicate that this bread should be eaten in remembrance of Him? The Lord's Supper, then, as Paul calls it, is a commemoration of Christ's death, not a remitting of sins, for that is the province of Christ's death alone. For He says: "This which I now bid you eat and drink shall be a symbol unto you which ye shall make commemoration of me." And that nothing needful for the true understanding of this commemoration may be lacking, Paul, in I Cor. 11:26, after having said with regard to the bread as well as with regard to the wine, "This do in remembrance of me," explains as follows: "For as often as you eat this bread" (symbolical bread, namely, for no one of them all calls it flesh), "and drink this cup, proclaim the Lord's death till he come." But what is it to "proclaim the Lord's death"? To preach, surely, to give thanks and praise, as Peter says, I Pet. 2:9: "That ye should shew forth the excellencies of him who called you out of darkness into his marvelous light." Paul, therefore, reminds us that even unto the end of the world, when Christ will return and contend in judgment with the human race, this commemoration of Christ's death should be so made that we proclaim the death of the Lord, that is preach praise, and give thanks.[3]

That Christ provided a fully sufficient atoning sacrifice in His death on the cross, and that we proclaim the Lord's coming in our eating of the Lord's Supper until the day of His return, join together, then, to bear witness that no further work need be done. Christ's atoning work is complete. The purpose of the Lord's Supper, then, must be seen most fundamentally in its commemorative function, of remembering just what has already happened in fullness, the reality of which is attested to further by Christ's future coming in glory. As Jesus said, when you take the bread, and drink the cup—recall, both elements stress this point—we must partake of these "in remembrance" of Him.

And furthermore, precisely because the Lord's Supper brings to mind the accomplished work of Christ, the Eucharist is exactly that, an act of celebration and thanksgiving in light of all that Christ has done. One of Zwingli's definitions of the Lord's Supper conveys this theme. He writes, "We therefore now understand from the very name what the Eucharist, that is, the Lord's Supper, is: namely, the thanksgiving and common rejoicing of those who declare the death

[3] U. Zwingli, *Commentary on True and False Religion*, ed. S. M. Jackson and C. N. Heller (Durham, NC: The Labyrinth Press, 1929, reprinted, 1981), 228.

of Christ, that is, trumpet, praise, confess, and exalt His name above all others."[4] In the Lord's Supper, then, the believer principally brings to mind, relishes, rejoices over, and gives thanks for sins forgiven, sin and Satan defeated, and eternal life granted, all through the finished work of Christ whose broken body and shed blood are remembered afresh through the bread and wine which are received with joy at the Table of the Lord until Christ returns. Remembering what Christ has done, while not being itself all that is entailed in the Lord's Supper, is the essential central element that makes possible all else that happens at the Lord's Table.

The Lord's Supper as the Signification of the Broken Body and Shed Blood of the Christ of Calvary

Closely tied to Zwingli's view of the Lord's Supper as a memorial is his view that the elements, rightly understood, cannot be the literal presence of the physical body of Christ—that literal flesh and blood was broken and poured out in His once-for-all sacrifice at Calvary—but rather these elements point to or signify the flesh and blood given fully in the past. The elements prompt us to *remember* as they *signify* the literal flesh sacrificed and the literal blood shed on the cross for sinners. But the bread and wine are not and cannot be themselves this literal flesh and blood.

In his letter to Matthew Alber written November 1524, Zwingli renders with greater precision than previously his linguistic theory of signification in regard to the Lord's Supper. Here, and in subsequent writings, he states clearly that the "is" in "This is my body" is an "is" of signification and not an "is" of identification or of substance. As such, the Dominical statement should be rendered, "This signifies my body."[5] In his *Commentary*, Zwingli appealed to biblical examples of this language of signification. Following some examples in the apostle Paul's writings, he turns to other claims made by Christ Himself. Zwingli writes,

> And when our Savior says, "I am the door" [Jn. 10:9], was He a door? Yet, according to the intolerance of those who refuse to admit any extension of the meaning of verbs and nouns, He must be a door. Of wood, then, or of stone, or of ivory or horn, as in Pliny and Homer? "I am the way" [Jn. 14:6], "I am

[4] Ibid., 200.

[5] Stephens, *Theology of Huldrych Zwingli*, 228.

> the vine" [Jn. 15:5], "I am the light" [Jn. 8:12], etc., force us in spite of ourselves to allow them a signification other than the literal one. Is He a vine? No, but He is like a vine. . . . So, also, in our passage we must consult faith, and if she says that in the expression, "This is my body," this verb "is" must not be taken in its literal meaning, we must by all means obey faith. . . . This verb "is," then, is in my judgment used here for "signifies."[6]

An important basis for the need that Zwingli felt to understand the "is" in "This is my body" as an "is" of signification was Zwingli's reading of John 6, and particularly John 6:63: "It is the Spirit who gives life; the flesh profits nothing. The words that I speak to you are spirit, and they are life" (NKJV). Just how Zwingli saw the connection between "This is my body" and "the flesh profits nothing" must be made clear. A superficial connection of these statements might lead one to think that Christ's body accomplished nothing as Christ died for human sin. Nothing, however, could be further from the truth. In fact, the death of Christ, involving essentially the sacrifice of His body on the cross, did profit much—it paid the penalty for our sin and brought to us salvation, to be received by faith. So, how can it be that the "flesh profits nothing"? Simply this: it is not the eating of the flesh of Christ, symbolized in the eating of the bread, that profits, but the profit comes fully and exclusively from what that eaten bread signifies, i.e., the actual, historical, once-for-all broken body and shed blood of the Savior. Or as Davis comments, "Christ's flesh did profit something—but not in the eating of it; rather, profit was in the recollection of its action."[7]

Zwingli makes a special point about the cup being a sign of the new testament (covenant). Even though Jesus says that the cup "is" the new testament in His blood, it is clear to all that a cup or a drink cannot literally be a testament. Rather, it bears witness to that testament which is His blood shed for sinners. In this sense, the cup signifies the truth and reality of the testament enacted through the blood of Christ shed on the cross. Concerning the cup as the new testament in Jesus' blood, Zwingli writes,

> "Testament," then is used here in an unusual sense for the "sign" or "symbol of the testament," just as a document is said to bear witness, though it does not breathe or speak, but is the sign of something said or done by somebody

[6] Zwingli, *Commentary on True and False Religion*, 227.

[7] T. J. Davis, *This Is My Body: The Presence of Christ in Reformation Thought* (Grand Rapids: Baker, 2008), 157.

> who did once breathe. . . . So also in this passage the testament is the death and blood of Christ, and the document, in which are contained the subject and description of the testament, is the sacrament in question; for in this we commemorate the blessings that Christ's death and the shedding of His blood have brought us, and enjoying these blessings we are grateful unto the Lord God for the testament which He has freely bestowed upon us.[8]

So, the "document" that points to the testament is the cup that represents Christ's blood, whereas the testament itself is the blood itself spilt for the forgiveness of sins and newness of life. The elements, then, are understood wrongly and inadequately if seen to be the literal reality of Christ's body and blood. Rather the elements signify—they are a sign pointing beyond themselves to—that reality which occurred on Calvary as Christ gave up His life for sinners.

A further reason why the cup Jesus offered to the disciples could not have been understood by them as the literal new testament or even the literal blood of that testament Christ came to inaugurate is Zwingli's simple observation that "when Christ offered the cup, His blood had not yet been shed. Therefore he did not offer them the blood of the testament to drink."[9] Zwingli continues,

> It becomes clear, therefore, that this cup was not the blood of the testament, nor the testament itself, but a symbol of the testament. The first remark or proposition, namely, "The blood of Christ, insofar as it was shed, is the blood of the new testament," gains strength in this way. Christ himself explains by his own words that this is the meaning when he says [Mt. 26:28], "which is shed for many for the remission of sins." The reason or purpose, therefore of the shedding of blood is the remission of sins? It is. But the free remission of sins through the blood of Christ is the new testament, as Jeremiah 31:31 foretold, and Paul explains in Hebrews 8:8 and 9:15 and Colossians 1:14. It follows, therefore, that the blood of Christ became the blood of the testament only when it was shed for us. . . . Hence today we drink not the blood itself of the testament, but a symbol of the blood of the testament.[10]

Both bread and cup, then, signify the glorious reality of what Christ has accomplished fully on the cross. Neither should be taken as containing the literal substance of Christ's body or blood, but both should be seen as pointing to or signifying the fullness of those substances given for us in Christ's sacrifice on the cross.

[8] Zwingli, *Commentary on True and False Religion*, 229.

[9] Zwingli, "Subsidiary Essay or Crown of the Work on the Eucharist," in *Huldrych Zwingli Writings, Vol. 2: In Search of True Religion: Reformation, Pastoral and Eucharistic Writings*, trans. H. W. Pipkin (Allison Park, PA: Pickwick Publications, 1984), 199.

[10] Ibid., 199–200.

The Lord's Supper to Be Received by Faith in What Christ Has Accomplished by His Death at Calvary

In "An Account of the Faith of Huldreich Zwingli, Submitted to the German Emperor Charles V, at the Diet of Augsburg, July 3, 1530," Zwingli states,

> I believe that the holy Eucharist, i.e., the supper of thanksgiving, the true body of Christ is present by the contemplation of faith. This means that they who thank the Lord for the benefits bestowed on us in His Son acknowledge that He assumed true flesh, in it truly suffered, truly washed away our sins by His blood; and thus everything done by Christ becomes as it were present to them by the contemplation of faith. But that the body of Christ in essence and really, i.e., the natural body itself, is either present in the supper or masticated with our mouth and teeth, as the Papists or some who look back to the fleshpots of Egypt assert, we not only deny, but constantly maintain to be an error, contrary to the Word of God.[11]

Precisely because the Lord's Supper was a commemorative celebration of the once-for-all death of Christ, and precisely because the body of Christ was not literally contained within the elements of the bread and wine, those elements signify the historical reality of a fully accomplished atonement, and the "contemplation of faith" is what brings to the faithful the renewed realization of sins forgiven. Here Zwingli was insistent that no sacramentalism enter our understanding of the Eucharist. No eating bread *per se*, or drinking wine *per se*, could benefit those partaking of the elements. Only as the faithful made the proper use of these elements—i.e., as they saw them for what they really are, signposts of or pointers to the death Christ paid for all sin, for all time—only then could the faithful be led into a contemplative faith that remembers, cherishes, and trusts in the fullness of the accomplished work of Christ. Recalling, through the elements, the once-for-all forgiveness and renewal accomplished by Christ's death becomes then the soul's meditation, and through this, its faith expression.

[11] Zwingli, "An Account of the Faith of Huldreich Zwingli, Submitted to the German Emperor Charles V, at the Diet of Augsburg, July 3, 1530," in *On Providence and Other Essays*, ed. S. M. Jackson and W. J. Hinke (Eugene, OR: Wipf and Stock, 2000), 49. Stephens, *Theology of Huldrych Zwingli*, 242, writes, "The main issue for Zwingli is that Luther puts 'the chief point of salvation in the bodily eating of the body of Christ,' for he sees it as strengthening faith and remitting sins. Zwingli attacks the bodily eating of the body of Christ in effect on two grounds: faith and scripture. It conflicts with the understanding and use of faith and with the testimony of scripture."

To bring this point home stronger, Zwingli endeavors to show how foolish and self-defeating it is to consider eating the actual body and blood of Christ, but to do so by faith. He writes,

> Observe, therefore, what a monstrosity of speech this is: I believe that I eat the sensible and bodily flesh. For if it is bodily, there is no need of faith, for it is perceived by sense; and things perceived by sense have no need of faith, for by sense they are perceived to be perfectly sure. On the other hand, if your eating is a matter of belief, the thing you believe cannot be sensible or bodily. Therefore what you say is simply a monstrosity.[12]

Since the Lord's Supper is to be entered into by faith, and since the elements are meant to promote faith not to remove the very grounding or necessity of faith, it follows then that the elements cannot be the physical and bodily presence of Christ, whose literal presence would preclude true faith. Rather, as we have seen, the elements *signify* the historical reality of sins forgiven in the crucified Savior, whose *contemplation* elicits *faith* within the thoughtful, trusting believer's heart.

One can see, then, how closely tied are the concepts of the Lord's Supper as *memorial*, the Lord's Supper as *signification*, and the Lord's Supper that is to be received by *faith*. It is precisely as believers, through the tangible bread and wine, reflect upon and call to mind the reality of Christ's historical sacrifice for their sin that they are led, through this very commemorative act, to trust afresh what Christ has done for them. Commemoration, then, involves reflection, musing, meditation, which activity evokes faith in the heart of those truly contemplating what Christ has done. Therefore, far from thinking that the bread and wine in themselves elicit grace or evoke faith, rather it is what the bread and wine signify, i.e., the actual death of Christ for sin, whose thoughts and meditations bring forth a fresh expression of faith. Quoting from Zwingli on this subject, Stephens writes,

> There is, however, nothing in the bread or wine apart from the Spirit and faith "for in vain we eat the flesh of your Son and drink the blood, unless through faith in your word we firmly believe before all things that this same Son of yours, our Lord Jesus Christ, nailed to the cross for us, atoned for the transgressions of the whole world. For he himself said the flesh is of no avail, it is the Spirit who gives life." The cross remains the fundamental reality in Zwingli's thinking about the eucharist and his concern is that people should meditate on the cross. . . .[13]

[12] Zwingli, *Commentary on True and False Religion*, 213–14.

[13] Stephens, *Theology of Huldrych Zwingli*, 224. Stephens quotes from Zwingli's *Works*, II,

Or as Davis puts it, "It was not the eating itself that was tied to the remission of sin but the meditation on Christ's work, a bodily work."[14]

The Lord's Supper Contemplating the True and Full Humanity of Christ, Offered as Sacrifice on the Cross and Commemorated in the Eucharist

A fundamental conviction that drove Zwingli to reject the literal presence of Christ's body and blood in the elements of the Lord's Supper was his insistence on appreciating the reality of the full and uncompromised humanity of Christ. Ironically, Zwingli believed that it was Luther's view—the view that saw the literal flesh and blood of Christ's human body conjoined with the substances of bread and wine, respectively—and not his own that actually diminished the fullness of the humanity of Christ. A human body cannot be truly human and be ubiquitous, pure and simple. To attribute to the human body of Christ the divine quality of ubiquity or omnipresence such that the body of Christ is literally present in the elements at the mass, is to render this body not genuinely human. No, if the fully human Christ died for our sins, rose again, and now is seated at the right hand of the Father as the exalted Lord over all, then Christ literally is "there," not "here." Concerning this, Zwingli writes,

> But I return to the subject, since from that reasoning which rests upon the holy Scriptures it is established that Christ's body must in a natural, literal and true sense be in one place, unless we venture foolishly and impiously to assert that our bodies also are in many places, we have wrung from our opponents the admission that Christ's body, according to its essence, naturally and truly sits at the right hand of the Father, and it is not in this way in the Supper, so that those who teach the contrary drag Christ down from heaven and the Father's throne. For all the learned have condemned as exploded and impious the opinion which some have ventured to maintain that Christ's body is just as much everywhere as His divinity. For it cannot be everywhere unless in virtue of being infinite in nature, and what is infinite is also eternal. Christ's humanity is not eternal; therefore it is not infinite.[15]

606.22–28, 597.28–598.1.

[14] Davis, *This Is My Body*, 158. Cf. D. R. Moore-Crispin, "'The Real Absence': Ulrich Zwingli's View?" in *Union and Communion, 1529–1979*, Papers read at the 1979 Westminster Conference (London: Westminster Conference at Westminster Chapel, 1979), 28–29.

[15] Zwingli, *An Exposition of the Christian Faith*, in Jackson and Hinke, *Providence and Other Essays*, 249–50.

The integrity of Christ's humanity requires that we see the elements of the Lord's supper, then, not as literal "pieces" of Christ's flesh and "drops" of Christ's blood, but as representations of the once-for-all sacrifice Christ accomplished when He died on the cross for sinners. As Stephens writes, Zwingli "insists that to hold that the humanity of Christ must be essentially and bodily where the divinity is, is to deny the whole new testament witness or to fall into Marcionism. The charge of Marcionism is in effect a charge that the body of Christ was not a real human body."[16]

As Zwingli understood Luther's view, the real presence of the body and blood of Christ was essential according to Luther if the Eucharist is truly to offer to us Christ and His salvation. In this sense, the gospel itself was at stake in the dispute Luther had with Zwingli, as Luther saw it. Zwingli, for his part, agreed that the gospel was at stake, but for nearly opposite reasons. Salvation is not found in the Eucharist but in the atonement itself, an atonement that could only be accomplished if Christ were both fully and truly human and fully and truly divine. Although Christ had to be divine for salvation to occur,[17] He also had to be human in order to bear our sin when He died on the cross. Zwingli, then, stressed the importance of distinguishing the natures in Christ, whereas Luther moved in the direction of seeing the human nature receiving divine qualities through the communication of divine attributes (i.e., the *communicatio idiomatum*) in its union with the divine nature.[18] Stephens explains that for Zwingli, if Christ's human body possesses the divine quality of ubiquity, then "Christ's humanity and saving work are denied, for the bodily presence of Christ in the sacrament would imply that His body unlike ours can be in more places than one at a time, and bodily eating would call in question the necessity of Christ's death for salvation, as the disciples ate the Last Supper before Christ died."[19]

[16] Stephens, *Theology of Huldrych Zwingli*, 247. Stephens quotes from Zwingli's *Works*, V, 918.12–919.26, 941.23–942.7.

[17] See Zwingli's discussion of the necessity of the deity of Christ for the efficacy of the atonement, in Zwingli, *Commentary on True and False Religion*, 205–6.

[18] T. George, *Theology of the Reformers* (Nashville: Broadman, 1988), 153, comments, "At heart the basic theological difference between the two reformers [Luther and Zwingli] was Christological. Both formally affirmed the definition of the Council of Chalcedon (451) that Christ was 'one person in two natures.' Luther, however, consistently stressed the unity of the person (like the Monophysites in the early church) while Zwingli emphasized the distinction between the two natures (like the Nestorians)."

[19] Stephens, *Introduction to His Thought*, 110.

Wandel provides further insight into Zwingli's insistence on the true humanity of Christ precluding the real physical presence of Christ in the elements of the Eucharist, along with Luther's strong disagreement with Zwingli on this point:

> As Zwingli said to Luther, according to witnesses who were there, "It is wonderfully consoling to me, each time I think of it, Christ had flesh like I do." For Zwingli and Oecolampadius both, "my body" was the body that each and every human being had. Christ's body was bounded just as our bodies are bounded: finite in space and time. . . . Zwingli's argument—that the body had its own integrity which God would not alter, that its very materiality was itself theologically significant—that argument, for Luther, was heretical. It was to divide the two natures. . . . For Luther, it was inconceivable for God to have taken on a *human* body, in other words, precisely because that body was bounded, materially finite. . . . For Luther, Christ's body had to be there in the bread for the Eucharist to be materially received. And that body could not be governed by what Luther called "mathematics," what we might today call physics. Christ's body was not the same as the human body. God took on a body which looked like a human body, but was different, materially different. Physics might apply to human bodies, but not to Christ's.[20]

Zwingli found Luther's view here appalling. Its docetic overtones render the humanity of Jesus spurious, and following from this, the atoning efficacy of Jesus' death for sin cannot help but be called into question. The full and true humanity of Jesus could not be compromised, yet attributing a divine quality to that humanity—the ubiquity of Christ, as proposed by Luther to account for Christ's physical presence in the mass wherever and whenever it takes place—disqualifies Christ from having had integral humanity in His earthly life and death on the cross. For the sake of the gospel, for the sake of the efficacy of the atonement, and for the sake of having a Savior who lives a fully human life in every respect as we do—for all these reasons, Zwingli rejected the literal presence of Christ's body and blood in the elements of the Lord's Supper in order to uphold and not compromise the reality of the full and unqualified humanity of Christ.

[20] L. P. Wandel, "The Body of Christ at Marburg, 1529," in *Image and Imagination of the Religious Self in Late Medieval and Early Modern Europe*, ed. R. Falkenburg, W. S. Melion, and T. M. Richardson (Turnhout, Belgium: Brepols NV, 2007), 198, 201.

The Lord's Supper as the Spiritual Presence of Christ through Eating the Bread and Drinking the Wine for All Who Partake in Faith

In the early confrontation that Zwingli had with Luther over the physical presence of Christ in the elements of the Eucharist, Zwingli labored hard to demonstrate that the elements signify the once-for-all offering of Christ such that they do not contain the literal and physical body and blood of Christ. But as a consequence of this debate with Luther, Zwingli then began to make even more clear what had been implicit in his argument all along, viz., that although Christ was not physically present through the substance of the body and blood of Christ intermingled with the substance of bread and wine (as Luther proposed), Christ was nonetheless meaningfully present with the faithful as they partook of these elements. His presence, though not physical, was real through His spiritual presence with them as they ate and drank in faith.[21] So, while the earlier Zwingli was more inclined to deny the presence of Christ in the elements—i.e., the physical presence of Christ's body and blood as Luther insisted—in his confrontation with Luther, the latter Zwingli was more inclined to stress the very and real presence of Christ in the Eucharist. This has led some[22] to think Zwingli has held to a "bare" form of memorialism in the Lord's Supper, but this is a misreading of Zwingli's intent.

As a result, one of the most common misperceptions of Zwingli's position relates to how Zwingli would answer the question, "Is Christ truly present in the observance of the Supper when taken in faith?" Because the term "present" might be interpreted to mean strictly and only the substance of Christ's body and blood as "physically present," some would say that Zwingli would answer this question, No. And as we have seen, Zwingli surely would reject the physical and literal presence of Christ's body and blood in the elements of the Lord's Table. But if "present" can be broadened to include "spiritually present," then Zwingli would give instead a hearty, Yes, as his reply to this question. Geoffrey Bromiley writes,

[21] Stephens, *Introduction to His Thought*, 105–6.

[22] A. McGrath, "The Eucharist: Reassessing Zwingli," *Theology* (Jan–Feb 1990), 14, cites the following as an example of an "influential but inaccurate study" of Zwingli that misunderstands Zwingli in a "hostile and superficial" manner, as denying the real presence of Christ in the Eucharist: D. G. Dix, *The Shape of the Liturgy* (London: A&C Black, 2000).

> Zwingli had no intention of denying a spiritual presence of Christ in the sacrament [of the Lord's Supper]. . . . This presence certainly means that the communion is more than a "bare" sign, at any rate to the believing recipient. . . . For in the sacrament we have to do not merely with the elements but with the spiritual presence of Christ himself and the sovereign activity of the Holy Spirit.[23]

And Bromiley adds:

> Zwingli does not dispute that Christ is truly present in the Supper. What he disputes is that he is substantially present, present in the substance of his flesh and blood, present after his human nature. . . . He had no wish to deny the presence of Christ altogether, and the reality of the spiritual presence of Christ involves something far more than a bare memorialism. The Supper cannot be merely a commemorative rite when the one commemorated is himself present and active amongst those who keep the feast.[24]

So far from a bare or empty memorialism, Zwingli saw the Lord's Supper as the occasion for believers to meet with Christ, by faith, through and not apart from the very elements that signify His broken body and shed blood for their sins. Although he had labored for years to deny the literal presence of Christ in the elements, he then labored to affirm the real and spiritual presence of this very crucified, risen, and exalted Christ who communes with His faithful followers at the Table of the Lord. Stephens conveys the importance of this theme for Zwingli:

> At this point[25] he was more concerned to affirm the presence of Christ than to deny it. Indeed in the appendix to *An Exposition of the Faith*, he asserted, "We believe Christ to be truly present in the Supper, indeed we do not believe that it is the Lord's Supper unless Christ is present." In support, however, he used a text that has nothing to do explicitly with the eucharist: "Where two or three are gathered together in my name, there am I in the midst of them." He asserted that the true body of Christ and everything done by him is present by the contemplation of faith, before denying the bodily presence and bodily eating. He could even say that he had never denied that Christ's body is truly, sacramentally, and mysteriously present in the Supper. As the body is present sacramentally, it can be eaten sacramentally.[26]

[23] G. W. Bromiley, ed., *Zwingli and Bullinger*, LCC 24 (Philadelphia: Westminster, 1953), 179.

[24] Ibid., 183.

[25] Here Stephens has referred to Zwingli's writings in 1530–31 following the colloquy with Luther. These writings include Zwingli's *An Account of the Faith* written for the Diet of Augsburg, *The Letter to the Princes of Germany* written following Eck's attack on Zwingli's views, and *An Exposition of the Faith* written for the King of France.

[26] Stephens, *Introduction to His Thought*, 106. Stephens refers to Zwingli's writings in his *Works*, VI. ii. 806.6–17; iii. 263.3–265.19.

To be sure, Zwingli did not hold that the only time believers experienced the spiritual presence of Christ was in the eating of the elements at the Lord's Table. Rather, believers could enter into the spiritual presence of Christ whenever, by faith, they looked to Christ as their Savior and Lord, trusting in His accomplished work and continued grace. But the Eucharist was an especially profound "moment" of the spiritual presence of Christ as the elements themselves would bring to their minds the suffering and death of the Christ who now lives and moves, by His Spirit, in their very hearts by faith. As Moore-Crispin explains, "The believer can experience such communion with Christ at any time. But in the sacrament of the Lord's Table, even the senses, which usually distract the mind when it seeks to contemplate Christ, are brought into line and actually aid the contemplation. The presence of Christ, therefore, is felt more intimately and intensely."[27] So, in this sense, Zwingli distinguished between the *spiritual presence* of Christ, which can be experienced apart from the Eucharist, even if it is experienced most prominently through that institution, and the *sacramental presence* of Christ which is the exclusive presence of Christ coming in and through the participation at the Lord's Table.[28] As Stephens writes, Zwingli "distinguished eating Christ's body spiritually, which is trusting in the mercy and goodness of God through Christ, and eating it sacramentally which is eating the body of Christ with the mind and spirit in conjunction with the sacrament. But without faith we do not eat sacramentally."[29]

Zwingli could not be clearer that Christ is experientially present by faith when partaking of the elements of the Supper. Permit me to end this section hearing from Zwingli himself, from two different passages. In the first, Ligon Duncan cites one of the most explicit statements of Zwingli's affirmation of the spiritual presence of Christ in the Eucharist:

> If I have called this a commemoration, I have done so in order to controvert those who would make of it a sacrifice. . . . We believe that Christ is truly present in the Lord's Supper; yea, that there is no communion without such

[27] Moore-Crispin, "'The Real Absence,'" 32.

[28] It should be noted that Zwingli does not maintain this distinction rigorously. Sometimes, instead, he uses "spiritual" and "sacramental" presence as virtual synonyms. For example, in his *Exposition of the Christian Faith*, p. 251, he writes, "The body of Christ is, therefore, not eaten by us, literally or in substance, and all the more not quantitatively, but only sacramentally and spiritually."

[29] Stephens, *Introduction to His Thought*, 106.

> presence. . . . We believe that the true Body of Christ is eaten in Communion, not in a gross and carnal manner, but in a spiritual and sacramental manner, by the religious, believing, and pious heart.[30]

The second passage comes from Zwingli's *Exposition of the Christian Faith*, published posthumously in 1536. Here, he writes,

> By this commemoration all the benefits which God has displayed in his Son are called to mind. And by the signs themselves, the bread and wine, Christ himself is as it were set before our eyes, so that not merely with the ear, but with eye and palate we see and taste that Christ whom the soul bears within itself and in whom it rejoices.[31]

The Lord's Supper as Communion with Christ and with Those of the Community of Faith Who Partake, in Faith, at the Lord's Table

Because the Lord's Supper pictures in visible, physical, tangible, even "tasteable" fashion the Great Story of the death of Christ for human sin, it functions then as the means of a double kind of Christian Communion. Since Christ is spiritually present at the Lord's Table to the faithful, as we have just seen, Communion with Christ Himself, spiritually yet really, takes place. We can rightly call the institution of the Lord's Supper both a Eucharist and a Communion, because through the contemplation of faith on the elements, the believer is brought to thankful meditation of Christ, and renewed experience of the spiritual presence of Christ. But the Lord's Supper as Communion also includes the joining together of the community of faith who participate together in celebration of what Christ has done not merely for one but for all the faithful. Communion with Christ, and Communion within the community of faith—this dual sense of Communion occurs at the Table of the Lord.

[30] Zwingli, *Exposition to the Christian Faith to King Francis I of France (1531)*, as quoted in L. Duncan, "True Communion with Christ in the Lord's Supper: Calvin, Westminster and the Nature of Christ's Sacramental Presence," in *The Westminster Confession into the 21st Century: Essays in Remembrance of the 350th Anniversary of the Westminster Assembly*, ed. J. L. Duncan (Ross-shire, Scotland: Christian Focus, 2004), 2:432, n. 5, as cited in E. S. Freeman, *The Lord's Supper in Protestantism* (New York: Macmillan, 1945), 62.

[31] Zwingli, *Exposition of the Christian Faith*, quoted in H. W. Pipkin, "The Positive Religious Values of Zwingli's Eucharistic Writings," in *Huldrych Zwingli, 1484–1531: A Legacy of Radical Reform*, ed. E. J. Furcha (Montreal: McGill University Faculty of Religious Studies, 1985), 127.

Moore-Crispin expresses well this dimension of Zwingli's theology of the Lord's Table. With quotes from Zwingli, he writes,

> Zwingli applied "the body of Christ" in Paul's phrase "a participation in the body of Christ" [1 Cor 10:16] to the community of believers, who are "members of his body." Those who share in the communion bread and wine "*become one body and bread.*" By eating the symbolical bread they "certainly show that they *are the body of Christ*, that is, members of his church, which, as it has one faith and eats the symbolical bread, *so is one body and one bread.*" To reinforce this, he adds that Christ chose to give us bread and wine to illustrate this very point, "because as these two are combined each into one body from numberless grains and atoms of flour or grapes of the vine, so we come together into one faith and body. Here, then, is Zwingli's answer to transubstantiation—the transformation, not of the bread, but of the community of true believers who have come together around the bread.[32]

Communion with Christ, and Communion with one another in Christ—both senses are seen in Zwingli's theology of the Table of the Lord, in which we meet with Christ spiritually yet no less really, and we meet with one another, sharing the Table together in love in the one body of Christ. Moore-Crispin again comments on Zwingli, that "he saw the sacrament as a divinely ordained means through which Christ may manifest himself to His gathered people, and by which their unity in the body of Christ may be expressed and, indeed, increased." Communion in both senses, then, is at the heart of Zwingli's understanding and practice of the Lord's Supper.[33]

Summary and Assessment

After surveying Zwingli's theology of the Lord's Supper, Timothy George certainly is correct to say, "Such a lofty view of the Eucharist cannot fairly be characterized as 'mere memorialism.'"[34] While Zwingli's conviction was central that the Lord's Supper served to bring to mind the once-for-all accomplishment of Christ, his memorialism proved to function more as the hub of a wheel with spokes extend-

[32] Moore-Crispin, "'The Real Absence,'" 32–33.

[33] Cf. McGrath, "The Eucharist: Reassessing Zwingli," 13–19, where McGrath shows that Zwingli's communitarian view of the Lord's Supper draws from his own social and cultural context within the Swiss Confederation. This does not diminish the biblical basis for Zwingli's dual-communion understanding of the Table, but it shows parallels in his experience as a Swiss national.

[34] George, *Theology of the Reformers*, 157.

ed out, than as an island disconnected and isolated from all other reality.

At least five spokes (i.e., five other themes) extend from the hub of Zwingli's commitment to the Lord's Supper as a memorial of the broken body and shed blood of Christ. His literary understanding of the nature of the language of *signification* gave him the linguistic resources by which he could account for Jesus' eucharistic statements while avoiding Luther's literalistic reading that had numerous problems, as he assessed the matter. Furthermore, the necessity of *faith* in the partaking of the elements warned against a sacramentalist understanding of the Eucharist, showing that the benefits of the Table are reserved exclusively for those who truly trust in Christ for the forgiveness of their sins by His death on the cross. The full *humanity* of Christ was also central to Zwingli's view since the Lord's Supper pointed to that which truly effected salvation. For Zwingli, the concept of a ubiquitous human was an oxymoron. For Christ to be genuinely human, He had to be localized as all humans are. In His full humanity Christ died on the cross and rose again, and no part of the human Jesus could be contained in the elements of the Supper. And although Christ was not physically present in the elements, His real presence was nevertheless experienced by the faithful. The *spiritual presence* of Christ, particularly His sacramental presence, was manifest within the hearts of those who contemplated in faith the death of Christ for them. And as Christ's presence was manifest, the believer's *communion* with Christ and with one another in Christ was established. As faith contemplates the elements of bread and wine, it gives rise to other attributes of the Lord's Table, all of which express the more full-orbed eucharistic theology of Ulrich Zwingli.

A few comments assessing Zwingli's theology of the Lord's Supper are in order. First, one of the key issues raised by the debate between Zwingli and Luther is the question of the most appropriate hermeneutical approach to Christ's eucharistic statements, "This is my body," and "This cup is the new covenant in my blood." Luther insisted consistently and without backing down that these statements must be taken in their straightforward and plain meanings, indicating that the "is" in these statements should be taken as an "is" of identity, or an "is" of substance. Luther followed here a literalist hermeneutic. He wrote, "Every single word should be permitted to stand in its natural meaning; no deviation should be allowed unless faith compels it."[35] As we have seen, Zwingli appealed to many other such statements by Jesus and other biblical writers to show that a metaphorical understanding of these statements provides the most reasonable understanding. So, while Luther saw no reason from faith to interpret the "is" metaphorically, Zwingli saw abundant reason from linguistics to take these statements as tropes. On this issue, it seems that the vast majority of Protestantism has sided with Zwingli. Just as Jesus is not a door or a rock or a vine literally, so the bread is not literally His body nor the cup literally the new covenant. Zwingli's argument here is compelling, to be sure.

Second, the issue of the humanity of Christ, also central to the differences between Zwingli and Luther, has significant implications as well. If it is true that Luther was unable to affirm the full and unqualified true humanity of Jesus in order for the communication of divine attributes also to be predicated of that humanity, then Zwingli is correct: for Luther, Jesus was not human in the way we are human. This is no trivial matter, as the Councils at Constantinople (AD 381), Ephesus (AD 431), and Chalcedon (AD 451) made clear. The Chalcedonian affirmation that the two natures of the person of Christ coexist within Him "without confusion" shows Luther's view here to be at odds with the orthodox tradition. Confusion of natures involves either a "divinized humanity" or a "humanized deity," neither of which is possible if Christ is truly and fully God and truly and fully man. But does not Luther's view of the *communication idiomatum* posit exactly the confusion of natures in the form of a divinized humanity? Zwingli rightly resisted this view of Christ's humanity and upheld the orthodox view essential to our salvation.

Third, Zwingli rightly emphasized the Lord's Supper as a memorial of the completed and perfect work of Christ, finished in its fullness on the cross. Paul's recounting of the words of Jesus in 1 Corinthians 11 has Jesus say "do this in remembrance of me" in relation to both the bread and the wine. While other spokes may connect to and extend from this central aspect of the Eucharist, Zwingli was right to insist on its centrality. Since the Lord's Supper is not a re-enactment of the sacrifice of Christ, or a new expression of that sacrifice, it of necessity functions to call to the believer's mind the once-for-all sacrifice Christ

[35] Luther, *The Adoration of the Sacrament*, *LW* 36.281.

has accomplished. Its fundamental purpose, much as the Passover did in relation to the exodus from Egypt, is to help believers remember God's greatest work ever done, as God in Christ paid the full penalty for our sin (2 Cor 5:21).

Fourth, Zwingli's support for the spiritual, even sacramental, presence of Christ in the Eucharist seems strained. Perhaps owing to his affinities with the young John Calvin and the Geneva school of Reformed teaching, Zwingli sought to uphold also the spiritual presence of Christ for those who partake of the elements in faith. And while he affirmed this clearly, as we have seen, he did not support his views biblically here to the extent that he did so strongly elsewhere.

Finally, one can appreciate how committed Zwingli was to his own position, since he not only received strong denunciation from the Catholics, but he also did from Martin Luther, whom he respected so very highly. It is hard for most in our age to appreciate the level of criticism and public ridicule that controversy brought to the lives of many of the Reformers, and Zwingli was certainly no exception. His courage and conviction, based on long hours of biblical study and reflection, led him to hold and defend views that were not widely appreciated in his own day. His contribution to the understanding of the Lord's Supper is among his strongest influences on subsequent generations of Christians. We may be grateful to God for working in and through this committed Christian man to help all of us consider more carefully just what takes place when believers gather to partake again of the Table of the Lord.[36]

[36] I am grateful to Mr. Matthew Barrett for offering to me his gracious and competent research assistance.

THE REFORMED VIEW OF THE LORD'S SUPPER

Shawn D. Wright*

Introduction and Thesis

The Reformed tradition emphasizes the Lord's Supper in its worship because of Christ's command and for the comfort of Christ's people.[1] Christ required His people—by example and by apostolic instruction—to celebrate the Eucharist, and for their comfort they should do this. We note this dominant pastoral and assuring function of the Eucharist in one of John Calvin's simplest definitions of the Lord's Supper:

> God has received us, once for all, into his family, to hold us not only as servants but as sons. Thereafter, to fulfill the duties of a most excellent Father concerned for his offspring, he undertakes also to nourish us throughout the course of our life. And not content with this alone, he has willed, by giving his pledge, to assure us of this continuing liberality. To this end, therefore, he has, through the hand of his only-begotten Son, given to his church another sacrament, that is, a spiritual banquet, wherein Christ attests himself to be the life-giving bread, upon which our souls feed unto true and blessed immortality.[2]

Similarly, the Westminster Confession of Faith (WCF) highlights the pastoral role of the Supper in two of its paragraphs:

> Our Lord Jesus, in the night wherein He was betrayed, instituted the sacrament of His body and blood . . . to be observed in His Church, unto the end of the world, for the perpetual remembrance of the sacrifice of Himself in His death; the sealing all benefits thereof unto true believers, their spiritual nourishment and growth in Him . . . ; and, to be a bond and pledge of their communion with Him, and with each other, as members of His mystical body (29.1).

* Shawn D. Wright received his Ph.D. from The Southern Baptist Theological Seminary. He is associate professor of Church History at The Southern Baptist Theological Seminary, Louisville, Kentucky.

[1] I will use "Lord's Supper," "Supper," "Eucharist," and "Communion" synonymously in this chapter. Matthew Barrett, secretary to the Library at Southern Seminary, helped immensely in gathering resources for this chapter.

[2] Calvin, *Institutes* 4.17.1.

> Worthy receivers, outwardly partaking of the visible elements, in this sacrament, do then also, inwardly by faith, really and indeed, yet not carnally and corporally but spiritually, receive and feed upon, Christ crucified, and all benefits of His death (29.7).

In this chapter I am going to note the way in which the Reformed tradition (RT) applies the Supper pastorally. Others have given broad overviews of the tradition's view of the Supper.[3] My concern will be to show the manner in which the Supper is applied for the edification of believers. Calvin is more detailed than Westminster in his exposition, and he makes more unguarded assertions than the WCF.[4] In fact, their pastoral motivations—which are the tremendous strength of their view—lead the RT to overstate the efficacy of the Eucharist. Calvin, especially, is guilty in this regard; Westminster is more careful but still not free from fault.

One of the problems inherent in attempting to speak about *the* Reformed tradition, of course, is to define that tradition, for there are too many Reformed confessions and theologians for us to consider. Confessions—weightier than any one theologian's views—might be examined,[5] but even this task would be too large.[6] In this chapter, then, we examine the two most important sources (after the Bible) to the RT in the English-speaking world: John Calvin and the WCF.[7]

[3] See, e.g., R. D. Phillips, "The Lord's Supper: An Overview" in *Give Praise to God: A Vision for Reforming Worship*, ed. P. G. Ryken, D. W. H. Thomas, and J. L. Duncan III (Phillipsburg, NJ: P&R, 2003), 193–221.

[4] Venema argues that WCF is more reserved than Calvin in its statements regarding Christ's presence in the Supper, saying nothing, for instance, about the Spirit's role in making Christ present (C. P. Venema, "The Doctrine of the Lord's Supper in the Reformed Confessions," *Mid-America Journal of Theology* 12 [2001]: 127–28).

[5] Cf. J. L. Duncan, "True Communion with Christ: Calvin, Westminster, and Consensus on the Lord's Supper," in *The Westminster Confession in the 21st Century*, ed. J. L. Duncan (Fearn, Scotland: Mentor, 2004), 2:448–49.

[6] Helpful overviews of Reformed confessions on the Lord's Supper include B. Gerrish, *The Old Protestantism and the New: Essays on the Reformation Heritage* (Chicago: University of Chicago, 1982), 118–30, and Venema, "The Doctrine of the Lord's Supper in the Reformed Confessions," 81–145.

[7] For example, two conservative Presbyterian denominations in the US—the Presbyterian Church in America (www.pcanet.org/general/cof) and the Orthodox Presbyterian Church (www.opc.org/beliefs.html)—use the WCF as their doctrinal standard. Much recent discussion has focused on discerning similarities and differences between Calvin's and Westminster's views of the Supper. One position sees Calvin's view as better than later changes in Reformed doctrine and practice, including those reflected in Westminster. For a representative, see K. A. Mathison, *Given for You: Reclaiming Calvin's Doctrine of the Lord's Supper* (Phillipsburg, NJ: P&R, 2002). Another position sees general agreement, although it recognizes that Calvin is more speculative than Westminster. See Duncan, "True Communion." A third position argues that there is dissimilarity between Calvin and Westminster and that Westminster's view is better. See W. R. Spear, "The Nature of the Lord's Supper According to Calvin and the Westminster Assembly,"

In order to elucidate the pastoral focus of the Lord's Supper in the RT, we will follow several paths. First of all, we will note the historical context of Calvin and Westminster relative to the Lord's Supper. Second, we will observe the churchly character of the Supper. Third, the RT's view of the Eucharist itself will be delineated. Last will be an evaluation of the RT's pastoral emphasis on the Lord's Supper. Calvin especially, and Westminster to a lesser degree, detracted from the centrality of the gospel by over-emphasizing the power of the Eucharist.

The Importance of the Eucharist in the Sixteenth and Seventeenth Centuries

The Lord's Supper dominated the sixteenth century. This may seem counter-intuitive to us, for we often think that the nature of a sinner's justification before the holy God was central to the Reformation enterprise. And, of course, it was. Our problem, though, comes in our tendency to juxtapose justification by faith alone and the Eucharist as if they were two separate, isolated topics up for discussion. Justification, we may presume, was the doctrinal debate; the Eucharist was merely an issue of practice, akin to Luther's appropriation of the mass or Calvin's refusal to allow instruments in worship. They are interesting historic phenomena, but not at the heart of Protestantism. But to view the Lord's Supper debates as simply a debate about *adiaphora* is to miss the centrality of the doctrinal-practical concerns that revolved around the Supper in the sixteenth and seventeenth centuries. Before we attempt to understand the *what* of the Reformed discussion of the Supper, we must try to understand *why* it mattered.

In the first place, we need to remember that the Eucharist was central to medieval piety. Indeed, according to Robert Godfrey, "The sacraments stood at the center of the worship and life of the medieval church."[8] What had been central to the Reformers' piety when they were Catholics affected their thinking about the Supper. One does not wake up one morning a Protestant and immediately leave all his Catholic upbringing behind. Some modern expositors of the

and id., "Calvin and Westminster on the Lord's Supper: Exegetical and Theological Considerations," in Duncan, *The Westminster Confession in the 21st Century*, 3:355–84 and 3:385–414. Of these three options, I believe that Spear's evaluation is the best.

[8] W. R. Godfrey, "Calvin, Worship, and the Sacraments: *Institutes* 4.13–19," in *A Theological Guide to Calvin's Institutes: Essays and Analysis*, ed. D. W. Hall and P. A. Lillback (Phillipsburg, NJ: P&R, 2008), 372.

Reformed tradition have asked how much Calvin's Catholic eucharistic upbringing influenced his subsequent exposition of the Supper.[9] Regardless of how one answers that question, the Supper dominated sixteenth-century discussions. According to Brian Gerrish, "No theological theme, not even justification, was more keenly debated in the Reformation era than the meaning of the central Christian rite, variously called, 'the Eucharist,' 'the Mass,' 'the Sacrament of the Altar,' 'the Breaking of Bread,' 'Holy Communion,' or 'the Lord's Supper.'"[10]

The doctrine of the Lord's Supper could not be isolated from a whole host (forgive the pun!) of other doctrines that were intricately linked to it. On the one hand, the Eucharist was related to fundamental issues of Christian piety. It was a major picture of God's grace to believers—in saving them, in accommodating Himself to their limitations, in visibly portraying His promises to them, in spiritually nourishing them, in assuring them of His continued love for them, in their experience of His fatherly concern for their good, and in their ongoing communion with the body of the risen Christ. More than that, one's doctrine of the Supper is closely connected with several other major doctrines that are of paramount importance in Christian theology. How one views the Bible, who Jesus is in His divinity and humanity, what the church is, how one is saved—all of these questions are wrapped up in a church's doctrine of the Lord's Supper.[11] This is essential for us to understand. What Timothy George noted about Luther and Zwingli we can apply to Calvin as well: "The very essence of the gospel was at stake in the debate over the supper. They were not merely arguing over words or being stubborn."[12] Thomas Davis has noted this well:

> From a modern point of view, the eucharistic controversies of the sixteenth century seem unchristian. Yet that is exactly part of the problem; for the participants, those controversies were about what it meant to be a Christian, how to worship as a Christian, how to live in the world as a Christian. Indeed,

[9] E.g., Duncan, "True Communion," 473; Spear, "Nature of the Lord's Supper," 357.

[10] B. A. Gerrish, "Eucharist," in *The Oxford Encyclopedia of the Reformation*, ed. H. J. Hillerbrand (New York: Oxford University Press, 1996), 2:71–72. Cf. Scott Clark: "Who should participate in the Lord's Supper and how they should do it were two of the most hotly contested questions of the sixteenth-century Reformation" (R. S. Clark, "The Evangelical Fall from the Means of Grace: The Lord's Supper," in *The Compromised Church: The Present Evangelical Crisis*, ed. J. H. Armstrong [Wheaton: Crossway, 1998], 134).

[11] D. J. Engelsma, "Martin Bucer's 'Calvinistic' Doctrine of the Lord's Supper," *Mid-America Journal of Theology* 3.2 (1987): 170–71.

[12] T. George, *Theology of the Reformers* (Nashville: Broadman, 1988), 145.

> what one finds is that Eucharistic theology was not simply about church ritual but, rather, it was about who God is, how God operates, how humanity is saved, where God might be found, what the Christian's duty is to others, and so forth. In other words, the Eucharist was a topic so wound up in Christian faith, doctrine, and practice that it impinged on all the important themes of Christianity.[13]

The Lord's Supper was central because it concerned matters of piety and doctrine essential to being a Christian.

John Calvin (1509–64) served as a pastor in Geneva (1536–38, 1541–64) well after Luther and Zwingli disagreed with each other at Marburg in 1529. Willem van't Spijker has noted that Calvin's goal was to chart a *via media* between Lutherans and Zwinglians and thus "prevent a new controversy over the Lord's Supper."[14] On the one side stood Luther and his followers who believed "the great error of Rome" was "the doctrine of Eucharistic sacrifice and turning the Supper into a human work rather than a divine gift." Zwingli's followers, on the other side, saw Rome's great error to be "the doctrine of transubstantiation and the idolatry of bread and wine that flowed from it."[15] These two vantage points led to distinct emphases. The Lutherans stressed the objective gift of God in the Eucharist; the Zwinglians emphasized that the meal was a memorial of Christ's cross work since Christ was in heaven. Calvin had affinities for both these views, believing they "were not fundamentally different" and trying "tirelessly to bring the two sides together."[16] His doctrine was closer to Luther's than to Zwingli's.[17]

[13] T. J. Davis, *This Is My Body: The Presence of Christ in Reformation Thought* (Grand Rapids: Baker, 2008), 13–14.

[14] W. van't Spijker, *Calvin: A Brief Guide to His Life and Thought*, trans. L. D. Bierma (Louisville: Westminster John Knox, 2009), 118–19. This is the common view. See, e.g., Gerrish, who calls Calvin's a "mediating position" ("Eucharist," 2:76), and A. E. McGrath, *Reformation Thought: An Introduction*, 3rd ed. (Malden, MA: Blackwell, 1999), 191.

[15] Godfrey, "Calvin, Worship, and the Sacraments," 372.

[16] Ibid. Janse suggests that Calvin's views were not stable but underwent change over time, sometimes reflecting a desire to move closer to the Zwinglians and other times trying to bridge the gap with the Lutherans (W. Janse, "The Sacraments," trans. G. W. Sheeres, in *The Calvin Handbook*, ed. H. J. Selderhuis [Grand Rapids: Eerdmans, 2009], 344–45, 352). Janse explicitly disagrees with Gerrish (Janse, "Sacraments," 346–46). Godfrey notes that Calvin believed that "two errors must be avoided. One error, that of the radical Zwinglians in his day, gave too little meaning and power to the sacraments. The other, the dominant error of Calvin's day [i.e., the Lutheran view] and of the medieval church, gave too much power to the sacraments" ("Calvin, Worship, and the Sacraments," 372–73). Anthony Lane provocatively argues that Calvin's heart was more Lutheran while his head was more Zwinglian (A. N. S. Lane. "Was Calvin a Crypto-Zwinglian?" in *Adaptations of Calvinism in Reformation Europe: Essays in Honour of Brian G. Armstrong*, ed. M. P. Holt, St. Andrews Studies in Reformation History [Burlington, VT: Ashgate, 2007], 41).

[17] This is the common view. See, e.g., Clark, "Evangelical Fall," 134; Godfrey, "Calvin,

The Westminster Assembly in England (1643–52) was a grand Puritan project to finally make the church in England wholly Reformed by writing a confessional statement that was wholeheartedly Calvinistic, and by creating a liturgy that reflected the tradition of Geneva instead of the pseudo-Catholicism of the Church of England's *Book of Common Prayer*. The result was an impressive doctrinal summation including the WCF approved by parliament in 1647, and the Larger Catechism (WLC) and Shorter Catechism (WSC), both of which were approved in 1648. Liturgically, the assembly produced the Directory for the Public Worship of God (1645). The Puritan situation was very different from Calvin's, not only in time but also in culture. The main opponents, sacramentally, to the Assembly were Catholics, whose presence was always feared by English Protestants. Apparently, though, the representatives at Westminster were not much concerned with opposing the details of Lutheran or memorialistic thought.[18] If nothing else, this fact makes the Westminster documents more direct in their exposition than Calvin's polemic-saturated writings.[19]

Worship, and the Sacraments," 383–84; I. J. Hesselink, "Reformed View: The Real Presence of Christ," in *Understanding Four Views on the Lord's Supper*, ed. J. H. Armstrong (Grand Rapids: Zondervan, 2007), 62–63; Lane, "Was Calvin a Crypto-Zwinglian?" 21–23; P. J. Leithart, "What's Wrong with Transubstantiation? An Evaluation of Theological Models," *WTJ* 53 (1991): 318; D. C. Steinmetz, *Calvin in Context* (New York: Oxford University Press, 1995), 172, 176–77. As Davis has noted, "What Calvin said he experienced in the eucharistic celebration, the presence of Christ, even when that had to do with the matter of the ascended Christ's body, sounds closer to Luther than to Zwingli. He experienced Christ bodily" (*This Is My Body*, 137). We should note, however, that Calvin's proximity to Luther's view was not, and is not, satisfying to Lutherans who saw Calvin as being more memorialist due to his denial of the bodily presence of Christ in the Eucharist. On this, see Duncan, "True Communion," 430; Lane, "Was Calvin a Crypto-Zwinglian?" 25; Hesselink, "Reformed View," 76–77. More could be said about the historical character of Calvin's doctrine, especially the important place of the *Consensus Tigurinus* (1549). On this see, e.g., T. George, "John Calvin and the Agreement of Zurich (1549)," in *John Calvin and the Church: A Prism of Reform*, ed. T. George (Louisville: Westminster/John Knox, 1990), 42–58; P. Rorem, "The Consensus Tigurinus (1549): Did Calvin Compromise?" in *Calvinus Sacrae Scripturae Professor*, ed. W. H. Neuser (Grand Rapids: Eerdmans, 1994), 72–90.

[18] Spear ("Calvin and Westminster," 400–408) overviews the eucharistic theology of four Westminster divines. To see the way in which a Puritan pastor in the Westminster tradition applied WCF's doctrine to bring assurance to his congregation, see J. Flavel, *Sacramental Meditations Upon Divers Select Places of Scripture: wherein Believers are assisted in preparing their Hearts, and exciting their Affections and Graces, when they draw nigh to God in that most awful and solemn Ordinance of the Lord's Supper*, in *The Works of John Flavel* (1820; rpt. Carlisle, PA: Banner of Truth, 1968), 6:328–460.

[19] For helpful overviews of the historical context of the Westminster assembly see R. S. Paul, *The Assembly of the Lord: Politics and Religion in the Westminster Assembly and the "Grand Debate"* (Edinburgh: T&T Clark, 1985); R. Letham, *The Westminster Assembly: Reading Its Theology in Historical Context* (Phillipsburg, NJ: P&R, 2009), 11–98.

The Church: The Boundary of the Eucharist

The church is paramount to the RT, and no more so than in its role to administer God's grace to His people. Regarding the Lord's Supper, we note three important ecclesiastical matters. The first concerns the role of the church in edifying and sustaining believers on their earthly pilgrimage. The other two concern how the church is to edify Christians through the Lord's Supper: the Supper as a "means of grace" and the Supper as a "sacrament." These three emphases highlight the ecclesiastical and pastoral character of the Eucharist in the RT.

The Church's Role in Edifying and Sustaining Christians

First, the church as a mother protects and nourishes her children. So Calvin says, "There is no other way to enter into life unless this mother [i.e., the church] conceive us in her womb, give us birth, nourish us at her breast, and lastly, unless she keep us under her care and guidance until, putting off mortal flesh, we become like the angels. Our weakness does not allow us to be dismissed from her school until we have been pupils all our lives."[20] Due to the weakness of our flesh, and also because of the spiritual battle that constantly rages around believers, God has graciously given us means to be encouraged in our faith, to keep us walking with Christ.[21] One of the most significant of these means is the church. The church, through its ministries, was designed to nourish and support Christians during their pilgrimage to heaven.[22]

The WCF also prioritizes the church, calling it "the kingdom of the Lord Jesus Christ, the house and family of God, out of which there is no ordinary possibility of salvation."[23] The Lord gives the church means to aid Christians on their quest for heaven. To the church

[20] Calvin, *Institutes* 4.1.4. I have decided to limit my interaction with Calvin to his *magnum opus*, the final 1559 edition of the *Institutio*. Much more could, and should, be said about Calvin's views. See R. A. Muller, *The Unaccommodated Calvin: Studies in the Foundation of a Theological Tradition* (Oxford: Oxford University Press, 2000). For the best short summary by Calvin himself, see his 1540 *Short Treatise on the Supper of our Lord* in *Selected Works of John Calvin: Tracts and Treatises*, ed. and trans. H. Beveridge (1849; rpt. Grand Rapids: Baker, 1983), 2:163–98. M. E. Osterhaven summarizes the *Short Treatise* well in "Eating and Drinking Christ: The Lord's Supper as an Act of Worship in the Theology and Practice of Calvin," *RefR* 37.2 (1984): 85.

[21] See my "John Calvin as Pastor," *SBJT* 13.4 (2009): 4–17.

[22] The church and the Lord's Supper are bound closely together in Reformed thought. See R. N. Gleason, "Calvin and Bavinck on the Lord's Supper," *WTJ* 45 (1983): 274.

[23] WCF 25.2.

"Christ hath given the ministry, oracles, and ordinances of God, for the gathering and perfecting of the saints in this life to the end of the world; and doth by His own presence and Spirit, according to His promise, make them effectual thereunto."[24] Pastors, the preaching of the gospel, and the ordinances of baptism and the Eucharist are God's means of perfecting His people because they are Christ's effectual means, through the ministry of the Spirit, of communicating His presence to believers.

The Lord's Supper as a "Means of Grace"

Second, the RT identifies the Lord's Supper as a "means of grace." Louis Berkhof explains,

> Strictly speaking, only the Word and the sacraments can be regarded as means of grace, that is, as objective channels which Christ has instituted in the Church, and to which He ordinarily binds Himself in the communication of His grace. Of course these may never be dissociated from Christ, nor from the powerful operation of the Holy Spirit, nor from the Church which is the appointed organ for the distribution of the blessings of divine grace. They are in themselves quite ineffective and are productive of spiritual results only through the efficacious operation of the Holy Spirit.[25]

Christ works through these means to give grace to His people. Power does not flow from the word or the sacrament per se, but through the powerful operation of His Spirit who communicates God's grace to His people through them.[26]

Westminster defines these means in WLC, question 154: "The outward and ordinary means whereby Christ communicates to his church the benefits of his redemption are all his ordinances; especially the word, sacraments, and prayer, all which are made effectual to the elect for their salvation."[27] In this tradition Robert Reymond has delineated

[24] WCF 25.3.

[25] L. Berkhof, *Systematic Theology* (Grand Rapids: Eerdmans, 1984), 604–5. See also H. Bavinck, *Reformed Dogmatics, Vol. 4: Holy Spirit, Church, and New Creation*, trans. J. Vriend (Grand Rapids: Baker, 2008), 541. As travelers on our earthly journey, we need grace to keep pursuing Christ. The Supper is one of those means, a gracious gift of God to keep us pursuing Christ because it communicates more of Christ's reality to us.

[26] For Calvin's view of the Supper as a "means of grace," see Spear, "Nature of the Lord's Supper," 364.

[27] Hodge noted that "means of grace" indicates "those institutions which God has ordained to be the ordinary channels of grace, i.e., of the supernatural influences of the Holy Spirit, to the souls of men. The means of grace, according to the standards of our Church, are the word, sacraments, and prayer" (C. Hodge, *Systematic Theology* [Grand Rapids: Eerdmans, 1986], 3:466).

three aspects of means of grace.[28] First, they are God's special grace to His elect; they do not refer to His common grace for all persons. Second, God is the efficient cause of grace in these means. All *ex opere operato* notions in which the act itself mechanically brings grace must be eschewed.[29] God, not the means, is the author and bestower of grace. Third, although the means of the sacraments is very important to healthy Christian living, they are not so essential that saving grace is unavailable apart from them.[30] We see here the pastoral focus on the Supper in the RT. It is one of God's ordained means to be gracious to His people and draw them close to Himself.

Definition of Sacraments

Third, now we are in the position to examine the RT's view of the sacraments.[31] John Calvin stood in a long ecclesiastical tradition in his efforts to understand the significance of Christ's two ordinances. Rather than create a new understanding of "sacrament," Calvin had recourse to the formative Augustine who called a sacrament "a visible sign of a sacred thing" or "a visible form of an invisible grace."[32] Since he thought that Augustine's brevity might lead to misunderstanding, Calvin offered two "simple and proper" definitions of a "sacrament." First, it could be considered "an outward sign by which the Lord seals on our consciences the promises of his good will toward us and we in turn attest our piety toward him in the presence of the Lord and of his angels and before men." Or more briefly it might be labeled simply "a

[28] Reymond began his discussion of means of grace with this apology: "Just as [a Christian's] physical body requires nutritious food to grow physically, so also he needs spiritual food to grow spiritually. This spiritual 'food' that God has provided for the Christian's growth in grace theologians refer to as the 'means of grace'" (R. Reymond, *A New Systematic Theology of the Christian Faith* [Nashville: Thomas Nelson, 1998], 911).

[29] For a helpful discussion of the meaning of *ex opere operato* see R. A. Muller, *Dictionary of Latin and Greek Theological Terms: Drawn Principally from Protestant Scholastic Theology* (Grand Rapids: Baker, 1985), 108.

[30] Reymond, *New Systematic Theology*, 913.

[31] Godfrey argues that Calvin's doctrine of the sacraments was "not inherently difficult to understand, but so many alternative theologies had to be analyzed and answered that the subject as a whole became difficult" ("Calvin, Worship, and the Sacraments," 373). This may be true, for we have already noted how central the Eucharist was in the sixteenth century. But it seems one could argue in this way about other aspects of Calvin's theology, which, though occasional, are more lucid. If Calvin is opaque on the sacraments, it may just be because he was opaque.

[32] Calvin, *Institutes* 4.14.1. See G. R. Evans, "Calvin on Signs: An Augustinian Dilemma," *Renaissance Studies* 3 (1989): 35–45; J. Fitzer, "The Augustinian Roots of Calvin's Eucharistic Thought," *Augustinian Studies* 7 (1976): 69–98.

testimony of divine grace toward us, confirmed by an outward sign, with mutual attestation of our piety toward him."[33]

Three elements of Calvin's definition merit our attention. First, we must note the outward character of sacraments. Sacraments are not primarily about one's personal dedication of heart and life to Jesus. They are external, earthy, and real things that one can see and touch.[34] Second, a sacrament is useful because in it specifically God promises to do something through the agency of the Holy Spirit.[35] Foremost, in it God graciously does something for us, sealing on our consciences the promise of His good will toward us in order to sustain the weakness of our faith. In this sense, a sacrament cannot be separated from the word of the gospel that explains it.[36] This truth—that God will be our God in Christ—is sealed to believers' experience when they partake of the sacraments.[37] Third, believers must respond to sacraments in faith. By receiving the sacrament a Christian attests his piety, expressing his love and trust in God his Father.[38]

WCF also stresses the importance of the sacraments, which it defines as "holy signs and seals of the covenant of grace, immediately instituted by God" for four reasons. They are, first, "to represent Christ and His benefits" to us. Second, they "confirm our interest in Him." Third, they visibly distinguish between believers and unbelievers.

[33] Calvin, *Institutes* 4.14.1.

[34] In this sense, Calvin refers to a sacrament as a "token" of God's covenant with His people; they are "exercises which make us more certain of the trustworthiness of God's Word," or, quoting Augustine, "a visible word" (*Institutes* 4.14.6). "Calvin's theology is . . . a theology of the Sacrament. God will not encounter man directly but by means of that which is already a human term of reference, the human means of communication and visible symbols" (T. H. L. Parker, *John Calvin: A Biography* [Philadelphia: Westminster, 1975], 42).

[35] On the role of the Holy Spirit in making the sacrament a reality see Godfrey, "Calvin, Worship, and the Sacraments," 375–76; Hesselink, "Reformed View," 61.

[36] "The sacrament requires preaching to beget faith" (Calvin, *Institutes* 4.14.4). On the priority of the word, see Godfrey, "Calvin, Worship, and the Sacraments," 375; T. Hart, "Calvin and Barth on the Lord's Supper," in *Calvin, Barth, and Reformed Theology*, ed. N. B. MacDonald and C. Trueman, Paternoster Theological Monographs (Milton Keynes, UK: Paternoster, 2008), 41.

[37] "The promise is sealed by the sacraments. . . . The sacraments bring the clearest promises; and they have this characteristic over and above the word because they represent them for us as painted in a picture from life" (Calvin, *Institutes* 4.14.5). On sign and seal in Calvin's sacramental theology see R. S. Wallace, *Calvin's Doctrine of the Word and Sacraments* (Edinburgh: Oliver and Boyd, 1953), 133–42.

[38] On the necessity of faith to receive the sacraments see Godfrey, "Calvin, Worship, and the Sacraments," 375; Hesselink, "Reformed View," 61. Much of Calvin's theology, I think, can be understood as an effort to promote God-honoring piety among Christians. See J. R. Beeke, "Calvin on Piety," in *The Cambridge Companion to John Calvin*, ed. D. K. McKim (New York: Cambridge University Press, 2004), 125–52.

Fourth, they engage believers to work in "the service of God in Christ, according to His Word."[39] In addition, WCF premises that "There is, in every sacrament, a spiritual relation, or sacramental union, between the sign and the thing signified" so that "the names and effects of the one are attributed to the other."[40] In other words, the element of the sacrament is so united with Christ that when one takes the Eucharist one is actually communing with Christ due to the "spiritual relation" between Him and the sacrament. Sean Lucas explains that "there is a spiritual relationship between Christ's ascended and glorified body and the bread by which we are enabled, by God's grace and his Spirit, to feed upon Christ's presence and receive his benefits."[41]

Here we encounter a pastoral tension in the RT. On the one hand, Calvin and the tradition stress the objective, grace-giving work of God by means of the sacraments. As Calvin argued, sacraments are fundamentally testimonies "of divine grace toward us, confirmed by an outward sign."[42] Thus Michael Horton avers,

> The sacraments were instituted by God chiefly as means of grace. Whatever other blessings may result from their lawful use, this must be recognized as their principal object: to convey Christ and all his benefits to poor sinners who every hour depend on the continuing intercession of the Savior so that their faith will not fail. Faith is weak, not strong, in the believer. It therefore needs to be regularly nourished by the means of grace which God alone has prescribed for that benefit.[43]

As promises of the grace of God and as manifestations of the presence of Christ to believers, sacraments objectively bring grace to Christians.[44] On the other hand, though, in receiving the sacraments believers subjectively exercise faith. So, sacraments are "exercises of piety" which "foster our faith, strengthen it, and help us offer ourselves as a living sacrifice to God."[45] The end result of receiving the sacraments, then, "is found in one's advancing in communion with Christ."[46]

[39] WCF 27.1.

[40] WCF 27.2.

[41] S. M. Lucas, *On Being Presbyterian: Our Beliefs, Practices, and Stories* (Phillipsburg, NJ: P&R, 2006), 84.

[42] Calvin, *Institutes* 4.14.1.

[43] M. S. Horton, "At Least Weekly: The Reformed Doctrine of the Lord's Supper and Its Frequent Celebration," *Mid-America Journal of Theology* 11 (2000): 162–63. Cf. Duncan, "True Communion," 470.

[44] See Janse, "Sacraments," 346–48.

[45] Beeke, "Calvin on Piety," 133–34.

[46] Van't Spijker, *Calvin*, 141.

This objective-subjective tension is seen in the "signing" and "sealing" functions of the sacraments. The Eucharist is first of all a "sign" of God's gracious goodwill to His people. God sends it to us due to our dullness and ignorance. The Lord gave the church sacraments as a means of accommodating Himself to our limitations so that we might better know and experience His fatherly care for us in Christ. Calvin says this explicitly:

> Our merciful Lord, according to his infinite kindness, so tempers himself to our capacity that, since we are creatures who always creep on the ground, cleave to the flesh, and, do not think about or even conceive of anything spiritual, he condescends to lead us to himself even by these earthly elements, and to set before us in the flesh a mirror of spiritual blessings . . . because we have souls engrafted in bodies, he imparts spiritual things under visible ones. Not that the gifts set before us in the sacraments are bestowed with the natures of the things, but that they have been marked with this signification by God.[47]

The net result of receiving the sacraments is that our faith is strengthened and we are fortified to continue on our pilgrimage.[48]

Sacraments also "seal" God's grace in the experience of Christians. Calvin argues that they "are truly named the testimonies of God's grace and are like seals of the good will that he feels toward us, which by attesting that good will to us, sustain, nourish, confirm, and increase our faith."[49] The sacraments are empty by themselves. But they function to verify the promises God gives us in the gospel. So, says Calvin, "the promise is sealed by the sacraments."[50] The sacraments do not seal apart from the word, but they make the word plainer to us; we do not just hear of God's love, but we also see it. Thus Calvin

[47] Calvin, *Institutes* 4.14.3. See Hart, "Calvin and Barth," 38. Beeke has well noted that sacraments "minister to our weakness by personalizing the promises for those who trust Christ for salvation" (Beeke, "Calvin on Piety," 135).

[48] Note Godrey's discussion of the increase of faith (Godfrey, "Calvin, Worship, and the Sacraments," 375). As T. H. L. Parker argues, for Calvin, "in the Sacraments God accommodates himself to our grasp, 'leads us down in the same fleshly elements—to himself! And makes us behold in the very flesh—the things of the Spirit!' The sole office of the Sacraments is to turn our eyes to beholding God's promises; that is, they make the Word perceptible to other senses than the ears" (*John Calvin*, 42).

[49] Calvin, *Institutes* 4.14.7. Gerrish argues that Calvin's tack was "to interpret the sacramental signs as bearers of the reality they signify. . . . Christ once gave his body to be crucified: he gives it to us daily, and in the Supper he inwardly fulfills what he outwardly signifies" (B. A. Gerrish, "The Place of Calvin in Christian Theology," in *The Cambridge Companion to John Calvin*, ed. D. K. McKim [New York: Cambridge University Press, 2004], 298–99).

[50] Calvin, *Institutes* 4.14.5.

can even claim that "the sacraments bring the clearest promises; and they have this characteristic over and above the word because they represent them for us as painted in a picture from life."[51]

WCF also emphasizes the "sign" and "seal" character of sacraments. Lucas notes that a sacrament "pictures or *signs* God's promises." Specifically, it points us to Christ, directing us "to the one who is the savior of our souls."[52] Lucas suggests, then, that the sacrament has no inherent power but rather serves as a pointer, leading us to look away from it to Christ. A sacrament also "seals" God's promises and in so doing "gives you confidence that his promises can be trusted." This assurance-producing effect of sacraments leads us to "confirm our interest in God and his promises."[53]

Intent on guarding against an over-emphasis on the objective character of the sacraments, both Calvin and WCF insist that an *ex opere operato* view of the sacraments is incorrect. The word is essential. Even more fundamentally, the Holy Spirit alone can apply the sacrament for the good of a Christian.[54] The Spirit is necessary to awaken our affections to the Lord so that "our souls" are "opened for the sacraments to enter in." Apart from His working, "the sacraments can accomplish nothing more in our minds than the splendor of the sun shining upon blind eyes, or a voice sounding in deaf ears." The sacraments are efficacious only when "the Spirit works within and manifests his power."[55]

WCF agrees, insisting that "the grace which is exhibited in or by the sacraments" depends "upon the work of the Spirit, and the word of institution, which contains, together with a precept authorizing the use thereof, a promise of benefit to worthy receivers."[56] The Spirit and the gospel make the sacrament effective. Stressing the strength of the verb, "exhibited," in WCF, Letham notes, "In the sacraments, union and communion with Christ are not only symbolized, but also exhibited visibly to our eyes and conferred by the Holy Spirit according to

[51] Ibid. For Calvin, the sacraments convince us of the Father's good will toward us even more vividly than the word preached. They are, he noted, "mirrors in which we may contemplate the riches of God's graces, which he lavishes upon us. For by them he manifests himself to us . . . as far as our dullness is given to perceive, and attests his good will and love toward us more expressly than by word" (ibid., 4.14.6).

[52] Lucas, *On Being Presbyterian*, 83.

[53] Ibid., 83–84.

[54] See Godfrey, "Calvin, Worship, and the Sacraments," 375–76.

[55] Calvin, *Institutes* 4.14.9.

[56] WCF 27.3.

the promise of God. In them we encounter the Holy Trinity."[57] Lucas helpfully draws a distinction between "valid" and "efficacious." A sacrament is valid, on the one hand, "because it is based on God's command and promise, contained in the words of institution." But this must be distinguished from its efficacy. A sacrament is efficacious, "it 'works,' if you will—because the Spirit applies Christ and his benefits to the individual who responds in faith to the promise."[58]

Where, then, does this leave us? We have seen the historical context of the Reformed discussion of the Lord's Supper, and we have noted the way in which all discussions of the Supper must be bound by the churchly character of this sacrament. Our discussion of the nature of sacraments has highlighted that, for the Reformed, sacraments have a promissory and assuring role especially. They do so because they bring Christ to His people. They promise participants their place in the gospel—with its forgiveness of sins—in a similar way to the gospel preached; and by consequence they assure believers of their acceptance with the holy God. In other words, all we have seen so far highlights the pastoral character of the Eucharist to Reformed Christians.

The Reformed Doctrine and Practice of the Lord's Supper

Now we will outline the RT's pastoral doctrine of the Lord's Supper. First, we will try to understand how God's grace objectively benefits Christ's people in the Eucharist since Jesus is present there. In the Eucharist God offers Christ, who is present to feed His people in the sacrament. And Christ's presence confirms God's gracious promises to His people. Second, the Supper—given its objective and pastoral character—must be orderly administered in the church by a rightly ordained pastor.

The Objective Promises of God and the Presence of Christ

The objective character of the Eucharist dominates the RT, especially Calvin's thought. We will note four aspects of this objectivity. The

[57] Letham, *Westminster Assembly*, 324–25.

[58] Lucas, *On Being Presbyterian*, 85. In this context he argues that it is valid to baptize an infant even though the baptism will only become efficacious later when the baptized child puts his faith in Jesus. Reymond comments on Westminster's doctrine of the sacraments in some detail (*New Systematic Theology*, 917–23).

Supper is, first and fundamentally, a gift of God to His people. Second, believers have union with Christ through the meal. Third, they must eat and drink Christ who is present in the Eucharist. Fourth, these things can happen in the Supper because Christ is present with His people and they with Him, through the agency of the Holy Spirit.[59]

First, Calvin and Westminster are united in viewing the Supper fundamentally as a gracious gift of God to His people. My feelings, my doubts, my ongoing sins—none of these can change the fact that at its core the Supper is a meal set by the Lord for His people. As the gospel is something done outside of believers by God, so the Supper is a gracious gift. It has divine authority, and perfect promise-keeping, as its foundation.[60] In the Supper God gives Christ to His people.

The Supper mirrors the gospel and convinces us that the gospel is true, and true for us. And the gospel—the cross work of Christ—is objectively done outside of us, showing us God's promise of grace to us. Calvin stresses that the foundation for the Supper of Christ is His cross: "The present distribution of the body and blood of the Lord would not greatly benefit us unless they had once for all been given for our redemption and salvation."[61] As Christ once "gave his body to be made bread when he yielded himself to be crucified for the redemption of the world," so in the same way "daily he gives it when by the word of the gospel he offers it for us to partake, inasmuch as it was crucified, when he seals such giving of himself by the sacred mystery of the Supper, and when he inwardly fulfills what he outwardly designates."[62] Without the gospel of Christ, the Supper would be pointless: "For, as Christ would not have been the bread of life for us if he had not been born and had not died for us, and if he had not arisen for us, so this would not now be the case at all if the effectiveness and result of his birth, death, and resurrection were not something eternal and immortal."[63] Indeed, the very purpose of the sacrament is to send "us to the cross of Christ" as we in "living ex-

[59] Calvin objectively titled his chapter on the Lord's Supper, "The Sacred Supper of Christ, and What It Brings to Us" (Calvin, *Institutes* 4.17).

[60] L. J. Vander Zee, *Christ, Baptism and the Lord's Supper: Recovering the Sacraments for Evangelical Worship* (Downers Grove, IL: InterVarsity, 2004), 176.

[61] Calvin, *Institutes* 4.17.3.

[62] Ibid., 4.17.5.

[63] Ibid.

perience" grasp the efficacy of His death for us.[64] The gospel of God's grace grounds the Supper.

Westminster agrees with Calvin here. Christ instituted the Supper for the purposes of "the perpetual remembrance of the sacrifice of Himself in His death" as well as "the sealing all benefits thereof unto true believers."[65] Similarly, the Eucharist is not an actual sacrifice of Christ, but is rather "a commemoration of that one offering up of Himself, by Himself, upon the cross, once for all."[66] The RT, then, highlights that the Supper is a gift from God founded on the once-for-all death of Christ on the cross.

Second, Calvin, especially, contends that in partaking of the Supper believers have true union with Christ.[67] WCF is not silent on this point, saying, for example, that the Supper is "a bond and pledge of their communion with" Christ.[68] And WLC, question 168, says that in the Supper participants have "union and communion" with Christ. But Calvin emphasizes this union.[69] The essence of the Supper is the "mystery of Christ's secret union with the devout."[70] The result of

[64] Ibid., 4.17.4.

[65] WCF 29.1.

[66] WCF 29.2.

[67] Helm, especially, connects union of the "whole Christ" to believers by means of the Holy Spirit. Believers have union with the risen Christ, a real union, but this only takes place through the mysterious working of the Spirit (P. Helm, *Calvin: A Guide for the Perplexed* [New York: T&T Clark, 2008], 119–23). He helpfully articulates Calvin's view in this way: "The presence does not consist in subjective changes in the believer's psyche, nor in physical presence, but in a Spirit-induced union with Christ. The Lord's Supper is not magical, but it is most certainly mysterious: 'incomprehensible' in Calvin's technical understanding of that term: something that though we may have some apprehension of, we cannot get our minds around, but which nonetheless leads him to expressions of the deepest feeling" (Helm, *Calvin*, 123). Following Mathison's interpretation, Mason urges that Calvin was reviving a central Pauline theme when he stressed union with Christ: "The Supper therefore reaffirms this union as, by the working of the Spirit, it signs and seals to us God's gracious promises in Christ, strengthening our faith, and so raising us up to feed once again on Christ. It is not that we ever stop being united to Christ; rather, this ongoing union is strengthened and nourished as we feed on him spiritually even as we feed on the bread and wine physically. . . . Put crudely, the Spirit bridges the vast physical gap that separates Christ from the believer. Therefore, Christ's presence in the Supper is not physical and ontological, versus Rome and Luther; but it is a true presence, versus Zwingli" (M. W. Mason, "A Spiritual Banquet: John Calvin on the Lord's Supper," *Churchman* 117.4 [2003]: 337).

[68] WCF 29.1.

[69] Many scholars have pointed out that union with Christ is one of Calvin's central emphases in his work. See, e.g., D. E. Tamburello, *Union with Christ: John Calvin and the Mysticism of St. Bernard*, Columbia Series in Reformed Theology (Louisville: Westminster John Knox, 1994), especially 84–101; J. T. Billings, *Calvin, Participation, and the Gift: The Activity of Believers in Union with Christ* (Oxford: Oxford University Press, 2008).

[70] Calvin, *Institutes* 4.17.1. M. Horton has recently stressed this in his "Union and Communion: Calvin's Theology of Word and Sacrament," *International Journal of Systematic Theology*

this union is assurance for Christians as "they have a witness of our growth into one body with Christ such that whatever is his may be called ours."[71] Driving home the salutary effects of this union, Calvin eloquently reflects on the "wonderful exchange" that is ours at the Table:

> This is the wonderful exchange which, out of his measureless benevolence, he has made with us; that, becoming Son of man with us, he has made us sons of God with him; that, by his descent to earth, he has prepared an ascent to heaven for us; that, by taking on our mortality, he has conferred his immortality upon us; that, accepting our weakness, he has strengthened us by his power; that, receiving our poverty unto himself, he has transferred his wealth to us; that, taking the weight of our iniquity upon himself (which oppressed us), he has clothed us with his righteousness.[72]

When believers take the Supper, they have union with Christ.

In explicating his view of union, while distancing himself from both transubstantiationists and consubstantiationists, Calvin asserts that Christ's flesh is life-giving.[73] So if one hopes to have spiritual life, one must have communion with His flesh: "The signs are bread and wine, which represent for us the invisible food that we receive from the flesh and blood of Christ."[74] Christians must experience this union because "*As* it is not the seeing but the eating of bread that suffices to feed the body, *so* the soul must truly and deeply become partaker of Christ that it may be quickened to spiritual life by his power." Relying on John 6, Calvin explains that "salvation for us rests on faith in his death and resurrection, but also that, by true partaking of him, his life passes into us and is made ours—*just as* bread when taken as food imparts vigor to the body."[75] There is a parallel, then, between believers as physical beings needing to ingest food and as spiritual beings needing to partake of Christ through union with Him. With John 6 in the

11.4 (2009): 398–414. But see Reymond, *New Systematic Theology*, 962–64, for a critique of Calvin's view, especially his use of John 6.

[71] Calvin, *Institutes* 4.17.2.

[72] Ibid. Calvin had used similar imagery to describe the manner in which Christ's righteousness is ours by faith. See, e.g., ibid., 3.11.10.

[73] On Calvin's doctrine of union see Wallace, *Calvin's Doctrine*, 143–74, 197–216. Calvin refuted transubstantiation in *Institutes* 4.17.12–15 and consubstantiation in *Institutes* 4.17.16–17, 29–31. Letham characterizes the four views (Catholic, Lutheran, memorial, and Reformed) as follows: "physical presence: transubstantiation; physical presence: consubstantiation; real absence: memorialism; and real spiritual presence: communion" (R. Letham, *The Lord's Supper: Eternal Word in Broken Bread* [Phillipsburg, NJ: P&R: 2001], 19–29).

[74] Calvin, *Institutes* 4.17.1.

[75] Ibid., 4.17.5 (my italics).

background again, Calvin teaches that as the eternal Word made flesh Jesus "poured that power upon the flesh which he took in order that from it participation in life might flow unto us."[76] This participation in, or communion with, Christ is essential: "God's promises," Calvin asserts, offer us Christ "not for us to halt in the appearance and bare knowledge alone, but to enjoy true participation in him" because His flesh is life-giving.[77]

Third, Calvin stresses the necessity of eating the body of Christ and drinking His blood in order to have this communion with Him, to participate in His flesh.[78] Calvin avers that Christ "in some measure renews, or rather continues, the covenant which he once for all ratified with his blood (as far as it pertains to the strengthening of our faith) whenever he proffers that sacred blood for us to taste."[79] Again using

[76] Ibid., 4.17.8.

[77] Ibid., 4.17.11. This discussion involves Calvin's understanding of the "substance" of Christ. Exactly with what, or whom, do believers participate in the Supper? Lane nicely articulates Calvin's view when he writes, "We have communion with and are fed from the substance of Christ's flesh and blood, which is the source of the benefits that we receive. At the same time he denies any transfusion or transference of the substance into the bread and wine, or any substantial presence in the bread and wine. In particular, the substance of Christ's flesh and blood is not swallowed or digested. . . . But through the work of the Holy Spirit the believer is enabled to have a spiritual communion with Christ's flesh and blood, to feed upon them and to receive from them the benefits won by Christ" ("Calvin a Crypto-Zwinglian?" 31). The tension in Calvin's language is largely responsible for the different interpretations of him, perhaps expressed most pointedly in the debates between John Williamson Nevin and Charles Hodge in the nineteenth century on how correctly to understand Calvin. For a fair-minded review of Nevin's reading of Calvin, see Davis, *This Is My Body*, 130. Also see M. L. Moore-Keish, *Do This in Remembrance of Me: A Ritual Approach to Reformed Eucharistic Theology* (Grand Rapids: Eerdmans, 2008), 55–58.

[78] Duncan, "True Communion," 444; Spear, "Nature of the Lord's Supper," 360–62; Osterhaven, "Eating and Drinking Christ," 87–88. After noting that Calvin's strong language about eating and drinking Christ has offended many, Hesselink admits that "the real presence and partaking of Christ's flesh and blood in the Supper should not be interpreted materialistically but spiritually; but 'spiritual' in this sense does not mean unreal or that Christ is present only in spirit. At the same time, Calvin resists the notion that the body and blood of Christ are contained in the elements. Rather, the elements 'are as instruments by which our Lord Jesus Christ distributes them to us.' Nevertheless, Christ is present to us in the Supper even though physically distant to us. The clue to Calvin's theology of the sacrament here, as with so many doctrines, is the Holy Spirit" ("Reformed View," 64). Horton does not flinch from the force of Calvin's argument, noting his similarity with Eastern patristic thought, including its doctrine of "theosis or divinization" ("Calvin's Theology," 401–3).

[79] Calvin, *Institutes* 4.17.1; cf. 4.17.5. Calvin did not stress the covenant ratifying nature of the Supper, but Clowney has, noting that fundamentally the Supper is a covenant meal practiced by the Lord Christ to inaugurate the New Covenant (E. P. Clowney, *The Church*, Contours of Christian Theology [Downers Grove, IL: InterVarsity, 1995], 284–90). See also S. B. Ferguson, *The Holy Spirit*, Contours of Christian Theology (Downers Grove, IL: InterVarsity, 1996), 200–201.

John 6 in his reflection, he notes that Christ here stressed the necessity of eating His flesh and drinking His blood.[80] Calvin comments, "As though all these things were said in vain: that his flesh is truly food, that his blood is truly drink; that none have life except those who eat his flesh and drink his blood; and other passages pertaining to the same thing!"[81] Taking these words of Jesus literally leads Calvin famously to say he is unable to comprehend with his mind, let alone communicate with words, the truth Jesus here taught.[82] We have to participate in Christ's flesh—really—if we are to have communion with Him: "the flesh of Christ is like a rich and inexhaustible fountain that pours into us the life springing forth from the Godhead into itself. Now who does not see that communion of Christ's flesh and blood is necessary for all who aspire to heavenly life?"[83]

This explains Calvin's emphasis on Christ's humanity. The real flesh of Christ is essential in our salvation.[84] Davis argues that for Calvin this real eating of Christ's flesh was necessary because of the manner in which it was tied to a sinner's justification before the holy God:

> To speak of eating the body of Christ meant for Calvin that the Christian is nourished by and gains union with a real human body. There is, literally, a fleshly body involved in the Christian's spirit feeding on Christ (though the body is literal, the feeding itself, however, must be understood spiritually in the sense of nourishment rather than manducation [chewing]). That is why Calvin insisted on substantial partaking of the body of Christ in the Eucharist, for it is the human body of Christ that is the accommodated instrument of God's salvation. It is the thing by which righteousness comes to believers.[85]

[80] Trimp disagrees with my assessment, claiming, rather, that "eating and drinking Christ" is intensive language used to express a love relationship the believer has with Christ (C. Trimp, "The Sacrament of the Lord's Supper," *Mid-America Journal of Theology* 12 [2001]: 176–81).

[81] Calvin, *Institutes* 4.17.7.

[82] Ibid.

[83] Ibid., 4.17.9.

[84] See, e.g., D. F. Wells, *The Person of Christ: A Biblical and Historical Analysis of the Incarnation* (Westchester, IL: Crossway, 1984), 120–25.

[85] Davis, *This Is My Body*, 87. Davis earlier insisted that this explains much of Calvin's polemics versus the Catholics and Lutherans since they seemed to downplay the reality of Christ's humanity in the Supper which, for Calvin, jeopardized the doctrine of salvation: "Every bit as much as Luther, Calvin tied the Christian's salvation to the presence of Christ's body, and he did so in a way thoroughly worked out in his commentary on the book of John. . . . There was much more to Calvin's thought than some barren understanding of 'Word.' Indeed, Calvin thought that Christ, bodily, was given in the Word and the Sacrament; he believed that the bodily mediation of Christ was essential to the Christian's salvation, and he insisted that, to take advantage of that mediation, the Christian must somehow or other participate in Christ's body and that such participation hinged, in large part, on *knowing* that such union with Christ was not simply a joining of the Christian's spirit to Christ's spirit but also to Christ's body" (*This Is My Body*, 16).

Thus in the Lord's Supper, believers commune with the real body and blood of Christ.

Fourth, Calvin's emphasis on union with Christ and the necessity of eating and drinking Him leads us to consider the RT's doctrine of Christ's presence in the Eucharist.[86] Calvin believed not that Christ is brought down, but, rather, that through the ministry of the Holy Spirit believers are brought to Christ, who is in heaven.[87] "In this Sacrament," he insists, we must know it is "as if Christ here present were himself set before our eyes and touched by our hands."[88] The soul is truly fed by the Supper because the body of Christ is really present and really given to believers due to the relation of sign to seal: "The godly ought by all means to keep this rule: whenever they see symbols appointed by the Lord, to think and be persuaded that the truth of the thing signified is surely present there. . . . If it is true that a visible sign is given us to seal the gift of a thing invisible, when we have received the symbol of the body, let us no less surely trust that the body itself is also given to us."[89] Calvin offers this as his final word on the subject: "I freely accept whatever can be made to express the true and substantial partaking of the body and blood of the Lord, which is shown to believers under the sacred symbols of the Supper—and so to express it that they may be understood not to receive it solely by imagination or understanding of mind, but to enjoy the thing itself as nourishment of eternal life."[90] Christ's "true and substantial" presence in the Lord's Supper is essential for the believer's spiritual nourishment.

Later he states, "According to Calvin, Christ's body is life-giving because it has been ordained as an instrument of God for that purpose. Thus Calvin insisted that the Christian must partake of the substance of Christ's body, for in it 'have all the parts of salvation [been] accomplished" (*This Is My Body*, 86).

[86] See Duncan, "True Communion," 442–45.

[87] There has been much discussion concerning whether Calvin believed Christians "ascend" to Christ in heaven or He "descends" to us, both through the agency of the Spirit. See, for example, Davis, *This Is My Body*, 128–33; Hesselink, "Reformed View," 66–67. Horton emphasizes the role of the Spirit in establishing the union between Christ and His people ("Calvin's Theology," 404–6). He writes, "The gift in the Supper is nothing less than Christ; not just his memory, nor even merely the benefits of Christ, but Jesus Christ himself, and not just his divinity, but the whole Christ. However, Christ is communicated to the believer in the sacrament in precisely the same manner as the union itself; namely, through the agency of the Spirit. . . . It is not simply Christ's divinity but the Spirit who makes Christ's reign universally present, so that even Christ's true and natural body and blood can be communicated to believers" ("Calvin's Theology," 408–9).

[88] Calvin, *Institutes* 4.17.3.

[89] Ibid., 4.17.10.

[90] Ibid., 4.17.19.

But how is Christ present in the Supper if consubstantiation and transubstantiation are both wrong?[91] Calvin's answer is that the Holy Spirit "truly unites things separated in space," a separation caused by the fact that Jesus has ascended and is in heaven.[92] Calvin agreed with the Zwinglians on the location of the ascended body of Christ: "Not Aristotle, but the Holy Spirit teaches that the body of Christ from the time of his resurrection was finite, and is contained in heaven even to the Last Day."[93] Jesus' human nature marks Him as spatially bound to one place. But as God, Jesus is omnipresent. Therefore, Calvin concludes, "since the whole Christ is everywhere, our Mediator is ever present with his own people, and in the Supper reveals himself in a special way, yet in such a way that the whole Christ is present, but not in his wholeness. For, as has been said, in his flesh he is contained in heaven until he appears in judgment."[94] Jesus' body, located in heaven, is present to believers in the Supper.

In the Eucharist believers have communion with the real flesh of Christ, which is in heaven. This happens due to the mysterious work of the Holy Spirit, who ushers believers into Christ's presence in

[91] Numerous scholars have struggled to understand the complexities of Calvin's language about how the signs can "represent" Christ while also "presenting" Him to us. Pruett notes that "for the Reformers, the risen Christ was indeed present and received *realiter*. An 'objective' presence, that is a presence *granted* to faith rather than *identified* with faith, is a critical concept in the Reformed Eucharistic doctrine. The Holy Spirit grants the body and blood of Christ to the believer; and therefore it is the body and blood of Christ that is received. Here is the key to an understanding of the consistent usage of realist terminology by men who struggled against the notions of corporal inclusion, sacrifice, and transubstantiation" (G. E. Pruett, "A Protestant Doctrine of the Eucharistic Presence," *CTJ* 10 [1975]: 155). Zachman well identifies the tension in Calvin here: "Calvin insists that what God represents (*repraesentat*) in the symbol of the Supper God simultaneously presents (*exhibeat*) in reality. This is the reason the symbol is given the name of the thing symbolized, for it not only represents the thing itself by analogy but also truly exhibits and presents the reality it represents." As part of this "irreducible tension" Calvin first "insists that the Lord not only represents and figures but also exhibits and presents the body and blood of Christ in the bread and wine of the Supper." But, on the other hand, "Calvin insists that Christ is not to be sought in the symbols of bread and wine but in heaven. Christ gives us the symbols as vehicles or ladders to help us in our weakness, so that we might ascend from earth to heaven, to seek the reality symbolized there. If we do not mount up to heaven on these ladders, the reality simply will not be given to us" (R. C. Zachman, *Image and Word in the Theology of John Calvin* [Notre Dame, IN: University of Notre Dame Press, 2007], 334, 340–41). I think the tension in Calvin is insurmountable and the WCF is better for not speculating about the nature of Christ's presence.

[92] Calvin, *Institutes* 4.17.10.

[93] Ibid., 4.17.26. Calvin had to be careful here, given the union of divine and human natures in Christ, so he wrote that "although the whole Christ is everywhere, still the whole of that which is in him is not everywhere" (*Institutes* 4.17.30).

[94] Ibid.

heaven when they in faith receive the Lord's Supper. Calvin stresses the Spirit's role: "Christ feeds his people with his own body, the communion of which he bestows upon them by the power of his Spirit."[95] Out of honor to the Spirit's power and authority, lest we commit "a serious wrong," we must "believe that it is through [the Spirit's] incomprehensible power that we come to partake of Christ's flesh and blood."[96] The Spirit's work is essential in Calvin's thought, for the Spirit makes it possible for Christians to have union with Christ who has ascended to heaven: "The bond of this connection is therefore the Spirit of Christ, with whom we are joined in unity, and is like a channel through which all that Christ himself is and has is conveyed to us."[97] Therefore, in the Supper Christians are raised by the power of the Spirit to heaven where we have real communion with the flesh of Christ.[98]

This is a mystery, to be sure, but Calvin thinks this is the best way to understand what takes place in the Eucharist. In summarizing his doctrine, he draws attention to the fact that the Holy Spirit must bring us to Christ in heaven to have communion with Him there:

> I wish to warn my readers to consider diligently the purport of our doctrine: whether it depends upon common sense or, having surmounted the world on the wings of faith, soars up to heaven. We say Christ descends to us both by the outward symbol and by his Spirit, that he may truly quicken our souls by the substance of his flesh and of his blood. He who does not perceive that many miracles are subsumed in these few words is more than stupid. For nothing is more beyond the natural than that souls should borrow spiritual and heavenly life from a flesh that had its origin from earth, and underwent death. There is nothing more incredible than that things severed and removed from one another by the whole space between heaven and earth should not only be connected across such a great distance but also be united, so that souls may receive nourishment from Christ's flesh.[99]

Calvin believed that this doctrine of Christ's presence in the Lord's Supper was essential for healthy Christian living. After explicating his

[95] Ibid., 4.17.18.

[96] Ibid., 4.17.33.

[97] Ibid., 4.17.12.

[98] Ibid., 4.17.36. See Lane, "Was Calvin a Crypto-Zwinglian?," 34.

[99] Calvin, *Institutes* 4.17.24. See this summary of Calvin's view by Walker: "Although communion is a spiritual act, it involves an actual sharing in Christ's flesh and blood, and although his body has now ascended physically into heaven, we are none the less able to make contact with it through the Spirit. How these things can be remains a mystery, to be treated with reverence and accepted in faith" (G. S. M. Walker, "The Lord's Supper in the Theology and Practice of Calvin," in *John Calvin*, ed. G. E. Duffield [Grand Rapids: Eerdmans, 1966], 133–34).

doctrine, he summarized it for his readers. We note Calvin's four pastoral and doctrinal summary statements. First, in the Supper believers feed on Christ:

> Our souls are fed by the flesh and blood of Christ in the same way that bread and wine keep and sustain physical life. For the analogy of the sign applies only if souls find their nourishment in Christ—which cannot happen unless Christ truly grows into one with us, and refreshes us by the eating of his flesh and the drinking of his blood.[100]

Second, the Spirit is the agent who makes this happen:

> Let us remember how far the secret power of the Holy Spirit towers above all our senses. . . . What, then, our mind does not comprehend, let faith conceive: that the Spirit truly unites things separated in space.[101]

Third, the body of Christ is truly given to Christians:

> The godly ought by all means to keep this rule: whenever they see symbols appointed by the Lord, to think and be persuaded that the truth of the thing signified is surely present there. . . . If it is true that a visible sign is given us to seal the gift of a thing invisible, when we have received the symbol of the body, let us no less surely trust that the body itself is also given to us.[102]

Fourth, believers truly participate in Christ for their assurance:

> In the mystery of the Supper, Christ is truly shown to us through the symbols of bread and wine, his very body and blood, in which he has fulfilled all obedience to obtain righteousness for us. Why? First, that we may grow into one body with him; secondly, having been made partakers of his substance, that we may also feel his power in partaking of all his benefits.[103]

The WCF is more chaste than Calvin in explaining Christ's presence in the Supper.[104] WCF notes that the Supper was given partly for Christians' "spiritual nourishment and growth in" Christ.[105] Later, in its most Calvin-like section, the WCF asserts,

[100] Calvin, *Institutes* 4.17.10.

[101] Ibid.

[102] Ibid.

[103] Ibid., 4.17.11.

[104] But see Duncan, "True Communion," 441–42. It is for good reason, I think, that Lucas says, about WCF 29.8, "Sometimes, the qualifications and caveats in the Standards are so confusing that it is hard to understand what is at stake or even what Presbyterians are trying to say." Lucas also labels the "spiritual feeding" section in WCF 29.7 "the somewhat tortured section" (*On Being Presbyterian*, 90, 92). At the very least, as Lucas acknowledges, these parts of WCF are difficult to exegete.

[105] WCF 29.1.

> Worthy receivers, outwardly partaking of the visible elements, in this sacrament, do then also, inwardly by faith, really and indeed, yet not carnally and corporally but spiritually, receive and feed upon, Christ crucified, and all benefits of His death: the body and blood of Christ being then, not corporally or carnally, in, with, or under the bread and wine; yet, as really, but spiritually, present to the faith of believers in that ordinance, as the elements themselves are to their outward senses.[106]

Although it does not detail how it happens, the WCF teaches the real, spiritual presence of Christ in the Lord's Supper.

In this section we have not stressed another aspect of the RT's eucharistic teaching, the requirement that Christians vigorously put their trust in Christ while taking the Supper in order to benefit by it.[107] This "subjective" emphasis in the RT is biblically accurate and pastorally significant. We have, rather, noted those aspects of the RT that differentiate it from many evangelical Protestants—its objective focus. In the RT the Lord's Supper is a gift from God to His people. By eating it, Christians have union with Christ who is present in the Eucharist. The union and presence occur through the agency of the Holy Spirit. This objective focus is the key to the RT's view of the Supper.

The Ecclesiastical Character of the Eucharist

Now we will examine the Supper through the lens of the church, for to Calvinists that is the only locus for the practice of the Supper. This aspect of the Supper is closely connected with the former

[106] WCF 29.7. The Princeton tradition has tended to downplay the evident meaning of this section of WCF. For example, commenting on this section, A. A. Hodge asserts, "The body and blood are present [in the Supper], therefore, only virtually; that is, the virtues and effects of the sacrifice of the body of the Redeemer on the cross are made present and are actually conveyed in the sacrament to the worthy receiver by the power of the Holy Ghost. . . . When it is said, therefore, that believers receive and feed upon the body and blood of Christ, it is meant that they receive, not by the mouth, but through faith, the benefits secured by Christ's sacrificial death upon the cross—that this feeding upon Christ is purely spiritual, accomplished through the free and sovereign agency of the Holy Ghost and through the instrumentality and in the exercise of faith alone; so that in no case is it ever done by the unbeliever. . . . Hence, also, it follows that believers do, in the same sense, receive and feed upon the body and blood of Christ at other times without the use of the sacrament, and in the use of other means of grace—as prayer, meditation on the Word, etc." (A. A. Hodge, *The Confession of Faith* [1869; rpt. Carlisle, PA: Banner of Truth, 1958], 362–63). For a similar assessment of WCF's meaning, see G. I. Williamson, *The Westminster Confession of Faith for Study Classes* (Philadelphia: P&R, 1964), 227.

[107] It is unfortunate that we have not been able to elaborate on this in the RT since this is one of the tradition's emphases. We see this in Calvin even in his discussion of sacraments in *Institutes* 4.14.7. For Calvin's prioritizing of faith in the Supper, see, e.g., *Institutes* 4.17.5. WCF likewise stressed the importance of faith; see WCF 29.7.

exposition, for Christ is present not just to the individual believer but to the church as a whole when it receives the Supper. Not only does the Supper bind the believer closer to Christ, but it also binds Him closer to the church as a whole.[108] Therefore, the Eucharist is a church ordinance.

In the *Institutes* Calvin included a short order describing how the Eucharist should be practiced:

> First, then, it should begin with public prayers. After this a sermon should be given. Then, when bread and wine have been placed on the Table, the minister should repeat the words of institution of the Supper. Next, he should recite the promises which were left to us in it; at the same time, he should excommunicate all who are debarred from it by the Lord's prohibition. Afterward, he should pray that the Lord, with the kindness wherewith he has bestowed this sacred food upon us, also teach and form us to receive it with faith and thankfulness of heart, and, inasmuch as we are not so of ourselves, by his mercy make us worthy of such a feast. But here either psalms should be sung, or something be read, and in becoming order the believers should partake of the most holy banquet, the ministers breaking the bread and giving the cup. When the Supper is finished, there should be an exhortation to sincere faith and confession of faith, to love and behavior worthy of Christians. At the last, thanks should be given, and praises sung to God. When these things are ended, the church should be dismissed in peace.[109]

The Westminster divines echoed many of these themes in their instructions for the celebration of the Supper in their churches. The service was largely focused on the minister who was first to preach, then to pray, and then to exhort the congregation in this manner:

> Expressing the inestimable benefit we have by this sacrament, together with the ends and use thereof: setting forth the great necessity of having our comforts and strength renewed thereby in this our pilgrimage and warfare: how necessary it is that we come unto it with knowledge, faith, repentance, love, and with hungering and thirsting souls after Christ and his benefits: how great the danger to eat and drink unworthily.[110]

Then the pastor is to warn unworthy persons not to partake, while encouraging those who are putting their hope in Christ "assuring them, in the same name, of ease, refreshing, and strength to their weak and

[108] Janse, "Sacraments," 352.

[109] Calvin, *Institutes* 4.17.43. A complete Lord's Day service with the Lord's Supper by Calvin is included in E. A. McKee, ed. and trans., *John Calvin: Writings on Pastoral Piety*, The Classics of Western Spirituality (New York: Paulist, 2001), 111–34.

[110] *The Directory for the Publick Worship of God*, in *Westminster Confession of Faith* (Glasgow: Free Presbyterian, 1976), 384.

wearied souls." After inviting the listeners to come, the pastor should proceed with reading the words of institution from the Gospels or 1 Corinthians. Then he should thank God for redemption in Christ, His work, "and for this sacrament in particular, by which Christ, and all his benefits, are applied and sealed up unto us, which, notwithstanding the denial of them unto others, are in great mercy continued unto us." He is to conclude his prayer, beseeching God "to vouchsafe his gracious presence, and the effectual working of his Spirit in us." Then he is to ask God "that we may receive by faith the body and blood of Jesus Christ, crucified for us, and so to feed upon him, that he may be one with us, and we one with him; that he may live in us, and we in him." In presenting the Supper and in praying, the minister should do this "with suitable affections, answering to such an holy action, and to stir up the like in the people." The pastor then should repeat the words of Christ in the upper room over both the bread and wine, and give them to the people. Finally, he should remind the people "of the grace of God in Jesus Christ, held forth in this sacrament; and exhort them to walk worthy of it." Then he should give thanks to God for the sacrament and dismiss the people.[111]

Four issues come to the fore in the ecclesiastically focused direction of the Supper in the RT.[112] First, the ceremony is to be simple, and it is to closely follow the NT's example. Calvin noted this several times. One of his guiding principles was that the worship and organization of the church must conform to Scripture. God has not left this up to human invention, since it is of supreme importance because He and His glory are paramount.[113] Although there certainly are elements of the Supper's administration that Scripture does not address, to adorn the ceremony with unbiblical additions is both to denigrate God and also to revert to superstition.[114] The guiding principle to the Reformed, then, has been to keep the liturgy of the Eucharist "scriptural and

[111] Ibid., 385–86.

[112] For an overview of this, see Letham, *Lord's Supper*, 49–60.

[113] On the so-called "regulative principle" in the RT see, J. L. Duncan III, "Does God Care How We Worship?" in *Give Praise to God: A Vision for Reforming Worship*, ed. P. G. Ryken, D. W. H. Thomas, and J. L. Duncan III (Phillipsburg, NJ: P&R, 2003), 17–50; J. L. Duncan III, "Foundations for Biblically Directed Worship," in *Give Praise to God*, 51–73; D. W. H. Thomas, "The Regulative Principle: Responding to Recent Criticism," in *Give Praise to God*, 74–93. Baptists have also operated ecclesiologically on the basis of the "regulative principle." See, e.g., M. E. Dever, "The Church," in *A Theology for the Church*, ed. D. L. Akin (Nashville: B&H, 2007), 811.

[114] Godfrey, "Calvin, Worship, and the Sacraments," 373–74.

simple."[115] Since the Supper was not a mystery to be adored but was, rather, comfort for the weary Christian, the church should practice the Supper "simply, solemnly, and serially."[116]

The second issue of note is the frequency with which the Lord's Supper should be practiced in the church. Since the Eucharist feeds believers "with Christ and all his benefits" and since it also creates unity and love among the people of God, Calvin desired frequent Communion.[117] As Gerrish has noted, "Calvin upheld the ancient rule that no meeting of the church should take place without also partaking of the Lord's Supper."[118] The Geneva city council, though, would not permit this so that "quarterly Communion became the norm in Geneva and Scotland."[119]

The question of frequency is a live discussion in Reformed churches. Although the practice in the past has been monthly or even more infrequent celebrations of the Supper, there is a growing movement advocating weekly celebration.[120] Cornelis Venema, for example, argues that the issue of frequency is bound up with how often the gospel is preached. Since gospel proclamation must accompany the Eucharist (the Lord's Supper "*ordinarily accompanies* the preaching of the Word"), and since the Eucharist symbolizes the gospel, the two should accompany each other:

> Though the Reformed confessions do not explicitly comment on the frequency of the administration of the Lord's Supper, they in principle favor a practice where the sacrament of the Lord's Supper ordinarily accompanies the preaching of the gospel. . . . the burden of the confessions' statements respecting this sacrament argues for a practice that, in obedience to Christ's institution, administers the Supper as a regular accompaniment of the preaching of the Word.[121]

[115] Reymond, *New Systematic Theology*, 958.

[116] Clark, "Evangelical Fall," 142. See Godfrey, "Calvin, Worship, and the Sacraments," 377.

[117] Horton, "At Least Weekly," 150. See Godfrey, "Calvin, Worship, and the Sacraments," 374; Hesselink, "Reformed View," 67–68.

[118] Gerrish, "Eucharist," 77.

[119] Ibid. See P. Benedict, *Christ's Churches Purely Reformed: A Social History of Calvinism* (New Haven: Yale University Press, 2002), 86; W. de Greef, "Calvin's Writings," in *The Cambridge Companion to John Calvin*, ed. D. K. McKim (New York: Cambridge University Press, 2004), 52–53; Parker, *John Calvin*, 46.

[120] On the historical infrequency of practice, see Benedict, *Christ's Churches*, 502.

[121] Venema, "The Doctrine of the Lord's Supper in the Reformed Confessions," 132–33, 141 (his italics). Others arguing for at least weekly Communion include Clark, "Evangelical Fall," and Horton, "At Least Weekly."

Proceeding more cautiously, Phillips avers that "the biblical data is helpful but indecisive."[122] First Corinthians 11:20–22 shows that the Eucharist seems to have been "a regular feature of [the Corinthians'] frequent meetings," but it is not clear "that Paul commends this practice." Phillips concludes that "it seems that [Paul] would be happier with less frequent and more careful partaking of the supper of the Lord."[123]

Third, the RT prioritizes the role of a rightly-ordained pastor in administering the Supper. It does so for two reasons. First, a pastor's ordination shows that he has been set apart for his work both by God and by the church. So Reymond notes that "in the Reformed churches the administration of the sacrament is restricted to ministers of the Word, not because it is thought that any sacerdotal power is resident in them by virtue of their ordination, but first, because (on the analogy of the high priest's admission to his office) 'no one takes this honor upon himself; he must be called of God' (Heb. 5:4), and, second, from the desire to insure good order."[124] This rightly ordained pastor should administer the sacrament only when the church gathers together, based on 1 Cor 11:18. The Supper is for the church, to be administered by an ordained pastor.[125]

A second reason is that an ordained pastor is qualified and able rightly to preach the gospel. The tie between the gospel and the Eucharist is as tight as the connection between the Word and the Holy Spirit. Calvin's "settled principle," according to Osterhaven, was that the sacraments have "the same office as the Word of God: to offer and set forth Christ to us, and in him the treasures of heavenly grace."[126]

[122] Phillips, "Lord's Supper," 219.

[123] Ibid., 220. Examining two streams within the Reformed tradition—the one arguing for weekly, frequent Communion, and the other advocating "great infrequence, perhaps only once a year"—Phillips notes that the biblical support for frequent Communion is much stronger than for its infrequent practice, and it has the added benefit of having historical precedent in the desire of Calvin (Phillips, "Lord's Supper," 220).

[124] Reymond, *New Systematic Theology*, 958. Erickson defines "sacerdotalism" as the belief "that only certain persons are qualified to administer the sacraments" (M. J. Erickson, *Christian Theology* [Grand Rapids: Baker, 1985], 1114). Reymond denies this is sacerdotalism in the strict sense of believing that grace comes through the sacraments via the ordained administrators. Yet, with a view toward some modern Reformed thinkers, Phillips warns of a "neo-sacerdotalism" in Reformed circles that implies the Lord's Supper is the way to receive Christ, rather than that placing trust in Him is what saves ("Lord's Supper," 209).

[125] Hesselink, though, notes a rising practice from the late twentieth century to have the Eucharist celebrated in non-church settings without the preaching of the gospel ("Reformed View," 71).

[126] Osterhaven, "Eating and Drinking Christ," 88, quoting Calvin, *Institutes* 4.14.17.

As such, the sacraments need explanation. Therefore, Calvin insists that without the preached word, "the sacrament is but a dumb show; the Word must go before."[127] Trevor Hart observes:

> The bread and wine are "seals" and "confirmations" of a promise already given, and make sense only when faith apprehends them as such. There must therefore always be some preaching or form of words which interprets the "bare signs" and enables us to make sense of them, and the "faith" which apprehends them, while not mere intellectual assent, has nonetheless a vital cognitive dimension.[128]

This is a corrective to a potential misunderstanding of the objective character of the Supper we have noted above. As Calvin argued, from the human perspective sacraments are "attestation[s] of our piety."[129] Stressing human responsibility in the proper reception of the Supper, the RT teaches that there needs to be proper preaching of the gospel and the exercise of faith by the recipients to make the Supper effective. Apart from gospel preaching and explanation the elements of the Eucharist are "bare signs." But the Holy Spirit empowers gospel preaching to make the promises real to the experience of believers who hear so that their faith is enabled to receive God's grace offered there.[130] The pastor presiding at the Eucharist should say the words of institution in the service so that, according to Davis, the words of institution may "give meaning to the signs. By themselves, bread and wine are mute; joined to the Words of Institution, they speak God's truth and promise; indeed, they point to where God may be found and experienced."[131] Or, as Calvin argues, "You see bread, and nothing else, but you hear that it is a sign of the body of Christ. Be quite sure that the Lord will carry out what you understand the words to mean: that his body, which you do not see at all, is spiritual food for you."[132] The pastor's role is paramount in the Eucharist since he proclaims the word of God.

The fourth and final issue of note in the churchly character of the Eucharist is the preparation required for one to take the sacrament and the church's obligation to "fence" the Table from unworthy

[127] Calvin, *Institutes* 4.17.39. See Clark, "Evangelical Fall," 141.

[128] Hart, "Calvin and Barth," 41.

[129] Calvin, *Institutes* 4.14.1.

[130] See J. D. Hannah, *Our Legacy: The History of Christian Doctrine* (Colorado Springs: NavPress, 2001), 291–92.

[131] Davis, *This Is My Body*, 67.

[132] Ibid., 68.

participants. This matter flows from Paul's warning in 1 Cor 11:27–29. Not only is active faith required on the part of the one who receives the Eucharist, but also there are serious consequences if one wrongly takes the sacrament.[133] As Letham comments, "Since faith is necessary to feed on Christ, . . . those without faith or godliness do not receive Christ at all, even though they may receive the sacrament. . . . They are guilty of the body and blood of Christ and so are liable to damnation."[134]

Thus, the church has the duty to determine the proper recipients of the Supper. Phillips represents the majority view of the RT when he argues the Supper should be withheld from several classes of persons: unbelievers; believers who are living in unrepentant sin; believers living out of communion with fellow Christians; and children of Christian parents who have not yet professed faith in Christ.[135] Only believers who are seeking Christ and striving after Him may take the Supper worthily. In Berkhof's words, they need to be believers who "earnestly repent of their sins, trust that these have been covered by the atoning blood of Jesus Christ, and are desirous to increase their faith, and to grow in true holiness of life."[136] Countering the concern that preparation for rightly taking the Supper may lead to legalism, Phillips comments, "Worthy partaking, then, does not mean making the sacrament work in our own spiritual strength or presenting a

[133] See, e.g., Lucas, *On Being Presbyterian*, 92.

[134] Letham, *Westminster Assembly*, 355.

[135] Phillips, "Lord's Supper," 215–16. The question of paedo-Communion has been discussed at length in the tradition. Arguing forcefully against it are Lucas, *On Being Presbyterian*, 94–95; Phillips, "Lord's Supper," 216; Reymond, *New Systematic Theology*, 958–59; Venema, "The Doctrine of the Lord's Supper in the Reformed Confessions," 141–42. John Murray well represents this position: "We cannot, on any scriptural basis, get away from the notion of restricted communion. The Lord's supper is not for all indiscriminately as the gospel is. The Lord's supper is chiefly commemoration and communion. It is for those who discern the Lord's body, who can commemorate his death in faith and love. And since the supper is also communion it is obviously for those who commune with Christ and with one another in the unity of the body which is the church. There can be no communion without union and therefore the central qualification for anticipation is union with Christ. The Lord's supper is for those who are his" (J. Murray, *Collected Writings of John Murray* [Carlisle, PA: Banner of Truth, 1977], 2:381). Hesselink avers that it is only "conservative" Reformed denominations that prohibit paedo-Communion; others allow it (Hesselink, "Reformed View," 70). For recent dialogue between two different groups of Reformed theologians, one arguing for the traditional view and the newer "federal vision" adherents arguing, among other things, for paedo-Communion, see *The Auburn Avenue Theology, Pros and Cons: Debating the Federal Vision*, ed. E. C. Beisner (Fort Lauderdale: Knox Theological Seminary, 2004).

[136] Berkhof, *Systematic Theology*, 656; cited in Phillips, "Lord's Supper," 217. See Osterhaven, "Eating and Drinking Christ," 89.

supposed righteousness of our own, but instead ensuring that ours is a faith that is credible and real."[137]

Therefore Christ's presence in the Supper (the objective focus we noted before) must be mediated through the ministry of the church. Christ has commanded the church—in simple ceremonies, frequently, via a rightly-ordained pastor, and while fencing the Table—to be the means of communicating His sacramental presence to His people. The church administers the sacrament, and in it Christ is present for His people.

Evaluation

In conclusion, there is a great deal to commend in the Reformed understanding of the Supper, especially its pastoral emphases. The RT is correct and wise to focus on assuring believers of Christ's once-for-all death on the cross for them and reminding them that their Savior's love and care continues. Right now—no matter what they see or feel—believers can trust in God's promises focused in Christ for their comfort and hope. The Lord's Supper effectively acts as a lens to focus their spiritual gaze and remind them of this.[138] Also, the RT is right to

[137] Phillips, "Lord's Supper," 218. Osterhaven points out that Calvin's pastoral emphasis was to assure weak believers, recognizing that faith was always imperfect in this life ("Eating and Drinking Christ," 90).

[138] Baptists have not disagreed with this. For example, the first writing theologian among Southern Baptists, John L. Dagg, noted that in the Supper a Christian "eats the bread, and drinks the wine, in token of receiving his spiritual sustenance from Christ crucified. . . . [Faith] discerns the Lord's body in the commemorative representation of it, and derives spiritual nourishment from the atoning sacrifice made by his broken body and shed blood" (J. L. Dagg, *Manual of Theology: Second Part, A Treatise on Church Order* [1858; rpt. Harrisonburg, VA: Gano, 1990], 210–11). While acknowledging that Baptists usually hold to a "memorial view," Dever says, "Baptists have historically used language so rich about Christ's presence in the Lord's Supper for those who come by faith that little difference is perceptible between their position and the Reformed idea of Christ's spiritual presence" ("The Church," 828). One sees this even in Augustus Strong's traditional Baptist memorial view because he argued that the Supper "sets forth, in general, the death of Christ as the sustaining power of the believer's life," i.e., it presently impacts the believer by reminding him of his continuing dependence on Christ (A. H. Strong, *Systematic Theology* [Valley Forge, PA: Judson, 1907; rpt, 1974], 962). Many Baptists, in fact, have held a spiritual presence view akin to the RT's. See, e.g., M. A. G. Haykin, "'His soul-refreshing presence': The Lord's Supper in Calvinistic Baptist Thought and Experience in the 'Long' Eighteenth Century," in *Baptist Sacramentalism*, ed. A. R. Cross and P. E. Thompson (Carlisle, UK: Paternoster, 2003), 177–93; C. W. Freeman, "'To Feed Upon by Faith': Nourishment from the Lord's Table," in *Baptist Sacramentalism*, ed. Cross and Thompson, 203–6; P. J. Morden, "The Lord's Supper and the Spirituality of C. H. Spurgeon," in *Baptist Sacramentalism 2*, ed. A. R. Cross and P. E. Thompson (Carlisle, UK: Paternoster, 2008), 175–96; and T. George, "SBJT Forum: The Lord's Supper," *SBJT* 6.3 (2002): 100–102. A helpful survey of Baptist controversies over Communion from the 1600s to the 1800s is found in P. Naylor, *Calvinism, Communion and*

call persons to exercise faith while receiving the Supper. In addition, the RT's emphasis on the churchly character and practice of the Supper is proper. In essence, the RT's supreme concern that the Supper both remind God's people of His objective love for them and also call on them to exercise faith and hope while receiving the Supper is sane, biblical, and pastorally sensitive.

However, there are several weaknesses with the RT's eucharistic theology, especially its emphasis on the spiritual presence of Christ. I begin with a simple observation. Although he distances himself from the most egregious errors of Rome, the Lutherans, and the Zwinglians, Calvin maintains a great deal in common with Rome and Luther especially. This does not necessarily mean he is wrong, but I note one instance of assumptions on his, and Westminster's, part here: their definition of sacraments. Scripture is silent on the sort of definition of a sacrament that we observed in the RT, both in Calvin and Westminster. Their understanding of sacraments seems as dependent on Augustine as on Scripture, for the Bible does not speak of sacraments as the RT does. Augustine developed his sacramental theology in controversy with the Donatists, and I suspect that he over-emphasized the objective nature of the sacraments to protect from the radicalism of his opponents. His sacramental theology led to much error in the medieval church. Baptists have been wiser in avoiding such careful, but extra-biblical definitions of sacraments. Thus in one of its most noticeable lacuna, the 1689 Second London Baptist Confession, which for the most part is a word-for-word adaptation of the WCF, does not even include a section on the sacraments.[139] So the Baptist

the Baptists: A Study of English Calvinistic Baptists from the Late 1600s to the Early 1800s (Carlisle, UK: Paternoster, 2003), 94–163.

[139] The confession skips from chap. 27, "Of the Communion of Saints," to chap. 28, "Of Baptism and the Lord's Supper," whereas WCF includes chap. 27, "Of the Sacraments." Instead of the elaborate sacramental discussion found in WCF, the Baptists simply asserted, "Baptism and the Lord's Supper are ordinances of positive and sovereign institution, appointed by the Lord Jesus, the only lawgiver, to be continued in his church to the end of the world" (*Second London Confession* 28.1). We should note that this does not preclude them from speaking of Christ's presence in the Supper in "spiritual" terms: "Worthy receivers, outwardly partaking of the visible elements in this ordinance, do then also inwardly by faith, really and indeed, yet not carnally and corporally, but spiritually receive and feed upon Christ crucified and all his benefits of his death; the body and blood of Christ being then not corporally or carnally, but spiritually present to the faith of believers in that ordinance, as the elements themselves are to their outward senses" (*Second London Confession* 30.7). The only differences from WCF 29.7 are that WCF calls this a "sacrament," whereas the Baptist confession labels it an "ordinance," and WCF includes "in, with, or under the bread and wine; yet, as really" to explain how Christ is not present corporally in the elements; the Second London Confession omits this wording.

divines were willing to use WCF. But they did so selectively. In leaving out WCF's elaborate discussion of the sacraments they were showing their biblicism. The Bible does not speak of the Supper as a "means of grace," a "sign," or a "seal." Nor does the Bible explicitly teach Christ's objective presence in the Supper.[140] These components of sacramental theology—the meaning of sacraments, means of grace, sign, seal, and the objective presence of Christ—are, it seems to me, largely imports from what the tradition assumes to be true about sacraments. Their understanding flows logically from their sacramental theology, but it does not flow necessarily from the Bible. This is important for us to note because it is largely on the basis of the RT's view of the sacraments that they arrive at their view of the objective nature of the Supper. But they do not derive this definition closely enough from Scripture.[141]

While the root problem with the RT is its definition of sacraments, it has three other shortcomings. One is theological, one pastoral, and one biblical.

Theologically, the RT is wrong to suggest that Jesus is present in the Supper in a way He is not present at other times. Jesus is especially present with His church when they exercise discipline, but since they are His body and are in Him, He is with them closely at all times. To zero in on the Lord's Supper as a place where Christ is especially available to them is theologically too narrow. There is a danger in too objectively focusing our gaze on Christ in the Lord's Supper. This may result either in down-playing the necessity of exercising our (God-imparted) faith or in forgetting that Christ is with His people at all times, not just as we celebrate the Lord's Supper.

A pastoral concern flows out of the theological issue I raised above. As Christians are assaulted continually by the world, their flesh, and

[140] Russell Moore rightly notes that "Christ is indeed 'really present' in the Lord's Supper. But it is not necessary to surmise that the Supper uniquely takes us to the heavenly places to commune with him there through the Spirit" since Jesus is always present with His people, especially in corporate worship and the exercise of church discipline. The blessings of the new covenant come to Christ's people through the gospel, and the ordinances and the word preached function to point Christians to Christ in the gospel (R. D. Moore, "The Reformed View: A Baptist Response," *Understanding Four Views on the Lord's Supper*, ed. J. H. Armstrong [Grand Rapids: Zondervan, 2007], 73).

[141] Even when Baptists have been happy to use the WCF's language on Christ's presence in the Supper, they have done so in order to balance carefully the objective with the subjective in the proper reception of the Eucharist. In this sense, I judge WCF to be more balanced and biblical than Calvin was.

the Devil, they are regularly in need of finding comfort for their weary souls. Much of the NT addresses this very issue. Where are we to look in times of trouble? Over and over, God's Word tells us to put our hope in the character of God supremely and to see that character of love and forgiveness exemplified in the cross of our Lord Jesus Christ. Christ, the cross, the gospel—these are what we are to put our hope in, even against what may seem to be the reality before our eyes. But the NT does not instruct us to look to the Supper for our hope.[142] Pastorally, we would be wiser to urge Christians to look to Christ, than to look for Christ in the Eucharist. If we are not careful, we may actually lead Christ's people to seek Him objectively where He has not said He will be found. Better for us to exhort Christ's people to seek Him by faith where He may always be found by the longing eyes of faith—on the cross. The gospel is certainly seen in the Supper. But the gospel is not the Supper. We need to seek our comfort in the gospel of Jesus Christ.

Finally, and most importantly, the Reformed tradition's emphasis on Christ's unique spiritual presence in the Lord's Supper lacks explicit biblical warrant. The gospel accounts assert that the bread "is" the body of Christ and the wine "is" the blood of Christ (Matt 26:26,28; Mark 14:22,24; Luke 22:19–20). Paul concurs (1 Cor 11:24–25). But, contrary to both the Catholic and Lutheran traditions, the RT has rightly viewed Jesus' statements here as instances of "metonymy."[143] Christ is not claiming to be in the elements of the Supper in a way that is unique.

That leaves just two other passages that bear on Christ's spiritual presence. The first is Jesus' bread of life discourse in John 6:22–59. Although Jesus did not clearly articulate a theology of the Eucharist here, few doubt that this passage has consequences for the church's understanding of the Supper because of Jesus' language regarding eating His flesh and drinking His blood (John 6:51,53–57).[144] Calvin

[142] Spear notes that one potential problem in Calvin's view is to encourage Christians to find a benefit in the Supper that is not found in the Word ("Nature of the Lord's Supper," 381).

[143] Calvin taught this explicitly, asserting that "this is my body" is a "metonymy, a figure of speech commonly used in Scripture when mysteries are under discussion. . . . For though the symbol differs in essence from the thing signified (in that the latter is spiritual and heavenly, while the former is physical and visible), still, because it not only symbolizes the thing that it has been consecrated to represent as a bare and empty token, but also truly exhibits it, why may its name not rightly belong to the thing?" (Calvin, *Institutes* 4.17.21). See Davis, *This Is My Body*, 74; Hart, "Calvin and Barth," 42–44.

[144] Schreiner believes this discourse has a secondary reference to the Eucharist: "When

acknowledged that this passage did not clearly articulate a spiritual presence view of the Eucharist, but again and again he used John 6 in his exposition of the Lord's Supper.[145] The context of the passage emphasizes over and over again that Jesus is pointing to His upcoming death on the cross. He is calling on His followers to put their trust in His future death.[146] D. A. Carson draws attention to the parallel between "eating" and "drinking" in v. 54, and "looking" and "believing" in the Son in v. 40: "The only substantial difference is that one speaks of eating Jesus' flesh and drinking Jesus' blood, while the other, in precisely the same conceptual location, speaks of looking to the Son and believing in him. The conclusion is obvious: the former is the metaphorical way of the referring to the latter."[147] In John 6, then, faith in Christ's finished work is emphasized. His spiritual presence in the Supper is not.[148]

Lastly, two Pauline statements in 1 Corinthians 10–11 have been used to support the idea of a spiritual presence.[149] In 10:16 Paul identifies the cup as "participation in the blood of Christ" and the bread as "participation in the body of Christ."[150] The apostle is addressing an

believers break the bread and drink the wine, they feed on the work of Jesus in giving his flesh and shedding his blood on their behalf" (T. R. Schreiner, *New Testament Theology: Magnifying God in Christ* [Grand Rapids: Baker, 2008], 712). Similarly Carson argues that although there are almost certainly allusions to the Supper here they "are set in the broader framework of Jesus' saving work, in particular his cross-work" (D. A. Carson, *The Gospel According to John* [Leicester, England: InterVarsity; Grand Rapids: Eerdmans, 1991], 297).

[145] E.g., Calvin, *Institutes* 4.17.5, 7, 8, 14. In his commentary on John, Calvin is unclear about how John 6 functions in the Supper. On the one hand, he writes, "This sermon does not refer to the Lord's Supper, but to the continual communication which we have apart from the reception of the Lord's Supper." On the other hand, he contends, "There is nothing said here that is not figured and actually presented to believers in the Lord's Supper" (John Calvin, *The Gospel According to St. John, 1–10*, CNTC 169–70).

[146] As Schreiner notes, Jesus used stark language requiring "a faith that eats [his] flesh and drinks his blood." What this means, though, is not a literal meal, or even a special spiritual encounter with Christ through the elements. Rather, it means "the life of the age to come becomes a reality as one trusts in the work of Jesus on the cross and in his resurrection" (Schreiner, *New Testament Theology*, 85). Elsewhere Schreiner argues, "This is almost certainly a reference to Jesus' death on the cross. . . . The offense of the cross is thereby communicated (John 6:61). The only way human beings can have life is to feed on Jesus as the crucified one. They must put their trust in him by relying on his body and blood as the only basis by which they could enjoy eternal life" (*New Testament Theology*, 285).

[147] Carson, *John*, 297.

[148] In addition Carson has noted several other problems—conceptual and chronological—with understanding this discourse to be about the Eucharist (Carson, *John*, 297).

[149] As Phillips claims, "The biblical institution mandates the true presence of Christ in some sense (see again 1 Cor. 10:16; 11:29). We do not merely reflect upon Christ's death, but we in some way eat what is offered" ("Lord's Supper," 203–4).

[150] Scripture quotations are from the ESV. Gordon Fee contends, "What the evidence [in

issue of conscience, whether or not believers are permitted to eat food offered to idols. Several contextual points argue against a sacramental understanding of Christ's spiritual presence here. First, the language in 10:2–4 alerts us that Paul is speaking symbolically. Second, he argues that Jews are "participants in the altar" (10:18) and that pagans are "participants with demons" who set a table for their followers (10:20–21). This "participation" does not argue for a special presence of demons in the idol feasts, for "the earth is the Lord's, and the fullness thereof" (10:26). Instead, those eating meals offered to demons are participating not in the demons themselves, but rather in the worship of demons. As Fee explains, "The food eaten at the pagan meals has been sacrificed to demons; that means that those at the table are sharers in what has been sacrificed to demons in the same way that Israel shared in what had been sacrificed to God. . . . Paul's point is simple: These pagan meals are in fact sacrifices to demons; the worship of demons is involved. One who is already bound to one's Lord and to one's fellow believers through participation at the Lord's Table cannot under any circumstances also participate in the worship of demons."[151] So, the apostle is here insisting, "Those who drink of the cup are partaking of the benefits of Christ's death on their behalf. Similarly, those who consume the broken bread share in the benefits of Christ's body. The broken bread symbolizes the body of Christ given for his people in his death."[152]

The second Pauline text is the apostle's warning against taking the Supper in "an unworthy manner" lest one be found "guilty of profaning the body and blood of the Lord" (1 Cor 11:27). Again, the context is the key to rightly understanding this verse. Paul warns the rich members of the community against bringing their own food to the Table and gorging themselves on their feast while the poor members of the community watch longingly. This is the "unworthy manner" of participation since it hinders one of the major reasons for celebrating

10:16] does not seem to allow is a sacramental understanding of the meal itself, as if they were 'participating in the Lord' by the actual eating of the food, as though the food were the Lord himself. Neither the language and grammar nor the example of Israel nor the examples from the pagan meals allow such a meaning. The 'fellowship,' therefore, was most likely a celebration of their common life in Christ, based on the new covenant in his blood that had previously bound them together in union with Christ by his Spirit" (G. D. Fee, *The First Epistle to the Corinthians* [Grand Rapids: Eerdmans, 1987], 467).

[151] Ibid., 472.

[152] Schreiner, *New Testament Theology*, 731.

the Supper—picturing the unity of brothers and sisters with one another.[153] Paul's point here then is largely to focus the Corinthians' eyes on their responsibilities to each other, not on Christ's presence in the Eucharist.

There is much to commend in the RT's understanding of the Lord's Supper, as we have already noted. But it has four weaknesses that call into question the validity of its teaching of the spiritual presence of Christ in the Supper. First, the RT lacks a biblically coherent understanding of sacraments. Second, it fails to prioritize Christ's presence with His people at all times. Third, it unwisely urges people to look to the Eucharist for hope. Fourth, it lacks clear biblical support.

Calvin teaches that the efficacy of the cross is applied to Christians "through the gospel but more clearly through the Sacred Supper, where [Christ] offers himself with all his benefits to us, and we receive him by faith."[154] This is an example of the out-of-focus pastoral motivations of the RT. Certainly the Eucharist should point us to the cross. But the cross of Jesus, not the Supper, is where we see Christ most clearly.

[153] On this interpretation, see Schreiner, *New Testament Theology*, 731–33.

[154] Calvin, *Institutes* 4.17.5. This is a common view in the RT. E.g., Venema says, "The preaching of the Word is a holy and awesome affair, for Christ dwells among his people through the preaching of the gospel. But no less holy and awesome are the sacramental signs and seals that accompany the gospel. For in the sacraments Christ is pleased to give himself to his people, in a manner distinct from that of preaching but not to be ignored" ("The Doctrine of the Lord's Supper in the Reformed Confessions," 84).

SOUNDS FROM BAPTIST HISTORY

Gregory A. Wills*

Between 1850 and 1950, Baptist churches in the United States altered in their Communion practices in a number of significant ways. They gave up leavened bread for unleavened, fermented wine for unfermented, and the common cup for individual cups. They also gave up close Communion for open Communion. Close Communion meant that scriptural baptism—the immersion of a professing believer—was prerequisite to participation in the Lord's Supper. Open Communion meant that faith alone was prerequisite. Baptist churches traditionally insisted on close Communion and until the 1890s disfellowshipped any pastors or churches that adopted open Communion. By 1900 Northern Baptists tolerated open Communion churches and the practice spread. Around 1950 Southern Baptists experienced a similar transformation.[1]

The acceptance of open Communion was an important step toward a more progressive religion among Baptists. For several generations American religion had been moving toward greater tolerance and individual freedom in religion, but these values had limited success among Baptists until the late nineteenth century. Baptists supported full religious liberty and tolerance in civil society, but in their churches they enforced orthodox belief and behavior, including commitment

* Gregory A. Wills received his Ph.D. from Emory University. He is professor of Church History, associate dean of Theology and Tradition, and director of the Center for the Study of the Southern Baptist Convention at the Southern Baptist Theological Seminary in Louisville, Kentucky.

[1] Terminology has varied somewhat over the years. "Close Communion" broadly referred to the practice of any denomination that limited participation in the Lord's Supper to its own fellowship, i.e., to persons belonging to the congregations of that denomination. Since most Baptists believed that believer's baptism by immersion was prerequisite to participation in the Lord's Supper, this had the effect of limiting Communion to Baptists alone. Baptists referred to their own practice as "close Communion," "strict Communion," or "restricted Communion." The phrase "closed Communion" was almost unprecedented in any context before 1900 but slowly entered common usage, and always meant the same thing as "close Communion." Many writers used it to refer to the Lutherans of the Missouri Synod or of the Wisconsin Synod, to Mennonites, to New England Puritans, and to some Anglicans and Presbyterians, in reference to the fact that certain classes or communions of professing Christians were prohibited from participation. Baptists usually referred to the practice of welcoming to the Lord's Table all believers, whether baptized or not, as "open Communion," but sometimes as "mixed Communion" or "intercommunion."

to close Communion.[2] As commitment to tolerance and individual freedom in religion grew, the practice of restricting Communion to the immersed appeared increasingly bigoted and tasteless. The acceptance of open Communion practice among Northern Baptists was an early indication of the broad transformation underway in American Protestantism. It strengthened the position of denominational progressives and prepared the denomination to tolerate other progressive developments, including the new modernist theology.

Leaven, Alcohol, and the Common Cup

The doctrine of close Communion dominated Baptist discussions of the Lord's Supper throughout most of their modern history, because it was controversial and because most Baptists judged that the Bible required it. Open Communion Baptists held that close Communion violated the Scripture's command of love. Other differences concerning Communion did not produce as much controversy because they did not seem to contradict biblical requirements.

Baptists, for example, differed on the preference for leavened or unleavened bread. Baptists before the late nineteenth century preferred leavened bread for use in Communion.[3] Like Reformed Protestants generally, Baptists used leavened bread because they held that Jesus appointed the use of bread merely, not of a specific kind of bread. They agreed with Baptist theologian Alexander Carson that Jesus used unleavened bread at the Last Supper only because "it was the bread that was present."[4] At the same time some churches used unleavened bread.[5] By 1900 unleavened bread was becoming more popular, and by midcentury, nearly all Baptist churches used unleavened bread.[6] The change may have been influenced by the paedobaptist argument that

[2] See G. A. Wills, *Democratic Religion: Freedom, Authority, and Church Discipline in the Baptist South, 1785–1900* (New York: Oxford University Press, 1997); N. Hatch, *The Democratization of American Religion* (New Haven: Yale University Press, 1989).

[3] The fact that Baptists used leavened bread in Communion was used to counter their insistence on immersion. See L. Woods, *Lectures on Infant Baptism* (Andover, MA: Flagg and Gould, 1829), 197; S. Miller, *Infant Baptism Scriptural and Reasonable* (Philadelphia: Joseph Whetham, 1835), 99–100; id., *Presbyterianism, the Truly Primitive and Apostolical Constitution of the Church of Christ* (Philadelphia: Presbyterian Board of Publication, 1835), 79.

[4] A. Carson, *Baptism in Its Mode and Subjects* (Philadelphia: American Baptist Publication Society, 1860), 379.

[5] J. A. Chambliss, "Administering the Lord's Supper," *Baptist Courier*, 3 November 1881, 1.

[6] See e.g. Ray Summers to J. Kenneth Clark, 6 February 1958, Ray Summers Papers, Southwestern Baptist Theological Seminary (SWBTS).

Baptists were inconsistent to insist on immersion in baptism while at the same time they did not insist on unleavened bread in Communion. But Protestants widely made the same change.

Baptists also relinquished the use of fermented wine, though for different reasons. Since about 1820 evangelicals opposed the use of alcohol as a beverage due to its tragic social consequences. As their efforts succeeded, alcoholic beverages became stigmatized and Communion wine was no exception. Baptist editor Joseph Baker recommended the change in 1848. He acknowledged that apostolic wine "often, if not always" contained alcohol, and that, therefore, there could be no justification for refusing alcoholic wine if served in Communion. But, he continued, it was best if "our churches, when practicable, should procure for sacramental purposes, wine without any alcoholic mixture."[7] Kentucky's Bracken Baptist Association recommended in 1860 that its churches purchase from vintners "unfermented wine for sacramental purposes."[8] By the early twentieth century Baptist churches in the North and the South had widely adopted the use of unfermented wine or grape juice. Temperance was now expected of evangelical Christians, and prohibition legislation was growing in popularity. The absence of alcohol, most Baptists concluded, had nothing to do with the form commanded, since Jesus commanded that his followers drink the fruit of the vine. Edgar Y. Mullins summarized the view in 1907: "The grounds on which the unfermented wine is substituted for the fermented is that Jesus, in the institution of the Lord's Supper, refers to it as the fruit of the vine, and the unfermented wine is regarded as sufficiently covering this statement of Christ."[9] By 1950 the use of fermented wine was very rare.[10]

The introduction of individual cups, though it provoked little controversy, altered the texture of the ceremony and suited broad cultural shifts. In the 1890s some Baptist churches began serving the wine in individual cups. The practice had been to use a common cup, or in larger congregations, several common cups.[11] The arguments in

[7] J. S. Baker, "The Sacramental Elements," *Christian Index*, 19 October 1848, 333.

[8] Bracken Baptist Association, *Minutes*, 1860, 4.

[9] Edgar Y. Mullins to M. L. Lawson, 16 January 1907, in Letterpress Book 31, p. 82, Letterpress Copybook Collection, Southern Baptist Theological Seminary (SBTS).

[10] See e.g. Ellis A. Fuller to H. P. Hoskins, 24 August 1949, box 18, Fuller Papers, SBTS; Ray Summers to J. Kenneth Clark, 6 February 1958, Ray Summers Papers, SWBTS.

[11] See e.g. Edgar Y. Mullins to W. H. Cannada, Letterpress Book 26, 23 February 1904, Letterpress Copybook Collection, SBTS; Edgar Y. Mullins to George Manning, ibid., 16 April 1904.

favor of the individual cup included taste and health. Passing the cup from mouth to mouth was unseemly or offensive to many persons—it violated good taste. Increasingly, many viewed it also as unsanitary.[12] Churches felt freedom to change the manner of distributing the wine, since it was the taking of the elements that was commanded, not the use of a single cup.[13]

But many churches hesitated to abandon the common cup. The use of individual cups seemed overly fastidious.[14] The refinement also seemed to some to lack warrant. The Bible spoke of "the cup" in the supper, and some believed that this indicated a scriptural norm. It was also cost prohibitive for poor congregations who could not afford to purchase individual service sets. It would further introduce a diversity of practice between wealthy and poor churches, which would promote alienation rather than unity among the churches. Some also doubted whether the single cup spread disease: "No one can produce an instance of disease contracted in the practice of the present plan. We all drink from the same dippers at wells, springs, hotels, etc., and will continue to do so notwithstanding our fastidiousness on the subject of germs."[15] In 1903, for example, only four or five North Carolina Baptist churches and only one South Carolina Baptist church were known to use individual cups.[16]

The influenza pandemic of 1918, in which over half a million Americans died, seems to have tipped the balance in the direction of the individual cups. The danger induced churches of many denominations, including Baptists, to adopt individual Communion sets. The William Dietz Company appealed to fears of the flu in its 1919 advertisements: "Did the 'flu' get you? No one was ever known to contract any contagion or infection of any kind by using Dietz Peerless Individual Communion Service."[17] Use of the common cup soon grew rare.

Baptists differed also on the frequency of observing Communion. Most churches observed the ceremony once per quarter, a smaller number observed it once per month, and a few observed it weekly.

[12] D. W. Key, "The Individual Cup," *Christian Index*, 2 May 1895, 2.

[13] J. W. Bailey, "Individual Cups in the Lord's Supper," *Biblical Recorder*, 5 August 1903, 8–9.

[14] Key, "The Individual Cup," 2.

[15] Bailey, "Individual Cups in the Lord's Supper," 8–9.

[16] Unsigned editorial, "Individual Communion Cups," *Baptist Courier*, 12 March 1903, 4; F. M. Satterwhite, "The Individual Cup," *Baptist Courier*, 19 March 1903, 16; Bailey, "Individual Cups in the Lord's Supper," 8–9.

[17] Advertisement, *Baptist Standard*, 20 March 1919, 24.

The vast majority held that the Bible required regular observance, but did not specify a precise frequency. In the early nineteenth century, however, a small number of preachers adopted the belief that the Bible required the churches to observe the Lord's Supper every Sunday. The most prominent among them was William B. Johnson, who afterward became the first president of the Southern Baptist Convention.[18] But Johnson convinced few. Practices regarding frequency changed little.[19]

Issues relating to the kind of bread, frequency, alcoholic content, and the kind of cup provoked little controversy among Baptists in America. Most Baptists held that these issues, while significant in their general bearings and ramifications, were not matters of moral duty. They decided these issues were based on such practical considerations as edification, decorum, and suitability. Baptist leaders believed that these issues did not affect their commitment to apostolic ecclesiology, biblical authority, traditional theology, or Baptist identity.

Close Communion, however, was a different matter. Baptists viewed the adoption of open Communion as a rejection of biblical ecclesiology. But it was more than that. It was a symptom of other errors. In fact, it generally indicated the adoption of progressive views of Scripture and theology. It indicated a different kind of Baptist.

Commitment to Close Communion

Until the Victorian era, most Baptists in England supported close Communion, though not without controversy. The two main groups of English Baptists emerging in the first half of the seventeenth century were the General Baptists and the Particular Baptists, and the majority of each group supported close Communion. In 1612 the English General Baptists residing in Amsterdam affirmed that "only baptized persons" could receive Communion. Their "Orthodox Creed" of 1678 asserted that "no unbaptized, unbelieving, or openly profane, or

[18] See W. B. Johnson, "Correspondence of W. B. Johnson, Letter VI," *Biblical Recorder*, 19 September 1846, 1. Joseph Baker was among the few who agreed (J. S. Baker, "Weekly Communion," *Christian Index*, 4 September 1861, 2).

[19] The 1953 report of the Committee on Relations with Other Religious Bodies, for example, indicated that 66 percent of churches observed Communion quarterly and 19 percent monthly (Southern Baptist Convention, *Annual*, 1953, 449).

wicked heretical persons ought to be admitted" to the Lord's Supper, since admitting them would "profane it."[20]

The Particular Baptists implicitly endorsed the practice in their 1644 First London Confession. Like the General Baptist confessions, the First London Confession taught that a scriptural church was composed only of persons who were baptized as believers by immersion, and Christ gave His ordinances to this church of baptized believers. "To this church," the First London Confession said, "he hath made his promises, and given the signs of his covenant." God had committed to this church the "practical enjoyment of the ordinances."[21]

But some Particular Baptists dissented. Several prominent and popular preachers opposed close Communion beginning in the seventeenth century. In 1671 John Bunyan, the influential preacher who wrote *Pilgrim's Progress* from the Bedford jail, published a defense of open Communion and open membership. He argued that baptism was not prerequisite to either church membership or Communion. A significant controversy ensued, but the majority of English Baptists retained close Communion practices until the nineteenth century, when Robert Hall's defense of open Communion made a deep impression and began to turn the tide in favor of open Communion. Particular Baptist Charles H. Spurgeon, England's most celebrated preacher in the second half of the nineteenth century, practiced open Communion and no doubt influenced many others in its favor. By 1900, open Communion was the common practice among English Baptists.[22]

In America, the great majority of Baptists practiced close Communion until the twentieth century. Baptists expressed their commitment to close Communion in their church documents. Most churches had

[20] "Propositions and Conclusions concerning True Christian Religion," in W. L. Lumpkin, *Baptist Confessions of Faith*, rev. ed. (Valley Forge, PA: Judson Press, 1969), 137; "Orthodox Creed," in Lumpkin, *Baptist Confessions*, 321. The General Baptists' "Standard Confession" of 1660 agreed and stated that it was the "duty of believers baptized" to observe the Lord's Supper ("Standard Confession," in Lumpkin, *Baptist Confessions*, 229).

[21] "The London Confession, 1644," in Lumpkin, *Baptist Confessions*, 165.

[22] When Particular Baptist ministers gathered in 1689 to issue a joint confession of faith, they produced the Second London Confession, a revision of the Westminster Confession. It omitted any statement on the matter for two apparent reasons. It was a revision of Presbyterians' Westminster Confession, which made no reference to the matter. And the Particular Baptists probably did not wish to exclude the open Communion minority from uniting in subscription to this statement at this critical time. For a fine discussion of the controversy between the open and the close communionists, especially in the nineteenth century, see M. J. Walker, *Baptists at the Table: The Theology of the Lord's Supper among English Baptists in the Nineteenth Century* (Didcot, UK: Baptist Historical Society, 1992), 32–81.

covenants or statements of "gospel order" that made this commitment explicit. The Phillips Mill Baptist Church in Georgia, for example, included commitment to close Communion in their 1785 covenant: "We believe that true believers only are the subjects of baptism, dipping is the mode, and that only those who have been baptized, and live agreeably to the rules of the gospel, have a right to Communion, to the Lord's Supper."[23]

Local associations expressed the same commitment and promoted uniformity in the practice. Associations played an important role in promoting orthodox faith and practice. When churches applied for admission, the association admitted only those whose "faith and practice" agreed with their understanding of the teaching of the NT. Typically a committee examined the candidate church's faith and practice and advised the association: "On examination, finding them orderly and orthodox, they were received."[24]

Associations held that open Communion was contrary to the apostolic church order and required close Communion as a condition of membership. Maine's Bowdoinham Baptist Association placed close Communion in its doctrinal statement when it organized in 1787—believer's baptism "was requisite" to the admission to the Lord's Supper.[25] The Philadelphia Baptist Association, organized in 1707 as the first association of Baptist churches in America, promoted close Communion also through the *Baptist Catechism*, which they adopted in 1742. The answer to Question 103 required believer's baptism, previously defined as immersion only, as prerequisite to participation in the Lord's Supper. It stated that the "proper subjects" of the Lord's Supper were "they who have been baptized upon a personal profession of their faith in Jesus Christ."[26]

The Separate Baptists, who originated in the First Great Awakening by separating from New Light Congregational churches, also insisted on baptism as prerequisite to immersion. The Sandy Creek Baptist

[23] Phillips Mill Baptist Church, "Church Covenant," *Christian Index*, 23 November 1859, 1.

[24] Kehukee Baptist Association, *Minutes*, 1789, 4, 6.

[25] See H. S. Burrage, *History of the Baptists in Maine* (Portland, ME: Marks Printing House, 1904), 89.

[26] *Baptist Catechism, or, A Brief Instruction in the Principles of the Christian Religion, Agreeably to the Confession of Faith Put Forth by Upwards of an Hundred Congregations in Great-Britain July the 3d, 1689; Adopted by the General Association of Philadelphia, September the 22d, 1742; and Now Received by Churches of the Same Denomination in Most of the United States, to Which Are Added, the Proofs from Scriptures* (Philadelphia: Robert Aitken, 1786), 17.

Association, the first association organized by the Separate Baptists, adopted a confession of faith that defined baptism as believer's baptism by immersion and required that only "regular baptized church members" could gain admission to the Lord's Supper.[27] When the Separate Baptists and Regular Baptists formally united, they made the practice of close Communion one of the eleven principles of their union: "Believer's baptism by immersion is necessary to receiving the Lord's Supper."[28]

The Problem of Close Communion

Baptists held that their practice was based on the simple proposition that baptism was prerequisite to participation in Communion. This was uncontroversial in principle, since all Christians agreed with it. The controversy arose because Baptists believed that baptizing infants was not baptism. Archibald T. Robertson, professor of NT at the Southern Baptist Theological Seminary, explained it this way in 1892:

> The New Testament teaches clearly by numerous examples that only baptized believers partook of the Lord's Supper. Instance the Apostles at its institution, Luke xxii:44ff.; the example of the early Christians, Acts ii:43, I. Cor. xi: 20–33. These passages show clearly that it was the baptized believers who celebrated the ordinance. . . . If we hold that immersion on profession of faith alone constitutes baptism, we are compelled as a matter of principle and consistency to invite only such persons to the Supper.[29]

Since close Communion involved rejecting ostensibly unbaptized believers from the Lord's Table, non-Baptists viewed the practice as uncharitable at best, and as bigoted at worst. English Baptist missionary William Ward argued in 1800 that the Baptist commitment to close Communion reflected a "moroseness of temper" that rendered Baptists "unlovely in the sight of the Christian world."[30] In the 1850s,

[27] Quoted in G. W. Purefoy, *History of the Sandy Creek Baptist Association* (New York: Sheldon and Co., 1859), 105. The association adopted this as its first confession of faith in 1816.

[28] Quoted in J. H. Spencer, *A History of Kentucky Baptists from 1769 to 1885*, ed. B. B. Spencer, (Cincinnati: J. H. Spencer, 1885), 1:546. See similarly R. B. Semple, *A History of the Rise and Progress of Baptists in Virginia*, ed. G. W. Beale (Richmond, VA: Pitt and Dickinson, 1894), 274, 427; Spencer, *A History of Kentucky Baptists*, 1:135, 362.

[29] A. T. Robertson, "Puzzling Questions," *Seminary Magazine* [Southern Baptist Theological Seminary] 5 (1892): 407–8.

[30] Ward, quoted in E. S. Wenger, *The Story of the Lall Bazar Baptist Church, Calcutta* (Calcutta: Edinburgh Press, 1908), 163. Under Ward's influence, the missionaries' church practiced

William Hooper, president of Wake Forest College, summarized the paedobaptist reproaches against the close Communion practice of Baptist churches: "This exclusiveness causes them to be thought and spoken of as narrow-minded, bigoted, and arrogating to themselves the claim of being the only true church of God."[31] When Basil Manly Jr. matriculated at the Princeton Theological Seminary in 1845, he felt the reproach. He sometimes worshipped in the Presbyterian church on Sundays, but since Manly's Baptist beliefs required him to view the Presbyterians as unbaptized and scripturally ineligible to participate in the Lord's Supper, he viewed their administration of Communion as unscriptural and disorderly. This did not make him popular among his fellow students. "Yesterday was communion Sabbath with the Presbyterians here, and I had my first trial. For a moment the thought rushed through my mind, 'These are Christians. This is the Lord's Supper. Can I not commune with my Lord in this ordinance?' But I felt that duty, honesty, and principle were not to be sacrificed—so I rose and took a seat where according to the pastor's request the non-communicants were seated. This was taking my stand." His stand provoked the criticism of fellow students.[32]

Some believers who were convinced of believer's baptism by immersion found close Communion sufficiently offensive and embarrassing that they refused to join a Baptist church. They sometimes asked the Baptist pastor to baptize them by immersion, but said that they did not intend to join the Baptist church because of their objection to close Communion. Baptist preachers rarely agreed to baptize such persons, because they knew the truth but were unwilling to act consistently with it and to identify with those who embraced it.[33] Richard Fuller, third president of the Southern Baptist Convention, explained that such a person was "plainly living in sin" since "he, by his public act, declares the Baptist church right, but joins (and throws his influence on the side of) a church which opposes the Baptist church, and which,

open Communion from 1800 to 1810, when it returned to close Communion practice against Ward's strong protest.

[31] W. H. Hooper, "Explanation," *Biblical Recorder*, 4 May 1854, 2. Hooper, an Englishman who embraced open Communion among the English Baptists, supported the close Communion practice of the Baptists in America.

[32] Basil Manly Jr. to Basil Manly Sr., 9 May 1845, quoted in Joseph P. Cox, "A Study of the Life and Work of Basil Manly Jr." (Th.D. dissertation, Southern Baptist Theological Seminary, Louisville, KY, 1954), 66.

[33] See Jesse Mercer's comments at Young Minister, untitled, *Christian Index*, 2 December 1834, 2.

if its doctrines could prevail, would utterly efface baptism from the earth and substitute the sprinkling of children."[34] It was a betrayal of acknowledged biblical principles and was motivated by the reproach of close Communion.

Baptists enforced commitment to close Communion by means of ordination standards, church discipline, and associational membership. Ordination councils required candidates for ordination to affirm close Communion, as an 1865 South Carolina council did: "Do you hold that a member of the Baptist church cannot partake with unbaptized persons at the Lord's Table, and do you intend to teach and practice restricted communion?"[35] Churches rebuked members who took Communion in a paedobaptist church, and sometimes rebuked their pastor. When John A. Chambliss, pastor of the prominent Second Baptist Church of Richmond, adopted open Communion principles in 1871, he had no choice but to resign. The church insisted on close Communion:

> Whereas, our pastor, Rev. J. A. Chambliss, gave notice to the church, on last Sunday, that for the future he could not "undertake to maintain and defend the practice of strict communion as it now prevails in the American Baptist churches," and has tendered his resignation as pastor of this church; and whereas this church holds now, as it ever has held since its organization, that none but baptized believers are authorized to partake of the Lord's Supper, and that immersion is the only scriptural mode of baptism; and believing that the pastor should be a faithful and fearless exponent and defender of the faith of his people, therefore, Resolved, That we accept the resignation of Brother J. A. Chambliss.

The editor of the Virginia Baptist newspaper approved: "Christian principle has triumphed over personal attachment, and the Second [Baptist] Church is entitled to a place in the foremost ranks of the great Baptist brotherhood as a defender of the faith once delivered to the saints."[36] Open Communion could find no foothold before the 1890s.

[34] R. Fuller, "Re-Baptism," *Biblical Recorder*, 30 August 1845, 1.

[35] Quoted in E. T. Winkler, "Case of Rev. J. C. C. Brandon," *Working Christian*, 23 December 1869, 2.

[36] Quoted in unsigned, "Action of the Second Baptist Church," *Working Christian*, 17 August 1871, 3. Not long afterward he became fully persuaded of the correctness of close Communion, received a call to Charleston, South Carolina's Citadel Square Baptist Church, and opposed open Communion from its pulpit. See T. Gaines, "Rev. J. A. Chambliss," *Working Christian*, 31 October 1872, 2; J. A. Chambliss, "Rev. Dr. Chambliss on Communion," *Working Christian*, 30 April 1874, 2; William D. Thomas to John A. Broadus, 26 August 1871, box 3, Broadus Papers; D. Shaver, "Hard Blows," *Christian Index*, 17 August 1871, 126.

Open Communion and the Long Island Baptist Association

John Chambliss, however, was not the only Baptist minister to embrace open Communion around 1870. Open Communion sentiments spread among Baptist clergy in the late nineteenth century as part of a broader movement that pitted a spirit of love and unity against orthodoxy. Although open Communion preachers experienced defeat in the 1870s when they challenged close Communion, by the 1890s they won toleration of open Communion among Northern Baptists. Toleration among Southern Baptists took longer.

In the late 1860s two respected Northern Baptist preachers publicly advocated open Communion. Charles H. Malcolm, pastor of the Newport, Rhode Island, Second Baptist Church, had quietly practiced open Communion in the church for some years when, in 1868, he decided to promote the adoption of open Communion among the Baptists.[37] Also in 1868, Crammond Kennedy, pastor of the Fifth Avenue Baptist Church in New York City, published a book advocating open Communion. The two succeeded in provoking considerable discussion of the matter in the Baptist newspapers of the North, but the weight of leadership, including the Baptist newspaper editors, opposed them.[38]

The greatest controversy over open Communion occurred in the 1870s in New York, particularly in Brooklyn. Several Baptist preachers in New York concluded that the time had now come to lead Baptists in a revolution, and they pressed for denominational toleration of open Communion. In the end they were unsuccessful. Crammond Kennedy's Fifth Avenue Baptist Church excluded him from fellowship.[39] George F. Pentecost, pastor of Brooklyn's Hanson Place Baptist Church, resigned his position in 1872 when it became clear that the church did not share his open Communion sentiments. Pentecost

[37] See e.g. D. Shaver, "The Open Communion Fiasco," *Christian Index*, 5 March 1868, 38; id., "The Open Communion Leader," *Christian Index*, 16 April 1868, 62.

[38] In 1871 Charlotte Broadus summarized the news and trends in America for her husband who was traveling in Europe and assessed the matter thus: "The Northern papers are full of articles on the question of open communion. The editors are all against it. Dr. Kendrick of R. wrote an article against it, wh. had been published in tract form and is selling by thousands; it is supposed to settle the question." Charlotte Broadus to John A. Broadus, 25 February 1871, box 3, John A. Broadus Papers, Archives and Special Collections, James P. Boyce Centennial Library, Southern Baptist Theological Seminary, Louisville, KY.

[39] See C. Kennedy, *Close Communion or Open Communion? An Experience and an Argument* (New York: American News Company, 1868); D. Shaver, "Discipline," *Christian Index*, 4 February 1869, 18; Shaver, untitled, ibid., 34.

afterward left the Baptists and joined the Congregationalist clergy.[40] His brother, H. O. Pentecost, similarly practiced open Communion as pastor of Long Island's Rockville Center Baptist Church, and like his brother was compelled to resign in 1873.[41]

Brooklyn pastor J. Hyatt Smith took center stage in the controversy. His decision to press for acceptance of open Communion provoked a controversy that continued for several years. In 1870 Smith, pastor of Brooklyn's Lee Avenue Baptist Church, published *The Open Door*, a fictional account of the Evansdale Baptist Church in which he portrayed close Communion as an obsolete relic of darker times.[42]

Most of the pastors in the Long Island Baptist Association, whose forty-two churches were anchored in Brooklyn but extended east to Sag Harbor, and to which the Lee Avenue church belonged, opposed open Communion. In 1873 Baptist preacher Justin D. Fulton accepted the call of the Hanson Place Baptist Church in order to lead the opposition to Smith and open Communion: "The chief reason why I was urged to come was because open communion was then sweeping like a tidal wave over the city and was threatening the weal of the denomination throughout the land. The battle was felt to be in Brooklyn."[43] Fulton began editing a newspaper dedicated to defending close Communion.

At the meeting of the Long Island Baptist Association in October 1873 the two forces collided. The contest began when some delegates raised objections to the open Communion position of Smith and his church. After extensive debate, the delegates voted in favor of E. T. Hiscox's motion to appoint a committee to investigate whether "the Lee Avenue church has departed from the faith and practices of the churches of this body in matters pertaining to the Lord's Supper."[44] The committee would recommend action the following year.

Smith predicted the triumph of open Communion. He told the press that the Lord's Supper was "free to all who desire to partake of it." And he believed that many other pastors in the association,

[40] From 1880 to 1886 Pentecost served as pastor of Brooklyn's Tompkins Avenue Congregational Church. Unsigned, "An Accession to the Brooklyn Pulpit," *Brooklyn Daily Eagle*, 9 May 1887, 4.

[41] Unsigned, "Personal," *Brooklyn Daily Eagle*, 9 June 1873, 4.

[42] J. H. Smith, *The Open Door; Or, Light and Liberty* (New York: T. E. Perkins, 1870).

[43] J. D. Fulton, "The Fulton Side of the Story," *Brooklyn Daily Eagle*, 5 December 1891, 5.

[44] Long Island Baptist Association, *Minutes*, 1873, 15–16; unsigned, "The Baptists," *Brooklyn Daily Eagle*, 22 October 1873, 4.

as well as most of the church members, supported his view. He expected, therefore, that the investigation would come to nothing and the association could not expel the church. "I tell you they dare not do it. It would create such a storm as would sweep them off their feet, and they know it." Smith believed that the cultural tide of individualism and enlightenment demanded greater liberty in denominational life and that it would soon overwhelm archaic doctrines and practices. Smith defied his opponents and led his church to participate in a Communion service with the Bedford Avenue Reformed Church, whose members were, according to Baptist beliefs, unbaptized.[45]

The Lee Avenue church claimed to accept close Communion in principle—they agreed that baptism must precede participation in the Lord's Supper. They agreed also that baptism was the immersion of professing believers. But they believed that God invited persons to the Table, not the church. They argued that God left the decision of eligibility to the individual conscience of each person present. The church had no authority to bar any believer from the Lord's Supper "simply on account of their conscientious differences from us concerning the mode and order of the ordinances, but on the contrary, we deem it consistent with the spirit of Christian charity and Gospel liberty to refrain from treating those whom God has cleansed as unclean merely because of their ceremonial irregularities."[46]

At the 1874 meeting of the Long Island Baptist Association, with a large crowd of spectators in attendance, it became evident that the majority disagreed with Smith and Lee Avenue church. The majority held that believer's baptism by immersion was a matter of fidelity to the Scripture's definite teaching, and that sprinkling infants as baptism was not merely a matter of ceremonial irregularity, but of disobedience to Christ, who commanded baptism as the first act of the new believer's discipleship. Close Communion was a natural and necessary corollary to the doctrines of believer's baptism and regenerate church membership. The committee concluded that the Lee Avenue church was, in fact, an "open communion church," and that close Communion was an "essential element in the basis of fellowship and cooperation" of the association. To remain in fellowship with the

[45] Unsigned, "J. H. Smith," *Brooklyn Daily Eagle*, 25 October 1873, 4; Long Island Baptist Association, *Minutes*, 1874, 20.

[46] Response of the Lee Avenue Baptist Church, quoted in Report of the Committee on the Lee Avenue church, in Long Island Baptist Association, *Minutes*, 1873, 19.

Lee Avenue church would implicate the association's other churches in their error and would countenance a "perversion of the gospel ordinances" and an assault against the "very grounds which justify our separate existence as a denomination." It would also destroy the association's harmony. The committee recommended expelling the Lee Avenue church from the association. The association voted 174–21 to expel the church.[47]

A minority agreed with Smith and the Lee Avenue Baptist Church. The members of the Gethsemane Baptist Church voted to withdraw from the association in sympathy. The First Baptist Church Brooklyn had a large contingent of members who supported open Communion, and its pastor and many of its delegates voted in support of Smith and the Lee Avenue church.[48] And open Communion sentiments were spreading among church members. The Strong Place Baptist Church and the Sixth Avenue Baptist Church had significant contingents of their membership who supported open Communion.[49] Even Fulton's Hanson Place church included an open Communion contingent who agitated against him.[50]

On the Sunday following the association action, Smith preached a sermon in which he gloried in being expelled from the "synagogue." Eligibility for participation in the Lord's Supper was, Smith said, "singly, simply, solely between the communicant and the Master of the Table," Jesus. To restrict fellow believers from the Table simply because they had different opinions concerning the ordinances of God's house, and to require all Baptist churches to impose this restriction, Smith said, was "bigotry" and "ecclesiastical tyranny," and disgraced the Baptist name. The Lee Avenue church had struck a blow for toleration and the "spirit of liberty," and joined the "triumphant of the liberalized and liberated church."[51]

The controversy did not end with the expulsion of the Lee Avenue Baptist Church. Also in 1874 the association refused to grant the request of the new Marcy Avenue Baptist Church for membership in the association because the new church would not affirm its commitment to close Communion. The pastor, Reuben Jeffrey, had refused to give

[47] Long Island Baptist Association, *Minutes*, 1873, 21–26.

[48] Unsigned, "J. H. Smith," *Brooklyn Daily Eagle*, 25 October 1873, 4; Long Island Baptist Association, *Minutes*, 1874, 26.

[49] Unsigned, "Open and Close," *Brooklyn Daily Eagle*, 30 November 1874, 4.

[50] Unsigned, "Baptist Broils," *Brooklyn Daily Eagle*, 29 September 1875, 4.

[51] J. H. Smith, "Rev. J. Hyatt Smith," *Brooklyn Daily Eagle*, 26 October 1874, 2.

a plain answer when the association's membership committee asked whether he held open Communion views. Delegates debated the matter for several hours until the church withdrew its application.[52] Jeffrey, in fact, did support open Communion. He argued that individual Christians were free to determine for themselves whether they were baptized. When it came to baptism and the Lord's Supper, Jeffrey held, "each disciple should be left to the exercise of his own liberty."[53]

After the association's 1874 actions against open Communion, the Lee Avenue and Marcy Avenue churches swelled with new members and visitors. Some were fleeing close Communion churches because they were "anxious to get clear of such bigots."[54] Smith concluded confidently that despite the church's expulsion, "the movement is spreading." It was indeed spreading, but too slowly and quietly to satisfy Smith. He soon resigned as pastor of the church. The congregation disbanded and sold their building. After a term in the United States Congress, Smith left the Baptist denomination and became pastor of Brooklyn's East Congregational Church.[55]

For the next two decades, open Communion made little noticeable progress among Northern Baptists. Marcy Avenue's Jeffrey finally decided against leading a revolution to establish open Communion. He submitted to the majority view of the ministers of the Long Island Baptist Association. In 1879, after five years of controversy, the Marcy Avenue Church gained admission to the association because the church finally satisfied the delegates that they sincerely pledged to uphold close Communion.[56] In 1883 a council of delegates from Long Island Baptist Association churches refused to recognize Brooklyn's new South Baptist Church because they believed that the church supported open Communion.[57] Long Island Baptists would not yield to open Communion.

[52] Unsigned, "The Baptists," *Brooklyn Daily Eagle*, 21 October 1874, 2. For a helpful overview of the entire affair from the open Communion perspective, see [Theodore M. Banta], *The Marcy Ave. Baptist Church, Brooklyn, N.Y. and the Long Island Baptist Association* (New York: Francis Hart and Co., 1880).

[53] R. Jeffrey, "Rev. Dr. Jeffrey," *Brooklyn Daily Eagle*, 26 October 1874, 2.

[54] Unsigned, "Open and Close," *Brooklyn Daily Eagle*, 30 November 1874, 4.

[55] Unsigned, "Open or Close," *Brooklyn Daily Eagle*, 20 November 1883, 4; unsigned, "Free Baptists," *Brooklyn Daily Eagle*, 25 October 1884, 6.

[56] Unsigned, "Baptist Association," *Brooklyn Daily Eagle*, 23 October 1879, 4.

[57] The church's articles of faith did not commit them to close Communion specifically, the pastor was evasive on the point, and many of the members of the church had been members at the recently disbanded Lee Avenue Baptist Church. The church afterward joined the open

The agitation for open Communion among Brooklyn Baptists provoked Baptists elsewhere to affirm their commitment to close Communion. The Baptist clergy of the Boston area adopted a statement affirming close Communion in 1872. The New York Baptist ministers association likewise voted in support of close Communion.[58] The majority among Northern Baptists refused to tolerate open Communion churches, and the most prominent leaders remained resolutely opposed to the practice.

The Baptist Congress and Open Communion Progress

In the years after the Brooklyn controversy most Baptist leaders believed that open Communion was making little progress and that Baptists in the North and South would remain solidly committed to close Communion.[59] Augustus H. Strong, the influential president of the Rochester Theological Seminary from 1872 to 1912, argued thoroughly for close Communion in all editions of his widely used *Systematic Theology*, and included a special section rebutting arguments in favor of open Communion.[60] The editor of the *Examiner*, the leading conservative voice among Northern Baptists, remained confident in the 1890s that Baptist orthodoxy stood firm. Its editor declared that the denomination's conviction in favor of close Communion was "settled and immovable."[61] But the appearance was deceiving.

The close Communion victory in the 1870s had shocked both progressive Baptists and the moderates who opposed driving the progressive men from the Baptist ranks. Open agitation for open Communion brought disastrous results. The moderates and progressives instead plotted a strategy designed to accustom Baptists to a policy of toleration.

Communion Free Baptist Association of New York and reorganized as the Hooper Street Free Baptist Church. Unsigned, "Open or Close," *Brooklyn Daily Eagle*, 20 November 1883, 4; unsigned, "Hard Shell," *Brooklyn Daily Eagle*, 23 November 1883, 2; unsigned, "Free Baptists," *Brooklyn Daily Eagle*, 25 October 1884, 6; unsigned, "Walks about the City," *Brooklyn Daily Eagle*, 11 August 1889, 10.

[58] Unsigned, "Pentecost," *Brooklyn Daily Eagle*, 15 November 1872, 2.

[59] See W. C. Wilkinson, *The Baptist Principle in Its Relation to Baptism and the Lord's Supper* (Philadelphia: American Baptist Publication Society, 1881), 239–44.

[60] See A. H. Strong, *Systematic Theology* (Philadelphia: Griffith and Rowland, 1909), 3:971–73, 977–80.

[61] Quoted in "Press Comment," *Public Opinion* 23 (1897): 753.

The chief obstacle was the conservative influence of the denominational newspapers, whose editors had great power in shaping consensus among Baptists and who nearly always promoted the traditional views. Their editorial consensus had helped to rout the open communionists in the 1870s and had discredited their pleas for toleration. When the editors declared progressives out of fellowship with the faith of the denomination, and demanded that they join another with whom they better agreed, they often followed J. Hyatt Smith's example and left the denomination. The loss of educated and gifted dissenters especially troubled the progressives. Due to the efforts of the editors to maintain the traditional view in the 1870s and 1880s, Crozer Theological Seminary professor E. H. Johnson observed, "the denomination at about that time lost a number of its brightest ministers."[62]

Open Communion functioned as the wedge issue for denominational progressives. Open Communion appealed to those clergy who sympathized most with the emerging liberal theology. It had little appeal to traditionalists. The denomination's commitment to close Communion was the point at which traditional orthodoxy effectively blocked the advance of the progressive ministers.

As progressive Northern Baptist clergy sought to establish tolerance of their views, therefore, they felt particularly "tormented by the communion question." A number of progressives consequently agreed in 1881 to organize a Baptist Congress, an annual meeting in which there would be freedom of discussion on both sides of important issues facing the denomination. They hoped particularly that it would serve as a platform on which progressive Baptists could express their views without condemnation and without being cast out of the denomination.[63] The congress was a place, progressive pastor Edwin M. Poteat said, where "free discussion" reigned "without fear of denominational councils," and where critics and censors alone were unwelcome.[64]

Success was not guaranteed. Since the congress privileged progressive views equally with the traditional views, most Baptists viewed

[62] E. H. Johnson, "Introductory Essay," *Eleventh Annual Session of the Baptist Congress* (New York: Baptist Congress Publishing Co., 1894), xii.

[63] Ibid., x–xvii. See also A. G. Lawson, "Historical Sketch of the Conference," in *Proceedings of the Second Annual Baptist Autumnal Conference* (Boston: Baptist Missionary Rooms, 1883), 100–101.

[64] E. M. Poteat, Address of Welcome, in *Ninth Annual Session of the Baptist Congress* (New York: Baptist Congress Publishing Co., 1890), 3.

the congress with suspicion. They judged it a "doubtful experiment," E. H. Johnson observed, because it welcomed "our sweet heretics."[65] They viewed it as an "irresponsible body" in which a few liberal Baptists typically expressed some "wild notions."[66]

The congress gained credibility by securing the support of conservative leaders. Such trusted conservatives as Alvah Hovey, president of Newton Theological Seminary, supported the congress and believed that it posed no threat to orthodoxy. Open discussion, Hovey thought, would clarify "what to fear" and what was "harmless" in the "new theology." The congress, for example, would discuss the new biblical criticism, he said, but Baptists were not likely to accept it, since that would mean "destroying root and branch our confidence in the writings of that volume as a revelation of the Lord's will." Hovey was confident that the congress would not promote liberal views because the leaders of the denomination were thoroughly committed to orthodoxy.[67]

Hovey was mistaken—the progressive strategy seemed to work. Progressive views on Communion and other points gradually achieved respectability among Northern Baptists. Indeed, by the 1890s, E. H. Johnson observed, it was the traditionalists who feared intolerance of their views: "For some years it has been the conservative who needed an assurance of respectful treatment from the progressive, rather than the progressive who needed a safe conduct home to assure him that indignant conservatives would not pounce upon him and lay him by the heels."[68]

By around 1900, close Communion was no longer credible for a growing number of Northern Baptist pastors. Those who supported close Communion were now on the defensive. Various observers recognized that a revolution had occurred on the matter. In 1897 New York's *Independent*, the popular advocate of liberalizing trends in religion, declared that "Christian charity and liberality" finally won a place for open Communion practice among Northern Baptists. Their

[65] E. H. Johnson, Response, in *Ninth Annual Session of the Baptist Congress* (New York: Baptist Congress Publishing Co., 1890), 5.

[66] From the *Christian Index*, quoted in "The Baptist Congress: What Our Baptist Papers Say about It," *Baptist Argus*, 2 December 1897, 93.

[67] A. Hovey, "Opening Address," in *Proceedings of the Second Annual Baptist Autumnal Conference for the Discussion of Current Questions* (Boston: Baptist Missionary Rooms, 1883), 5–6.

[68] E. H. Johnson, "Introductory Essay," *Eleventh Annual Session of the Baptist Congress* (New York: Baptist Congress Publishing Co., 1894), xv–xvi.

repression of open Communion in the 1870s was now "ancient history."[69] George A. Lofton, a prominent Southern Baptist pastor, noticed it too. After attending the 1897 meeting of the Baptist Congress in Chicago, Lofton remarked that "there is a growing sentiment among our northern brethren towards higher criticism, looseness in doctrine, open communionism in practice, and to the extinction of creedal authority as a bond of denominational authority among the churches."[70] An 1899 survey of Northern Baptist ministers suggested that only one-third of the Baptist pastors in the northeastern United States supported close Communion.[71] The editors of Chicago's *Standard* observed correctly in 1904 that "among northern Baptists the 'communion question' is no longer an issue."[72]

The Meaning of Open Communion

Open Communion represented the advance of a liberal and enlightened faith. Intellectual and cultural progress had discredited many elements of the traditional Baptist orthodoxy. Its Calvinist theology, its traditional view of inspiration, its strict church discipline, and its close Communion were giving way before the new liberal theology, privatized religion, robust individualism, and open Communion. E. H. Johnson characterized the trends among Northern Baptists in 1890 in terms of the quiet but rapid spread of belief in open Communion, Arminianism, future probation, and a progressive view of inspiration.[73]

Progressive Baptists felt that open Communion was a missiological imperative. The progressive clergy recognized that "the spirit of liberty is in the air" and sought to free the churches from their bondage to the outdated dogmas that crippled their effectiveness in the new age of liberty. J. Hyatt Smith committed the pulpit of the Lee Avenue church to expressing the love of Christ without the dogma: "This pulpit shall never be a hammer place where doctrines shall be wrought out. The demand today is—what? More Christ and less creed, and it is

[69] Quoted in "Press Comment," *Public Opinion* 23 (1897): 752.
[70] G. A. Lofton, "The Baptist Congress at Chicago," *Baptist Argus*, 25 November 1897, 69.
[71] W. C. Bitting, "From Greater New York," *The Standard* [Chicago], 9 December 1899, 26.
[72] Unsigned, "Diversity in Unity," *The Standard* [Chicago], 23 April 1904, 5.
[73] E. H. Johnson, quoted in "The Religious Press," *Christian Index*, 27 March 1890, 1.

to be our maxim until some early day when it shall be published from the walls of the church: 'All Christ and no creed.'"[74]

Close Communion jeopardized the future of the denomination. "This clinging to the old ideas," Smith explained, "is drawing people away from the Baptist churches. I see it every day. People feel the need of more liberty and go where they can find it. Whole families go away, particularly in the cities." Close Communion, Smith believed, may have been a useful practice for Baptists two centuries earlier, but "the world is advancing and we believe in keeping up with the world." The close communionists in the denomination "cling to their old beliefs that are out of date. The world's advance meant that the church could no longer "cling to old doctrines and dogmas, for "the time for creeds has past."[75]

Many Americans found close Communion's exclusivism offensive. Progressive clergy like Smith held that close Communion was part of the restrictive dogmatic religion. It derived from "bigotry" and "intolerance." Open Communion advanced under the banner of "light, liberty, and love."[76] Close Communion repulsed people from Baptist churches. H. F. Buckner, a Georgia Baptist pastor, reported that many persons had complained to him, "I have but one objection to you Baptists: I can't believe in your close communion."[77] The traditional Baptist practice was "driving away many good people who would otherwise connect themselves with that church."[78]

When George Dana Boardman, pastor of the Philadelphia First Baptist Church from 1864 to 1894 and president of the American Baptist Missionary Union, the foreign mission agency of the Northern Baptists, advocated open Communion in his 1901 volume on *The Church*, he appealed to the same individualist cultural trends. The Lord's Supper, he said, was "not so much an ecclesiastical, public rite as it is a personal, private privilege." Close Communion resulted from the logic of the letter of Scripture, but open Communion resulted from the charity of the spirit of Scripture. Churches should not judge

[74] Unsigned, "J. Hyatt Smith," *Brooklyn Daily Eagle*, 25 October 1873, 4; J. Hyatt Smith, "Rev. J. Hyatt Smith," *Brooklyn Daily Eagle*, 26 October 1874, 2.

[75] Unsigned, "J. Hyatt Smith," *Brooklyn Daily Eagle*, 25 October 1873, 4.

[76] See e.g. J. H. Smith, *The Open Door, or Light and Liberty*, 2nd ed. (Brooklyn, NY: D. S. Holmes, 1874), v, xiii.

[77] H. F. Buckner, "Thoughts on Close Communion," *Christian Index*, 16 October 1873, 2.

[78] Guy Sibley to John Broadus, note appended to Broadus to Sibley, 26 March 1888, box 12, Broadus Papers.

the qualifications of communicants, but "leave the responsibility where it belongs, with the listener himself." The only qualification was "Christian character."[79]

Traditionalists also recognized the affinities between open Communion and theological liberalism. Since the 1850s they viewed open Communion as a leading indicator of heresy. For nearly two years, from 1857 to 1859, James R. Graves, the Landmark editor of the *Tennessee Baptist*, kept up an attack on the orthodoxy of the Baptist clergy of Charleston, South Carolina. They were unsound, he claimed, because they tolerated an open Communion pastor among them. Although Graves finally conceded that his informant was mistaken, both he and the Charleston ministers connected open Communion with heresy.[80] When Sylvanus Landrum and Samuel Boykin assumed their duties as co-editors of Georgia Baptists' *Christian Index* in 1859, they presented their bona fides to the paper's subscribers: "We are Calvinistic, strict communion Baptists, and deeply interested in all our state denominational interests."[81] Commitment to Calvinism and to close Communion marked them as orthodox.

When John Broadus, founding professor at Southern Baptist Theological Seminary, defended the seminary's creed in 1859 also, he claimed that the most salient dangers to Baptist orthodoxy were "Campbellitish, or Arminian, or Open Communionist" principles.[82] M. B. Wharton, editor of the *Christian Index*, in 1884 similarly placed open Communion in his catalog of fundamental errors: "Unitarianism, Universalism, Antimissionism, Open communionism, Pedobaptism, Arminianism, Campbellism, Spiritualism."[83] Open Communion still meant disobedience to Christ, but it meant more than that. It was the entering wedge of a broad progressive movement and a leading indicator of heresy.

[79] G. D. Boardman, *The Church (Ecclesia)* (New York: Charles Scribner's Sons, 1901), 80, 86, 89–90. Churches increasingly left the judgment of Christian character also to the "listener himself."

[80] See e.g. J. P. Tustin, "The Tennessee Baptist," *Southern Baptist*, 26 May 1857, 2; J. R. Kendrick, "The Nashville Inquisitor," *Southern Baptist*, 22 September 1857, 2; unsigned, "The Quietus of a Report," *Southern Baptist*, 22 September 1859, 2. For a similar episode, see J. S. Baker, "An Apparent Impeachment," *Christian Index*, 28 April 1858, 2; Perryman, DeVotie et al., "Vindication of Rev. J. E. Dawson," *Christian Index*, 21 July 1858, 2.

[81] Sylvanus Landrum and Samuel Boykin, "Salutatory," *Christian Index*, 6 July 1859, 2.

[82] J. A. Broadus, "Southern Baptist Theological Seminary," *Religious Herald*, 25 August 1859, 1.

[83] M. B. Wharton, "The Religious Press," *Christian Index*, 7 February 1884, 1.

Open Communion and the Secession of Northern Baptist Conservatives

These connections alienated many traditional Baptists from the Northern Baptist Convention as open Communion spread in the denomination. After 1900, consequently, Northern Baptist conservatives from Illinois to California switched their affiliation to the Southern Baptist Convention, where commitment to close Communion was still strong. They held that to condone open Communion was effectively to condone liberalism and heresy.[84]

The traditionalists in southern Illinois were the first to make the switch. They organized a separate state convention in 1907 and affiliated it with the Southern Baptist Convention. They judged that the old state convention, which was affiliated with Northern Baptists, was unsound because it tolerated Unitarianism and open Communion. In 1906 George B. Foster, professor at the University of Chicago Divinity School and a member of the Chicago Baptist Minister's Conference, published a book in which he denied the deity of Christ. Also in 1906 prominent Illinois pastor John Aitchison published a book arguing in favor of open Communion. When the old convention rejected a resolution repudiating these two positions, conservative pastors in the southern part of the state formed the new convention to "wash their hands of these Unitarian and open communion heresies."[85] As a protection against liberalism and open Communion, they adopted the New Hampshire Confession and required member churches to agree with it.

In 1910 a group of New Mexico Baptists initiated a secession from the Northern Baptist Convention that resulted two years later in the convention's affiliation with the Southern Baptist Convention. The agitators believed that the Northern Baptists' Home Mission Society was promoting open Communion and tolerance of liberal theology. They accused the new pastor of the Albuquerque First Baptist Church, a recent graduate of Rochester Theological Seminary, of holding liberal and open Communion views.[86]

[84] See e.g. J. M. Dawson to W. W. Hamilton, 23 May 1942, Fuller Papers, SBTS; Floyd Looney to Ellis A. Fuller, 13 August 1948, box 18, Fuller Papers, SBTS.

[85] "Historical Preface," in Illinois State Baptist Association, Minutes, 1907, 6. For a fuller discussion, see M. Dillow, *Harvesttime on the Prairie: A History of Baptists in Illinois 1796–1996* (Franklin, TN: Providence House Publishers, 1996), 327–54.

[86] See e.g. Harriet B. Runyan to Edgar Y. Mullins, 21 August 1911, box 14, Edgar Y.

In 1928 a group of Arizona Baptists formed a new convention and affiliated it with the Southern Baptist Convention. The old convention's affiliation with the Northern Baptist Convention troubled conservatives because of the trend among Northern Baptists toward acceptance of liberal theology, open Communion, and ecumenical alliances. In their apology for forming the new convention, they indicted the old convention for its refusal to stand against open Communion and alien immersion. Opposing open Communion and alien immersion, they believed, was "the best way we can guard against the menace of liberalism." They too adopted the New Hampshire Confession.[87]

Many Baptists in California similarly dropped affiliation with Northern Baptists because of the spread of open Communion and the acceptance of alien immersions. They organized a new state convention in 1940 and affiliated with the Southern Baptist Convention.[88] Others in Oregon and Washington followed suit in 1948, when they organized a convention that affiliated with the Southern Baptist Convention. The departure of Northern Baptist churches from orthodoxy justified their action, they said. That departure began with the practice of receiving alien immersions and practicing open Communion. "This practice opens the Baptist churches to all the heresies of Protestantism and gives the Baptist churches a strong urge to interdenominational cooperation and affiliation," which was leading them toward the Federal Council of Churches, liberalism, and Unitarianism.[89] For Baptists, the road to apostasy began at open Communion.

Southern Baptists and Open Communion

In the twentieth century, after Northern Baptists generally had committed themselves to tolerance of open Communion practice, Southern Baptists continued to insist in principle on close Communion.

Mullins Papers, SBTS. The presenting issue in the controversy was whether New Mexico's Baptist churches were free to cease affiliation with the Northern Baptist's Home Mission Society and join the Southern Baptist Convention. The most important reason that they wanted to disassociate with Northern Baptists was the spread of liberalism and open Communion among them.

[87] Baptist General Convention of Arizona, Minutes, 1928, 10, 27. For a more extensive discussion, see C. L. Pair, *A History of the Arizona Southern Baptist Convention, 1928–1984* (n.p.: Arizona Southern Baptist Convention, 1989), 4–35.

[88] See F. Looney, *History of California Southern Baptists* (Fresno, CA: Southern Baptist General Convention of California, 1954), 10–29.

[89] R. E. Milam, "Application for Membership in the Southern Baptist Convention by the Baptist Convention of Oregon," in Southern Baptist Convention, *Annual*, 1948, 46.

The Southern Baptist Convention adopted its first statement of faith in 1919 to explain their opposition to ecumenical alliances, since alliances required broad agreement on doctrine and practice. It included commitment to close Communion as a fundamental practice: baptism was "the immersion in water of a believer" and was "prerequisite to participation in the Lord's Supper." In 1925, when the convention adopted a more thorough confession of faith, the Baptist Faith and Message, it retained the commitment to close Communion. It affirmed that baptism, "the immersion of a believer in water," was "prerequisite to the privileges of a church relation and to the Lord's Supper." The convention adopted thorough revisions of the confession in 1963 and in 2000, but both retained the commitment to close Communion in the exact terminology of the 1925 version. In principle Southern Baptists did not relax their commitment to close Communion in the twentieth century, but, in fact, after midcentury the practice diminished rapidly.[90]

Around 1940 a progressive movement began among Southern Baptist ministers, and it included a rejection of close Communion. Like the progressive movement among Northern Baptists, it initially appeared to have little chance of success. Many Southern Baptists suspected that the Southern Baptist Theological Seminary supported the movement and promoted open Communion. President John R. Sampey assured them that the seminary remained committed to close Communion:

> In recent years there has been in our country a growing number of Baptists who advocated open communion. This has been especially true of the northern states. So far as my observation goes, most of our Southern Baptist churches still practice restricted communion. I have always belonged to a Baptist church that adhered to restricted communion. Baptists have grown wherever they have adhered to restricted communion. . . . In the southern states of our own country where restricted communion is the rule, our people are still growing rapidly. . . . This is the position of all the teachers in the Southern Baptist Theological Seminary. Not one of us practices open communion or advocates it."[91]

That soon changed.

[90] "Fraternal Address of Southern Baptists to Those of 'Like Precious Faith with Us' Scattered Abroad, Beloved in the Lord," *Baptist Standard*, 26 February 1920, 5, 20, 24; Baptist Faith and Message 1925, 1963, and 2000, in *Readings in Baptist History: Four Centuries of Selected Documents*, ed. J. Early (Nashville: B&H Academic, 2008), 252.

[91] John R. Sampey to John W. Welch, 29 November 1941, box 17, Sampey Papers, SBTS.

In 1949 the state conventions in Arkansas and Oklahoma were sufficiently worried about the spread of open Communion views that they adopted resolutions prohibiting the seating of messengers from churches that practiced open Communion. And when Southern Baptists established a committee in 1947 to maintain cordiality between the Southern Baptist Convention and the Northern Baptist Convention, it became a controversial effort to reinforce orthodoxy among Southern Baptists by rejecting ecumenical alliances and maintaining close Communion. Progressive Southern Baptists were relieved when the committee did not recommend excluding open Communion churches. It did so in part because open Communion views had spread sufficiently, especially in Virginia and Maryland, that the convention could not bear the loss of open Communion churches. The committee took consolation in the fact that 89 percent of Southern Baptist churches practiced close Communion, but the adoption of their report effectively established the convention's toleration of open Communion.[92] It meant, observed Southern Seminary president Duke McCall, "that Southern Baptists recognize these differences and have determined to walk together despite them."[93] Open Communion views spread significantly after the 1940s.

Progressive leaders urged the adoption of open Communion as part of a larger program to enlighten and reform Southern Baptist churches out of their traditional narrowness and backwardness. L. L. Gwaltney, the liberal editor of the *Alabama Baptist*, worked to overthrow "the doctrine of close communion" and recognized that by the 1940s Southern Baptists were relinquishing their commitment to it.[94] A young Bill Moyers, studying for the ministry at the Southwestern Baptist Theological Seminary in the late 1950s, chafed amid the confident conservatism of his fellow Southern Baptists. He found close Communion particularly repulsive: "I hated the closed tables of communion."[95] Progressive pastor W. W. Finlator acknowledged in 1961 that "the matter of closed communion is repugnant to me," and led his Pullen Memorial Baptist Church in Raleigh, North Carolina, to adopt open Communion.[96]

[92] Southern Baptist Convention, *Annual*, 1951, 459–61; ibid., 1953, 446–51.

[93] Duke K. McCall, untitled, *The Tie*, June 1953, 2.

[94] L. L. Gwaltney to Ellis A. Fuller, 15 March 1948, box 17, Fuller Papers, SBTS.

[95] Bill Moyers to Carlyle Marney, 30 January 1960, box 33, Carlyle Marney Papers, Manuscripts Division, Perkins Library, Duke University.

[96] W. W. Finlator to Herschel H. Hobbs, 7 August 1961, SBTS Dale Moody Affair folder,

Professors at Southern Baptist colleges and seminaries gave considerable support to overthrowing close Communion. Dale Moody, professor of theology at the Southern Baptist Theological Seminary, was the best known. He promoted open Communion and confessed that he had more in common ecclesiologically with Oxford's Benedictines and Jesuits than with Baptists.[97] In 1961 he criticized close Communion at the same Oklahoma Baptist Bible conference in which he criticized the doctrine of perseverance. The Oklahoma County Pastors' Conference passed a resolution of protest:

> We seriously disagree with, and object to, the teaching of a teacher in one of our seminaries, who in a recent Bible conference at Shawnee, Okla., expressed himself both publicly and in private conversation with some of us and our brethren that he believed it possible for a person once saved to be lost, that he favored receiving members into our churches by alien immersion, and that he accepted the practice of open communion. We further disagree and object to his position favoring the ecumenical movement. . . . We call upon the boards of trustees and administrations of all our Baptist colleges, universities and seminaries to take appropriate action to prevent these and other false teachings from being taught as truths in our institutions.[98]

Other Oklahoma Baptists agreed. The Muskogee Baptist Association affirmed that they held to the perseverance of the saints and rejected open Communion, alien immersions, and evolution. They were determined "to hold fast these fundamental teachings" and called on the seminaries to "rid themselves of teachers who are not loyal to our Baptist beliefs."[99]

Commitment to close Communion remained strongest in Arkansas, Oklahoma, Texas, and new western conventions, but even there open Communion was spreading. In 1968 the Arkansas Baptist Convention voted to withdraw fellowship from four of its churches because they practiced open Communion or recognized alien immersions.[100] By 1969 many of California's Southern Baptists thought that the time had come to drop the state convention's constitutional prohibition against

Hobbs Papers, Southern Baptist Historical Library and Archives (SBHLA).

[97] Dale Moody to Carlyle Marney, 28 June 1962, box 29, Carlyle Marney Papers, Manuscripts Division, Perkins Library, Duke University.

[98] Oklahoma County Pastors' Conference, "Text of Resolution Passed by Oklahoma County Pastors' Conference," *Baptist Courier*, 24 August 1961, 6.

[99] Jewell M. Green to Herschel H. Hobbs, 13 October 1961, SBTS Dale Moody Affair folder, Hobbs Papers, SBHLA.

[100] Unsigned, "Arkansas Accepts College, Rejects Four Churches," *Baptist Courier*, 28 November 1968, 9.

seating messengers from churches that practiced open Communion or recognized alien immersions. A study committee recommended abolishing the restrictions but the vote fell short of the required two-thirds majority.[101]

By the 1970s many conservatives had acquiesced and no longer resisted open Communion. Such trusted leaders as Herschel Hobbs and W. A. Criswell continued to support close Communion in principle, but unlike earlier conservatives, they did not insist on it. They seemed to view it more as a private conviction than as a scriptural requirement. Hobbs, in fact, effectively practiced open Communion. He told a South Carolina pastor in 1970,

> For years I have not made any reference to "closed" or "open" communion when we have observed the Lord's Supper. We simply observe it without asking anyone of other faiths to leave or not to participate. I feel that only baptized believers have the right to participate, but I also feel that this is the Lord's Table and that only He has the right to invite or deny as He speaks in one's heart. This simply means that I have definite beliefs about it, but feel that it is something that I must not impose upon another."[102]

By the late twentieth century, most conservative Southern Baptist pastors practiced open Communion. Some, like Hobbs, accepted close Communion in principle but practiced open Communion. Others adopted open Communion in principle and practice. A 1990 poll of Southern Baptist pastors revealed that 45 percent of pastors invited all professing believers, and 31 percent left the Table open to any individual who felt invited. Three-quarters of the Southern Baptist pastors in the poll were practicing open Communion.[103]

The widespread adoption of open Communion among conservative Southern Baptists indicated that they did not cross the twentieth century unscathed by the progressive currents against which they struggled. Progressive Baptists, in the 1890s North and the 1940s South, sought to overthrow traditional commitment to Calvinism, confessional narrowness, plenary inspiration, and close Communion. Conservatives successfully resisted part of the progressive agenda, but

[101] Unsigned, "California Has Close Vote," *Baptist Courier*, 27 November 1969, 13; unsigned, "California Celebrates 30th Anniversary; Debates Alien Immersion, Communion Issues," *Baptist Courier*, 26 November 1970, 15.

[102] Herschel H. Hobbs to J. L. Goldman, 16 June 1970, Baptist Beliefs folder, Hobbs Papers, SBHLA.

[103] Cited in A. Wardin Jr., *Tennessee Baptists* (Brentwood, TN: Executive Board of the Tennessee Baptist Convention, 1999), 504.

in other areas they too adopted the conclusions or practices of their progressive opponents.

The progressive commitment to pragmatism in religion played a particularly important role. Religious pragmatism argued that genuine spiritual vitality and effectiveness required churches to overcome their ineffective traditional forms and creeds. They were ineffective, progressives said, because they were historically conditioned, belonging to a former age, and the times had changed. Although conservative Baptists finally were not persuaded to abandon their creeds, they did abandon many of their traditional forms, in particular their traditional ecclesiology, in the course of the twentieth century. Close Communion was not the only victim. Broadly conservative Baptists relinquished the conviction that God commanded specific forms and structures in the visible church. The traditional church practices and structures lost their basis in a "thus saith the Lord." The old practices were relinquished or transformed, and new ones adopted, because they promised to increase spiritual vitality and missional effectiveness. Regenerate church membership, church discipline, baptism as immersion, congregationalism, and close Communion were sustained only to the extent that they seemed to promote spiritual vitality and missional effectiveness. And in many ways they no longer seemed to do so.

THE LORD'S SUPPER: CELEBRATING THE PAST AND FUTURE IN THE PRESENT

Brian J. Vickers*

In virtually every tradition, Christians gather weekly, monthly, quarterly, or in some cases annually and hear the words "Do this in remembrance of me," or something like them. Then they eat a bit of bread and drink a sip of wine or juice. In spite of the commonplace nature of the Supper, for many Christians it is a mystery—not just in the biblical-theological sense of what is or is not happening in or with the bread and the cup, nor in what way(s) Christ is or is not present, but "mystery" in the popular sense of mysterious, unknown, inexplicable. What are we doing when we gather around the Table? What does it all mean? Put those questions to any Christian and the answers will vary from the utterly vague to the theologically precise and all points in between. Most people would say that the Supper somehow symbolizes Christ's death on the cross, the forgiveness of our sins, and perhaps has something to do with Christ's second coming. Beyond these objective observations there is also an experiential side of the Supper full of aspects more difficult to explain.

For some Christians the Table is a time of intense personal introspection sometimes associated with unrelenting guilt. Doubts give rise to questions that crowd the mind of the communicant: Have I committed too many sins? Have I repented enough? Am I taking this in a worthy manner? These are certainly not bad questions if taken in the right biblical measure. Those coming to the Table are told to "examine" themselves, an exhortation often accompanied by reading these words: "Therefore, whoever eats the bread or drinks the cup of the Lord in an unworthy manner will be guilty of sinning against the body and blood of the Lord. . . . For anyone who eats and drinks without recognizing the body of the Lord eats and drinks judgment on himself" (1 Cor 11:27–29).[1] Then the presiding minister may reinforce Paul's warning, encouraging believers to remain in their seats or

* Brian Vickers received his Ph.D. from The Southern Baptist Theological Seminary. He is associate professor of New Testament Interpretation at The Southern Baptist Theological Seminary in Louisville, Kentucky.

[1] Unless otherwise indicated, Scripture quotations are from the NIV.

to let the elements pass—not easy things to do—if we harbor sins for which we are not repentant. Even when reminded that the Table is a place for sinners and a place for repentance, some go away filled with remorse wondering whether they now stand under Paul's condemnation for "sinning against the body and blood of the Lord." A week or a month later, the whole experience is played out again.

On the other hand, for some Christians taking the Supper amounts to going through the motions without awareness or thoughtfulness. The warning text in 1 Corinthians 11, even if read, may make little impression. The words of institution are perhaps read, maybe heard, and then the Supper is over, a hymn is sung, and it's back to daily life. Such experience of the Supper is sometimes associated with traditions (such as Roman Catholicism) that view the elements as themselves efficacious, or with churches that observe the Supper weekly. In turn, the danger of this unplugged experience of the Supper is often given as a reason not to take the Supper on a weekly basis—as though taking the Supper monthly will solve the problem or lend it more significance or solemnity. It is entirely wrong to think that taking the Supper by rote is a symptom exclusive to Roman Catholics, Orthodox, or Lutherans, or other churches that observe the Lord's Supper weekly.[2] Such experience of the Supper is not at all tradition-bound.

Overwhelming guilt and thoughtless routine are the extremes of experience at the Lord's Supper. Obviously there is another way, because countless Christians enjoy the Supper without the bonds of an overwrought conscience or a dull pattern of thoughtless routine. Yet it is not a stretch to say that all Christians have walked the gamut of experience, and perhaps during a single observance of the Supper. It is probably true that too much emphasis is placed on individual experience of the Supper. Experience does not define or authenticate the Supper. Part of the glory of the Supper is that, like the truth of the gospel, the believer can lay hold of Christ's death for sinners by faith regardless of shifting moods, emotions, and thoughts. Nevertheless, the Supper is an experience, a central event in the church, and each believer is called to take the bread and cup and remember the death of Christ on their behalf.

[2] I realize that various traditions use different terms for the Lord's Supper. However, for simplicity's sake, as well as by conviction, I will use "the Lord's Supper" or "the Supper" and "The Lord's Table" or "the Table."

There is no single response that will answer all the questions or solve all the experiential issues associated with the Lord's Supper. There is, however, a place to begin; namely by considering the biblical theme of remembrance and then faith which rests on God's work in the past that guarantees the future. Laying hold of the convergence of the past and the future is what fuels life in the present, and can assuage the guilt that comes from making the Supper only a matter of personal experience and also animate the dull heart that merely goes through the motions. This perspective can also deepen the objective understanding of what we do when we approach the Table set by our Lord and to which He calls us to eat and drink freely in remembrance of Him.

Memory and Remembering

We give little thought to memory. Typically, if we do think about it, it is only in a casual way like saying, "I remember the time when I went to the beach" or negatively, "I can't remember where I put my keys." Memory, however, is anything but casual. Through memory we know things, judge actions, and make decisions and future plans.[3] For better or worse, we rely on memory. We remember the past, but memory itself is not in the past because in the act of remembering the past is brought up to the present. When we remember a past action or event (whether we experienced it personally is often inconsequential), we remember it *now* in the present; on that basis we consider the future, a future also known (to us) only in the present. In this way memory is a kind of crossroads of past and future in the present. As Augustine put it,

> Here [in memory] are all the things I experienced myself or took on trust of others. From this store of things there are new and ever-newer representations of my experiences or of things accepted in the past on the basis of trust. These I recombine with representations of the past to ponder future actions, their consequences and possibilities, all considered (once more) as present.[4]

[3] I take into account that memory can be faulty, and we can remember things incorrectly, and that sin invades our memory, as it does every other aspect of our being. The point here is simply to consider the vital place of memory biblically and theologically.

[4] G. Wills, *Saint Augustine's Memory* (New York: Viking Penguin, 2002), 53. This work is Book 10 of Augustine's famous, *Confessions* (10.8.14), translated with introduction and commentary by Garry Wills, who renders *confessio* as "testimony." The excerpt quoted here is also cited by Wills in his introduction, 14–15.

This is, as Garry Wills points out, Augustine's concept of "the three presents—the present of the past, the present of the present and the present of the future (recollection, observation, anticipation)."[5] All this may have an esoteric sound to it, but considering a few biblical texts that focus on memory will help show that what Augustine is speaking about is right in line with the act and purpose of remembering in the Bible and will also provide a biblical and conceptual context for what we are remembering in the Lord's Supper.

Remembrance in the Old Testament

The Promise-Keeping God

In the OT there are numbers of texts that express the essential place of remembering for the people of God. Before looking at a few significant examples, consider the special promise-keeping title that God uses for Himself. When God appears to Moses in the burning bush, He says, "I am the God of your fathers, the God of Abraham, Isaac, and the God of Jacob" (Exod 3:5). God is the God who has acted and kept His promises made to the patriarchs, and now will act again on behalf of His people. It is the past that guarantees the future—the God who promised Abraham that He would rescue his descendents from slavery (Gen 15:16) has Himself remembered His covenant (Exod 2:25) and comes to fulfill it. Moses is to give this message to the elders of Israel (Exod 3:16–17):

> "Go, assemble the elders of Israel and say to them, 'The LORD, the God of your fathers—the God of Abraham, Isaac and Jacob— appeared to me and said: I have watched over you and have seen what has been done to you in Egypt. And I have promised to bring you up out of your misery in Egypt into the land of the Canaanites, Hittites, Amorites, Perizzites, Hivites and Jebusites—a land flowing with milk and honey.'"

The assurance flowing from the past and reaching toward the future—*I* am the God *of your fathers*—is meant to generate faith in God in the present. They are called to remember who God is, what He has done and promised, and to trust that He will again keep His word.

[5] Ibid., 15.

A History of Remembering

Later Israelites will be called upon to remember the Exodus—God's work in the past that guarantees His word about the future (whether blessing or warning). Through collective memory, later Israelites constantly relive the past of their ancestors, and through memory it becomes *their* past guiding their future.[6] In Augustine's terms, in their memory events that happened to their ancestors that they accept on trust is ever (re)combined with their own experiences (of God's faithfulness) leaving them to "ponder future actions, their consequences and possibilities."

Psalm 78 recounts the trajectory of Israel's history. Asaph teaches them "things from of old—what we have heard and known, what our fathers have told us. We will not hide them from their children; we will tell the next generation the praiseworthy deeds of the LORD, his power, and the wonders he has done" (vv. 2–4). In Deuteronomic fashion he recounts the experience of the Exodus generation, their children, and the early experiences of the Israelites in the land. The vast majority of the Psalm focuses on Israel's unfaithfulness, which serves as a backdrop to God's unswerving commitment to His promises. The Psalm ends with the choice and establishment of David the king, a crowning testimony to God's faithfulness. This sets the context for Psalm 79, a psalm that tells of invasion, the destruction of Jerusalem and the temple, and the slaughter of the people of Israel (vv. 1–4). In response, Asaph cries out (vv. 5a,8–10a),

> How long, O LORD? Will you be angry forever? . . . Do not hold against us the sins of the fathers; may your mercy come quickly to meet us, for we are in desperate need. Help us, O God our Savior, for the glory of your name; deliver us and forgive our sins for your name's sake. Why should the nations say, "Where is their God?"

The Psalm concludes with a further call for God to act against the nations, to save His people, with the (future) result that "from generation to generation we will proclaim your praise" (v. 13b). If we read these psalms together, and certainly we are meant to do so, Psalm 78

[6] I mean "collective memory" in the sense Richard Bauckham uses it in his important book, *Jesus and the Eyewitnesses: The Gospels as Eyewitness Testimony* (Grand Rapids: Eerdmans, 2006), 314–18. As Bauckham states, "I use the term 'collective memory' to refer to the traditions of a group about events not personally recollected by any of the group's members" (314). In this sense, "collective memory" *does not* refer to how people in a society "construct their collective pasts in ways that are meaningful and useful in the present" (315).

provides the assurance of God's faithfulness in the past, culminating in the establishment of the king. They need this assurance for living through events such as the psalmist describes in Psalm 79, and for believing that God will once again act to save His people. By remembering the past the people can believe the future in the midst of the present, a present that if left by itself holds little if any hope.

Signs for Remembering

Two episodes in the life of Israel in particular combine remembering with visual signs. In 1 Sam 7:12, after the Lord gives the Philistines over to the Israelites, Samuel sets up a stone in Mizpah and names it "Ebenezer," which means, "Thus far has the Lord helped us." The stone is a visual symbol, a physical reminder of what God did for Israel, and also of Israel's experience of God at Mizpah. Before the Israelites went out to battle they repented of their idolatry (7:3–4), and Samuel gathered them at Mizpah to fast and confess their sins. So the stone is a witness to God's salvation and Israel's repentance of sin and recommitment to serve God.

The stone at Mizpah was not the first visual symbol used to remind Israel of God's mighty acts. Upon crossing the Jordan to enter the land, the Lord commanded men from each tribe to lay a stone, twelve stones for twelve tribes, where the priests had stood with the ark of the covenant as the people passed by on dry land—and that not for the first time (Josh 4:4–9). The cairn stands to remind Israel of what God had done for them, "to serve as a sign among you" (Josh 4:6a). It will also be a pointer for future generations, for Joshua tells them (4:21–24),

> "In the future when your descendants ask their fathers, 'What do these stones mean?' tell them, 'Israel crossed the Jordan on dry ground.' For the LORD your God dried up the Jordan before you until you had crossed over. The LORD your God did to the Jordan just what he had done to the Red Sea when he dried it up before us until we had crossed over. He did this so that all the peoples of the earth might know that the hand of the LORD is powerful and so that you might always fear the LORD your God."

The future component, implicit at Mizpah, is explicit in this text. By remembering God's work on their behalf, with a visual symbol to help them do so, the future generations of Israel are not only instructed about *what* to do, namely, "fear the Lord," but most importantly, *why* they ought to fear the Lord—because of His deliverance, power, and faithfulness. He proved Himself in the past, therefore He can and will prove Himself in the future, and this is the foundation for their life in the present.

A Sign of Hope

In Numbers 13 Moses sends spies into the Promised Land to scout it out.[7] They are meant to take a look at the people living there, what the land and towns are like, whether the land is arable, and what grows there (vv. 17–20). The foray ended with a majority voting "no" to conquest, and the report resulted in a nationwide act of unbelief and disobedience. The spies did, however, bring back symbols which, though ignored at the time, were later recalled. They brought back a cluster of grapes cut from the Valley of Eshcol ("Eshcol" means "cluster") so large that it took two men to carry it, along with some pomegranates and figs. These signs of "a land flowing with milk and honey" (Exod 13:5) made no impression. But later, recounting their history of rebellion, Moses reminded them of the fruit from Eshcol as well as the minority report that they ignored: "It is a good land that the LORD our God is giving us" (Deut 1:25). The symbolic fruit could have urged them on to take God at His word and go in and take the land. The fruit symbolized what God had promised about the land, and what He had in store for them. It was a symbol of hope for the future.

"Remember This Day"

One event above all others sets the pattern of remembrance as a fundamental part of life in Israel. It recounts history, teaches future generations, and is filled with visual and edible signs. This feast is the ultimate reminder of who the Lord is, what He has done, and what He promises to do. It also continually reestablishes the identity of the Israelites as the people of God, as those who are wholly dependent on the Lord for their lives past, present, and future. The feast of Passover is the ultimate old-covenant remembrance.

Here is what the Lord commands the Israelites: "When the LORD brings you into the land of the Canaanites, Hittites, Amorites, Hivites

[7] This text did not cross my mind in connection with the Supper or regarding symbols in the OT until reading N.T. Wright, *The Meal that Jesus Gave Us: Understanding Holy Communion* (Louisville: John Knox, 2002). I am retelling the story and making the same observations and emphases that Wright does.

and Jebusites—the land he swore to your forefathers to give you, a land flowing with milk and honey—you are to observe this ceremony in this month" (Exod 13:5). Once a year the nation is to relive the experience of the first Passover when every firstborn male in Egypt was killed unless the blood of the Passover lamb was smeared over the door on the night before the Lord rescued them from slavery. All the facets of memory discussed earlier are here. The Israelites are commanded to remember God's saving work on their behalf. As a symbol of their salvation, they will eat unleavened bread together with bitter herbs just as they ate it on the night of the first Passover (Exod 12:8; 13:7). By eating the bread and herbs, future generations will relive the exodus experience of their ancestors, and it will be part of their collective memory that forms their identity. Though they were not there that night in Egypt, they are *there* in the memorial feast, and whether in the wilderness (Num 9:1–13) or in the Promised Land, that night lives on in the present of their memory.

The visual symbols of Passover are joined with teaching that interprets the symbols. Fathers are to tell their children, "I do this because of what the LORD did for me when I came out of Egypt" (Exod 13:8b). Through these symbols and their interpretation, the children of Israel, particularly the post-exodus generations, were also taught how they ought to live. The Passover serves as a perpetual foundation for living, as the ceremony reminds them that prior salvation undergirds a response of obedience to the God who redeemed them: "This observance will be for you like a sign on your hand and a reminder on your forehead that the law of the LORD is to be on your lips. For the LORD brought you out of Egypt with his mighty hand" (13:9).[8]

Faith in God's future is woven into the feast as well. God tells them they are to observe Passover in the land—a land now inhabited by opposing nations (13:5). God will keep His promises made to their forefathers. This thought is repeated a few verses later, as God tells Moses that once the people are in the land (13:11) they must "give over to the Lord the first offspring of every womb. All the firstborn males of your livestock belong to the LORD" (13:12). Again the sign is interpreted, for when the children ask what this act means the fathers

[8] Stuart comments, "It [Passover] triggered remembrance of the covenant law by which the Israelites were kept in proper relationship with God and for which he had brought them out of Egypt in the first place (to *serve* him, not just to go to a nicer place to live)" (D. K. Stuart, *Exodus*, NAC [Nashville: B&H, 2006], 315).

are to tell them of the first Passover and say, "When Pharaoh stubbornly refused to let us go, the LORD killed every firstborn in Egypt, both man and animal. This is why I sacrifice to the LORD the first male offspring of every womb and redeem each of my firstborn sons" (13:15). This sacrifice and redemption serves as "a constant reminder to Israel that their life came from death."[9] Salvation comes at the price of blood.[10]

There is also something implicit in the offering of the firstborn livestock. By freely offering costly and needful livestock, they show that they can (or at least that they ought to) trust the God who rescued them from slavery and believe that He will provide for them and keep His promises.[11]

The biblical pattern of remembering, established in the OT, means actively calling God's grace and salvation to mind, to bring the past into the present with hope for the future. It is anything but a casual reminiscence about the past, or casting a few wistful thoughts to what happened "back there" somewhere. For the generations living in the times after the events themselves, there is, in fact, nothing "back there" in terms of their personal experience.

The objective knowledge that these things happened is absolutely necessary. The feast, the cairn, and the stone, all point back to moments in history. But to remember them is not merely to list some historical facts, or to recall a piece of personal, experienced history; it is to take part in those events *now* in the remembering of them. That's why the symbols are meant to be interpreted: Why are we in the land now eating unleavened bread, bitter herbs, and sacrificing these animals? Because of what God did *for us* in Egypt. Why are those rocks piled up on the river bank? Because of what God did *for us* there. This kind of remembering was meant to inform, shape, sustain, and give hope to the Israelites. And that is the pattern we are meant to apply when we hear the words, "Do this in remembrance of me."

[9] P. Enns, *Exodus*, NIVAC (Grand Rapids: Zondervan, 2000), 254.

[10] Ibid., 255.

[11] "As a symbol of their belief in this God of past, present and future history, the Israelites will redeem their firstborn to demonstrate their faith in the God who has elected Israel as Yahweh's firstborn" (P. R. House, *Old Testament Theology* [Downers Grove: InterVarsity, 1998], 103).

Invitation to the Table

In 1 Cor 11:23 Paul says that he "passed on" to the Corinthians what he "received from the Lord." He then proceeds to recount the tradition, quite similar to that found in the Synoptic Gospels and particularly in Luke, of the Last Supper. He uses almost identical language in 15:1 when he speaks of his preaching of the gospel: "I want to remind you of the gospel I preached to you, which you received." Just as Moses passed on the Lord's instructions to the Israelites, so too Paul passed on what he received from the Lord. Just as the Passover became a central part of Israel's life and experience, even so far as that month marking the beginning of their calendar year (Exod 12:2), so the Lord's Supper becomes central to life in the new covenant. As the Israelites celebrated release from slavery in Egypt, deliverance through blood, so too members of the new covenant celebrate deliverance from bondage to sin—salvation through the body and blood of Christ. Along with baptism, the Lord's Supper is *the* defining and shaping event in the life of the church. It is a reminder that we were "bought with a price" (1 Cor 6:20; 7:23), the price being the life of our Lord Jesus Christ, who also promises never to leave us (Matt 28:20; John 14:3). When we take the bread and the cup, we relive (not reenact) and take part in what God has done, is doing, and is yet to do for us.

Inauguration Meal

The symbolism in the Lord's Supper—breaking and eating the bread (Matt 26:26; Mark 14:22; Luke 22:19; 1 Cor 11:23) and drinking the cup (Matt 26:27–28; Mark 14:23–24; Luke 22:20; 1 Cor 11:25)—points explicitly and implicitly to the death of Jesus for the forgiveness of sins. Explicitly we read in the Synoptics and in Paul that Jesus said the bread is the symbol of "my body" and is given "for you" and the cup is "my blood." Matthew includes that the cup is "for the forgiveness of sins" (26:28), a phrase which though not found in the other texts is undoubtedly implied. The words of institution mark a turning point in redemption. The long awaited promise that includes the gift of the Spirit, forgiveness, and a new relationship with God is fulfilled.

A Promise Sealed in Blood

All the accounts of the Lord's Supper in the NT allude to Exodus 24 and the inauguration of the old covenant. On the morning of the confirmation Moses builds an altar at the bottom of Sinai, has twelve stones set up to symbolize the twelve tribes of Israel, and directs men to offer burnt and fellowship offerings (24:4–5). Moses sprinkles half the blood on the altar, reads the Book of the Covenant to the people (who promise to do everything in it), and then taking the other half of the blood he sprinkles it on the people and says, "This is the blood of the covenant that the LORD has made with you in accordance with all these words" (v. 8). The Sinai covenant is inaugurated and sealed in blood. This same generation of Israelites already experienced redemption through blood. They were those who took the blood of the Paschal lamb and spread it on the top beam of their doors on the night of the Passover. Now away from Egypt the idea is reinforced as they enter into a covenant relationship with the Lord. On their part, after hearing the Book of the Covenant, they pledge, "We will do everything the LORD has said; we will obey" (24:7).

This covenant was inaugurated with the blood of bulls and later maintained with the blood of bulls and goats, but it is "impossible" for such blood "to take away sins" (Heb 10:4). The story of the inauguration of the Sinai covenant is not complete; it is promise but not fulfillment. But when we hear the words, "This cup is the new covenant in my blood, which is poured out for you" (Luke 22:20), we are reminded that a new relationship has been established, one built on "better promises" (Heb 8:6), established in the blood of Christ who "was sacrificed once to take away the sins of many people" (Heb 9:28).[12]

A New Meal for a New Relationship

The Lord's Supper testifies that God keeps His promises. When Jesus called the cup "the new covenant in my blood," He signaled that the time had come, the long awaited fulfillment of a promise of a new relationship, a new covenant. In Jer 31:31–34 God promises that this new covenant will not, like the first, be broken (v. 32). Unlike

[12] "As the first redeemer made a sacrifice for the people so that they might enter into a new covenant with God, so does the last redeemer inaugurate another covenant by offering his blood—that is, his life—for the forgiveness of sins" (D. C. Allison Jr., ed., *Matthew: A Shorter Commentary* [London: T&T Clark, 2004], 474).

the Sinai covenant, the members of this covenant will have God's law written on their minds and hearts (v. 33). God promises to forgive sins once and for all (v. 34).

Ezekiel spoke of the same promise (36:25–29a):

> I will sprinkle clean water on you, and you will be clean; I will cleanse you from all your impurities and from all your idols. I will give you a new heart and put a new spirit in you; I will remove from you your heart of stone and give you a heart of flesh. And I will put my Spirit in you and move you to follow my decrees and be careful to keep my laws. You will live in the land I gave your forefathers; you will be my people, and I will be your God. I will save you from all your uncleanness.

The Supper affirms the reality of the fulfillment of these prophecies. Those invited to the Table are cleansed from sin, indwelt by the Holy Spirit, and have new hearts.

Calling it a new covenant distinguishes it from the previous covenants but does not demolish all continuity with them. For instance, Jesus comes as the fulfillment of the promise to Abraham that was sealed with an oath by God (Genesis 15), and He is the fulfillment of the covenant God made with David; He is the promised Davidic heir who will sit on the throne forever (2 Sam 7:13). And while it is vital not to think of it simply as a *newer* version of Sinai or other redemptive covenants—being the thing to which they pointed—the essential covenantal character of the relationship cannot be undermined.[13] As with prior biblical eras, redemption comes through covenant.[14] The redemption secured in this covenant establishes a relationship guaranteed by the One who gave His life to secure it unconditionally. When Jesus says, "This cup is the new covenant in my blood," He seals the covenant, He fulfills the promise.[15] The Supper is a firm reminder of the forgiveness of sins guaranteed by

[13] "There is much that is new, unique, and transcendent, and all this is involved in the unprecedented fact that Christ is given to be the covenant. He embodies in himself all of the grace and faithfulness that covenant, at the zenith of its revelation and realization, involves. But we must not so emphasize the newness that we overlook the covenantal character of Christ's institution. And when Jesus says, 'the new covenant in my blood,' he means that all that covenant represents as oath certified confirmation, and covenant at the zenith of realization, comes to men in his shed blood" (J. Murray, "The Lord's Supper," in *Collected Writings of John Murray* [Carlisle, PA: Banner of Truth, 1977], 2:376–77).

[14] Ibid.

[15] Again, Murray writes, "Covenant is not to be equated with promise; it is confirmatory and similar to an oath. It is the oath-certified confirmation of promise" (ibid., 377). Of course, the cup is a symbol; the covenant was sealed by the blood of Jesus shed on the cross.

the words of institution. When believers take up the cup, they drink as the people of God in a new relationship with Him, sealed by the blood of Christ.[16]

The Sacrifice of the Servant

In the words "poured out for many" is an allusion to a well-known OT figure: Isaiah's Servant of Yahweh. The Servant is "pierced for our transgressions" and "crushed for our iniquities" and "by his wounds we are healed" (53:5). The life of the servant is given as a "guilt offering" (53:10). The servant will be vindicated "because he poured out his life unto death" and "bore the sin of many" (53:12).[17] The Servant imagery is made more explicit in Mark, for instance, because the "blood of the covenant . . . poured out *for many*" (14:24) echoes Mark 10:45 where Jesus' role as the servant who dies in the place of others is spelled out: "For even the Son of Man did not come to be served, but to serve, and to give his life as a ransom for many."[18] The main theme of the Servant passage is vicarious atonement. That is, the life of the servant is sacrificed for the sin of others. He stands in their place and receives the punishment that ought to fall on them. The invitation to the Supper is made possible by Christ the servant of God who also served us in His death.

A Somber Reminder

A dark chord resonates in the words of institution: The night of the Supper was a night of betrayal. The death of Jesus was set in motion by one of His close companions. The fact that all four Gospel

[16] In regard to what was inaugurated at the Last Supper, Schlatter writes, "By his death the community's new relationship to God was born, to which God granted a new revelation of his will. The act of God by which he initiated the new community into its close relationship with him was Christ's surrender to death. Jesus gave his blood cheerfully so that the new covenant would come into being" (A. Schlatter, *The History of the Christ: The Foundation of New Testament Theology*, trans. A. Köstenberger [Grand Rapids: Baker, 1997], 356).

[17] France points out that the phrase "poured out" in Mark 14:24 not only alludes to Exod 24:8 (see below) but also to Isa 53:12 and the pouring out of the life of the servant of God (R. T. France, *The Gospel of Mark*, NIGTC [Grand Rapids: Eerdmans, 2002], 570).

[18] "Jesus' words over the cup thus pick up the concept of vicarious death which he has already presented in 10:45, with a deliberate further echo of that same remarkable passage in Isaiah" (ibid., 571). There are other connections in Mark as well: "The broken bread recalls the loaves shared on the mountains, and the body to be shattered on the hill; Jesus is the body language of servanthood. The cup recalls the suffering promised to the disciples (10:39), which Jesus himself must now face" (L. T. Johnson, *The Writings of the New Testament*, 3rd ed. [Minneapolis: Fortress, 2010], 161).

writers emphasize the betrayal of Jesus, and Paul includes the phrase, "on the night he was betrayed," should get our attention. It is another reminder that the forgiveness celebrated at the Supper came at a cost. Judas accompanied Jesus through His public ministry; he heard the teaching and received private explanations and instructions; he saw the blind receive sight, the lame walk, and demons cast out of the possessed. Yet he betrayed Jesus for a pocketful of money (Matt 26:14–16). The believer coming to the Table understands, or should understand, that the same sin that caused Judas to sell Jesus for thirty pieces of silver potentially lurks in every heart. Perhaps the reminder of Judas's betrayal of Jesus is meant to make each one coming to the Table say something like, "That could be me." At the least Judas reminds us that our sins betray the Christ who died for us and show ongoing tendencies toward rebellion and unfaithfulness. As such we can combine the reminder of Judas with Paul's warning that whoever eats the Supper "in an unworthy manner will be guilty of sinning against the body and blood of the Lord" (1 Cor 11:27).

Worthy and Unworthy

Every person coming to the Table with Paul's words in mind has wondered at some point whether to refrain from participating in the Supper. More than one Christian has taken the Supper with concerns that he or she is doing so in a worthy manner. But what does it mean to be worthy? Does it mean that some point of near perfection, however temporary, must be reached? While most people do not believe in perfection as a prerequisite for the Table, a practical perfectionism can creep in. Is there a quantifiable limit on how sinful one may be before crossing the line to unworthiness? Of course, the person living in sin, refusing to repent, and having no real intention of dealing with the sin fits the description of "unworthy." The person harboring unchecked anger, lust, greed, or dissension (to list a few of the practices characteristic of those who will not inherit the kingdom of God, Gal 5:19–21) is clearly "guilty of sinning against the body and blood of the Lord." Not everyone who struggles with the issue of worthiness, however, is living in demonstrably unrepentant sin.

Community Concerns

Though discussion of being worthy or unworthy to take the Supper is often linked exclusively to personal, hidden, or private sins, Paul's concern is not limited to individual sin. There are other problems afoot in Corinth as well. The examining that Paul speaks of, the eating in an unworthy manner, and being guilty of the body and blood of the Lord, is immediately directed to the community and not just to each person as a private entity. A word of caution is needed before going further. It is not strictly correct to speak of "corporate" and "individual" sin as though they are unrelated, and even worse to speak of sin exclusively in one category and dismiss the other. Of course, corporate bodies can and do sin, but every group is made up of individuals each of whom is responsible for his or her own sins. At the same time, sin in one member affects the whole body, and in a sense all sin has a public aspect. It is nevertheless convenient to separate community and individual matters for the sake of discussion.

The Corinthians are sinning against one another and doing so at a time when they ought to be the most united.[19] In this regard, Paul says, "I have no praise for you, for your meetings do more harm than good" (1 Cor 11:17).[20] Rather than their diversity being a source of fruitfulness and strength in the community, as Paul will teach them in chap. 12, the Corinthians are making unfair distinctions, taking advantage of and humiliating those of lower social status, and generally turning the Lord's Supper into a sham (1 Cor 11:19–22).

Paul begins the letter by reminding the Corinthians of who they are and from where they came. They are not the elite of society, nor the smartest, nor the most impressive (1:26). For the most part, in the world's eyes they are weak, lowly, and despised (1:27–28)—yet they are the ones God chose. Their identity is not found in themselves but in Christ who is the wisdom of God shown on the cross, and through whom they have righteousness, holiness, and redemption (1:30). In themselves the Corinthians have nothing about which to boast, but

[19] "Paul was incensed that such a callous disregard of poorer brothers and sisters in Christ occurred at the Lord's Supper. Indeed, the behavior exhibited indicates that what was being celebrated was not truly the Lord's Supper (1 Cor. 11:20). To say that they were meeting in honor of the Lord while at the same time the poor were being despised and some of the rich were getting drunk is a contradiction. Such behavior amounts to a despising of God's church and humiliation of the poor (1 Cor. 11:21)" (T. R. Schreiner, *New Testament Theology: Magnifying God in Christ* [Grand Rapids: Baker, 2008], 732).

[20] See the chapter in this volume, "The Lord's Supper in Paul" by Jim Hamilton.

they can exalt in God in Christ (1:29–31). Later he reminds them that whatever they are, whatever they have as believers, is a gift: "For who makes you different from anyone else? What do you have that you did not receive? And if you did receive it, why do you boast as though you did not?" (4:7).[21] However many problems there were at Corinth, at or near the center was the sin of pride that leads to judging and acting according to worldly standards. When they would come to the Lord's Supper, the event that should remind them of God's pure grace and mercy in Christ toward sinners, they were forgetting what is most fundamental to being a believer: "Now you are the body of Christ, and each one of you is a part of it" (12:27). When Paul warns them of "sinning against the body of Christ," he is using a kind of double meaning. They are sinning against Christ's own body and blood sacrificed for them, but their particular sin is committed against those for whom Christ died, that is, His body, the church.[22]

The Supper is *the* ultimate symbolic act of unity in the Church, as the body of Christ gathers around common symbols of the one Lord who died for all and in whom all are united. As Ursinus says,

> The Lord's supper was instituted . . . that it might be a bond of love, declaring that all who partake of it aright, are made members of one body whose head is Christ. 'For we being many are one bread and one body; for we are all partakers of that one bread' (1 Cor 10:17). Those now who are members of the same body have a mutual love one for another.[23]

We must, therefore, as Christians, reemphasize Paul's community focus in regard to the Lord's Supper. It is easy to devalue the body of Christ in lieu of personal, individual matters, but it is not so in the NT. The Christlike behavior that should adorn the Church is evident: "Do nothing out of selfish ambition or vain conceit, but in humility consider others better than yourselves" (Phil 2:3). Likewise, Peter says, "Each one should use whatever gift he has received to serve others, faithfully administering God's grace in its various forms" (1 Pet 4:10). This kind of teaching follows in the footsteps of Jesus who said

[21] After writing this section I found that Keener makes the same connections from chaps. 1 and 4 in his treatment of chap. 11 (C. S. Keener, *1–2 Corinthians*, in The New Cambridge Bible Commentary [New York: Cambridge, 2005], 99).

[22] Their transgression was a failure to recognize the "body" (11:29)—not just the bread pointing to Jesus' physical body on the cross (11:24), but the spiritual body of those who died with Him (10:16–17; 12:12) (ibid.).

[23] *The Commentary of Dr. Zacharias Ursinus on the Heidelberg Catechism*, trans. G. W. Willard, reprint edition (Phillipsburg, NJ: P&R, n.d.), 379.

that the greatest in the kingdom are servants of all (Mark 10:43–44). Given the other-centeredness of the Christian life, which takes Christ Himself as the pattern, sins that break the unity of the church must be taken seriously in the discussion of worthiness to take the Lord's Supper. Sins with a noticeably corporate aspect such as slander, factionalism, selfish promotion, neglect of those in need, and the relegation of church members to second-class status on the basis of income, gifts, education, interests, clothing, or perceived usefulness, render one unworthy to take the Lord's Supper.

Personal Concerns

The discussion of "worthiness" must not, however, be limited to corporate ideas. First, there is the practical reality that when this is done, the need for personal examination and repentance may be overlooked. Then there is the biblical reality that the larger church body and the individuals in it are never separated. It is easy to speak of repentance just in corporate terms, and it is quite ineffective too if individuals are not confronted with biblical truth: "For we must all appear before the judgment seat of Christ, that each one may receive what is due him for the things done while in the body, whether good or bad" (2 Cor 5:10). The body and its members individually are one. For example, when Paul condemns the Corinthians for their pride in allowing sexual immorality (in regard to the man who "has his father's wife" [1 Cor 5:1]), there is nevertheless a great deal of emphasis on disciplining the individual—both for his ultimate benefit personally (5:4–5) and corporately for the whole church (5:6). Secondly, the situation Paul describes in 1 Corinthians 11 is not just a general discussion of corporate sin but is aimed at a specific context. In Corinth the Supper was part of a larger common meal, and the specific sins Paul condemns (e.g., that some go away still hungry and others get drunk) are connected immediately to that context. Moreover, Paul says that each person is responsible for self-examination before coming to the Table (11:28). Limiting this text to sins such as oppression and discrimination is shortsighted and does not take seriously the larger context of 1 Corinthians, much less the rest of the NT. The NT is full of epistles, some quite negative in tone, written to church bodies, though the apostles do not separate the churches and the individuals that compose them. They address the churches at both levels.

All this is to say that a balance between corporate and individual realities must be maintained.

What then shall we say about the individual and his or her worthiness to take the Lord's Supper? Pastorally, it is difficult to strike a balance. In some evangelical churches the question of eating in an unworthy manner focuses so exclusively on what amounts to works-righteousness that it is a wonder that anyone takes the Supper, at least with a clear conscience. This is not without irony. Evangelical churches are, by name, meant to be about the gospel. The unifying belief—at least theoretically—is that salvation is through faith in Christ on the cross. "Nothing in my hand I bring, simply to thy cross I cling" we sing, or used to, with regularity. Without intending to do so, churches that do not otherwise believe in salvation by works can give the impression that only those who have overcome sin, those free from all lustful, greedy, covetous, and hateful thoughts and actions may come to the Table. Granted, this is often done with good intentions in an effort on the part of pastors presiding over the Supper to take sin and the sanctity of the Lord's Table seriously. On the other hand, wishing to avoid works-righteousness or guilt-driven ethics and to emphasize grace and forgiveness, pastors may inadvertently open the door for people to partake of the body and blood of Jesus though they live in and with habitual, unrepentant, sin.

The answer to the question of worthiness begins with the gospel. Long ago the prophet Isaiah made this proclamation (55:1–3):

> Come, all you who are thirsty, come to the waters; and you who have no money, come, buy and eat! Come, buy wine and milk without money and without cost. Why spend money on what is not bread, and your labor on what does not satisfy? Listen, listen to me, and eat what is good, and your soul will delight in the richest of fare.

Centuries later Jesus called out, "Come to me, all you who are weary and burdened, and I will give you rest. Take my yoke upon you and learn from me, for I am gentle and humble in heart, and you will find rest for your souls. For my yoke is easy and my burden is light" (Matt 11:28–30). And Paul tells us how it is that the poor, thirsty, and hungry can drink and eat, and how the weary can find rest (Rom 3:25–26):

> God presented him as a sacrifice of atonement, through faith in his blood. He did this to demonstrate his justice, because in his forbearance he had left the

> sins committed beforehand unpunished—he did it to demonstrate his justice at the present time, so as to be just and the one who justifies those who have faith in Jesus.

The invitation to the Supper is an invitation to remember the gospel, promised by the prophets, fulfilled in Christ, and proclaimed by the apostles. The thirsty, hungry, and tired are welcome, for God makes them worthy by the blood of Jesus Christ; they can come through faith, grasping promises kept and promises awaiting fulfillment.

At this point, an illustration from the parable of the Great Banquet (Luke 14:1–24) may help. Jesus is having dinner at the house of one of the leaders of the Pharisees. While there, Jesus observes how the guests choose the best seats at the table, and He tells them a short parable to warn them that if they choose the best seats for themselves they may well be embarrassed when asked to move. He then tells the Pharisee who invited Him that he should not invite friends, or family, or the rich so as to get an invitation in return, but to "invite the poor, the crippled, the lame, the blind" (14:13) so as to receive a reward at the resurrection. One guest responds by saying, "Blessed is everyone who will eat bread in the kingdom of God" (v. 15, ESV). Jesus counters with the parable of the Banquet. A man gives a banquet and invites many people to come (v. 16). When everything is ready he sends a servant to call the invited guests, but each one has a different excuse not to come. The excuses are hard to comprehend, and even more so in comparison to the invitation to the banquet.[24] We might well hear Jesus saying, "What good is it for a man to gain the whole world, yet forfeit his soul?" (Mark 8:36; cf. Matt 16:26). The man becomes angry and sends the servant out to the streets and roads "and bring in the poor, the crippled, the blind and the lame" (v. 21). Having still more room, he sends the servant out to "the roads and country lanes" to "make them come in" (v. 23). The parable ends with the man saying that none of the original guests will get a bite from the banquet.

This parable is not about the Lord's Supper, but it does illustrate related themes. The original invited guests likely represent historical-redemptive eras, the original invitation in v. 16 being the calling of God through the prophets, and then the sending out of the servant

[24] As Blomberg says, "The specific excuses which the three guests give illustrate how 'all alike' refused (v. 18). They need not stand for any particular type of reason for rejecting the kingdom; others might just as easily have been listed. What all three share is an extraordinary lameness" (C. L. Blomberg, *Interpreting the Parables* [Downers Grove: InterVarsity, 1990], 235).

represents the ministry of Jesus and His followers.[25] In both instances God's invitation is met with self-assurance, unbelief, and rejection. Spoken as it is to those gathered at the Pharisee's home, and given that Luke tells us there was more than an air of suspicion on the part of the guests toward Jesus (14:1), the implications are (1) those in the house are like the invited guests who do not come and are finally excluded from the banquet; (2) that the people jockeying for the best seats assume they are worthy of them; and (3) they do not feel themselves in danger of suffering the judgment in the parable. In His words to the Pharisee and in the parable, Jesus mentions not the worthy but those thought to be unworthy, perhaps thought of as such by themselves. It is not the presumptuous—assuming the places of honor are theirs, counting on their lineage or status, and entangled with worldly pursuits—who end up at the banquet, but the poor, crippled, lame, and blind. In a dramatic reversal, the "worthy" become unworthy and the unworthy become worthy, or as Jesus says, "For everyone who exalts himself will be humbled, and he who humbles himself will be exalted" (Luke 14:11). Two things may be applied from this parable. First, in the context, the ones caught up in worldly affairs are comparable to the guests at the Pharisee's house who appear not to see that for all their self-assurance they are not worthy of the banquet, not worthy of the kingdom of God. Secondly, those who come to the Table are not worthy because they make themselves so; they are made worthy by one who invites them.[26]

Assurance, not Presumption

At the same time, the Lord's Supper is not a place for presuming upon grace and forgiveness. The theme of judgment that arises in the Great Banquet (Luke 14:24) is implicit in the Synoptics and in Paul. As seen earlier, the reminder that the Supper was instituted on a night of betrayal sounds an implicit word of warning. Both Matthew and Luke place particular emphasis on the judgment and condemnation

[25] Cf. A. J. Hultgren, *The Parables of Jesus: A Commentary* (Grand Rapids: Eerdmans, 2000), 337.

[26] The parable obviously does not spell out a full soteriology. No mention is made of the faith or repentance of the people who ended up at the banquet. That consideration is beyond the scope of the parable. The "worthy" who have no need in their own eyes of repentance and forgiveness are not members of the kingdom, quite contrary to their opinion. The kingdom will be filled with the "unworthy." This matches well with Luke's common theme of the outsiders in society being the ones who come to Jesus in faith and gladly accept Him.

of Judas, pronouncing woe upon the one who betrays Jesus (Matt 26:24; Luke 22:22), with Matthew including the further malediction, "It would be better for him if he had not been born." The warning from Paul is clear in regard to sinning against the body of Christ (1 Cor 11:27), but the previous verse underscores the danger of ignoring the warning: the One against whom they are sinning will return.[27] This thought should give pause to any who come to the Table with unchecked sin or with careless disregard for the One whose body and blood provide the Supper.

As with the gospel, the only requisite for coming to the Table is faith—faith that confesses sin and lays hold of forgiveness through the sacrifice of Christ. However, the biblical emphasis on grace and salvation by faith cannot be turned into an excuse to hold on to sin, that is, refuse to confess and live by faith. The Supper is a powerful, symbolic reminder of the gospel. It is one of the clearest (baptism being the other) visible pictures of the gospel given to the church. On the cross the blood of Jesus was shed for the forgiveness of sins and to set people free from bondage to sin. His body was broken as a sacrifice. This is why taking the Supper in an unworthy manner is such a serious matter. One must come to the Table *believing* the gospel promises, for whatever "does not come from faith is sin" (Rom 14:23). The Lord's Supper, which symbolically puts the body and blood of Christ before us, is a place for sinners who know their unworthiness but believe in the promise of Christ and confess their sins, then rejoice in the forgiveness accomplished at Calvary. Taking the Supper depends on resting completely in Christ's finished work with confidence in His promised future. We do not confess and repent in order to lay hold of Christ—thus turning repentance into a work—we can only confess and repent *by* laying hold of Christ and finding the satisfaction in Him that releases us from sin. It is not a choice between promising to do good works tomorrow or to hold on to sin. It is seeing the gospel in the Supper through the eyes of faith and receiving from the hand of Jesus who bought us with His blood and invites us to His Table—the One who, through faith, is present with us today and can be trusted for tomorrow.

[27] Cf. D. E. Garland, *1 Corinthians*, BECNT (Grand Rapids: Baker, 2003), 550.

Communing with Christ

In what sense can it be said that Christ is present at the Supper? The question has been answered in many ways.[28] On one end of the spectrum, the answer is that Christ is somehow actually present in or around the elements themselves. On the other end, the Supper is purely a memorial. The key to the presence of Christ is the same as the key to the gospel, namely, faith.

Luke tells of the encounter between the risen Christ and the disciples walking on the road to Emmaus (Luke 24:13–32). When He joins the disciples they do not recognize Him and proceed to tell Him everything that happened lately in Jerusalem. He listens to them for a while and then He, a stranger in their eyes, chides them for not believing the Scripture and goes on to show them, beginning with Moses, that the Christ had to suffer, die, and rise from the dead. Later the disciples would say that while He talked their hearts were burning (24:32). When they sit down to eat together, a strange thing happens. Jesus, still hidden from them, takes the bread, gives thanks (as Luke tells us He did on the night He was betrayed), breaks it, then hands some to them. At that moment "their eyes were opened and they recognized him" (24:31), and then He was gone. When the disciples go tell the others what happened, Luke recounts it like this: "Then the two told what had happened on the way, and how Jesus was recognized by them when he broke the bread" (24:35).[29]

Echoes of the Lord's Supper are evident in the encounter between Jesus and the two disciples in Luke 24. Verse 30 is nearly identical to Luke's account of the Last Supper: "And he took bread, gave thanks and broke it, and gave it to them" (22:19). In the Emmaus Road account, Luke draws attention to the disciples' response to Jesus' teaching—their hearts were burning—and to the revelation of Him in the breaking of bread. As Christ is made known through faith in the preaching of the gospel ("faith comes from hearing and hearing through the word of Christ," Rom 10:17), so Christ is present to us

[28] For an analysis and critique of the Roman Catholic conception of the real presence of Christ in the Supper see the chapter in this book by Gregg Allison. For analysis of other perspectives see the chapters in this book by Matthew Crawford on Luther's view, Bruce Ware on Zwingli, and Shawn Wright on Calvin and the Westminster tradition.

[29] A good discussion of the connections between Luke's account of the Last Supper and the meeting on the Emmaus Road can be found in J. R. Kimbell, "The Atonement in Lukan Theology" (Ph.D. diss., The Southern Baptist Theological Seminary, 2008), 44–54.

by faith when we take up the symbols that He Himself described as His body and blood. Though Jesus is not revealed visibly to us in the Supper, He is seen by faith through the analogy of the bread and the cup. Just as the body is sustained by food and drink, so we are made and kept alive by the sacrifice of Christ.[30]

The symbols may be said to *reveal* Jesus as they serve to remind believers that salvation comes only through His body and blood, and that only those who partake of Him will be saved.[31] John records Jesus' shocking words that turned many followers away: "Whoever eats my flesh and drinks my blood has eternal life, and I will raise him up at the last day" (John 6:54). Though this text is not about the Lord's Supper *per se,* it does shed light on what the Supper is about: namely, believing in Jesus for forgiveness of sin and the gift of eternal life.[32] Eternal life comes through the crucifixion of Jesus, and those who believe in Him will gain it.[33]

Going a step further with John, partaking in Jesus by faith is intrinsically bound to *remaining* in Jesus: "Whoever eats my flesh and drinks

[30] "For this very familiar comparison penetrates into even the dullest minds: just as bread and wine sustain physical life, so are souls fed on Christ. We now understand the purpose of this mystical blessing, namely, to confirm for us the fact that the Lord's body was once for all so sacrificed for us that we may now feed upon it, and by feeding feel in ourselves the working of that unique sacrifice" (Calvin, *Institutes* [4.17.1], 1361).

[31] The word "reveal" is in italics because I do not mean it in terms of "special revelation," i.e., as God is specially revealed in Scripture.

[32] As Carson says, "In short, John 6 does not directly speak of the eucharist; it does expose the true meaning of the Lord's Supper as clearly as any passage in Scripture" (D. A. Carson, *The Gospel According to John* [Grand Rapids: Eerdmans, 1991], 298). Connecting v. 54, where eating flesh and drinking blood result in eternal life, with v. 40, where believing in Jesus the Son results in eternal life, Carson concludes, "The former is the metaphorical way of referring to the latter" (ibid., 297). In other words, "believing" is the meaning of "eat" and "drink." Köstenberger, agreeing with Carson that a eucharistic or sacramental interpretation does not fit the context of John adds, "On a secondary level, however, John may expect his readers to read Jesus' words in light of the church's observance of the Lord's Supper, though not necessarily in a sacramental sense" (A. Köstenberger, *John*, BECNT [Grand Rapids: Baker, 2004], 217).

[33] Koester points out that the "centrality of faith" is established prior to John 6:54. In 6:28–29, people in the crowd ask Jesus about doing the works of God, and Jesus responds by saying that the work of God is "to believe in the one he has sent." Then in v. 40 Jesus says, "Everyone who looks to the Son and believes in him shall have eternal life," and in v. 47, "I tell you the truth, he who believes has everlasting life." From this it follows that eating Jesus' flesh and drinking His blood, which results in eternal life, means to believe in Jesus: "To partake of Jesus as the bread of life is to believe that the crucified Messiah is the source of eternal life with God" (C. R. Koester, *Symbolism in the Fourth Gospel: Meaning, Mystery, Community*, 2nd ed. [Minneapolis: Fortress, 2003], 103). Major commentaries on John discuss the longstanding debate over a possible sacramental background for chap. 6, but for a good summary and analysis of "sacramental symbolism" in John see the section in Koester's appendix (pp. 301–9). See also the discussion in Jonathan Pennington's chapter in this volume.

my blood remains in me, and I in him" (6:56). Without unpacking John's theology of *remaining/abiding* in Christ, it is enough here to say that the language of "remaining" points to a real relationship with Christ and not simply a mental grasp of the truth of the gospel. Of course, faith is impossible without hearing the spoken word of the gospel and agreeing that it is true, but *through* faith the believer enters into a spiritual reality of mutual abiding with Jesus.[34] Later in John 15, abiding in Jesus is linked to various facets of the Christian life such as prayer, obedience, joy, love, and witness.[35] Taken together and applied to the Lord's Supper, the vivid imagery of eating, drinking, and abiding indicates the comprehensive nature of what is remembered and celebrated at the Table. The Supper celebrates union with Jesus through whom we receive the gift of eternal life that transforms life in the present.

It is important to point out that the symbols do not add "sight" to faith; they draw our minds and hearts to the crucified and risen Christ who is known only by faith. The believer does not hold the bread and say, "Now I see Christ," but rather, "I believe that Christ died for my sins." Nor does the believer take the cup and imagine that it is full of Christ's blood, but he drinks while hearing, "This cup is the new covenant in my blood; do this, whenever you drink it, in remembrance of me" (1 Cor 11:23). When Christ said, "This is my body" and "This is my blood," it was not so the disciples would fixate on the bread and cup, but so they would fixate on the breaking of Christ's body and the shedding of His blood. The bread and cup contain the story of the gospel, and the Supper is a means of reinforcing that story in the lives of believers.[36] Understood in this way, the elements are not incidental or immaterial, much less can they be disposed with—they are tangible reminders that Christ came down to us in flesh and blood and died for our sins to bring us to God. The visible evidence of the bread and cup actually reminds us that we live by faith rather than by what is

[34] "Mutual" does not imply "equal." See Carson, *The Gospel According to John*, 298; and Köstenberger, *John*, 216, n. 79. In John, *remaining/abiding in Jesus* is connected to the relationship between Jesus the Son and the Father (e.g., 6:57; 15:23; 17:21,23).

[35] Cf. Carson, *The Gospel According to John*, 517.

[36] "This God-given success of his death explained why the blood should be drunk by the disciples and why the body should be eaten by them. They were for them the means of life which entered them with effective power, since his death provided for them the new relationship with God that had its characteristic feature in the forgiveness of sins" (Schlatter, *History of the Christ*, 356–57).

seen, since Christ incarnate now sits enthroned at the right hand of God. In the material elements, Christ left us a physical reminder of His continually abiding spiritual presence.[37] Therefore, the bread and cup do not create faith or make faith possible; but must be grasped in faith so as to remind us that in Christ we are forgiven, rest in a covenant relationship with God, are made alive in Christ, freed from bondage to sin, and await the day when we will see the One who died, rose again, and ascended into heaven. In this way, at the Supper the believer may be strengthened for life in the present, not by seeing the elements alone, but through what they represent: the gospel of salvation by faith through Christ crucified, risen, and coming again.

There is another thing to consider regarding the presence of Christ in the Supper. The risen Christ is seen when people of every conceivable background, social status, race, and ethnicity gather around the Table confessing the death of Jesus for the forgiveness of their sins. In other words, He is present in His body, the church. Of course, He is present in and with His people at all times, but the Supper affords a special glimpse into that reality as believers indwelt by the same Spirit, having the same baptism, commune together, confessing the same Lord and Savior. Christ is recognized among believers each week in the breaking of bread. As believers approach the Supper, they may look around and consider the others coming to the Table and say to themselves, "Christ died for her. His sins were forgiven on the cross. These brothers and sisters are all part of Christ's body."

The very nature of the Supper, being a corporate experience, should focus attention on the community of believers. It is not a time only for individual contemplation and personal communion with Christ; the communion is between Christ and His body with individuals as members of that body.[38]

[37] By "spiritual" I mean through the Spirit. Calvin's comment on 1 Cor 11:27 is similar: "For, in view of the fact that he is not present with us in visible form, we need to have some symbol of His spiritual presence, with which to occupy our minds" (Calvin, *1 Corinthians*, CNTC 250).

[38] Schlatter, commenting on the corporate nature of the Supper that "lent visibility to the church's continual union with Jesus," puts it like this: "The celebration of the Lord's Supper also did not merely associate individuals with him [Christ] but took place in the gathered community and thereby further strengthened its union" (A. Schlatter, *The Theology of the Apostles*, trans. A. Köstenberger [Grand Rapids: Baker, 1999], 48).

The Future and the Past in the Present

The Supper proclaims the death of Christ through the apostolic word of the gospel that interprets its symbolism. Similar to most of the OT examples considered earlier, the symbols are filled with content through explanation. Jesus referred *explicitly* to the bread and the cup being His body and blood. Likewise, Paul repeated the received tradition to the Corinthians. In the Gospels and in Paul, there is an eschatological thread woven through the Lord's Supper. In the Synoptic Gospels Jesus makes mention of a future meal with His disciples. In Matthew's account, Jesus says, "I tell you, I will not drink of this fruit of the vine from now on until that day when I drink it anew with you in my Father's kingdom" (26:29).[39] He implied His resurrection even while initiating a meal for remembering His death. As the Supper points back to the death of Jesus, so also it points forward to the return of the resurrected Lord. In the same vein Paul says that every time believers come to the Table and eat the bread and drink the cup they "proclaim the Lord's death *until he comes*" (1 Cor 11:26).[40]

The gospel that proclaims Jesus' death also proclaims His resurrection, making the Supper not a memorial service in remembrance of the dead, but a remembrance of the dead and buried Jesus who rose from the grave and who is coming again. The constant interaction of the past, present, and future is nowhere more evident than in the Lord's Supper. The death and resurrection of Christ guarantees the future and transforms the present as believers are reminded through the interpreted symbols that their lives are not just an endless loop of days; the One who gave Himself for His people abides with them and is coming again for them. In the Supper, believers are called to step into the reality of a future that invades the present.[41] Because Christ is raised and by faith we are raised with Him (Eph 2:6; Col 3:1), the future is already here in the present. As the cluster of grapes from Eshcol

[39] Mark's account is quite similar though not surprisingly has "kingdom of God" (14:25) instead of Matthew's "my Father's kingdom." Luke refers to the eschatological Passover that awaits fulfillment in the kingdom of God (22:16).

[40] Garland is right to point out that Paul's "focus is *on the past*—what Jesus did on the night he was handed over" (*1 Corinthians*, 549, his emphasis). The point here is simply that theologically the Lord's Supper is inherently eschatological.

[41] "This is the food," notes Wright, "which will assure us we are on the right road, and that the God who began a good work in us, and now feeds us with his own life, the life of his own Son, will bring that work to completion when all things are made new and we stand at last in the presence of Jesus himself" (*The Meal that Jesus Gave Us*, 58).

was a sign of hope for life in the Land, so the bread and the cup are signs of a future banquet, already set by Jesus in His resurrection and ascension, the new heavens and new earth.

In Rev 19:9, John is told to write, "Blessed are those who are invited to the marriage supper of the Lamb" (ESV), and the Lord's Supper is a foretaste, a sign of hope, for the coming day when all believers are called to eat and drink with Jesus in the kingdom of God. The writer to the Hebrews says that "faith is the assurance of things hoped for, the conviction of things not seen" (11:1, ESV). Just as the OT saints, resting on God's past faithfulness and thereby fixing their hope on God's future, lived by faith in the present, so believers may come to the Table today and celebrate the past with hope fixed on the future.

Conclusion

The Lord's Supper calls the death of Jesus powerfully to mind through the visible signs of the bread and the cup. In fact, the physical act of taking the Supper is itself a reminder that our help comes from outside ourselves. Just as we reach out to take the bread and the cup, so too must we reach out, away from ourselves, and lay hold of Christ through faith. Ultimately the Supper proclaims that in the gospel of Christ, God is *for us*. The believer might well say upon coming to the Table, "I do this because of what the LORD did for me when I came out of Egypt" (Exod 13:8b), but replace "Egypt" with, "when I was forgiven and released from my slavery to sin." The Table is a sign of the salvation God brings in Christ and which is proclaimed, "so that all the peoples of the earth might know that the hand of the LORD is powerful and so that you might always fear the LORD your God" (Josh 4:24). The Table is not merely an invitation to a history lesson; it is a sign that God keeps His promises.

Recently a friend told me about a church in which many members would not take Communion. As far as I know, the people in this church profess faith in Christ; they are from a tradition that puts particular emphasis on God's sovereignty and grace; and they do not believe that their works in any way contribute to their salvation. The problem is that when the Table was set most members in the church simply would not come forward. Their apprehension was not, apparently, based on rampant sin or a refusal to repent—it just seems that most people could not find enough worthiness in themselves to take the Supper. This is, admittedly, a fairly radical example, but it helps make a point that applies to all believers. The problem with excessive introspection is that it leads us only back to ourselves. Once there, left to ourselves, we will never find enough worthiness. What the members of that church need to hear and what we all need to hear is this: "You are exactly right. You are not worthy. But Christ is, and His body and blood, broken and shed for you, make you worthy and by faith He abides with you. Now come, confess and repent of your sins and proclaim His death until He comes." The Supper, as a proclamation of the gospel, leads us away from ourselves to Christ who invites us to come to His Table to remember Him, believe in Him, and wait for Him.

THE LORD'S SUPPER AND WORKS OF LOVE

Gregory Alan Thornbury*

Introduction

In 1911, Karl Barth took up a new life as a country parson in the little village of Safenwil, Switzerland. Three months after he arrived, he was invited to deliver a series of lectures to the local Workers Association. *Der Freie Aargauer*, a socialist newspaper, published the series in December of that year under the title, "Jesus Christ and the Movement for Social Justice." The result was a somewhat clumsy attempt by Barth to apply the liberal theology that he had learned at the University of Berlin under the tutelage of Adolf Von Harnack to the conditions in which he currently found himself ministering. In Barth's early account, Jesus opposed private property, and the kingdom of God was intended to provide deliverance from the plight of the proletariat. If Jesus were alive today, Barth went on to say, He would have been a Social Democrat.

Over time, Barth realized that his political message was failing to reach his blue-collar audience. He began preaching more simple, biblical messages, and in the process of doing so, he discovered what he called "a strange new world within the Bible." In it, he maintained, we find not simply the history of men or of class struggle. The Word of God is not merely an aid to "godly living." Jesus did not merely come to change a political order, but instead "he is the redeemer of a humanity gone astray and ruled by evil demons and powers. He is the redeemer of the groaning creation about us."[1]

What some readers might find a bit perplexing is that Barth never really changed his view of economics, his advocacy for the poor, or his opposition to fascism. He remained politically engaged until his death in 1968, and always sought to make theological connections to the

* Gregory Alan Thornbury received his Ph.D. from The Southern Baptist Theological Seminary. He is associate professor of Christian Thought & Tradition, vice president for Spiritual Life, Campus Ministries, and dean of the School of Theology & Missions at Union University in Jackson, Tennessee.

[1] K. Barth, "The Strange New World Within the Bible," as cited in C. E. Braaten and R. W. Jensen, ed., *A Map of Twentieth-Century Theology: Readings from Karl Barth to Radical Pluralism* (Minneapolis: Fortress, 1995), 30.

field of justice issues.[2] But what changed about Barth's hermeneutic is that he began to see that only traditional theological categories contained within them the power to precipitate the kind of social revolution which he hoped for the downtrodden. In 1934, when he penned the Barmen Declaration, the Swiss thinker openly opposed the Third Reich not out of some ad hoc attempt to connect the Scripture to modern life, but from the resources of the gospel itself.

For most Southern Baptists today, our problem is functionally the reverse of the early Barth. While the contemporary pastor might occasionally address justice issues, unlike that once-young pastor in Safenwil he is not likely to feel the "dangerous" nature of preaching biblical truth. The class and social distinctions in the congregation will very likely go undisturbed, and if there are feathers ruffled, there is only a squawk behind the protest, and not an SS storm trooper awaiting you in the foyer. Barth wanted to unsettle the bourgeoisie with the claims of the Bible. And he found a much more potent weapon in the gospel than he ever found in socialist politics.

In Baptist congregational life in our time, the challenge will not be to find a strange new world within the Bible, but to become strange Christians within a new secular world. The willingness of the church to be a prophetic social presence in a community has always been a leading indicator of biblical fidelity. This was the case, for example, in the struggle for civil rights. As Martin Luther King wrote in his "Letter from a Birmingham Jail,"

> In the midst of a mighty struggle to rid our nation of racial and economic injustice, I have heard many ministers say: "Those are social issues, with which the gospel has no real concern." And I have watched many churches commit themselves to a completely other worldly religion which makes a strange, un-Biblical distinction between body and soul, between the sacred and the secular. . . .
>
> In deep disappointment I have wept over the laxity of the church. . . .
>
> But the judgment of God is upon the church as never before. If today's church does not recapture the sacrificial spirit of the early church, it will lose its authenticity, forfeit the loyalty of millions, and be dismissed as an irrelevant social club with no meaning for the twentieth century. . . .
>
> Is organized religion too inextricably bound to the status quo to save our nation and the world?[3]

[2] See, e.g., F. Jehle, *Ever Against the Stream: The Politics of Karl Barth, 1906–1968,* trans. R. Burnett and M. Burnett (Grand Rapids: Eerdmans, 2002).

[3] Martin Luther King Jr., "Letter from a Birmingham Jail," in *The American Intellectual Tra-*

King's words possess a prophetic ring because they represent the heart of the Lord Jesus and the apostles themselves. What does it mean to refer to "the sacrificial spirit of the early church"? I would like to suggest that it has to do with radical declaration of belonging to Christ found in the NT and made known preeminently in the gospel (Gal 3:28–29). That understanding created new cultural identification markers that transcended racial, ethnic, and political boundaries. Commitment to this manifestation of God's power stiffened the resolve of the early church and produced a solidarity within the body of Christ that Caesar could not defeat. That sacrificial spirit was most preeminently put on display in the practice of Communion, the celebration that the Christian's identity is to be found nowhere else than in Christ Himself and in His body, the church. The meal itself challenged the very notion of identity in the dawning era of the Christian community's witness. To a Roman culture with seemingly intractable social hierarchies, it brought to an end the notion that one's worth came from birth, possessions, or class.[4] For the people of God, everything centered on Christ.

The Lord's Supper and the Modern World

Interrupting this role that the Lord's Supper played in the early church's life and witness, however, is the history of the development and debate about the nature of the meal itself. And the nature of what precisely is going on during the celebration of the Supper has become almost the sole emphasis on the meaning of the meal, to the exclusion of its impact upon social justice and its evangelistic aspect. The shift, of course, was inevitable because the stakes are so high. The question of whether or not the actual body and blood of the Lord Jesus are present at the Table goes to the heart of the church's claims about reality. Theological claims about epistemology and metaphysics are thus brought under examination.

For this very reason, the debate about what exactly happens during Communion was the defining issue that gave birth to the modern world. That may come as a surprise to modern inquirers, but an entire

dition, Volume Two: 1865 to the Present, ed. D. A. Hollinger and C. Capper (New York: Oxford University Press, 1989), 242–43.

[4] See, e.g., R. M. Grant, *Early Christianity and Society* (San Francisco: Harper & Row, 1977), 130–34; R. Vander Laan, *In the Dust of the Rabbi* (Grand Rapids: Zondervan, 2006), 109ff.

philosophical tradition was birthed as a result of it. In the High Middle Ages, the debate centered around how the words of the priest spoken in the Eucharist could actually be transformed into something corporeal with respect to the body and blood of Christ. Were the words spoken somehow inextricably bound to the elements themselves? This brought up an even greater philosophical matter which involved whether or not words themselves are real signs of the things that they represent. Or were they merely conventions?[5]

In the eleventh century, Berengar of Tours ignited a controversy when he simply raised the question of how it was that the prayer of the priest made at the altar precipitates an ontological and substantial change of the bread and wine into "real" body and blood. Anticipating Aristotelian distinctions about which he would not have known at the time, he seemed to be suggesting that accidents (i.e., that which exists in and is said of another) cannot exist without its supporting substance (that which is, and cannot be said of another). Stated differently, Berengar appeared to be saying that "the body and blood of Christ" cannot be said of "bread and wine" on the grounds that Christ Himself is not literally on the altar.[6]

Lanfranc, Anselm's predecessor as Archbishop of Canterbury, considered the very query itself to be impious. Of course, Christ's body in its quality, quantity, relation, and affect can exist in the host and the wine in the time and place of the moment of transubstantiation, he said. It was heresy to deny that. How else could the believer receive the gift of Christ from the church? He thus charged Berengar with replacing the authoritative teaching of the church with reason. Lanfranc wrote:

> On the one hand, there is the sacrament; on the other, there is the "thing of the sacrament (*res sacramenti*)." The "thing" (or the "reality") of the sacrament is the body of Christ. Yet Christ is risen from the dead. He does not die, and death has no more power over him (Romans 6:9). So, as the Apostle Andrew says, while the bits of [Christ's] flesh (*carnes*) are really eaten and his blood is really drunk, he himself nevertheless continues in his totality

[5] For a clear discussion of these issues, see D. Knowles, *The Evolution of Medieval Thought* (Baltimore, MD: Helicon, 1962), 93–130. For a concise and clear discussion of the Aristotelian distinction of substance and accident as read through a Thomistic lens, see "Natural Philosophy: Substance and Accident." Accessed 11 November 2009. Online: http://www.aquinasonline.com/Topics/substacc.html; also *The Catholic Encyclopedia,* ed. C. G. Herbermann, et al., s.v. "Eucharist" (New York: The Encyclopedia Press, 1913), 580–83.

[6] J. F. McCue, "The Doctrine of Transubstantiation from Berengar Through Trent: The Point at Issue," *HTR* 61.3 (July 1968): 386–88.

> (*integer*), living in the heavens at the right hand of the Father until such time as when all will be restored. If you ask me how this is possible, I can only reply briefly as follows: it is a mystery of faith. To believe it can be healthy; to investigate it cannot be of any use.[7]

The papacy sided with Lanfranc and demanded that Berengar recant of his line of thinking, which he did at the Synod of Rome in 1059.

Berengar's impieties did not die with him, but they did prompt continual revisitations of the doctrine. By 1215, the Fourth Lateran Council established that transubstantiation was the accepted doctrine of the church.[8] But the Council did not settle how the mechanism by which the miracle of the elements of the Eucharist becoming the body and blood of Christ Himself was metaphysically possible. Aquinas modified Abelardian conceptualism, and contended that the substance of Christ's body replaces the substance of the bread, and so on.[9] To maintain anything less than that would be to propound heresy. In other words, as soon as the Mass is performed the bread and wine cease to be physical food and become the food of Christ Himself.[10]

But if ever there was an "elephant in the room" being ignored in Christian doctrine, it was this account of the Lord's Supper. The obvious question still remaining, despite the sophisticated account of Thomas, remains "Why does the bread and wine still in every way taste, smell, and feel like nothing more than bread and wine, and not flesh and blood?" What most interpreters of transubstantiation had argued before William of Ockham was that when the Mass was performed, the elements of the bread and wine remained inherent in their quantity, but that the actual substances changed from ordinary food to the real spiritual food of Christ Himself. And *that is* why the bread and the wine taste the same. But there is something deeply unsatisfying about that explanation. It seems to be far too complicated.

[7] Lanfranc of Bec, *De corpore et sanguine Christi*; in *Beati Lanfranci archiepiscopi Cantuarensis opera*, ed. J. A. Giles (Oxford: Clarendon, 1844), 2:167; as cited in A. McGrath, *The Christian Theology Reader* (Oxford: Blackwell, 1995), 298. Though obscure, the reference to the apostle Andrew is almost certainly a paraphrase of a citation in the *Acts of the Apostle Andrew* in the NT Apocrypha. Accessed 21 September 2010. Online: http://www.newadvent.org/fathers/0819.htm.

[8] See J. Pelikan, *The Growth of Medieval Theology (600–1300)*, vol. 3, *The Christian Tradition: A History of the Development of Doctrine* (Chicago: The University of Chicago Press, 1978), 185–214.

[9] Betty Radice defines Abelardian conceptualism in the following way: "Universals were neither realities nor mere names but the concepts formed by the intellect when abstracting the similarities between perceived individual things." Cited in B. R. Hergenhahn, ed., *An Introduction to the History of Psychology*, 5th ed. (Belmont, CA: Thomson Wadsworth, 2005), 78–79.

[10] Pelikan, *The Growth of Medieval Theology*, 268–69.

William of Ockham took up this subject matter in his lectures on the *Sentences* of Peter Lombard in his treatise *De Corpus Christi*. The Oxford theologian, true to the law of parsimony which now bears his name, eliminated almost all of the conventional renderings of the Aristotelian categories. For him, only substance and quality existed. Further, he contended that universal essences do not exist. What we take for these are merely names (hence the term "nominalism"). Only individual substances exist in reality. As such, for example, quantity (i.e., one of the Categories Ockham eliminated) is not a thing in-and-of-itself. Therefore, with respect to the Mass, substances are not exchanged *ex opere operato*. Rather, the substance of bread and wine and the substance of Christ and His body are partaken of simultaneously. The former we perceive with our senses. The latter we receive by faith in what the Scripture says and the theological tradition instructs us to believe. Thus, the sacrifice of Christ is accepted on the basis of faith alone.[11]

Such a conclusion appeared in the eyes of the papacy to be dangerous. Ockham was summoned to Avignon to give testimony to a panel of inquisitors about his theological innovations. After his censure, he redirected his scholarship toward political theory, but his work continued to have ramifications throughout the fifteenth and sixteenth centuries. As I have argued elsewhere, Ockham is often cited as a bogeyman of sorts who is the villain giving rise to the modern attack on objective truth based on his nominalist metaphysics.[12] But it was Ockham—who himself never denied transubstantiation—who cracked the door in favor of the proposition that certain things may be believed simply on the basis of faith in the Scriptures. He drew into question the basis upon which authority rests. Is it with the priest? With Aristotle? With the papacy in Avignon?

Gabriel Biel, a follower of Ockham, continued to insist upon the correctness of transubstantiation as the true doctrine of the church.

[11] See F. Copelston, *Late Medieval and Renaissance Philosophy*, *Part Two: The Revival of Platonism to Suárez*, vol. 3, *A History of Philosophy* (Garden City, NY: Image Books/Doubleday, 1963), 56–133; McCue, "Transubstantiation," 407ff; see also M. Rubin, *Corpus Christi: The Eucharist in Late Medieval Culture* (New York: Cambridge University Press, 1991; reprint 1992), 32–25; W. J. Courtenay, "Cranmer as a Nominalist: *Sed Contra*," *HTR* 57.4 (October, 1964): 372–73; P. V. Spade, "Ockham's Nominalist Metaphysic: Some Main Themes," in *The Cambridge Companion to Ockham*, ed. P. V. Spade (New York: Cambridge University Press, 1999), 105–6.

[12] G. A. Thornbury, "Prolegomena: Introduction to the Task of Theology," in *A Theology for the Church*, ed. D. L. Akin (Nashville: B&H, 2007), 29–36.

But Biel accomplished something strategic with his discussion of the Mass. As Heiko Oberman asserts, "Though he does not deny that it can be fruitful to be present and hear the Mass, it is Communion, along with faith and baptism, which makes one a Christian."[13] The Reformers picked up on this theme and developed a robust view of the communion of the saints.[14] Whatever their differences were on the precise nature of the Lord's Supper, their principle of *scriptura prima* drove them back to the perspicacious teaching of the NT itself—that the Lord's Supper is not fundamentally a rite about which to engage in metaphysical speculations. Rather, it is a statement about what Christ's death on the cross has accomplished on behalf of, and in the midst of, a new community of believers.

Remarkably, one could argue with some force that virtually every crucial development in the transition from medieval to modern philosophy was occasioned by an exploration of the meaning of the Lord's Supper. The debate over realism versus nominalism began there, and quickly extended to the rest of the syllabus of philosophical inquiry. It is hard for modern inquirers to realize just how high the stakes were. If what was happening on that altar was not actually a supernatural intervention into the physical world, then Christianity could possibly be seen as a sham, and the church a fraud, continually making unkept promises. But while the controversy over Communion may have proved to be fruitful soil for discussion with respect to what is meant by the term "miracle," and whether words sufficiently correspond to a fixed universal point of reference, the debate that ensued probably did not do justice to the biblical materials themselves. We can, however, find the original intent through the study of biblical backgrounds in general and particularly with specific reference to the ministry of the apostle Paul.

The Simplicity of the Lord's Supper

In the fall of 2005, in the city of Megiddo in North Israel, archaeologists uncovered a site that is precipitating a rediscovery of the early church. In what is now widely regarded as the earliest Christian church ever discovered, those involved with discoveries at Megiddo,

[13] H. Oberman, *The Harvest of Medieval Theology: Gabriel Biel and Late Medieval Nominalism* (Grand Rapids: Baker Academic, 2000), 278.

[14] G. C. Berkouwer, *Studies in Dogmatics: The Sacraments*, trans. H. Bekker (Grand Rapids: Eerdmans, 1969), 56–89.

report the uncovering of "a detailed and well-preserved mosaic, the foundations of a rectangular building, and pottery dated to the third and fourth century." Within the mosaic stands the *icthus*, the pre-Constantinian symbol for Christianity. Yotam Tepper, an archaeologist with the Israeli Antiquities Authority, reports, "There are no crosses on the mosaic floor."[15] The cross, of course, did not achieve prominence as a Christian symbol of identification until the fourth century.

The discovery at the church at Megiddo also included a table, evidently donated by a woman named Akeptous, with an inscription stating that she donated funds "in the memory of the God, Jesus Christ." In addition to the testimony of Akeptous, there is also an inscription regarding the testimony of a Roman soldier who had become a Christian. Those familiar with the dig emphasize that this was indeed a table and not an altar. The memorial language with respect to Jesus Christ at the sight of the table appears to indicate something far less theologically sophisticated and elaborate than what has come to be associated with the concept of an altar. Simply put, no mass was apparently celebrated here, at least in any form reminiscent of what has now come to characterize the rite.[16]

The archaeological findings at Megiddo give us a glimpse into what both the biblical evidence and early church tradition confirmed to us regarding the place of the Lord's Supper in the life of the church of the Lord Jesus Christ. The Agape Feast and the Eucharist were first and foremost about remembering who Christ was and what He had done. Additionally, it solidified the community of faith and the witness of a local church to the reality of the gospel. What does not seem to characterize the goings-on—at least in this particular piece of archaeological evidence—was any hint about how one achieves or maintains grace or standing with God.

This volume has attempted a foray into understanding the Lord's Supper. The contributors have considered the larger tradition of the church, the debates between the Reformers, and the unique contributions that Baptists have and continue to make to the Lord's ordinance. But where Baptists have been at their best, they have stated that the

[15] C. McGreal, "Holy Land's 'oldest church' found at Armageddon," *The Guardian*, 7 November 2005 Accessed 12 August 2009. Online: http://www.guardian.co.uk/world/2005/nov/07/israel.artsnews.

[16] V. Tzaferis, "Inscribed to God Jesus Christ," *BAR*. Accessed 11 November 2009. Online: http://www.bib-arch.org/online-exclusives/oldest-church-02.asp.

power of institutions such as the Lord's Supper and baptism lie not in the performance of the rite or in the actions of the clergy, but in the testimony of a local body of people committed to the truth of the gospel.

Baptist theology at its best is a theology of humility, prioritizing the needs of the community and deference toward one's brother and sister. Indeed, both early General and Particular Baptist statements related to Communion emphasize "Christ's call for union with each other and the view that the Supper was primarily 'a perpetual remembrance'" of Christ's sacrifice.[17] Baptist ecclesiology points away from the church as an institution of power, and directs our attention toward the Word that is to be preached, believed in, and trusted. Traditional theological interpretations of the Lord's Supper focus on the presence of Christ in the meal according to denominational position.[18] But of similar importance is the way in which the rite of Communion forms a presence of Christ within the congregation itself which, in turn, transfigures the whole assembly gathered into a Spirit-led community.

The ideal of a church community living in peace with one another is foundational to the evangelistic witness for the local congregation. It stands to reason that the Lord's Supper, then, is not just an observance but a declaration about the way things are to be among God's people. The meal contains a message not only about who Christ is and what He has done for the church, but who is included in the gospel story and in the benefits of Christ's glory. It is a story of belonging, and a radical message that God intends for His people to identify with all believers, whether they are poor, weak, or forgotten. This revolutionary social message came into focus as the apostles planted churches and slowly began to untangle the mess of the oppressive class social structure of the Greco-Roman world.

The Lord's Supper as a Hermeneutical Key to Paul's Understanding of Culture

When we check the news, read a magazine, or turn on our radio, we quickly find ourselves immersed in a world of political turmoil, social tension, and even violence. For some reason, by way of contrast,

[17] W. Brackney, *The Baptists* (Westport, CT: Praeger, 1994), 61.

[18] See, e.g., the traditional discussion of this type in M. Erickson, *Christian Theology*, 2nd ed. (Grand Rapids: Baker, 1998), 1123–34.

we approach the Bible in such a way as to ignore that this was also the case in the ancient world. This reticence stems from some right motivations and concerns. It is, after all, tricky business to get too far afield from the text itself and delve into a world of historical-cultural and psycho-social research. We likewise want to get to the important business of thinking theologically, and understanding the intertextual connections in Scripture that transcend time and place. For others, modern interpretation has reached a point of despair with respect to the possibility of developing an imaginative sympathy with the author of ancient texts. We have read Gadamer's trenchant critique of Schleiermacher in *Truth and Method* and are tempted to feel jaded about the prospects of recovering authorial intent.[19] We ask ourselves just how much can be gained by attempting to recreate the world in which the apostles lived, taught, and gave their lives for the gospel. Such concerns deserve to be addressed, but not at the expense of losing our connection with the fabric of the biblical narrative and the very real historical pathos which prompted the epistolary writings. What is at stake is losing the prophetic power of passages like 1 Corinthians 13—texts that are familiar to people of faith but have been domesticated into something sweet that could be printed on a Hallmark card or a merely poetic addition to a wedding program. The Lord's Supper is a declaration about how to love one another in light of the gospel that heralds a new order that Jesus brought with Him when He came declaring that the kingdom of God was at hand.

Paul's discussion of Communion arose from a specific context in ancient Corinth to which the first letter to the Corinthians was written. The locus of Paul's concerns for that context related to the treatment of one class of Christians by those of another class.[20] The apostle certainly found himself adjudicating sources of strife and divisions of various kinds in the congregation. But by the time he gets to

[19] H.-G. Gadamer, *Truth and Method*, 2nd. ed, trans. J. Weinsheimer and D. G. Marshall (New York: Crossroad, 1989), 184–97. Here I have in mind Gadamer's discussion of the "questionableness of Romantic hermeneutics" that involves Schleiermacher's suggestion that an interpreter can accurately reproduce the world of the original author of a text via an imaginative sympathy. There is much to learn from Gadamer's position that one always approaches a text from a particular horizon, with certain prejudices in place that cannot be set aside, thus making a purely inductive study of any text, let alone the Bible, nearly impossible.

[20] In this connection, I have been persuaded by the account offered by A. C. Thiselton in *The First Epistle to the Corinthians*, NIGTC (Grand Rapids: Eerdmans, 2000), 23–29. Thiselton's analysis is further supported by D. Garland with his discussion of "haves" and "have nots" in *First Corinthians*, BECNT (Grand Rapids: Baker Academic, 2003), 533–44.

chap. 13—the perhaps too familiar "love chapter"—one might think that Paul needs a break from the depressing problems of his troublesome Corinthian congregation. He needs a distraction. So he pens this beautiful poem on love to try to get their minds off the problems that are at hand.[21] On the contrary, when the apostle speaks of love it is never a distraction, nor is it an abstraction. For Paul, love exhibits two primary characteristics. First, love is not a matter of metaphysical speculation, as it was with the Greek philosophers. Love finds meaning in the accomplishments of Jesus Christ alone as expressed in the gospel. Secondly, as an extension of its rooting in the gospel, Paul believed that true Christian affection toward a brother and sister in Christ always finds its expression in the concrete day-to-day practice of the local church. He intended to teach them that behavior is the primary indicator of what and upon whom one has actually believed and trusted. For Paul, love means nothing if it is not wedded to concrete acts of compassion, service, and sacrifice in deference to one's brother in Christ. For this reason, Krister Stendahl defined love in this context as "concern for the community."[22]

By treating the topic of love in this way, the apostle set a different course for how the church would treat the great philosophical question of love that bewitched the minds of the Greek philosophers before him, and continues to do the same today. In the documentary *Derrida*, filmmaker Amy Ziering Kofman requested that the French *philosophe* comment on the subject of love. Derrida demurred, "I have nothing to say about love. At least pose a question. I cannot examine 'love' just like that. I'm not capable of talking in generalities about love."[23] Neither could Paul, but he was willing to define the word in active verbs. In the context of the Corinthian church that he planted, the apostle knew where first to look to determine whether or not love was actually being practiced: at the Agape feast and the Lord's Table. To this end, he carefully investigated reports that something was awry during the memorial meal celebrating Christ's death, resurrection, and ongoing power in the assembly of the people of God.

[21] Garland, *First Corinthians*, 605–8.

[22] K. Stendahl, as cited in Garland, *First Corinthians*, 606.

[23] *Derrida*, prod. Amy Ziering and Gil Kofman; dir. Amy Ziering and Kirby Dick, 84 min., Zeitgeist Films, 2004, DVD.

Revisiting the Corinthian Situation

The Corinthian church deserves its reputation as the most infamous church in the Bible. As students taking a NT Survey course will learn, the city of Corinth itself was notorious. But the place did not start off that way. Originally, the locale did not have much to commend itself until eventually a highway known as the *dioklos* was built across the isthmus.[24] All of the sudden, you could get from one coast line to the other with relative ease. As a result, Corinth became a very important port city because you wouldn't have to sail around the Peloponnesus to make a delivery of goods. You could access the city either from the Gulf of Corinth or the Saronic Gulf, making it a natural stopping point for both commerce and official Roman business. This boon to infrastructure meant big business.

In modern society, we have all seen cities like this—metroplexes that just grow up overnight because of some upsurge in the economy that has suddenly taken place. Images come to mind of the oil boom that occurred in the state of Texas in the 1920s and 1930s. Corinth was very much like that. As a result, the people who gained wealth and power were those that previously had not been as wealthy. They were mostly from the social status of the freedmen class, people who had been slaves, then freed, and ultimately had been allowed by the Roman government to come settle the city and do business. So in essence, they were what we call "new money"—the *nouveau riche*.[25]

The problem with the *nouveau riche* usually stems from the fact that they do not know how to behave with their abundance. Elvis's decor at Graceland in Memphis happens. Every age deals with the challenges of the newly rich, and the phenomenon occurs every time an economy rapidly expands in a given sector. In his history of the Morgan banking dynasty, Ron Chernow chronicles how the Morgan family themselves disdained the arrival of the Vanderbilts into Manhattan, with their "gaudy palaces" in uptown on Fifth Avenue.[26]

[24] D. W. J. Gill, "1 Corinthians," in *Zondervan Illustrated Bible Backgrounds Commentary*, ed. C. E. Arnold (Grand Rapids: Zondervan, 2002), 104. See also J. E. Stambaugh and D. L. Balch, *The New Testament in Its Social Environment* (Philadelphia: Westminster, 1986), 157–60.

[25] A good review of the history of interpretation is provided in Thiselton, *The First Epistle to the Corinthians*, 23–29, and Garland, *First Corinthians*, 1–9.

[26] R. Chernow, *The House of Morgan: An American Banking Dynasty and the Rise of Modern Finance* (New York: Grove, 1990), 46–47.

One does not need to take the matter out of context to see Corinth serves as an ancient picture of this timeless phenomenon. The Corinthian *nouveau riche* showed off their success by living in lavish homes. Worse still, they boasted about their wealth, status, and power.[27] At the same time, they still had people from the slave class who were the average, ordinary, everyday workers in Corinth. A deepening classism seems to have resulted, with the wealthy prizing their status and accomplishments. These individuals seemed to have brought their attitudes with them right into the church after they professed faith in Jesus. They devised categories to make distinctions among themselves. They juxtaposed possessing honor as opposed to shame, and power versus exhibiting weakness. Most of all, they prided themselves in being rich as opposed to being poor. Those trademarks—honor, power, and wealth—were signs to them of the blessings of God.

When Paul came to Corinth, he seemed to defy expectations for a man of his office. Soon after his arrival, Paul started working with Priscilla and Aquila as a leather worker or fabric weaver.[28] Although Rabbis of Paul's level of skill and training would have been accustomed to using their talents in a trade in addition to being a teacher, these particular Greeks held different expectations.[29] Evidently, they wanted somebody who represented the status that they thought was so important. They surmised that if you were really a great teacher, if you were a dynamic pastor, you could make your living simply by talking and not doing anything else. They wanted to make a celebrity out of Paul. They wanted somebody who delivered his orations with beautiful, flowing rhetoric like the pagan philosophers. This expectation, of course, characterized more than just the Corinthians. Augustine, after all, expressed his initial disappointment with the prose of the NT after he judged it in light of the standards for rhetoric found in Cicero's *Hortensius*.[30]

Paul understood that such cultural snootiness could kill the prospects for evangelistic witness. And so what did Paul do when he

[27] Surely Paul is responding to extant Corinthian prejudices at the time when he mounts his argument, e.g., in 1 Corinthians 1:26ff.

[28] R. F. Hock, *The Social Context of Paul's Ministry: Tentmaking and Apostleship* (Philadelphia: Fortress, 1980), 14ff.

[29] For a helpful discussion of this, see B. Winter, *After Paul Left Corinth* (Grand Rapids: Eerdmans, 2001), 32–43.

[30] A. D. Fitzgerald, ed., *Augustine Through the Ages: An Encyclopedia* (Grand Rapids: Eerdmans, 1999), 437.

arrived at Corinth? It is at least curious to note that it is not until Acts 18 that one receives any mention of Paul taking up the practice of tentmaking. He no doubt knew the craft before he arrived in Corinth and may have been referencing the skill in 2 Thess 2:9. Luke, however, uniquely draws attention to it. While it is very likely the case that a Rabbi or teacher of Paul's ability would have plied a trade in addition to his teaching ministry, Paul was also a great cultural strategist. He would have been aware of how his every action would be scrutinized and interpreted in each new social situation. In light of this supposition, it seems that Paul's strategy may very well have been as follows: (1) Do not give in to an attitude about wealth, status, and power. Confront it directly with the gospel. (2) Identify with the working classes. Work with your hands as the Lord Jesus Himself did. (3) When planting a church in a new city, reach all levels of society. Use your trade or skill or storefront as a staging ground for evangelism. (4) Shame those people who say that Christianity is all about wealth and power and status. These are themes that Paul would return to throughout his ministry, as when he exhorted the Romans, "Live in harmony with one another. Do not be haughty, but associate with the lowly" (Rom 12:16).[31] At no time in his ministry did the apostle practice what he preached more than in the year and a half that he spent in the city of Corinth. So he opened up a little shop with Priscilla and Aquila and started working with his hands. This would have likely been an offense to the *nouveau riche* in Corinth. To them, a great preacher and miracle worker who was supposedly a powerful herald of this message of the resurrected Christ should not stoop to a "finger nails dirty" lifestyle reminiscent of the slave class. As a result, Paul's theology of the cross created a stumbling block not only for the message that he preached, but in the gospel that he lived. In Corinth, the seemingly intractable divisions that broke out among the new believers in Christ centered around answering this central question: What does it mean to have status in Christianity?

Paul weighed into the debate with an eye toward the ordinance that most publicly makes the church a community: the Lord's Supper. The focal passage of concern is 1 Cor 11:27. Many Christians will recognize references from this passage about the matter of taking the Lord's Supper "in an unworthy manner" and eating and drinking damnation

[31] Unless otherwise indicated, biblical quotations are from the ESV.

upon oneself. It is an enigmatic statement, and one that has precipitated much introspection. After all, what does it mean for a man to eat and drink damnation on himself? While the background of the situation in Corinth surely does not exhaust the possibilities of broader applications of the apostle's warning, the truth is probably that Paul is addressing the meaning of the Lord's Supper in light of the social divisions in his troubled Corinthian congregation. Paul lamented, "In the following instructions I do not commend you, because when you come together, it is not for the better but for the worse" (1 Cor 11:17). Essentially, their "father" in the faith (1 Cor 4:15) was telling them that they would be better off not coming to church, than to act like they were acting. Paul elaborated further:

> For, in the first place, when you come together as a church, I hear that there are divisions among you. And I believe it in part, for there must be factions among you in order that those who are genuine among you may be recognized. When you come together, it is not the Lord's supper that you eat. For in eating, each one goes ahead with his own meal. One goes hungry, another gets drunk. What! Do you not have houses to eat and drink in? Or do you despise the church of God and humiliate those who have nothing? What shall I say to you? Shall I commend you in this? No, I will not. For I received from the Lord what I also delivered to you, that the Lord Jesus on the night when he was betrayed took bread, and when he had given thanks, he broke it, and said, "This is my body which is for you. Do this in remembrance of me." In the same way also he took the cup, after supper, saying, "This cup is the new covenant in my blood. Do this, as often as you drink it, in remembrance of me." For as often as you eat this bread and drink the cup, you proclaim the Lord's death until he comes. Whoever, therefore, eats the bread or drinks the cup of the Lord in an unworthy manner will be guilty concerning the body and blood of the Lord. Let a person examine himself, then, and so eat of the bread and drink of the cup. For anyone who eats and drinks without discerning the body eats and drinks judgment on himself. That is why many of you are weak and ill, and some have died. (1 Cor 11:18–30)

Paul directed his criticism toward certain well-to-do people in the Corinthian congregation. As Roger Gehring explains, "Paul apparently took it for granted that not only the more affluent but also the poorer Christians, who were not able to bring anything, would be able to eat to their satisfaction from the food brought by others."[32] The affluent could have eaten as much as they wanted at their home,

[32] R. W. Gehring, *House Church and Mission: The Importance of Household Structures in Early Christianity* (Peabody, MA: Hendrickson, 2000), 173. For a more detailed description of what was happening at the Agape Feast and Lord's Supper, see 171–79.

but instead, they chose to display their status and lives of blessing in whatever wealthy person's home the church was meeting in that week. Evidently, here is what was happening. The "money party" would gather together early and claim that they were celebrating the Agape feast that preceded the Lord's Table. But what they were really doing was having a sumptuous feast at which they came and gorged themselves in this large dining room of the hosts' home, who would have no doubt been complicit in the display. After which point, the lower classes, the "have nots" would gather together in the atrium and begin a long wait for those who were eating to finish up before church could take place. The effect is that some of the congregation were not participating in the fellowship meal. Not everybody in Christ's body was included. So the select few were satiating themselves with fine food and wine, and then afterward, almost as an afterthought, they say they're going to have the Lord's Supper. If any portions of the food are left over, they concluded, that can be given to the folks in the atrium.[33] The juxtaposition surely would have driven home a lesson about status and honor, as opposed to shame and loneliness. And so, Paul, himself a blue-collar worker, said, "If anyone is hungry, let him eat at home." He is obviously not talking to the poor people. That would have been cruel. He is talking to those who used weekly worship as a staging ground for a banquet. In essence, he told them, if you have something to eat, then stay home and eat it in the privacy of your own home. One must not "show off" the fact that his position and place is greater than his neighbor. This practice perverted the use and meaning of the very meal which Jesus instituted as a sign of His humiliation on the cross and His identification with poor sinners.

To take such an ordinance and turn it into a parable on your new-found wealth, status, and power betrayed a wickedness of the most incorrigible kind. You do that, the apostle said, and you will eat and drink damnation on yourself. Further, he remarked that for this reason, "some have died." When people are separated from one another, when members of Christ are socially isolated from each other, God will not honor it. He will bring into judgment any community who takes His gospel of forgiveness and righteousness and turns it into some sort of perverse social structure. This theological insight comports with extant sociological data that points to the supporting

[33] Thiselton, *The First Epistle to the Corinthians,* 848–53, 860–63.

conclusion that social structures that facilitate radical individualism, loneliness, and isolation contribute to higher incidences of disease and death.[34] On the contrary, places that privilege community, belonging, and family promote health and human flourishing. Paul looked at the dissension created by the new money class in his Corinthian church, recognized it immediately as being at cross purposes with the gospel, and concluded: This must stop.

Two chapters later we get Paul's beautiful paean to love in 1 Corinthians 13. When D. A. Carson wrote *Exegetical Fallacies*, he skewered those who turn simple Greek word studies into programmatic theological position statements.[35] Everyone who has read C. S. Lewis's *The Four Loves* is familiar with his archetypal definition of love as "Gift-Love"—love as self-giving sacrifice.[36] Certainly that meaning is possible for the semantic range of 1 Corinthians 13, but it is best to understand Paul's sense of the term in light of the immediate historical context of his relationship with the Corinthian church, and in light of their harmful and hurtful congregational practices. So what does *agape* mean in light of these circumstances? For Paul, in his pastoral work, love entails something more like giving a community what it needs. It's not an abstract concept. And what a community needs is concrete and practical expressions of care. This definition fits as well with other places where Paul talks about love. For example, in Rom 12:9, he tells the church, "Let love be genuine." Paul elaborates on what he means: "Love one another with brotherly affection. Outdo one another in showing honor. . . . Contribute to the needs of the saints and seek to show hospitality" (vv. 10,13). Of course, the Corinthians loved to boast in their gifts of prophecies and tongues and all their spiritual powers. The apostle rejoiced that they possessed these phenomena. But if in the end people walked away from the Lord's Supper feeling dispossessed, lowly, and rejected from Christ as consequence, then what was happening was little more than nihilism in

[34] One fascinating study in this connection can be found in D. Leader and D. Corfield, *Why People Get Sick* (New York: Pegasus, 2008).

[35] D. A. Carson, *Exegetical Fallacies* (Grand Rapids: Baker, 1984), 30–32.

[36] "But Divine Gift-love—Love Himself working in a man—is wholly disinterested and desires what is simply best for the beloved. Again, natural Gift-love is always directed to objects which the lover finds in some way intrinsically lovable—objects which Affection or Eros or a shared point of view attracts him, or, failing that, to the grateful and the deserving, or perhaps to those whose helplessness is of a winning and appealing kind. But Divine Gift-love in the man enables him to love what is not naturally lovable; lepers, criminals, enemies, morons, the sulky, the superior and the sneering" (C. S. Lewis, *The Four Loves* [New York: Harcourt, 2005], 128).

religious garb. It was nothing. In this section of the Pauline correspondence, we are being told that ground zero for learning how to be a Christian is at the Lord's Table. If you cannot get it right there, you will not get it right anywhere. "For the kingdom of God does not consist in talk," Paul says, "but in power" (1 Cor 4:20). The doing of it is all that counts.

This imperative to love is not something that comes from natural law. From reason we might learn the tack of self-preservation and the advantages of politics. Jesus addressed such matters in the Sermon on the Mount. It makes eminent sense to say, "Love your tribe," "be good to your kin," "follow the crowd." It takes a God-man to say, "Love your enemies" (Matt 5:44). This was a central assertion made by the Danish philosopher Søren Kierkegaard in his treatise *Works of Love*. He contends that you can read all the poetry that has ever been written about love and all the most beautiful, lyrical exercises. You can read the greatest works of philosophy about the subject, and you can hear the greatest songs ever written about love. You can be inspired by all of these. But here is the one marker in the Hebrew-Christian worldview thinking about love that none of the pagan philosophers shall say, and the world does not say on its own accord: "Thou shalt love."[37] It is a divine command. You have to actually do it, not just talk about it. You must love your neighbor as yourself. It is the least thing we can do, and the least thing God requires: true love for God and love for our brothers and sisters. And it is that—the actual demonstration of these tangible acts of kindness and acceptance—that gives the Christian community the credibility necessary to do evangelism. And Paul seemed to be telling the Corinthians that if you can't love one another while memorializing Christ's death and resurrection, then you will never be able to do it at all.

The Hard Truth of the Baptist Vision

This volume has explored the biblical, hermeneutical, historical and theological understandings of Communion held by the church through the ages. The majority Baptist view, however, a modification of the Zwinglian position, leaves some younger Baptists today feeling cold. Indeed, there is a romanticism to sacramental theology that

[37] S. Kierkegaard, *Works of Love* in *A Kierkegaard Anthology*, ed. Robert Bretali (Princeton: Princeton University Press, 1951), 284–306.

cannot be ignored and must be confronted straight on. Transubstantiation, Consubstantiation, and Real Presence views hold the attraction that when a person approaches the altar that offers Christ's body and blood, the church has something to offer that cannot be found anywhere else: grace. This perspective especially possesses an attraction for those of us in the clergy. As we seek to keep our place in an increasingly secular age, we long to hold on to elements of our faith that cannot be found outside the established church. To the modern man, it seems like an ever-shrinking piece of territory. The appeal of sacramentalism rests in its assertion that the church can offer something to the individual that cannot be found anywhere else: God's grace, blessing, and favor. It is an exclusive to the people of God. As Pope Pius X once put it succinctly, "Holy Communion is the shortest and safest way to heaven."[38] As such, in the sacerdotalist tradition, the sacrament becomes a primary focus of worship. Even those traditions that highly esteem the preaching of the Word of God and reject the Roman Catholic understanding still in some manner appear to claim that one must come to the altar in order to receive a blessing from God that is unique to the ministry of the church.

In the Baptist tradition, however, the memorial view of the Lord's Supper has been the majority position. The Second London Baptist Confession of 1689 deems the Lord's Supper to be "only a memorial," although some Baptists have, of course, dissented from this point of view.[39] But if the Lord's Supper *is* "simply commemorative" as the nineteenth century Baptist stalwart J. L. Reynolds so forthrightly put it, then the emphasis moves away from Communion itself and focuses instead on the gospel that is preached and the holiness of the Christian community assembled in that place.[40] To be certain, the latter depends upon the former. Indeed, the entire concept of a regenerate church membership is established upon the reality of hearing and responding to the faithful exposition of Scripture. When the gathered church celebrates Communion, they are not simply confessing something

[38] Pope Pius X, cited in http://blog.catholicscomehome .org/?p=143. See R. de Sola Chervin, *Quotable Saints* (Oak Lawn, IL: CMJ Marian), 79.

[39] Others interpret the Second London Baptist Confession as presenting a more Reformed view of the Supper in light of its similar terminology to the Westminster Confession, but I think the key word in the Baptist Confession is the word "only."

[40] J. L. Reynolds, *Church Polity or the Kingdom of Christ* in *Polity: Biblical Arguments on How to Conduct Church Life*, ed. M. E. Dever (Washington, D.C.: Center for Church Reform, 2001), 389.

about themselves. They are proclaiming certain truths about Christ. They are taking themselves in hand and preaching to themselves that Christ's substitutionary work on the cross was efficacious, objective, and finished. Further, the church is committing herself to the proposition that the promises in the OT are true, and that the history of redemption has reached its fulfillment in the work of Christ. Indeed, Jesus announced the arrival of the new covenant when He instituted the Supper, and in so doing confirmed that His Father was indeed the God of Promise and the God of Abraham, Isaac, and Jacob (Jeremiah 31; Matt 22:30). Further, in Mark's Gospel Communion forces us to look beyond this world and anticipate the final triumph of Christ and the full consummation of His kingdom (Mark 14:25). If the Supper's role is primarily to stand as an immovable marker of that gospel, then God's power rests in the quality of discipleship and the preaching of the Word.

That is a difficult thing to accept because discipleship is hard. And despite all caricatures to the contrary, hearing the gospel, believing in it and responding to it is also hard. With this said, then, Communion exhibits power only insofar as it points to the new humanity begun by Jesus' life, death, and resurrection. There is no magic in the elements served or in the words spoken. It is just you in the room with God's people at the mercy and behest of the Holy Spirit to transform you. Earlier in this chapter, I recounted how the story of fourteenth-century metaphysics raised an uncomfortable question for the church at the time. Is the Mass an authentic miracle? Is there any way of conceiving of the bread and the wine as being the literal body and blood of Christ without resorting to some fancy discussion of Aristotelian accidentals? Is there some other euphemism to explain where Christ is in the elements? A genuine epistemological and theological crisis emerged from these questions, and the answers to them were not forthcoming until the work of Wycliffe, Hus, and the Protestant Reformers. The Reformation underscored the truth that one's relationship with Christ depended upon grasping the gospel by faith alone. It proclaimed that God's acceptance of us was dependent upon the finished work of Christ, and not the ongoing performance of certain rites by the church. Despite this, more than half a millennium later, believers struggle to understand how the practice of Communion should influence their lives with respect to their daily relationship with God and their ongoing life together with other believers. We are still haunted by what might be lost if there is no miracle taking place in the sacrament. Younger evangelicals hunger for liturgy, and see example after example of evangelical leaders who leave the Reformation tradition to return to Rome with its fully developed sacramental theology.[41] And while a new generation of Baptists may not ever convert to Catholicism, some will wonder if they want to serve in churches that will remain in the low-church tradition for the foreseeable future when higher liturgical traditions possess a powerful attraction for them.[42]

The defining question related to the Lord's Supper comes down to this. Do we have the courage to believe that the only miracle happening during the act of Communion is that the Supper bears witness to the saving grace found at Calvary and reflected in the lives of those around us? We must ask ourselves if we can be content with celebrating the reality of that good news alongside those who have believed on Jesus' name and trusted in Him to save them from their sins. Are we willing to admit that we have nothing else to offer the world except a little gathering of like-minded believers who confess one Lord, one faith, and one Baptism? This may be a hard truth for a new generation of Baptists to embrace, but one I am convinced we must accept without hesitation or fear.

We should not, of course, reckon that only Baptists can confess these convictions with sincerity. After all, Dietrich Bonhoeffer contended for the sufficiency of the church living life together in light of the gospel in his magnificent works in tandem *Sanctorum Communio* and *Act and Being*. And what was the central argument of both those works? Just this: "God is free not from human beings but for them. Christ is the word of God's freedom. God is present, that is, not in eternal non-objectivity but—to put it quite provisionally for now—'haveable,' graspable in the Word within the church."[43] That "graspability" of Christ in His Word and within the fellowship of believers must be taught, preached, exampled, and believed upon wherever the church is to be found. To the unconverted person, the Lord's incarnation, grisly death, and bodily resurrection seem *prima facie* impossible

[41] R. Webber, *The Younger Evangelicals* (Grand Rapids: Baker, 2002), 195–201; F. Beckwith, *Return to Rome: Confessions of an Evangelical Catholic* (Grand Rapids: Brazos, 2009).

[42] S. R. Harmon, *Towards a Baptist Catholicity* (Waynesboro, GA: Paternoster, 2006).

[43] D. Bonhoeffer, *Act and Being*, vol. 2, *Dietrich Bonhoeffer Works*, ed. W. W. Floyd (Minneapolis: Fortress, 1996), 90–91.

to believe. And what does God give us as the means through which we might know, tangibly, that this message is true? Really, perhaps even absurdly, the answer to that question is found in the face of our brother in Christ, the one preaching the gospel to us, and forgiving us of our debts against him, even as God also in Christ forgave him (Matt 6:12–14; Eph 4:32). The Christian that we see now before us is a promissory note that the resurrected Christ is real, sitting at the right hand of God the Father Almighty in heaven. He is ours, and His righteousness is ours. It is not a cheapening or lessening of the meaning of Communion to say that it is a sermon, a reminder to us of what Christ has done. On the contrary, the Lord's Supper sets His church aright by bringing unity from party spirit, joy from sorrow, and forgiveness where sin had once ruptured one's fellowship with another. It takes courage to live out this view in the church because one need not retreat into sacerdotalism when the going gets tough.

In 1707, Isaac Watts published some 200 hymns in a collection entitled *Hymns and Spiritual Songs*. One-third of the volume contained hymns to be sung during the Lord's Supper. One of Watts's most famous contributions in this respect is "How Sweet and Awful Is the Place," a song filled with great pathos and confidence in the gathered church. It expresses the heart of the Nonconformist minister in his time, and the realization of the goodness of the gospel that results from the church gathered to celebrate the Lord's Supper without vestments, pronouncements over the elements, or rite:[44]

How sweet and awful is the Place
With Christ within the Doors,
While everlasting Love displays
The choicest of her Stores!

While all our Hearts and all our Songs
Join to admire the Feast,
Each of us cry with thankful Tongues,
"Lord, why was I a Guest?

"Why was I made to hear thy Voice,
"And enter while there's Room;
"When Thousands make a wretched Choice
"And rather starve than come!"

[44] Isaac Watts, *Hymns and Spiritual Songs* (London: W. Strahan, J. and F. Rivington, J. Buckland, G. Keith, L. Hawes, W. Clarke and B. Collins, T. Longman, T. Field, and E. and C. Dilly, 1773), 296.

'Twas the same Love that Spread the Fest,
That sweetly forc'd us in;
Else we had still refus'd to taste,
And perish'd in our Sin.

Pity the Nations, O our God!
Constrain the Earth to come;
Send thy victorious Word abroad,
And bring the Strangers home.

We long to see thy Churches full,
That all the chosen Race
May with one Voice, and Heart, and Soul,
Sing thy Redeeming Grace.

THE LORD'S SUPPER IN THE CONTEXT OF THE LOCAL CHURCH

Ray Van Neste*

The practice of Communion in Baptist churches has certainly fallen on hard times. Baptist churches affirm the practice and often know what it is not (or even why it is not "too" important), but in many settings there is little passion in the practice. People are often unclear on what the value of Communion is. We know the Bible says to do it, and we want to obey the Bible, but we don't really know what benefit to expect. We understand our duty but frankly don't take much delight in it.

The previous essays in this book have explored the meaning of Communion. If we want to practice this ordinance well in our churches, this meaning has to be taught and taught well so that the people of God can obey with understanding, in order that their hearts can be moved by the truth manifested in Communion. Here I will consider how we practice this ordinance in the local church and suggest some ways to improve our practice. But first, I want to suggest a few reasons I think are central to the problem of our current lack of appreciation of Communion.

Reasons the Lord's Supper Is Undervalued

Lack of Appreciation of Ritual

First, we have bought our culture's line that ritual is bad. We typically do not have the ability to see the value and beauty of traditional practices. Instead we tend to think that spontaneity and change are always best. But we should examine critically this assumption. Why do we assume that having a regular pattern to our worship is necessarily bad and that "changing things up" is necessarily good? Probably part of the reason is that generations before us failed to reflect on what they practiced, and so failed to teach us why we did what we did. As a result we may have seen empty tradition and ritual. However, we

* Ray Van Neste received his Ph.D. from the University of Aberdeen, Scotland. He is associate professor of Biblical Studies and director of the R. C. Ryan Center for Biblical Studies at Union University in Jackson, Tennessee.

must not let a bad example turn us away from the real thing. As we search the Scriptures we find that God is pleased with tradition and ritual properly done. Paul warns us not to let man-made traditions obscure Scripture, but Scripture itself gives us some rituals, particularly baptism and Communion.[1] We must seek to recover the value of community traditions, things done regularly with rich meaning. This is what the two ordinances are supposed to be, visible reminders of the gospel. These are the divinely ordained dramatic and illustrative portrayals of the gospel.

Lack of Appreciation of Symbolism

This leads to a second and related point. Our culture has largely lost its ability to appreciate symbolism, and this is no less true in the church than in the wider culture. In short we have lost our poetry and as a result have little appreciation for the symbolic. As people are realizing this, many try all sorts of ways to integrate the use of the symbolic and dramatic into our worship, but often miss what Christ Himself has instituted for us in the two symbolic practices which are dramatic portrayals of the gospel.

Our general failure to appreciate symbols is seen in our language when Communion is described as a "mere" symbol. "Mere"?! Why "mere"? This is not a "mere" symbol, but a Christ-ordained, holy, precious symbol which portrays for us the gospel. We ought never speak like the pastor who "regularly admonished his congregation upon observing the Supper: 'Now, remember that this doesn't mean anything. These are just symbols.'"[2] If we are going to properly appreciate Communion—indeed if we are going to properly appreciate Scripture—we must reclaim a sympathy for and appreciation of symbolism.

J. B. Phillips commented on this 50 years ago when writing his little book on how "for Christians who are prepared to use their minds and imaginations, it [Communion] can deepen and enrich their spiritual lives."[3] One reason so many people fail to see the value of

[1] Paul warns against the encroachment of human traditions in Col 2:8, as does Jesus in Matt 15:1–9. However, Paul calls for obedience to God-given, apostolic tradition (1 Cor 11:2; 2 Thess 2:15) and calls for discipline against those who disregard apostolic tradition (2 Thess 3:6).

[2] C. W. Freeman, "'To Feed Upon by Faith': Nourishment from the Lord's Table," in *Baptist Sacramentalism*, ed. A. R. Cross and P. E. Thompson (Milton Keynes: Paternoster, 2003), 206.

[3] J. B. Phillips, *Appointment with God: Some Thoughts on Holy Communion* (New York: Macmillan, 1956), vii.

Communion is that they have not been trained in the biblical value of and use of the imagination. We have abandoned this important aspect of the mind and are the poorer for it.

Focus on Negative

For too long Baptists have focused more on what the Supper does not mean than what it does. In opposing those who make too much of the Supper we have failed to esteem it enough. Millard Erickson once winsomely and wisely quipped,

> Out of a zeal to avoid the conception that Jesus is present in some sort of magical way, certain Baptists among others have sometimes gone to such extremes as to give the impression that the one place where Jesus most assuredly is not to be found is the Lord's Supper. This is what one Baptist leader termed 'the doctrine of the real absence' of Jesus Christ.[4]

This is one reason why this book is needed. We need to engage afresh this ordinance which our good, wise, and caring Savior gave us for our benefit. We need to embrace the value of this ritual without fear of esteeming it too much.

Lack of Substantive Teaching

We have had a serious downgrade in substantive biblical teaching in the church. The ordinances, precisely because they are symbols, were never intended to exist apart from the Word—Word and Sacraments.[5] In a day when biblical teaching is at a low ebb in the church, there should be no surprise that the ordinances are not prized. Without strong, intentional biblical teaching, confusion sets in, and people are unable to appreciate what they do not understand.

Entertainment Culture

If our entertainment culture shapes our approach to corporate worship (e.g., the need to "keep things moving"), then Communion (and sometimes baptism as well) will be viewed as something which takes up too much time and gets in the way of our show. Communion does

[4] M. Erickson, *Christian Theology* (Grand Rapids: Baker, 1985), 1123.

[5] I use the term "sacrament" here in a Protestant sense (as did B. H. Carroll, A. H. Strong, etc.) without intending Catholic overtones.

not make for good television. Too often events commanded by Christ are viewed merely as impediments to things desired by us.

Joyless Observance

Too often Communion has been treated as a time to beat ourselves up again for our sins, almost a Protestant version of medieval self-flagellation. I have wondered for some time, "Why do so many observances of Communion seem so morose?" Jesus said to do this "in *remembrance* of Me" not "in *remorse* of Me." Joy is a key element in the Lord's Supper. The point is not to focus on our sin or even on Christ's suffering. Both of these are in view, but not as the center. Rather they are steps along the way to the true center—the grace of God in redeeming us through the death of Christ.

I discovered, though, that this more morose view has significant roots in our Baptist history. It is not merely a modern ill. For example, in 1878 J. M. Pendleton in his *Baptist Church Manual* states, "If ever the *tragedy* of Calvary should engross the thoughts of the Christian to the exclusion of every other topic, it is when he sits at the table of the Lord."[6] He draws this conclusion from Paul's words in 1 Cor 11:26—"For as often as you eat this bread and drink the cup, you proclaim the Lord's death until he comes."[7] I think Pendleton has improperly applied this verse, and the results of such application are widely seen. Very often people do, in fact, approach the Lord's Table in this way, focusing exclusively on the *tragedy* of Christ's death. The sense is that the purpose of this exercise is for us to focus on our sin, to remember afresh the depth of our wickedness and how much this cost God. It is as if God is that mother who constantly reminds the family how much she has suffered for everyone and wants to make sure you never forget it! But this most certainly is *not* the point Paul is making. Pendleton (and others after him) unnecessarily infers the word "tragedy" from the death of Christ. Yes, the Table proclaims Christ's death, but not simply—or even primarily—the *tragedy* of His death. The point is that this is "proclamation." Elsewhere in the NT what is being proclaimed when Christ's death is in view? It is not tragedy but hope! It is the fact that the death of Christ has made possible the forgiveness

[6] J. M. Pendleton, *Baptist Church Manual* (Nashville: Broadman, 1966), 89. See also the same wording in J. M Pendleton, *Christian Doctrines: A Compendium of Theology* (Philadelphia: American Baptist Publication Society, 1878), 358.

[7] Unless otherwise indicated, all Scripture quotations are from the ESV.

of sin, reconciliation with God, transference from being enemies of God to being children of God! What is proclaimed is good news, the gospel. We do wrong when our participation in Communion is a self-flagellating focus on tragedy.[8] We do not gather merely to tell God we're sorry He had to go through this. We are reminded of our sin and how far God in His love went to reach us, but the focus is on celebrating and giving thanks for God's amazing grace. The taking of the elements is the tangible proclamation of the forgiveness of sins. It is one of God's prescribed means of reminding His people that He has forgiven their sins. This is good news which should bring great joy to all God's people.[9]

This celebratory element has too often been eclipsed in Baptist history, but there have been exceptions. For example, M. E. Dodd speaks of Communion as "that glad, joyous occasion when our memories are refreshed and when our gratitude is enlarged as we meditate upon the things that Christ did for us as represented in this supper."[10]

Furthermore, Michael Haykin has referenced the diary of a young Baptist man in London in 1771 who described his church's Communion service where the congregants "came around the table of our dear dying Lord to feast on the sacrifice of his offered body, show his death afresh, to claim and recognize our interest therein, to feast on the sacrifice of his offered body *as happy members of the same family of faith and love*."[11] We need to reclaim this biblical focus on the redemptive work of the gospel in order to reinvigorate our practice of Communion.[12]

As J. I. Packer has stated,

[8] This is actually just one more way we turn the gospel into law which, as Luther said is "the supreme art of the devil" (*Table Talk*, *LW* 54.106).

[9] The nineteenth-century pastor Melancthon W. Jacobus, in a different context, expressed this well, stating, "The Gospel is good news—glad tidings. To whomsoever it is glad tidings and good news, to him it is the gospel. It has come to make troubled consciences peaceful, and wounded hearts whole, and anxious distressed spirits glad. Sinner! does this doctrine of Christ crucified and risen to give repentance and forgiveness, make you glad? Then it is yours" (*Notes, Critical and Explanatory, on The Acts of the Apostles* [1859; repr., Birmingham, AL: Solid Ground, 2006], 82).

[10] M. E. Dodd, *Baptist Principles and Practices* (Alexandria, LA: Chronicle, 1916), 75.

[11] Cited in M. A. G. Haykin, "'His soul-refreshing presence': The Lord's Supper in Calvinistic Baptist Thought and Experience in the 'Long' Eighteenth Century," in Cross and Thompson, *Baptist Sacramentalism*, 185.

[12] Spurgeon made a similar point as noted by T. Grass and I. Randall, "C. H. Spurgeon on the Sacraments," 55–75, in Cross and Thompson, *Baptist Sacramentalism*. They state, "Spurgeon did not want the solemnity of the occasion of communion to be oppressive. . . . Ultimately, as Spurgeon saw it, a note of joy needed to be struck at the Lord's Supper" (73).

> What we need more than anything else at the Lord's Table is a fresh grasp of the glorious truth that we sinners are offered mercy through faith in the Christ who forgives and restores, out of which faith comes all the praise that we offer and all the service that we render. . . . For this everlasting gospel of salvation for sinners is what in Scripture the Lord's Supper is all about. . . . At the Holy Table, above all, let there be praise.[13]

Having discussed some of the common hindrances to our practice of the Lord's Supper, we must now turn our attention to several pertinent questions that arise concerning how we actually go about the practice in the local church setting.

Practicing the Lord's Supper

Church Ordinance

Many of the following questions or issues will be affected by the point that the Lord's Supper is a *church* ordinance, so this point needs to be discussed first. To describe the Lord's Supper as a church ordinance is to assert that this rite was given to the church to practice and not simply to individual Christians. This is the understanding of the great majority of Christians across the history of the church. The Supper assumes a gathered community each time it is mentioned in the NT (e.g., Acts 20:7; 1 Cor 11:17–34). In Acts 20 Paul and his companions were in Troas for a full week, but the Lord's Supper is celebrated on the first day of the week when they were gathered together (v. 7). Furthermore, Paul's admonitions in 1 Corinthians 11 discuss the Lord's Supper as something which occurs "when you come together as a church" and "when you come together" (vv. 18,20). From these observations it seems that the NT assumes the Lord's Supper is a church event.

Who Presides and Serves?

The NT never directly addresses the issue of who presides at Communion or who serves the elements. As a significant part of the church's worship, it should be led by someone with recognized authority in the congregation. This would seem typically to be pastors, though others could be authorized to lead.

[13] J. I. Packer, "The Gospel and the Lord's Supper," in *Serving the People of God: The Collected Shorter Writings of J. I. Packer* (Carlisle, UK: Paternoster, 1998), 2:49, 51.

In many Baptist churches the deacons serve the elements. This is often connected to the service of the deacons in distributing food in Acts 6. This is certainly fine practice, though we ought to be clear that the service in Acts 6 (keeping widows from starving) is significantly different from serving Communion. If the practice of deacons serving in this way helps to illustrate their role as servants, then this can be very fitting. However, we ought to be clear that others could also serve Communion. In my church, various men serve Communion.

This also raises the issue of whether or not women can serve Communion. Since this service does not include teaching or exercising authority over men (1 Tim 2:12), there is no biblical prohibition against women serving. This, in many ways, will depend on various elements of the context in specific churches. In my church, for example, we have no policy against women serving Communion. We have simply decided to enlist men to do this work as part of their overall leadership and service.

Frequency?

As is commonly noted, there is no specific command given on how frequently we ought to celebrate Communion. Baptist churches, then, have typically said the issue is up to the churches with practice varying widely, quarterly or monthly being more common. In some places Communion has been even less frequent. I have known of churches where, since Communion did not have a regularly scheduled time, a year or more went by without it being celebrated.

I am convinced that our churches will benefit from celebrating Communion more, rather than less, often. In fact, I think there is a clear pattern of weekly observance in the NT.

Already in Acts 2:42, we see Communion listed as a central piece of Christian worship. The four activities listed here are not four separate things but the four elements which characterized a Christian gathering.[14] One of the key things the early church "devoted" itself to was the "breaking of bread," i.e., the Lord's Supper.[15] The wording suggests that each of these activities occurred when they gathered.

[14] I. H. Marshall, *Acts*, TNTC (Grand Rapids: Eerdmans, 1980), 83.

[15] It is widely agreed that "the breaking of bread" is a technical term in Luke-Acts for the Lord's Supper. So F. F. Bruce states, "The 'breaking of bread' here denotes something more than ordinary partaking of food together: the regular observance of the Lord's Supper is no doubt indi-

Perhaps the most striking reference to the frequency of the Lord's Supper occurs in Acts 20:7.

> On the first day of the week, when we were gathered together to break bread, Paul talked with them, intending to depart on the next day, and he prolonged his speech until midnight.

Paul, on his way to Jerusalem has stopped at Troas. Here "on the first day of the week" he meets with the local church, and Luke directly states that the purpose of their gathering was "to break bread," i.e., to celebrate the Lord's Supper![16] Marshall writes,

> The breaking of bread is the term used especially in Acts for the celebration of the Lord's Supper (2:42; cf. 1 Cor. 10:16), and this passage is of particular interest in providing the first allusion to the Christian custom of meeting *on the first day of the week* for the purpose.[17]

This passage need not mean the Lord's Supper was the only purpose of their gathering, but it certainly is one prominent purpose and the one emphasized here. The centrality of Communion to the weekly gathering is stated casually without explanation or defense, suggesting this practice was common among those Luke expected to read his account. These early Christians met *weekly* to celebrate the Lord's Supper.

Of course, the longest discussion of the practice of the Lord's Supper is in 1 Corinthians. Many issues can be raised here, but the fact that abuse of the Lord's Supper was such a problem in Corinth strongly suggests the Supper was held frequently. Could it have been such a problem if it only occurred quarterly? Is this the sense which arises from the passage? According to 11:20, "When you come together, it is not the Lord's Supper that you eat." It is widely agreed that the terminology "come together" here is used as a technical term for gathering as the church.[18] This wording suggests that when they gathered they ate a meal which they intended to be the Lord's Supper.[19] Though they

cated" (*The Book of the Acts*, revised, [Grand Rapids: Eerdmans, 1988], 79). See also Marshall, *Acts*, 83; J. B. Polhill, *Acts*, NAC (Nashville: Broadman and Holman, 1992), 119.

[16] The construction is an infinitive denoting purpose. Cf. W. D. Mounce, *Basics of Biblical Greek*, 2nd ed. (Grand Rapids: Zondervan, 2003), 306; H. E. Dana and J. R. Mantey, *A Manual Grammar of the Greek New Testament* (New York: Macmillan, 1927), 214.

[17] Marshall, *Acts*, 325.

[18] Cf. G. D. Fee, *The First Epistle to the Corinthians*, NICNT (Grand Rapids: Eerdmans, 1987), 535–36; D. Garland, *1 Corinthians*, BECNT (Grand Rapids: Baker, 2003), 539.

[19] So also I. H. Marshall, "The Biblical Basis of Communion," *Interchange* 40 (n.d.): 54: "It

were abusing the Supper, their practice (which was not considered odd by Paul) was to celebrate each time they gathered. Even the wording in 11:25, "As often as you drink it," which is often used to suggest frequency is unimportant, in context actually suggests a frequent celebration of the Lord's Supper. Commenting on this verse, Gordon Fee notes, "This addition in particular implies a frequently repeated action, suggesting that from the beginning the *Last* Supper was for Christians not an annual Christian Passover, but a regularly repeated meal in 'honor of the Lord,' hence the *Lord's* Supper."[20]

From these passages a clear pattern emerges of a weekly celebration of Communion in the NT.[21] I am not here arguing that weekly celebration is a direct biblical command so that if we fail to do this we sin. I am arguing that this is the pattern in the NT and therefore would be the best practice. In our man-centered age where so many services are shamefully devoid of any meaningful reference to the cross, could we not benefit from a move to a regular use of the Christ-ordained means for reminding us of the cross? In an increasingly "visual" age, might we not benefit from regular use of the visible, tangible portrayal given to us by Christ? In a day when we are so captivated by the allures of this age and seemingly interested merely in *Our Best Life Now*, do we not need regularly the Christ-ordained means of reminding us of the Lord's return and the wedding feast of the Lamb? Might not "the Bride" (cf. Rev 21:9; 22:17) be more pure if regularly reminded of the coming wedding?[22]

Questions will quickly arise on how to do this. Some doubt that this can be done well. Many of the Baptist churches in Scotland do

would seem that when the members assembled 'as a church' it was specifically to eat the Lord's Supper."

[20] Fee, *The First Epistle to the Corinthians*, 555.

[21] Though Hammett does not argue for weekly Communion, he does conclude with this statement: "For most of Christian history, the Eucharist or Lord's Supper has been the central act of Christian worship" (J. S. Hammett, *Biblical Foundations for Baptist Churches* [Grand Rapids: Kregel, 2005], 294). If it is "the central act" of our worship, should we not do it each Lord's Day?

[22] Cf. John Brown, *An Apology for the More Frequent Administration of the Lord's Supper: With Answers to the Objections Urged Against It* (Edinburgh: Printed by J. Ritchie for Ogle & Aikman, 1804), 16: "If the conscientious improvement of this ordinance tend so remarkably to the advantage of believers, ought they not frequently to partake of it? Ought they not, if possible, to go to the uttermost extent of frequency that Christ allows? It will not be denied, that Christ allows conscientious communicating every Sabbath." Brown also states, "As often as the church of Christ has been in a flourishing state, greater frequency has been practiced or pushed. . . . On the other hand, a declension toward the unfrequent [sic] celebration of this ordinance, has been generally the close attendant of apostasy and backsliding" (12).

this, and the practice flourishes. Also, my church has practiced weekly Communion for about six years, and the consistent testimony of members is that their appreciation of Communion has only increased. We are often told by people who move away that they particularly miss weekly Communion.

A typical argument against this idea is, "If we do this so often it will become less meaningful." At first this has the appearance of wisdom; but with just a little pondering the illusion fades. Do we apply this reasoning to other means of grace? Are we worried about praying too frequently? Reading the Bible too much? Shall we be safe and make biblical preaching less frequent?[23] Well, perhaps some are using this reasoning! These practices become rote not because of frequency but because of laziness of mind and heart on our part and the lack of robust biblical proclamation alongside the ordinance.

Some also say we can appreciate Communion more when we set aside only certain Sundays for it and on those days focus directly on Communion. However, what we need is not more elaborate observance or contrived production, but regular observance of this simple rite tied into the regular preaching of the Word. We do not need to "build it up" with any extras. We need to preach the gospel and then display and participate in the gospel in Communion. I am in agreement with Spurgeon who stated,

> So with the Lord's Supper. My witness is, and I think I speak the mind of many of God's people now present, that coming as some of us do, weekly, to the Lord's table, we do not find the breaking of bread to have lost its significance—it is always fresh to us. I have often remarked on Lord's-day evening, whatever the subject may have been, whether Sinai has thundered over our heads, or the plaintive notes of Calvary have pierced our hearts, it always seems equally appropriate to come to the breaking of bread. Shame on the Christian church that she should put it off to once a month, and mar the first day of the week by depriving it of its glory in the meeting together for fellowship and breaking of bread, and showing forth of the death of Christ till he come. They who once know the sweetness of each Lord's-day celebrating his Supper, will not be content, I am sure, to put it off to less frequent

[23] I was pleased to discover that this very point was made over 200 years ago by John Brown of Haddington who wrote, "If the abuse of an ordinance is any reason against the frequent use of it, why preach we any more than one Sabbath in the year, since to many our preaching is the savour of death unto death, and gives men an occasion to trample under foot the blood of the Son of God? . . . Ought Christ's children to be starved, because the dogs will snatch at their food . . . ?" (*Apology*, 29–30).

> seasons. Beloved, when the Holy Ghost is with us, ordinances are wells to the Christian, wells of rich comfort and of near communion.[24]

The Elements—Real Wine? One Loaf?

Though this topic has at times been contentious, we must be careful to stress what the Scriptures themselves stress. It is not uncommon to hear a preacher argue that we need pure, unfermented grape juice because Jesus' blood is pure. However, M. E. Dodd, father of the Southern Baptist Cooperative Program, argued for real wine, stating, "I have always been of the opinion that it ought not to be grape juice but ought to be pure, fermented wine."[25] My point is that an argument based on purity is unhelpful since it can be turned either way. The Scriptures make no point concerning the purity of the liquid used. In fact, the biblical emphasis does not fall on fermentation or the lack thereof. Rather this element is typically referred to simply as "the cup." That is the term used consistently by Paul in 1 Corinthians. It is also the term used by Jesus in the Gospels (cf. Matt 26:26–29; Mark 14:22–25; Luke 22:14–20) as He instituted this rite. Jesus then referred back to the cup as the "fruit of the vine." I am not saying that wine was not used. Surely it was, since some of the Corinthians got drunk (1 Cor 10:21). Rather, my point is that the biblical symbolism is not so much caught up in the term "wine" or fermentation but the OT concept of the "cup of God's wrath."[26] Christ drank the cup of God's wrath, leaving us only the "cup of blessing" (1 Cor 10:16).[27] Therefore, I do not think fermentation or the lack thereof is of particular importance.

As a point of practice, "wine" today typically means fermented grape juice. Therefore, if you are not using wine it is best not to refer

[24] "Songs of Deliverance," Sermon no. 763, July 28, 1867. Accessed 21 December 2009. Online: http://www.spurgeon.org/sermons/0763.htm. Spurgeon was preaching from Judg 5:11—another reminder that any passage properly preached points to the gospel, and therefore to the Supper, God's ordained means for portraying the gospel.

[25] Dodd, *Baptist Principles and Practices*, 79.

[26] See Ps 75:8; Isa 51:17,22; Jer 25:15–17,28; 49:12; 51:7; Hab 2:16; Zech 2:12. This same imagery is picked up in Revelation as well. See Rev 14:10; 16:19; 18:6.

[27] "The 'cup of blessing' was the technical term for the final blessing offered at the end of the meal. This was the cup that our Lord blessed at the Last Supper (cf. 11:25, 'after supper') and interpreted as 'the new covenant in my blood.' Hence the early church took over the language of this blessing to refer to the cup of the Lord's Table" (Fee, *The First Epistle to the Corinthians*, 467–68).

to it as wine. It just seems to me that this is confusing or at least sounds odd to others. I have made it my practice to refer to this element as "the cup," which fits biblical terminology and prevents misunderstanding.

In regards to the bread, Scripture makes one main symbolic point—the single loaf. In 1 Corinthians 10 Paul draws a point about unity from the "one loaf" of Communion: "Because there is one bread, we who are many are one body, for we all partake of the one bread" (10:17). This significant point often finds no representation in our practice. Surely our practice is deficient if the symbolism intended by Scripture is obscured or simply absent. W. A. Criswell stated,

> The Lord's Supper served as a visible demonstration of the fellowship of the body of Christ as all members partook of one loaf and one cup. The use of "many crumbs and many cups" is more sanitary, but the significant symbolism pictured by the one loaf and one cup is lost in our modern practice.[28]

This is a fair point (winsomely put), though Scripture does not make the point about unity from a common cup. It only mentions the one loaf.

The practical problems of the "one loaf" include hygiene and quantity; serving even a moderately sized congregation with one loaf would be difficult. The symbolism can be preserved, however, if one portion of the bread is broken before the people and then the plates which are passed contain pieces of the same sort of bread. The goal is to maintain the symbolism which Scripture draws from the elements.

Is the Location Important?

Should the Lord's Supper be celebrated in church only, or may it also be practiced in small groups, or at parachurch gatherings? Baptists, like the majority of Christendom, have most often argued that the Lord's Supper should be celebrated in the worship of a specific church and not in other independent settings. This seems to me to be the best practice. I see no compelling reason, on any regular basis, of having Communion in settings outside of the local church. I know of settings where Communion is observed in seminary chapels or theological meetings, but this strikes me as unhelpful and unnecessary.[29] Communion is, as stated earlier, a church ordinance.

[28] W. A. Criswell, *The Doctrine of the Church* (Nashville, TN: Convention, 1980), 101.
[29] So also Criswell, *Doctrine of the Church*, 105.

Communion really only makes sense in the setting of believers who know one another and are covenanted together in submission to the Word of God seeking conformity to Christ. Outside of such a setting it is difficult to imagine what "discerning the body" (1 Cor 11:29) would mean. The Corinthian church is rebuked for failing to take note of and care for one another. Furthermore, exclusion from the Table is a significant aspect of discipline. Removing Communion from the local church then makes it difficult to uphold the discipline of the church.

Only When the Church Is Gathered?

Should we serve it privately to individuals in nursing homes or shut-ins? Should we serve it to nursery workers (or others unable to be in corporate worship due to service in the church) after the service? This question is related to the previous one. In the Scriptures, Communion is part of the gathered worship. It is not merely a private act. It is a corporate confession of faith and gospel proclamation. The inference of 1 Cor 10:17 on the unity of the church ("the body") and the entire flow of 1 Corinthians 11 only really make sense in a corporate gathering. Thus Communion is not fitting in individual situations.[30]

First, then, I do not think it is appropriate to serve Communion to a couple in their wedding ceremony as everyone else simply watches. This is done in some traditions and has been picked up more recently by some Baptists. Communion is to be celebrated by a congregation, not by a few for others to watch.

Secondly, this would mean it is not appropriate to serve Communion to individual shut-ins at home or in nursing homes. I understand that it may seem harsh, for example, to say to a shut-in lady, "No, I will not come and administer this ordinance," particularly if she has requested it. But I think it is simply not possible any more than it is possible for her to "just get up and come to church." The perceived harshness arises from the assumption that I could bring Communion to her if I just would. However, my point is that I cannot bring Communion to her even if I tried. It cannot be re-created apart

[30] J. L. Dagg aptly states, "It [communion] could not serve as a token of fellowship between the disciples of Christ, if it were performed in solitude" (*Manual of Church Order* [Harrisonburg, VA: Gano, 1990], 212).

from the gathered body. So, as we lament the fact that she cannot attend church, part of that lament is our pity that she thus cannot come to the Lord's Table with us. This can and should lead us to pity and compassion, but we cannot alter the reality.[31]

In one church I pastored, nursery workers requested that on Communion Sundays, I meet with them (about 10 people) and serve them Communion after the service. I appreciated their desire to partake of the Lord's Supper, but this practice always seemed artificial to me. The celebration was cut off from the corporate worship service. I do not think we sinned in this, but I would not now repeat the practice because I don't think it is best. In fact, this situation can be remedied by having Communion more frequently (as argued above) so that even when people miss one Sunday due to service, they will be able to partake soon.

How to Serve?

Because this corporate and congregational element is so important, it must be evidenced in the way in which we practice Communion. It seems one practice that is becoming more popular is that of having families celebrate Communion as family units with the father of each family serving. I affirm wholeheartedly the importance of the family and the role of the father. I like the Puritan idea of each father serving as the pastor of his family. However, when we gather as the church, we ought to gather as one and not simply a collection of families. The corporate, unified idea stressed by Paul in 1 Corinthians 10 and 11 will be best exemplified as the whole congregation partakes together.

For the same reason I do not favor the practice of presenting the elements and then allowing individuals to come forward as they are ready and take the elements on their own. Particularly in our individualistic

[31] Criswell states that because the local church is responsible for the administration of the Lord's Supper, "the pastor should not take the Lord's Supper to individuals and administer it personally" (Criswell, *Doctrine of the Church*, 105). So also G. W. Truett, "The Supper of Our Lord," in *Some Vital Questions / The Inspiration of Ideals*, vol. 3 of *George W. Truett Library* (Nashville, TN: Broadman, 1980), 76. That this is not simply a Baptist idea is illustrated by the comments of John Angell James, English Non-conformist Congregational minister of the nineteenth century in his book, *The Church Members' Guide* (1822; repr., Vestavia Hills, AL: Solid Ground, 2003), 175–79. In taking up some specific questions of concern, James raises the topic, "On the Propriety of occasionally administering the Lord's Supper in private Houses, for the Sake of sick Persons who are incapable of attending the Solemnities of Public Worship." He answers firmly in the negative with arguments similar to those given here, including the point that Communion is a church ordinance.

age, this does not seem to be healthy. We are to take this as a church together. Anything which allows us to consider ourselves alone, apart from the rest of the body, seems to fly in the face of the unity called for in 1 Corinthians 11. We do not have the luxury of preparing ourselves on our own schedule. We need to walk in step with our brothers and sisters, which, though more difficult and complex, is part of the point of Communion.

Therefore, I favor having the congregation wait until everyone is served each element and then taking it together.[32] Together, we once more affirm our need, Christ's provision, and our faith in Him. I also favor doing this with our eyes open in awareness of one another. We are not to imagine ourselves "alone with the Lord" shutting everyone else out. One of the key points of the Supper is to be mindful of one another.[33]

Who Can Partake?

It is clear in the NT that only believers are to partake of the Lord's Supper, and this has been the understanding of the church through the centuries. In 1 Cor 10:16–18 Paul states that in taking Communion we "participate" in the body and blood of Christ. Whatever this phrase might mean, it certainly involves professing that we share in the benefits of Christ's death. This is Paul's point later in 10:21 when he states that one cannot partake of "the table of the Lord and the table of demons." You cannot be connected to Christ and the Devil simultaneously. Only the Lord's people come to fellowship with the Lord at the Lord's Table.[34]

[32] J. T. Wayland connected the partaking together with the church being a democracy ("Lord's Supper, Administration of," in *Encyclopedia of Southern Baptists*, ed. N. Cox [Nashville: Broadman, 1982], 2:794). The Bible never makes this point, however. The point, rather, is our corporate connection with one another to Christ.

[33] J. I. Packer mentions a problem in some Anglican settings which is also too often found in Baptist circles: "A strange perverse idea has got into Anglican hearts that the Lord's Supper is a flight of the alone to the Alone; it is my communion I come to make, not our communion in which I come to share. You can't imagine a more radical denial of the Gospel than that" ("The Gospel and the Lord's Supper," 50).

[34] Some writers have been unnecessarily concerned to argue that Judas, an unbeliever, left the upper room before the Last Supper was taken. Even if Judas was present at that time, it would not matter. The point is that only "professing" believers can come to the Table. We know that some partake of Communion while professing to be believers only later to show that they never truly were believers. Surely this would have been the case of the immoral man of 1 Corinthians 5. He had been a part of the church in Corinth but was now to be put out because he was show-

This also means that people who have been excommunicated (i.e., removed from membership by church discipline) cannot partake of Communion. The act of excommunication declares that a person is by all appearances an unbeliever, so he must be barred from the Table. This is a significant part of the person's removal from the community (cf. 1 Cor 5:9–13).

From time to time there have been those who argue that unbelievers *should* be allowed to partake as a gospel witness. While it is true that the Lord's Supper proclaims the gospel, the receiving of the elements suggests believing and appropriating this gospel and its benefits. This is simply untrue for an unbeliever. Part of faithful proclamation is telling people the truth about their alienation from God. Thus, the Table is evangelistic to unbelievers (including our unconverted children) as they see they do not yet have access to the benefits of the gospel.

It may be useful to comment here a bit more on children. It is not uncommon today for people to be concerned not to make others, particularly children, feel "left out." I have talked with parents in Baptist churches who did not want their children to feel like "they were not part of the church." However, this is precisely what we are saying, and what I want my children to hear. Part of the instructive element for children is for them to see that while they participate in this community of people, they are not automatically part of the church. As they are not allowed to partake of the elements each time, the point is made that they are outside of Christ and need to be reconciled to Him.

Pastorally, then, one way we make the most of the evangelistic element of Communion is by reminding unbelievers that the incredible benefits illustrated in Communion are not currently theirs. Each time I lead in Communion I make this point and call unbelievers to repent and believe.[35] The ordinance they need, then, is baptism.

Baptism a Requirement?

This leads to the question of whether or not one has to be baptized before partaking of Communion. This issue is not directly addressed in Scripture, though there are principles to apply. In fact, the various

ing by his life that he did not know Christ. Surely he had in the past taken Communion with the church.

[35] J. L. Dagg makes a similar point in *Manual of Church Order*, 213.

traditions of Christianity have almost universally affirmed that baptism should precede Communion.

If we understand baptism correctly—that it is *the* public profession of faith—then it makes sense for baptism to precede participating in Communion.[36] Someone ought not come to the Table unless he is recognized as a believer. We make this difficult in situations where we intentionally delay baptism, creating the situation where you have believers who have given a credible profession of faith before the church but have not been baptized. We can rectify this problem by returning to the NT pattern of baptizing people as soon as possible after their conversion.[37]

The debate, however, does not concern people who refuse baptism, but centers on those who consider themselves baptized although they were not immersed as believers (i.e., paedobaptists).[38] Can people who have not been properly baptized (i.e., immersed upon a profession of faith) be invited to partake of Communion? This is a longstanding controversy. Richard Furman, first president of the Triennial Convention,[39] could write in an 1806 circular letter, "On this subject, however, there is a variety of sentiment among enlightened and pious men." He describes this as a "delicate question" but argues that paedobaptists are not qualified to participate in Communion.[40] This position, which has been the majority opinion in Southern Baptist history, is typically labeled "close Communion." The position that all true believers, even those with "improper" baptisms, are qualified to partake in Communion is typically labeled "open Communion."[41]

The "close" position centers on the assertion that baptism must precede Communion. Since Baptists do not recognize the sprinkling of infants as true baptism, they believe paedobaptists have not truly

[36] For a good explanation of this understanding of baptism see R. H. Stein, "Baptism and Becoming a Christian in the New Testament," *SBJT* (Spring 1998): 6–17. See also R. Van Neste, "Reinvigorating Baptist Practice of the Ordinances," *Theology for Ministry* 1 (2006): 78–91.

[37] See Stein, "Baptism," esp. 16–17.

[38] Some may object that paedobaptists do, in fact, refuse baptism. That claim is dealt with later in this section.

[39] The Triennial Convention was the first concerted effort of Baptists in America on a national scale. Furman was also the first president of the first Baptist state convention in America, the South Carolina Baptist Convention.

[40] "Circular Letter No. XIII: On the Communion of Saints—1806," in *Life and Works of Dr. Richard Furman, D.D.*, ed. G. W. Foster Jr. (Harrisonburg, VA: Sprinkle, 2004), 565–66.

[41] While the terms vary a little, "closed Communion" is also often used to refer to the position that one ought to take Communion only at the church where he is a member.

been baptized and are thus not qualified to partake of Communion. The historical literature is full of acknowledgments that this sounds harsh to many but that we must obey Scripture even if it seems harsh.

While I respect the proponents of close Communion, I am thoroughly unconvinced by their arguments. Therefore, here I will examine the arguments for excluding some Christians from the Table and argue instead for inclusion of all true Christians at the Lord's Table.

The primary issue is whether or not Scripture requires baptism as a prerequisite for Communion. Many Baptist confessions of faith assert that baptism is such a prerequisite, but there is no direct scriptural statement of this point. If Scripture clearly required baptism before partaking Communion, I would accept the close position. However, that is not the case. Appeal is made to patterns and inferences which I do not think are valid.

One very common argument (appearing in almost every articulation of the close position I have seen) is appeal to the order of the commands in the Great Commission where Jesus says (Matt 28:19–20a),

> Go therefore and make disciples of all nations, baptizing them in the name of the Father and of the Son and of the Holy Spirit, teaching them to observe all that I have commanded you.

The argument runs like this. The order of the commands is (1) make disciples, (2) baptize them, (3) teach them to obey Christ. Taking Communion is part of what Christ taught, thus it follows baptism. However, surely this strains the text. There is no emphasis in the text on temporal order. One command ("make disciples") is explained by two participles ("baptizing" and "teaching").[42] The word order does not necessarily say anything about temporal order in Greek. Jesus is not here commanding His followers to make sure converts are baptized before they obey any of His teachings. Are we to say that converts must be baptized before they are qualified to love one another or to pray? These are part of what Christ commanded us, just like Communion. If this text makes baptism a prerequisite for Communion, why does it not also make baptism a prerequisite for these other commands? Surely we do not say, "If you are not yet immersed you cannot learn to obey Christ in any other way." In fact, if one presses it,

[42] Both participles are also present tense. There would be no grammatical basis for arguing that one action is required before the other.

baptism itself is part of what Christ commands, so technically we will have to do command three before we can do command two—i.e., we have to teach people the need to be baptized before we baptize them.

Some will protest that it is surely clear that baptism comes first as the initiatory rite of Christianity. That is true, and that is all that is being asserted in the Great Commission. Disciples are to be baptized. There is a natural order here of being baptized as soon as one is converted, but this text cannot be turned into a law prohibiting from the Table those who seek baptism but misinterpret the practice of baptism. Of course, if someone refused baptism outright, this would call into question their allegiance to Christ. However, our paedobaptist brothers and sisters are not refusing baptism but simply hold to a faulty understanding of baptism.

Appeal is also often made to Acts 2:41–42 where new converts are baptized and then the church devotes itself to "the apostles' teaching and the fellowship, to the breaking of bread and the prayers." Here again people are baptized and then participate in Communion ("breaking bread"). This pattern is neither surprising nor disturbing to an open Communion advocate. The passage does not speak to the issue where some believers understand baptism differently. We observe a pattern which is typically observed. No command though is given about appropriate practice of baptism before participation in Communion.

Baptist writers often note that there is no command about the frequency of celebrating the Lord's Supper, and therefore the frequency is a matter of choice. Yet, when it comes to baptism as a prerequisite for Communion, the absence of a command is rarely noted. There is more and stronger evidence of a pattern of weekly Communion in the NT than of baptism being required before Communion. Why, in practice, have we often overlooked one pattern and treated the other pattern as law? This is inconsistent. Earlier in this chapter I argued that there is a clear pattern of weekly observance in the NT. I thus argued that weekly Communion would be the best practice, but I sought to be clear that since this is not directly commanded we cannot say that something less than weekly observance is sin. So also here we do see that converts were baptized before participating in community observances. Of course, this is the pattern we expect. It is not, however, a law requiring us to bar those who, due to misunderstanding, have improper baptisms. We must be careful not to create laws where we have only patterns.

A number of writers have also argued that close Communion is the safest course. The argument is that if we bar some from the Table they are not really harmed since no special grace is communicated at the Table. On the other hand, if we allow some to the Table who are not fit, we endanger them before God. O. L. Hailey, for example, argued that inviting non-Baptists to the Table "would be to encourage individuals to their own condemnation."[43] This, he says, is true because such people are not capable of taking the Supper in line with 1 Cor 11:27—"Whoever, therefore, eats the bread or drinks the cup of the Lord in an unworthy manner will be guilty concerning the body and blood of the Lord." He goes on to state, "One not baptized [i.e., not immersed] is not prepared to 'do this [receive Communion] in remembrance' of the Lord."[44]

There are at least two problems here. First, does 1 Cor 11:27 really fit our paedobaptist brethren? How can we say that one would partake in an unworthy manner simply because he has an improper baptism? First Corinthians 11 has in view serious neglect of the rest of the congregation. To apply this to paedobaptists is a violation of the text. Those excluded from Communion in the Scriptures are those engaged in flagrant, unrepentant sin (see 1 Corinthians 5, esp. v. 11). Exclusion from Communion is a mark of discipline, which is itself a declaration that one shows no evidence of being a believer. This is simply not true of our faithful paedobaptist brothers and sisters.

Now some have sought to argue that paedobaptists are, in fact, in direct rebellion against Christ because they refuse to be immersed. Christ's command is to be "baptized," which means to be immersed after conversion, and they do not do so. Of course, they have not fulfilled this command, but is this really rebellion? Are they really on par with someone who refuses baptism in any form, under any interpretation? Their problem is one of scriptural interpretation. They seek to obey the command of baptism, believing the Bible instructs them to administer this ordinance to infants of believers and therefore their incorrect interpretation leads them to an incorrect practice.

[43] O. L. Hailey, "Why Close Communion and Not Open Communion," in *Baptist Why and Why Not*, ed. J. M. Frost (Nashville: Sunday School Board of the Southern Baptist Convention, 1900), 203.

[44] Ibid.

First, we might then ask if every incorrect interpretation of Scripture should be construed as sin. After all, surely incorrect beliefs manifest themselves in incorrect practice. Also, surely at some level we interpret incorrectly because our hearts which are prone to going astray in so many ways refuse to see the truth (e.g., the men on the road to Emmaus were rebuked not because they didn't have good hermeneutics classes to show them where Christ was in the OT but were told that they were slow of heart to believe). Therefore, there is perhaps a sense in which all incorrect interpretation should be labeled sin. We might say that this is not right because we of course want to understand the text correctly. Dare we say, though, that our paedobaptist brethren do not want to understand the text correctly? The problem is that we can point to a situation where their incorrect interpretation is manifested in practice. What if, however, the cessationist is incorrect in his interpretation concerning the gifts of the Spirit? By direct consequence, then, he will not "earnestly desire the spiritual gifts, especially that [he] may prophesy" (1 Cor 14:1), if he thinks that prophecy does not take place in this age. If the cessationist is wrong in his interpretation, he is disobeying a direct command of Scripture. Thus, John Piper has noted, "I would ask all of us: are we so sure of our hermeneutical procedure for diminishing the gifts that we would risk walking in disobedience to a plain command of Scripture? 'Earnestly desire spiritual gifts, especially that you may prophesy.'"[45] Surely we would have to consider such individuals to be walking in sin if their interpretation that the gifts have ceased is incorrect. However, it seems that most believers would quickly oppose such a conclusion and point out that the cessationist (even if he is wrong) is striving to obey the Scripture and should not be identified as one whose heart is hardened and refuses to obey the commands of Christ. More than that, most would agree that he should never be banned from the Table because "he is walking in disobedience to God's Word." What then differentiates the evangelical paedobaptist from the cessationist in this situation?[46]

Second, is this really the "safe" option? It is true that we disobey God and thus endanger ourselves and others if we invite to the Table

[45] J. Piper, "Signs and Wonders: Then and Now." Accessed 2 September 2009. Online: http://www.desiringgod.org/resource-library/resources/signs-and-wonders-then-and-now.

[46] We could also apply this to the commands concerning head coverings (1 Cor 11:2–16) or for greeting one another with a holy kiss (Rom 16:16; 1 Cor 16:20; 2 Cor 13:12; 1 Thess 5:26; 1 Pet 5:14).

those whom the Lord Himself does not invite. I affirm the close Communionist's statement that this is the Lord's Table, and the issue is not simply whom we want to invite. This is precisely the point, because it is also a serious sin to bar from the Table one whom the Lord invites. Just as it is not our place to invite beyond the Lord's invitation, neither is it our place to exclude those whom Christ has made clean.

We have wrongly created a new category regarding Communion—those who are faithful believers but are denied the Table. All we see in the NT are faithful Christians who come to the Table. Those who are denied the Table are those in rebellion against Christ, who need church discipline, who are by all indications not true believers. Barring from the Table is supposed to be an indication that people are not considered Christians. Close Communion muddies these waters.

Lastly, appeal is often made to Baptist history, that the most common Baptist position has been "close" Communion. It is true that the "close" position has a strong showing in Baptist history, but the Second London Confession (1677–78), arguably the most influential of the Baptist confessions, did not restrict Communion to those properly baptized, and the First London Confession did not include such restricting language in its earliest editions.[47] Even the later editions of the First London, with more restrictive language, were signed by churches which continued practicing open Communion.[48] The first Particular Baptist church, under pastors John Spilsbury and Hercules Collins, practiced open Communion. Hercules Collins taught that "none are to be excluded but those who in Confession and Life declared themselves Infidels, profane, and ungodly."[49] After surveying British Baptist history, Hilburn stated that close membership and open Communion were present from the beginnings of the Baptist movement and "has been the prevalent practice among English Baptist

[47] See W. L. Lumpkin, *Baptist Confessions of Faith* (Valley Forge: Judson, 1969), 167 (First London Confession), 237 (Second London Confession).

[48] G. Hilburn, "The Lord's Supper: Admission and Exclusion Among English Baptists" (Th.D. thesis, Southwestern Baptist Theological Seminary, 1960), 44. Hilburn's thesis is very informative on the open/close question in early Baptist history.

[49] G. Gould, *Open Communion and the Baptists of Norwich* (Norwich: Josiah Fletcher, 1860), cxxvi–cxxvii, summarizing Collins, *An Orthodox Confession* (1680). A nice overview of Hercules Collins can be found in the recent book edited by M. A. G. Haykin and S. Weaver, *Devoted to the Service of the Temple: Piety, Persecution, and Ministry in the Writings of Hercules Collins* (Grand Rapids: Reformation Heritage, 2007).

churches since the time of Charles Haddon Spurgeon" (a prominent advocate of open Communion).[50]

Still, the close position has historically held sway in Southern Baptist life. However, W. A. Criswell, in his book on the church, dodged the open/close question by simply stating, "Baptists have been so busy talking about who should be excluded from the Lord's table that we have forgotten to insist that all believers should be in regular attendance at the Lord's Supper."[51] Many others—including conservatives—can be found who have practiced open Communion. The witness of Baptist history is mixed, and we must be willing to respectfully differ with our forebears if their arguments cannot be upheld by the Scriptures themselves.

Therefore, when at our church we come to Communion we warn unbelievers not to partake, and we invite all Christians "who are members in good standing of an evangelical church" (i.e., those not under discipline).

Should One Ever Abstain from Communion?

It is a fairly common practice for believers voluntarily to abstain from Communion because they feel they are not properly prepared at that given time. They think they should not partake of Communion if they are struggling with sin. This, though, arises from a misunderstanding of the call to examine ourselves in 1 Cor 11:28. The warning in v. 11 is against partaking in an unworthy manner, referring to the unrepentant self-centeredness of the Corinthians who were ignoring other members of the body. The warning does not apply to those who are struggling with sin but are looking to the cross in repentance, hating their sin and yearning to be pleasing to God. When the understanding of the people is that you must wait until you have been "good enough" or have gotten yourself into a moment of being "good enough," we have turned this amazing reminder of grace into an ogre of legalism. No one is worthy. That is the point. Melancthon again says it well:

> Some will not venture to profess Christ until they can rather profess themselves. They wait for worthiness to come to the Lord's table, not consider-

[50] Hilburn, "The Lord's Supper," 207.
[51] Criswell, *Doctrine of the Church*, 106.

> ing that it is unworthiness which they are to profess, along with Christ's worthiness—their sins, along with His name for remission of sins.[52]

In the Supper we are reminded again that Christ died for sinners like us. The requirement is that we come in faith and repentance. Too often, having stripped the Supper of any positive meaning, we are left only with the threat of divine judgment if we do it incorrectly. It is no wonder in such cases that many do not want to have Communion more frequently. They believe it won't actually *do* anything for them if they take it correctly, and, what's worse, they might suffer if they do it incorrectly. Judgment is real, but so is the truth of grace for the repentant.

If we have struggled this week and sinned (and we have), that is all the more reason we need the Lord's Supper. We need to be reminded in a tangible way that Christ has made provision for that sin. The only pre-condition for a believer is that he be repentant. To refuse Communion is symbolically to refuse the work of Christ. Thus, the only time that one should keep himself from the Table is if he refuses to repent. Then, that person should realize he is declaring that he refuses to submit to Christ and is beginning to show himself an unbeliever.[53]

I tell our people that the Scriptures are not barring any who have ever danced with the Devil. We all have. You simply cannot come to the Table still holding the Devil's hand. As long as you are repentant, come. Be reminded of the cost of your sin, hate it afresh, and be reminded that your Savior has paid the debt. Be reminded of the grace of God that is greater than your sin. Be humbled anew by grace which is staggeringly beyond what you could expect, ask, or think. Allow

[52] Jacobus, *Notes, Critical and Explanatory, on The Acts of the Apostles*, 82.

[53] Jesus' statement in Matt 5:23–24 about the need to reconcile with your brother is used by some as reason to abstain from Communion. It is odd that this verse has become especially attached to Communion. What is in view in this text is worship in old covenant terms. We must not associate the mention of the "altar" with Communion. The NT makes clear that worship must be seen in terms of all of life. Jesus' call is to orient our minds to staying reconciled with others. This sort of living is foundational to any true worship. When we apply this to formal public worship, then the point of contact is not Communion per se but the corporate worship itself. Jesus' call is exactly what has been stated above—repent and come. Of course, repentance is needed. Jesus does not give the option of perpetually abstaining from worship. Trouble has been caused when, using this text and others, Communion has been made into a special and infrequent time for self-examination. We ought rather to be daily asking whether we are living in harmony with God and man, that we are living a lifestyle of repentance. We cannot live lives of worship to God any other way.

the truth of free grace to melt your heart and cause you to long all the more for holiness.

J. I. Packer says it well:

> We are also to learn the divinely intended discipline of drawing assurance from the sacrament. We should be saying in our hearts, "As sure as I see and touch and taste this bread and this wine, so sure is it that Jesus Christ is not a fancy but a fact, that he is for real, and that he offers me himself to be my Saviour, my Bread of Life, and my Guide to glory. He has left me this rite, this gesture, this token, this ritual action as a guarantee of this grace; He instituted it, and it is a sign of life-giving union with him, and I'm taking part in it, and thus I know that I am his and he is mine forever." That is the assurance that we should be drawing from our sharing in the Lord's Supper every time we come to the table.[54]

Closing Thoughts on Practice

I have argued that it would be best to celebrate Communion weekly and to invite to participate all those who trust Christ and are members in good standing with an evangelical church. Let me close now by describing how we approach Communion in our church. My point is not to say that the way we do it is the only way, but to provide a concrete example of putting these ideas into practice.

In our church we always celebrate Communion at the close and climax of the service. Having prayed at the close of the sermon, we sing a fitting hymn together while both elements are distributed. We distribute both elements at the same time.[55] If the Word is rightly preached, then no matter the text, the gospel is expounded. Communion is then a fitting response. It gives us a way to respond to the Word—a biblical way, without creating something from our own minds. Having heard the Word preached, we come once more to the Table, confessing again our need of a Savior, our faith in this Christ, and our intention by His grace to live out His commands, including the portion just preached. Rather than an altar call, it is a Table call, allowing each of us, in a sense, to rededicate ourselves each week.

[54] Packer, "The Gospel and the Lord's Supper," 50.

[55] Distributing the elements together works smoothly and conserves some time. We are not in a hurry but want to use our time well. I like to have both elements in hand and not to have a break between the taking of one element and the taking of the other. This also prevents a large gap of time between the preaching and the taking of the elements, supporting the sense of response to the Word. I mention this not as a biblical requirement, but as one practical step we take which has been helpful to us.

If the Word preached that day has been particularly convicting and we have seen our sin exposed, then with Communion we are tangibly reminded that atonement has been made for our sins. The pastoral value of this is too rarely considered. It is deeply meaningful, having been rebuked and humbled and perhaps being tempted with despair by a condemning conscience, to see again the physical reminders of Christ's body broken and His blood spilled for us. We are not simply told again of His sacrifice, but we are reminded visibly, tangibly, that Christ has decisively dealt with our sin. In J. B. Phillips words, we "accept the cordial of God's forgiveness and reinstatement."[56]

The Supper is not for those who have it all sorted out. In fact, it is for sinners only. By taking the elements we confess we are sinners in need of a Savior, and we confess again that we take Christ, with His work at the cross, as our Savior. Among the many benefits of this practice is that it keeps us from even sounding legalistic and after the rebuke of sin allows us to close on the note of sins forgiven. People deeply struggle to believe that God loves them, to receive the amazing word that in Christ *all* our sins are forgiven. In Communion we have the truth of Christ's redeeming love portrayed, showing us that His forgiveness is so real we can taste it.

If that day the Word has been especially encouraging, then Communion roots that encouragement in the work of Christ. Why is it that we can have any encouragement, hope, or peace? Because Christ's body was broken and His blood spilled for us. Our hope is tangibly rooted in the work of Christ.

Furthermore, this use of Communion at the close of the service is powerfully evangelistic. An unbeliever sitting in the service will have heard the gospel expounded and will have been called to repent and believe. The elements will have been explained with a call to repent and believe but a warning that if he does not repent and believe, then the elements are not for him. Then the elements of Christ come to him, and he is forced to encounter the symbols of Christ's body and blood. Week after week he is confronted with the work of Christ. The symbol of the broken body of Christ will be passed by him and he must say, "I refuse to trust in this Christ!" And again comes the symbol of Christ's poured out blood and again the unbeliever must say, "This is not for me. I will not receive!" I think it is more powerfully

[56] Phillips, *Appointment with God*, 57.

and properly evangelistic than many other things that we do, as well as deeply edifying to believers who at the close of each time are reminded, "This is what has been done for me."

Conclusion

There are a number of disputes concerning how we practice Communion in our local churches, and I have tried to address most of them here. However, while it is important to think carefully about the details, we must be careful not to miss the big picture. Christ has given us a rite for regular use to remind us in physical terms that He loves us and gave Himself for us. In a time focused only on the here and now, it points to the past and the future. In this present evil age, it reminds us of the coming wedding feast. In a hectic world, it forces us to slow down. In a setting of increasingly virtual communication, it brings us back to the physical and corporeal. In a culture dominated by the odd mixture of individualism and loneliness, it reminds us we are part of a family. We need this celebration. Our God thinks so, or He would not have commanded it. We need to return to thinking deeply, carefully, and pastorally about how to reinvigorate our practice of this wonderful ordinance for the good of the church and the glory of God.[57]

[57] Portions of this chapter previously appeared in my article "Ponderings on Our Practice of the Ordinances," *Theology for Ministry* 1 (November 2006): 75–87. Also, thanks are due to Brian Denker who was such a help to me in tracking down items and in providing many helpful suggestions. I am also indebted to my fellow pastor, Lee Tankersley, who has challenged and shaped my thoughts in this chapter.

EPILOGUE

Thomas R. Schreiner
Matthew R. Crawford

The chapters of this book have surveyed far and wide the biblical, historical, theological, and pastoral issues relevant to the Lord's Supper. All four approaches to the issue are necessary for a proper understanding of the Supper. We begin with Scripture. We then see how the church has interpreted Scripture throughout her history. Next we attempt to put the words of Scripture together into a coherent and logical system. Finally we place the doctrine in its proper context within the life of the church. Through this process of reflection we gain a better and more faithful understanding of the Lord's Supper. Yet, all such reflection will have been in vain if this book does not influence what actually happens in the pulpit and the pew as local churches regularly partake of the Supper of our Lord. The scholarly contributions of this book are intended by their authors to contribute to a renewed awareness of the significance of the Eucharist in the life of the church.

This is a book written by Baptists for Baptists, a fact that we make no apology for. By our very name, Baptists are distinguished from other branches of the Christian church for our particular view of the water-rite associated with salvation. Indeed, many imply that the Baptist view of baptism is *the* most central element of our identity and theology, or at least the first one that springs to mind when attempting to explain who we are to outsiders. Such an identity is not wrong per se, and indeed fits nicely with the Baptist emphasis upon conversion. Yet, if the emphasis upon baptism leads to a denigration or dismissal of the other great rite of the Christian church—the Lord's Supper—surely something is amiss. Believer's baptism by immersion is central to Baptist identity, but let us not forget that the partaking of the Supper in obedience to our Lord is central to our identity as Christians. Baptists are known by their view of baptism, but if we wish to be biblical, we must make the Supper as integral to our theology and praxis as the immersion of those who have believed in Christ. Baptism is inextricably tied to conversion, but Christ did not call us simply to see people be converted, but rather, to make disciples, that is, to see people persevere in the faith once for all delivered to the saints. The

Lord's Supper is crucial in the perseverance of the saints until the return of Christ as King, as it brings the gospel again and again to the forefront of the church's reflection. It would seem that many Southern Baptist churches have lost or forgotten the connection between the Supper and the ongoing life of the Christian and the local church. It is out of a desire to remedy such a loss that this book was born.

As this book draws to a close, perhaps one final, simple observation is in order. The name of the meal-rite commanded by Christ on the eve of His death contains within it the meaning of the event. Thus, when we think of the Lord's Supper we should remember at least two things. First, and foremost in importance, it is the Supper *of the Lord.* That is, the meal that we gather to partake of together is fundamentally a meal about our Lord Jesus Christ, and therefore, a meal fundamentally about the gospel. The message of the Supper is not something added on to the message of the New Testament. Nor is it a vague metaphysical mystery about which we are not permitted to speak. Rather, the message of the Lord's Supper is the message of the New Testament—the life, death, burial, resurrection, ascension, and final return of the incarnate Son of God to redeem His people. If the gospel is not in view when the Supper is celebrated by churches, then it is not the Supper *of the Lord* that we partake of. If gospel-less preaching would not be tolerated in Baptist churches, then neither should gospel-less celebrations of the Supper. It is in light of the gospel that another common name for this event arises—the Eucharist—since as the church remembers the gospel it gives thanks for the wonderful grace of God.

Secondly, when we consider the Lord's Supper, we must remember that it is the *Supper* of our Lord. That is, it is a rite that consists of a communal meal, celebrated by a group of believers, not simply isolated Christians. Jesus enjoyed the Last Supper amidst a group of His followers, and surely it was His intention that the ongoing celebration of that meal take place amidst a gathered community, as the practice of the early church in Acts and in the epistles makes clear. One of the strengths of Baptist ecclesiology is its insistence on the primacy of the local church, and oddly enough the Lord's Supper serves this emphasis quite well. It is not odd to find such a correlation since it was intended by our Lord, but it is odd that so few Baptists seem to have exploited this connection. If Baptists want to uphold the primacy of the local church in the life of the Christian and in the providential ordering of God, then a recovery of the theology and practice of the Supper is essential. For it is here in the Supper that the church is confronted again and again with the gospel event that brought this community of faith into existence, which sustains it through the tribulations of this world, and which promises a glorious end to its earthly sojourn. Moreover, as the church remembers and celebrates what God has done for her, then individual Christians are inspired to demonstrate that same kind of love and care for one another. Thus, the communal nature of the meal that we share serves to remind us that the gospel is not merely about us as individual persons, but fundamentally about a community of the redeemed who live even now as citizens of the kingdom of heaven while they await the full reality of His reign in the age to come. The Supper is about us as we relate to God, but also about us as we relate to one another. It is the *Lord's* Supper, and it is the *Supper* of the Lord.

We would like to thank all the contributors who have taken time away from their other commitments to write the essays contained in this book. We would also like to thank B&H for their support of this project from its inception to its completion. Finally, we would like to thank our Lord who purchased us with His own precious blood, and who commanded us to remember His sacrifice until His return.

Soli deo gloria

SELECTED BIBLIOGRAPHY

Primary Sources

Ambrose. *On the Sacraments and On the Mysteries*. Edited by J. H. Srawley. Translated by T. Thompson. London: SPCK, 1950.

Aquinas, Thomas. *The Eucharistic Presence*. Vol. 58 of *Summa Theologiae*. Translated by William Barden. New York: McGraw-Hill, 1964.

Brown, John. *An Apology for the More Frequent Administration of the Lord's Supper: With Answers to the Objections Urged Against It*. Edinburgh: Ogle & Aikman, 1804.

Cajetan, Thomas. *The Celebration of the Mass*. In *Forerunners of the Reformation: The Shape of Late Medieval Thought Illustrated by Key Documents*. Edited by Heiko A. Oberman. Translated by Paul L. Nyhus. New York: Holt, Rinehart and Winston, 1966.

Calvin, John. *Short Treatise on the Supper of Our Lord*. In *Selected Works of John Calvin: Tracts and Treatises*, vol. 2, part 2. Edited and translated by Henry Beveridge. Grand Rapids: Baker, 1983; reprinted as *Treatises on the Sacraments: Catechism of the Church in Geneva, Forms of Prayer, and Confessions of Faith*. Fearn, Scotland: Christian Heritage, 2002.

Flavel, John. *Sacramental Meditations Upon Divers Select Places of Scripture: wherein Believers are assisted in preparing their Hearts, and exciting their Affections and Graces, when they draw nigh to God in that most awful and solemn Ordinance of the Lord's Supper*. In *The Works of John Flavel*, vol. 6. Carlisle, PA: Banner of Truth, 1968.

Gould, George. *Open Communion and the Baptists of Norwich*. Norwich: Josiah Fletcher, 1860.

Hoen, Cornelisz. "A Most Christian Letter." In *Forerunners of the Reformation: The Shape of Late Medieval Thought Illustrated by Key Documents*. Edited by Heiko A. Oberman. Translated by Paul L. Nyhus. New York: Holt, Rinehart and Winston, 1966.

Kennedy, Crammond. *Close Communion or Open Communion? An Experience and an Argument*. New York: American News Company, 1868.

Lehmann, Martin E., ed. "The Marburg Colloquy and the Marburg Articles." In *LW* 38, *Word and Sacrament: IV*. Translated by Martin E. Lehmann. Philadelphia: Fortress, 1971.

Luther, Martin. *The Babylonian Captivity of the Church*. In LW 36, *Word and Sacrament: II*. Edited by Abdel Ross Wentz. Translated by A. T. W. Steinhauser and revised by Frederick C. Ahrens and Abdel Ross Wentz. Philadelphia: Muhlenberg, 1959.

Pascasius Radbertus of Corbie. "The Lord's Body and Blood." In *Early Medieval Theology*. Edited and translated by George E. McCracken and Allen Cabaniss. LCC 9. London: SCM, 1957.

Ratramnus of Corbie. "Christ's Body and Blood." In *Early Medieval Theology*. Edited and translated by George E. McCracken and Allen Cabaniss. LCC 9. London: SCM, 1957.

Wilkinson, W. C. *The Baptist Principle in Its Relation to Baptism and the Lord's Supper*. Philadelphia: American Baptist Publication Society, 1881.

Wyclif, John. *On the Eucharist*. In *Advocates of Reform: From Wyclif to Erasmus*. Edited by Matthew Spinka. Translated by Ford Lewis Battles. LCC 14. Philadelphia: Westminster, 1953.

Zwingli, Ulrich. *On the Lord's Supper*. In *Zwingli and Bullinger*. Edited and translated by G. W. Bromiley. LCC 24. Philadelphia: Westminster, 1953.

Secondary Sources

Armstrong, John H., ed. *Understanding Four Views on the Lord's Supper*. Grand Rapids: Zondervan, 2007.

Bagchi, David. "Diversity or Disunity: A Reformation Controversy over Communion in Both Kinds." In *Unity and Diversity in the Church: Papers Read at the 1994 Summer Meeting and the 1995 Winter Meeting of the Ecclesiastical History Society*. Edited by R. N. Swanson. Cambridge, MA: Blackwell, 1996.

Barclay, William. *The Lord's Supper*. Philadelphia: Westminster, 1967.

Barrett, C. K. "Luke XXII.15: To Eat the Passover." *JTS* 9 (1958): 305–7.

Barth, Markus. *Rediscovering the Lord's Supper: Communion with Israel, with Christ, and Among the Guests*. Atlanta: John Knox, 1988.

Pope Benedict XVI. *The Sacrament of Charity = Sacramentum Caritatis: Post-synodal Apostolic Exhortation*. Washington, D.C.: United States Conference of Catholic Bishops, 2007.

Berkouwer, G. C. *The Sacraments*. Translated by Hugo Bekker. Grand Rapids: Eerdmans, 1969.

Blinzler, Josef. "Qumran-Kalendar und Passionchronologie." *ZNW* 49 (1958): 238–51.

Blue, Bradley B. "The House Church at Corinth and the Lord's Supper: Famine, Food Supply, and the Present Distress." *CTR* 5 (1991): 221–39.

Bridge, Donald, and David Phypers. *Communion: The Meal That Unites?* Wheaton, IL: Harold Shaw, 1981.

Chadwick, Henry. "Eucharist and Christology in the Nestorian Controversy." *JTS* 2 (1951): 145–64.

Chwolson, Daniel. *Das letzte Passamahl Christi und der Tag seines Todes*. 2nd ed. Leipzig: H. Haessel, 1908.

Clark, R. Scott. "The Evangelical Fall from the Means of Grace: The Lord's Supper." In *The Compromised Church: The Present Evangelical Crisis*. Edited by John H. Armstrong. Wheaton: Crossway, 1998.

Clements, R. E., et al. *Eucharistic Theology Then and Now*. London: S.P.C.K., 1968.

Collins, C. John. "The Eucharist as Christian Sacrifice: How Patristic Authors Can Help Us Read the Bible." *WTJ* 66 (2004): 1–23.

Daly-Denton, Margaret M. "Water in the Eucharistic Cup: A Feature of the Eucharist in Johannine Trajectories through Early Christianity." *ITQ* 72 (2007): 356–70.

Davis, Thomas J. *This Is My Body: The Presence of Christ in Reformation Thought*. Grand Rapids: Baker, 2008.

Dugmore, C. W. "Sacrament and Sacrifice in the Early Fathers." *JEH* 2 (1951): 24–37.

Duncan, J. Ligon. "True Communion with Christ in the Lord's Supper: Calvin, Westminster and the Nature of Christ's Sacramental Presence." In *The Westminster Confession into the 21st Century: Essays in Remembrance of the 350th Anniversary of the Westminster Assembly*. Vol. 2. Edited by J. Ligon Duncan. Ross-shire, Scotland: Christian Focus, 2004.

Engelsma, David J. "Martin Bucer's 'Calvinistic' Doctrine of the Lord's Supper." *Mid-America Journal of Theology* 3 (1987): 169–95.

Fitzer, Joseph. "The Augustinian Roots of Calvin's Eucharistic Thought." *Augustinian Studies* 7 (1976): 69–98.

Fitzpatrick, P. J. "Present and Past in a Debate on Transubstantiation." In *The Philosophical Assessment of Theology: Essays in Honour of Frederick C. Copleston*. Edited by Gerard J. Hughes. Washington, D.C.: Georgetown University Press, 1987.

Freeman, Curtis W. "'To Feed Upon by Faith': Nourishment from the Lord's Table." In *Baptist Sacramentalism*. Edited by Anthony R. Cross and Philip E. Thompson. Carlisle, UK: Paternoster, 2003.

George, Timothy. "John Calvin and the Agreement of Zurich (1549)." In *John Calvin and the Church: A Prism of Reform*. Louisville: Westminster/John Knox, 1990.

Gerrish, Brian. "Gospel and Eucharist: John Calvin on the Lord's Supper." In *The Old Protestantism and the New: Essays on the Reformation Heritage*. Chicago: University of Chicago Press, 1982.

Gleason, Ronald N. "Calvin and Bavinck on the Lord's Supper." *WTJ* 45 (1983): 273–303.

Grappe, Christian, ed. *Le Repas de Dieu/Das Mahl Gottes: 4. Symposium Strasbourg, Tübingen, Upsala, 11–15 Septembre 2002*. WUNT 169. Tübingen: Mohr Siebeck, 2004.

Hailey, O. L. "Why Close Communion and Not Open Communion." In *Baptist: Why and Why Not*. Edited by J. M. Frost. Nashville: Sunday School Board of the Southern Baptist Convention, 1900.

Hall, Basil. "Hoc est Corpus Meum: The Centrality of the Real Presence for Luther." In *Luther: Theologian for Catholics and Protestants*. Edited by George Yule. Edinburgh: T&T Clark, 1985.

Halliburton, R. J. "The Patristic Theology of the Eucharist." In *The Study of Liturgy*. Edited by Cheslyn Jones, Geoffrey Wainwright, and Edward Yarnold. London: SPCK, 1978.

Hart, Trevor. "Calvin and Barth on the Lord's Supper." In *Calvin, Barth, and Reformed Theology*. Edited by Neil B. MacDonald and Carl Trueman. Paternoster Theological Monographs. Milton Keynes, UK: Paternoster, 2008.

Haykin, Michael A. G. "'His soul-refreshing presence': The Lord's Supper in Calvinistic Baptist Thought and Experience in the 'Long' Eighteenth Century." In *Baptist Sacramentalism*. Edited by Anthony R. Cross and Philip E. Thompson. Carlisle, UK: Paternoster, 2003.

Heron, Alasdair I. C. *Table and Tradition*. Philadelphia: Westminster, 1983.

Higgins, A. J. B. "Origins of the Eucharist." *NTS* 1 (1955): 200–209.

Hilburn, Glen. "The Lord's Supper: Admission and Exclusion Among English Baptists." Th.D. thesis, Southwestern Baptist Theological Seminary, 1960.

Hinson, Glenn. "The Lord's Supper in Early Church History." *RevExp* 64 (1969): 15–24.

Howard, J. K. "Passover and Eucharist in the Fourth Gospel." *SJT* 20 (1967): 329–37.

Hovey, Michael S. "At Least Weekly: The Reformed Doctrine of the Lord's Supper and Its Frequent Celebration." *Mid-America Journal of Theology* 11 (2000): 147–69.

Jalland, T. G. "Justin Martyr and the President of the Eucharist." *StPatr* 5 (1962): 83–85.

Jaubert, Annie. *The Date of the Last Supper*. New York: Alba House, 1965.

Jeremias, Joachim. *The Eucharistic Words of Jesus*. Translated by Norman Perrin. London: SCM, 1966.

Johanny, Raymond. *L'eucharistie, centre de l'histoire du salut chez saint Ambroise de Milan*. Paris: Beauchesne, 1968.

Pope John Paul II. *On the Mystery and Worship of the Eucharist*. Boston: St. Paul Editions, 1980.

Jorissen, Hans-Joachim. *Die Entfaltung der Transsubstantiationslehre bis zum Beginn der Hochscholastik*. Münsterische Beiträge zur Theologie, Heft 28, 1. Münster: Aschendorffsche Verlagsbuchhandlung, 1965.

Lane, Anthony N. S. "Was Calvin a Crypto-Zwinglian?" In *Adaptations of Calvinism in Reformation Europe: Essays in Honour of Brian G. Armstrong*. Edited by Mack P. Holt. St. Andrews Studies in Reformation History. Burlington, VT: Ashgate, 2007.

Leithart, Peter J. "What's Wrong with Transubstantiation? An Evaluation of Theological Models." *WTJ* 53 (1991): 295–324.

Letham, Robert. *The Lord's Supper: Eternal Word in Broken Bread*. Phillipsburg, NJ: P&R: 2001.

MacDonald, A. J. *Berengar and the Reform of the Sacramental Doctrine*. London: Longmans, Green and Co., 1930.

Macy, Gary. *The Theologies of the Eucharist in the Early Scholastic Period: A Study of the Salvific Function of the Sacrament according to the Theologians c.1080–c.1220*. Oxford: Clarendon Press, 1984.

Marshall, I. Howard. *Last Supper and Lord's Supper*. Grand Rapids: Eerdmans, 1980.

Mathison, Keith A. *Given for You: Reclaiming Calvin's Doctrine of the Lord's Supper*. Phillipsburg: P&R, 2002.

McCue, James F. "The Doctrine of Transubstantiation from Berengar Through Trent: The Point at Issue." *HTR* 61 (1968): 385–430.

McGowan, Andrew. *Ascetic Eucharists: Food and Drink in Early Christian Ritual Meals*. Oxford: Clarendon Press, 1999.

———. "Eating People: Accusations of Cannibalism Against Christians in the Second Century." *JECS* 2 (1994): 413–42.

———. "'Is There a Liturgical Text in This Gospel?': The Institution Narratives and Their Early Interpretive Communities." *JBL* 118 (1999): 73–87.

McGrath, Alister. "The Eucharist: Reassessing Zwingli." *Theology* 93 (1990): 13–19.

Meyer, Ben F., ed. *One Loaf, One Cup: Ecumenical Studies of 1 Cor 11 and Other Eucharistic Texts: The Cambridge Conference on the Eucharist, August 1988*. Macon: Mercer University Press, 1993.

Moore-Crispin, Derek R. "'The Real Absence': Ulrich Zwingli's View?" In *Union and Communion, 1529–1979: Papers read at the 1979 Westminster Conference*. London: Westminster Conference, 1979.

Moore-Keish, Martha L. *Do This in Remembrance of Me: A Ritual Approach to Reformed Eucharistic Theology*. Grand Rapids: Eerdmans, 2008.

Morden, Peter J. "The Lord's Supper and the Spirituality of C. H. Spurgeon." In *Baptist Sacramentalism* 2. Edited by Anthony R. Cross and Philip E. Thompson. Milton Keynes, UK: Paternoster, 2008.

Naylor, Peter. *Calvinism, Communion and the Baptists: A Study of English Calvinistic Baptists from the Late 1600s to the Early 1800s*. Carlisle, UK: Paternoster, 2003.

Packer, J. I. "The Gospel and the Lord's Supper." In *Serving the People of God: The Collected Shorter Writings of J. I. Packer*, vol. 2. Carlisle, UK: Paternoster, 1998.

Phillips, J. B. *Appointment with God: Some Thoughts on Holy Communion*. New York: Macmillan, 1956.

Phillips, Richard D. "The Lord's Supper: An Overview." In *Give Praise to God: A Vision for Reforming Worship*. Edited by Philip Graham Ryken, Derek W. H. Thomas, and J. Ligon Duncan III. Phillipsburg, NJ: P&R, 2003.

Pipkin, H. Wayne. "The Positive Religious Values of Zwingli's Eucharistic Writings." In *Huldrych Zwingli, 1484–1531: A Legacy of Radical Reform*. Edited by E. J. Furcha. Montreal: McGill University Faculty of Religious Studies, 1985.

Pruett, Gordon E. "A Protestant Doctrine of the Eucharistic Presence." *CTJ* 10 (1975): 142–74.

Rorem, Paul. "The Consensus Tigurinus (1549): Did Calvin Compromise?" In *Calvinus Sacrae Scripturae Professor*. Edited by Wilhelm H. Neuser. Grand Rapids: Eerdmans, 1994.

Rubin, Miri. *Corpus Christi: The Eucharist in Late Medieval Culture*. Cambridge: Cambridge University Press, 1991.

Sasse, Hermann. *This Is My Body: Luther's Contention for the Real Presence in the Sacrament of the Altar*. Minneapolis: Augsburg, 1959.

Schürmann, Heinz. *Der Paschamahlbericht: Lk 22, (7–14.) 15–18: Teil einer quellenkritischen Untersuchung des lukanischen Abendmahlsberichtes Lk 22, 7–38*. Neutestamentliche Abhandlungen, Bd. 19, Heft 5. Münster: Aschendorffsche Verlagsbuchhandlung, 1953.

Schweizer, Eduard. *The Lord's Supper According to the New Testament*. Translated by James M. Davis. Philadelphia: Fortress, 1967.

Smit, Peter-Ben. *Fellowship and Food in the Kingdom: Eschatological Meals and Scenes of Utopian Abundance in the New Testament*. WUNT 2. Tübingen: Mohr-Siebeck, 2008.

Smith, Gordon T., ed. *The Lord's Supper: Five Views*. Downers Grove, IL: IVP Academic, 2008.

Spear, Wayne R. "The Nature of the Lord's Supper According to Calvin and the Westminster Assembly." In *The Westminster Confession in the 21st Century*, vol. 3. Edited by J. Ligon Duncan. Fearn, Scotland: Mentor, 2009.

Stephenson, John. "Martin Luther and the Eucharist." *SJT* 36 (1983): 447–61.

Stoffer, Dale R., ed. *The Lord's Supper: Believers Church Perspectives*. Scottdale, PA: Herald, 1997.

Thompson, Mark D. "Claritas Scripturae in the Eucharistic Writings of Martin Luther." *WTJ* 60 (1998): 23–41.

Trimp, Cornelis. "The Sacrament of the Lord's Supper." *Mid-America Journal of Theology* 12 (2001): 147–201.

Vander Zee, Leonard J. *Christ, Baptism and the Lord's Supper: Recovering the Sacraments for Evangelical Worship*. Downers Grove, IL: InterVarsity, 2004.

Venema, Cornelis P. "The Doctrine of the Lord's Supper in the Reformed Confessions." *Mid-America Journal of Theology* 12 (2001): 81–145.

Walker, Michael J. *Baptists at the Table: The Theology of the Lord's Supper among English Baptists in the Nineteenth Century*. Didcot, UK: Baptist Historical Society, 1992.

Wandel, Lee Palmer. "The Body of Christ at Marburg, 1529." In *Image and Imagination of the Religious Self in Late Medieval and Early Modern Europe*. Edited by Reindert Falkenburg, Walter S. Melion, and Todd M. Richardson. Turnhout, Belgium: Brepols Publishers, 2007.

Wenham, David. "How Jesus Understood the Last Supper: A Parable in Action." *Them* 20 (1995): 11–16.

Winter, Bruce W. "'Private' Dinners and Christian Divisiveness (1 Corinthians 11:17–34)." In *After Paul Left Corinth: The Influence of Secular Ethics and Social Change*. Grand Rapids: Eerdmans, 2001.

Witherington, Ben, III. *Making a Meal of It: Rethinking the Theology of the Lord's Supper*. Waco, TX: Baylor University Press, 2007.

Wright, N.T. *The Meal that Jesus Gave Us: Understanding Holy Communion*. Louisville: Westminster John Knox, 2002.

NAME INDEX

SCRIPTURE INDEX